Lecture Notes in Computer Science 6808

Commenced Publication in 1973
Founding and Former Series Editors:
Gerhard Goos, Juris Hartmanis, and Jan van Leeuwen

Markus Holzer   Martin Kutrib
Giovanni Pighizzini (Eds.)

Descriptional Complexity of Formal Systems

13th International Workshop, DCFS 2011
Gießen/Limburg, Germany, July 25-27, 2011
Proceedings

 Springer

Volume Editors

Markus Holzer
Universität Gießen, Institut für Informatik
Arndtstraße 2, 35392 Gießen, Germany
E-mail: holzer@informatik.uni-giessen.de

Martin Kutrib
Universität Gießen, Institut für Informatik
Arndtstraße 2, 35392 Gießen, Germany
E-mail: kutrib@informatik.uni-giessen.de

Giovanni Pighizzini
Università degli Studi di Milano
Dipartimento di Informatica e Comunicazione
Via Comelico 39, 20135 Milano, Italy
E-mail: pighizzini@dico.unimi.it

ISSN 0302-9743   e-ISSN 1611-3349
ISBN 978-3-642-22599-4   e-ISBN 978-3-642-22600-7
DOI 10.1007/978-3-642-22600-7
Springer Heidelberg Dordrecht London New York

Library of Congress Control Number: 2011931777

CR Subject Classification (1998): F.1, D.2.4, F.3, F.4.2-3

LNCS Sublibrary: SL 1 – Theoretical Computer Science and General Issues

Typesetting: Camera-ready by author, data conversion by Scientific Publishing Services, Chennai, India

Printed on acid-free paper

Springer is part of Springer Science+Business Media (www.springer.com)

Preface

The 13th International Workshop of Descriptional Complexity of Formal Systems (DCFS 2011) was organized by the Institut für Informatik of the Universität Giessen and took place in the vicinity of Giessen, in Limburg, Germany. It was a three-day workshop starting July 25 and ending July 27, 2011. The city of Limburg lies in the west of the province Hessen between the Taunus and the Westerwald in the beautiful Lahn valley and it looks back on a history of more than 1, 100 years.

The DCFS workshop is the successor workshop and the merger of two related workshops, Descriptional Complexity of Automata, Grammars and Related Structures (DCAGRS) and Formal Descriptions and Software Reliability (FDSR). The DCAGRS workshop took place in Magdeburg, Germany (1999), London, Ontario, Canada (2000), and Vienna, Austria (2001), while the FDSR workshop took place in Paderborn, Germany (1998), Boca Raton, Florida, USA (1999), and San Jose, California, USA (2000). The DCFS workshop has previously been held in London, Ontario, Canada (2002), Budapest, Hungary (2003), London, Ontario, Canada (2004), Como, Italy (2005), Las Cruces, New Mexico, USA (2006), Nový Smokovec, Slovakia (2007), Charlottetown, Prince Edward Island, Canada (2008), Magdeburg, Germany (2009), and Saskatoon, Saskatchewan, Canada (2010).

This volume contains the invited contributions and the accepted papers of DCFS 2011. Special thanks go to the invited speakers:

- Jarkko Kari (Unversity of Turku, Finland)
- Friedrich Otto (Universität Kassel, Germany)
- Stefan Schwoon (ENS de Cachan, France)
- Denis Thérien (McGill University, Quebec, Canada)

for accepting our invitation and presenting their recent results at DCFS 2011. The papers were submitted to DCFS 2011 by a total of 54 authors from 16 different countries, from all over the world, Canada, Czech Republic, Finland, France, Germany, Hungary, India, Italy, Republic of Korea, Latvia, Malaysia, Portugal, Romania, Slovakia, Spain, and USA. From these submissions, on the basis of three referee reports each, the Program Committee selected 21 papers—the submission and refereeing process was supported by the EasyChair conference management system. We warmly thank the members of the Program Committee for their excellent work in making this selection. Moreover, we also thank the additional external reviewers for their careful evaluation. All these efforts were the basis for the success of the workshop. We are indebted to Alfred Hofmann and Anna Kramer, from Springer, for their efficient collaboration in making this volume available before the conference. Their timely instructions were very helpful to our preparation of this volume.

We are grateful to the Organizing Committee consisting of Susanne Gretschel, Markus Holzer (Co-chair), Sebastian Jakobi, Martin Kutrib (Co-chair), Andreas Malcher, Katja Meckel, Heinz Rübeling, and Matthias Wendlandt (Co-chair) for their support of the sessions, the excursion and the other accompanying events. Thanks also go to the staff of the Dom Hotel in Limburg, where the conference took place, and all the other helping hands that were working in the background for the success of this workshop.

Finally, we would like to thank all the participants for attending the DCFS workshop. We hope that this year's workshop stimulated new investigations and scientific co-operations in the field of descriptional complexity, as in previous years. Looking forward to DCFS 2012 in Porto, Portugal.

July 2011   Markus Holzer
                                                              Martin Kutrib
                                                         Giovanni Pighizzini

Organization

DCFS 2011 was organized by the Institut für Informatik of the Universität Giessen, Germany. The conference took place at the Dom Hotel in Limburg, Germany.

Program Committee

Jean-Marc Champarnaud	Université de Rouen, France
Erzsébet Csuhaj-Varjú	MTA SZTAKI, Hungary
Zoltan Ésik	University of Szeged, Hungary
Markus Holzer	Universität Giessen, Germany (Co-chair)
Galina Jirásková	Slovak Academy of Sciences, Slovakia
Martin Kutrib	Universität Giessen, Germany (Co-chair)
Carlos Martín-Vide	Roviri i Virgili University, Spain
Tomáš Masopust	Czech Academy of Sciences, Czech Republic; Centrum Wiskunde & Infromatica, The Netherlands
Ian McQuillan	University of Saskatoon, Canada
Carlo Mereghetti	Università degli Studi di Milano, Italy
Victor Mitrana	Universitatea din Bucureşti, Romania
Alexander Okhotin	University of Turku, Finland
Giovanni Pighizzini	Università degli Studi di Milano, Italy (Co-chair)
Bala Ravikumar	Sonoma State University, USA
Rogério Reis	Universidade do Porto, Portugal
Kai Salomaa	Queen's University, Canada
Bianca Truthe	Universität Magdeburg, Germany

External Referees

Alberto Bertoni	Christof Löding	Rama Raghavan
Sabine Broda	Andreas Malcher	Shinnosuke Seki
Flavio D'Alessandro	Florin Manea	Ralf Stiebe
Mike Domaratzki	Wim Martens	Maurice H. ter Beek
Stefan Gulan	Giancarlo Mauri	Sandor Vagvolgyi
Yo-Sub Han	Katja Meckel	Lynette Van Zijl
Szabolcs Ivan	Nelma Moreira	György Vaszil
Sebastian Jakobi	Zoltan L. Nemeth	Claudio Zandron
Tomasz Jurdzinski	Dana Pardubska	
Lakshmanan Kuppusamy	Xiaoxue Piao	

Sponsoring Institutions

Universität Giessen

Table of Contents

Invited Papers

Regular Papers

Linear Algebra Based Bounds for One-Dimensional Cellular Automata

Jarkko Kari[*]

Department of Mathematics, University of Turku
FI-20014 Turku, Finland
jkari@utu.fi

Abstract. One possible complexity measure for a cellular automaton is the size of its neighborhood. If a cellular automaton is reversible with a small neighborhood, the inverse automaton may need a much larger neighborhood. Our interest is to find good upper bounds for the size of this inverse neighborhood. It turns out that a linear algebra approach provides better bounds than any known combinatorial methods. We also consider cellular automata that are not surjective. In this case there must exist so-called orphans, finite patterns without a pre-image. The length of the shortest orphan measures the degree of non-surjectiveness of the map. Again, a linear algebra approach provides better bounds on this length than known combinatorial methods. We also use linear algebra to bound the minimum lengths of any diamond and any word with a non-balanced number of pre-images. These both exist when the cellular automaton in question is not surjective. All our results deal with one-dimensional cellular automata. Undecidability results imply that in higher dimensional cases no computable upper bound exists for any of the considered quantities.

A one-dimensional *cellular automaton* (CA) over a finite alphabet A is a transformation $F : A^{\mathbb{Z}} \longrightarrow A^{\mathbb{Z}}$ that is defined by a local update rule $f : A^m \longrightarrow A$ applied uniformly across the cellular space $\mathbb{Z}$. Bi-infinite sequences $c \in A^{\mathbb{Z}}$ are *configurations*. For every *cell* $i \in \mathbb{Z}$, the *state* $c(i) \in A$ will be denoted by c_i. The local rule is applied at all cells simultaneously on the pattern around the cell to get the state of the cell in the next configuration: For all $c \in A^{\mathbb{Z}}$ and $i \in \mathbb{Z}$

$$F(c)_i = f(c_{i+k}, c_{i+k+1}, \dots, c_{i+k+m-1}). \tag{1}$$

Here, $k \in \mathbb{Z}$ is a constant offset and m is the *range* of the neighborhood $\{k, k+1, \dots, k+m-1\}$ of the CA.

The case of the smallest non-trivial range $m = 2$ is termed the *radius-$\frac{1}{2}$* neighborhood. Any neighborhood range m can be simulated by a radius-$\frac{1}{2}$ neighborhood by blocking segments of $m-1$ cells into "super cells" that take their values over the alphabet A^{m-1}. Therefore we mostly consider the radius-$\frac{1}{2}$ case.

Cellular automata are much studied complex systems and models of massively parallel computation. Viewing them as discrete dynamical systems often involves

---

[*] Research supported by the Academy of Finland Grant 131558.

M. Holzer, M. Kutrib, and G. Pighizzini (Eds.): DCFS 2011, LNCS 6808, pp. 1–7, 2011.
© Springer-Verlag Berlin Heidelberg 2011

considering a natural compact topology on the configuration space $A^{\mathbb{Z}}$. The topology is defined by a subbase consisting of sets $\mathcal{S}_{a,i}$ of configurations that assign a fixed state $a \in A$ in a fixed cell $i \in \mathbb{Z}$. Cellular automata transformations are continuous under this topology. Also the converse is true: cellular automata maps are precisely those transformations $A^{\mathbb{Z}} \longrightarrow A^{\mathbb{Z}}$ that are continuous and that commute with translations [1].

Cellular automaton $F : A^{\mathbb{Z}} \longrightarrow A^{\mathbb{Z}}$ is called *reversible* if it is bijective and the inverse function is also a CA. A compactness argument directly implies that for bijective CA the inverse function is automatically a CA. It is also easy to see that an injective CA function is automatically surjective, so reversibility, bijectivity and injectivity are equivalent concepts on CA. If a cellular automaton is not surjective then there exist configurations without a pre-image, known as *Garden-Of-Eden* configurations.

An application of a range m local CA rule on a finite word of length l yields – by applying (1) in the obvious way – a word of length $l - m + 1$. Compactness of $A^{\mathbb{Z}}$ implies that in non-surjective CA there must exist finite words without a pre-image, so that an occurrence of such a word in a configuration forces the configuration to be a Garden-Of-Eden. We call these words *orphans*. One can also prove that in surjective one-dimensional CA all finite words have exactly $|A|^{m-1}$ pre-images. In measure theoretic terms this *balance* property states that the uniform Borel measure is preserved by all surjective CA. We see that all non-surjective CA have *unbalanced* words whose number of pre-images is different from the average $|A|^{m-1}$. Clearly, there is a word of length l with too many pre-images if and only if there is another one with too few pre-images.

A pair of configurations $c, e \in A^{\mathbb{Z}}$ is called *asymptotic* if the set $diff(c, e) = \{i \in \mathbb{Z} \mid c_i \neq e_i\}$ of cells where they differ, is finite. A CA is *pre-injective* if no two distinct asymptotic configurations can have the same image. The celebrated *Garden-Of-Eden-theorem* by Moore and Myhill states that a cellular automaton is surjective if and only it is pre-injective [6,7]. In particular, a non-surjective, radius-$\frac{1}{2}$ cellular automaton has a *diamond*: a pair aub and avb of distinct words of equal length ($u \neq v$ and $|u| = |v|$) that begin and end in identical states $a, b \in A$, and that are mapped to the same word by the CA. We define the *length* of the diamond to be the common length of the words u and v.

These fundamental concepts and results can be extended to higher dimensional CA, where the cellular space $\mathbb{Z}$ is replaced by $\mathbb{Z}^d$, for dimension d. See [3] for more basic facts about cellular automata.

The topological approach outlined above provides the existence of the following values. Consider the set $CA(n)$ of radius-$\frac{1}{2}$ cellular automata with n states. Let

- $inv(n)$ denote the smallest number m such that the inverse map of every reversible CA in $CA(n)$ can be defined using range-m neighborhood,
- $bal(n)$ denote the smallest number l such that every non-surjective CA in $CA(n)$ has an unbalanced word of length l,
- $orph(n)$ denote the smallest number l such that every non-surjective CA in $CA(n)$ has an orphan of length l, and

- $diam(n)$ denote the smallest number l such that every non-surjective CA in $CA(n)$ has a diamond of length l.

The topological approach, however, does not provide any upper bound on these numbers, nor any means of computing them. In fact, in two- and higher dimensional spaces the analogous values exist by similar topological arguments, but the undecidability of the injectivity and surjectivity properties of two-dimensional CA [2] implies that none of these can be bounded by any computable function in the two-dimensional set up.

We discuss bounding the values in the one-dimensional case. A classic approach is based on de Bruijn -representations of one-dimensional CA [8]. This method, however, only provides quadratic bounds on $inv(n)$, and $diam(n)$, and an exponential bound on $orph(n)$. A linear algebra based approach was introduced in [4,5] that easily provides

$$inv(n) \leq n - 1,$$
$$bal(n) \leq n,$$
$$orph(n) \leq n^2, \text{ and}$$
$$diam(n) \leq 2n\lfloor\sqrt{n}\rfloor - 2n + 2.$$

The bound $n - 1$ of $inv(n)$ is known to be tight [4], but the other three bounds are not tight: small improvements for $orph(n)$ and $diam(n)$ were provided in [5]. Exhaustive computer search shows that for $n = 2, 3, 4$ we have $orph(n) = 2n - 1$ and $diam(n) = bal(n) = n - 1$, and it remains an interesting open problem to see whether these formula extend to all n.

1 De Bruijn -Graph Based Bounds

This section briefly outlines the combinatorial methods based on de Bruijn - graphs. See [8] for more details.

The de Bruijn -graph representation of a one-dimensional cellular automaton over the alphabet A and with neighborhood range $m \geq 2$ is a directed graph with vertex set $V = A^{m-1}$ and edge set $E = A^m$. For every $a, b \in A$ and $u \in A^{m-2}$ the edge aub is from vertex au into vertex ub. Note that in the case $m = 2$, the graph has $n = |A|$ vertices and the full edge set. We assign each edge aub two labels from the alphabet: the input label $i(aub) = a$ and the output label $o(aub) = f(aub)$ where f is the local update rule of the CA. For a bi-infinite path $p \in E^{\mathbb{Z}}$ in the graph, we denote by $i(p) \in A^{\mathbb{Z}}$ (by $o(p)$, respectively) the sequences of input labels (output labels, respectively) along path p. It is clear that i provides then a bijective correspondence between $A^{\mathbb{Z}}$ and the bi-infinite paths in the graph. The edges along the path represent the views in the corresponding configuration through a window of width m that slides over the configuration. The output labeling o provides the image under the CA function of this configuration, possibly shifted by fixed amount k which is given by the offset of the neighborhood of the CA, as in (1).

It is now clear that the de Bruijn -graph representation and the output labeling of the edges is a non-deterministic finite automaton (NFA) that recognizes precisely those words that are not orphans. All vertices are taken as initial and final states. The NFA can be determinized and complemented to make it recognize orphans. However, in the worst case, determinizing an NFA may increase the number of states exponentially, so that the upper bound that can be obtained on the length of the shortest orphan (that is, the shortest word not accepted by the NFA) is exponential on the number of vertices.

To recognize diamonds and to test reversibility, a *pair graph* is used. The pair graph is obtained by taking the intersection of the de Bruijn automaton with itself: Its vertex set is $V \times V$, and for any two edges $u_1 \longrightarrow v_1$ and $u_2 \longrightarrow v_2$ whose output label is the same $a \in A$ we put the edge $(u_1, u_1) \longrightarrow (v_1, v_2)$ in the pair graph, and label the new edge with a. States $(v, v) \in V \times V$ are called the *diagonal states*. It is easy to see that the CA is not reversible if and only if the pair graph contains a cycle through a non-diagonal state, and it is not pre-injective if and only if it contains a cycle that goes through a diagonal and a non-diagonal node. In the latter case, the cycle provides a diamond of the CA. Hence the number of vertices in the pair graph provides an upper bound on the length of the shortest diamond. In the case of $m = 2$, this number is quadratic on the number of states.

If the CA is non-reversible, then the longest path that contains at most one diagonal vertex gives the neighborhood range of the inverse CA. Again, in the $m = 2$ case, the upper bound we obtain for this number is quadratic on the number of states.

Observe that the de Bruijn -graph methods outlined above provide fast, polynomial time algorithms to determine if a given one-dimensional CA is injective or surjective. The method also provides a polynomial time algorithm to find a diamond in a non-surjective CA, but not any fast method for finding an orphan.

2   The Linear Algebra Approach

Let $n = |A|$ so that we can denote $A = \{1, 2, \ldots, n\}$, and let us assume that the CA has neighborhood range $m = 2$. Our linear algebra approach is based on viewing sets of states as n-dimensional 0/1-vectors. We associate to a set $X \subseteq A$ the vector $\boldsymbol{X} = (x_1, x_2, \ldots, x_n)$ where $x_i = 1$ for $i \in X$ and $x_i = 0$ otherwise. Let $\boldsymbol{e}_i$ be the i'th unit coordinate vector associated to the singleton set $\{i\}$, and let $\boldsymbol{1} = (1, 1, \ldots, 1)$. Finally, we denote by $w : \mathbb{R}^n \longrightarrow \mathbb{R}$ the linear functional $w(x_1, x_2, \ldots, x_n) = x_1 + x_2 + \cdots + x_n$, and we call $w(\boldsymbol{x})$ the *weight* of vector $\boldsymbol{x}$. Clearly, for any set $X \subseteq A$ the weight of the corresponding vector $\boldsymbol{X}$ is the same as the cardinality of the set X.

To each $a \in A$ we associate the linear transformation ψ_a that maps $\boldsymbol{e}_i \mapsto \boldsymbol{X}_i$ where $X_i = \{b \in A \mid f(i, b) = a\}$. Compositions of linear transformations ψ_a are denoted as follows: For any word $u = a_1 a_2 \ldots a_j$ we write ψ_u for the composition $\psi_{a_1} \circ \psi_{a_2} \circ \cdots \circ \psi_{a_j}$, where the functions are applied in the left-to-right order.

Now it is easy to see that $\psi_u(\boldsymbol{e}_i) = (x_1, x_2, \ldots x_n)$ where x_j is the number of pre-images of word u that begin with state $i \in A$ and end in state $j \in A$. In particular, if $x_j > 1$ there is a diamond beginning and ending in states i and j, respectively, whose image is word u. The length of the diamond is then $|u| - 1$. It also follows that the weight of $\psi_u(\mathbf{1})$ is the same as the number of pre-images of word u. Hence u is unbalanced if and only if the weight of $\psi_u(\mathbf{1})$ is different from n, and u is an orphan if and only if $\psi_u(\mathbf{1})$ is the zero vector.

The following two simple lemmas are all we need in order to obtain small bounds on the lengths of the orphans, unbalanced words and diamonds [5]:

Lemma 1. *Let $V \subseteq \mathbb{R}^n$ be an affine space of dimension d, let ψ_a be linear transformations $\mathbb{R}^n \longrightarrow \mathbb{R}^n$ for all $a \in A$, and let $\mathbf{x} \in V$ be such that there exists a word u with the property $\psi_u(\mathbf{x}) \notin V$. Then there exists such a word u whose length is at most $d + 1$.* □

Lemma 2. *Let ψ_a be the linear transformations associated to a CA over the alphabet A and let $\mathbf{x} \in \mathbb{R}^n$ and $u \in A^*$ be such that the weights of $\mathbf{x}$ and $\psi_u(\mathbf{x})$ are not the same. Then there exist words u' and u'' that have the same length as u such that the weights of $\psi_{u'}(\mathbf{x})$ and $\psi_{u''}(\mathbf{x})$ are strictly less and strictly greater than the weight of $\mathbf{x}$, respectively.* □

The second lemma follows from the fact that for every $i, j \in A$ there is precisely one $a \in A$ such that $f(i, j) = a$. So the average weight of vectors $\psi_a(\mathbf{x})$ over all $a \in A$ is the same as the weight of $\mathbf{x}$.

Consider now the $(n-1)$-dimensional affine spaces V_r consisting of all vectors of weight r. Recall that $\mathbf{1} \in V_n$, and that a word u is balanced if and only if $\psi_u(\mathbf{1})$ is in V_n. A non-surjective CA has some unbalanced words, so by Lemma 1 there is an unbalanced word of length at most $\dim V_n + 1 = n$. We have that

$$bal(n) \leq n.$$

To find a short orphan one finds a word u_1 of length at most n such that the weight of $\mathbf{x}_1 = \psi_{u_1}(\mathbf{1})$ is strictly less than n. Such a word exists by Lemmas 1 and 2. Since $\mathbf{x}_1$ is an integer vector, we have that the weight of $\mathbf{x}_1$ is at most $n - 1$. Repeat the reasoning on vector $\mathbf{x}_1$ in place of $\mathbf{1}$, and observe that there exists a word u_2 of length at most n such that the weight of $\mathbf{x}_2 = \psi_{u_1}(\mathbf{x}_1)$ is at most $n - 2$. After $j \leq n$ steps we reach a vector $\mathbf{x}_j$ whose weight is at most zero, so that $\mathbf{x}_j$ is the zero vector. The concatenation $u_1 u_2 \ldots u_j$ of the discovered words is then an orphan of length at most n^2. We have that

$$orph(n) \leq n^2.$$

It is easy to see [5] that the described process also provides a polynomial-time algorithm to find an orphan of length at most n^2. The discovered orphan, however, is not necessarily the shortest orphan for the CA.

To find a bound on the length of the shortest diamond we begin with $\mathbf{x} = \psi_a(\mathbf{e}_i)$ that has non-zero values in more than one coordinate position. Such $i, a \in A$ necessarily exist if the CA is non-surjective. We now use Lemmas 1 and 2 to find words that increment the weight of the vector $\mathbf{x}$ step by step, and observe that there exists a word u of length at most $l = n(\lfloor \sqrt{n} \rfloor - 1)$ such that either $\psi_u(\mathbf{x})$ is not a 0/1-vector (in which case there exists a diamond whose image is the word au), or $\psi_u(\boldsymbol{x})$ is a 0/1-vector whose weight is greater than $\sqrt{n}$. In the latter case, there is a collection of more than $\sqrt{n}$ words v ending in different letters such that the CA maps all iv into the same word au.

Analogously, working to the opposite direction from some $\boldsymbol{e}_j$ and a suitable last letter b, we find a word u' of length at most l such that either there is a diamond whose image is $u'b$, or there are more than $\sqrt{n}$ words v' that begin with different letters such that the CA maps all $v'j$ into the same word $u'b$.

Combining the latter cases, we can see that some pair of words $ivv'j$ must be a diamond: there are more than n pairs $(c,d) \in A^2$ such that some v word ends in letter c and some v' word ends in letter d. So there are two different pairs (c_1, d_1) and (c_2, d_2) with the same image $f(c_1, d_1) = f(c_2, d_2)$. Then $iv_1v_1'j$ and $iv_2v_2'j$ form a diamond, where v_1, v_2 and v_1', v_2' are the discovered words that end in c_1, c_2 and begin with d_1, d_2, respectively. The length of this diamond is at most $2l + 2$, showing that

$$diam(n) \leq 2n\lfloor \sqrt{n} \rfloor - 2n + 2.$$

The linear algebra techniques to bound $inv(n)$ are slightly different, and require some additional concepts. Now we assume the cellular automaton is reversible and has neighborhood range $m = 2$. For any word u, let us denote by L_u and R_u the sets of states that appear as the leftmost symbol and the rightmost symbol, respectively, of some pre-images of u. It follows from reversibility that for sufficiently large integers l and r we have that $L_u \cap R_v$ is a singleton for all $u \in A^l$ and all $v \in A^r$. Let us take r and l to be the smallest such integers. Clearly, the inverse CA can then use neighborhood range $l + r$. The sets L_u for $u \in A^l$ are called the *left Welch sets* and the sets R_v for $v \in A^r$ are the *right Welch sets* of the CA. One can easily infer (see [1]) that all left Welch sets (all right Welch sets) have the same cardinality w_L, called the *left Welch index* (w_R, called *right Welch index*, respectively). Moreover, $w_L w_R = n$.

Let $\mathcal{L}$ and $\mathcal{R}$ denote the collections of all left and right Welch sets, respectively. As above, we denote by $\boldsymbol{L}$ and $\boldsymbol{R}$ the 0/1-vectors corresponding to sets $L \in \mathcal{L}$ and $R \in \mathcal{R}$. One can easily see that r is the smallest number such that $\psi_u(\boldsymbol{R_1}) = \psi_u(\boldsymbol{R_2})$, for all $u \in A^r$ and all $R_1, R_2 \in \mathcal{R}$. Similar observation holds for the number l. Let us consider the vector spaces V_i that are generated by vectors $\psi_u(\boldsymbol{R_1}) - \psi_u(\boldsymbol{R_2})$ over $u \in A^i$ and all $R_1, R_2 \in \mathcal{R}$. Then

- $V_0 \supseteq V_1 \supseteq V_2 \supseteq \ldots$,
- $V_r = \{\boldsymbol{0}\}$, and
- if $V_{k+1} = V_k$ then $V_{k+i} = V_k$ for all $i \geq 0$,

from which we can infer that $r \leq \dim V_0$. See [4] for the detailed proofs of these facts. Analogous consideration can be done on the left to conclude that l is not greater that the dimension of the space U_0 generated by the vectors $\boldsymbol{L_1} - \boldsymbol{L_2}$, over all $L_1, L_2 \in \mathcal{L}$. Our final observation, based on the properties of the Welch sets, is that spaces U_0 and V_0 are orthogonal to each other and to the vector

1. Indeed, the inner product of generators $L_1 - L_2$ and $R_1 - R_2$ of U_0 and V_0, respectively, is

$$(L_1 - L_2) \cdot (R_1 - R_2) = L_1 \cdot R_1 - L_2 \cdot R_1 - L_1 \cdot R_2 + L_2 \cdot R_2 = 1 - 1 - 1 + 1 = 0.$$

Here we used the fact that, because the intersections of left and right Welch sets are singletons, $L \cdot R = 1$ for all $L \in \mathcal{L}$ and $R \in \mathcal{R}$. The inner product of the generator $R_1 - R_2$ with 1 is $w_R - w_R = 0$, and analogously we see that $L_1 - L_2$ is orthogonal to 1. This means that

$$r + l \leq \dim V_0 + \dim U_0 \leq n - 1,$$

so that

$$inv(n) \leq n - 1.$$

3   Conclusions

It remains an interesting problem to determine the exact values of $bal(n)$, $orph(n)$ and $diam(n)$. In [5] we provided a family of CA that verifies $orph(n) \geq 2n - 1$ for all n, and we conjectured that, in fact, $orph(n) = 2n - 1$. Computer search confirms this for $n = 2, 3$ and 4. As for $bal(n)$ and $diam(n)$, we are not aware of a non-constant lower bounds but we conjecture that both values are equal to $n - 1$.

References

1. Hedlund, G.: Endomorphisms and automorphisms of shift dynamical systems. Mathematical Systems Theory 3, 320–375 (1969)
2. Kari, J.: Reversibility and surjectivity problems of cellular automata. Journal of Computer and System Sciences 48, 149–182 (1994)
3. Kari, J.: Theory of Cellular Automata: a survey. Theoretical Computer Science 334, 3–33 (2005)
4. Czeizler, E., Kari, J.: A tight linear bound on the neighborhood of inverse cellular automata. In: Caires, L., Italiano, G.F., Monteiro, L., Palamidessi, C., Yung, M. (eds.) ICALP 2005. LNCS, vol. 3580, pp. 410–420. Springer, Heidelberg (2005)
5. Kari, J., Vanier, P., Zeume, T.: Bounds on non-surjective cellular automata. In: Královič, R., Niwiński, D. (eds.) MFCS 2009. LNCS, vol. 5734, pp. 439–450. Springer, Heidelberg (2009)
6. Moore, E.F.: Machine Models of Self-reproduction. In: Proceedings of the Symposium in Applied Mathematics, vol. 14, pp. 17–33 (1962)
7. Myhill, J.: The Converse to Moore's Garden-of-Eden Theorem. Proceedings of the American Mathematical Society, 14, 685–686 (1963)
8. Sutner, K.: De Bruijn Graphs and Linear Cellular Automata. Complex Systems 5, 19–30 (1991)

On Restarting Automata with Window Size One*

Friedrich Otto

Fachbereich Elektrotechnik, Informatik
Universität Kassel, 34109 Kassel, Germany
otto@theory.informatik.uni-kassel.de

Abstract. The *restarting automaton* is a machine model that is motivated by the technique of *analysis by reduction* from linguistics. It consists of a finite-state control, a flexible tape with end markers and a read/write window of fixed size. This paper begins with a short description of the general model of the restarting automaton and its major variants. In particular, the question for the influence of the size of the *read/write window* on the expressive power of the various types of restarting automata is addressed. The main part then focuses on the weakest model of the restarting automaton and its variants: the so-called R-*automaton* with a read/write window of size one (R(1)-automaton for short). It is well-known that R(1)-automata only accept regular languages, but it will be shown that several seemingly rather powerful extensions have just the same expressive power. Accordingly it is of interest to study the descriptional complexity of these types of restarting automata in relation to the R(1)-automata on the one hand and the (deterministic and nondeterministic) finite-state acceptors on the other hand. Then various types of cooperating distributed systems (CD-systems) of deterministic R(1)-automata are presented. If all components of such a system are stateless, then the language accepted by the system has a semi-linear Parikh image, and actually the rational trace languages and the context-free trace languages have been characterized in terms of certain CD-systems of stateless deterministic R(1)-automata. Also for these devices the question for their descriptional complexity will be addressed in short.

Keywords: Restarting automaton, stateless device, cooperating distributed system, language hierarchy, descriptional complexity.

1 Introduction

Analysis by reduction is a technique used in linguistics to analyze sentences of natural languages that have a free word order [52,53]. This analysis consists of a stepwise simplification of a sentence in such a way that the syntactical correctness or incorrectness of the sentence is not affected. After a finite number

---

* This paper reports on joint work with Norbert Hundeshagen from the University of Kassel and Benedek Nagy from the University of Debrecen.

M. Holzer, M. Kutrib, and G. Pighizzini (Eds.): DCFS 2011, LNCS 6808, pp. 8–33, 2011.
© Springer-Verlag Berlin Heidelberg 2011

of steps either a correct simple sentence is obtained, or an error is detected. In the former case the given sentence is accepted as being syntactically correct; if, however, all possible sequences of simplifications yield errors, then the given sentence is not syntactically correct. In this way it is also possible to determine dependencies between various parts of the given sentence, and to disambiguate between certain morphological ambiguities contained in the sentence.

A generative device capable of simulating the analysis by reduction is the *sorted dependency 1-contextual grammar with regular selectors* by Gramatovici and Martín-Vide [15], which combines the *contextual grammars* of Marcus (see, e.g., [13,31]) with dependency grammars (see, e.g., [12]).

As illustrated by Jančar et al. (cf., e.g., [25]) the restarting automaton was invented to model the analysis by reduction. As defined in [22] the *restarting automaton* is a nondeterministic machine model that processes strings which are stored on a flexible tape (or in a list) with end markers. It has a finite-state control, and it has a read/write window of fixed size that is working on the list of symbols. As such it can be seen as a modification of the *list automaton* presented in [7] and the *forgetting automaton* [20,21]. However, the restarting automaton can only perform two kinds of operations: *move-right transitions*, which shift the read/write window one position to the right, thereby changing the actual state, and combined *delete/restart transitions*, which delete some symbols from the read/write window, place this window over the left end of the tape, and put the automaton back into its initial state. Hence, after performing a delete/restart transition a restarting automaton has no way to remember that it has already performed some steps of a computation. Further, by each application of a delete/restart transition the tape is shortened. In this aspect the restarting automaton is similar to the *contraction automaton* [55]. It follows that restarting automata are linearly space-bounded.

Subsequently Jančar et al. extended their model in various ways. Instead of simply deleting some symbols from the actual content of the read/write window during a delete/restart transition, a restarting automaton *with rewriting* has combined *rewrite/restart* transitions that replace the content of the read/write window by a shorter string [23]. Further, the use of auxiliary (that is, non-input) symbols was added to the model in [24], which yields the so-called RWW-*automaton*. Also in [24] the restart transition was separated from the rewrite transition so that, after performing a rewrite step, the automaton can still read the remaining part of the tape before performing a restart transition. This gives the so-called RRWW-*automaton*, which is required to execute exactly one rewrite transition between any two restart transitions. In addition, various notions of *monotonicity* have been discussed for the various types of restarting automata. It turned out that monotone RWW- and RRWW-automata accept exactly the context-free languages, and that all the various types of monotone deterministic RWW- and RRWW-automata accept exactly the deterministic context-free languages. Finally, the deterministic RWW- and RRWW-automata characterize the so-called *Church-Rosser languages* [46,48]. In [17,18] the descriptional complexity of deterministic RWW- and RRWW-automata was studied, establishing non-recursive trade-offs from nondeterministic pushdown automata to deterministic RWW- and RRWW-automata and vice versa.

Many parameters have been studied for various types of restarting automata, restricting the form of the rewrite operations or the use of auxiliary symbols (see, e.g., [39,54]). One parameter that is of interest to us is the size of the read/write window. Already in 2001 Mráz proved that for all types of restarting automata without auxiliary symbols, the size of the read/write window induces an infinite strictly increasing hierarchy of language classes [38]. For restarting automata with window size 1, auxiliary symbols are useless, as each rewrite operation simply deletes a single letter. In fact, R-automata with window size 1, denoted as R(1)-automata, and deterministic RR-automata with window size 1, denoted as det-RR(1)-automata, only accept regular languages [29,30,38], while already monotone RR(1)- and deterministic R(2)-automata accept non-regular languages. In [29,30] the descriptional complexity of R(1)- and deterministic RR(1)-automata is studied, establishing an exponential trade-off between these types of restarting automata and finite-state acceptors.

In the present paper we will proceed as follows. After introducing the main variants of the restarting automaton in Section 2, we concentrate on restarting automata with window size 1 in Section 3. Then we consider an extension of the restarting automaton, the so-called *nonforgetting* restarting automaton (with window size 1) in Section 4. Such an automaton behaves like a standard restarting automaton with the one exception that a restart operation is combined with a change of the internal state just like the move-right and rewrite operations. Nonforgetting restarting automata were introduced by Messerschmidt and Stamer in [37]. They were studied in more detail in [33], and in [34,35,36] they are shown to be closely related to the so-called *cooperating distributed systems* (CD-systems) of restarting automata. Here we present a recent result showing that monotone nonforgetting R(1)- and monotone deterministic nonforgetting RR(1)-automata only accept regular languages, while deterministic nonforgetting R(1)-automata that are not monotone are already much more expressive. Finally in Section 5 we consider CD-systems of deterministic R(1)-automata that are *stateless*, that is, each of these automata has a single state only. Stateless types of restarting automata were first studied in [27,28], and in [41] CD-systems of stateless deterministic R(1)-automata were introduced. Here we present the main results on these CD-systems, address in short the question for their descriptional complexity, and also present some recent extentions of these systems.

2   Restarting Automata

As indicated above a restarting automaton is a nondeterministic machine that has a finite-state control and a read/write window that works on a list of symbols delimited by end markers. Formally, a *restarting automaton*, RRWW-automaton for short, is a one-tape machine that is described by an 8-tuple $M = (Q, \Sigma, \Gamma, \mathmissing{c}, \$, q_0, k, \delta)$. Here Q is a finite set of states, Σ is a finite input alphabet, Γ is a finite tape alphabet containing Σ, the symbols $\mathic{c}, \$ \notin \Gamma$

serve as markers for the left and right border of the work space, respectively, $q_0 \in Q$ is the initial state, $k \in \mathbb{N}_+$ is the size of the *read/write window*, and δ is a *transition relation* that assigns finite sets of possible transitions to pairs of the form (q, u), where $q \in Q$ is a state and u is a possible contents of the read/write window. There are four different types of transition steps:

(1) A *move-right step* is of the form $(q', \mathsf{MVR}) \in \delta(q, u)$, where $q' \in Q$. It causes M to shift its read/write window one position to the right and to enter state q'. However, if the content u of the read/write window is only the symbol \$, then no shift to the right is possible.

(2) A *rewrite step* is of the form $(q', v) \in \delta(q, u)$, where $q' \in Q$ and $|v| < |u|$. It causes M to replace the content u of the read/write window by the string v, and to enter state q'. Further, the read/write window is placed immediately to the right of the string v. However, some additional restrictions apply in that the border markers ¢ and \$ must not disappear from the tape nor that new occurrences of these markers are created. Further, the read/write window must not move across the right border marker \$.

(3) A *restart step* is of the form $\mathsf{Restart} \in \delta(q, u)$. It causes M to move its read/write window to the left end of the tape, so that the first symbol it sees is the left border marker ¢, and to reenter the initial state q_0.

(4) An *accept step* is of the form $\mathsf{Accept} \in \delta(q, u)$. It causes M to halt and accept.

If $\delta(q, u) = \emptyset$ for some pair (q, u), then M necessarily halts, and we say that M *rejects* in this situation. The letters in $\Gamma \setminus \Sigma$ are called *auxiliary symbols*.

A *configuration* of M is a string $\alpha q \beta$, where $q \in Q$, and either $\alpha = \lambda$ (the empty word) and $\beta \in \{¢\} \cdot \Gamma^* \cdot \{\$\}$ or $\alpha \in \{¢\} \cdot \Gamma^*$ and $\beta \in \Gamma^* \cdot \{\$\}$; here $q \in Q$ represents the current state, $\alpha\beta$ is the current content of the tape, and it is understood that the read/write window contains the first k symbols of β or all of β when $|\beta| \leq k$. A *restarting configuration* is of the form $q_0 ¢ w \$$, where $w \in \Gamma^*$; if $w \in \Sigma^*$, then $q_0 ¢ w \$$ is an *initial configuration*. Thus, initial configurations are a particular type of restarting configurations. Further, we use Accept to denote *accepting configurations*, which are those configurations that M reaches by executing an accept instruction. A configuration of the form $\alpha q \beta$ such that $\delta(q, \beta_1) = \emptyset$, where β_1 is the current content of the read/write window, is a *rejecting configuration*. A *halting configuration* is either an accepting or a rejecting configuration.

In general, the automaton M is *nondeterministic*, that is, there can be two or more instructions with the same left-hand side (q, u), and thus, there can be more than one computation for an input word. If this is not the case, the automaton is *deterministic*. We use the prefix det- to denote deterministic types of restarting automata.

We observe that any finite computation of a restarting automaton M consists of certain phases. A phase, called a *cycle*, starts in a restarting configuration, the head moves along the tape performing move-right and rewrite operations until a restart operation is performed and thus a new restarting configuration is reached. If no further restart operation is performed, any finite computation necessarily finishes in a halting configuration – such a phase is called a *tail*. We require that M performs *exactly one* rewrite operation during any cycle – thus each new phase starts on a shorter word than the previous one. During a tail at most one rewrite operation may be executed. By $x \vdash^c_M y$ we denote the execution of a cycle that transforms the restarting configuration $q_0 \mathrm{c} x \$$ into the restarting configuration $q_0 \mathrm{c} y \$$, and $\vdash^{c*}_M$ is the reflexive transitive closure of this relation. It can be seen as the *rewrite relation* on Γ^* that is realized by M.

An input $w \in \Sigma^*$ is accepted by M, if there exists a computation of M which starts with the initial configuration $q_0 \mathrm{c} w \$$, and which finally ends with executing an accept instruction. By

$$L(M) = \{\, w \in \Sigma^* \mid M \text{ has an accepting computation on input } w \,\}$$

we denote the *(input) language* of M. Given an input of length n, an RRWW-automaton can execute at most n cycles. Thus, we have the following result, where NP and P denote the well-known complexity classes, and DCSL denotes the class of *deterministic context-sensitive languages*, that is, the space complexity class DSPACE(n). Further, for a type X of restarting automaton, $\mathcal{L}(\mathsf{X})$ denotes the class of input languages that are accepted by X-automata.

Proposition 1. (a) $\mathcal{L}(\mathsf{RRWW}) \subseteq \mathsf{NP} \cap \mathsf{CSL}$.

(b) $\mathcal{L}(\mathsf{det\text{-}RRWW}) \subseteq \mathsf{P} \cap \mathsf{DCSL}$.

Next we restate some basic facts about computations of restarting automata. These facts are often used in proofs.

Proposition 2. (Error Preserving Property)
Let $M = (Q, \Sigma, \Gamma, \mathrm{c}, \$, q_0, k, \delta)$ be an RRWW-automaton, and let x, y be words over its input alphabet Σ. If $x \vdash^{c*}_M y$ holds and $x \notin L(M)$, then $y \notin L(M)$, either.

Proposition 3. (Correctness Preserving Property)
Let $M = (Q, \Sigma, \Gamma, \mathrm{c}, \$, q_0, k, \delta)$ be an RRWW-automaton, and let x, y be words over its input alphabet Σ. If $x \vdash^{c*}_M y$ is an initial segment of an accepting computation of M, then $y \in L(M)$.

Also the following fact is very useful in proofs.

Proposition 4. (Pumping Lemma)
For any RRWW-automaton $M = (Q, \Sigma, \Gamma, \mathrm{c}, \$, q_0, k, \delta)$, there exists a constant p such that the following holds. Assume that $uvw \vdash^c_M uv'w$, where $u = u_1 u_2 u_3$ and $|u_2| = p$. Then there exists a factorization $u_2 = z_1 z_2 z_3$ such that z_2 is non-empty, and

$$u_1 z_1 (z_2)^i z_3 u_3 v w \vdash^c_M u_1 z_1 (z_2)^i z_3 u_3 v' w$$

holds for all $i \geq 0$, that is, z_2 is a 'pumping factor' in the above cycle. Similarly, such a pumping factor can be found in any factor of length p of w. Such a pumping factor can also be found in any factor of length p of a word accepted in a tail computation.

Based on the fact that each cycle (and also the tail) of a computation of an RRWW-automaton can be seen to consist of three phases, the transition relation of an RRWW-automaton can be described through so-called *meta-instructions* [47] of the form $(E_1, u \to v, E_2)$, where E_1 and E_2 are regular languages, called the *regular constraints* of this instruction, and u and v are strings such that $|u| > |v|$. The rule $u \to v$ stands for a rewrite step of the RRWW-automaton M considered. On trying to execute this meta-instruction M will get stuck (and so reject) starting from the restarting configuration $q_0 \text{¢} w \$$, if w does not admit a factorization of the form $w = w_1 u w_2$ such that $\text{¢} w_1 \in E_1$ and $w_2 \$ \in E_2$. On the other hand, if w does have a factorization of this form, then one such factorization is chosen nondeterministically, and $q_0 \text{¢} w \$$ is transformed into $q_0 \text{¢} w_1 v w_2 \$$. In order to describe the tails of accepting computations we use meta-instructions of the form $(\text{¢} \cdot E \cdot \$, \mathsf{Accept})$, where the strings from the regular language E are accepted by M in tail computations.

Finally, we introduce some restricted types of restarting automata. A restarting automaton is called an **RWW-***automaton* if it makes a restart immediately after performing a rewrite operation. In particular, this means that it cannot perform a rewrite step during the tail of a computation. A cycle of a computation of an RWW-automaton M consists of two phases only. Accordingly, the transition relation of an RWW-automaton can be described by *meta-instructions* of the form $(E, u \to v)$, where E is a regular language, and u and v are strings such that $|u| > |v|$, and meta-instructions of the form $(\text{¢} \cdot E \cdot \$, \mathsf{Accept})$ for describing tail computations.

An RRWW-automaton is called an **RRW-***automaton* if its tape alphabet Γ coincides with its input alphabet Σ, that is, if no auxiliary symbols are available. It is an **RR-***automaton* if it is an RRW-automaton for which each rewrite step $(q', v) \in \delta(q, u)$ satisfies the property that v is a scattered subword of u. Analogously, we obtain RW- and R-automata from the RWW-automaton.

Let M be an RRWW-automaton. Each computation of M can be described by a sequence of cycles $C_1, C_2 \ldots, C_n$, where C_n is the last cycle, which is followed by the tail of the computation. Each cycle C_i of this computation contains a unique configuration of the form $\text{¢} x q u y \$$ such that q is a state and $(q', v) \in \delta(q, u)$ is the rewrite step that is applied during this cycle. By $D_r(C_i)$ we denote the *right distance* $|u y \$|$ of this cycle. The sequence of cycles $C_1, C_2, \ldots, C_n$ is called *monotone* if $D_r(C_1) \geq D_r(C_2) \geq \cdots \geq D_r(C_n)$ holds. A computation of M is called *monotone* if the corresponding sequence of cycles is monotone. Observe that the tail of the computation is not taken into account here. Finally, the RRWW-automaton M itself is called *monotone* if each of its computations that starts from an initial configuration is monotone. We use the prefix mon- to denote monotone types of restarting automata.

The following fundamental results have been obtained on the expressive power of restarting automata with auxiliary symbols. Here CRL denotes the class of Church-Rosser languages [32], and GCSL is the class of growing context-sensitive languages [9].

Theorem 5. [25,26,46,48]

(a) $\mathcal{L}(\text{det-mon-R}) = \mathcal{L}(\text{det-mon-RRWW}) = $ DCFL.
(b) $\mathcal{L}(\text{mon-RWW}) = \mathcal{L}(\text{mon-RRWW}) = $ CFL.
(c) $\mathcal{L}(\text{det-RWW}) = \mathcal{L}(\text{det-RRWW}) = $ CRL.
(d)   GCSL $\subsetneq$ $\mathcal{L}(\text{RWW})$ $\subseteq \mathcal{L}(\text{RRWW}) \subseteq$ DCSL.

As the restarting automaton is a 'new' automata model that specifies certain classes of formal languages, the question arises of whether this model may give more concise descriptions than previously studied models (like, e.g., phrase-structure grammars or other types of automata).

Following [18] we say that a *descriptional system* S is a recursive set of finite descriptors, where each descriptor $D \in S$ describes a formal language $L(D)$. Further, there must exist an effective procedure that converts a descriptor D into a Turing machine for $L(D)$. Then $\mathcal{L}(S) = \{ L(D) \mid D \in S \}$ is the class of languages that are described by the descriptional system S, and for each $L \in \mathcal{L}(S)$, $S(L) = \{ D \in S \mid L(D) = L \}$ is the set of descriptors from S for L. A *complexity measure* for S is a total recursive function $c : S \to \mathbb{N}$ such that, for any alphabet A, the set of descriptors in S that describe languages over A is recursively enumerable in order of increasing size, and it does not contain infinitely many descriptors of size n for any $n \in \mathbb{N}$.

Definition 6. *Let* S_1 *and* S_2 *be two descriptional systems, and let* c *be a complexity measure for* S_1 *and* S_2. *A function* $f : \mathbb{N} \to \mathbb{N}$ *satisfying* $f(n) \geq n$ *for all* $n \in \mathbb{N}$ *is called an* upper bound *for the increase in complexity when changing from a minimal description in* S_1 *to an equivalent minimal description in* S_2, *if, for all* $L \in \mathcal{L}(S_1) \cap \mathcal{L}(S_2)$, *the following inequality holds:*

$$\min\{ c(D) \mid D \in S_2(L) \} \leq f(\min\{ c(D) \mid D \in S_1(L) \}).$$

If no such recursive upper bound exists, then it is said that the trade-off *for changing from a minimal description in* S_1 *to an equivalent minimal description in* S_2 *is* non-recursive.

The following non-recursive trade-offs have been obtained for restarting automata.

Theorem 7. [17,18]

(a) *The trade-off for changing from a nondeterministic pushdown automaton to a deterministic* RWW- *or* RRWW-*automaton is non-recursive.*
(b) *The trade-off for changing from a deterministic* RWW- *or* RRWW-*automaton to a nondeterministic pushdown automaton is non-recursive.*
(c) *The trade-off for changing from a deterministic* RWW-*automaton to a deterministic monotone* RRWW-*automaton is non-recursive.*
(d) *The trade-off for changing from a deterministic* RWW-*automaton to a deterministic* RRW-, RW-, RR-, *or* R-*automaton is non-recursive.*

3   Restarting Automata with Window Size One

One of the most obvious parameters for restarting automata is the size of the read/write window. For a type X of restarting automata and a positive integer $k \geq 1$, let $X(k)$ denote the restarting automata of type X that have a read/write window of size k. Concerning this parameter the following results have been obtained.

Theorem 8. [38] *For all $k \geq 1$ and all $X \in \{R, RR, RW, RRW\}$,*

(a) $\mathcal{L}(\text{det-mon-X}(k)) \subsetneq \mathcal{L}(\text{det-mon-X}(k+1))$.
(b) $\mathcal{L}(\text{det-X}(k))$ $\subsetneq$ $\mathcal{L}(\text{det-X}(k+1))$.
(c) $\mathcal{L}(\text{mon-X}(k))$ $\subsetneq$ $\mathcal{L}(\text{mon-X}(k+1))$.
(d) $\mathcal{L}(X(k))$ $\subsetneq$ $\mathcal{L}(X(k+1))$.

Thus, when no auxiliary symbols are available, then the expressive power of the various types of restarting automata increases with the size of the read/write window. If, however, auxiliary symbols are available, then the situation changes.

Theorem 9. [50,51]

(a) $\mathcal{L}(\text{mon-RWW}(k))$ =   CFL   *for all $k \geq 3$.*
(b) $\mathcal{L}(\text{mon-RRWW}(k))$ =   CFL   *for all $k \geq 2$.*
(c) $\mathcal{L}(\text{RRWW}(k))$ $= \mathcal{L}(\text{RRWW}(k+1))$ *for all $k \geq 2$.*

Here we are particularly interested in restarting automata with read/write window of size 1. Obviously, for these restarting automata auxiliary symbols cannot be used, and all rewrite operations are simply deletions of single letters. Thus, we see that $R(1) = RW(1) = RWW(1)$ and $RR(1) = RRW(1) = RRWW(1)$ hold. Concerning the expressive power of these restarting automata, the following results have been established.

Theorem 10. [29,30,38]

(a) $\mathcal{L}(\text{det-mon-R}(1)) = \mathcal{L}(\text{mon-R}(1)) = \mathcal{L}(\text{det-R}(1)) =$ $\mathcal{L}(R(1))$ = REG.
(b) $\mathcal{L}(\text{det-mon-RR}(1)) = \mathcal{L}(\text{det-RR}(1)) =$ REG $\subsetneq \mathcal{L}(\text{mon-RR}(1))$.

Proof outline. It is obvious that each of the given types of restarting automata can simulate a deterministic finite-state acceptor, and hence, REG is included in all the other language classes mentioned in the statement of the theorem. Conversely, Mráz has shown in [38] that an $R(1)$-automaton M can be simulated by a nondeterministic finite-state acceptor A. Essentially, A simulates all cycles of M in parallel. Analogously, Kutrib and Reimann have shown in [29,30] that a deterministic $RR(1)$-automaton M' can be simulated by a deterministic finite-state acceptor A'. Here the idea is as follows. If M' executes a cycle $w = xay \vdash^c_{M'} xy$, then in the next cycle M' will again read the prefix x of the current tape content completely, as it is deterministic. Thus, when simulating M', there is no need for A' to reread this prefix; instead it can simply continue with processing the suffix y.

Finally, in order to prove the fact that monotone $RR(1)$-automata already accept some non-regular languages, we consider the following example. Let M_0

be the RR(1)-automaton on $\Sigma = \{a, b\}$ that is given through the following meta-instructions:

(1) $(\mathbb{c} \cdot (aa)^* \cdot a, a \to \lambda, (bb)^+ \cdot \$)$,   (4) $(\mathbb{c} \cdot (aa)^*, b \to \lambda, (bb)^* \cdot \$)$,
(2) $(\mathbb{c} \cdot (aa)^*, a \to \lambda, (bb)^* \cdot b \cdot \$)$,   (5) $(\mathbb{c} \cdot (aa)^* \cdot a, b \to \lambda, b \cdot (bb)^* \cdot \$)$.
(3) $(\mathbb{c} \cdot \$, \mathsf{Accept})$,

The automaton M_0 processes inputs of the form $a^m b^n$. In fact, it alternatingly removes the last occurrence of the letter a and the first occurrence of the letter b, and to distinguish between these two cases it uses the parity of the number of a's and the parity of the number of b's. It follows that M_0 is monotone, and that it accepts the language $L(M_0) = \{\, a^m b^n \mid m = n \text{ or } m + 1 = n \,\}$, which is not regular.   □

It is easily seen that all types of restarting automata accept non-regular languages when they have a read/write window of size at least 2. For example, the *restricted Dyck language* (see, e.g., [2])

$$D_1'^* = \{\, w \in \{a, b\}^* \mid |w|_a = |w|_b, \text{ and } \forall w = uv : |u|_a \geq |u|_b \,\}$$

is easily seen to be accepted by a deterministic monotone R(2)-automaton.

As R(1)- and deterministic RR(1)-automata accept exactly the regular languages, it is only natural to ask for the succinctness with which these automata describe regular languages. Kutrib and Reimann have investigated this question in [29,30,49]. Their results are summarized in the table in Figure 1, which has been taken from [29].

	DFA	NFA	R(1)	det-RR(1)
NFA	2^n	–	n	$2^n - 1$
R(1)	$2^n + 1$	2^n	–	$2^n - 1$
det-RR(1)	$\Omega((n-1)!) \leq \cdot \leq O(n!)$	$(2n - k + 2) \cdot 2^{k-1}$	$(2n - k + 2) \cdot 2^{k-1}$	–

Fig. 1. Trade-offs when changing from an automaton of the leftmost column to an automaton of the topmost row. Here n denotes the number of states, and k is the number of states that are reachable after executing a rewrite (that is, delete) step.

4   Nonforgetting Restarting Automata

In 2004, Messerschmidt and Stamer defined a generalization of the restarting automaton which they called *nonforgetting restarting automaton* [37]. The nonforgetting restarting automaton is obtained from the standard restarting automaton by combining the restart operation with a change of the internal state just like the move-right and the rewrite operations. Thus, when executing a restart operation, a nonforgetting restarting automaton is not necessarily reset to its initial state, but it enters the internal state that is given by the corresponding restart operation. Accordingly, a rewriting meta-instruction for a nonforgetting RRWW-automaton is written as $(q, E_1, u \to v, E_2, q')$. It applies to restarting configurations of the form $q¢xuy\$$, where $¢x \in E_1$ and $y\$ \in E_2$, and it transforms this restarting configuration into the restarting configuration $q'¢xvy\$$. Analogously, an accepting meta-instruction has the form $(q, ¢ \cdot E \cdot \$, \mathsf{Accept})$. It accepts the strings from the regular language E when applied to a restarting configuration of the form $q¢w\$$.

Example 11. Let M be the deterministic nonforgetting R-automaton on $\Sigma = \{a, b, \#\}$ that is given by the following meta-instructions:

(1) $(q_0, ¢ \cdot \{a, b\}^*, a\#a \to \#, q_a)$,
(2) $(q_0, ¢ \cdot \{a, b\}^*, b\#b \to \#, q_b)$,
(3) $(q_0, ¢ \cdot \# \cdot \# \cdot \$, \mathsf{Accept})$,
(4) $(q_a, ¢ \cdot \{a, b\}^* \cdot \# \cdot \{a, b\}^* \cdot \# \cdot \{a, b\}^*, a\$ \to \$, q_0)$,
(5) $(q_b, ¢ \cdot \{a, b\}^* \cdot \# \cdot \{a, b\}^* \cdot \# \cdot \{a, b\}^*, b\$ \to \$, q_0)$.

It is easily seen that $L(M) = \{w\#w^R\#w \mid w \in \{a, b\}^*\}$, that is, $L(M)$ is the so-called *Gladkij language* L_{Glad} which is known to be not even growing context-sensitive [5,6,14].

Together with Theorem 5 this example clearly demonstrates that nonforgetting restarting automata are much more expressive than the corresponding (standard) restarting automata. Surprisingly, this is not the case for monotone R(1)- and monotone deterministic RR(1)-automata. Here the prefix nf- is used to denote types of nonforgetting restarting automata.

Theorem 12. [19]
$\mathcal{L}(\text{det-mon-nf-R}(1)) = \mathcal{L}(\text{mon-nf-R}(1)) = \mathcal{L}(\text{det-mon-nf-RR}(1)) = \mathsf{REG}$.

Proof outline. Let $M = (Q, \Sigma, \Sigma, ¢, \$, q_0, 1, \delta)$ be a deterministic monotone nf-R(1)-automaton that accepts a language $L \subseteq \Sigma^*$. Without loss of generality we may assume that $Q = \{q_0, q_1, \ldots, q_{n-1}\}$, and that M executes accept instructions only on reading the $\$$-symbol. The computations of M can be simulated by a deterministic finite-state acceptor $A = (Q_A, \Sigma \cup \{\$\}, q_0^{(A)}, F, \delta_A)$ for $L \cdot \$$. In its finite-state control A stores the following information on the computation of M that it currently tries to simulate:

- The *current restart state* CRS that contains the state $q \in Q$ with which the cycle of M starts that is currently active. Initially CRS is set to q_0.
- A *state table* T that contains pairs of the form (q_i, q_i') $(i = 0, 1, \ldots, n - 1)$, where q_i' is the state that M reaches from state q_i after reading across the prefix $¢u$ of the given tape contents that has already been processed. Initially T contains the list of all pairs (q_i, q_i') $(i = 0, 1, \ldots, n-1)$, where q_i' is the state that M enters from state q_i on seeing the $¢$-symbol. Thus, (q_i, q_i') belongs to T if $\delta(q_i, ¢) = (q_i', \mathsf{MVR})$. If $\delta(q_i, ¢)$ is undefined, which means that M cannot restart in state q_i, then T contains the item $(q_i, -)$.

- A *buffer* B of length n that is initially empty. It will be used to store information on possible rewrite (that is, delete) operations encountered during the current simulation. The items stored in B will consist of an input letter a and a list of 4-tuples of the form (q_i, p_i, q_i', T'), where T' is a table of the form above, and q_i, p_i, q_i' are states of M that satisfy the following conditions: Restarting in state q_i, M reaches state p_i on encountering the letter a, and $\delta(p_i, a) = (q_i', \lambda)$. Observe that there may be several such 4-tuples, as M may restart in any of its n internal states.

The intended simulation of M by A crucially depends on the property that M is monotone. Consider an accepting computation of M on input w, and assume that this computation consists of a sequence of at least two cycles that is followed by a tail computation, that is, it has the following form:

$$
\begin{aligned}
q_0 \mathophat{c} w\$ &= q_0 \mathophat{c} uav\$ \vdash^+_{\mathsf{MVR}} \mathophat{c} u p_0 av\$ \vdash_M q_{i_1} \mathophat{c} uv\$ \\
&= q_{i_1} \mathophat{c} xby\$ \vdash^+_{\mathsf{MVR}} \mathophat{c} x p_{i_1} by\$ \vdash_M q_{i_2} \mathophat{c} xy\$ \\
\vdash^*_M \ q_{i_m} \mathophat{c} z\$ &\vdash^+_{\mathsf{MVR}} \mathophat{c} z p_{i_m}\$ \vdash_M \mathsf{Accept}.
\end{aligned}
$$

The right distance of the first cycle is $d_1 = |v| + 2$, and the right distance of the second cycle is $d_2 = |y| + 2$. As M is monotone, we have $d_1 \geq d_2$, that is, $|v| \geq |y|$. Since $uv = xby$, this means that y is a suffix of v. If y is a proper suffix of v, then $v = x_2 by$ for a suffix x_2 of x. In this case $w = uav = uax_2by$, which implies that the second delete operation is executed at a place that is strictly to the right of the place where the first delete operation was executed. In this situation A first encounters the letter a deleted in the first cycle and later it encounters the letter b deleted in the second cycle.

If, however, $v = y$, then $uv = xby = xbv$ implies that $u = xb$, and so $w = uav = xbav$. Thus, in this situation the second delete operation is executed immediately to the *left* of the place where the first delete operation was executed. Hence, in this case the b deleted in the second cycle is encountered by A before the a that is deleted in the first cycle. However, this can happen only if M completes the first cycle by restarting in the correct state q_{i_1}. In addition, as M is deterministic, we have $q_{i_1} \neq q_0$.

Obviously, the second case above can occur more than once in a row. However, as all the corresponding restarting states must differ from one another, the length of such a sequence is bounded from above by the number n of states of M. Based on this observation A can now be designed in such a way that it simulates the accepting computations of M.

In fact, it can even be shown that the above simulation extends to nondeterministic monotone nf-R(1)-automata. Finally, by introducing a preprocessing stage for A, it can be shown that a deterministic monotone nf-RR(1)-automaton can be simulated by a deterministic two-way finite-state acceptor. ☐

From Theorem 10 we see that Theorem 12 does not extend to monotone nf-RR(1)-automata that are nondeterministic. In Section 5 we will shortly consider deterministic nf-R(1)-automata that are non-monotone.

As monotone nf-R(1)- and det-nf-RR(1)-automata accept just the regular languages, the question for their descriptional complexity arises: Do these more involved types of automata offer more succinct representations for regular languages than (standard) R(1)- and det-RR(1)-automata? A first preliminary result concerning this question is the following.

Proposition 13. [19] *For each $n \geq 2$, there exists a language $L_n \subseteq \{a,b\}^*$ that is accepted by a det-mon-nf-RR(1)-automaton with $O(n)$ states, but every (standard) det-RR(1)-automaton accepting L_n has at least $O(2^n)$ many states.*

Proof. For $n \geq 2$, let $L_n = \{ w \in \{a,b\}^m \mid m > n,\ w_n = a,$ and $w_{m+1-n} = b \}$, where w_i $(1 \leq i \leq |w|)$ denotes the i-th symbol of w. A det-mon-nf-RR(1)-automaton M for L_n can be described by the following meta-instructions, where $x \in \{a,b\}$:

$$(1)\ (q_0, \mathrm{\mathvarphi}, x \rightarrow \lambda, \{a,b\}^{n-2} \cdot a \cdot \{a,b\}^+ \cdot \$, q_1),$$
$$(2)\ (q_1, \mathrm{\mathvarphi} \cdot a^*, b \rightarrow \lambda, \{a,b\}^{n-1} \cdot \{a,b\}^+ \cdot \$, q_1),$$
$$(3)\ (q_1, \mathrm{\mathvarphi} \cdot a^*, b \rightarrow \lambda, \{a,b\}^{n-1} \cdot \$, \mathsf{Accept}).$$

For realizing these meta-instructions $O(n)$ states suffice, as M must be able to count from 1 to n. On the other hand, a deterministic RR(1)-automaton M' for L_n must accept each word $w \in L_n$ satisfying $|w| = m \leq 2n$ in a tail computation because of the correctness preserving property. Hence, it behaves essentially just like a deterministic finite-state acceptor, which implies that it needs $O(2^n)$ states to check the condition $w_{m+1-n} = b$. □

It remains to study the descriptional complexity of (deterministic) mon-nf-R(1)- and det-mon-nf-RR(1)-automata in more detail.

5 CD-Systems of Stateless Deterministic R(1)-Automata

In [34] *cooperating distributed systems* (CD-systems) of restarting automata were introduced, and it was shown that these CD-systems closely correspond to non-forgetting restarting automata. These CD-systems can be interpreted as an adaptation of the notion of *CD grammar system with external control* (see, e.g., [8]) to the setting of restarting automata.

A *cooperating distributed system* of RRWW-*automata* (or a CD-RRWW-system, for short) consists of a finite collection $\mathcal{M} = ((M_i, \sigma_i)_{i \in I}, I_0)$ of RRWW-automata $M_i = (Q_i, \Sigma, \Gamma_i, \mathrm{\mathvarphi}, \$, q_0^{(i)}, k, \delta_i)$ $(i \in I)$, *successor relations* $\sigma_i \subseteq I$ $(i \in I)$, and a subset $I_0 \subseteq I$ of *initial indices*. Here it is required that $Q_i \cap Q_j = \emptyset$ for all $i, j \in I$, $i \neq j$, that $I_0 \neq \emptyset$, and that $\sigma_i \neq \emptyset$ for all $i \in I$.

As for CD-grammar systems (see, e.g., [8,10]) various modes of operation like $= j$, $\leq j$, $\geq j$ for $j \geq 1$ and t have been introduced and studied for CD-RRWW-systems, but here we are only interested in mode $= 1$ computations. The computation of $\mathcal{M}$ in mode $= 1$ on an input word w proceeds as follows. First an index $i_0 \in I_0$ is chosen nondeterministically. Then the RRWW-automaton M_{i_0} starts the computation with the initial configuration $q_0^{(i_0)} \mathrm{\mathvarphi} w \$$, and executes a single cycle. Thereafter an index $i_1 \in \sigma_{i_0}$ is chosen nondeterministically, and

M_{i_1} continues the computation by executing a single cycle. This continues until, for some $l \geq 0$, the machine M_{i_l} accepts. Should at some stage the chosen machine M_{i_l} be unable to execute a cycle or to accept, then the computation fails.

By $L_{=1}(\mathcal{M})$ we denote the language that the CD-RRWW-system $\mathcal{M}$ accepts in mode $= 1$. It consists of all words $w \in \Sigma^*$ that are accepted by $\mathcal{M}$ in mode $= 1$ as described above. If X is any of the above types of restarting automata, then a CD-X-system is a CD-RRWW-system for which all component automata are of type X. By $\mathcal{L}_{=1}(\text{CD-X})$ we denote the class of languages that are accepted by CD-X-systems in mode $= 1$.

In [34] the following correspondence has been established between CD-systems of restarting automata and nonforgetting restarting automata.

Theorem 14. *For all types* $\text{X} \in \{\text{R}, \text{RR}, \text{RW}, \text{RRW}, \text{RWW}, \text{RRWW}\}$, $\mathcal{L}_{=1}(\text{CD-X}) = \mathcal{L}(\text{nf-X})$.

A CD-RRWW-system $\mathcal{M} = ((M_i, \sigma_i)_{i \in I}, I_0)$ is called *locally deterministic* if all component automata M_i $(i \in I)$ are deterministic, and it is called *globally deterministic* if, in addition, I_0 is a singleton and if, for each $i \in I$, each restart operation of M_i is combined with an index from the set σ_i. In a globally deterministic system, when M_i finishes a cycle by executing a particular restart operation (Restart, j), where $j \in \sigma_i$, then the component automaton M_j takes over. This ensures that computations of a globally deterministic CD-RRWW-system are completely deterministic, while in general those of a locally deterministic CD-RRWW-system are not. We use the prefix det-global- to denote globally deterministic types of CD-RRWW-systems. In [36] the following correspondence has been established between globally deterministic CD-systems of restarting automata and nonforgetting restarting automata.

Theorem 15. *For all types* $\text{X} \in \{\text{R}, \text{RR}, \text{RW}, \text{RRW}, \text{RWW}, \text{RRWW}\}$, $\mathcal{L}_{=1}(\text{det-global-CD-X}) = \mathcal{L}(\text{det-nf-X})$.

Here we are interested in CD-systems of stateless deterministic R(1)-automata. Stateless types of restarting automata were introduced in [27,28], where an RWW-automaton $M = (Q, \Sigma, \Gamma, \text{¢}, \$, q_0, k, \delta)$ is called *stateless* if $Q = \{q_0\}$. Thus, in this situation M can simply be written as $M = (\Sigma, \Gamma, \text{¢}, \$, k, \delta)$. Obviously, the most restricted type of stateless restarting automaton is the *stateless deterministic* R(1)-*automaton*, which was first studied in [41].

Definition 16. *If* $M = (\Sigma, \Sigma, \text{¢}, \$, 1, \delta)$ *is a stateless deterministic* R(1)-*automaton, then its alphabet* Σ *can be partitioned into four disjoint subalphabets:*

(1.) $\Sigma_1 = \{ a \in \Sigma \mid \delta(a) = \text{MVR} \}$,   (3.) $\Sigma_3 = \{ a \in \Sigma \mid \delta(a) = \text{Accept} \}$,
(2.) $\Sigma_2 = \{ a \in \Sigma \mid \delta(a) = \lambda \}$,   (4.) $\Sigma_4 = \{ a \in \Sigma \mid \delta(a) = \emptyset \}$,

where $\delta(a) = \emptyset$ *is used to denote the fact that the transition function* δ *is undefined for the symbol* a. *Thus,* Σ_1 *is the set of letters that* M *just moves across,* Σ_2 *is the set of letters that* M *deletes,* Σ_3 *is the set of letters which cause* M *to accept, and* Σ_4 *is the set of letters on which* M *will get stuck.*

Then the following characterization can be established quite easily.

Proposition 17. [41] *Let* $M = (\Sigma, \Sigma, \mathfrak{c}, \$, 1, \delta)$ *be a stateless deterministic R(1)-automaton, and assume that the subalphabets* $\Sigma_1, \Sigma_2, \Sigma_3, \Sigma_4$ *are defined as above. Then the language* $L(M)$ *is characterized as*

$$
L(M) = \begin{cases}
\emptyset, & \text{if } \delta(\mathfrak{c}) = \emptyset, \\
\Sigma^*, & \text{if } \delta(\mathfrak{c}) = \mathsf{Accept}, \\
(\Sigma_1 \cup \Sigma_2)^* \cdot \Sigma_3 \cdot \Sigma^*, & \text{if } \delta(\mathfrak{c}) = \mathsf{MVR} \text{ and } \delta(\$) \neq \mathsf{Accept}, \\
(\Sigma_1 \cup \Sigma_2)^* \cdot ((\Sigma_3 \cdot \Sigma^*) \cup \{\lambda\}), & \text{if } \delta(\mathfrak{c}) = \mathsf{MVR} \text{ and } \delta(\$) = \mathsf{Accept}.
\end{cases}
$$

We use the prefix stl- to denote stateless types of restarting automata. In [40] it is shown that the language classes $(\mathcal{L}(\mathsf{stl\text{-}det\text{-}R}(k)))_{k \geq 1}$ form an infinite strictly increasing hierarchy, and that for all $k \geq 2$, the class $\mathcal{L}(\mathsf{stl\text{-}det\text{-}R}(k))$ is incomparable to REG under inclusion, and for all $k \geq 9$, $\mathcal{L}(\mathsf{stl\text{-}det\text{-}R}(k))$ is incomparable to CFL under inclusion.

A stl-det-local-CD-R(1)-system $\mathcal{M} = ((M_i, \sigma_i)_{i \in I}, I_0)$ is a CD-system of stateless deterministic R(1)-automata. By $\mathcal{L}_{=1}(\mathsf{stl\text{-}det\text{-}local\text{-}CD\text{-}R}(1))$ we denote the class of languages that are accepted by mode = 1 computations of these systems. The following examples illustrate the expressive power of these systems.

Example 18. Let $\mathcal{M} = ((M_i, \sigma_i)_{i \in I}, I_0)$, where $I = \{a, b\}$, $I_0 = \{a\}$, $\sigma_a = \{b\}$, $\sigma_b = \{a\}$, and the stateless deterministic R(1)-automata M_a and M_b are defined by the following transition functions:

$$
\begin{aligned}
M_a : &(1)\ \delta_a(\mathfrak{c}) = \mathsf{MVR}, & M_b : &(4)\ \delta_b(\mathfrak{c}) = \mathsf{MVR}, \\
&(2)\ \delta_a(a) = \lambda, & &(5)\ \delta_b(a) = \mathsf{MVR}, \\
&(3)\ \delta_a(\$) = \mathsf{Accept}, & &(6)\ \delta_b(b) = \lambda.
\end{aligned}
$$

Then it is easily seen that $L_{=1}(\mathcal{M})$ is the restricted Dyck language $D_1'^*$ (see the last paragraph of Section 3).

Example 19. Let $\mathcal{M} = ((M_i, \sigma_i)_{i \in I}, I_0)$, where $I = \{a, b, c, +\}$, $I_0 = \{a, +\}$, $\sigma_a = \{b\}$, $\sigma_b = \{c\}$, $\sigma_c = \{a, +\}$, $\sigma_+ = \{a\}$, and M_a, M_b, M_c, and M_+ are the stateless deterministic R(1)-automata that are given by the following transition functions:

$$
\begin{aligned}
M_a : &(1.)\ \delta_a(\mathfrak{c}) = \mathsf{MVR}, & M_c : &(9.)\ \delta_c(\mathfrak{c}) = \mathsf{MVR}, \\
&(2.)\ \delta_a(b) = \mathsf{MVR}, & &(10.)\ \delta_c(a) = \mathsf{MVR}, \\
&(3.)\ \delta_a(c) = \mathsf{MVR}, & &(11.)\ \delta_c(b) = \mathsf{MVR}, \\
&(4.)\ \delta_a(a) = \lambda, & &(12.)\ \delta_c(c) = \lambda, \\
M_b : &(5.)\ \delta_b(\mathfrak{c}) = \mathsf{MVR}, & M_+ : &(13.)\ \delta_+(\mathfrak{c}) = \mathsf{MVR}, \\
&(6.)\ \delta_b(a) = \mathsf{MVR}, & &(14.)\ \delta_+(\$) = \mathsf{Accept}. \\
&(7.)\ \delta_b(c) = \mathsf{MVR}, & & \\
&(8.)\ \delta_b(b) = \lambda, & &
\end{aligned}
$$

Then $L_{=1}(\mathcal{M})$ is the non-context-free language $L_{abc} = \{ w \in \{a, b, c\}^* \mid |w|_a = |w|_b = |w|_c \geq 0 \}$.

As defined above the stl-det-local-CD-R(1)-systems look rather complicated and technically involved. The advantage of the technical definition is certainly the fact that proofs can be based on the large body of technical results and methods that have been developed for restarting automata. However, there is a much simpler, more illustrative way of looking at these systems.

Definition 20. [44] *A finite-state acceptor with translucent letters (NFAwtl) is defined as a 7-tuple $A = (Q, \Sigma, \$, \tau, I, F, \delta)$, where Q is a finite set of internal states, Σ is a finite alphabet of input letters, $\$ \notin \Sigma$ is a special symbol that is used as an* endmarker, $\tau : Q \to 2^{\Sigma}$ *is a translucency mapping, $I \subseteq Q$ is a set of initial states, $F \subseteq Q$ is a set of final states, and $\delta : Q \times \Sigma \to 2^Q$ is a transition relation. For each state $q \in Q$, the letters from the set $\tau(q)$ are translucent for q, that is, in state q the automaton A does not see these letters. A is called* deterministic, *abbreviated as* DFAwtl, *if $|I| = 1$ and if $|\delta(q, a)| \leq 1$ for all $q \in Q$ and all $a \in \Sigma$.*

An NFAwtl $A = (Q, \Sigma, \$, \tau, I, F, \delta)$ works as follows. For a word $w \in \Sigma^*$, it starts in a nondeterministically chosen initial state $q_0 \in I$ with the word $w\$$ on its input tape. Assume that $w = a_1 \cdots a_n$ for some $n \geq 1$ and $a_1, \ldots, a_n \in \Sigma$. Then A looks for the first occurrence from the left of a letter that is not translucent for state q_0, that is, if $w = uav$ such that $u \in (\tau(q_0))^*$ and $a \notin \tau(q_0)$, then A nondeterministically chooses a state $q_1 \in \delta(q_0, a)$, erases the letter a from the tape thus producing the tape contents $uv\$$, and switches to its internal state q_1. In case $\delta(q_0, a) = \emptyset$, A halts without accepting. Finally, if $w \in (\tau(q_0))^*$, then A reaches the $\$$-symbol and the computation halts. In this case A accepts if q_0 is a final state; otherwise, it does not accept. Thus, A executes the following computation relation on its set $Q \cdot \Sigma^* \cdot \{\$\}$ of configurations:

$$qw\$ \vdash_A \begin{cases} q'uv\$, & \text{if } w = uav, \ u \in (\tau(q))^*, \ a \notin \tau(q), \ \text{and } q' \in \delta(q, a), \\ \text{Accept}, & \text{if } w \in (\tau(q))^* \text{ and } q \in F. \end{cases}$$

Observe that this definition also applies to configurations of the form $q\$$, that is, $q \cdot \lambda \cdot \$ \vdash_A$ Accept holds if and only if q is a final state. A word $w \in \Sigma^*$ is *accepted by* A if there exists an initial state $q_0 \in I$ such that $q_0 w\$ \vdash_A^*$ Accept holds, where $\vdash_A^*$ denotes the reflexive transitive closure of the single-step computation relation $\vdash_A$. Now $L(A) = \{ w \in \Sigma^* \mid w$ is accepted by $A \}$ is the *language accepted by* A, $\mathcal{L}(\mathsf{NFAwtl})$ denotes the class of all languages that are accepted by NFAwtls, and $\mathcal{L}(\mathsf{DFAwtl})$ denotes the class of all languages that are accepted by DFAwtls.

The classical *nondeterministic finite-state acceptor* (NFA) is obtained from the NFAwtl by removing the endmarker $\$$ and by ignoring the translucency relation τ, and the *deterministic finite-state acceptor* (DFA) is obtained from the DFAwtl in the same way. Thus, the NFA (DFA) can be interpreted as a special type of NFAwtl (DFAwtl).

If $A = (Q, \Sigma, \$, \tau, I, F, \delta)$ is an NFAwtl, then we can assign a stl-det-local-CD-R(1)-system $\mathcal{M}$ to it by defining $\mathcal{M} = ((M_j, \sigma_j)_{j \in J}, J_0)$ as follows. The set of indices is $J = Q \times \Sigma$, and $J_0 = I \times \Sigma$. For all pairs $(q, a) \in J$,

$M_{(q,a)} = (\Sigma, \Sigma, \math€, \$, 1, \delta_{(q,a)})$ is defined by the following transition relation and successor set:

$$\delta_{(q,a)}(\math€) = \mathsf{MVR},$$
$$\delta_{(q,a)}(b) = \mathsf{MVR} \quad \text{for all } b \in \tau(q),$$
$$\delta_{(q,a)}(\$) = \mathsf{Accept}, \text{ if } q \in F,$$
$$\delta_{(q,a)}(a) = \lambda, \qquad \text{if } a \notin \tau(q) \text{ and } \delta(q,a) \neq \emptyset,$$
$$\sigma_{(q,a)} = \begin{cases} \delta(q,a) \times \Sigma, & \text{if } \delta(q,a) \neq \emptyset, \\ Q \times \Sigma, & \text{otherwise.} \end{cases}$$

Further, $\delta_{(q,a)}(c) = \emptyset$ for all letters $c \in (\Sigma \setminus (\tau(q) \cup \{a\}))$, and $\delta_{(q,a)}(\$) = \emptyset$, if q is not a final state of A. Observe that the automaton $M_{(q,a)}$ cannot make any rewrite/restart step, and hence, its successor set is never used, if $a \in \tau(q)$ or $\delta(q,a) = \emptyset$.

A computational step $q_1 uav\$ \vdash_A q_2 uv\$$ of A is simulated by the component $M_{(q_1,a)}$ of $\mathcal{M}$ as $q_{(q_1,a)}\math€ uav\$ \vdash^* \math€ uq_{(q_1,a)}av\$ \vdash q_{(q_2,b)}\math€ uv\$$, where q_j denotes the unique state of M_j, $j \in J$, and $(q_2, b) \in \sigma_{(q_1,a)}$. Further, an accepting step of A of the form $q_1 u\$ \vdash_A \mathsf{Accept}$ is simulated by a component $M_{(q_1,a)}$ as $q_{(q_1,a)}\math€ u\$ \vdash^* \math€ uq_{(q_1,a)}\$ \vdash \mathsf{Accept}$. Thus, in order to simulate an accepting computation of A, one must guess the next letter to be deleted in each step, and choose the corresponding component of $\mathcal{M}$. It now follows easily that $L_{=1}(\mathcal{M}) = L(A)$ holds.

Conversely, if $\mathcal{M} = ((M_j, \sigma_j)_{j \in J}, J_0)$ is a stl-det-local-CD-R(1)-system, where $M_j = (\Sigma, \Sigma, \math€, \$, 1, \delta_j)$ $(j \in J)$, then we can associate an NFAwtl $A = (J \cup \{+\}, \Sigma, \$, \tau, J_0, F, \delta)$ to $\mathcal{M}$ as follows. For each index $j \in J$, we define the translucency mapping τ and the transition function δ as follows:

$$\tau(j) = \begin{cases} \Sigma, & \text{if } \delta_j(\math€) = \mathsf{Accept}, \\ \Sigma_1^{(j)}, & \text{otherwise,} \end{cases}$$
$$\delta(j, a) = \sigma_j \quad \text{for all } a \in \Sigma_2^{(j)},$$
$$\delta(j, b) = \{+\} \quad \text{for all } b \in \Sigma_3^{(j)}.$$

Here $\Sigma_1^{(j)}$, $\Sigma_2^{(j)}$, and $\Sigma_3^{(j)}$ are the subsets of Σ described in Definition 16 that correspond to the stateless R(1)-automaton M_j. Further, we define $\tau(+) = \Sigma$ and

$$F = \{ j \in J \mid \delta_j(\$) = \mathsf{Accept} \} \cup \{+\}.$$

It can now be verified that A can simulate the accepting computations of $\mathcal{M}$ in a stepwise fashion. Thus, it follows that $L(A) = L_{=1}(\mathcal{M})$ holds. Hence, we have the following correspondences.

Proposition 21. (a) $\mathcal{L}(\mathsf{NFAwtl}) = \mathcal{L}_{=1}(\mathsf{stl\text{-}det\text{-}local\text{-}CD\text{-}R}(1))$.
(b) $\mathcal{L}(\mathsf{DFAwtl}) = \mathcal{L}_{=1}(\mathsf{stl\text{-}det\text{-}global\text{-}CD\text{-}R}(1))$.

From a DFA one can easily design a DFAwtl that accepts the same language. Thus, together with Example 18 we have the following proper inclusion.

Corollary 22. REG $\subsetneq \mathcal{L}_{=1}$(stl-det-global-CD-R(1)).

If $\Sigma = \{a_1, \ldots, a_n\}$ is an alphabet, then the morphism $\psi : \Sigma^* \to \mathbb{N}^n$ defined by $w \mapsto (|w|_{a_1}, \ldots, |w|_{a_n})$ is called the *Parikh mapping* for Σ. Two languages $L_1, L_2 \subseteq \Sigma^*$ are said to be *letter-equivalent* if $\psi(L_1) = \psi(L_2)$ holds. Finally, L_1 is called *semi-linear* if $\psi(L_1)$ is a semi-linear subset of $\mathbb{N}^n$ (see, e.g., [16]).

The following result is a very useful tool for proving that a language is not accepted by a stl-det-local-CD-R(1)-system.

Theorem 23. [41] *Each language* $L \in \mathcal{L}_{=1}$(stl-det-local-CD-R(1)) *contains a regular sublanguage* E *such that* $\psi(L) = \psi(E)$ *holds. In fact, an NFA for* E *can be constructed effectively from a* stl-det-local-CD-R(1)-*system for* L.

From this result we obtain the following immediate consequences.

Corollary 24. *The language class* $\mathcal{L}_{=1}$(stl-det-local-CD-R(1)) *only contains semi-linear languages.*

Corollary 25. *The language* $L = \{a^n b^n \mid n \geq 0\}$ *is not accepted by any* stl-det-local-CD-R(1)-*system working in mode* $= 1$.

Together with Example 19 this gives the following incomparability results, where DLIN denotes the class of *deterministic linear languages*, that is, the class of languages that are accepted by deterministic one-turn pushdown automata, and LIN is the class of *linear languages*.

Corollary 26. *The language class* $\mathcal{L}_{=1}$(stl-det-local-CD-R(1)) *is incomparable to the classes* DLIN, LIN, DCFL, *and* CFL *with respect to inclusion.*

Next we will show that $\mathcal{L}_{=1}$(stl-det-local-CD-R(1)) includes a rather large superclass of the regular languages. Let Σ be a finite alphabet, and let D be a binary relation on Σ that is reflexive and symmetric, that is, $(a, a) \in D$ for all $a \in \Sigma$, and $(a, b) \in D$ implies that $(b, a) \in D$, too. Then D is called a *dependency relation* on Σ, and the relation $I_D = (\Sigma \times \Sigma) \setminus D$ is called the corresponding *independence relation*. Obviously, the relation I_D is irreflexive and symmetric. The dependency relation D (or rather its associated independence relation I_D) induces a binary relation $\equiv_D$ on Σ^* that is defined as the smallest congruence relation containing the set of pairs $\{(ab, ba) \mid (a, b) \in I_D\}$. For $w \in \Sigma^*$, the congruence class of $w \bmod \equiv_D$ is denoted by $[w]_D$, that is, $[w]_D = \{z \in \Sigma^* \mid w \equiv_D z\}$. These equivalence classes are called *traces*, and the factor monoid $M(D) = \Sigma^*/\equiv_D$ is a *trace monoid*. In fact, $M(D)$ is the *free partially commutative monoid* presented by (Σ, D) (see, e.g., [11]). By φ_D we denote the morphism $\varphi_D : \Sigma^* \to M(D)$ that is defined by $w \mapsto [w]_D$ for all words $w \in \Sigma^*$.

A subset S of a trace monoid $M(D)$ is called *recognizable* if there exist a finite monoid N, a morphism $\alpha : M(D) \to N$, and a subset P of N such that $S = \alpha^{-1}(P)$ (see, e.g., [2]). By REC($M(D)$) we denote the set of recognizable subsets of $M(D)$. A subset S of a trace monoid $M(D)$ is called *rational* if it can be obtained from singleton sets by a finite number of unions, products, and star operations (see, e.g., [2]). This property can be characterized more conveniently as follows.

Proposition 27. *Let $M(D)$ be the trace monoid presented by (Σ, D), and let $\varphi_D : \Sigma^* \to M(D)$ be the corresponding morphism. Then a set $S \subseteq M(D)$ is rational if and only if there exists a regular language R over Σ such that $S = \varphi_D(R)$.*

By $\mathsf{RAT}(M(D))$ we denote the set of rational subsets of $M(D)$. Concerning the relationship between the recognizable subsets of $M(D)$ and the rational subsets of $M(D)$ the following results are known (see, e.g., [11]).

Proposition 28. *For each trace monoid $M(D)$, $\mathsf{REC}(M(D)) \subseteq \mathsf{RAT}(M(D))$, and these two sets are equal if and only if $I_D = \emptyset$.*

Thus, the free monoids are the only trace monoids for which the recognizable subsets coincide with the rational subsets.

We call a language $L \subseteq \Sigma^*$ a *rational trace language*, if there exists a dependency relation D on Σ such that $L = \varphi_D^{-1}(S)$ for a rational subset S of the trace monoid $M(D)$ presented by (Σ, D). From Proposition 27 it follows that L is a rational trace language if and only if there exist a trace monoid $M(D)$ and a regular language $R \subseteq \Sigma^*$ such that $L = \varphi_D^{-1}(\varphi_D(R)) = \bigcup_{w \in R}[w]_D$. By $\mathcal{LRAT}(D)$ we denote the set of rational trace languages $\varphi_D^{-1}(\mathsf{RAT}(M(D)))$, and $\mathcal{LRAT}$ is the class of all rational trace languages. The next theorem states that all these languages are accepted by stl-det-local-CD-R(1)-systems.

Theorem 29. [41] $\mathcal{LRAT} \subset \mathcal{L}_{=1}(\text{stl-det-local-CD-R}(1))$, *that is, if D is a dependency relation on the finite alphabet Σ, then the language $\bigcup_{w \in R}[w]_D$ is accepted by a stl-det-local-CD-R(1)-system working in mode $= 1$ for each regular language $R \subseteq \Sigma^*$.*

As the Dyck language $D_1'^*$ (see Example 18) is not a rational trace language, we see that the inclusion $\mathcal{LRAT} \subset \mathcal{L}_{=1}(\text{stl-det-local-CD-R}(1))$ is actually strict. In fact, in [41] a subclass of stl-det-local-CD-R(1)-systems is described that characterizes the rational trace languages.

From Proposition 21 we know that each stl-det-global-CD-R(1)-system can be simulated by a stl-det-local-CD-R(1)-system. On the other hand, there is the following negative result.

Proposition 30. [45] *The rational trace language*

$$L_\vee = \{ w \in \{a, b\}^* \mid \exists n \geq 0 : |w|_a = n \text{ and } |w|_b \in \{n, 2n\} \}$$

is not accepted by any globally deterministic stateless CD-R(1)-system.

Thus, we have the following proper inclusion.

Corollary 31. $\mathcal{L}_{=1}(\text{stl-det-global-CD-R}(1)) \subsetneq \mathcal{L}_{=1}(\text{stl-det-local-CD-R}(1))$.

As the Dyck language $D_1'^*$ is accepted by a stl-det-global-CD-R(1)-system (see Example 18), we can conclude that the language class $\mathcal{L}_{=1}(\text{stl-det-global-CD-R}(1))$ is incomparable to the class of rational trace languages with respect to inclusion.

Concerning closure and non-closure properties for the language classes $\mathcal{L}_{=1}(\text{stl-det-local-CD-R}(1))$ and $\mathcal{L}_{=1}(\text{stl-det-global-CD-R}(1))$ the following results have been derived in [40,45]:

Type of CD-System	Operations								
	$\cup$	$\cap_{REG}$	c	$\cdot$	$*$	h	h^{-1}	com	R
stl-det-local-CD-R(1)	+	−	−	+	+	−	?	+	?
stl-det-global-CD-R(1)	−	−	+	−	−	−	?	−	−

Here the operations are abbreviated as follows:

- $\cup$ denotes the operation of union,
- $\cap_{REG}$ denotes the intersection with a regular language,
- c denotes the operation of complementation,
- $\cdot$ denotes the product operation,
- $*$ denotes the Kleene star,
- h denotes the application of an alphabetic morphism,
- h^{-1} denotes the operation of taking the preimage with respect to a morphism,
- com denotes the operation of taking the commutative closure,
- R denotes the operation of taking the reversal,

and "+" denotes the fact that the corresponding class is closed under the given operation, "−" denotes the fact that it is not closed, and "?" indicates that the status of this property is still open.

It remains to study the descriptional complexity of stl-det-global-CD-R(1)- and stl-det-local-CD-R(1)-systems.

Example 32. Let $\Sigma = \{a, b, c\}$, and let $n \geq 1$. We define the language $L_{=n} \subseteq \Sigma^*$ as follows:

$$L_{=n} = \{ w \in \Sigma^* \mid |w|_a = n = |w|_b \}.$$

We can easily construct a stl-det-global-CD-R(1)-system $\mathcal{M}$ with $2n+1$ components that accepts the language $L_{=n}$ in mode $= 1$. We just need n component automata that each simple delete one occurrence of the letter a, while moving right across occurrences of the letters b and c, we need another n component automata that each simply delete one occurrence of the letter b, while moving right across occurrences of the letter c, and we need a final component that accepts all words from c^*.

Now assume that $A = (Q, \Sigma, q_0, F, \delta)$ is an NFA for $L_{=n}$. We claim that A has at least $(n + 1)^2$ many states. Just consider the words $x_{i,j} = a^i b^j$ and $y_{i,j} = a^{n-i} b^{n-j}$ for all $i, j = 0, 1, \ldots, n$. Then $x_{i,j} y_{i,j} = a^i b^j a^{n-i} b^{n-j} \in L_{=n}$

for all i, j, while $x_{i,j} y_{i',j'} \notin L_{=n}$, whenever $i' \neq i$ or $j' \neq j$. Thus, the set of pairs $(x_{i,j}, y_{i,j})_{i,j=0,\ldots,n}$ is a fooling set for $L_{=n}$. Accordingly it follows that $|Q| \geq (n+1)^2$ [4].

Analogously for the finite language

$$L'_{=n} = \{ w \in \Sigma^* \mid |w|_a = |w|_b = |w|_c = n \}$$

we have a stl-det-global-CD-R(1)-system consisting of $3n + 1$ component automata, while an NFA for this language needs at least $(n+1)^3$ many states.

Thus, we can realize a polynomial trade-off of any degree from stl-det-global-CD-R(1)-systems to nondeterministic finite-state acceptors. Can we even realize an exponential trade-off between stl-det-global-CD-R(1)-systems (or stl-det-local-CD-R(1)-systems) and nondeterministic finite-state acceptors?

As globally deterministic CD-systems of R(1)-automata working in mode $= 1$ correspond to deterministic nonforgetting R(1)-automata (Theorem 15), it follows that $\mathcal{L}_{=1}(\text{stl-det-global-CD-R(1)}) \subseteq \mathcal{L}(\text{det-nf-R(1)})$ holds. Here we investigate this inclusion in a little more detail.

Proposition 33. [19] $\mathcal{L}_{=1}(\text{stl-det-global-CD-R(1)}) \subsetneq \mathcal{L}(\text{det-nf-R(1)})$.

Proof. It remains to show that the above inclusion is proper. Consider the language $L_{pr} = \{ wc \mid w \in \{a,b\}^*, |w|_a \geq |w|_b \geq 0 \}$. It is easily seen that L_{pr} is the language that is accepted by the det-nf-R(1)-automaton M_{pr} that is given through the following meta-instructions:

(1) $(q_0, \mathtext{¢} \cdot a^* \cdot c\$, \text{Accept})$, (2) $(q_0, \mathtext{¢} \cdot a^*, b \to \lambda, q_1)$, (3) $(q_1, \mathtext{¢} \cdot b^*, a \to \lambda, q_0)$.

On the other hand, it is shown in [45] that L_{pr} is not accepted by any stl-det-global-CD-R(1)-system. □

In addition, the following result holds.

Theorem 34. [19] *The language class $\mathcal{L}(\text{det-nf-R(1)})$ is incomparable to the class $\mathcal{L}_{=1}(\text{stl-det-local-CD-R(1)})$ and to the class of semi-linear languages with respect to inclusion.*

Proof. On the one hand, it can be shown that the rational trace language $L_\vee = \{ w \in \{a,b\}^* \mid \exists n \geq 0 : |w|_a = n \text{ and } |w|_b \in \{n, 2n\} \}$ is not accepted by any det-nf-R(1)-automaton. On the other hand, $\mathcal{L}(\text{det-nf-R(1)})$ contains the language $L_{ex2} = \{ (ab)^{2^n}(cd)^n e^2 \mid n \geq 0 \}$, which is not semi-linear, as $\psi(L_{ex2}) = \{ (2^n, 2^n, n, n, 2) \mid n \geq 0 \}$ is not a semi-linear subset of $\mathbb{N}^5$. □

Finally, it can be shown that

$$L_{\text{pal}} = \{ w \in \{a,b\}^* \mid w = w^R \} \in \mathcal{L}(\text{det-nf-R(2)}) \setminus \mathcal{L}(\text{det-nf-R(1)}),$$

implying that window size one is a real restriction for det-nf-R-automata. In summary, we have the hierarchy of language classes depicted in the diagram in Figure 2.

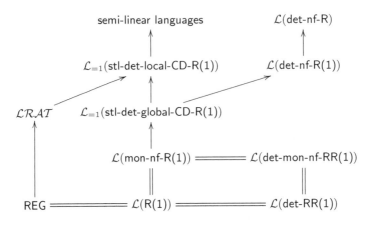

Fig. 2. Hierarchy of language classes accepted by various types of nonforgetting R-automata with window size 1. Each arrow represents a proper inclusion.

6   Extensions and Concluding Remarks

We have studied restarting automata with window size one, where we concentrated on various types of R(1)-automata. Even the nonforgetting version of these automata accepts only regular languages, if it is required to be monotone (Theorem 12). On the other hand, without this requirement already deterministic R(1)-automata accept some quite complicated languages (see the proof of Theorem 34). Further, by combining several stateless deterministic R(1)-automata into a CD-system, we obtain a device that is quite powerful, as all rational trace languages are accepted by CD-systems of this form (Theorem 29). In fact, we have seen that these CD-systems correspond to a generalization of the NFA, the *finite-state acceptor with translucent letters*.

Naturally the latter concept can be generalized to other types of automata. For example, one can consider *pushdown automata with translucent letters*, which, in analogy to the NFAwtl, do not necessarily process the leftmost input symbol, but which may read across a prefix consisting of letters that are translucent for the current internal state and the current topmost symbol on the pushdown. Formally, such a system can be defined as a *pushdown CD-system of stateless deterministic* R(1)-*automata* (PD-CD-R(1)-system, for short). It consists of a CD-system of stateless deterministic R(1)-automata and an external pushdown store. Formally, it is defined as a tuple $\mathcal{M} = (I, \Sigma, (M_i, \sigma_i)_{i \in I}, \Gamma, \perp, I_0, \delta)$, where

- I is a finite set of indices,
- Σ is a finite input alphabet,
- for all $i \in I$, $M_i = (\Sigma, \Sigma, \mathfrak{c}, \$, 1, \delta_i)$ is a stateless deterministic R(1)-automaton on Σ, and $\sigma_i \subseteq I$ is a non-empty set of possible successors for M_i,
- Γ is a finite pushdown alphabet,
- $\perp \notin \Gamma$ is the bottom marker of the pushdown store,
- $I_0 \subseteq I$ is a set of initial indices, and

- $\delta : (I \times \Sigma \times (\Gamma \cup \{\bot\})) \rightarrow 2^{I \times (\Gamma \cup \{\bot\})^*}$ is a finite successor relation. For each $i \in I$, $a \in \Sigma$, and $A \in \Gamma$, $\delta(i, a, A)$ is a subset of $\sigma_i \times \Gamma^{\leq 2}$, and $\delta(i, a, \bot)$ is a subset of $\sigma_i \times (\bot \cdot \Gamma^{\leq 2})$.

A *configuration* of $\mathcal{M}$ is a triple $(i, \mathfrak{c}w\$, \alpha)$, where $i \in I$ is the index of the active component automaton M_i, the word $\mathfrak{c}w\$$ ($w \in \Sigma^*$) is the tape content of a restarting configuration of M_i, and the word $\alpha \in \bot \cdot \Gamma^*$ is the current content of the pushdown store with the first symbol of α at the bottom and the last symbol of α at the top. For $w \in \Sigma^*$, an *initial configuration* of $\mathcal{M}$ on input w has the form $(i_0, \mathfrak{c}w\$, \bot)$ for any $i_0 \in I_0$, and an *accepting configuration* has the form $(i, \mathsf{Accept}, \bot)$ for any $i \in I$.

The *single-step computation relation* $\Rightarrow_\mathcal{M}$ that $\mathcal{M}$ induces on the set of configurations is defined by the following three rules, where $i \in I$, $w \in \Sigma^*$, $\alpha \in \bot \cdot \Gamma^*$, $A \in \Gamma$, and, for each $i \in I$, $\Sigma_1^{(i)}$, $\Sigma_2^{(i)}$, and $\Sigma_3^{(i)}$ are the subsets of Σ according to Definition 16 that correspond to the automaton M_i:

(1) $(i, \mathfrak{c}w\$, \alpha A) \Rightarrow_\mathcal{M} (j, \mathfrak{c}w'\$, \alpha\eta)$ if $\exists u \in {\Sigma_1^{(i)}}^*, a \in \Sigma_2^{(i)}, v \in \Sigma^*$ such that
$$w = uav, w' = uv, \text{ and } (j, \eta) \in \delta(i, a, A);$$

(2) $(i, \mathfrak{c}w\$, \bot) \Rightarrow_\mathcal{M} (j, \mathfrak{c}w'\$, \bot\eta)$ if $\exists u \in {\Sigma_1^{(i)}}^*, a \in \Sigma_2^{(i)}, v \in \Sigma^*$ such that
$$w = uav, w' = uv, \text{ and } (j, \bot\eta) \in \delta(i, a, \bot);$$

(3) $(i, \mathfrak{c}w\$, \bot) \Rightarrow_\mathcal{M} (i, \mathsf{Accept}, \bot)$ if $\exists u \in {\Sigma_1^{(i)}}^*, a \in \Sigma_3^{(i)}, v \in \Sigma^*$ such that
$$w = uav, \text{ or } w \in {\Sigma_1^{(i)}}^* \text{ and } \delta_i(\$) = \mathsf{Accept}.$$

By $\Rightarrow_\mathcal{M}^*$ we denote the *computation relation* of $\mathcal{M}$, which is simply the reflexive and transitive closure of the relation $\Rightarrow_\mathcal{M}$. The language $L(\mathcal{M})$ accepted by $\mathcal{M}$ consists of all words for which $\mathcal{M}$ has an accepting computation, that is,

$$L(\mathcal{M}) = \{\, w \in \Sigma^* \mid \exists i_0 \in I_0 \, \exists i \in I : (i_0, \mathfrak{c}w\$, \bot) \Rightarrow_\mathcal{M}^* (i, \mathsf{Accept}, \bot) \,\}.$$

By $\mathcal{L}(\mathsf{PD\text{-}CD\text{-}R}(1))$ we denote the class of languages that are accepted by PD-CD-R(1)-systems. On these systems the following main results have been obtained.

Theorem 35. [42] *Each language $L \in \mathcal{L}(\mathsf{PD\text{-}CD\text{-}R}(1))$ contains a context-free sublanguage E that is letter-equivalent to L. In fact, a pushdown automaton for E can be constructed effectively from a* PD-CD-R(1)*-system for L.*

It follows that the class $\mathcal{L}(\mathsf{PD\text{-}CD\text{-}R}(1))$ only contains semi-linear languages. Further, we see that the language $L = \{\, a^n b^n c^n \mid n \geq 0 \,\}$ is not accepted by any PD-CD-R(1)-system. On the other hand, the following positive result has been shown, where a language $L \subseteq \Sigma^*$ is called a *context-free trace language*, if there exist a dependency relation D on Σ and a context-free language $R \subseteq \Sigma^*$ such that $L = \varphi_D^{-1}(\varphi_D(R)) = \bigcup_{w \in R}[w]_D$ [1,3]. By $\mathcal{LCF}$ we denote the class of all context-free trace languages.

Theorem 36. [42] $\mathcal{LCF} \subsetneqq \mathcal{L}(\mathsf{PD\text{-}CD\text{-}R}(1))$.

Here the strictness of the inclusion follows from the facts that the language $L' = \{\, wa^m \mid |w|_a = |w|_b = |w|_c \geq 1, m \geq 1 \,\}$ is accepted by a stl-det-local-CD-R(1)-system [40], but that L' is not a context-free trace language [42].

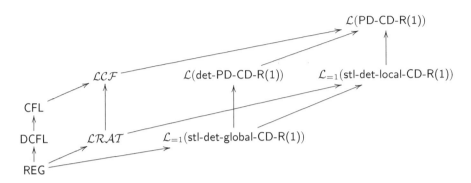

Fig. 3. Hierarchy of language classes accepted by various types of CD-R(1)-systems. Each arrow represents a proper inclusion, and classes that are not connected by a sequence of arrows are incomparable under inclusion.

Finally, in [43] also *deterministic pushdown CD-systems of stateless deterministic* R(1)*-automata* are introduced and studied. These systems can be interpreted as *deterministic pushdown automata with translucent letters*. Concerning the language classes accepted by these CD-systems the hierarchy displayed in the diagram in Figure 3 has been obtained, where $\mathcal{L}(\text{det-PD-CD-R}(1))$ denotes the class of languages that are accepted by deterministic PD-CD-R(1)-systems.

For the various CD-systems of stateless deterministic R(1)-automata, also the emptiness problem, the finiteness problem, and the universe problem have been studied [40,42,45]. However, the question of the succinctness of these CD-systems as descriptional systems for (regular or context-free) languages still remains to be studied.

References

1. Aalbersberg, I., Rozenberg, G.: Theory of traces. Theor. Comput. Sci. 60, 1–82 (1988)
2. Berstel, J.: Transductions and Context-Free Languages. Leitfäden der angewandten Mathematik und Mechanik 38. Teubner Studienbücher. Teubner, Stuttgart (1979)
3. Bertoni, A., Mauri, G., Sabadini, N.: Membership problems for regular and context-free trace languages. Inform. Comput. 82, 135–150 (1989)
4. Birget, J.C.: Intersection and union of regular languages and state complexity. Inform. Proc. Letters 43, 185–190 (1992)
5. Book, R.: Grammars with time functions. PhD thesis. Harvard University, Cambridge, Massachusetts (1969)
6. Buntrock, G., Otto, F.: Growing context-sensitive languages and Church-Rosser languages. Inform. Comput. 141, 1–36 (1998)
7. Chytil, M., Plátek, M., Vogel, J.: A note on the Chomsky hierarchy. Bull. EATCS 27, 23–30 (1985)

8. Csuhaj-Varjú, E., Dassow, J., Kelemen, J., Păun, G.: Grammar Systems. A Grammatical Approach to Distribution and Cooperation. Gordon and Breach, London (1994)
9. Dahlhaus, E., Warmuth, M.: Membership for growing context-sensitive grammars is polynomial. J. Comput. Syst. Sci. 33, 456–472 (1986)
10. Dassow, J., Păun, G., Rozenberg, G.: Grammar systems. In: Rozenberg, G., Salomaa, A. (eds.) Handbook of Formal Languages, vol. 2, pp. 155–213. Springer, Berlin (1997)
11. Diekert, V., Rozenberg, G.: The Book of Traces. World Scientific, Singapore (1995)
12. Dikovsky, A., Modina, L.: Dependencies on the other side of the curtain. Traitement Automatique des Langues 41, 79–111 (2000)
13. Ehrenfeucht, A., Păun, G., Rozenberg, G.: Contextual grammars and formal languages. In: Rozenberg, G., Salomaa, A. (eds.) Handbook of Formal Languages, vol. 2, pp. 237–293. Springer, Berlin (1997)
14. Gladkij, A.: On the complexity of derivations for context-sensitive grammars. Algebra i Logika 3, 29–44 (1964) (in Russian)
15. Gramatovici, R., Martín-Vide, C.: 1-contextual grammars with sorted dependencies. In: Spoto, F., Scollo, G., Nijholt, A. (eds.) 3rd AMAST Workshop on Language Processing, Proc. Universiteit Twente, Enschede, pp. 99–109 (2003)
16. Harrison, M.: Introduction to Formal Language Theory. Addison-Wesley, Reading (1978)
17. Holzer, M., Kutrib, M., Reimann, J.: Descriptional complexity of deterministic restarting automata. In: Meregetti, C., Palano, B., Pighizzini, P., Wotschke, D. (eds.) DCFS 2005, pp. 158–169. Proc. Università degli Studi di Milano, Milan (2005)
18. Holzer, M., Kutrib, M., Reimann, J.: Non-recursive trade-offs for deterministic restarting automata. J. Autom. Lang. Comb. 12, 195–213 (2007)
19. Hundeshagen, N., Otto, F.: Characterizing the regular languages by nonforgetting restarting automata. In: Leporati, A. (ed.) DLT 2011. LNCS, vol. 6795, pp. 288–299. Springer, Heidelberg (2011)
20. Jančar, P., Mráz, F., Plátek, M.: A taxonomy of forgetting automata. In: Borzyszkowski, A., Sokolowski, S. (eds.) MFCS 1993. LNCS, vol. 711, pp. 527–536. Springer, Heidelberg (1993)
21. Jančar, P., Mráz, F., Plátek, M.: Forgetting automata and context-free languages. Acta. Inf. 33, 409–420 (1996)
22. Jančar, P., Mráz, F., Plátek, M., Vogel, J.: Restarting automata. In: Reichel, H. (ed.) FCT 1995. LNCS, vol. 965, pp. 283–292. Springer, Heidelberg (1995)
23. Jančar, P., Mráz, F., Plátek, M., Vogel, J.: On restarting automata with rewriting. In: Păun, G., Salomaa, A. (eds.) New Trends in Formal Languages. LNCS, vol. 1218, pp. 119–136. Springer, Heidelberg (1997)
24. Jančar, P., Mráz, F., Plátek, M., Vogel, J.: Different types of monotonicity for restarting automata. In: Arvind, V., Ramanujam, S. (eds.) FST TCS 1998. LNCS, vol. 1530, pp. 343–355. Springer, Heidelberg (1998)
25. Jančar, P., Mráz, F., Plátek, M., Vogel, J.: On monotonic automata with a restart operation. J. Autom. Lang. Comb. 4, 287–311 (1999)
26. Jurdziński, T., Otto, F.: Shrinking restarting automata. Intern. J. Found. Comp. Sci. 18, 361–385 (2007)
27. Kutrib, M., Messerschmidt, H., Otto, F.: On stateless two-pushdown automata and restarting automata. In: Csuhaj-Varjú, E., Ésik, Z. (eds.) AFL 2008, pp. 257–268. Proc. Computer and Automation Research Institute, Hungarian Academy of Sciences (2008)

28. Kutrib, M., Messerschmidt, H., Otto, F.: On stateless two-pushdown automata and restarting automata. Intern. J. Found. Comp. Sci. 21, 781–798 (2010)

29. Kutrib, M., Reimann, J.: Optimal simulations of weak restarting automata. In: Geffert, V., Pighizzini, G. (eds.) Workshop Descriptional Complexity of Formal Systems, Proc., Košice, Slovakia, Institute of Computer Science, P.J. Šafàrik University, pp. 81–92 (2007)

30. Kutrib, M., Reimann, J.: Succinct description of regular languages by weak restarting automata. Inform. Comput. 206, 1152–1160 (2008)

31. Marcus, S.: Contextual grammars and natural languages. In: Rozenberg, G., Salomaa, A. (eds.) Handbook of Formal Languages, vol. 2, pp. 215–235. Springer, Berlin (1997)

32. McNaughton, R., Narendran, P., Otto, F.: Church-Rosser Thue systems and formal languages. J. Assoc. Comput. Mach. 35, 324–344 (1988)

33. Messerschmidt, H., Otto, F.: On nonforgetting restarting automata that are deterministic and/or monotone. In: Grigoriev, D., Harrison, J., Hirsch, E. (eds.) CSR 2006. LNCS, vol. 3967, pp. 247–258. Springer, Heidelberg (2006)

34. Messerschmidt, H., Otto, F.: Cooperating distributed systems of restarting automata. Intern. J. Found. Comp. Sci. 18, 1333–1342 (2007)

35. Messerschmidt, H., Otto, F.: Strictly deterministic CD-systems of restarting automata. In: Csuhaj-Varjú, E., Ésik, Z. (eds.) FCT 2007. LNCS, vol. 4639, pp. 424–434. Springer, Heidelberg (2007)

36. Messerschmidt, H., Otto, F.: On deterministic CD-systems of restarting automata. Intern. J. Found. Comp. Sci. 20, 185–209 (2009)

37. Messerschmidt, H., Stamer, H.: Restart-Automaten mit mehreren Restart-Zuständen. In: Bordihn, H. (ed.) Proceedings of two Workshop 'Formale Sprachen in der Linguistik und 14.Theorietag Automaten und Formale Sprachen' pp. 111–116. Proc. Institut für Informatik, Universität Potsdam (2004)

38. Mráz, F.: Lookahead hierarchies of restarting automata. J. Autom. Lang. Comb. 6, 493–506 (2001)

39. Mráz, F., Otto, F., Plátek, M.: On the gap-complexity of simple RL-automata. In: Ibarra, O., Dang, Z. (eds.) DLT 2006. LNCS, vol. 4036, pp. 83–94. Springer, Heidelberg (2006)

40. Nagy, B., Otto, F.: CD-systems of stateless deterministic R-automata with window size one. Kasseler Informatikschriften 2/2010, Universität Kassel (April 2010), https://kobra.bibliothek.uni-kassel.de/handle/urn:nbn:de:hebis:34-2010042732682

41. Nagy, B., Otto, F.: CD-systems of stateless deterministic R(1)-automata accept all rational trace languages. In: Dediu, A., Fernau, H., Martín-Vide, C. (eds.) LATA 2010. LNCS, vol. 6031, pp. 463–474. Springer, Heidelberg (2010)

42. Nagy, B., Otto, F.: An automata-theoretical characterization of context-free trace languages. In: Černá, I., Gyimóthy, T., Hromkovič, J., Jefferey, K., Královič, R., Vukolić, M., Wolf, S. (eds.) SOFSEM 2011. LNCS, vol. 6543, pp. 406–417. Springer, Heidelberg (2011)

43. Nagy, B., Otto, F.: Deterministic pushdown CD-systems of stateless deterministic R(1)-automata. In: Dömösi, P. (ed.) AFL 2011, Proc. Computer and Automation Research Institute, Hungarian Academy of Sciences (to appear, 2011)

44. Nagy, B., Otto, F.: Finite-state acceptors with translucent letters. In: Bel-Enguix, G., Dahl, V., De La Puente, A. (eds.) BILC 2011, pp. 3–13. Proc. SciTePress, Portugal (2011)

45. Nagy, B., Otto, F.: Globally deterministic CD-systems of stateless R(1)-automata. In: Dediu, A., Inenaga, S., Martín-Vide, C. (eds.) LATA 2011. LNCS, vol. 6638, pp. 390–401. Springer, Heidelberg (2011)
46. Niemann, G., Otto, F.: Restarting automata, Church-Rosser languages, and representations of r.e. languages. In: Rozenberg, G., Thomas, W. (eds.) Proc. DLT 1999, pp. 103–114. World Scientific, Singapore (2000)
47. Niemann, G., Otto, F.: On the power of RRWW-automata. In: Ito, M., Păun, G., Yu, S. (eds.) Words, Semigroups, and Transductions. Essays in Honour of Gabriel Thierrin, On the Occasion of His 80th Birthday, pp. 341–355. World Scientific, Singapore (2001)
48. Niemann, G., Otto, F.: Further results on restarting automata. In: Ito, M., Imaoka, T. (eds.) Proc. on Words, Languages and Combinatorics III, pp. 353–369. World Scientific, Singapore (2003)
49. Reimann, J.: Beschreibungskomplexität von Restart-Automaten. PhD thesis, Naturwissenschaftliche Fachbereiche, Justus-Liebig-Universität Giessen (2007)
50. Schluter, N.: On lookahead hierarchies for monotone and deterministic restarting automata with auxiliary symbols (Extended abstract). In: Gao, Y., Lu, H., Seki, S., Yu, S. (eds.) DLT 2010. LNCS, vol. 6224, pp. 440–441. Springer, Heidelberg (2010)
51. Schluter, N.: Restarting automata with auxiliary symbols and small lookahead. In: Dediu, A., Inenaga, S., Martín-Vide, C. (eds.) LATA 2011. LNCS, vol. 6638, pp. 499–510. Springer, Heidelberg (2011)
52. Straňáková, M.: Selected types of pg-ambiguity. The Prague Bull. Math. Ling. 72, 29–57 (1999)
53. Stranáková, M.: Selected types of pg-ambiguity: Processing based on analysis by reduction. In: Sojka, P., Kopeček, I., Pala, K. (eds.) TSD 2000. LNCS (LNAI), vol. 1902, pp. 139–144. Springer, Heidelberg (2000)
54. Černo, P., Mráz, F.: Clearing restarting automata. Fund. Inform. 104, 17–54 (2010)
55. von Solms, S.: The characterization by automata of certain classes of languages in the context sensitive area. Inform. Contr. 27, 262–271 (1975)

Construction and SAT-Based Verification of Contextual Unfoldings

Stefan Schwoon and César Rodríguez

LSV, ENS de Cachan & CNRS, INRIA
61 avenue du Président Wilson, 94230 Cachan, France
{schwoon,rodrigue}@lsv.ens-cachan.fr

Abstract. Unfoldings succinctly represent the set of reachable markings of a Petri net. Here, we shall consider the case of contextual nets, which extend Petri nets with read arcs, and which are more suitable to represent the case of concurrent read access. We discuss the problem of (efficiently) constructing unfoldings of such nets. On the basis of these unfoldings, various verification problems can be encoded as satisfiability problems in propositional logic.

1 Introduction

Petri nets are generally recognized as an adequate formal model for concurrent, distributed systems. The unfolding of a Petri net is, essentially, an acyclic version of the net in which the loops have been unrolled. While in general infinite, one can construct a finite "complete" prefix of it that represents all its behaviours, and whose acyclic structure permits easier analysis. The resulting object is typically larger than the net, but much smaller than the number of its reachable markings. The idea of using unfoldings for verifying properties of Petri nets was first employed by McMillan [7] and subsequently greatly expanded by many other works, see [3] for a survey. On 1-safe Petri nets, for instance, the reachability problem is PSPACE-complete, whereas the corresponding problem is only NP-complete for complete prefixes. Notwithstanding the fact that the size of the unfolding is rather larger than the net itself, this opens avenues for efficient reachability checking [5].

The success of unfolding-based techniques is due to the fact that unfoldings exploit the inherently concurrent nature of the underlying system; loosely speaking, the more concurrency there is in the net, the more advantages unfoldings have when compared to reachability-graph techniques.

However, Petri nets are not expressive enough to adequately model concurrent read accesses to the same resource, that is, if multiple actions at the same time require non-exclusive access to one common resource. Consequently, the unfolding technique becomes inefficient in the presence of such situations.

Contextual nets address this problem. They extend Petri nets with *read arcs*, which allow transitions to require the presence of a token on certain places without actually consuming them. They have been used, e.g., to model concurrent

M. Holzer, M. Kutrib, and G. Pighizzini (Eds.): DCFS 2011, LNCS 6808, pp. 34–42, 2011.

database access [9], concurrent constraint programs [8], priorities [6], and asynchronous circuits [12]. Modelling using read arcs allows unfolding-based techniques to take advantage of concurrency in the model, resulting in unfoldings that are up to exponentially smaller in the presence of multiple readers.

This advantage comes at a price: read arcs introduce a phenomenon known as *asymmetric conflict*, meaning that an event e may not be necessary for another event e' to happen, but if both e and e' happen, then e must happen first. (This phenomenon is absent in the Petri net case.) Asymmetric conflicts complicate the theoretical foundations by no small amount, which explains why contextual unfolding techniques were slow to be developed. A first approach by Vogler, Semenov, and Yakovlev proposed an unfolding procedure for a restricted subclass [12]. Winkowski proposed a general but non-constructive procedure [13]. A constructive, general solution was finally given in [2], and steps towards a concrete implementation were undertaken in [1] and more recently in [11], resulting in the tool Cunf [10].

Experiments in [11] show that contextual unfoldings are not only more succinct but can generally be constructed more quickly then Petri unfoldings. Moreover, as we shall see, the reachability problem remains in NP, and we shall discuss an encoding of this and related problems in SAT.

The rest of the paper is structured as follows. In Section 2 we define contextual nets and their unfoldings. In Section 3 we summarize the salient points about their construction, and in Section 4, we discuss SAT-based approaches to some verification problems.

2   Contextual Nets and Their Unfoldings

In this section, we introduce contextual nets and their unfoldings. We also discuss an example showing the greater succinctness of contextual unfoldings when compared to normal unfoldings. A more expanded treatment of the subject can be found, e.g., in [2] or [11].

2.1   Contextual Nets

A *contextual net (c-net)* is a tuple $N = \langle P, T, F, C, m_0 \rangle$, where P and T are disjoint sets of *places* and *transitions*, $F \subseteq (P \times T) \cup (T \times P)$ is the *flow relation*, and $C \subseteq P \times T$ is the *context relation*. A pair $(p, t) \in C$ is called *read arc*. Any function $m \colon P \to \mathbb{N}$ is called a *marking*, and m_0 is the *initial marking*. A *Petri net* is a c-net without any read arcs.

For $x \in P \cup T$, we call $^\bullet x := \{ y \in P \cup T \mid (y, x) \in F \}$ the *preset* of x, and $x^\bullet := \{ y \in P \cup T \mid (x, y) \in F \}$ the *postset* of x. The *context* of a place p is defined as $\underline{p} := \{ t \in T \mid (p, t) \in C \}$, and the context of a transition t as $\underline{t} := \{ p \in P \mid (p, t) \in C \}$. These notions are extended to sets in the usual fashion.

A marking m is *n-safe* if $m(p) \le n$ for all $p \in P$. A set $A \subseteq T$ of transitions is *enabled* at a marking m if for all $p \in P$,

$$m(p) \geq |p^\bullet \cap A| + \begin{cases} 1 & \text{if } \underline{p} \cap A \neq \emptyset \\ 0 & \text{otherwise} \end{cases}$$

Such A may *fire*, leading to a new marking m', where $m'(p) = m(p) - |p^\bullet \cap A| + |^\bullet p \cap A|$ for all $p \in P$. We call $\langle m, A, m' \rangle$ a *step* of N.

A finite sequence of transitions $\sigma = t_1 \ldots t_n \in T^*$ is a *run* if there exist markings $m_1, \ldots, m_n$ such that $\langle m_{i-1}, \{t_i\}, m_i \rangle$ is a step for $1 \leq i \leq n$, and m_0 is the initial marking of N; if such a run exists, m_n is said to be *reachable*. A c-net N is said to be *n-safe* if every reachable marking of N is *n-safe*.

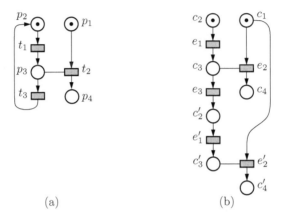

(a)   (b)

Fig. 1. (a) A 1-safe c-net; (b) One of its unfolding prefixes (right)

Fig. 1 (a) depicts a 1-safe c-net. Read arcs are drawn as undirected lines. For t_2, we have $\{p_1\} = {}^\bullet t_2$, $\{p_3\} = \underline{t_2}$ and $\{p_4\} = t_2^\bullet$.

In this treatment, we restrict our interest to finite 1-safe c-nets and treat markings as sets of places. Notice, however, that the general theory of contextual unfolding developed in [2] extends to semi-weighted nets.

2.2   Unfoldings

Let $N = \langle P, T, F, C, m_0 \rangle$ be a c-net. Intuitively, the unfolding of N is a 1-safe acyclic c-net where loops of N are "unrolled".

Definition 1. *The unfolding of N, written $\mathcal{U}_N$, is a c-net $(B, E, G, D, \widehat{m}_0)$ equipped with a mapping $f \colon (B \cup E) \to (P \cup T)$, which we extend to sets and sequences in the usual way. We call the elements of B conditions, and those of E events; f maps conditions to places and events to transitions.*

Conditions will take the form $\langle p, e' \rangle$, where $p \in P$ and $e' \in E \cup \{\bot\}$, and events will take the form $\langle t, M \rangle$, where $t \in T$ and $M \subseteq B$. We shall assume $f(\langle p, e' \rangle) = p$ and $f(\langle t, M \rangle) = t$, respectively. A set M of conditions is called concurrent iff $\mathcal{U}_N$ has a reachable marking M' s.t. $M' \supseteq M$.

$\mathcal{U}_N$ is the smallest net containing the following elements:

- *if $p \in m_0$, then $\langle p, \perp \rangle \in B$ and $\langle p, \perp \rangle \in \widehat{m}_0$;*
- *for any $t \in T$ and disjoint pair of sets $M_1, M_2 \subseteq B$ such that $M_1 \cup M_2$ is concurrent, $f(M_1) = {}^\bullet t$, $f(M_2) = \underline{t}$, we have $e := \langle t, M_1 \cup M_2 \rangle \in E$, and for all $p \in t^\bullet$, we have $\langle p, e \rangle \in B$. Moreover, G and D are such that ${}^\bullet e = M_1$, $\underline{e} = M_2$, and $e^\bullet = \{ \langle p, e \rangle \mid p \in t^\bullet \}$.*

For example, Fig. 1 (b) shows the beginning of the unfolding of the c-net from Fig. 1 (a). In general, unfoldings are infinite. We shall study finite portions of them that contain all information about reachable markings:

Definition 2. *Let x, y be nodes. We write $x < y$ if either $(x, y) \in G$, or x, y are events such that $x^\bullet \cap \underline{y} \neq \emptyset$, or (x, y) is in the transitive closure of the first two cases. We define $[x] := \{ e \in E \mid e \leq x \}$ as the set of* causes *of x. A set $X \subseteq E$ is called* causally closed *if $[e] \subseteq X$ for all $e \in X$. A* prefix *of $\mathcal{U}_N$ is a net $\mathcal{P} = \langle B', E', G', D', \widehat{m}_0 \rangle$ such that $E' \subseteq E$ is causally closed, $B' = \widehat{m}_0 \cup (E')^\bullet$, and G', D' are the restrictions of G, D to $(B' \cup E')$.*

In Fig. 1 (b), we have, e.g., $c_2 < e_1$, $e_1 < e_2$, and $c_2 < e_2$. If e, e' are two events with $e < e'$, then e must occur before e' in any run that fires e'. A prefix is a causally-closed subnet of $\mathcal{U}_N$. We are interested in prefixes that have the same markings as N itself, modulo f.

Definition 3. *A prefix $\mathcal{P}$ is called* complete *if for all markings m, m is reachable in N iff there exists a marking $\widehat{m}$ reachable in $\mathcal{P}$ such that $f(\widehat{m}) = m$.*

2.3   Succintness of Contextual vs. Petri Net Unfoldings

For Petri nets, there are methods of constructing complete finite prefixes that may be exponentially smaller than the reachability graph, and at worst no larger than it [4]. Here, we shall make another observation: the unfolding of a c-net may be exponentially more succinct than the unfolding of a Petri net that has the same set of reachable markings.

Consider the c-net N depicted in Fig. 2 (a). The place p has two transitions b, c in its context. This models a situation where, e.g., two processes are read-accessing a common resource modelled by p. Notice that $\{b, c\}$ can fire in N. Fig. 2 (b) shows a Petri net N' in which read arcs have been replaced by read/write loops. Evidently, N' has the same set of reachable markings as N.

However, $\{b, c\}$ cannot fire in N': the encoding step does not preserve the concurrency between b and c. As a result, the unfolding of N' enumerates both the sequence "first b, then c" and the inverse, whereas the unfolding of N is actually identical to N itself, see Fig. 3. One easily sees that if b and c were replaced by n transitions reading from p, the unfolding of N' would become exponentially larger than the one of N.

We note in passing that this blowup can be mitigated, but not completely avoided, by a less naïve transformation into Petri nets provided by Vogler et al [12].

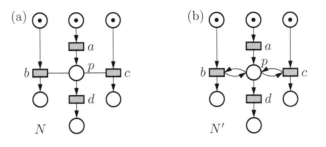

Fig. 2. C-net N and Petri net N'

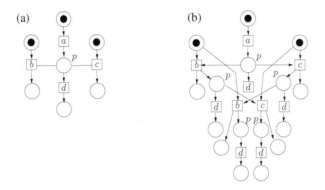

Fig. 3. Unfoldings of N and N' from Fig. 2

3 Constructing Contextual Unfoldings

We sketch the main ideas for the algorithms behind efficiently constructing complete finite unfolding prefixes. Again, an expanded treatment can be found in [2,11]. Notice that Definition 7 and Proposition 8 follow a new and slightly more elegant approach than was put forward in [11].

For the rest of the section, let us fix a 1-safe c-net $N = \langle P, T, F, C, m_0 \rangle$ and its unfolding $\mathcal{U}_N = \langle B, E, G, D, \widehat{m}_0 \rangle$. We first elaborate on the notion of asymmetric conflict that is characteristic for c-nets.

Definition 4. *Two events $e, e' \in E$ are in* asymmetric conflict, *written $e \nearrow e'$, iff (i) $e < e'$, or (ii) $\underline{e} \cap {}^\bullet e' \neq \emptyset$, or (iii) $e \neq e'$ and ${}^\bullet e \cap {}^\bullet e' \neq \emptyset$. For a set of events $X \subseteq E$, we write $\nearrow_X$ to denote the relation $\nearrow \cap\, X \times X$. A configuration of $\mathcal{U}_N$ is a finite, causally closed set of events $\mathcal{C}$ such that $\nearrow_\mathcal{C}$ is acyclic. A history of an event e is a configuration H such that $e'(\nearrow_H)^* e$ for all $e' \in H$. For a configuration $\mathcal{C}$ we define $\mathsf{Cut}(\mathcal{C}) := (\widehat{m}_0 \cup \mathcal{C}^\bullet) \setminus {}^\bullet\mathcal{C}$, and its marking as its image through $f \colon \mathsf{Mark}(\mathcal{C}) := f(\mathsf{Cut}(\mathcal{C}))$.*

Asymmetric conflict can be thought of as a scheduling constraint: if both e, e' occur in a run, then e must occur first (in case (iii) this is vacuously the case, as e, e' cannot both occur). The notion of configuration captures sets of events that can be arranged to form a run that respects $\nearrow$; naturally, such a set must be free of cyclic scheduling constraints. A history of e is a configuration in which e necessarily fires last.

Definition 5. *Configurations $\mathcal{C}$, $\mathcal{C}'$ are said to be in* conflict, *written $\mathcal{C} \# \mathcal{C}'$, if there exists some $e \in \mathcal{C}$ and $e' \in \mathcal{C}' \setminus \mathcal{C}$ such that $e' \nearrow e$, or the inverse condition holds.*

Intuitively, $\mathcal{C} \# \mathcal{C}'$ means that $\mathcal{C}$ and $\mathcal{C}'$ represent "diverging" runs of the unfolding; from either $\mathcal{C}$ or $\mathcal{C}'$ it is no longer possible to obtain a run that contains the elements of $\mathcal{C} \cup \mathcal{C}'$.

Definition 6. *Let c be a condition. A* generating history *of c is $\emptyset$ if $c \in \widehat{m}_0$, or H if $\{e\} = {}^\bullet c$ and H is a history of e. A* reading history *of c is any H such that $e \in \underline{c}$ and H is a history of e. A* history *of c is any of its generating or reading histories or $H_1 \cup H_2$, where H_1 and H_2 are histories of c verifying $\neg(H_1 \# H_2)$.*

The key idea of [2], in order to construct a complete prefix of $\mathcal{U}_N$, is to consider pairs $\langle e, H \rangle$, where H is a history of e. Definition 7 in combination with Proposition 8 gives a unique characterization of these pairs.

Definition 7. *A pair $\langle c, H \rangle$, where H is a history of c, is called an* enriched condition. *The pair $\rho = \langle c, H \rangle$ is said to be* asymmetrically concurrent *to $\rho' = \langle c', H' \rangle$ iff (i) $\neg(H \# H')$, (ii) $c, c' \in \mathsf{Cut}(H \cup H')$, and (iii) $\underline{c} \cap H' \subseteq H$. If this is the case, we write $\rho \mathbin{/\!/} \rho'$.*

Proposition 8. *Let e be an event of $\mathcal{U}_N$ such that ${}^\bullet e = \{c_1, \ldots, c_k\}$ and $\underline{e} = \{c_{k+1}, \ldots, c_n\}$. Then H is a history of e iff there exist enriched conditions $\rho_i = \langle c_i, H_i \rangle$, for $i = 1, \ldots, n$, such that*

1. *$H = \{e\} \cup \bigcup_{i=1}^n H_i$;*
2. *$H_{k+1}, \ldots, H_n$ are generating histories of $c_{k+1}, \ldots, c_n$;*
3. *$\rho_i \mathbin{/\!/} \rho_j$ for $i = 1, \ldots, k$ and $j = 1, \ldots, n$;*
4. *$\rho_i \mathbin{/\!/} \rho_j$ or $\rho_j \mathbin{/\!/} \rho_i$ for $i, j \in k+1, \ldots, n$.*

The binary relation $\mathbin{/\!/}$ is efficiently computable [11,10] and allows to discover algorithmically the histories and therefore the events that constitute $\mathcal{U}_N$. Moreover, [2,11] provide criteria for determining which event and histories need to be considered when constructing a complete prefix of $\mathcal{U}_N$; experimental results with Cunf are reported in [11].

4   Verifying Properties about Contextual Nets Using SAT

In this section we briefly give some examples showing how the complete prefix of a c-net unfolding can be used to answer questions about the c-net itself. For this, we adapt the SAT-based reductions of [3] to the contextual case.

We start by recalling that the following problem is NP-complete, see e.g. [3]:

Given a complete prefix of $\mathcal{U}_N$, where N is a 1-safe *Petri* net, and a marking m of N, is m reachable in N?

It is straightforward to see that the result extends to the case where N is a general c-net (with read arcs).

This result suggests that the reachability problem can be encoded as a satisfiability problem in propositional logic, using a formula whose size is proportional to that of $\mathcal{U}_N$. The key idea is to first construct a formula ϕ_N that characterizes the configurations and markings of $\mathcal{U}_N$. More precisely, for every condition c and event e of $\mathcal{U}_N$, ϕ_N will contain a variable $\mathbf{c}$ and $\mathbf{e}$, respectively; the models of ϕ_N will be those assignments in which the event variables with value true correspond to some configuration $\mathcal{C}$ and the true condition variables to $\mathsf{Mark}(\mathcal{C})$.

ϕ_N will be a conjunction of formulae ensuring that $\mathcal{C}$ is indeed a configuration, that is, causally closed and free of asymmetric-conflict cycles; variable $\mathbf{c}$ will be true iff condition c is produced but not consumed by $\mathcal{C}$. For instance, suppose that condition c has $^\bullet c = \{e\}$, $c^\bullet = \{f_1, \ldots, f_m\}$, and $\underline{c} = \{g_1, \ldots, g_k\}$. Then we define

$$\phi_c := \left(\bigvee_{i=1}^{m} \mathbf{f}_i \vee \bigvee_{i=1}^{k} \mathbf{g}_i \right) \rightarrow \mathbf{e} \quad \wedge \quad \mathbf{c} \leftrightarrow \left(\mathbf{e} \wedge \bigwedge_{i=1}^{m} \neg \mathbf{f}_i \right)$$

Moreover, let $\mathsf{Cycles}(\mathcal{U}_N) := \{\, e_1, \ldots, e_n \mid e_1 \nearrow \cdots \nearrow e_n \nearrow e_1 \,\}$ and

$$\phi_C := \bigwedge_{e_1, \ldots, e_n \in \mathsf{Cycles}(\mathcal{U}_N)} \neg(e_1 \wedge \cdots \wedge e_n)$$

We now set $\phi_N := \phi_C \wedge \bigwedge_{c \in B} \phi_c$.

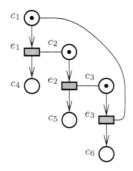

Fig. 4. e_1, e_2, e_3 form an asymmetric-conflict cycle of length 3

The main difference between ϕ_N and the corresponding construction for Petri nets in [3] is the treatment of asymmetric-conflict cycles. In Petri nets, all conflicts are symmetric and between pairs of events e, e' with $^\bullet e \cap \, ^\bullet e' \neq \emptyset$. In contrast, conflict cycles in c-nets can be of arbitrary length as exemplified by Fig. 4. Nonetheless, they give rise to the same type of constraint in the SAT encoding.

Using ϕ_N, and following the example of [3], one can encode many questions about the set of reachable markings of N in terms of propositional logic, for instance:

- Is there any reachable marking in N that contains both places p and q?
  Let f is the mapping from Definition 1, and suppose that $c_1, \ldots, c_m \in B$ are those conditions with $f(c_i) = p$, for $i = 1, \ldots, m$, and $d_1, \ldots, d_k \in B$ those with $f(d_i) = q$, for $i = 1, \ldots, k$. Let $\phi_p = \mathbf{c}_1 \vee \cdots \vee \mathbf{c}_m$ and $\phi_q = \mathbf{d}_1 \vee \cdots \vee \mathbf{d}_k$. Then, a marking that contains both p and q exists in N iff

$$\phi_N \wedge \phi_p \wedge \phi_q$$

  is satisfiable.
- Is $\{p, q\}$ a P-invariant of N?
  This means that every reachable marking puts exactly one token into either p or q. Under the same assumptions as above, this is the case iff

$$\phi_N \rightarrow (\phi_p \oplus \phi_q)$$

  is valid, i.e., its negation is unsatisfiable.
- Does N contain a deadlock?
  Suppose that t is a transition of N with $^\bullet t = \{p, q\}$, and otherwise make the same assumptions as above. Let $\phi_t = \phi_p \wedge \phi_q$, then any model of $\phi_N \wedge \phi_t$ corresponds to a marking in which t is enabled. Assuming that we construct corresponding formulae for all other transitions of N, then a deadlock exists iff

$$\phi_N \wedge \bigwedge_{t \in T} \neg \phi_t$$

  is satisfiable.

References

1. Baldan, P., Bruni, A., Corradini, A., König, B., Schwoon, S.: On the computation of mcMillan"s prefix for contextual nets and graph grammars. In: Ehrig, H., Rensink, A., Rozenberg, G., Schürr, A. (eds.) ICGT 2010. LNCS, vol. 6372, pp. 91–106. Springer, Heidelberg (2010)
2. Baldan, P., Corradini, A., König, B., Schwoon, S.: McMillan's complete prefix for contextual nets. In: Jensen, K., van der Aalst, W.M.P., Billington, J. (eds.) Transactions on Petri Nets and Other Models of Concurrency I. LNCS, vol. 5100, pp. 199–220. Springer, Heidelberg (2008)
3. Esparza, J., Heljanko, K.: Unfoldings - A Partial-Order Approach to Model Checking. EATCS Monographs in Theoretical Computer Science. Springer, Heidelberg (2008)
4. Esparza, J., Römer, S., Vogler, W.: An improvement of McMillan's unfolding algorithm. Formal Methods in System Design 20, 285–310 (2002)
5. Heljanko, K.: Combining Symbolic and Partial-Order Methods for Model-Checking 1-Safe Petri Nets. Ph.D. thesis. Helsinki University of Technology (2002)

6. Janicki, R., Koutny, M.: Invariant semantics of nets with inhibitor arcs. In: Groote, J.F., Baeten, J.C.M. (eds.) CONCUR 1991. LNCS, vol. 527, pp. 317–331. Springer, Heidelberg (1991)

7. McMillan, K.L.: Using unfoldings to avoid the state explosion problem in the verification of asynchronous circuits. In: Probst, D.K., von Bochmann, G. (eds.) CAV 1992. LNCS, vol. 663, pp. 164–177. Springer, Heidelberg (1993)

8. Montanari, U., Rossi, F.: Contextual occurrence nets and concurrent constraint programming. In: Ehrig, H., Schneider, H.-J. (eds.) Dagstuhl Seminar 1993. LNCS, vol. 776. Springer, Heidelberg (1994)

9. Ristori, G.: Modelling systems with shared resources via Petri nets. Ph.D. thesis. University of Pisa (1994)

10. Rodríguez, C.: The Cunf tool, `http://www.lsv.ens-cachan.fr/~rodriguez/tools/cunf/`

11. Rodríguez, C., Schwoon, S., Baldan, P.: Efficient contextual unfolding. Tech. rep., LSV, ENS de Cachan (2011)

12. Vogler, W., Semenov, A.L., Yakovlev, A.: Unfolding and finite prefix for nets with read arcs. In: Sangiorgi, D., de Simone, R. (eds.) CONCUR 1998. LNCS, vol. 1466, pp. 501–516. Springer, Heidelberg (1998)

13. Winkowski, J.: Reachability in contextual nets. Fundamenta Informaticae 51(1-2), 235–250 (2002)

The Power of Diversity

Denis Thérien

School of Computer Science, McGill University,
Montréal (Québec), H3A 2A7 Canada
denis@cs.mcgill.ca

Abstract. In computations realized by finite automata, a rich understanding has come from comparing the algebraic structure of the machines to the combinatorics of the languages being recognized. In this
expository paper, we will first survey some basic ideas that have been
useful in this model. In the second part, we sketch how this dual approach
can be generalized to study some important class of boolean circuits,
what results have been obtained, what questions are still open. The intuition gained in the simple model sometimes carry through, sometimes
not, so that one has to be careful on what conjectures to make.

1 Introduction

The mathematical formalization of the notion of computation is one of the important intellectual achievements of the last century. This concept serves as one of
the theoretical foundations for the technological revolution that has transformed
so radically our society in the last years; it is also at the heart of a sophisticated
scientific theory where challenging problems abound. Although theory of computation may not be universally accepted to be "core mathematics", we can take
comfort in the fact that our P vs NP question has been elevated by the Clay
Institute to the rank of a "millennium" problem, on equal footing with e.g. The
Riemann Hypothesis (see www.claymath.org/millenium).

P vs NP is deep and difficult, and it is not exaggerated to view the problem as
the main driver for our field. There are of course several simplified models that
are being studied in order to increase our understanding of computations. For
example, one that has met with some success is the model of finite automata.
Finite state machines represent an appealing model for analyzing computations,
albeit in a very simplified context. An elegant theory has developed that connects
fruitfully a structural algebraic point of view of the machines with a descriptive
logico-combinatorial understanding of the computations that can be realized.
This duality gives rise to several nice results that provide good intuitions on
important computational properties.

The finite automata model provides a single fixed machine, with fixed amount
of resources, that handles inputs of all lengths, reading once the string left to
right. It is an example of a (very!) uniform model of computation. This has been
generalized to a more interesting and more challenging version of the model, by
allowing a length-dependent "program" to translate the input into a new string

M. Holzer, M. Kutrib, and G. Pighizzini (Eds.): DCFS 2011, LNCS 6808, pp. 43–54, 2011.
© Springer-Verlag Berlin Heidelberg 2011

which is then processed by the machine; various notions of uniformity can be imposed on how efficiently the translating program can be constructed for a given length, but we will not be interested in this question. We rather concentrate on combinatorial constraints that are consequences of restrictions on the algebraic structure in which the computation takes place.

In this expository paper we will first review some computational concepts which appear to be fundamental in the world of finite automata, pointing out in particular the connections derived from carrying in parallel the structural and the descriptive point of view. We will then show how these concepts translate to the general non-uniform version. Our presentation will give examples where the behaviour is preserved as we do the generalization, and other examples where it is not. One of the points we wish to make is that algorithms can be very surprising and that one should be careful on how intuition is being used. Our paper does not attempt to be completely rigorous, and several concepts and proofs are only sketched; for all terms not properly defined here, the reader will find them, and much more, in the excellent book of Straubing [14]

2   Setting Up the Table

Our presentation will be in terms of computations realized by finite monoids, which are equivalent to finite automata, but more convenient to manipulate. But we first briefly introduce boolean circuits which serve as a universal model, to which we can compare our algebraic framework.

For a finite set A, we write A^* to represent the set of all strings of finite length over A, including the empty string ϵ; a language L is a subset of A^*, which we identify with its characteristic function $L : A^* \to \{0, 1\}$.

2.1   Boolean Circuits

Circuits provide an intuitive computational model. An n-input circuit C_n is given by a directed acyclic graph: in order to make it possible to work over a non-binary alphabet, we allow vertices of in-degree 0 (the input nodes) to be labelled by "$x_i = a$?" for some $1 \leq i \leq n$, $a \in A$; vertices of in-degree k are labelled by some "elementary" function $f : \{0, 1\}^k \to \{0, 1\}$, and we assume a unique vertex of out-degree 0 (the output node). Such an object naturally computes a function from A^n to $\{0, 1\}$, and we can recognize a language $L \subseteq A^*$ by considering a sequence $(C_n)_{n \geq 0}$.

The size of C_n is the number of vertices in the graph, and the depth is the length of the longest path from an input node to the output node. Typically we allow as elementary functions AND, OR and MOD_q where $\text{AND}(Y_1, \cdots, Y_k) = 1$ iff all Y_i's are 1, $\text{OR}(Y_1, \cdots, Y_k) = 1$ iff at least one Y_i is 1, and $\text{MOD}_q(Y_1, \cdots, Y_k) = 1$ iff the sum of the Y_i's is not divisible by q. We define a language L to be in the class $\mathsf{P}/poly$ if there exists $(C_n)_{n \geq 0}$ where, for each n, C_n has size n^d for some constant d, and C_n recognizes the set $L \cap A^n$;

no relationship is required between the different C_n's and P/*poly* is the non-uniform version of the polynomial-time complexity class classically defined via Turing machines.

We will be interested in the following subclasses of P/*poly*. The class $\mathsf{AC^0}$ comprises circuits of polynomial size, constant depth, constructed with AND/OR gates. The class $\mathsf{CC_q^0}$ is similar but uses MOD_q gates instead; $\mathsf{ACC_q^0}$ allows all three types of gates. We write $\mathsf{CC^0}$ for $\cup_q \mathsf{CC_q^0}$ and $\mathsf{ACC^0}$ for $\cup_q \mathsf{ACC_q^0}$. Finally, we denote by $\mathsf{NC^1}$ the class of circuits of $O(\log n)$ depth constructed with binary gates. We use the same notation for the class of languages that can be recognized by the given circuit class. A simple divide-and-conquer argument shows that $\mathsf{ACC^0}$ is contained in $\mathsf{NC^1}$. The inclusion of $\mathsf{AC^0}$ into $\mathsf{ACC^0}$ is known to be proper, but not that of $\mathsf{CC^0}$; in fact it is not known if $\mathsf{CC^0} = \mathsf{NP}$ or not.

2.2   Finite Monoids

A monoid is a set M, with a binary associative operation defined on it, and admitting a 2-sided identity element, denoted 1_M. Finite monoids are closely related to finite automata and have appeared early on as a model for computations realized by machines with fixed amount of memory.

Monoids recognize languages as follows: given a homomorphism $\phi : A^* \to M$, and a subset $F \subseteq M$ of accepting elements, the recognized language is $L = \phi^{-1}(F)$. In other words there is a mapping $\phi : A \to M$ that transforms an input string $x = a_1 a_2 \ldots a_n$ into a sequence of monoid elements $\phi(a_1)\phi(a_2)\ldots\phi(a_n)$ and this sequence is evaluated using the monoid operation; the input is accepted iff the resulting value $\phi(x)$ belongs to the accepting set F. This is equivalent to viewing the set-up as a deterministic finite automaton where M is the set of states, 1_M is the initial state and the transition function $\delta : M \times A \to M$ is given by $\delta(m, a) = m\phi(a)$.

The theorem of Kleene gives a beautiful description of the languages recognized in this framework. The class of regular languages over the alphabet A is the smallest family of subsets of A^* containing the finite sets and closed under union, concatenation and star.

Theorem 1. *L is regular iff L can be recognized by a finite monoid M.*

It follows that the class of regular languages is also closed under complement.

A natural ordering on monoids is given by division: M divides N, denoted $M \prec N$, iff M is a homomorphic image of a submonoid of N. If M divides N, then any language recognizable with M is also recognizable with N; hence $\prec$ can really be interpreted as a measure of computing power.

The notion of variety is central in universal algebra, it is adapted here in the following way. A (pseudo)variety of finite monoids is a class $\mathbf{V}$ of finite monoids closed under division and direct product. It turns out that the family of languages that can be recognized by monoids in a variety $\mathbf{V}$ has nice closure properties. Classifying monoids (and languages) in terms of varieties is a central tool in analyzing computations in the finite-state model [7].

In the 80's, finite automata were generalized to a model introduced under the name "bounded-width branching programs" [5]. These computations can be also considered to be taking place in a finite monoid. An n-input program P_n over monoid M is a sequence $P_n = (i_1, f_1) \ldots (i_s, f_s)$ where $1 \leq i_j \leq n$ and $f_j : A \rightarrow M$ for each j. This program transforms an input string of length n, $x = a_1 \ldots a_n$, into a sequence of length s of monoid elements $f_1(a_{i_1}) \ldots f_s(a_{i_s})$, which can be evaluated using the operation of M; we will use the notation $P_n(x)$ to denote both the string of length s in M^* and the resulting value in M. Thus, fixing a set $F \subseteq M$ of accepting elements, we can use a sequence of n-input programs over M, $(P_n)_{n \geq 0}$, to recognize a language L where $L \cap A^n = \{x : P_n(x) \in F\}$; in a totally equivalent way, we can request the string $P_n(x)$ to belong to the language $\{z \in M^* : z$ evaluates to some $m \in F\}$. We consider here only programs of polynomial length, i.e. sequences $(P_n)_{n \geq 0}$ where the length of P_n is n^d for some fixed d. We will then say that L is p-recognized by M .

A program is thus a mechanism to transform an input string over A into a sequence of monoid elements, and then let the monoid process the transformed sequence according to its internal operation. In contrast a homomorphism ϕ is a special case of a program $(\phi_n)_{n \geq 0}$ where $\phi_n = (1, \phi)(2, \phi) \ldots (n, \phi)$. The question we are interested in is to understand how the algebraic structure of the monoid M constrains the combinatorial intricacy of the languages being recognized.

3 Computations in Monoids via Homomorphisms

3.1 The Idea of Counting

Counting is of course central in any computational model. We have for example defined boolean circuits directly in terms of counters. Counting also plays a role in algebraic computations.

It is easy to see that in any finite monoid there exist integers $t \geq 0$, $q \geq 1$, such that $m^t = m^{t+q}$ for every m in M. If $q = 1$, i.e. $m^t = m^{t+1}$, we say that M is an aperiodic; if $t = 0$, i.e. $m^q = 1_M$, we say that M is a group. Both the class **A** of aperiodics and the class **G** of groups form varieties. The two cases are in a sense "orthogonal" to each other.

Fact 1 *The language* $1^* \subseteq \{0,1\}^*$ *cannot be recognized by a group, i.e. groups cannot realize the* AND *function.*

Proof. Let $\phi : \{0,1\}^* \rightarrow G$ where G satisfies $g^q = 1_G$. Let $\phi(1) = g$; then $\phi(1) = \phi(10^q) = g$ so g must be both accepting and rejecting, a contradiction. □

Fact 2 *The language* $((0^*10^*)^q)^* \subseteq \{0,1\}^*$ *cannot be recognized by an aperiodic monoid, i.e. aperiodics cannot realize the* MOD$_q$ *function.*

Proof. Let $\phi : \{0,1\}^* \rightarrow M$ where M satisfies $m^t = m^{t+1}$. Let $\phi(1) = m$, and write e for m^t. Then $\phi(1^{tq}) = \phi(1^{tq+1}) = e$ so that e must be both accepting and rejecting, a contradiction. □

Let us next consider decomposing arbitrary monoids into simpler components. In the case of groups, there is a natural opportunity to do this, arising from the presence of normal subgroups. Recall that a subgroup $H \subseteq G$ is normal if $Hg = gH$ for all $g \in G$; in this case the set of distinct cosets $G/H = \{Hg_1, \ldots, Hg_k\}$ inherits a group structure in a natural way. One can define an operation to combine groups, the *wreath product*, denoted $\circ$, that allows to reconstruct G from H and G/H, in the sense that $G \prec H \circ G/H$. The wreath product can also be defined on arbitrary monoids. Both **A** and **G** are closed under wreath product and the fundamental Krohn-Rhodes Theorem stresses again the importance of these two varieties.

Theorem 2 ([9]). *For any finite monoid M, there exists aperiodics M_0, M_1, ..., M_k and groups $G_0, G_1, \ldots, G_k$ such that $M \prec M_0 \circ G_0 \circ M_1 \circ \cdots \circ G_k \circ M_k$. Furthermore, the G_i's can always be chosen so that $G_i \prec M$ for each i.*

Commutative monoids, i.e. those satisfying $mn = nm$ for all elements m, n, are in many ways the easiest to analyze, as they can be shown to be essentially direct product of cyclic counters, i.e. they "count" in the most transparent way. We will write $\mathbf{A}_{\mathrm{com}}$ for the family of commutative aperiodics, and $\mathbf{G}_{\mathrm{com}}$ for the family of commutative groups; both classes form varieties. The wreath product has a 2-sided analogue, called the *block product* and denoted $\square$, which is often more interesting to use. In the case of groups, the block operation is identical to the wreath, but it is more powerful in the general case; both **A** and **G** are closed under block. It turns out that every aperiodic decomposes, under block product but not under wreath, into commutative components.

Theorem 3. *M is aperiodic iff $M \prec M_1 \square \cdots \square M_k$ where each M_i is a commutative aperiodic monoid; in fact each M_i can be taken to be the 2-element commutative idempotent monoid, i.e. each M_i can be taken to satisfy $m = m^2$.*

Monoids that are both idempotent and commutative are also called semi-lattices, and the theorem can be rephrased to say that the closure of the two-element semi-lattice under block product is the variety of all aperiodics.

The case of groups is more complicated. For g, h in G, let $[g, h] = g^{-1}h^{-1}gh$. We then write $[G, G]$ for the subgroup generated by all $[g, h]$. This subgroup is called the derived subgroup of G and is always normal. We next define the derived series of G to be the sequence $G_0 \triangleright G_1 \triangleright \cdots$ where $G_0 = G$ and $G_i = [G_{i-1}, G_{i-1}]$, and we say that G is solvable if this sequence terminates with the trivial subgroup. Solvable groups decompose, under block or wreath, into commutative components.

Theorem 4. *G is a solvable group iff $G \prec G_1 \square \cdots \square G_k$ where each G_i is a commutative group. In fact, each G_i can be taken to be a cyclic counter that satisfies $m^{p_i} = 1_{G_i}$ for some prime p_i.*

To be complete, we mention that, unsurprizingly, the block product closure of commutative monoids is exactly the variety of solvable monoids, i.e. all monoids M

having the property that any group G which divides M is a solvable group. Unfortunately, it is not true that all groups are solvable. There exist so called simple non-commutative groups which cannot be decomposed into commutative parts using block product. The smallest example is the group of even permutations on 5 points, which comprises 60 elements. If one adopts the religious position that all computations should reduce to counting, then this happens for simple non-commuative groups in a mysterious, and as yet incomprehensible, way.

3.2   The Idea of Nesting

We next look at a question which arises more naturally when we start with the combinatorial description of the computations realized by finite automata. Recall that a language is recognized by a finite monoid iff it is regular, i.e. it belongs to the smallest boolean algebra containing the finite subsets of A^* that is closed under concatenation and star. Schützenberger investigated the question of what happens when star is disallowed: the answer is deservedly famous. Let the class of star-free languages be the smallest boolean algebra containing the finite subsets of A^* and that is closed under concatenation.

Theorem 5 ([12]). *A language is star-free iff it can be recognized by a finite aperiodic.*

It becomes natural to parametrize star-free sets by counting how many levels of concatenation are needed to express them. It is convenient to do it as follows. Let $\mathcal{D}_0 = \{\emptyset, A^*\}$; for $d \geq 1$, let $\mathcal{D}_d$ be the boolean algebra generated by the languages of the form $L_0 a_1 L_1 \ldots a_s L_s$ where $a_i \in A$ and L_i is in $\mathcal{D}_{d-1}$. Clearly L is star-free iff it belongs to some $\mathcal{D}_d$. We can write $\mathbf{D_d}$ for the class of monoids that can recognize only languages in $\mathcal{D}_d$, and we call them monoids of *dot-depth* d: it can be shown that each $\mathbf{D_d}$ is a variety. The levels of the hierarchy $\mathcal{D}_0 \subseteq \mathcal{D}_1 \subseteq \mathcal{D}_2 \cdots$ are not known to be decidable for $d \geq 2$, but each inclusion is known to be strict. Consider the language L_d recognized by the partial automaton

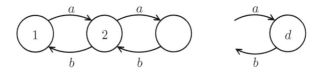

where we take 1 to be the initial and accepting state. It is clear that we have $L_1 = \{\epsilon\}$ and $L_d = (aL_{d-1}b)^*$, which yields a regular expression with $d-1$ stars nested one in the other. On the other hand the language must be star-free since the transformation monoid of the automaton, which recognizes L_d, can be verified to be aperiodic: actually Schützenberger Theorem produces an explicit star-free expression from an aperiodic, but not necessarily with the minimum number of nested concatenations. It requires some work to produce an expression of depth d. We concentrate here on sketching the lower bound, which is a variation on the result of [6].

Theorem 6. *For $d \geq 1$, L_d is not in $\mathcal{D}_{d-1}$.*

Proof. It is trivial that $L_0 = \{\epsilon\}$ is not in $\mathcal{D}_0$ Let $\mu_0 = \epsilon$ and for $d \geq 1$,

$$\mu_d = (\mu_{d-1}a\mu_{d-1}b\mu_{d-1})^\omega$$

$$\nu_d = (\mu_{d-1}b\mu_{d-1}a\mu_{d-1})^\omega$$

where ω is an integer chosen large enough. It is easy to see by induction that $\mu_d \in L_{d+1}$, $\nu_d \notin L_{d+1}$. We prove the theorem by showing that no language in $\mathcal{D}_d$ can distinguish between the two words. We will need to prove as a lemma that for any language L in $\mathcal{D}_d$, μ_d is in L iff $\mu_d a \mu_d$ is in L iff $\mu_d b \mu_d$ is in L. For $d = 1$, consider $L = A^* a_1 A^* \cdots a_s A^*$; by choosing ω suitably large, we can insure that $a_1 \cdots a_s$ appears as a subword of $\mu_1 = (ab)^\omega$ iff it also appears as a subword of $\nu_1 = (ba)^\omega$, i.e. both words are in L or both words are not in L. It easily follows that no language in $\mathcal{D}_1$ can separate μ_1 from ν_1. For $d > 1$, let $L = J_0 a_1 J_1 \cdots , a_s J_s$ be such that $J_0, \ldots, J_s$ are in $\mathcal{D}_{d-1}$ and $a_1, \ldots, a_s$ are in A. We need to check that μ_d is in L iff ν_d also is. We can do this by induction on s. If $s = 0$, we are fine since μ_d and ν_d both behave as μ_{d-1} for any $\mathcal{D}_{d-1}$-language. If $s > 0$, write $\mu_d = y_0 a_1 y_2 \ldots a_s y_s$ with $y_i \in J_i$ for each i. A straightforward case analysis of the position of the marker a_s in the word μ_d will yield the result. The proof that $\mu_d a \mu_d$, $\mu_d b \mu_d$ and μ_d behaves the same for any $\mathcal{D}_d$-language is using the same idea. $\square$

Membership of a word x in a language of $\mathcal{D}_d$ depends on the existence, or not, of certain factorizations of the form $x = x_0 a_1 x_1 \ldots a_s x_s$, where, for each i, word x_i belongs to L_i for some L_i in $\mathcal{D}_{d-1}$. We get a "group equivalent" of this hierarchy by counting, modulo q, the number of times that x can be factorized in such manner, instead of simply testing for existence. Formally, let $\mathcal{C}$ be a class of languages over A^* and let $\alpha = (L_0, a_1, L_1, \ldots, a_s, L_s)$ where the L_i's are languages in $\mathcal{C}$ and the a_i's are letters in A. We next let $|x|_\alpha$ be the number of times a string x can be factorized in the form $x = x_0 a_1 x_1 \ldots a_s x_s$ where x_i is in L_i for each i, and define $L(\alpha, i, q) = \{x : |x|_\alpha \equiv i \mod q\}$. Starting with $\mathcal{F}_0 = \{\emptyset, A^*\}$ we let $\mathcal{F}_d$ be the boolean algebra generated by $L(\alpha, i, q)$ where α is using languages from $\mathcal{F}_{d-1}$, and $\mathbf{F_d}$ be the class of monoids that recognize only languages in $\mathcal{F}_d$. Each $\mathbf{F_d}$ is a variety, and contrary to $\mathbf{D_d}$, the membership question is here decidable, in the following way. Let $G = G_0$ and for each $k \geq 1$, $G_k = [G_{k-1}, G]$ be the subgroup generated by elements of the form $g^{-1}h^{-1}gh$ with $g \in G_{k-1}$, $h \in G$. Note that this is not the same G_k as in the previous section where we had $G_k = [G_{k-1}, G_{k-1}]$. But in this new case again G_k is normal in G_{k-1} and the group G is said to be nilpotent if the sequence $G_0 \triangleright G_1 \triangleright G_2 \triangleright \cdots$ terminates with the trivial group. It is clear that every commutative group is nilpotent and that every nilpotent group is solvable. In particular, if G is solvable, we can consider the shortest sequence $G = H_0 \triangleright H_1 \triangleright \cdots \triangleright H_d = \{1\}$ where each H_i/H_{i+1} is required to be nilpotent. Such sequence is called a Fitting series and G is then said to have Fitting length d. It is well-known that the Fitting hierarchy for groups is strict.

Theorem 7 ([15]). *A language L is in $\mathcal{F}_d$ iff it can be recognized by a solvable group of Fitting length $\leq d$. Since we can calculate all chains of subgroups and test which ones are Fitting series, the property is decidable.*

4   Computations in Monoids via Programs

In this section, we revisit the ideas of the last chapter in the more general context of programs. Recall that $L \subseteq A^*$ is p-recognized by M if there exist a sequence $(P_n)_{n \geq 0}$ of polynomial length programs over M and a subset $F \subseteq M$ of accepting elements such that $L \cap A^n = \{x : P_n(x) \in F\}$ for each n. We do not impose any constructability condition on the P_n's and thus position the discussion in the non-uniform setting.

We first observe that all p-recognizable languages are in NC^1: using divide-and-conquer, we can construct with binary gates a logarithmic depth circuit that will simulate directly a polynomial-length program; for a program P, and an element $m \in M$, the language $L(P, m) = \{x : P(x) = m\}$ is

$$\cup_{(m_1, m_2):\, m_1 m_2 = m}(L(P_1, m_1) \cap L(P_2, m_2)),$$

where P_1 is the first half of the program and P_2 is the second half of the program. With some more work, using the close kinship between semilattices and AND/OR gates, it can be shown that programs over aperiodic monoids ($=$ block product of a fixed number of semilattices) can be recognized by AC^0 circuits (fixed depth arrangement of AND/OR's); similarly programs over solvable groups ($=$ wreath product of a fixed number of commutative groups) can be recognized by CC^0 circuits (fixed depth arrangement of MOD_q's). Indeed the kinship between counting gates and cyclic monoids is deep enough that the converse of these facts also hold and we have the

Theorem 8 ([4]). *A language L is in AC^0 iff it can be p-recognized by an aperiodic monoid. L is in CC^0 iff it can be p-recognized by a solvable group. L is in ACC^0 iff it can be p-recognized by a solvable monoid.*

There remains the case of programs over monoids that cannot be decomposed into a block product of commutative monoids, in particular the case of simple non-commutative groups. As mentioned previously, languages p-recognized by such monoids can be verified to be in NC^1. One may have the intuition that the converse has to be false: an NC^1 circuit can for example compute the MAJORITY function, which seems to require to keep track of the exact sum of the bits, an unbounded integer, a mission that apparently cannot be accomplished with a fixed finite monoid, even with the help of a polynomial length program. A surprise was thus caused when Barrington proved that every language in NC^1 is p-recognizable. The magic is reusing a trick that had been discovered more than 20 years earlier by Maurer and Rhodes [10].

Theorem 9 ([2]). *If L is in NC^1, then L is p-recognizable.*

Proof. Let G be a simple non-commutative group. For any element $t \in G$, we can write an $O(1)$-length 2-input program Π_t that will compute the binary AND function in the sense that $\Pi_t(11) = t, \Pi_t(01) = \Pi_t(10) = \Pi_t(00) = 1_G$. Indeed we can do this for at least some $t \neq 1_G$ by taking two elements g, h that do not commute and letting $t = g^{-1}h^{-1}gh$; the way to do this is to consider $\Pi_t = (1, \alpha)(2, \beta)(1, \gamma)(2, \delta)$ where $\alpha(1) = g^{-1}$, $\beta(1) = h^{-1}$, $\gamma(1) = g$, $\delta(1) = h$ and $\alpha(0) = \beta(0) = \gamma(0) = \delta(0) = 1_G$. We next observe that the set of elements t of G for which a fixed length program can be written to behave as AND forms a normal subgroup; it must be the whole of G since it is non-trivial and G is simple. In a similar way we can write an $O(1)$-length 1-input program to compute the NOT function, hence we can compute binary OR, using de Morgan rule. It is then easy to combine these ingredients to transform a logarithmic-depth circuit into a polynomial-length program over G. □

Note that Theorem 8 does not preclude the AND function being realizable with a solvable group (i.e. a CC^0 circuit) or the MOD$_q$ function being realizable with an aperiodic (i.e. an AC^0 circuit). That would run counter to our intuition but we have just seen, in Theorem 9, that programs can allow strange behaviours. At least in the second case, a deep and difficult theorem shows this cannot happen.

Theorem 10 ([8]). *The language $((0^*10^*)^q)^*$ is not p-recognizable by an aperiodic, i.e. the MOD$_q$ function cannot be computed in AC^0.*

Thus an aperiodic cannot simulate any group computation, even with the help of a polynomial-length program. We have seen with the theorem of Barrington that the dual statement is not true, i.e. groups can simulate aperiodic computation. It is tempting to conjecture that non-solvability is needed in order to "cheat", but the case of the language 1^* with respect to programs over solvable groups is completely open. The best result we have in that direction is the consequence of a beautiful theorem of Barrington and Straubing.

Theorem 11 ([3]). *A program of length $o(n \log \log n)$ over a solvable group cannot p-recognize 1^*.*

The authors in fact show that, in general, such a short program over any M can p-recognize only regular languages that are recognizable via homomorphims by a direct product of copies of M and copies of the reversal of M.

   The relationship stated in Theorem 8 between AC^0 circuits and aperiodics on the one hand, and CC^0 circuits and solvable groups on the other hand can be verified to take exact depth into account; the hierarchy induced corresponds, essentially, to the dot-depth for aperiodics, and to the Fitting length for solvable groups. To state precisely the results, let AC^0_d represent the languages that are fixed-size boolean combinations of sets, each of which recognizable by an AC^0 circuit of depth exactly d. Let CC^0_d be similarly defined.

Theorem 12 ([11]). *L is in AC_1^0 iff L can be p-recognized by a semilattice; for $d \geq 2$, L is in AC_d^0 iff L can be p-recognized by a monoid of depth d. L is in CC_1^0 iff L can be recognized by a commutative group; for $d \geq 2$, L is in CC_d^0 iff L can be recognized by a solvable group of Fitting length d.*

Proof. We sketch the proof for the AC^0 case. For depth 1, the claim follows easily from the observation that OR (AND) defines an idempotent commutative monoid. In fact, for any OR gate, one can write a program P such that the gate accepts input x iff $P(x)$ is a string in $\{a,b\}^*a\{a,b\}^*$; a similar statement can be made for AND and the language a^*. For $d > 1$, it is an exercise to see that any regular language L of dot-depth d is computable in AC_d^0, and that the same is true for a language that reduces to L by a program of polynomial length. Conversely, assume inductively the existence of a language K of dot-depth $d - 1$ such that any circuit C of depth $d-1$ whose output gate is an AND is such that there exists a program P_C having the property that C accepts x iff $P_C(x)$ is a string in K; consider a circuit of the form $\mathrm{OR}(C_1, \ldots, C_s)$, where each C_i is of depth $d - 1$ with the output gate being AND. One can form the program $P = \$P_1\$ \cdots \$P_s\$$, where $\$$ is a new symbol, and it has the property that the circuit accepts an input x iff the string $P(x)$ is in the language $A^*\$K\$A^*$, which has dot-depth d. A similar argument can be given when the output gate is an AND.   □

In this case again, it does not directly follow that p-recognizability by a monoid of dot-depth d is strictly weaker than p-recognizability by a monoid of dot-depth $d + 1$, nor the corresponding statement for Fitting length. In the first case we can show the statement to hold, the second case is open. The first one to prove that the depth hierarchy in AC^0 is strict was Sipser in [13]. It follows from the proof of the previous theorem that we can actually separate the levels with regular languages. Indeed, if the regular language constructed in the proof of Theorem 12 for depth d was actually computable in depth $d - 1$, then the whole of AC_d^0 would be contained in AC_{d-1}^0, since that regular language is complete for the d-th level in a natural sense, thus contradicting Sipser. It is an intriguing open question to determine if the language L_d of Section 3.2, which has dot-depth d but not $d-1$ is also a witness of the strict inclusion of the AC^0 levels, as it does not appear to be complete in the sense of the discussion just mentioned.

Getting results on the depth hierarchy in CC^0 seems to be a hard question, our understanding of nesting of modular gates being extremely sketchy at this point. It is known that programs over nilpotent groups (i.e. solvable groups of Fitting length 1) cannot do AND, and the same for certain very specific examples of groups of Fitting length 2. A next example to tackle could be the variety of supersolvable groups, an interesting subclass of Fitting length 2. A theorem of Auinger and Steinberg [1] describes this variety as the join, over all primes p, of groups that can be decomposed as a wreath product $G \circ H$ with G a p-group and H a commutative group of exponent $p-1$. These thus correspond to circuits of polynomial size and constant depth constructed with MOD_p gates, except the bottom level which comprises MOD_{p-1} gates. These groups in particular have very constrained representations; since the tool of representations has been used in some cases to derive lower bounds, the hope exists that this restricted situation can also be handled by this method. Here again, it is tempting to conjecture that the Fitting hierarchy being strict in the world of computations via homomorphisms, the same should be true for programs as well. We really dont have that much ground to argue in this way.

5   Conclusion

The objective of this paper was two-fold. First, we wanted to review some nice examples within the world of regular languages where the duality between algebra and combinatorics on words was interestingly present to explain some computational behaviors. Second, we wished to remind ourselves that we understand rather little about computing when the machines gets a bit sophisticated; hence we should be careful when defending conjectures that are based on intuition that has been generated in simpler models. The theorem of Barrington is a good example that this intuition can be wrong; even after seeing the proof, it is still quite mysterious how a simple group actually performs the calculation to solve a problem like MAJORITY. It is certain that many surprizing upper bounds are yet to be discovered.

References

1. Auinger, K., Steinberg, B.: Varieties of finite supersolvable groups with the M. Hall property. Math. Ann. 335, 853–877 (2006)
2. Barrington, D.A.: Bounded-width polynomial-size branching programs recognize exactly those languages in NC^1. Journal of Computer and System Sciences 38(1), 150–164 (1989)
3. Barrington, D.A.M., Straubing, H.: Superlinear lower bounds for bounded-width branching programs. Journal of Computer and System Sciences 50(3), 374–381 (1995)
4. Barrington, D.A.M., Thérien, D.: Finite monoids and the fine structure of NC^1. Journal of the ACM 35(4), 941–952 (1988)
5. Borodin, A., Dolev, D., Fich, F.E., Paul, W.: Bounds for width two branching programs. SIAM Journal on Computing 15(2), 549–560 (1986)
6. Brzozowski, J., Knast, R.: The dot-depth hierarchy of star-free languages is infinite. Journal of Computer and System Sciences 16(1), 37–55 (1978)
7. Eilenberg, S.: Automata, Languages and Machines, vol. B. Academic Press, New York (1976)
8. Furst, M., Saxe, J.B., Sipser, M.: Parity, circuits, and the polynomial-time hierarchy. Mathematical Systems Theory 17(1), 13–27 (1984)
9. Krohn, K., Rhodes, J.: The algebraic theory of machines I. Trans. Amer. Math. Soc. 116, 450–464 (1965)
10. Maurer, W., Rhodes, J.: A property of finite simple non-Abelian groups. Proc. Amer. Math. Soc 16, 552–554 (1965)
11. McKenzie, P., Péladeau, P., Thérien, D.: NC^1: The automata theoretic viewpoint. Computational Complexity 1, 330–359 (1991)

12. Schützenberger, M.P.: On finite monoids having only trivial subgroups. Information and Computation 8(2), 190–194 (1965)
13. Sipser, M.: Borel sets and circuit complexity. In: Proceedings of the Fifteenth Annual ACM Symposium on the Theory of Computing, pp. 61–69 (1983)
14. Straubing, H.: Finite Automata, Formal Logic and Circuit Complexity. Birkhauser, Boston (1994)
15. Thérien, D.: Classification of finite monoids: The language approach. In: Theoretical Computer Science, vol. 14, pp. 195–208 (1981)

Decidability and Shortest Strings in Formal Languages

Levent Alpoge[1], Thomas Ang[2], Luke Schaeffer[2], and Jeffrey Shallit[2]

[1] Harvard College
Cambridge, MA 02138, USA
levent.alpoge@gmail.com
[2] School of Computer Science, University of Waterloo
Waterloo, ON N2L 3G1, Canada
angthomas@gmail.com, l3schaef@uwaterloo.ca, shallit@cs.uwaterloo.ca

Abstract. Given a formal language L specified in various ways, we consider the problem of determining if L is nonempty. If L is indeed nonempty, we find upper and lower bounds on the length of the shortest string in L.

1 Introduction

Given a formal language L specified in some finite way, a common problem is to determine whether L is nonempty. And if L is indeed nonempty, then another common problem is to determine good upper and lower bounds on the length of the shortest string in L, which we write as $\mathrm{lss}(L)$. Such bounds can be useful, for example, in estimating the state complexity $\mathrm{sc}(L)$, since $\mathrm{lss}(L) < \mathrm{sc}(L)$.

As an example, we start with a simple result often stated in introductory classes on formal language theory. Here, as usual, we let $L(M)$ denote the language accepted by the machine M.

Proposition 1. *Let M be an NFA with n states and t transitions. Then we can decide whether $L(M)$ is nonempty in time $O(n + t)$. If $L(M)$ is nonempty, then $\mathrm{lss}(L(M)) < n$. Further, this bound is tight.*

Proof. Clearly M accepts some string if and only if there is a walk from q_0, the start state, to some final state. Using either the usual depth-first or breadth-first search, we can determine which states are reachable in $O(n + t)$ time.

Now assume $L \neq \emptyset$. Let x be a shortest string in L, and let $p_0, p_1, \ldots, p_r$ be the states encountered in some accepting computation for x. If $r \geq n$, then by the pigeonhole principle some state must be repeated, forming a loop in the accepting walk. We can then cut out this loop to get a shorter accepted string, a contradiction. Hence $r < n$.

The bound is tight because the language $\{a^{n-1}\}$ can be accepted by an NFA with n states. $\qquad\square$

We now turn to a more challenging example. Here L is specified as the *complement* of a language accepted by an NFA.

M. Holzer, M. Kutrib, and G. Pighizzini (Eds.): DCFS 2011, LNCS 6808, pp. 55–67, 2011.
© Springer-Verlag Berlin Heidelberg 2011

Theorem 2. *Let L be accepted by an NFA with n states. Then it is PSPACE-complete to determine whether $\overline{L} \neq \emptyset$. If $\overline{L} \neq \emptyset$, then $\mathrm{lss}(\overline{L}) < 2^n$. Further, for some constant c, $0 < c \leq 1$, there is an infinite family of NFA's that accept all words shorter than 2^{cn}.*

Proof. For the PSPACE-completeness, see [1].

The upper bound is easy and follows from the subset construction. The lower bound is significantly harder; see [5]. □

These two examples set the theme of the paper. We examine several problems about shortest strings in regular languages and prove bounds for $\mathrm{lss}(L)$. Some of the results have appeared in the master's thesis of the second author [3].

2   The First Problem

Recall the following classical result about intersections of regular languages.

Proposition 3. *Let M_1 be an NFA with s_1 states and t_1 transitions, and let M_2 be an NFA with s_2 states and t_2 transitions. Then $L(M_1) \cap L(M_2)$ is accepted by an NFA with $s_1 s_2$ states and $t_1 t_2$ transitions.*

Proof. Use the usual direct product construction as shown in [6, p. 59]. □

This suggests the following natural problems. Given NFA's M_1 and M_2 as above, decide if $L(M_1) \cap L(M_2) \neq \emptyset$. This can clearly be done in $O(s_1 s_2 + t_1 t_2)$ time, by using the direct product construction followed by breadth-first or depth-first search.

Now assume $L(M_1) \cap L(M_2) \neq \emptyset$. What is a good bound on $\mathrm{lss}(L(M_1) \cap L(M_2))$? Combining Propositions 1 and 3, we immediately get the upper bound $\mathrm{lss}(L(M_1) \cap L(M_2)) < s_1 s_2$. However, is this bound tight? For $\gcd(s_1, s_2) = 1$ an obvious construction shows it is, even in the unary case: choose $L_1 = a^{s_1-1}(a^{s_1})^*$ and $L_2 = a^{s_2-1}(a^{s_2})^*$. However, this idea no longer works for $\gcd(s_1, s_2) > 1$. Nevertheless, the bound $s_1 s_2 - 1$ is tight for binary and larger alphabets, as the following result shows.

Theorem 4. *For all integers $m, n \geq 1$ there exist DFAs M_1, M_2 over a binary alphabet $\Sigma = \{0, 1\}$ with m and n states respectively, such that $L(M_1) \cap L(M_2) \neq \emptyset$, and $\mathrm{lss}(L(M_1) \cap L(M_2)) = mn - 1$.*

Proof. The proof is constructive. Without loss of generality, assume $m \leq n$, and set $\Sigma = \{0, 1\}$. Let M_1 be the DFA given by $(Q_1, \Sigma, \delta_1, p_0, F_1)$, where $Q_1 = \{p_0, p_1, p_2, \ldots, p_{m-1}\}$, $F_1 = \{p_0\}$, and for each a, $0 \leq a \leq m - 1$, and $c \in \{0, 1\}$ we set

$$\delta_1(p_a, c) = p_{(a+c) \bmod m}.$$

Then

$$L(M_1) = \{x \in \Sigma^* : |x|_1 \equiv 0 \pmod{m}\},$$

where, as usual, $|x|_a$ denotes the number of occurrences of the symbol a in the word x.

Let M_2 be the DFA $(Q_2, \Sigma, \delta_2, q_0, F_2)$, shown in Figure 1, where $Q_2 = \{q_0, q_1, \ldots, q_{n-1}\}$, $F_2 = \{q_{n-1}\}$, and for each a, $0 \le a \le n - 1$,

$$\delta_2(q_a, c) = \begin{cases} q_{a+c}, & \text{if } 0 \le a < m - 1; \\ q_{(a+1) \bmod n}, & \text{if } c = 0 \text{ and } m - 1 \le a \le n - 1; \\ q_0, & \text{if } c = 1 \text{ and } m - 1 \le a \le n - 1. \end{cases}$$

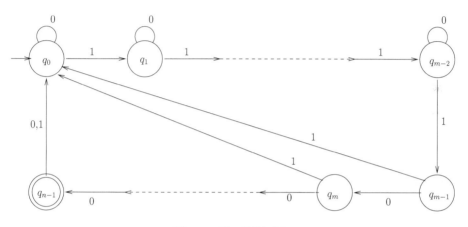

Fig. 1. The DFA M_2

Focusing solely on the 1's that appear in some accepting computation in M_2, we see that we can return to q_0

(a) via a simple path with m 1's, or
(b) (if we go through q_{n-1}), via a simple path with $(m - 1)$ 1's and ending in the transition $\delta(q_{n-1}, 0) = q_0$.

After some number of cycles through q_0, we eventually arrive at q_{n-1}. Letting i denote the number of times a path of type (b) is chosen (including the last path that arrives at q_{n-1}) and j denote the number of times a path of type (a) is chosen, we see that the number of 1's in any accepted word must be of the form $i(m - 1) + jm$, with $i > 0$, $j \ge 0$. The number of 0's along such a path is then at least $i(n - m + 1) - 1$, with the -1 in this expression arising from the fact that the last part of the path terminates at q_{n-1} without taking an additional 0 transition back to q_0.

Thus

$$L(M_2) \subseteq \{x \in \Sigma^* : \exists i, j \in \mathbb{N}, \text{ such that } i > 0, j \ge 0, \text{ and } \\ |x|_1 = i(m - 1) + jm, |x|_0 \ge i(n - m + 1) - 1\}.$$

Furthermore, for every $i, j \in \mathbb{N}$, such that $i > 0, j \geq 0$, there exists an $x \in L(M_2)$ such that $|x|_1 = i(m-1) + jm$, and $|x|_0 = i(n-m+1) - 1$. This is obtained, for example, by cycling j times from q_0 to q_{m-1} and then back to q_0 via a transition on 1, then $i - 1$ times from q_0 to q_{n-1} and then back to q_0 via a transition on 0, and finally one more time from q_0 to q_{n-1}.

It follows then that

$$L(M_1) \cap L(M_2) \subseteq \{x \in \Sigma^* : \exists i, j \in \mathbb{N}, \text{ such that } i > 0, j \geq 0, \text{ and}$$
$$|x|_1 = i(m-1) + jm, \ |x|_0 \geq i(n-m+1) - 1$$
$$\text{and } i(m-1) + jm \equiv 0 \pmod{m}\}.$$

Further, for every such i and j, there exists a corresponding element in $L(M_1) \cap L(M_2)$. Since $m - 1$ and m are relatively prime, the shortest such word corresponds to $i = m$, $j = 0$, and satisfies $|x|_0 = m(n-m+1) - 1$. In particular, a shortest accepted word is $(1^{m-1}0^{n-m+1})^{m-1}1^{m-1}0^{n-m}$, which is of length $mn - 1$. □

We can also obtain a bound for the unary case. Let

$$F(m, n) = \max_{\substack{1 \leq i \leq m \\ 1 \leq j \leq n}} \big(\max(m - i, n - j) + \text{lcm}(i, j) \big),$$

as defined in [7].

Theorem 5. *Let M_1 and M_2 be unary DFA's with m and n states, respectively. Assume $L(M_1) \cap L(M_2) \neq \emptyset$. Then $\text{lss}(L(M_1) \cap L(M_2)) \leq F(m, n) - 1$. Furthermore, for all $m, n \geq 1$ there exist unary DFA's of m and n states achieving this bound.*

Proof. In [7, Thm. 4] it is shown that, given unary DFA's with m and n states, one can construct a unary DFA with at most $F(m, n)$ states for the intersection. This proves the first result. In [7, Thm. 5] it is shown that for all m and n there exist DFA's with m and n states such that the minimal DFA has exactly $F(m, n)$ states. Inspection of the construction shows that for the constructed DFA M we have $\text{lss}(M) = F(m, n) - 1$.

3   The Second Problem

Recall the Post correspondence problem: we are given two finite nonempty languages $L_1 = \{x_1, x_2, \ldots, x_n\}$ and $L_2 = \{y_1, y_2, \ldots, y_n\}$, and we want to determine if there exist $r \geq 1$ and a finite sequence of indices $i_1, i_2, \ldots, i_r$ such that $x_{i_1} \cdots x_{i_r} = y_{i_1} \ldots y_{i_r}$. As is well-known, this problem is undecidable.

Alpoge [2] asked about the variant where we throw away the "correspondence": determine if there exist $r, s \geq 1$ and two finite sequences of indices $i_1, \ldots, i_r$ and $j_1, \ldots, j_s$ such that $x_{i_1} \cdots x_{i_r} = y_{j_1} \cdots y_{j_s}$. In other words, we want to decide if $L_1^+ \cap L_2^+ \neq \emptyset$, where $L^+ := \bigcup_{i=1}^{\infty} L^i$ denotes positive closure.

This variant is, of course, decidable. In fact, even a more general version is decidable, where the languages need not be finite.

Proposition 6. *Let M_1 be an NFA with s_1 states and t_1 transitions, and let M_2 be an NFA with s_2 states and t_2 transitions. Then we can decide in $O(s_1 s_2 + t_1 t_2)$ time whether $L(M_1)^+ \cap L(M_2)^+ \neq \emptyset$.*

Proof. Given NFA M_1, we can create an ϵ-NFA M_1' accepting $L(M_1)^+$ by adding an ϵ-transition from every final state of M_1 back to its initial state. We can apply a similar construction to create M_2' accepting $L(M_2)^+$. Then we can create an ϵ-NFA M accepting $L(M_1)^+ \cap L(M_2)^+$ using the usual direct product construction as shown in [6, p. 59], and adding some additional edges.

These extra edges account for edges in which one machine performs an explicit ϵ-transition, and the other machine performs an implicit ϵ-transition by staying in its own state. There are $s_1 s_2$ such ϵ-transitions that we add and we end up with an ϵ-NFA accepting $L(M_1)^+ \cap L(M_2)^+$ that has at most $t_1 t_2 + 2 s_1 s_2$ transitions.

Now we can use the usual breadth-first or depth-first search to solve the emptiness problem. □

Corollary 7. *Let M_1 and M_2 be NFA's of m and n states, respectively. Suppose $L(M_1)^+ \cap L(M_2)^+ \neq \emptyset$. Then the shortest string in $L(M_1)^+ \cap L(M_2)^+$ is of length at most $mn - 1$.*

Suppose $n \geq m \geq 1$. Then there exist NFA's M_1 and M_2 of m and n states, respectively, with $L(M_1)^+ \cap L(M_2)^+ \neq \emptyset$ such that the shortest string in $L(M_1)^+ \cap L(M_2)^+$ is of length $\geq m(n-1)$.

Proof. The first assertion follows from Proposition 3.

For the second assertion, we can take M_1 and M_2 as in the proof of Theorem 4. Clearly $L(M_1) = L(M_1)^+$. When we apply our construction to M_2 to create the ϵ-NFA that accepts $L(M_2)^+$, we add an ϵ-transition from q_{n-1} back to q_0. The effect is to allow one less 0 in each cycle through the states. As in the proof of Theorem 4, to get the proper number of 1's, we must have $i = m$, and hence the shortest string in $L(M_1)^+ \cap L(M_2)^+$ is of length $m(n-1)$. □

We can improve the upper bound to $mn - 2$ as follows:

Theorem 8. *Suppose $n \geq m \geq 2$. Then for any m-state DFA M_1 and n-state DFA M_2 such that $L(M_1)^+ \cap L(M_2)^+ \neq \emptyset$ we have $\mathrm{lss}(L(M_1)^+ \cap L(M_2)^+) < mn - 1$.*

Proof. Assume, contrary to what we want to prove, that we have DFAs M_1 and M_2 with m and n states, respectively, such that $\mathrm{lss}(L(M_1)^+ \cap L(M_2)^+) = mn - 1$. Let M_1 be the DFA given by $(Q_1, \Sigma, \delta_1, p_0, F_1)$, where $Q_1 = \{p_0, p_1, p_2, \ldots, p_{m-1}\}$, and let M_2 be the DFA given by $(Q_2, \Sigma, \delta_2, p_0, F_2)$, where $Q_2 = \{q_0, q_1, q_2, \ldots, q_{n-1}\}$. Then let M_1' and M_2' be the ϵ-NFA's obtained by adding ϵ-transitions from the final states to the start states in M_1 and M_2, respectively. Let M be the ϵ-NFA obtained by applying the cross-product construction to M_1' and M_2'. Then M accepts $L(M_1)^+ \cap L(M_2)^+$.

If M has more than one final state, a shortest accepting path would only visit one of them, and this immediately gives a contradiction. So, assume each of M_1 and M_2 has only one final state; that is $F_1 = \{p_x \in Q_1\}$ and $F_2 = \{q_y \in Q_2\}$. Then $M = (Q_1 \times Q_2, \Sigma, \delta, [p_0, q_0], [p_x, q_y])$, where for all $p_i \in Q_1, q_j \in Q_2, a \in \Sigma, \delta([p_i, q_j], a) = [\delta_1(p_i, a), \delta_2(q_j, a)]$. Note that M has ϵ-transitions from $[p_x, q_j]$ to $[p_0, q_j]$ for all $q_j \in Q_2$ and $[p_i, q_y]$ to $[p_i, q_0]$ for all $p_i \in Q_1$.

Let w_1 be a shortest word accepted by M_1 and w_2 be a shortest word accepted by M_2. Then $\delta([p_0, q_0], w_1) \supseteq [p_x, q_i]$ for exactly one i such that $q_i \in Q_2$, and while carrying out this computation we never pass through two states $[p_a, q_b]$ and $[p_c, q_d]$ such that $a = c$. Likewise, $\delta([p_0, q_0], w_2) \supseteq [p_j, q_y]$ for exactly one j such that $p_j \in Q_1$, and while carrying out this computation we never pass through two states $[p_a, q_b]$ and $[p_c, q_d]$ such that $b = d$. If both $x = 0$ and $y = 0$ the shortest accepted string is ϵ, so without loss of generality, assume $x \neq 0$. Then $i = 0$ or else we can visit $|w_1| + 2$ states with $|w_1|$ symbols by using an ϵ-transition and we get a contradiction. If $y = 0$, w_1 is the shortest string accepted by M and we have a contradiction. So, $y \neq 0$ and $j = 0$. It follows that reading w_1 from the initial state brings us to $[p_x, q_0]$ without passing through $[p_0, q_y]$, and reading w_2 from the initial state brings us to $[p_0, q_y]$ without passing through $[p_x, q_0]$. So, a shortest accepting path need only visit one of $[p_x, q_0]$ and $[p_0, q_y]$, and again we have a contradiction. □

We do not know an exact bound for this problem. However, for the unary case, we can obtain an exact bound based on a function G introduced in [7]. Define $G(m, n) = \max_{\substack{1 \leq i \leq m \\ 1 \leq j \leq n}} \mathrm{lcm}(i, j)$, and define the variant

$$G'(m, n) = \max_{\substack{1 \leq i \leq m \\ 1 \leq j \leq n \\ (i, j) \neq (m, n)}} \mathrm{lcm}(i, j).$$

Then $G'(m, n) = \max(G(m - 1, n), G(m, n - 1))$. Here, as usual, the max over an empty set is defined to be 0 so that, for example, $G'(1, 1) = 0$. The function G is a very difficult one to estimate, although deep results in analytic number theory give some upper and lower bounds [7].

Theorem 9. *Let M_1 (resp., M_2) be a unary NFA with m states (resp., n states). Suppose $\mathrm{lss}(L(M_1)^+ \cap L(M_2)^+) \neq \emptyset$. Then $\mathrm{lss}(L(M_1)^+ \cap L(M_2)^+) \leq G'(m, n)$. Furthermore, for all $m, n \geq 1$ there exist unary DFA's of m and n states, respectively, achieving this bound.*

Proof. Assume the input alphabet of both M_1 and M_2 is $\Sigma = \{a\}$. If $L(M_i) = \{\epsilon\}$ for $i = 1$ or $i = 2$, the result is trivial. So assume both M_1 and M_2 accept some nonempty string.

Let c_1 (resp., c_2) be the length of the shortest nonempty string in $L(M_1)$ (resp., $L(M_2)$). Clearly $c_1 \leq m$ and $c_2 \leq n$. Furthermore, if $c_1 = m$, then $L(M_1) = (a^m)^*$, and similarly if $c_2 = n$ then $L(M_2) = (a^n)^*$. Hence if $(c_1, c_2) = (m, n)$, then $\epsilon \in L(M_1)^+ \cap L(M_2)^+$, and hence $\mathrm{lss}(L(M_1)^+ \cap L(M_2)^+) = 0 \leq G'(m, n)$. Otherwise either $c_1 < m$ or $c_2 < n$. Without loss of generality, assume $c_2 < n$.

Then $a^{\text{lcm}(c_1,c_2)} \in L(M_1)^+ \cap L(M_2)^+$, so $\text{lss}(L(M_1)^+ \cap L(M_2)^+) \leq \text{lcm}(c_1, c_2) \leq G(m, n-1) \leq G'(m, n)$.

Now suppose we are given m and n. Let i, j be the integers maximizing $\text{lcm}(i, j)$ over $1 \leq i \leq m$, $1 \leq j \leq n$ with $(i, j) \neq (m, n)$. If $i < m$, choose $L_1 = (a^i)^+$, which can be accepted by a DFA with $i + 1 \leq m$ states, and choose $L_2 = (a^j)^*$, which can be accepted by a DFA with $j \leq n$ states. Otherwise, reverse the roles of m and n. Thus we get DFA's of m and n states, respectively, achieving $\text{lss}(L(M_1)^+ \cap L(M_2)^+) = G'(m, n)$. □

4   The Third Problem

Another variation on the Post correspondence problem, also proposed by Alpoge [2], is more interesting. Here we throw away only *part* of the "correspondence": given $L_1 = \{x_1, x_2, \ldots, x_n\}$ and $L_2 = \{y_1, y_2, \ldots, y_n\}$, we want to decide if there exist $r \geq 1$ and two finite sequences of indices $i_1, i_2, \ldots, i_r$ and $j_1, j_2, \ldots, j_r$ such that $x_{i_1} \cdots x_{i_r} = y_{j_1} \ldots y_{j_r}$. In other words, we only demand that the number of words on each side be the same.

This case is also efficiently decidable, even when L_1 or L_2 is a possibly infinite regular language.

Theorem 10. *Let M_1 (resp., M_2) be an NFA with s_1 states and t_1 transitions (resp., s_2 states and t_2 transitions). We can decide in polynomial time (in s_1, s_2, t_1, t_2) whether there exists k such that $L(M_1)^k \cap L(M_2)^k \neq \emptyset$.*

Proof. First, we prove the (possibly surprising?) result that

$$L = \bigcup_{k \geq 1} \left(L(M_1)^k \cap L(M_2)^k \right)$$

is a context-free language.

We construct a pushdown automaton M accepting L. On input x, our PDA attempts to construct two same-length factorizations of x: one into elements of $L(M_1)$, and one into elements of $L(M_2)$. To ensure the factorizations are really of the same length, we use the stack of the PDA to maintain a counter that records the absolute value of the difference between the number of factors in the first factorization and the number of factors in the second. The appropriate sign of the difference is maintained in the state of the PDA.

As we read x, we simulate the NFA's M_1 and M_2. If we reach a final state in either machine, then we have the option (nondeterministically) to deem this the end of a factor in the appropriate factorization, and update the stack accordingly, or continue with the simulation. We accept if the stack records a difference of 0 — that is, if the stack contains no counters and only the initial stack symbol Z_0 — and we are in a final state in both machines (indicating that the factorization is complete into elements of both L_1 and L_2).

Thus we have shown that L is context-free. Furthermore, our PDA has $O(s_1 s_2)$ states and $O(t_1 t_2)$ transitions. It uses only two distinct stack symbols — the

counter and the initial stack symbol — and never pushes more than one additional symbol on the stack in any transition. Such a PDA can be converted to a
context-free grammar G, using the standard "triple construction" [6, Thm. 5.4],
using $O(s_1^2 s_2^2)$ states and $O(s_1^2 s_2^2 t_1 t_2)$ transitions. Now we can test the emptiness
of the language generated by a context-free grammar of size t in $O(t)$ time, by
removing useless symbols and seeing if any productions remain [6, Thm. 4.2].

We conclude that it is decidable in polynomial time whether there exists k
such that $L(M_1)^k \cap L(M_2)^k \neq \emptyset$.   □

Remark 11. There exist simple examples where $L = \bigcup_{k \geq 1} \left(L(M_1)^k \cap L(M_2)^k \right)$
is not regular. For example, take $L(M_1) = b^* a b^*$ and $L(M_2) = a^* b a^*$. Then
$L = \{ x \in \{a,b\}^* : |x|_a = |x|_b \geq 1 \}$, the language of nonempty strings with the
same number of a's and b's.

Furthermore, if M_1, M_2, M_3 are all NFA's, then the analogous language

$$L = \bigcup_{k \geq 1} \left(L(M_1)^k \cap L(M_2)^k \cap L(M_3)^k \right)$$

need not be context-free. A counterexample is given by taking $L(M_1) =
\{b,c\}^* a \{b,c\}^*$, $L(M_2) = \{a,c\}^* b \{a,c\}^*$, and $L(M_3) = \{a,b\}^* c \{a,b\}^*$. Then

$$L = \{ x \in \{a,b,c\}^* : |x|_a = |x|_b = |x|_c \geq 1 \},$$

which is clearly not context-free.

Remark 12. Mike Domaratzki (personal communication) observes that the decision problem "given M_1, M_2, does there exist $k \geq 1$ such that $L(M_1)^k \cap
L(M_2)^k \neq \emptyset$" becomes undecidable if M_1 and M_2 are pushdown automata, by
reduction from the problem "given CFG's G_1, G_2, is $L(G_1) \cap L(G_2) \neq \emptyset$"
[6, Theorem 8.10]. Given G_1 and G_2, we can easily create PDA's accepting
$L_1 := L(G_1)\#$ and $L_2 := L(G_2)\#$, where $\#$ is a new symbol not in the alphabet of either G_1 or G_2. Then $L_1^k \cap L_2^k \neq \emptyset$ for some $k \geq 1$ if and
only if $L(G_1) \cap L(G_2) \neq \emptyset$. A similar result holds for the linear context-free
languages [4].

We now turn to the question of, given regular languages L_1 and L_2, determining
the shortest string in $L = \bigcup_{k \geq 1} \left(L_1^k \cap L_2^k \right)$, given that it is nonempty. Actually,
we consider a more general problem, where we intersect more than two languages.
We start by proving a result about directed graphs.

Lemma 13. *Suppose* $G = (V, E)$ *is a directed graph with edge weights in* $\mathbb{Z}^d$,
where the components of the edge weights are all bounded in absolute value by K.
Let $\sigma(p)$ *denote the weight of a path* p, *obtained by summing the weights of all associated edges. If* G *contains a cycle* $C: u \to u$ *such that* $\sigma(C) = \mathbf{0} = (0,0,\ldots,0)$,
then G *also contains a cycle* $C': u \to u$ *with* $\sigma(C') = \mathbf{0} = (0,0,\ldots,0)$ *and length
at most* $|V|^{d+1} K^d d^{d/2} (|V|^2 + d)$.

Proof. For each vertex v in the cycle C, break C at the first occurrence of v. This gives us

$$C = P_1 P_2 P_3 \cdots P_k$$

such that $P_1 \colon v_1 \to v_2, P_2 \colon v_2 \to v_3, \ldots, P_k \colon v_k \to v_{k+1}$ where $\{v_1, \ldots, v_k\}$ is the set of vertices visited by C. The final vertex, v_{k+1}, is the same as v_1 because C is a cycle. Notice that $k \leq |V|$ because each vertex appears at most once in the list $v_1, \ldots, v_k$.

For each $P_i \colon v_i \to v_{i+1}$, generate a new path $\hat{P}_i \colon v_i \to v_{i+1}$ by removing all simple subcycles. The length of $\hat{P}_i$ is at most $|V|$; otherwise some vertex is repeated, so we have not removed all subcycles. Recombine the $\hat{P}_i$'s into a cycle $T = \hat{P}_1 \cdots \hat{P}_k$ having length $|T| \leq |V|k \leq |V|^2$. In addition to T, we have a list of simple subcycles $B_1, \ldots, B_\ell$ that we removed while generating the $\hat{P}_i$'s.

Consider the cycles we can construct using $T, B_1, B_2, \ldots, B_\ell$. For any B_i, we know T visits the starting vertex of B_i because T visits all the vertices in C. Therefore we can splice B_i into T at its starting vertex. Since B_i is a cycle, we can insert it into T any positive number of times. We can also append T to the whole cycle as many times as we like. These techniques allow us to construct a cycle with weight

$$t\sigma(T) + b_1\sigma(B_1) + \cdots + b_\ell\sigma(B_\ell)$$

where $t \geq 1$ and $b_1, \ldots, b_n \geq 0$ are all integers.

Recall that $T, B_1, \ldots, B_\ell$ were constructed by decomposing C. Each edge from C exists somewhere in $T, B_1, \ldots, B_\ell$, so we have

$$\mathbf{0} = \sigma(C) = \sigma(T) + \sigma(B_1) + \cdots + \sigma(B_\ell).$$

This shows that it is possible to write $\mathbf{0}$ as an integer linear combination of $\sigma(T), \sigma(B_1), \ldots, \sigma(B_\ell)$. Unfortunately, for each nonzero b_i we have at least one copy of B_i, with length at most $|V|$. Since all the b_i's are nonzero and ℓ is unbounded, the corresponding cycle has unbounded length. If we hope to find a bounded cycle by this technique then we need to bound the number of nonzero b_i's. Let us approach the problem with linear programming. Construct a matrix $A \in \mathbb{R}^{d \times \ell}$ where the ith column is given by $A^{(i)} = \sigma(B_i)$. Let $b \in \mathbb{R}^d$ be the column vector $\sigma(T)$. We are looking for solutions to the problem

$$Ax = b, \quad x \geq 0, \quad x \in \mathbb{R}^\ell.$$

This is just the feasible set of a linear program in standard equality form. We saw earlier that it has the feasible solution $x = \begin{pmatrix} 1 & 1 & \cdots & 1 & 1 \end{pmatrix}^T$. Note that if A is not full rank then we remove linearly dependent rows until we have a full rank matrix, and proceed with a matrix of rank $d' \leq d$.

Linear programming theory tells us a feasible problem of this form has a *basic* feasible solution x^* with at most d nonzero entries. Without loss of generality (relabelling if necessary), take all but the first d entries of x^* to be zero. Letting $\hat{A}$

be the first d columns of A, the basic solution x^* satisfies the following equation:

$$\hat{A} \begin{pmatrix} x_1^* \\ \vdots \\ x_d^* \end{pmatrix} = b;$$

$$\sigma(B_1)x_1^* + \cdots + \sigma(B_d)x_d^* = -\sigma(T).$$

We are not done yet because the x_i^*s are real numbers and we need an integer linear combination. Cramer's rule gives an explicit solution for each coefficient, $x_i^* = \frac{\det(\hat{A}_i)}{\det(\hat{A})} = \frac{|\det(\hat{A}_i)|}{|\det(\hat{A})|}$, where $\hat{A}_i$ is the matrix $\hat{A}$ with the ith column replaced by b. Note that $\hat{A}$ and $\hat{A}_i$ are integer matrices, so their determinants are integers and x_i^* is a rational number. When we multiply through by $|\det(\hat{A})|$, all the coefficients will be positive integers:

$$\sigma(B_1)|\det(\hat{A}_1)| + \cdots + \sigma(B_d)|\det(\hat{A}_d)| + \sigma(T)|\det(\hat{A})| = \mathbf{0}.$$

We can bound the determinants with Hadamard's inequality, which says that the determinant of a matrix M is bounded by the product of the norms of its columns. Each B_i is a simple cycle, so $|B_i| \leq |V|$. It follows that any entry of $\sigma(B_i)$ is at most $|V|K$, so $\|\sigma(B_i)\| \leq |V|K\sqrt{d}$. On the other hand, T has length at most $|V|^2$, giving $\|\sigma(T)\| \leq |V|^2 K \sqrt{d}$. Combining these estimates gives $|\det(\hat{A}_i)| \leq |V|^d K^d d^{d/2}$ for all i and $|\det(\hat{A})| \leq |V|^{d+1}K^d d^{d/2}$. Now we construct the cycle C' from this linear combination, with $|\det(\hat{A})|$ copies of T and $|\det(\hat{A}_i)|$ copies of each B_i. By construction, C' has weight $\mathbf{0}$ and its length is bounded as follows:

$$|C'| = |\det A||T| + \sum_{i=1}^{d} |\det A_i||B_i|$$

$$\leq |V|^{d+1}K^d d^{d/2}|V|^2 + \sum_{i=1}^{d}|V|^d K^d d^{d/2}|V|$$

$$= |V|^{d+1}K^d d^{d/2}(|V|^2 + d).$$

$\square$

We consider a generalization of the third problem to d languages.

Corollary 14. *Let $L_1, L_2, \ldots, L_d$ be languages accepted by NFA's having $s_1, \ldots, s_d$ states, respectively. If*

$$\bigcup_{k \geq 1}(L_1^k \cap \cdots \cap L_d^k)$$

is nonempty, then the shortest string in the language has length bounded by

$$O(s^d(d-1)^{(d-1)/2}(s^2 + d - 1)),$$

where $s := (s_1 + 1)(s_2 + 1)\ldots(s_n + 1)$.

Proof. We discuss the case $d = 2$, and then briefly indicate how this is generalized to the general case.

First we discuss an automaton $M_K = (Q_K, \Sigma, \delta_K, q_K, F_K)$ accepting $K = L_1^* \cap L_2^*$ which is a slight variant of the construction given in the proof of Theorem 3.

Suppose we are given a regular language L_1 (resp., L_2) accepted by an NFA M_1 (resp., M_2). Without loss of generality, we will assume that M_1 (resp., M_2) has no transitions into its initial state. This can be accomplished, if necessary, by adding one new state with transitions out the same as the transitions out of the initial state, and redirecting any transitions into the initial state to the new state. If the original machine had s states, then the new machine has at most $s + 1$ states. Call these new machines $M_1' = (Q_1, \Sigma, \delta_1, q_1, F_1)$ and $M_2' = (Q_2, \Sigma, \delta_2, q_2, F_2)$.

Next we create an NFA-ϵ $M_1'' = (Q_1, \Sigma, \delta_1', q_1, F_1')$ by adding an ϵ-transition from every final state of M_1' back to its initial state, and by changing the set of final states to be $F_1' = \{q_1\}$. This new machine M_1'' accepts L_1^*. We carry out a similar construction on M_2' obtaining M_2'' accepting L_2^*.

Finally, mimicking the construction of Theorem 3 we create an NFA-ϵ M_K accepting $K = L_1^* \cap L_2^*$ using the direct product construction outlined above on M_1'' and M_2''. Note that M_K has at most $(s_1 + 1)(s_2 + 1)$ states and has exactly one accepting state, which is its initial state.

We define the edge weights of M_k to be $\mathbb{Z}$ as follows. An explicit ϵ-transition in M_1' or M_2' marks the end of a word, so each explicit ϵ-transition taken in M_1' back to the start gets weight $+1$, while each explicit ϵ-transition in M_2' back to the start gets weight -1. In this way we keep track of the difference between the number of factors used in $L(M_1')$ and $L(M_2')$.

For the general case, we form the intersection automaton as before, and define the i'th coordinate of $\sigma(P)$, for $1 \le i < d$, to be the difference in the number of ϵ-transitions taken in M_1' and M_{i+1}'. Now just apply Lemma 13 to get the desired bound. □

When $d = 2$, we can improve on the result of the previous lemma:

Theorem 15. *If $d = 2$, then the length of the cycle C' in Lemma 13 is at most $2K|V|^2$.*

Proof. We say a cycle c is simple if it has no subcycles. Start by removing simple cycles $B_1, B_2, \ldots, B_\ell$ from C until we are left with R which contains no subcycles, therefore R is also a simple cycle. Thus, we have decomposed C into simple subcycles, so note that the weight of C is the sum of the weights of all the B_i's and R.

If R has weight 0 then take $C' = R$. We are done because R has length at most $|V|$, which is smaller than $2K|V|^2$. If R has nonzero weight then the positive and negative cases are identical so take R to have positive weight without loss of generality. Then there must be some B_i with negative weight, otherwise the sum of the weights of the B_i's and R would be positive, but C has weight 0. Call the negative weight cycle S.

If R and S have some vertex in common, then we can splice $\sigma(R)$ copies of S into $-\sigma(S)$ copies of R to get a cycle C' of weight 0. Since $\sigma(R) \leq K|R|$ and $\sigma(S) \leq K|S|$, the cycle has length $|\sigma(R)||S| + |\sigma(S)||R| \leq 2K|R||S| \leq 2K|V|^2$.

Otherwise, R and S have no vertex in common so we need to find some way to get from R to S and back again. Clearly C passes through every vertex in R and S, but we want a shorter cycle. Let T be the shortest cycle that passes through some vertex in R and some vertex in S. We will split T into α, the piece from R to S, and β, the piece from S to R.

We know that R, S are simple, and α, β must be simple or we could make a shorter cycle T by making them shorter. Therefore, any vertex in V occurs at most four times in R, S and T, once for each of R, S, α, β. But R and S have no vertices in common, so each vertex occurs at most three times in R, S and T.

Now if some vertex v occurs three times in R, S and T, then it must be in α, β and either R or S (without loss of generality, let it be in R). Then we can remove a prefix of α up to v, producing $\hat{\alpha}$. Similarly, remove a suffix of β starting from v, giving $\hat{\beta}$. Then $\hat{\alpha}\hat{\beta}$ is a shorter cycle that visits $v \in R$ and still visits S, contradicting the minimality of T. Therefore any vertex v occurs at most twice in R, S and T, so $|R| + |S| + |T| \leq 2|V|$.

Let us combine T with R if T has positive weight or with S if T has negative weight to produce a cycle Y. Either R or S is left over, call it X. Note that X and Y have opposite sign weights, and also have a vertex in common. As before, we combine $|\sigma(X)|$ copies of Y with $|\sigma(Y)|$ copies of X to produce a cycle C' of length at most $2K|X||Y|$. Under the constraint $|X|+|Y| = |R|+|S|+|T| \leq 2|V|$, the length $2K|X||Y|$ is maximized when $|X| = |Y| = |V|$, with maximum value $2K|V|^2$, completing the proof. $\square$

Finally, we prove an improvement for the unary case.

Proposition 16. *Let L_1, L_2 be nonempty finite languages over a unary alphabet, say $L_1 = \{a^{m_1}, \ldots, a^{m_r}\}$ and $L_2 = \{a^{n_1}, \ldots, a^{n_s}\}$. Then $L_1^k \cap L_2^k \neq \emptyset$ for some $k \geq 1$ iff $\min_{1 \leq i \leq r} m_i \leq \max_{1 \leq j \leq s} n_j$ and $\min_{1 \leq j \leq s} n_j \leq \max_{1 \leq i \leq r} m_i$. If both conditions hold, then $L_1^k \cap L_2^k \neq \emptyset$ for some $k < \max(m_1, \ldots, m_r, n_1, \ldots, n_s)$, and this bound is tight.*

Proof. Suppose $\min_{1 \leq i \leq r} m_i > \max_{1 \leq j \leq s} n_j$. Then every element of L_1^k will be of length greater than every element of L_2^k. Similarly, if $\min_{1 \leq j \leq s} n_j \leq \max_{1 \leq i \leq r} m_i$, then every element of L_2^k will be of length greater than every element of L_1^k. Hence if either condition holds, we have $L_1^k \cap L_2^k = \emptyset$ for all $k \geq 1$.

Now suppose $\min_{1 \leq i \leq r} m_i \leq \max_{1 \leq j \leq s} n_j$ and $\min_{1 \leq j \leq s} n_j \leq \max_{1 \leq i \leq r} m_i$. Then there exist $a^l, a^n \in L_1$ and $a^m \in L_2$ such that $l \leq m \leq n$. Choose $i = n-m$ and $j = m - l$. Then L_1^{i+j} contains $(a^l)^i (a^n)^j = a^{li+nj} = a^{ln-lm+nm-nl} = a^{m(n-l)}$. And L_2^{i+j} contains $(a^m)^{i+j} = a^{m(n-l)}$. So for $k = i+j$ we get $L_1^k \cap L_2^k \neq \emptyset$. Now $i - j = n - l < n \leq \max(m_1, \ldots, m_r, n_1, \ldots, n_s)$.

The bound is tight, as can be seen by taking $L_1 = \{a, a^n\}$ and $L_2 = \{a^{n-1}\}$. Then the least k such that $L_1^k \cap L_2^k \neq \emptyset$ is $k = n - 1$. $\square$

5   The Fourth Problem

Suppose we have a set of pairs of strings $(a_1, b_1), \ldots, (a_n, b_n)$, as in the Post correspondence problem. Let $L_1 = \{a_1, \ldots, a_n\}$ and $L_2 = \{b_1, \ldots, b_n\}$. In the third problem we looked at strings in $L_1^+ \cap L_2^+$ with the same number of words in the L_1^+ decomposition as the L_2^+ decomposition. Here we ask that for each i, a_i occurs in the L_1^+ decomposition as often as b_i occurs in the L_2^+ decomposition.

Corollary 17. *If the language defined in the fourth problem is nonempty then Lemma 13 gives us a bound on the length of the shortest string. We can decide if the language is nonempty by enumerating all strings and decompositions up to this bound.*

6   Conclusions

In this paper we examined some natural questions about the length of the shortest string in the intersection of formal languages. We introduced the lss function, which gives the length of the shortest string in a nonempty language. Our most significant results were Theorem 4, which gives a tight bound for $\mathrm{lss}(L(M_1) \cap L(M_2))$ in terms of the number of states of M_1 and M_2; and Corollary 14, which gives an upper bound on $\mathrm{lss}(\bigcup_{k \geq 1}(L_1^k \cap \cdots \cap L_d^k))$. The most significant problem we could not fully resolve is the exact upper bound for $\mathrm{lss}(L(M_1)^+ \cap L(M_2)^+)$.

References

1. Aho, A.V., Hopcroft, J.E., Ullman, J.D.: The Design and Analysis of Computer Algorithms. Addison-Wesley, Reading (1974)
2. Alpoge, L.: Post correspondence problem variant. Posted to (January 12, 2011), http://cstheory.stackexchange.com/questions/4284/post-correspondence-problem-variant
3. Ang, T.: Problems related to shortest strings in formal languages. M. Math. thesis. University of Waterloo (2010)
4. Baker, B.S., Book, R.V.: Reversal-bounded multipushdown machines. J. Comput. System Sci. 8, 315–332 (1974)
5. Ellul, K., Krawetz, B., Shallit, J., Wang, M.-W.: Regular expressions: new results and open problems. J. Autom. Lang. Combin. 10, 407–437 (2005)
6. Hopcroft, J.E., Ullman, J.D.: Introduction to Automata Theory, Languages, and Computation. Addison-Wesley, Reading (1979)
7. Pighizzini, G., Shallit, J.: Unary language operations, state complexity, and Jacobsthal's function. Int. J. Found. Comput. Sci. 13, 145–159 (2002)

On the Degree of Team Cooperation in CD Grammar Systems

Fernando Arroyo[1], Juan Castellanos[2], and Victor Mitrana[3,*]

[1] Department of Languages, Projects and Computer Information Systems
University School of Informatics
Polytechnic University of Madrid, Crta. de Valencia km. 7, 28031 Madrid, Spain
farroyo@eui.upm.es
[2] Department of Artificial Intelligence, Faculty of Informatics
Polytechnic University of Madrid, 28660 Boadilla del Monte, Madrid, Spain
jcastellanos@fi.upm.es
[3] Department of Organization and Structure of Information
University School of Informatics
Polytechnic University of Madrid, Crta. de Valencia km. 7, 28031 Madrid, Spain
victor.mitrana@upm.es

Abstract. In this paper, we introduce a dynamical complexity measure, namely the *degree of team cooperation*, in the aim of investigating "how much" the components of a grammar system cooperate when forming a team in the process of generating terminal words. We present several results which strongly suggest that this measure is trivial in the sense that the degree of team cooperation of any language is bounded by a constant. Finally, we prove that the degree of team cooperation of a given cooperating/distributed grammar system cannot be algorithmically computed and discuss a decision problem.

1 Introduction

A cooperating grammar system, as introduced in [8] with motivations related to two level grammars, is a set of usual Chomsky grammars, which rewrite, in turn, the same sentential form. Initially, this is a common axiom. At each moment, a grammar is active, that means it is authorized to rewrite the common string, and the others are inactive. The conditions under which a component can become active or disabled and leaves the sentential form to the other components are specified by the cooperation protocol. The language of terminal strings generated in this way is the language generated by the system.

A rather intensive study of cooperating grammar systems has been started after relating them in [3] with artificial intelligence notions, such as the blackboard models in problem solving [10]. Along these lines, more conditions for components enabling and disabling were considered, namely step limitations (a component can work a prescribed number of steps, at least or at most a prescribed number), and the maximal competence strategy, similar in some extent

---

* Work partially supported by the Alexander von Humboldt Foundation.

M. Holzer, M. Kutrib, and G. Pighizzini (Eds.): DCFS 2011, LNCS 6808, pp. 68–79, 2011.

to the stopping condition in [8]: a component must work as long as it can (in [8] a component must work until it introduces a non-terminal which cannot be rewritten by the same component). CD grammar systems working under the last mentioned strategy characterize one of the most important language classes in the L-systems area, namely the *ET0L* language family [3]. The same strategy of cooperation is considered in [1], where modular grammars were introduced with motivations from the regulated rewriting area.

An important part of the theory of grammar systems is the theory of cooperation protocols; the focus is not on the generative capacity, but on the functioning of the systems, and on its influence on the generative capacity and on other specific properties. For a survey, the reader may want to consult [6].

In order to increase the power of such mechanisms, a simple and natural idea is to allow several components to become active during a time unit, see [7]. The sets of grammars which become active at each unit time, are called *teams.*

In [9], teams which rewrite strings in a synchronized manner, are considered: at each step when the team is working, each member of the team uses one of its rules. The teams considered in [9] differ essentially from the other types of teams already considered in [5,7,11], where the size of teams is a prescribed constant. In [9], the number of components in teams is not prescribed, moreover, at different steps the team that processes the sentential form is dynamically formed by components having the same *level of excitation.* More precisely, all components that can rewrite each nonterminal appearing in the sentential form constitute a team. This strategy increases considerably the computational power of CD grammar systems. Thus, important classes, e.g. *ET0L* and the class of matrix grammars, are strictly included in the class of languages generated by teams in CD grammar systems [9]. It is worth mentioning work [2], where hybrid CD grammar systems with teams of different derivation modes, possibly of variable size and/or formed automatically were considered.

In this paper, we introduce a dynamical complexity measure, namely the *degree of team cooperation,* in the aim of investigating "how much" cooperate the components of a grammar system forming a team in the process of generating terminal words. We present several results that suggest that this measure is trivial in the sense that the degree of team cooperation of any language is bounded by a constant. These results are:

(i) The degree of team cooperation of every *ET0L* language is 1.

(ii) Every language having the degree of team cooperation equal to 1 belongs to the class of languages generated by random context grammars with forbidding contexts only.

(iii) Every language generated by random context grammars with forbidding contexts only has the degree of team cooperation at most 2.

Finally, we consider a few computability and decidability issues. More precisely, we prove that the degree of team cooperation of a given CD grammar system is not algorithmically computable. We also show that deciding whether or not a team plays in a CD grammar system is algorithmically equivalent to the emptiness problem for the language generated by teams in a CD grammar system.

2   Preliminaries

The reader is referred to [14] for basic elements of formal language theory. If V is an alphabet then V^* is the set of all words over V. The empty word is denoted by λ and the set of all nonempty words is $V^+ = V^* - \{\lambda\}$. Denote by $\mid x \mid$ the length of $x \in V^*$ and by $(x)_U$ the string obtained from x by erasing all symbols that are not in U. For a finite set A, $card(A)$ denotes the number of elements in A.

A *cooperating distributed (shortly CD) grammar system* [3] is a construct :

$$\Gamma = (N, T, w_0, P_1, \ldots, P_n),$$

where N, T are disjoint finite alphabets, $w_0 \in (N \cup T)^*$, and $P_i, 1 \leq i \leq n$, are finite sets of context-free rules over $(N \cup T)^*$. These sets are called the *components* of Γ.

A *team* in a *CD* grammar system is a set $\mathcal{T} = \{P_{i_1}, \ldots, P_{i_m}\}, m \geq 1, i_j \in \{1, 2, \ldots, n\}, 1 \leq j \leq m$.

Let $\mathcal{T} = \{P_{i_1}, \ldots, P_{i_m}\}$ be a team and $x \in (N \cup T)^*$. Define the derivation relation :

$$x \Longrightarrow_{\mathcal{T}} y \text{ if and only if } \quad x = x_0 A_1 x_1 \ldots A_m x_m, x_k \in (N \cup T)^*, 0 \leq k \leq m,$$

$$y = x_0 y_1 x_1 \ldots y_m x_m, \text{ and } A_j \to y_j \in P_{i_j}, 1 \leq j \leq m.$$

Observe that $\mathcal{T}$ is a set (though two components may be identical but they are identified by their names that are different) and, thus, the members P_{i_j} can be considered in any sequence. In other words, each member of a team rewrites exactly one nonterminal in an arbitrary order. In the sequel, we consider the following way of constituting dynamically a team. This is the so-called *total level of excitation* in [9].

Let $dom(P_i)$ be the set of all symbols in the left-hand side of the rules from P_i, i.e.,

$$dom(P_i) = \{A \mid A \to x \in P_i\}.$$

For a string $x \in (N \cup T)^*$ the *level of excitation* of $P_i, 1 \leq i \leq n$, with respect to x, is the maximal set of symbols from $dom(P_i)$ that appear in x. The level of excitation of P_i with respect to x is *total* if $(x)_N \in dom(P_i)^*$. The team consisting of all components which have a total level of excitation with respect to x, is denoted $\mathcal{T}_x$. Formally

$$\mathcal{T}_x = \{P_i \mid (x)_N \in (dom(P_i))^*\}$$

The language generated by teams in the CD grammar system $\Gamma = (N, T, w_0, P_1, \ldots, P_n)$ is

$$L(\Gamma) = \{w \in T^* \mid w_0 \Longrightarrow_{\mathcal{T}_{w_0}} w_1 \Longrightarrow_{\mathcal{T}_{w_1}} w_2 \Longrightarrow \ldots \Longrightarrow_{\mathcal{T}_{w_{m-1}}} w_m = w, m \geq 1\}.$$

Example 1. *Assume that Γ_1 is the following CD grammar system :*

$$\Gamma_1 = (\{S, A, B, C, X\}, \{a\}, S, P_1, P_2, P_3, P_4, P_5, P_6)$$

$P_1 = \{S \rightarrow a, S \rightarrow aa, S \rightarrow AA\}, \qquad\qquad P_2 = \{A \rightarrow BB, B \rightarrow B\}$

$P_3 = \{B \rightarrow C, C \rightarrow C\}, \qquad\qquad\qquad P_4 = \{C \rightarrow A, C \rightarrow X, A \rightarrow A\}$

$P_5 = \{C \rightarrow A, C \rightarrow X, X \rightarrow X, X \rightarrow a\}, \qquad P_6 = \{X \rightarrow a\}$

The language generated by teams in Γ_1 is $L(\Gamma_1) = \{a^{2^n} \mid n \geq 0\}$. Let us list below a derivation for the word a^4.

$$S \implies_{\{P_1\}} AA \implies_{\{P_2, P_4\}} BBA \implies_{\{P_2\}} BBBB \implies_{\{P_2, P_3\}}$$

$$CBBB \implies_{\{P_3\}} CCBB \implies_{\{P_3\}} CCCB \implies_{\{P_3\}} CCCC \implies_{\{P_3, P_4, P_5\}}$$

$$XXCC \implies_{\{P_5\}} XXXC \implies_{\{P_5\}} XXXX \implies_{\{P_5, P_6\}}$$

$$aXXX \implies_{\{P_5, P_6\}} aaXX \implies_{\{P_5, P_6\}} aaaa$$

Example 2. *Let Γ_2 be the CD grammar system :*

$$\Gamma_2 = (\{S, A\}, \{a, b\}, S, P_1, P_2, P_3)$$

$$P_1 = \{S \rightarrow AA\}, \qquad P_2 = P_3 = \{A \rightarrow aAb, A \rightarrow ab\}$$

Note that the language generated by teams in Γ_2 is $L(\Gamma_2) = \{a^n b^n a^n b^n \mid n \geq 1\}$. Observe that the sentential form $a^k Ab^k a^k Ab^k$ may be rewritten by the team $\{P_2, P_3\}$ into $a^{k+1}b^{k+1}a^{k+1}Ab^{k+1}$, but the derivation is blocked as in the next step the same team $\{P_2, P_3\}$ cannot be applied though it is activated by the sentential form. Furthermore, it is worth mentioning that two components of the aforementioned grammar system are identical and if we remove one of them, then the generated language is completely different which is not the case of usual grammar systems.

As far as the generative capacity of these devices is concerned, in [9] it was proved that they are strictly stronger then the matrix grammars and at least as powerful as $ET0L$ systems.

Now, we are going to define a dynamical measure, namely the *degree of team cooperation*, with the aim of investigating "how much" the components of a grammar system cooperate when forming a team in the process of generating terminal words. Let $\Gamma = (N, T, w_0, P_1, P_2, \ldots, P_n)$ be a CD grammar system and w be a terminal string and D be the following derivation for w:

$$w_0 \implies_{T_{w_0}} w_1 \implies_{T_{w_1}} w_2 \implies \ldots \implies_{T_{w_{m-1}}} w_m = w.$$

The degree of team cooperation in the derivation D for w is

$$Tcoop_\Gamma(w, D) = max\{card(\mathcal{T}_{w_i}) | 0 \leq i \leq m - 1\},$$

while the degree of team cooperation in the generation of $x \in T^*$ is

$$Tcoop_\Gamma(x) = \begin{cases} min\{Tcoop_\Gamma(x, D) | D \text{ is a derivation for } x\}, & \text{if } x \in L(\Gamma), \\ 0, & \text{if } x \notin L(\Gamma) \end{cases}$$

Although we used the same name for the two mappings defined above, there is no risk of confusion as they have a different arity.

We further set

$$Tcoop(\Gamma) = max\{Tcoop_\Gamma(x) \mid x \in L(\Gamma)\}.$$

Clearly, if Γ is a CD grammar system of degree n, then $1 \leq Tcoop(\Gamma) \leq n$.

For instance, in the case of grammar system from Example 1 we have

$$Tcoop_{\Gamma_1}(a^{2^n}) = \begin{cases} 1, & \text{if } n \in \{0,1\} \\ 3, & \text{if } n \geq 2 \end{cases}$$

whilst in Example 2 we have $Tcoop_{\Gamma_2}(a^n b^n a^n b^n) = 2$, for any $n \geq 1$. Consequently, $Tcoop(\Gamma_1) = 3$ and $Tcoop(\Gamma_2) = 2$.

For a language L generated by teams in a CD grammar system, we define the degree of team cooperation of L by

$$TCOOP(L) = min\{Tcoop(\Gamma) \mid L = L(\Gamma)\}.$$

3   Is the Degree of Team Cooperation a Trivial Measure?

It is obvious that the degree of team cooperation of any context-free language is 1. A natural problem is whether the converse of this assertion is true, namely whether or not each language having the degree of team cooperation equal to 1 is context-free. The answer is negative which is not surprising. However, it is rather unexpected that the class of languages having the degree of team cooperation equal to 1 is very large. This class includes $ET0L$ which strongly suggests that this measure is trivial, that is there exists a natural number n such that $TCOOP(L) \leq n$ for any language L generated by teams in a CD grammar system. More surprisingly, this number seems to be 1.

We recall the following derivation mode in a CD grammar system. Given a CD grammar system $\Gamma = (N, T, w_0, P_1, P_2, \ldots, P_n)$, we denote by $\Longrightarrow_{P_i}$ the usual one step derivation with respect to P_i. Now we write $x \Longrightarrow^t_{P_i} y$ iff $x \Longrightarrow^*_{P_i} y$ and there is no $z \in (N \cup T)^*$ such that $y \Longrightarrow_{P_i} z$. The language generated by Γ with the t-mode of derivation is denoted by $L(\Gamma, t)$. It is known (see [1,3]) that the class of languages generated by CD grammar systems in the t-mode of derivation is exactly $ET0L$.

Theorem 3. *If L is an ET0L language, then $TCOOP(L) = 1$.*

Proof. Let L be the language generated by the CD grammar system $\Gamma = (N, T, w_0, P_1, P_2, \ldots, P_n)$ with the t-mode of derivation. Without loss of generality, we may assume that each successful derivation in Γ ends in P_n and that P_n is used exactly once in this derivation. We construct a new CD grammar system

$$\Gamma' = (N', T, w_0 X, P_0, P'_1, P''_1, P'_2, P''_2, \ldots, P'_n, P''_n),$$

where X is a new symbol, $X \notin (N \cup T)$,

$$N' = N \cup \{X\} \cup \{X_i, X_i' \mid 1 \le i \le n\} \cup \{A_i, A_i' \mid A \in N, 1 \le i \le n-1\}$$
$$\cup \{A_n \mid A \in N\},$$

and the sets of rules are defined as follows:

$$P_0 = \{X \to X_i \mid 1 \le i \le n\} \cup \{A \to A \mid A \in N\},$$
$$P_i' = \{X_i \to X_i, X_i \to X_i'\} \cup \{A \to A_i \mid A \in N\} \cup \{A_i \to A_i \mid A \in N\}$$
$$\cup \{A_j' \to A_i \mid A \in N, 1 \le j \ne i \le n-1\},$$
$$\text{for all } 1 \le i \le n,$$
$$P_i'' = \{X_i' \to X_i'\} \cup \{A_i \to h_i(\alpha) \mid A \to \alpha \in P_i,\ h_i \text{ is a morphism defined by}$$
$$h_i(Z) = \begin{cases} Z, & \text{if } Z \in T \\ Z_i, & \text{if } Z \in N \end{cases} \} \cup \{A_i \to A_i' \mid A \notin dom(P_i)\}$$
$$\cup \{A_i' \to A_i' \mid A \notin dom(P_i)\} \cup \{X_i' \to X_j \mid 1 \le j \ne i \le n\},$$
$$\text{for all } 1 \le i \le n-1,$$
$$P_n'' = \{X_n' \to \lambda, X_n' \to X_n'\} \cup \{A_n \to h_n(\alpha) \mid A \to \alpha \in P_n\},$$

where h_n is defined similarly to each morphism h_i.

Assume that

$$w_0 \Longrightarrow_{P_{i_1}}^t w_1 \Longrightarrow_{P_{i_2}}^t w_2 \Longrightarrow_{P_{i_3}}^t \cdots \Longrightarrow_{P_{i_k}}^t w_k \Longrightarrow_{P_n}^t w$$

is a derivation in the t-mode of the terminal word w in Γ. We describe below how this derivation is simulated by teams in Γ'. One starts with $w_0 X \Longrightarrow_{\{P_0\}} w_0 X_{i_1}$. Now, the team formed by P_{i_1}' only will be iteratively activated until each occurrence of any nonterminal in w_0 is substituted by its copy with the index i_1. In other words,

$$w_0 X \Longrightarrow_{\{P_0\}} w_0 X_{i_1} \Longrightarrow_{\{P_{i_1}'\}}^* h_{i_1}(w_0) X_{i_1}'. \tag{1}$$

In the next derivation steps, the team $\{P_{i_1}''\}$ is to be activated until the sentential form $h_{i_1}(w_0) X_{i_1}'$ is transformed into $h_{i_1}'(w_1) X_{i_2}$, where each morphism h_j' is defined as follows:

$$h_j' : (T \cup (N \setminus dom(P_j)))^* \to (N' \cup T)^*, \quad h_j'(Z) = \begin{cases} Z, & \text{if } Z \in T, \\ Z_j', & \text{if } Z \in (N \setminus dom(P_j)). \end{cases}$$

The derivation continues with the team $\{P_{i_2}'\}$ that is used for several times until $h_{i_1}'(w_1)$ becomes $h_{i_2}(w_1)$. Hence, $h_{i_1}'(w_1) X_{i_2} \Longrightarrow_{\{P_{i_2}'\}}^* h_{i_2}(w_1) X_{i_2}'$. In conclusion, we have

$$w_0 X \Longrightarrow_{\{P_0\}} w_0 X_{i_1} \Longrightarrow_{\{P_{i_1}'\}}^* h_{i_1}(w_0) X_{i_1}' \Longrightarrow_{\{P_{i_1}''\}}^* h_{i_1}'(w_1) X_{i_2}$$
$$\Longrightarrow_{\{P_{i_2}'\}}^* h_{i_2}(w_1) X_{i_2}'. \tag{2}$$

Inductively, the derivation continues with

$$h_{i_2}(w_1)X'_{i_2} \Longrightarrow^*_{\{P''_{i_2}\}} h'_{i_2}(w_2)X_{i_3} \Longrightarrow^*_{\{P'_{i_3}\}} \cdots \Longrightarrow^*_{\{P'_{i_k}\}} h_{i_k}(w_{k-1})X'_{i_k}$$
$$\Longrightarrow^*_{\{P''_{i_k}\}} h'_{i_k}(w_k)X_n \Longrightarrow^*_{\{P'_n\}} h_n(w_k)X'_n \Longrightarrow^*_{\{P''_n\}} w. \tag{3}$$

Consequently, $L(\Gamma, t) \subseteq L(\Gamma')$. From the above explanations it immediately follows that $Tcoop_{\Gamma'}(x) = 1$ for all $x \in L(\Gamma, t)$. It now suffices to prove the converse inclusion. To this aim, we analyze the other possible continuations at different steps of the above derivation. Here are two important observations that are very useful in the sequel:

(i) Due to the symbols X_i and X'_i, $1 \le i \le n$, there is no possibility to activate teams consisting of more than one component.
(ii) A sentential form containing X_i or X'_i will activate *at most* either the team $\{P'_i\}$ or $\{P''_i\}$, respectively.

Now, the strategy of a successful derivation is based on the following three principles:

(I) The symbol X_i of a sentential form cannot be replaced by X'_i until all non-terminals of the sentential form are indexed by i, otherwise the derivation is blocked.
(II) The symbol X'_i of a sentential form cannot be replaced by X_j until all rules from P''_i simulating rules from P_i are applied (this means that the sentential form does not contain any occurrence of A_i with $A \in dom(P_i)$) and all the other nonterminals of the sentential form (that is A_i with $A \notin dom(P_i)$) are substituted by their primed copies.
(III) By our assumption on Γ, as soon as the sentential form activates the team $\{P'_n\}$, the derivation goes to its end by iteratively activating $\{P''_n\}$.

By these explanations, one can easily infer that $L(\Gamma') \subseteq L(\Gamma, t)$ which completes the proof. $\square$

A question that naturally arises is whether Theorem 1 can be extended to a characterization of the class $ET0L$. If this were the case, then there would exist languages having a degree of team cooperation bigger than 1, as it is known that $ET0L$ is strictly included in the class of languages generated by teams in CD grammar systems. We cannot answer this question, however we can indicate a class of languages that contains all languages having a degree of team cooperation equal to 1. This is the class of languages generated by random context grammars with forbidden contexts only [13]. It is known that this class strictly includes $ET0L$ [13] (see also [12,15] for an earlier proof of a stronger form of this statement). If we denote by $TCCD(k)$, $k \ge 1$, and fRC the class of languages having a degree of team cooperation at most k and languages generated by random context grammars with forbidden contexts only, respectively, our result can be stated as follows.

Theorem 4. $ET0L \subseteq TCCD(1) \subseteq fRC$ and at least one of these inclusions is proper.

Proof. By the aforementioned considerations, it suffices to prove the inclusion $TCCD(1) \subseteq fRC$. The construction is rather simple, but we first need to briefly recall the definition of a random context grammar with forbidding contexts only. Such a grammar is a construct $G = (N, T, S, P)$, where N, T, S are the classic parameters of a context-free grammar and P is a set of pairs of the form $(A \rightarrow x, Q)$ where $A \rightarrow x$ is a context-free rule and Q is a set of nonterminals. We say that the rule $(A \rightarrow x, Q)$ is applied in the one step derivation $\alpha \Longrightarrow \beta$ in G, if β is obtained from α by applying $A \rightarrow x$ as usual in a context-free grammar provided that $(\alpha)_N \cap Q = \emptyset$. In other words, the rule can be applied to α if no symbol from Q appears in α. The generated language by G is defined as usual.

Let $\Gamma = (N, T, w_0, P_1, P_2, \ldots, P_n)$ be a CD grammar system with $Tcoop(\Gamma) = 1$. We construct the random context grammar with forbidding contexts only $G = (N \cup \{S\}, T, S, P)$, where S is a new symbol, $S \notin (N \cup T)$, and P is defined as follows:

$$P = \{S \rightarrow w_0\} \cup \bigcup_{i=1}^{n} \{(A \rightarrow x, N \setminus dom(P_i)) \mid A \rightarrow x \in P_i\}.$$

The fact that G and Γ generate the same language is immediate. $\square$

We finish this section by completing the picture we have emphasized so far with a final result.

Theorem 5. $fRC \subseteq TCCD(2)$.

Proof. Let $G = (N, T, S, P)$ be a random context grammar with forbidding contexts only. Assume that $P = \{r_1, r_2, \ldots, r_n\}$ for some $n \geq 1$. We construct the CD grammar system

$$\Gamma = (N', T, SX, P_0, P_1^1, P_1^2, P_1^3, P_2^1, P_2^2, P_2^3, \ldots, P_n^1, P_n^2, P_n^3, P_0'),$$

where the set of nonterminals is

$$N' = \{S, X\} \cup \{X_i, X_i' \mid 1 \leq i \leq n\} \cup \{A_i \mid A \in N, 1 \leq i \leq n\},$$

and the components are defined in the following way:

$P_0 = \{X \rightarrow X_i \mid 1 \leq i \leq n\} \cup \{S \rightarrow S\},$

$P_i^1 = \{X_i \rightarrow X_i, X_i \rightarrow X_i'\} \cup \{A \rightarrow A_i \mid A \in N\} \cup \{A_i \rightarrow A_i \mid A \in N\}$
$\qquad \cup \{A_j \rightarrow A_i \mid A \in N, 1 \leq j \neq i \leq n\},$
$\qquad$ for all $1 \leq i \leq n$,

$P_i^2 = \{X_i' \rightarrow X_i'\} \cup \{A_i \rightarrow h_i(\alpha) \mid r_i = (A \rightarrow \alpha, Q) \in P,\ h_i$ is a morphism

$\qquad$ defined by $h_i(Z) = \begin{cases} Z, & \text{if } Z \in T \\ Z_i, & \text{if } Z \in N \end{cases} \} \cup \{B_i \rightarrow B_i \mid B \in N \setminus (Q \cup \{A\})\},$

$\qquad$ for all $1 \leq i \leq n$,

$P_i^3 = \{X_i' \rightarrow X_j \mid 1 \leq j \neq i \leq n\} \cup \{A_i \rightarrow A_i \mid A \in N\}$, for all $1 \leq i \leq n$,

$P_0' = \{X_i \rightarrow \lambda \mid 1 \leq i \leq n\}.$

The argument for proving $L(G) = L(\Gamma)$ is rather similar to that from the proof of Theorem 1. More precisely, if

$$S \Longrightarrow_{r_{i_1}} w_1 \Longrightarrow_{r_{i_2}} w_2 \Longrightarrow_{r_{i_3}} \cdots \Longrightarrow_{r_{i_k}} w_k = w \in T^*,$$

for some $k \geq 1$, is a derivation in G, then the following derivation is possible in Γ:

$$SX \Longrightarrow_{\{P_0\}} SX_{i_1} \Longrightarrow^*_{\{P^1_{i_1}\}} S_{i_1} X'_{i_1} \Longrightarrow_{\{P^2_{i_1}, P^3_{i_1}\}} h_{i_1}(w_1) X_{i_2}$$
$$\Longrightarrow^*_{\{P^1_{i_2}\}} h_{i_2}(w_1) X'_{i_2} \Longrightarrow_{\{P^2_{i_2}, P^3_{i_2}\}} h_{i_2}(w_2) X_{i_3}$$
$$\Longrightarrow^*_{\{P^1_{i_3}\}} \cdots \Longrightarrow^*_{\{P^1_{i_k}\}} h_{i_k}(w_{k-1}) X'_{i_k} \Longrightarrow_{\{P^2_{i_k}, P^3_{i_k}\}} w_k X_j \Longrightarrow^*_{\{P'_0\}} w_k,$$

for some $1 \leq j \neq i_k \leq n$.

Therefore, $L(G) \subseteq L(\Gamma)$ holds. Furthermore, $Tcoop_\Gamma(x) \leq 2$ for every $x \in L(G)$.

A slightly modified version of the discussion from the second part of the proof of Theorem 1 holds for proving the inclusion $L(\Gamma) \subseteq L(G)$. It is worth mentioning that the construction from the proof of Theorem 1 cannot be used in this case because that construction cannot cope with the situation when x from a rule $(A \rightarrow x, Q) \in P$ contains a nonterminal in Q.   □

The following problems remain open:

1. Which of the inclusions in the statement of Theorem 2 is proper?
2. Are there languages having a degree of team cooperation larger than 1?
3. If the answer of the previous problem is affirmative, then is the degree of team cooperation a non-trivial measure? If this is not the case, what is the maximal degree of team cooperation?
4. Is the degree of team cooperation a connected measure, that is for any natural n does there exist a language L_n with $TCOOP(L_n) = n$?

4   Computability/Decidability Issues

This section is devoted to some computability and decidability issues. We first investigate the possibility of computing the degree of team cooperation of a CD grammar system.

Theorem 6. *Given a CD grammar system Γ, $Tcoop(\Gamma)$ fails to be algorithmically computable.*

Proof. Let

$$x = (x_1, x_2, \ldots, x_n)$$
$$y = (y_1, y_2, \ldots, y_n)$$

be an instance of the Post Correspondence Problem (PCP) over the alphabet V. Let further $G = (N, V \cup \{c\}, S, P)$, $c \notin (N \cup V)$, be a context-free grammar generating the language $L = \{vccw \mid v, w \in V^+, v \neq w^R\}$. We now construct the CD grammar system $\Gamma = (N \cup \{S_0, X, Y, Z\}, V \cup \{c\}, S_0, P_1, P_2, P_3, P_4)$, where

$$P_1 = P \cup \{S_0 \to S, S_0 \to X\},$$
$$P_2 = \{X \to x_i X y_i^R \mid 1 \leq i \leq n\} \cup \{X \to x_i Y Z y_i^R \mid 1 \leq i \leq n\},$$
$$P_3 = \{Y \to c, Z \to Z\}, \qquad P_4 = \{Z \to c, Y \to Y\}.$$

Clearly, $L(\Gamma) = L(G)$ if and only if $Tcoop(\Gamma) = 1$ if and only if PCP for the instance (x, y) has no solution. Therefore, one cannot compute $Tcoop(\Gamma)$. □

Another problem of interest is to investigate the possibility of computing the degree of team cooperation in the generation of a terminal word in a given CD grammar system. We do not have a solution, but a related problem is: Given a CD grammar system Γ and a terminal word x, is it decidable whether or not a team $\mathcal{T}$ is ever activated in a derivation of x in Γ? A first step towards a solution to this problem is presented in what follows.

Let $\Gamma = (N, T, w_0, P_1, \ldots, P_n)$ be a CD grammar system and let $\mathcal{T} = \{P_{i_1}, \ldots, P_{i_m}\}$ be a team in Γ. We say that $\mathcal{T}$ "plays" if there are $x, y \in (N \cup T)^*$, such that

$$w_0 \Longrightarrow^* x \Longrightarrow_{\mathcal{T}} y.$$

We say that a team $\mathcal{T}$ plays successfully if there are x, y, z with $x, y \in (N \cup T)^*, z \in T^*$, such that

$$w_0 \Longrightarrow^* x \Longrightarrow_{\mathcal{T}} y \Longrightarrow^* z.$$

Proposition 7. *If the problem "Does a team play successfully?" is decidable, then the emptiness problem for languages generated by teams in CD grammar systems is decidable.*

Proof. Let $\Gamma = (N, T, w_0, P_1, \ldots, P_n)$ be a CD grammar system with $T = \{a_1, a_2, \ldots, a_t\}$; we construct the CD grammar system

$$\Gamma' = (N', T, \bar{w}_0 Z, P_1', \ldots, P_n', P_{n+1}', P_{n+2}')$$

with $N' = N \cup N'' \cup \{Z, Z', Y, \Lambda\}$, where $N'' = \{A_i \mid 1 \leq i \leq t\}$, Z, Z', Y, Λ are new symbols, and the components P_j' are defined as follows:

$$P_j' = \bar{P}_j \cup \{A_i \to A_i \mid 1 \leq i \leq t\} \cup \{\Lambda \to \Lambda, Z \to Z, Z \to Z'\}, 1 \leq j \leq n,$$

where $\bar{P}_j$ is P_j in which the terminals a_i are renamed by A_i and λ is renamed by Λ. Further,

$$P_{n+1}' = \{A_i \to a_i \mid 1 \leq i \leq t\} \cup \{\Lambda \to \lambda, Z' \to Z', Z' \to Y\}, \quad P_{n+2}' = \{Y \to \lambda\}.$$

If $x \in (N \cup T)^*$, then $\bar{x}$ denotes the word obtained from x by renaming each terminal symbol a_i by A_i, $1 \leq i \leq t$, and leaving unchanged the nonterminals. Let $\mathcal{T} = \{P_{n+1}'\}$ be a team in Γ'.

It is easy to prove that if $w_0 \Longrightarrow_\Gamma^* w$, then $\bar{w}_0 Z \Longrightarrow_{\Gamma'}^* \bar{w} Z'$ and if $\bar{w}_0 Z \Longrightarrow_{\Gamma'}^*$ $X_1 X_2 \ldots X_m Z', X_i \in N', i = 1, \ldots, m$, then $w_0 \Longrightarrow_\Gamma^* X_1' \ldots X_m'$, where

$$X_j' = \begin{cases} X_j, & \text{if } X_j \in N, \\ a_i, & \text{if } X_j = A_i \in N", \\ \lambda, & \text{if } X_j = \Lambda. \end{cases}$$

Note that, if the team $\mathcal{T}$ plays in Γ' (it actually plays successfully), then there exists a sentential form $\bar{u} Z'$ with $\bar{u} \in (N" \cup \{\Lambda\})^*$ such that $\bar{w}_0 Z \Longrightarrow^* \bar{u} Z'$ in Γ'. Therefore, it follows that $w_0 \Longrightarrow_\Gamma^* u, u \in T^*$. Consequently, $L(\Gamma) \neq \emptyset$ holds.

Conversely, assume that $L(\Gamma) \neq \emptyset$. Hence, there is a $w \in T^*$ such that $w_0 \Longrightarrow_\Gamma^*$ w. Consequently, we obtain that $\bar{w}_0 Z \Longrightarrow_{\Gamma'}^* \bar{w} Z'$. Note that $\bar{w} \in (N" \cup \{\Lambda\})^*$ and therefore the team $\mathcal{T}$ can be applied to $\bar{w}$. Thus, $\mathcal{T}$ plays successfully in Γ' as the derivation successfully ends in the next step after $\mathcal{T}$ is disabled. Consequently, $\mathcal{T}$ plays successfully in Γ' if and only if $L(\Gamma) \neq \emptyset$. □

Is the converse true as well? In other words, is the decidability status of the problem "Does a team play successfully?" the same as that of the emptiness problem for languages generated by teams in CD grammar systems? We give below a proof for a weaker variant of this statement, namely the word "successfully" is removed.

Proposition 8. *If the emptiness problem for languages generated by teams in CD grammar systems is decidable, then the problem "Does a team play?" is decidable.*

Proof. Let $\Gamma = (N, T, w_0, P_1, \ldots, P_n)$ be a CD grammar system and let $\mathcal{T} = \{P_{i_1}, \ldots, P_{i_r}\}$ be a fixed team in Γ. In order to solve the problem if $\mathcal{T}$ plays in Γ, we consider the CD grammar system Γ',

$$\Gamma' = (N', T', w_0' Z, P_1', \ldots, P_n', P_{n+1}', P_{n+2}'),$$

where $N' = N \cup \{Z, Z', Y\}$ and T' is a disjoint copy of $N, T' = \{X' \mid X \in N\}$. The components of Γ' are:

$$P_i' = \{X \to \varphi(\alpha) \mid X \to \alpha \in P_i\} \cup \{X \to X' \mid X \in dom(P_i)\} \cup \{Z \to Z, Z \to Z'\},$$

for all $1 \leq i \leq n$, where φ is the morphism that erases all symbols from T and preserves symbols from N and

$$P_{n+1}' = \{X \to X' \mid X \in N\} \cup \{Z' \to Z', Z' \to Y\}, \qquad P_{n+2}' = \{Y \to \lambda\}.$$

Note that: $L(\Gamma') = \{\psi(u) \mid w_0 \Longrightarrow_\Gamma^* u\}$, where, $\psi(X) = \begin{cases} \lambda, & \text{if } X \in T, \\ X', & \text{if } X \in N. \end{cases}$ Now, for any nonempty subset $D, D \subseteq dom(P_{i_1}) \cap \cdots \cap dom(P_{i_r})$ consider the set $D' = \{X' \mid X \in D\}$ and the regular language $R_\mathcal{T}$:

$$R_\mathcal{T} = (D')^* - \left(\bigcup_{i=0}^{r-1} (D')^i \right) = \{v \in (D')^* : \mid v \mid \geq r\}.$$

Now, it is easy to notice that the team $\mathcal{T}$ plays if and only if

$$L_{\mathcal{T}} = (L(\Gamma') \cap R_{\mathcal{T}}) \neq \emptyset.$$

It is an easy exercise to show that $L_{\mathcal{T}}$ can be generated by teams in a CD grammar system. Thus, if we can decide whether or not $L_{\mathcal{T}}$ is empty, then we can decide whether or not $\mathcal{T}$ plays. $\square$

Although the emptiness for $ET0L$ is decidable we do not know the decidability status of the emptiness problem for languages generated by teams in CD grammar systems.

References

1. Atanasiu, A., Mitrana, V.: The modular grammars. International Journal of Computer Math. 30, 17–35 (1989)
2. ter Beek, M.H.: Teams in grammar systems: hybridity, and weak rewriting. Acta Cybernetica 12, 427–444 (1996)
3. Csuhaj-Varjú, E., Dassow, J.: On cooperating distributed grammar systems. J. Inform. Process. Cybern. EIK 26, 49–63 (1990)
4. Csuhaj-Varjú, E., Dassow, J., Kelemen, J., Păun, G.: Grammar Systems. Gordon and Breach (1994)
5. Csuhaj-Varjú, E., Păun, G.: Limiting the size of teams in cooperating grammar systems. Bulletin EATCS 51, 198–202 (1993)
6. Dassow, J., Păun, G., Rozenberg, G.: Grammar Systems. In: [14]
7. Kari, L., Mateescu, A., Păun, G., Salomaa, A.: Teams in cooperating grammar systems. Journal of Experimental & Theoretical Artificial Intelligence 7, 347–359 (1995)
8. Meersman, R., Rozenberg, G.: Cooperating grammar systems. In: Winkowski, J. (ed.) MFCS 1978. LNCS, vol. 64, pp. 364–374. Springer, Heidelberg (1978)
9. Mateescu, A., Mitrana, V., Salomaa, A.: Dynamical teams in cooperating distributed grammar systems. Ann. Univ. of Bucharest, 3–14 (1993-1994)
10. Nii, P.H.: Blackboard systems. In: Barr, A., Cohen, P.R., Feigenbaum, E.A. (eds.) The Handbook of AI, vol. 4. Addison-Wesley, London (1989)
11. Păun, G., Rozenberg, G.: Prescribed teams of grammars. Acta Informatica 31, 525–537 (1994)
12. Penttonen, M.: ET0L-grammars and N-grammars. Inform. Proc. Letters 4, 11–13 (1975)
13. Rozenberg, G., Vermeir, D.: On the relationships between context-free programmed grammars and $ET0L$ systems. Fundamenta Informaticae 1, 325–345 (1978)
14. Rozenberg, G., Salomaa, A. (eds.): Handbook of Formal Languages, vol. I-III. Springer, Berlin (1997)
15. von Solms, S.H.: On $T0L$ languages over terminals. Inform. Proc. Letters 3, 69–70 (1975)

The Size-Cost of Boolean Operations on Constant Height Deterministic Pushdown Automata*

Zuzana Bednárová[1], Viliam Geffert[1], Carlo Mereghetti[2], and Beatrice Palano[2]

[1] Department of Computer Science, P. J. Šafárik University,
Jesenná 5, 04154 Košice, Slovakia
{ivazuzu@eriv,viliam.geffert@upjs}.sk
[2] Dipartimento di Scienze dell'Informazione, Università degli Studi di Milano
via Comelico 39, 20135 Milano, Italy
{mereghetti,palano}@dsi.unimi.it

Abstract. We study the size-cost of boolean operations on *constant height deterministic pushdown automata*. We prove an *asymptotically optimal* exponential blow-up for union and intersection, as well as polynomial blow-up for complement.

Keywords: pushdown automata; boolean operations on languages; descriptional complexity.

1 Introduction

The model of constant height pushdown automata (PDA) is introduced in [2], where it is studied from a descriptional complexity viewpoint. Roughly speaking, a constant height PDA is a traditional PDA (see, e.g., [5]) with a built-in constant limit (i.e., not depending on the input length) on the height of the pushdown. It is a routine exercise to show that such devices accept exactly regular languages. Nevertheless, a representation of regular languages by constant height PDAs can potentially be more succinct than by standard formalisms. In fact, in [2], optimal exponential and double-exponential gaps are proved between the size of constant heigh deterministic and nondeterministic PDAs (DPDAs and NPDAs, resp.) and that of deterministic, nondeterministic finite state automata (DFAs and NFAs, resp.), and of classical regular expressions.

In this paper, we continue the investigation on the descriptional power of constant height PDAs by tackling a truly classical problem in descriptional complexity, namely, the *size-cost of boolean operations*. There exists a wide literature on this research issue with respect to, e.g., finite state automata [4,8], regular expressions [1,3], grammars [6,7], etc.. In our context, the problem can be expressed as: given constant height DPDAs A and B accepting the languages $L(A)$

---

* This work was partially supported by CRUI/DAAD under the project "Programma Vigoni: Descriptional Complexity of Non-Classical Computational Models", and by research grants VEGA 1/0035/09 and APVV-0035-10.

M. Holzer, M. Kutrib, and G. Pighizzini (Eds.): DCFS 2011, LNCS 6808, pp. 80–92, 2011.
© Springer-Verlag Berlin Heidelberg 2011

and $L(B)$, respectively, determine the size – as a function of the sizes of A and B – of constant height DPDAs accepting $L(A)^c$, $L(A) \cup L(B)$, and $L(A) \cap L(B)$.

In Section 3, we analyze the size-cost of complementing a constant height DPDA A working with a finite set Q of states and constant height h. A DPDA for $L(A)^c$ is proposed, working with $O(|Q| \cdot h)$ states and constant height h. Basically, the size increase directly reflects the cost of detecting and eliminating loops of pushdown moves plus other "non-conventional" rejection policies such as pushdown overflow/underflow and blocking situations.

In Section 4, we study the costs of union and intersection of constant height DPDAs A and B working with constant height h_A and h_B, respectively. We design DPDAs for $L(A) \cup L(B)$ and $L(A) \cap L(B)$ with a number of states exponential in h_A and pushdown height h_B. Moreover, we prove the asymptotical optimality of this exponential blow-up by exhibiting families $\{L_h\}_{h>1}$ of languages such that: (i) L_h is the union or intersection of two languages both accepted by DPDAs of pushdown height h, (ii) L_h cannot be accepted by any DPDA where both the number of states and pushdown height are bounded by a polynomial in h.

2   Preliminaries

The set of natural numbers, including zero, is denoted here by $\mathbf{N}$, while Σ^* is the set of words on an alphabet Σ, including the empty word ε. By $|w|$, we denote the length of a word $w \in \Sigma^*$ and by Σ^i the set of words of length $i \in \mathbf{N}$, with $\Sigma^0 = \{\varepsilon\}$ and $\Sigma^{\leq m} = \bigcup_{i=0}^{m} \Sigma^i$. By $|S|$, we denote the cardinality of a set S, and by S^c its complement. We assume the reader is familiar with the models of deterministic and nondeterministic finite state automata (DFA and NFA, for short) and pushdown automata (DPDA and NPDA, for short) (see, e.g., [5]).

For technical reasons, we shall introduce the NPDAs in the following form [2], where moves manipulating the pushdown store are clearly distinguished from those reading the input tape: an NPDA is a 6-tuple $A = \langle Q, \Sigma, \Gamma, H, q_0, F \rangle$, where Q is the finite set of states, Σ the input alphabet, Γ the pushdown alphabet, $q_0 \in Q$ the initial state, $F \subseteq Q$ (resp., $Q \backslash F$) the set of accepting (resp., rejecting) states, and $H \subseteq Q \times (\{\varepsilon\} \cup \Sigma \cup \{+, -\} \cdot \Gamma) \times Q$ the *transition relation* with the following meaning: (i) $(p, \varepsilon, q) \in H$: A reaches the state q from the state p without using the input tape or the pushdown store, (ii) $(p, a, q) \in H$: A reaches the state q from the state p by reading the symbol a from the input, not using the pushdown store, (iii) $(p, -X, q) \in H$: if the symbol on top of the pushdown is X, A reaches the state q from the state p by popping X, not using the input tape, (iv) $(p, +X, q) \in H$: A reaches the state q from the state p by pushing the symbol X onto the pushdown, not using the input tape.

Such a machine does not use any initial pushdown symbol. *An accepting computation begins in the state q_0 with the empty pushdown store and input head at the beginning of the input string, and ends in an accepting state $q \in F$ after reading the entire input.* As usual, $L(A)$ is the language accepted by A.

A *deterministic pushdown automaton* (DPDA), roughly speaking, is an NPDA for which there is at most one move for any configuration. In the next section, introducing the study on DPDA complementation, we will state conditions for determinism in more details.

It is not hard to see that any NPDA in the classical form can be transformed into this latter form and vice versa, preserving determinism in the case of DPDAs. Yet, the transformation increases the number of states by a constant multiplicative factor only.

Given a constant $h \in \mathbf{N}$, we say that the NPDA A is of pushdown height h if, for any word in $L(A)$, there exists an accepting computation along which the pushdown store never contains more than h symbols. From now on, we shall consider *constant height* NPDAs only. Such a machine will be denoted by a 7-tuple $A = \langle Q, \Sigma, \Gamma, H, q_0, F, h \rangle$, where $h \in \mathbf{N}$ is a constant denoting the pushdown height, and all other elements are defined as above. By definition, the meaning of the transitions in the form (iv) is modified as follows:

(iv') $(p, +X, q) \in H$: *if the current pushdown store height is smaller than h*, then A reaches the state q from the state p by pushing the symbol X onto the pushdown, not using the input tape; *otherwise* A halts and rejects.

The reader may easily verify that: (i) for $h = 0$, the definition of constant height NPDA exactly coincides with that of an NFA, (ii) the class of languages accepted by constant height NPDAs coincide with regular languages. For a constant height NPDA, a fair definition of size must account for the size of all the components the device consists of, i.e., the finite state control plus the pushdown store and its alphabet. So, according to [2], we state that

Definition 1. *The* size of a constant height NPDA $A = \langle Q, \Sigma, \Gamma, H, q_0, F, h \rangle$ *is the ordered triple* $\mathrm{size}(A) = (|Q|, |\Gamma|, h)$.

3   Complementing Constant Height DPDAs

In this section, we study the size-increase when complementing constant height DPDAs. More precisely, we deal with the following problem: given a constant height DPDA $A = \langle Q, \Sigma, \Gamma, H, q_0, F, h \rangle$, determine the size – as a function of $\mathrm{size}(A)$ – of a constant height DPDA accepting $L(A)^c$. Clearly, as a first direct approach, one may turn A into an equivalent DFA A' by storing possible pushdown contents of A in the finite control states. Then, by switching accepting with rejecting states in A', the desired machine A'' would be obtained, featuring $\mathrm{size}(A'') = (|Q| \cdot |\Gamma|^{\leq h}, 0, 0)$. However, we want to precisely evaluate how the cost of complementation impacts on the the size of both the finite control and the pushdown store. So, we build a full-featured constant height DPDA for $L(A)^c$.

We start with few considerations concerning acceptance and rejection on DPDAs. As observed in Section 2, our constant height DPDA A accepts an input string $x \in \Sigma^*$ by completely sweeping it, and entering an accepting state. On the other hand, in order to reject, A may adopt several policies:

(i) A completely consumes x and enters a rejecting state;

(ii) BLOCKING SITUATION: A gets into a situation where the input head is scanning one of the input cells and no move, either on the input and on the pushdown, is possible;

(iii) PUSHDOWN OVERFLOW AND UNDERFLOW: A pushes a symbol onto the pushdown but h symbols are already piled up (overflow), or A tries to pop an empty pushdown (underflow);

(iv) LOOP: A enters a *computation loop* which can be of three types:

- ε-LOOP: A performs an endless sequence of ε-moves, without moving the input head or acting on the pushdown,
- PUSHDOWN-LOOP: A performs an endless sequence of moves manipulating the pushdown only; in this computation, the input head is kept stationary and pushdown boundaries are never violated,
- MIXED-LOOP: A performs an infinite alternation of finite sequences of push and pop operations and finite sequences of ε-transitions; in this computation, the input head is kept stationary and pushdown boundaries are never violated.

If rejection took place according to policy (i) only, then we could complement A by simply switching accepting with rejecting states, as for DFAs. However, the presence of rejection policies (ii), (iii), and (iv) immediately implies that such a simple approach would not work. In what follows, we are going to eliminate policies (ii), (iii), and (iv) and *let constant height DPDAs reject by (i) only*. Yet, we will analyze the size cost of this operation which directly gives the cost of complementing constant height DPDAs.

Let us begin by introducing some notation that will turn out to be useful in our constructions. Given the constant height NPDA $A = \langle Q, \Sigma, \Gamma, H, q_0, F, h \rangle$, we define the following subsets of states: (i) $Q_\varepsilon = \{p \in Q : (p, \varepsilon, q) \in H\}$, i.e., those sets which ε-moves start from; (ii) $Q_\sigma = \{p \in Q : (p, \sigma, q) \in H\}$ for each $\sigma \in \Sigma$, i.e., those sets which moves upon consuming the input symbol σ start from. We let $Q_\Sigma = \cup_{\sigma \in \Sigma} Q_\sigma$; (iii) $Q_{+X} = \{p \in Q : (p, +X, q) \in H\}$ for each $X \in \Gamma$, i.e., those sets from which X is pushed onto the pushdown store. In a similar way, we define the set Q_{-X} of those states from which popping of X takes place. We let $Q_{+\Gamma} = \cup_{X \in \Gamma} Q_{+X}$, $Q_{-\Gamma} = \cup_{X \in \Gamma} Q_{-X}$, and $Q_\Gamma = Q_{+\Gamma} \cup Q_{-\Gamma}$. It is easy to see that A is deterministic if and only if all the following conditions are satisfied:

- For every $\alpha, \beta \in \{\varepsilon, \Sigma, \{+, -\} \cdot \Gamma\}$ with $\alpha \neq \beta$, then $Q_\alpha \cap Q_\beta = \emptyset$.
- For every $\alpha \in \{\varepsilon\} \cup \Sigma \cup \{+, -\} \cdot \Gamma$ and $p \in Q_\alpha$, then $|\{(p, \alpha, q) : q \in Q\}| \leq 1$.
- For every $X, Y \in \Gamma$ with $X \neq Y$, then $Q_{+X} \cap Q_{+Y} = \emptyset$.

We are now ready to show how to remove rejection policies (ii), (iii), (iv) from the constant height DPDA $A = \langle Q, \Sigma, \Gamma, H, q_0, F, h \rangle$ and make it reject according to (i) only. To get a "worst-case" upper bound on the size of the resulting machine, we assume that A *presents all rejection policies (ii), (iii), (iv)*, and we incrementally remove them.

3.1   Removal of Rejection Policy (ii): Blocking Situation

We start by removing situations in which A rejects by being blocked in a state p, with the input head scanning the symbol σ, the pushdown top being X, and $p \notin Q_\varepsilon \cup Q_\sigma \cup Q_{-X} \cup Q_{+\Gamma}$. We call this a *blocking situation*, which is dealt with as follows. First of all, we add a new rejecting state r to the set of states Q, and the new set of transitions $\{(r, \gamma, r) : \gamma \in \Sigma\}$ to the transition relation H. We further add a new transition according to the following rules:

- if $p \in Q_\Sigma$ or $p \notin Q_\Sigma \cup Q_{-\Gamma}$, then we add the new transition (p, σ, r),
- if $p \in Q_{-\Gamma}$, then we add the new transition $(p, -X, r)$.

For every blocking situation, we update the transition relation H according to the above rules, and obtain the new transition relation H'. It is easy to verify that the resulting machine $A' = \langle Q \cup \{r\}, \Sigma, \Gamma, H', q_0, F, h \rangle$ is still a constant height DPDA behaving exactly as A except when it reaches a situation that was blocking for A. In fact, in this situation, the new set of transitions now is easily seen to move the input head off the right end of the string, leading to the new rejecting state r. Hence, A' now rejects according to policy (i). We get that $\text{size}(A') = (|Q| + 1, |\Gamma|, h)$.

3.2   Removal of Rejection Policy (iii): Pushdown Overflow/Underflow

Let us now remove from A' rejection by pushdown overflow and underflow. To this end, we store the current pushdown height in the finite control states. Before any push or pop operation, we check whether the current pushdown height allows it. If this is not the case, we make A' completely sweep the input string, finally reaching the rejecting state r. Formally, the set of states of the new machine A'' consists of $Q'' = (Q \times \{0, \ldots, h\}) \cup \{r\}$, i.e., each state is associated with the current pushdown height which is a number in $\{0, \ldots, h\}$. Clearly, the initial state is $[q_0, 0]$, while the set of accepting states is $F'' = F \times \{0, \ldots, h\}$. The new set of transitions H'' is built out from H' as follows:

- MOVES ON THE INPUT: we replace any transition $(p, \alpha, q) \in H'$ with $\alpha \in \{\varepsilon\} \cup \Sigma$ by the set of transitions $\{([p, k], \alpha, [q, k]) : k \in \{0, \ldots, h\}\}$.
- PUSH OPERATIONS: we replace any transition $(p, +X, q) \in H'$ with $X \in \Gamma$ by the set of transitions $\{([p, k], +X, [q, k + 1]) : k \in \{0, \ldots, h - 1\}\}$. Moreover, to recover from pushdown overflow, we add the transition $([p, h], \varepsilon, r)$.
- POP OPERATIONS: we replace any transition $(p, -X, q) \in H'$ with $X \in \Gamma$ by transitions $\{([p, k], -X, [q, k - 1]) : k \in \{1, \ldots, h\}\}$. Moreover, to recover from pushdown underflow, we add the transition $([p, 0], \varepsilon, r)$.

The resulting constant height DPDA $A'' = \langle Q'', \Sigma, \Gamma, H'', [q_0, 0], F'', h \rangle$ is easily seen to act exactly as A' except when in situations previously causing pushdown overflow or underflow. In fact, for the former case, A'' now finds itself in a state $[p, h]$, and the new ε-transition $([p, h], \varepsilon, r)$ leads it to the rejecting state r. At this point, transitions $\{(r, \gamma, r) : \gamma \in \Sigma\}$, already introduced for removal of rejection policy (ii), make A'' sweep the whole input. Underflow recovery is performed in the symmetrical way. So, rejection by pushdown overflow and underflow is now substituted with type (i) rejection. We get that $\text{size}(A'') = (|Q| \cdot (h+1)+1, |\Gamma|, h)$.

3.3 Removal of Rejection Policy (iv): ε-Loop and Mixed-Loop

We now remove from A'' rejection by ε-loop, i.e., a sequence of ε-transitions of the form $\Lambda = (p_0, \varepsilon, p_1), (p_1, \varepsilon, p_2), \ldots, (p_n, \varepsilon, p_0)$ with $p_i \in Q''_\varepsilon$. Such kind of loops may be easily detected by constructing the digraph $D = (Q''_\varepsilon, E)$ where the set $E \subseteq Q''_\varepsilon \times Q''_\varepsilon$ of arcs is defined as $E = \{(p,q) : (p, \varepsilon, q) \in H''\}$. It is not hard to see that ε-loops correspond to elementary cycles in D.

So, given the ε-loop Λ, for any $0 \le i \le n$ define the set of transitions $\Lambda_i = \{(q, \alpha, p_i) \in H''\}$. Basically, Λ_i consists of all transitions in H'' leading A'' to enter the loop at the state p_i. Notice that, once in the loop, A'' cannot leave it due to determinism. We can remove the ε-loop Λ by simply deleting all the involved transitions from H'' and states from Q''. (Without loss of generality, we will always maintain $[q_0, 0]$ in Q''.). In addition, we replace in H'' each set Λ_i with the new set of transitions $\tilde{\Lambda}_i = \{(q, \alpha, r) : (q, \alpha, p_i) \in \Lambda_i\}$. The resulting constant height DPDA $A''' = \langle Q''', \Sigma, \Gamma, H''', [q_0, 0], F''', h \rangle$ is easily seen to behave as A'' except that, instead of entering an ε-loop, it directly reaches the rejecting states r. At this point, transitions $\{(r, \gamma, r) : \gamma \in \Sigma\}$, already present from previous removal operations, make A''' sweep the whole input. Thus, ε-loop rejection is now replaced with type (i) rejection.

For the sake of completeness, we can also remove from A''' all the ε-transitions as follows. After ε-loop elimination, A''' may only perform finite sequences of ε-transitions of the form $\Psi = (p_0, \varepsilon, p_1), (p_1, \varepsilon, p_2), \ldots, (p_{n-1}, \varepsilon, p_n)$ with $p_i \in Q'''_\varepsilon$ for $0 \le i \le n-1$ and $p_n \in Q'''_\Sigma \cup Q'''_\varepsilon$. Even these sequences may be easily detected by inspecting paths in the digraph built on Q'''_ε and H'''', as explained above. Again, let $\Psi_i = \{(q, \alpha, p_i) \in H'''\}$. We can remove the ε-path Ψ by simply deleting from H''' all the involved transitions, and from Q''' all the involved states except p_0. Next, we replace in H''' each set Ψ_i with the new set of transitions $\tilde{\Psi}_i = \{(q, \alpha, p_0) : (q, \alpha, p_i) \in \Psi_i\}$ and add the new transitions $\{(p_0, \alpha, q) : (p_n, \alpha, q) \in H'''\}$. In conclusion, the resulting constant height DPDA $A'''' = \langle Q'''', \Sigma, \Gamma, H'''', [q_0, 0], F'''', h \rangle$ is completely ε-transition free. Clearly, we get that $\text{size}(A'''')$ is bounded from above by $\text{size}(A'') = (|Q| \cdot (h+1)+1, |\Gamma|, h)$.

As a final observation, we notice that ε-transition removal clearly turns *mixed-loops* of A'''' into genuine pushdown-loops, whose removal will be approached in the next section.

3.4 Removal of Rejection Policy (iv): Pushdown-Loop

Let us finally operate on A'''' to delete rejection by pushdown-loop. A pushdown-loop may be formally defined by introducing the notion of internal configuration. We say that, at any given instant, A'''' is in the internal configuration (p, γ), with $p \in Q''''$ and $\gamma \in \Gamma^*$, if and only if it is in the state p and the pushdown content is γ. A pushdown-loop is a nonempty sequence of push and pop operations only, starting from and ending in the same internal configuration. An *upward pushdown-loop* is a pushdown-loop starting from and ending into an internal configuration (p, γ), along which the pushdown height never goes below $|\gamma|$. The following lemma states that, once in a pushdown-loop, A'''' will eventually enter an upward pushdown-loop.

Lemma 2. *Along any pushdown-loop, an internal configuration is eventually reached which an upward pushdown-loop starts from.*

Proof. Let c be the internal configuration with the lowest pushdown height along a pushdown-loop. It is not hard to see that the pushdown-loop starting from and ending into c is the desired upward pushdown-loop.   □

As an easy consequence of Lemma 2, *we can get rid of pushdown-loops in A'''' by eliminating upward pushdown-loops.* Moreover, one may easily observe that, along an upward pushdown-loop starting from pushdown height d, the deepest d symbols in the pushdown never come into play. Hence, to decide whether a given internal configuration will give rise to an upward pushdown-loop it suffices to focus on *the finite control state only*, regardless of the pushdown content.

The following procedure enables us to single out those states $U \subseteq Q''''$ which upward pushdown-loops start from. Given the state $[p, k] \in Q''''$, we must decide whether or not $[p, k] \in U$. First of all, it is easy to see that $[p, k]$ cannot belong to $Q'''_\Sigma \cup Q'''_{-\Gamma}$. Hence, it must be that $[p, k] \in Q'''_{+X}$ for some $X \in \Gamma$, and clearly we must have $0 \leq k < h$. Next, we initialize A'''' in the internal configuration $([p, k], \alpha)$ for some $\alpha \in \Gamma^k$, and run a nonempty sequence Π of at most $|Q| \cdot (h-k)$ push and pop moves only, starting by pushing X. If, along Π, the state $[p, k]$ will be reached again without passing through states $[q, t]$ with $t < k$ (thus meaning that an upward pushdown-loop took place from $[p, k]$), then $[p, k] \in U$.

Once determined $U \subseteq Q'''_{+\Gamma} \subseteq Q''''$, it is easy to build from A''' a constant height DPDA $A^v = \langle Q'''', \Sigma, \Gamma, H^v, [q_0, 0], F'''', h \rangle$ in which rejection by pushdown-loop is replaced by type (i) rejection. Basically, A^v coincides with A'''' except that, for any $[p, k] \in U$ with $[p, k] \in Q''''_{+X}$ and $0 \leq k < h$, the corresponding push move in H'''' is replaced by the new push transition $([p, k], +X, r)$. The resulting transition relation H^v makes A^v behave exactly as A'''' except when a state $[p, k] \in U$ is reached. In fact, the new transition $([p, k], +X, r) \in H^v$ now leads A^v into the rejecting state r, and the transitions $\{(r, \gamma, r) : \gamma \in \Sigma\}$, already present from previous removal operations, make A^v sweep the whole input. We get that the size of A^v coincides with that of A'''' which, in turn, is bounded from above by $(|Q| \cdot (h + 1) + 1, |\Gamma|, h)$.

3.5   The Cost of Complementing

In conclusion, the removal constructions so far explained enable us to state

Proposition 3. *Given a constant height DPDA $A = \langle Q, \Sigma, \Gamma, H, q_0, F, h \rangle$, there exists a constant height DPDA $A' = \langle Q', \Sigma, \Gamma, H', q'_0, F', h \rangle$ with $L(A') = L(A)$, such that: (i) H' always defines a valid move, (ii) computations never get into* *loops or violate pushdown boundaries, (iii) on any input string belonging to $L(A')$ (resp., $L(A')^c$), the computation ends in an accepting (resp., rejecting) state after reading the entire input, (iv) $|Q'| \leq |Q| \cdot (h + 1) + 1$.*

It is clear that Proposition 3 directly determines the size-cost of complementing constant height DPDAs:

Theorem 4. *Given a constant height DPDA $A = \langle Q, \Sigma, \Gamma, H, q_0, F, h \rangle$, there exists a constant height DPDA B accepting $L(A)^c$, such that $\mathrm{size}(B)$ is bounded from above by $(|Q| \cdot (h + 1) + 1, |\Gamma|, h)$.*

Proof. Start from A, and consider the equivalent constant height dpda A' in Proposition 3. The constant height DPDA B is identical to A' except that F' is replaced by $Q' \setminus F'$. □

4   Union and Intersection of Constant Height DPDAs

Let us now deal with the other two boolean operations, and tackle the following problem: given constant height DPDAs $A = \langle Q_A, \Sigma, \Gamma_A, H_A, q_A, F_A, h_A \rangle$ and $B = \langle Q_B, \Sigma, \Gamma_B, H_B, q_B, F_B, h_B \rangle$, determine the size – as a function of $\mathrm{size}(A)$ and $\mathrm{size}(B)$ – of constant height DPDAs accepting $L(A) \cup L(B)$ and $L(A) \cap L(B)$.

Clearly, also in this case one may transform A and B into equivalent DFAs, and operate as usual in order to obtain DFAs with at most $|Q_A| \cdot |\Gamma_A^{\leq h_A}| \cdot |Q_B| \cdot |\Gamma_B^{\leq h_B}|$ states performing the desired tasks. However, by actually exploiting the power of pushdown storage, we are going to provide a slightly improved construction.

Theorem 5. *Given constant height DPDAs $A = \langle Q_A, \Sigma, \Gamma_A, H_A, q_A, F_A, h_A \rangle$ and $B = \langle Q_B, \Sigma, \Gamma_B, H_B, q_B, F_B, h_B \rangle$, there exist constant height DPDAs C and D satisfying $L(C) = L(A) \cup L(B)$ and $L(D) = L(A) \cap L(B)$, respectively. Moreover, $\mathrm{size}(C)$ and $\mathrm{size}(D)$ are both bounded by $(|Q_A| \cdot |\Gamma_A^{\leq h_A}| \cdot (|Q_B| + 1), |\Gamma_B|, h_B)$.*

Proof. (sketch) The key idea is first to turn one of the two initial DPDAs, say A, into an equivalent DFA $\hat{A}$. Then, we build C and D with suitably fixed accepting states, which run in parallel $\hat{A}$ and B. □

The rest of this section is devoted to proving that the exponential cost highlighted in Theorem 5 is unavoidable. To this end, we exhibit two languages accepted by constant height DPDAs and show there cannot exist constant height DPDAs for their union and intersection having size lower than the limit established in Theorem 5. Let us first introduce some notations. For a string $x = x_1 \cdots x_n$, let $x^R = x_n \cdots x_1$ denote its reversal. We set the alphabet $\Sigma = \Gamma \cup \{\$\}$, for $\Gamma = \{0, 1\}$ and a special symbol $\$$. On Σ, we define two languages specified by two integers $h_1, h_2 > 0$:

$$L_{1,h_1} = \{u_1 \$ u_2 \$ v_1^R \$ v_2^R \$: u_1, u_2, v_1, v_2 \in \Gamma^*, u_1 = v_1 \text{ and } |u_1| = |v_1| \leq h_1\},$$
$$L_{2,h_2} = \{u_1 \$ u_2 \$ v_1^R \$ v_2^R \$: u_1, u_2, v_1, v_2 \in \Gamma^*, u_2 \neq v_2 \text{ and } |u_2| \leq h_2\}.$$

Lemma 6. *For any $h_1, h_2 > 0$, the languages L_{1,h_1} and L_{2,h_2} are accepted by* DPDA*s M_1 and M_2, respectively, with a constant number of states and pushdown height h_1 and h_2, respectively.*

We are now ready to examine constant height DPDAs accepting $L_{1,h_1} \cup L_{2,h_2}$. Let $h = \max\{h_1, h_2\}$, and denote the union of L_{1,h_1} and L_{2,h_2} as

$$L_h = L_{1,h_1} \cup L_{2,h_2} = \{ \, u_1 \$ u_2 \$ v_1^R \$ v_2^R : u_1, u_2, v_1, v_2 \in \Gamma^*,$$
$$u_1 = v_1 \text{ and } |u_1| = |v_1| \leq h_1, \text{ or } u_2 \neq v_2 \text{ and } |v_2| \leq h_2 \, \}.$$

The following theorem proves that the size of any constant height DPDA for the language L_h cannot be bounded by a polynomial in h, thus yielding the asymptotical optimality of the construction for the union in Theorem 5.

Theorem 7. *For any $h > 1$, any constant height* DPDA *accepting L_h cannot use a number of states and a pushdown height which are polynomial in h.*

Proof. Assume, by contradiction, the existence of a constant height DPDA $A = \langle Q, \Sigma, \Gamma, H, q_0, h' \rangle$ accepting L_h, with $|Q| < p(h)$ and $h' < p(h)$, for some polynomial $p(h) > h$. From now on, for the sake of readability, we simply write p instead of $p(h)$. We also assume, without loss of generality, a binary pushdown alphabet. Moreover, only to simplify mathematics, we choose $h = h_2 = 3h_1$. First, we define the set $V_0 = \{[u_1, u_2] : u_1, u_2 \in \Gamma^* \text{ and } |u_2| = 3|u_1| = h\}$. Since $h_2 = 3h_1$, we get $|V_0| = 2^{h_1} \cdot 2^{h_2} = 2^{\frac{4}{3}h_2}$. Let us consider the computation of A on an input $u_1 \$ u_2 \$ v_1^R \$ v_2^R \$$, where $[u_1, u_2] \in V_0$, and set the following parameters to be taken in the course of reading u_2 along the input: (i) ℓ_y the lowest height of pushdown store, (ii) q_ℓ the state in which the height ℓ_y is attained for the last time, (iii) ℓ_x the distance from the beginning of u_2 to the input position in which q_ℓ is entered. In addition, upon reading the second occurrence of the symbol $\$$ in the input word (i.e., at the end of the string u_2), we let: (iv) q_e be the state of A, and (v) $\bar{u}_1 \cdot \bar{u}_2$ be the pushdown content, where $\bar{u}_1$ denotes the initial (from the bottom) portion, of height ℓ_y, while $\bar{u}_2$ is the remaining part. For better understanding, see Fig. 1.

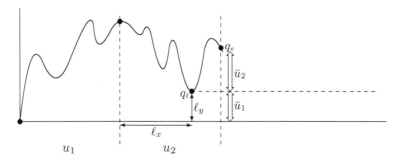

Fig. 1. Parameters and pushdown content along the first part of the computation

Note that $0 \leq \ell_x \leq h < p$ and $0 \leq \ell_y \leq h' < p$. So, the number of different triples $[q_e, l_x, l_y] \in Q \times \{0, \ldots, h\} \times \{0, \ldots, h'\}$ is bounded by p^3. Indeed, since A is deterministic, each pair $[u_1, u_2] \in V_0$ is associated with exactly one of these triples. Hence, a simple pigeonhole argument proves the existence of a set $V_1 \subseteq V_0$, with $|V_1| \geq \frac{|V_0|}{p^3} \geq \frac{2^{\frac{4}{3}h_2}}{p^3}$, such that all string pairs $[u_1, u_2] \in V_1$ share the same triple $[q_e, l_x, l_y]$. Let us now build the following sets from V_1:

$V_{1,1} = \{u_1 : \exists u_2, \text{ such that } [u_1, u_2] \in V_1\}$,
$V_{1,2} = \{u_2 : \exists u_1, \text{ such that } [u_1, u_2] \in V_1\}$.

Clearly, $|V_{1,1}| \leq 2^{h_1} = 2^{\frac{1}{3}h_2}$ and $|V_{1,2}| \leq 2^{h_2}$. Yet, we have $V_1 \subseteq V_{1,1} \times V_{1,2}$, and then $|V_1| \leq |V_{1,1}| \cdot |V_{1,2}|$. So, we get $V_{1,2} \neq \emptyset$, since $|V_{1,2}| \geq \frac{|V_1|}{|V_{1,1}|} \geq \frac{2^{h_2}}{p^3}$. Therefore, $V_{1,2}$ can be split into the following two disjoint sets:

$V_2 = \{u_2 : \text{there exist more than one } u_1 \in V_{1,1} \text{ such that } [u_1, u_2] \in V_1\}$,
$V_2^c = \{u_2 : \text{there exists exactly one } u_1 \in V_{1,1} \text{ such that } [u_1, u_2] \in V_1\}$.

Let $x = |V_2|$. To evaluate x, observe that $|V_2^c| = |V_{1,2}| - x \leq 2^{h_2} - x$. If $u_2 \in V_2^c$, then it is impossible to have $[u'_1, u_2] \in V_1$ and $[u''_1, u_2] \in V_1$ for two different strings $u'_1, u''_1 \in V_{1,1}$, while the opposite holds for $u_2 \in V_2$. In this latter case, the number of pairs in V_1 sharing the same u_2 is clearly bounded by $|V_{1,1}| \leq 2^{\frac{1}{3}h_2}$. So, we get $|V_1| \leq |V_2^c| + |V_2| \cdot |V_{1,1}| \leq (2^{h_2} - x) + x \cdot 2^{\frac{1}{3}h_2} = x \cdot (2^{\frac{1}{3}h_2} - 1) + 2^{h_2}$, whence

$$|V_2| = x \geq \frac{|V_1| - 2^{h_2}}{2^{\frac{1}{3}h_2} - 1} \geq \frac{\frac{2^{\frac{4}{3}h_2}}{p^3} - 2^{h_2}}{2^{\frac{1}{3}h_2}} = \frac{2^{h_2}}{p^3} - 2^{\frac{2}{3}h_2}. \tag{1}$$

Let us fix some lexicographical order on the set $V_{1,1}$ and, for each $u_2 \in V_2$, take the first two $u'_1 \neq u''_1$ in this ordering satisfying $[u'_1, u_2] \in V_1$ and $[u''_1, u_2] \in V_1$. The number of such $u'_1 \neq u''_1$ is clearly bounded by $|V_{1,1} \times V_{1,1}| \leq 2^{2h_1} = 2^{\frac{2}{3}h_2}$. This, together with (1) and a pigeonhole argument, yields the existence of a nonempty set $V_3 \subseteq V_2$, with cardinality

$$|V_3| \geq \frac{|V_2|}{|V_{1,1} \times V_{1,1}|} \geq \frac{\frac{2^{h_2}}{p^3} - 2^{\frac{2}{3}h_2}}{2^{\frac{2}{3}h_2}} = \frac{2^{\frac{1}{3}h_2}}{p^3} - 1, \tag{2}$$

such that all strings $u_2 \in V_3$ share the same pair $u'_1 \neq u''_1$ in $V_{1,1}$, with $[u'_1, u_2] \in V_1$ and $[u''_1, u_2] \in V_1$. By definition of V_1, we have that $[u'_1, u_2]$ and $[u''_1, u_2]$ share the common triple $[q_e, l_x, l_y]$, and hence $u'_1 \$ u_2 \$$ and $u''_1 \$ u_2 \$$ produce the same upper part $\bar{u}_2$ in the pushdown store.

Now, consider input strings of the form $z' = u'_1 \$ u_2 \$ u''_1{}^R \$ u_2^R \$$, enumerating all strings $u_2 \in V_3$, but using the fixed pair $u'_1 \neq u''_1$, taken according to the previous reasoning. Clearly, $z' \notin L_h$ since $u'_1 \neq (u''_1{}^R)^R$ and $u_2 = (u_2{}^R)^R$. Let us take a closer look at the computation of A right after consuming the first part of the input, namely, $u'_1 \$ u_2 \$$. At this point, A is in some state q_e (depending on u_2) and the pushdown content consists of the word $\bar{u}'_1$ (the same for all strings u_2) under the word $\bar{u}_2$ (depending on u_2), with $|\bar{u}'_1| = \ell_y$. Moreover, at the end of the computation on the whole input, A must reach some state $q \notin F$, since $z' \notin L_h$.

There are two possibilities for Π_{u_2}, the segment of the computation of A starting in the state q_e, in the course of reading $u''_1{}^R$, on input $z' = u'_1 \$ u_2 \$ u''_1{}^R \$ u_2^R \$$:

CASE I: *There exists some $u_2 \in V_3$ such that Π_{u_2} does not visit* the lower content of the pushdown store consisting of ℓ_y symbols, in the course of reading $u_1''^R$. This situation is depicted in Fig. 2.

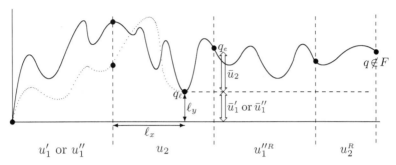

Fig. 2. The computation not visiting lower ℓ_y pushdown symbols

So, take the input string $z'' = u_1''\$u_2\$u_1''^R\$u_2^R\$$ (obtained from z' by replacing u_1' by u_1'') belonging to L_h since $u_1'' = (u_1''^R)^R$. However, $u_2 \in V_3$ and the pairs $[u_1', u_2]$ and $[u_1'', u_2]$ share the same triple $[q_\ell, l_x, l_y]$. By determinism of A and since we do not visit the lower ℓ_y pushdown symbols after the position ℓ_x in u_2, A does not distinguish between having $\bar{u}_1''$ instead of $\bar{u}_1'$ at the bottom of the pushdown store. Hence, the computation starting from the same state q_e and seeing the same right part of u_2 must lead to the same state q_e and push the same string $\bar{u}_2$ onto the pushdown store.

But then, since the computation segment Π_{u_2} does not visit the lower ℓ_y symbols in pushdown store even in the course of reading $u_1''^R$, the computation starting from q_e on z'', seeing the same symbols along the input, must lead to the same state $q \notin F$, thus rejecting z''. This gives a contradiction.

CASE II: *For each string $u_2 \in V_3$, the segment Π_{u_2} visits* the lower content of the pushdown store consisting of ℓ_y symbols in the course of reading $u_1''^R$. This situation is depicted in Fig. 3.

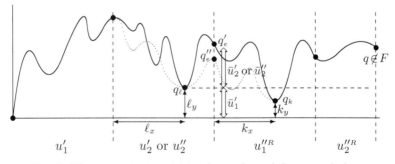

Fig. 3. The computation visiting lower ℓ_y pushdown symbols

Hence, for each $u_2 \in V_3$, A pops some symbols of the word $\bar{u}'_1$ from the pushdown store. With respect to Π_{u_2}, define: (i) k_y the lowest height of pushdown store, (ii) q_k the state in which the height k_y is attained for the last time, (iii) k_x the distance from the beginning of u''^R_1 to the input position in which q_k is entered. Notice that $0 \leq k_x \leq h_1 \leq h_2 \leq p$ and $0 \leq k_y \leq h_2 < p$. So, the number of different triples $[q_k, k_x, k_y]$ is bounded by p^3. This, together with (2) and a pigeonhole argument, shows the existence of a set $V_4 \subseteq V_3$, with

$$|V_4| \geq \frac{|V_3|}{p^3} \geq \frac{\frac{2^{\frac{1}{3}h_2}}{p^3} - 1}{p^3} = \frac{2^{\frac{1}{3}h_2}}{p^6} - \frac{1}{p^3} \geq 2, \qquad (3)$$

such that all $u_2 \in V_4$ share the same triple $[q_k, k_x, k_y]$. So, fix some $u'_2 \neq u''_2$ in V_4, and consider the input strings $v' = u'_1 \$ u'_2 \$ u''^R_1 \$ u''^R_2 \$ \in L_h$ and $v'' = u'_1 \$ u''_2 \$ u''^R_1 \$ u''^R_2 \$ \notin L_h$. On both v' and v'', A reaches the same state q_k at the same position k_x. Moreover, the reader may easily verify that, at this time, all the information previously stored in the upper part of the pushdown (i.e., $\bar{u}'_2$ or $\bar{u}''_2$, respectively) has been popped, since we have reached the pushdown height $k_y < \ell_y$. Intuitively, this prevents A from distinguishing between v' and v''. More formally, the remaining parts are the same on both inputs, the machine starts in the same state and, moreover, the remaining symbols stored in the pushdown will never be examined any more. (Recall that q_k is the state in which the height k_y is attained for the last time. Therefore, from this point forward, the stack height will always be above k_y.) Thus, the computation of A from q_k on both inputs leads to the same outcome (accept or reject), which is a contradiction.

In conclusion, A must have either a number of states which is exponential in h, or its pushdown height is exponential. $\qquad \square$

We end this section by also showing the asymptotical optimality of the construction for the intersection in Theorem 5. Let us take the languages L^c_{1,h_1} and L^c_{2,h_2}. The constructions in Section 3 show that L^c_{1,h_1} (resp., L^c_{2,h_2}) can be accepted by a DPDA with $O(h_1)$ (resp., $O(h_2)$) states and pushdown height h_1 (resp., h_2) obtained by complementing the constant height DPDA M_1 (resp., M_2) in Lemma 6. Again, we let $h = \max\{h_1, h_2\}$, and define the language $\tilde{L}_h = L^c_{1,h_1} \cap L^c_{2,h_2}$. Then:

Theorem 8. *For any $h > 1$, any constant height DPDA accepting $\tilde{L}_h$ cannot use a number of states and a pushdown height which are polynomial in h.*

Proof. Assume, by contradiction, that $\tilde{L}_h$ is accepted by a constant height DPDA A whose number of states and pushdown height are both bounded by a polynomial in h. By De Morgan's law, we have $L_h = \tilde{L}^c_h$. So, by complementing A, we would obtain a constant height DPDA A' for L_h. Moreover, by Theorem 4, we would get that the number of states of A', as well as its pushdown height, is bounded by a polynomial in h. This, clearly, contradicts Theorem 7. $\qquad \square$

Acknowledgements

The authors wish to thank the anonymous referees for useful and kind comments.

References

1. Ehrenfeucht, A., Zieger, P.: Complexity measures for regular expressions. J. Computer and System Sciences 12, 134–146 (1976)
2. Geffert, V., Mereghetti, C., Palano, B.: More concise representation of regular languages by automata and regular expressions. Inf. and Comp. 208, 385–394 (2010)
3. Gruber, H., Holzer, M.: Language operations with regular expressions of polynomial size. Theor. Comput. Sci. 410, 3281–3289 (2009)
4. Holzer, M., Kutrib, M.: Nondeterministic descriptional complexity of regular languages. Int. J. Found. Comput. Sci. 14, 1087–1102 (2003)
5. Hopcroft, J.E., Motwani, R., Ullman, J.D.: Introduction to Automata Theory, Languages, and Computation. Addison-Wesley, Reading (2001)
6. Kutrib, M., Malcher, A., Wotschke, D.: The Boolean closure of linear context-free languages. Acta Inf. 45, 177–191 (2008)
7. Meyer, A.R., Fischer, M.J.: Economy of description by automata, grammars, and formal systems. In: IEEE 12th Symp. Switching and Automata Theory, pp. 188–191 (1971)
8. Yu, S., Zhuang, Q., Salomaa, K.: The state complexities of some basic operations on regular languages. Theoret. Comp. Sci. 125, 315–328 (1994)

Syntactic Complexity of Prefix-, Suffix-, and Bifix-Free Regular Languages*

Janusz Brzozowski[1], Baiyu Li[1], and Yuli Ye[2]

[1] David R. Cheriton School of Computer Science, University of Waterloo
Waterloo, ON, Canada N2L 3G1
{brzozo,b5li}@uwaterloo.ca
[2] Department of Computer Science, University of Toronto
Toronto, ON, Canada M5S 3G4
y3ye@cs.toronto.edu

Abstract. The syntactic complexity of a regular language is the cardinality of its syntactic semigroup. The syntactic complexity of a subclass of the class of regular languages is the maximal syntactic complexity of languages in that class, taken as a function of the state complexity n of these languages. We study the syntactic complexity of prefix-, suffix-, and bifix-free regular languages. We prove that n^{n-2} is a tight upper bound for prefix-free regular languages. We present properties of the syntactic semigroups of suffix- and bifix-free regular languages, and conjecture tight upper bounds on their size.

Keywords: bifix-free, finite automaton, monoid, prefix-free, regular language, semigroup, suffix-free, syntactic complexity.

1 Introduction

A language is *prefix-free* (respectively, *suffix-free*) if it does not contain any pair of words such that one is a proper prefix (respectively, suffix) of the other. It is *bifix-free* if it is both prefix- and suffix-free. We refer to prefix-, suffix-, and bifix-free languages as *free* languages. Nontrivial prefix-, suffix-, and bifix-free languages are also known as prefix, suffix, and bifix codes, respectively [1] and, as such, have many applications in areas such as cryptography, data compression, and information processing.

The *state complexity* of a regular language is the number of states in the minimal deterministic finite automaton (DFA) recognizing that language. An equivalent notion is that of *quotient complexity,* which is the number of left quotients of the language. State complexity of regular operations has been studied quite extensively: for surveys of this topic and lists of references we refer the reader to [2,19]. With regard to free regular languages, Han, Salomaa and Wood [8]

* This work was supported by the Natural Sciences and Engineering Research Council of Canada under grant No. OGP0000871 and a Postgraduate Scholarship, and by a Graduate Award from the Department of Computer Science, University of Toronto.

M. Holzer, M. Kutrib, and G. Pighizzini (Eds.): DCFS 2011, LNCS 6808, pp. 93–106, 2011.

examined prefix-free regular languages, and Han and Salomaa [7] studied suffix-free regular languages. Bifix-, factor-, and subword-free regular languages were studied by Brzozowski, Jirásková, Li, and Smith [3].

The notion of quotient complexity can be derived from the Nerode congruence [14], while the Myhill congruence [13] leads to the syntactic semigroup of a language and to its *syntactic complexity*, which is the cardinality of the syntactic semigroup. It was pointed out in [4] that syntactic complexity can be very different for regular languages with the same quotient complexity. Thus, for a fixed n, languages with quotient complexity n may possibly be distinguished by their syntactic complexities.

In contrast to state complexity, syntactic complexity has not received much attention. In 1970 Maslov [12] dealt with the problem of generators of the semigroup of all transformations in the setting of finite automata. In 2003–2004, Holzer and König [9], and independently, Krawetz, Lawrence and Shallit [11] studied the syntactic complexity of automata with unary and binary alphabets. In 2010 Brzozowski and Ye [4] examined the syntactic complexity of ideal and closed regular languages. Here, we deal with the syntactic complexity of prefix-, suffix-, and bifix-free regular languages, and their complements.

Basic definitions and facts are stated in Sections 2 and 3. In Section 4 we obtain a tight upper bound for the syntactic complexity of prefix-free regular languages. In Sections 5 and 6 we study the syntactic complexity of suffix- and bifix-free regular languages, respectively, and we state conjectures about tight upper bounds for these classes. Section 7 concludes the paper.

2   Transformations

A *transformation* of a set Q is a mapping of Q into itself. In this paper we consider only transformations of finite sets, and we assume without loss of generality that $Q = \{1, 2, \ldots, n\}$. Let t be a transformation of Q. If $i \in Q$, then it is the image of i under t. If X is a subset of Q, then $Xt = \{it \mid i \in X\}$, and the *restriction* of t to X, denoted by $t|_X$, is a mapping from X to Xt such that $it|_X = it$ for all $i \in X$. The *composition* of two transformations t_1 and t_2 of Q is a transformation $t_1 \circ t_2$ such that $i(t_1 \circ t_2) = (it_1)t_2$ for all $i \in Q$. We usually drop the composition operator "$\circ$" and write $t_1 t_2$ for short. An arbitrary transformation can be written in the form

$$t = \begin{pmatrix} 1 & 2 & \cdots & n-1 & n \\ i_1 & i_2 & \cdots & i_{n-1} & i_n \end{pmatrix},$$

where $i_k = kt$, $1 \leqslant k \leqslant n$, and $i_k \in Q$. The *domain* dom t of t is Q. The *image* img t of t is the set img $t = Qt$. We also use the notation $t = [i_1, i_2, \ldots, i_n]$ for the transformation t above. A transformation t of Q is *injective* on a subset X of Q if, for all $i, j \in X$, $i \neq j$, we have $it \neq jt$.

A *permutation* of Q is a mapping of Q *onto* itself. In other words, a permutation π of Q is a transformation where img $\pi = Q$.

The *identity* transformation maps each element to itself, that is, $it = i$ for $i = 1, \ldots, n$. A transformation t contains a *cycle* of length k if there exist pairwise different elements $i_1, \ldots, i_k$ such that $i_1 t = i_2, i_2 t = i_3, \ldots, i_{k-1} t = i_k$, and $i_k t = i_1$. A cycle will be denoted by $(i_1, i_2, \ldots, i_k)$. For $i < j$, a *transposition* is the cycle (i, j), and (i, i) is the identity. A *singular* transformation, denoted by $\binom{i}{j}$, has $it = j$ and $ht = h$ for all $h \neq i$, and $\binom{i}{i}$ is the identity. A *constant* transformation, denoted by $\binom{Q}{j}$, has $it = j$ for all i.

The set of all transformations of a set Q, denoted by $\mathcal{T}_Q$, is a finite monoid. The set of all permutations of Q is a group, denoted by $\mathfrak{S}_Q$ and called the *symmetric group* of degree n. It was shown in [10] and [16] that two generators are sufficient to generate the symmetric group of degree n. In 1935 Piccard [15] proved that three transformations of Q are sufficient to generate the monoid $\mathcal{T}_Q$. In the same year, Eilenberg showed that fewer than three generators are not possible, as reported by Sierpiński [18]. We refer the reader to the book of Ganyushkin and Mazorchuk [5] for a detailed discussion of finite transformation semigroups. Let $Q = \{1, \ldots, n\}$. The following are well-known facts about generators of $\mathfrak{S}_Q$ and $\mathcal{T}_Q$:

Theorem 1 (Permutations, [10,16]). *The symmetric group $\mathfrak{S}_Q$ of size $n!$ can be generated by any cyclic permutation of n elements with any transposition. In particular, $\mathfrak{S}_Q$ can be generated by $c = (1, 2, \ldots, n)$ and $t = (1, 2)$.*

Theorem 2 (Transformations, [15]). *The complete transformation monoid $\mathcal{T}_Q$ of size n^n can be generated by any cyclic permutation of n elements together with a transposition and a "returning" transformation $r = \binom{n}{1}$. In particular, $\mathcal{T}_Q$ can be generated by $c = (1, 2, \ldots, n)$, $t = (1, 2)$ and $r = \binom{n}{1}$.*

3 Quotient Complexity and Syntactic Complexity

If Σ is a non-empty finite alphabet, then Σ^* is the free monoid generated by Σ, and Σ^+ is the free semigroup generated by Σ. A *word* is any element of Σ^*, and the empty word is ε. The length of a word $w \in \Sigma^*$ is $|w|$. A *language* over Σ is any subset of Σ^*. If $w = uv$ for some $u, v \in \Sigma^*$, then u is a *prefix* of w, and v is a *suffix* of w. A *proper* prefix (suffix) of w is a prefix (suffix) of w other than w.

The *left quotient*, or simply *quotient*, of a language L by a word w is the language $L_w = \{x \in \Sigma^* \mid wx \in L\}$. For any $L \subseteq \Sigma^*$, the *Nerode congruence* [14] $\sim_L$ of L is defined as follows:

$$x \sim_L y \text{ if and only if } xv \in L \Leftrightarrow yv \in L, \text{ for all } v \in \Sigma^*.$$

Clearly, $L_x = L_y$ if and only if $x \sim_L y$. Thus each equivalence class of this congruence corresponds to a distinct quotient of L.

The *Myhill congruence* [13] $\approx_L$ of L is defined as follows:

$$x \approx_L y \text{ if and only if } uxv \in L \Leftrightarrow uyv \in L \text{ for all } u, v \in \Sigma^*.$$

This congruence is also known as the *syntactic congruence* of L. The quotient set $\Sigma^+ / \approx_L$ of equivalence classes of the relation $\approx_L$, is a semigroup called the *syntactic semigroup* of L, and $\Sigma^*/\approx_L$ is the *syntactic monoid* of L. The *syntactic complexity* $\sigma(L)$ of L is the cardinality of its syntactic semigroup. The *monoid complexity* $\mu(L)$ of L is the cardinality of its syntactic monoid. If the equivalence class containing ε is a singleton in the syntactic monoid, then $\sigma(L) = \mu(L) - 1$; otherwise, $\sigma(L) = \mu(L)$.

A *deterministic finite automaton* (DFA) is a quintuple $\mathcal{A} = (Q, \Sigma, \delta, q_1, F)$, where Q is a finite, non-empty set of *states*, Σ is a finite non-empty *alphabet*, $\delta: Q \times \Sigma \to Q$ is the *transition function*, $q_1 \in Q$ is the *initial state*, and $F \subseteq Q$ is the set of *final states*. We extend δ to $Q \times \Sigma^*$ in the usual way. The DFA $\mathcal{A}$ accepts a word $w \in \Sigma^*$ if $\delta(q_1, w) \in F$. The set of all words *accepted* by $\mathcal{A}$ is $L(\mathcal{A})$. By the *language of a state* q of $\mathcal{A}$ we mean the language L_q accepted by the automaton $(Q, \Sigma, \delta, q, F)$. A state is *empty* if its language is empty.

Let L be a regular language. The *quotient automaton* or *quotient DFA* of L is $\mathcal{A} = (Q, \Sigma, \delta, q_1, F)$, where $Q = \{L_w \mid w \in \Sigma^*\}$, $\delta(L_w, a) = L_{wa}$, $q_1 = L_\varepsilon = L$, $F = \{L_w \mid \varepsilon \in L_w\}$. To simplify notation we write ε for the language $\{\varepsilon\}$. The number $\kappa(L)$ of distinct quotients of L is the *quotient complexity* of L. The quotient DFA of L is the minimal DFA accepting L, and so quotient complexity is the same as state complexity, but there are advantages to using quotients [2].

In terms of automata, each equivalence class $[w]_{\sim_L}$ of $\sim_L$ is the set of all words w that take the automaton to the same state from the initial state. In terms of quotients, it is the set of words w that can be followed by the same quotient L_w. In terms of automata, each equivalence class $[w]_{\approx_L}$ of $\approx_L$ is the set of all words that perform the same transformation on the set of states.

Let $\mathcal{A} = (Q, \Sigma, \delta, q_1, F)$ be a DFA. For each word $w \in \Sigma^*$, the transition function for w defines a transformation t_w of Q by the word w: for all $i \in Q$, $it_w \stackrel{\text{def}}{=} \delta(i, w)$. The set $T_{\mathcal{A}}$ of all such transformations by non-empty words forms a subsemigroup of $\mathcal{T}_Q$, called the *transition semigroup* of $\mathcal{A}$ [17] (p. 690). Conversely, we can use a set $\{t_a \mid a \in \Sigma\}$ of transformations to define δ, and so the DFA $\mathcal{A}$. When the context is clear we simply write $a = t$, where t is a transformation of Q, to mean that the transformation performed by $a \in \Sigma$ is t.

Let $\mathcal{A}$ be the quotient automaton of L. Then $T_{\mathcal{A}}$ is isomorphic to the syntactic semigroup T_L of L, and we represent elements of T_L by transformations in $T_{\mathcal{A}}$.

We attempt to obtain tight upper bounds on the syntactic complexity $\sigma(L) = |T_L|$ of L as a function of the state complexity $\kappa(L)$ of L. First we consider the syntactic complexity of regular languages over a unary alphabet, where the concepts, prefix-, suffix-, and bifix-free, coincide. So we may consider only unary prefix-free regular languages L with quotient complexity $\kappa(L) = n$. When $n = 1$, the only prefix-free regular language is $L = \emptyset$ with $\sigma(L) = 1$. For $n \geqslant 2$, a prefix-free regular language L must be a singleton, $L = \{a^{n-2}\}$. The syntactic semigroup T_L of L consists of $n - 1$ transformations t_w by words $w = a^i$, where $1 \leqslant i \leqslant n - 1$. Thus we have

Proposition 3 (Unary Free Regular Languages). *If L is a unary prefix-free (suffix-free, bifix-free) regular language with $\kappa(L) = n \geqslant 2$, then $\sigma(L) = n - 1$.*

The tight upper bound for regular unary languages [9] is n.

We assume that $|\Sigma| \geqslant 2$ in the following sections. Since the syntactic semigroup of a language is the same as that of its complement, we deal only with prefix-free, suffix-free, and bifix-free languages. All the syntactic complexity results, however, apply also to the complements of these languages.

4   Prefix-Free Regular Languages

Recall that a regular language L is prefix-free if and only it has exactly one accepting quotient, and that quotient is ε [8].

Theorem 4 (Prefix-Free Regular Languages). *If L is regular and prefix-free with $\kappa(L) = n \geqslant 2$, then $\sigma(L) \leqslant n^{n-2}$. Moreover, this bound is tight for $n = 2$ if $|\Sigma| \geqslant 1$, for $n = 3$ if $|\Sigma| \geqslant 2$, for $n = 4$ if $|\Sigma| \geqslant 4$, and for $n \geqslant 5$ if $|\Sigma| \geqslant n + 1$.*

Proof. If L is prefix-free, the only accepting quotient of L is ε. Thus L also has the empty quotient, since $\varepsilon_a = \emptyset$ for $a \in \Sigma$. Let $\mathcal{A} = (Q, \Sigma, \delta, 1, n-1)$ be the quotient DFA of L, where $Q = \{1, 2, \ldots, n\}$ and, without loss of generality, $n - 1 \in Q$ is the only accepting state, and $n \in Q$ is the empty state. For any transformation $t \in T_L$, $(n-1)t = nt = n$. Thus we have $\sigma(L) \leqslant n^{n-2}$.

The only prefix-free regular language for $n = 1$ is $L = \emptyset$ with $\sigma(L) = 1$; here the bound n^{n-2} does not apply. For $n = 2$ and $\Sigma = \{a\}$, the language $L = \varepsilon$ meets the bound. For $n = 3$ and $\Sigma = \{a, b\}$, $L = b^*a$ meets the bound. For $n \geqslant 4$, let $\mathcal{A}_n = (\{1, 2, \ldots, n\}, \{a, b, c, d_1, d_2, \ldots, d_{n-2}\}, \delta, 1, \{n-1\})$, where $a = \binom{n-1}{n}(1, 2, \ldots, n-2)$, $b = \binom{n-1}{n}(1, 2)$, $c = \binom{n-1}{n}\binom{n-2}{1}$, and $d_i = \binom{n-1}{n}\binom{i}{n-1}$ for $i = 1, 2, \ldots, n-2$. DFA $\mathcal{A}_6$ is shown in Fig. 1, where $\Gamma = \{d_1, d_2, \ldots, d_{n-2}\}$. For $n = 4$, input a coincides with b; hence only 4 inputs are needed.

Any transformation $t \in T_L$ has the form

$$t = \begin{pmatrix} 1 & 2 & 3 & \cdots & n-2 & n-1 & n \\ i_1 & i_2 & i_3 & \cdots & i_{n-2} & n & n \end{pmatrix},$$

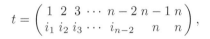

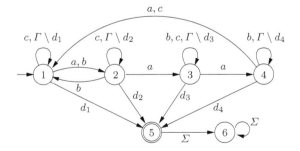

Fig. 1. Quotient DFA $\mathcal{A}_6$ of prefix-free regular language with 1,296 transformations

where $i_k \in \{1, 2, 3, \ldots, n\}$ for $1 \leqslant k \leqslant n - 2$. There are three cases:

1. If $i_k \leqslant n - 2$ for all k, $1 \leqslant k \leqslant n - 2$, then by Theorem 2, $\mathcal{A}_n$ can do t.

2. If $i_k \leqslant n - 1$ for all k, $1 \leqslant k \leqslant n - 2$, and there exists some h such that $i_h = n - 1$, then there exists some j, $1 \leqslant j \leqslant n - 2$ such that $i_k \neq j$ for all k, $1 \leqslant k \leqslant n - 2$. For all $1 \leqslant k \leqslant n - 2$, define i'_k as follows: $i'_k = j$ if $i_k = n - 1$, and $i'_k = i_k$ if $i_k \neq n - 1$. Let

$$s = \begin{pmatrix} 1 & 2 & 3 & 4 & \cdots & n - 2 & n - 1 & n \\ i'_1 & i'_2 & i'_3 & i'_4 & \cdots & i'_{n-2} & n & n \end{pmatrix}.$$

By Case 1 above, $\mathcal{A}_n$ can do s. Since $t = sd_j$, $\mathcal{A}_n$ can do t as well.

3. Otherwise, there exists some h such that $i_h = n$. Then there exists some j, $1 \leqslant j \leqslant n - 2$, such that $i_k \neq j$ for all k, $1 \leqslant k \leqslant n - 2$. For all $1 \leqslant k \leqslant n - 2$, define i'_k as follows: $i'_k = n - 1$ if $i_k = n$, $i'_k = j$ if $i_k = n - 1$, and $i'_k = i_k$ otherwise. Let s be as above but with new i'_k. By Case 2 above, $\mathcal{A}_n$ can do s. Since $t = sd_j$, $\mathcal{A}_n$ can do t as well.

Therefore, the syntactic complexity of $\mathcal{A}_n$ meets the desired bound.   □

We conjecture that the alphabet sizes cannot be reduced. As shown in Table 1, on p. 104, we have verified this conjecture by enumerating all prefix-free regular languages for $n \leqslant 5$ using *GAP* [6].

It was shown in [4] that for certain right, left, and two-sided ideals with maximal syntactic complexity, the reverse languages have maximal state complexity. This is also true for prefix-free languages.

Theorem 5. *The reverse of the prefix-free regular language accepted by automaton $\mathcal{A}_n$ of Theorem 4 restricted to $\{a, c, d_{n-2}\}$ has $2^{n-2} + 1$ quotients, which is the maximum possible for a prefix-free regular language.*

Proof. Let $\mathcal{B}_n$ be the automaton $\mathcal{A}_n$ restricted to $\{a, c, d_{n-2}\}$. Since $L(\mathcal{A}_n)$ is prefix-free, so is $L_n = L(\mathcal{B}_n)$. We show that $\kappa(L_n^R) = 2^{n-2} + 1$.

Let $\mathcal{N}_n$ be the NFA obtained by reversing $\mathcal{B}_n$. (See Fig. 2 for $\mathcal{N}_6$.) Apply the subset construction to $\mathcal{N}_n$. We prove that the following $2^{n-2} + 1$ sets of states of $\mathcal{N}_n$ are reachable and distinct: $\{n - 1\} \cup \{S \mid S \subseteq \{1, \ldots, n - 2\} \}$.

The singleton set $\{n - 1\}$ of initial states of $\mathcal{N}_n$ is reached by ε. From $\{n - 1\}$ we reach the empty set by a. The set $\{n - 2\}$ is reached by d_{n-2} from $\{n - 1\}$, and from here, $\{1\}$ is reached by a^{n-3}. From any set $\{1, 2, \ldots, i\}$, where $1 \leqslant i < n - 2$, we reach $\{1, 2, \ldots, i, i + 1\}$ by ca^{n-3}. Thus we reach $\{1, 2, \ldots, n - 2\}$ from $\{1\}$ by

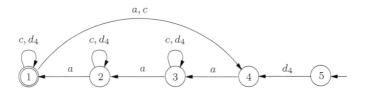

Fig. 2. NFA $\mathcal{N}_6$ of L_6^R with quotient complexity $\kappa(L_6^R) = 17$; empty state omitted

$(ca^{n-3})^{n-3}$. Now assume that any set S of cardinality $k \leqslant n-2$ can be reached; then we can get a set of cardinality $k-1$ by deleting an element j from S by applying $a^j d_{n-2} a^{n-2-j}$. Hence all subsets of $\{1, 2, \ldots, n-2\}$ can be reached.

The empty state accepts nothing, and the initial state $n-1$ is the only state accepting $d_{n-2} a^{n-3}$. For $1 \leqslant i \leqslant n-2$, the word a^{i-1} is accepted only by state i of $\mathcal{N}_n$. Suppose $S_1, S_2, S_1 \neq S_2$, are two non-empty subsets of $\{1, \ldots, n-2\}$. Then there exists $i \in S_1 \setminus S_2 \cup S_2 \setminus S_1$, and $w = a^i$ is accepted by one subset but not the other.

It was shown in [8] that the quotient complexity of reversal of prefix-free languages is at most $2^{n-2}+1$. Since all $2^{n-2}+1$ sets of states of $\mathcal{N}_n$ are reachable and pairwise distinguishable, L_n is a witness.   □

5   Suffix-Free Regular Languages

For any regular language L, a quotient L_w is *uniquely reachable* if $L_w = L_x$ implies that $w = x$. It is known from [7] that, if L is a suffix-free regular language, then $L = L_\varepsilon$ is uniquely reachable by ε, and L has the empty quotient. For $n \geqslant 1$, let $Q = \{1, 2, \ldots, n\}$. Without loss of generality, for any quotient automaton of a suffix-free regular language L with Q as its set of states, we assume that 1 is the initial state, and n is the empty state. Let

$$G_n = \{t \in \mathcal{T}_Q \mid 1 \notin \operatorname{img} t, nt = n, \text{ and } 1t = n \text{ or } 1t \neq it \text{ for } i \neq 1\}.$$

Note that G_n is not a semigroup for $n \geqslant 3$ because $s = [2, 3, 3, \ldots, 3, n] \in G_n$ but $s^2 = [3, 3, 3, \ldots, 3, n] \notin G_n$. Let $g(n) = |G_n|$.

Proposition 6. *If L is a regular language with quotient complexity n and syntactic semigroup T_L, then the following hold:*

1. *If L is suffix-free, then T_L is a subset of G_n.*
2. *If L is suffix-free and $n \geqslant 2$, then $\sigma(L) \leqslant g(n) = (n-1)^{n-2} + (n-2)^{n-1}$.*
3. *If L has only one accepting quotient, and $T_L \subseteq G_n$, then L is suffix-free.*

Proof. 1. Let L be suffix-free, and let $\mathcal{A}_n = (Q, \Sigma, \delta, 1, F)$ be its quotient DFA. Consider an arbitrary $t \in T_L$. Since the quotient L is uniquely reachable, $it \neq 1$ for all $i \in Q$. Since the quotient L_n is empty, $nt = n$. Furthermore, since L is suffix-free, for any two quotients L_v and L_{uv}, where $u, v \in \Sigma^+$ and $L_v \neq \emptyset$, we must have $L_v \cap L_{uv} = \emptyset$, and so $L_v \neq L_{uv}$. This means that, for any $t \in T_L$, if $1t \neq n$, then $1t \neq it$ for any $i \neq 1$. So $t \in G_n$, and $T_L \subseteq G_n$.

2. Since $T_L \subseteq G_n$, $\sigma(L) \leqslant |G_n| = g(n)$. Let $t \in G_n$ be any transformation. Note that $nt = n$ is fixed. There are two cases for t:

(a) $1t = n$: For any $i \neq 1, n$, there are $n-1$ choices for it: $2, 3, \ldots, n$. Thus there are $(n-1)^{n-2}$ such t's.

(b) $1t \neq n$: There are $n-2$ choices for $1t$: $2, 3, \ldots, n-1$. For any $i \neq 1, n$, it can be chosen from $\{2, 3, \ldots, n\} \setminus \{1t\}$. There are $(n-2)(n-2)^{n-2}$ such t's.

Altogether, we have $g(n) = (n-1)^{n-2} + (n-2)^{n-1}$.

3. Assume that $T_L \subseteq G_n$, and let f be the only accepting quotient. If L is not suffix-free, then there exist nonempty words u and v such that $v, uv \in L$. Let t_u and t_v be the transformations by u and v, and let $i = 1t_u$. Then $i \neq 1$, $f \neq n$, and $1t_v = f = 1t_{uv} = 1t_u t_v = it_v$, which contradicts the fact that $t_v \in G_n$. Therefore L is suffix-free. □

Next, we construct a large semigroup that can be the syntactic semigroup of a suffix-free regular language. Let C_k^n be the binomial coefficient, and let

$$P_n = \{t \in G_n \mid \text{ for all } i, j \in Q \text{ where } i \neq j, \text{ we have } it = jt = n \text{ or } it \neq jt\}.$$

Proposition 7. *For $n \geqslant 3$, P_n is a subsemigroup of G_n, and its cardinality is*

$$p(n) = |P_n| = \sum_{k=1}^{n-1} C_k^{n-1}(n-1-k)!C_{n-1-k}^{n-2}.$$

Proof. We know that a transformation t is in P_n if and only if the following hold:

(a) $it \neq 1$ for all $i \in Q$, and $nt = n$;
(b) for all $i, j \in Q$, such that $i \neq j$, either $it = jt = n$ or $it \neq jt$.

Clearly $P_n \subseteq G_n$. For any $t_1, t_2 \in P_n$, consider the composition $t_1 t_2$. Since $1 \notin \text{img } t_2$, then $1 \notin \text{img}(t_1 t_2)$. We also have $nt_1 t_2 = nt_2 = n$. Pick $i, j \in Q$ such that $i \neq j$. Suppose $it_1 t_2 \neq n$ or $jt_1 t_2 \neq n$. If $it_1 t_2 = jt_1 t_2$, then $it_1 = jt_1$ and thus $i = j$, a contradiction. Hence $t_1 t_2 \in P_n$, and P_n is a subsemigroup of G_n.

Let $t \in P_n$ be any transformation. Note that $nt = n$ is fixed. Let $Q' = Q \setminus \{n\}$, and $Q'' = Q \setminus \{1, n\}$. Suppose k elements in Q' are mapped to n by t, where $0 \leqslant k \leqslant n-1$; then there are C_k^{n-1} choices of these elements. For the set D of the remaining $n - 1 - k$ elements, which must be mapped by t to pairwise different elements of Q'', there are $C_{n-1-k}^{n-2}(n-1-k)!$ choices for the mapping $t|_D$. When $k = 0$, there is no such t since $|Dt| = n - 1 > n - 2 = |Q''|$. Altogether, the cardinality of P_n is $|P_n| = \sum_{k=1}^{n-1} C_k^{n-1}(n-1-k)!C_{n-1-k}^{n-2}$. □

We now construct a generating set of size n for P_n, which can be used to show that there exist DFA's accepting suffix-free regular languages with quotient complexity n and syntactic complexity $p(n)$.

Proposition 8. *When $n \geqslant 3$, the semigroup P_n can be generated by the following set I_n of transformations of Q: $I_3 = \{a, b\}$, where $a = [3, 2, 3]$ and $b = [2, 3, 3]$; $I_4 = \{a, b, c\}$, where $a = [4, 3, 2, 4]$, $b = [2, 4, 3, 4]$, $c = [2, 3, 4, 4]$; for $n \geqslant 5$, $I_n = \{a_0, \ldots, a_{n-1}\}$, where*

$$
\begin{aligned}
a_0 &= [\, n, \;\; 3, \;\; 2, \;\; 4, \quad \ldots, \quad n-1, n \,], \\
a_1 &= [\, n, \;\; 3, \;\; 4, \ldots, n-1, \;\; 2, \;\; n \,], \\
a_i &= [\, 2, \;\; \ldots, \;\; i, \;\; n, \;\; i+1, \quad \ldots, \quad n \,],
\end{aligned}
$$

for $i = 2, \ldots, n - 1$. That is, $a_0 = \binom{1}{n}(2, 3)$, $a_1 = \binom{1}{n}(2, 3, \ldots, n-1)$, and $ja_i = j+1$ for $j = 1, \ldots, i-1$, $ia_i = n$, and $ja_i = j$ for $j = i+1, \ldots, n$.

Proof. First note that I_n is a subset of P_n, and so $\langle I_n \rangle$, the semigroup generated by I_n, is a subset of P_n. We now show that $P_n \subseteq \langle I_n \rangle$.

Let t be any transformation in P_n. Note that $nt = n$ is fixed. Let $Q' = Q \setminus \{n\}$. Let $E_t = \{j \in Q' \mid jt = n\}$, $D_t = Q' \setminus E_t$, and $Q'' = Q \setminus \{1, n\}$. Then $D_t t \subseteq Q''$, and $|E_t| \geq 1$, since $|Q''| < |Q'|$. We prove by induction on $|E_t|$ that $t \in \langle I_n \rangle$.

First, note that $\langle a_0, a_1 \rangle$, the semigroup generated by $\{a_0, a_1\}$, is isomorphic to the symmetric group $\mathfrak{S}_{Q''}$ by Theorem 1. Consider $E_t = \{i\}$ for some $i \in Q'$. Then $ia_i = it = n$. Moreover, since $D_t a_i, D_t t \subseteq Q''$, there exists $\pi \in \langle a_0, a_1 \rangle$ such that $(ja_i)\pi = jt$ for all $j \in D_t$. Then $t = a_i \pi \in \langle I_n \rangle$.

Assume that any transformation $t \in P_n$ with $|E_t| < k$ can be generated by I_n, where $1 < k < n - 1$. Consider $t \in P_n$ with $|E_t| = k$. Suppose $E_t = \{e_1, \ldots, e_{k-1}, e_k\}$. Let $s \in P_n$ be such that $E_s = \{e_1, \ldots, e_{k-1}\}$. By assumption, s can be generated by I_n. Let $i = e_k s$; then $i \in Q''$, and $e_j(sa_i) = n$ for all $1 \leq j \leq k$. Moreover, we have $D_t(sa_i) \subseteq Q''$. Thus, there exists $\pi \in \langle a_0, a_1 \rangle$ such that, for all $d \in D_t$, $d(sa_i\pi) = dt$. Altogether, for all $e_j \in E_t$, we have $e_j(sa_i\pi) = e_j t = n$, for all $d \in D_t$, $d(sa_i\pi) = dt$, and $n(sa_i\pi) = nt = n$. Thus $t = sa_i\pi$, and $t \in \langle I_n \rangle$.

Therefore $P_n = \langle I_n \rangle$. $\qquad\square$

Proposition 9. *For $n \geq 5$, let $\mathcal{A}_n = \{Q, \Sigma, \delta, 1, F\}$ be the DFA with alphabet $\Sigma = \{a_0, a_1, \ldots, a_{n-1}\}$, where each a_i defines a transformation as in Proposition 8, and $F = \{2\}$. Then $L = L(\mathcal{A}_n)$ has quotient complexity $\kappa(L) = n$, and syntactic complexity $\sigma(L) = p(n)$. Moreover, L is suffix-free.*

Proof. First we show that all the states of $\mathcal{A}_n$ are reachable: 1 is the initial state, state n is reached by a_1, and for $2 \leq i \leq n - 1$, state i is reached by a_i^{i-1}. Also, the initial state 1 accepts a_2 while state i rejects a_2 for all $i \neq 1$. For $2 \leq i \leq n - 1$, state i accepts a_1^{n-i}, while state j rejects it, for all $j \neq i$. Also n is the empty state. Thus all the states of $\mathcal{A}_n$ are distinct, and $\kappa(L) = n$.

By Proposition 8, the syntactic semigroup of L is P_n. The syntactic complexity of L is $\sigma(L) = |P_n| = p(n)$. By Proposition 6, L is suffix-free. $\qquad\square$

As shown in Table 1 on p. 11, the size of Σ cannot be decreased for $n \leq 5$.

By Proposition 6, the upper bound on the syntactic complexity of suffix-free regular languages is achieved by the largest subsemigroup of G_n. We conjecture that P_n is such a subsemigroup.

Conjecture 10 (Suffix-Free Regular Languages). *If L is a suffix-free regular language with $\kappa(L) = n \geq 2$, then $\sigma(L) \leq p(n)$ and this is a tight bound.*

We prove the conjecture for $n \leq 4$:

Proof. By Proposition 6, the syntactic semigroup T_L of a suffix-free regular language L is contained in G_n. For $n \in \{2, 3\}$, $p(n) = g(n)$. So $p(n)$ is an upper bound, and it is tight by Proposition 9. For $n = 4$, there are 17 transformations in G_4 and 13 in P_4. Transformations $r_1 = [3, 2, 2, 4]$ and $r_2 = [2, 3, 3, 4]$ in G_4 are such that $\langle r_i \rangle \not\subseteq G_4$ for $i = 1, 2$. Thus T_L can contain neither r_1 nor r_2. Two other transformations, $s_1 = [4, 2, 2, 4]$ and $s_2 = [4, 3, 3, 4]$, in G_4 are such that s_1

conflicts with $t_1 = [3, 2, 4, 4] \in P_4$ ($t_1s_1 = [2, 2, 4, 4] \notin G_4$), and s_2 conflicts with $t_2 = [2, 3, 4, 4]$ ($t_2s_2 = [3, 3, 4, 4] \notin G_4$). Thus $\sigma(L) \leqslant 13$. By Proposition 9, the bound is tight.   □

6   Bifix-Free Regular Languages

Let L be regular and bifix-free with $\kappa(L) = n$. From Sections 4 and 5 we have:

1. L has ε as a quotient, and this is the only accepting quotient;
2. L has $\emptyset$ as a quotient;
3. L as a quotient is uniquely reachable.

Let $\mathcal{A}$ be the quotient automaton of L, with $Q = \{1, \ldots, n\}$ as the set of states. As in Section 5, we assume that $n - 1$ corresponds to the quotient ε, and n is the empty state. Consider the set

$$H_n = \{t \in G_n \mid (n - 1)t = n\}.$$

Let $h(n) = |H_n|$. The following is an observation similar to Proposition 6.

Proposition 11. *If L is a regular language with quotient complexity n and syntactic semigroup T_L, then the following hold:*

1. *If L is bifix-free, then T_L is a subset of H_n.*
2. *If L is bifix-free and $n \geqslant 3$, then $\sigma(L) \leqslant h(n) = (n - 1)^{n-3} + (n - 2)^{n-2}$.*
3. *If ε is the only accepting quotient of L, and $T_L \subseteq H_n$, then L is bifix-free.*

Proof. 1. Since L is suffix-free, $T_L \subseteq G_n$. Since L is also prefix-free, it has ε and $\emptyset$ as quotients. By assumption, $n - 1 \in Q$ corresponds to the quotient ε. Thus for any $t \in T_L$, $(n - 1)t = n$, and so $T_L \subseteq H_n$.
2. To calculate the size of H_n, we analyze the two possible cases of $t \in H_n$:
  (a) $1t = n$. For $i = 2, \ldots, n - 2$, it can be chosen from $\{2, \ldots, n\}$. There are $(n - 1)^{n-3}$ such transformations.
  (b) $1t \neq n$. For $i = 2, \ldots, n - 2$, it can be chosen from $\{2, \ldots, n\} \setminus \{1t\}$. There are $(n - 2)(n - 2)^{n-3} = (n - 2)^{n-2}$ such transformations.
  Altogether, we have $|T_L| \leqslant |H_n| = h(n) = (n - 1)^{n-3} + (n - 2)^{n-2}$.
3. Since ε is the only accepting quotient of L, L is prefix-free. Since $T_L \subseteq H_n \subseteq G_n$, L is suffix-free by Proposition 6. Therefore L is bifix-free.   □

We now find a large semigroup that can be the syntactic semigroup of a bifix-free regular language. Let

$$R_n = \{t \in H_n \mid it = jt = n \text{ or } it \neq jt \text{ for all } 1 \leq i, j \leq n\}.$$

Proposition 12. *For $n \geqslant 3$, R_n is a subsemigroup of H_n, and its cardinality is*

$$r(n) = |R_n| = \sum_{k=0}^{n-2} \left(C_k^{n-2}\right)^2 (n - 2 - k)!$$

Proof. First we show that R_n is a semigroup. Let t_1, t_2 be any transformations in R_n. Since $1 \notin \text{img } t_2$, also $1 \notin \text{img}(t_1 t_2)$. Since $nt_1 = nt_2 = n$, we have $nt_1 t_2 = nt_2 = n$. Since $(n-1)t_1 = n$, also $(n-1)t_1 t_2 = nt_2 = n$. Fix arbitrary $i, j \in Q$, where $i \neq j$. Note that $it_1 t_2 \neq n$ implies $it_1 \neq n$. If $it_1 t_2 = jt_1 t_2$, since $t_2 \in R_n$, then $it_1 = jt_1 \neq n$; because $t_1 \in R_n$, we have $i = j$, a contradiction. Thus $it_1 t_2 = jt_1 t_2 = n$ or $it_1 t_2 \neq jt_1 t_2$. So $t_1 t_2 \in R_n$, and R_n is a subsemigroup of H_n.

Pick any $t \in R_n$. Note that $(n-1)t = n$ and $nt = n$ are fixed, and $1 \notin \text{img } t$. Let $Q' = Q \setminus \{n-1, n\}$, $E = \{i \in Q' \mid it = n\}$, and $D = Q' \setminus E$. Suppose $|E| = k$, where $0 \leq k \leq n-2$; then there are C_k^{n-2} choices of E. Elements of D are mapped to pairwise different elements of $Q \setminus \{1, n\}$; then there are $C_{n-2-k}^{n-2}(n-2-k)!$ different $t|_D$. Altogether, we have $|R_n| = \sum_{k=0}^{n-2} \left(C_k^{n-2}\right)^2 (n-2-k)!$ $\square$

Proposition 13. *For* $n \geqslant 3$, *let* $Q' = Q \setminus \{n-1, n\}$ *and* $Q'' = Q \setminus \{1, n\}$. *Then the semigroup* R_n *can be generated by* $J_n = \{t \in R_n \mid Q't = Q'' \text{ and } it \neq jt \text{ for all } i, j \in Q'\}$.

Proof. We want to show that $R_n = \langle J_n \rangle$. Since $J_n \subseteq R_n$, we have $\langle J_n \rangle \subseteq R_n$. Let $t \in R_n$. By definition, $(n-1)t = nt = n$. Let $E_t = \{i \in Q' \mid it = n\}$. If $E_t = \emptyset$, then $t \in J_n$; otherwise, there exists $x \in Q''$ such that $x \notin \text{img } t$. We prove by induction on $|E_t|$ that $t \in \langle J_n \rangle$.

First note that, for all $t \in J_n$, $t|_{Q'}$ is an injective mapping from Q' to Q''. Consider $E_t = \{i\}$ for some $i \in Q'$. Since $|E_t| = 1$, $\text{img } t \cup \{x\} = Q''$. Let $t_1, t_2 \in J_n$ be defined by

$$t_1 = [\, 2,\ 3,\ \ldots,\quad i,\quad n-1,\quad i+1,\quad \ldots,\quad n-2,\ n, n \,],$$
$$t_2 = [\, x, 1t, 2t,\ \ldots,\ (i-1)t, (i+1)t, \ldots, (n-2)t, n, n \,].$$

That is, $jt_1 = j+1$ for $j = 1, \ldots, i-1$, $it_1 = n-1$, $jt_1 = j$ for $j = i+1, \ldots, n-2$, and $1t_2 = x$, $jt_2 = (j-1)t$ for $j = 2, \ldots, i$, $jt_2 = jt$ for $j = i+1, \ldots, n-2$. Then $t_1 t_2 = t$, and $t \in \langle J_n \rangle$.

Assume that any transformation $t \in R_n$ with $|E_t| < k$ can be generated by J_n, where $1 < k < n-2$. Consider $t \in R_n$ with $|E_t| = k$. Suppose $E_t = \{e_1, \ldots, e_{k-1}, e_k\}$, and let $D_t = Q' \setminus E_t = \{d_1, \ldots, d_l\}$, where $l = n-2-k$. By assumption, all $s \in R_n$ with $|E_s| = k-1$ can be generated by J_n. Let s be such that $E_s = \{1, \ldots, k-1\}$; then $1s = \cdots = (k-1)s = n$. In addition, let $ks = x$, and let $(k+j)s = d_j t$ for $j = 1, \ldots, l$. Let $t' \in J_n$ be such that $e_j t' = j$ for $j = 1, \ldots, k-1$, $kt' = n-1$, and $d_j t' = k+j$ for $j = 1, \ldots, l$. Then $t's = t$, and $t \in \langle J_n \rangle$. Therefore, $R_n = \langle J_n \rangle$. $\square$

Proposition 14. *For* $n \geqslant 3$, *let* $\mathcal{A}_n = \{Q, \Sigma, \delta, 1, F\}$ *be the automaton with alphabet* Σ *of size* $(n-2)!$, *where each* $a \in \Sigma$ *defines a distinct transformation* $t_a \in J_n$, *and* $F = \{n-1\}$. *Then* $L = L(\mathcal{A}_n)$ *has quotient complexity* $\kappa(L) = n$, *and syntactic complexity* $\sigma(L) = r(n)$. *Moreover,* L *is bifix-free.*

Proof. We first show that all the states of $\mathcal{A}_n$ are reachable. Note that there exists $a \in \Sigma$ such that $t_a = [2, 3, \ldots, n-1, n, n] \in J_n$. State $1 \in Q$ is the initial state, and a^{i-1} reaches state $i \in Q$ for $i = 2, \ldots, n$. Furthermore, for $1 \leq i \leq n - 1$, state i accepts a^{n-1-j}, while for $j \neq i$, state j rejects it. Also, n is the empty state. Thus all the states of $\mathcal{A}_n$ are distinct, and $\kappa(L) = n$.

By Proposition 13, the syntactic semigroup of L is R_n. Hence the syntactic complexity of L is $\sigma(L) = r(n)$. By Proposition 11, L is bifix-free. $\square$

We know by Proposition 11 that the upper bound on the syntactic complexity of bifix-free regular languages is reached by the largest subsemigroup of H_n. We conjecture that R_n is such a subsemigroup. Since $r(n) = h(n)$ for $n = 2, 3$, and 4, $r(n)$ is an upper bound, and it is tight by Proposition 14.

Conjecture 15 (Bifix-Free Regular Languages). If L is a bifix-free regular language with $\kappa(L) = n \geq 2$, then $\sigma(L) \leq r(n)$ and this is a tight bound.

The conjecture holds for $n = 5$ as we now show:

Proof. For $n = 5$, we have $h(5) = |H_5| = 43$, and $r(5) = |R_5| = 34$. There are two transformations $s_1 = [2, 3, 3, 5, 5]$ and $s_2 = [3, 2, 2, 5, 5]$ in H_5 such that $\langle s_i \rangle \not\subseteq H_5$ for $i = 1, 2$. Thus T_L cannot contain them, and we reduce the bound to $\sigma(L) \leq 41$. Let $U_5 = H_5 \setminus (R_5 \cup \{s_1, s_2\}) = \{\tau_1, \ldots, \tau_7\}$. We found for each τ_i a unique $t_i \in R_5$ such that the semigroup $\langle \tau_i, t_i \rangle$ is not a subset of H_5:

$$\begin{aligned}
\tau_1 &= [2, 4, 4, 5, 5], & t_1 &= [3, 4, 2, 5, 5]; \\
\tau_2 &= [3, 4, 4, 5, 5], & t_2 &= [3, 5, 2, 5, 5]; \\
\tau_3 &= [4, 2, 2, 5, 5], & t_3 &= [2, 4, 3, 5, 5]; \\
\tau_4 &= [4, 3, 3, 5, 5], & t_4 &= [2, 5, 3, 5, 5]; \\
\tau_5 &= [5, 2, 2, 5, 5], & t_5 &= [3, 2, 4, 5, 5]; \\
\tau_6 &= [5, 3, 3, 5, 5], & t_6 &= [2, 3, 4, 5, 5]; \\
\tau_7 &= [5, 4, 4, 5, 5], & t_7 &= [3, 2, 5, 5, 5].
\end{aligned}$$

Since $\langle \tau_i, t_i \rangle \subseteq T_L$, if both τ_i and t_i are in T_L, then $T_L \not\subseteq H_5$, and L is not bifix-free by Proposition 11. Thus, for $1 \leq i \leq 7$, at most one of τ_i and t_i can

Table 1. Syntactic complexities of prefix-, suffix-, and bifix-free regular languages

	$n = 2$	$n = 3$	$n = 4$	$n = 5$	$n = 6$
$|\Sigma| = 1$	1	2	3	4	5
$|\Sigma| = 2$	*	3/3/*	11/11/7	49/49/20	?
$|\Sigma| = 3$	*	*	14/13/*	95/61/31	?
$|\Sigma| = 4$	*	*	16/ * / *	110/67/32	?
$|\Sigma| = 5$	*	*	*	119/73/33	?
$|\Sigma| = 6$	*	*	*	125/ ? /34	? /501/ ?
$\cdots$					
$n^{n-2}/p(n)/r(n)$	1/1/1	3/3/2	16/13/7	125/73/34	1296/501/209
Suffix-free : $g(n)$	1	3	17	145	1,649
Bifix-free : $h(n)$	1	2	7	43	381

appear in T_L, and $|T_L| \leqslant 34$. Since $|R_5| = 34$ and R_5 is a semigroup, we have $\sigma(L) \leqslant 34 = r(5)$ as the upper bound for $n = 5$. This bound is reached by automaton $\mathcal{A}_5$ in Proposition 14. $\square$

7   Conclusions

Each cell of Table 1 shows the syntactic complexity bounds of prefix-, suffix-, and bifix-free regular languages, in that order, with a particular alphabet size. The figures in bold type are tight bounds verified by *GAP*. To compute the bounds for suffix- and bifix-free regular languages, we enumerate semigroups generated by elements of G_n and H_n that are subsemigroups of G_n and H_n respectively, and record the largest ones. By Propositions 6 and 11, we get the desired bounds from the enumeration. The asterisk $*$ indicates that the bound is already tight for a smaller alphabet. The last three rows include the tight upper bound n^{n-2} for prefix-free regular languages, conjectured upper bounds $p(n)$ for suffix-free and $r(n)$ for bifix-free regular languages, and weaker upper bounds (not tight in general) $g(n)$ for suffix-free and $h(n)$ for bifix-free regular languages.

References

1. Berstel, J., Perrin, D., Reutenauer, C.: Codes and Automata (Encyclopedia of Mathematics and its Applications). Cambridge University Press, Cambridge (2009)
2. Brzozowski, J.: Quotient complexity of regular languages. In: Dassow, J., Pighizzini, G., Truthe, B. (eds.) Proceedings of the 11th International Workshop on Descriptional Complexity of Formal Systems (DFS), Magdeburg, Germany, Otto-von-Guericke-Universität, pp. 25–42 (2009); to appear, J. Autom. Lang. Comb., Extended abstract at http://arxiv.org/abs/0907.4547
3. Brzozowski, J., Jirásková, G., Li, B., Smith, J.: Quotient complexity of bifix-, factor-, and subword-free regular languages. In: Proceedings of the 13th International Conference on Automata and Formal Languages, AFL (to appear, 2011), Full paper at http://arxiv.org/abs/1006.4843v3
4. Brzozowski, J., Ye, Y.: Syntactic complexity of ideal and closed languages. In: Mauri, G., Leporati, A. (eds.) Proceedings of the 15th International Conference on Developments in Language Theory (DLT). LNCS. Springer, Heidelberg (to appear, 2011), Full paper at http://arxiv.org/abs/arXiv:1010.3263
5. Ganyushkin, O., Mazorchuk, V.: Classical Finite Transformation Semigroups: An Introduction. Springer, Heidelberg (2009)
6. GAP-Group: GAP - Groups, Algorithms, Programming - a System for Computational Discrete Algebra (2010), http://www.gap-system.org/
7. Han, Y.S., Salomaa, K.: State complexity of basic operations on suffix-free regular languages. Theoret. Comput. Sci. 410(27-29), 2537–2548 (2009)
8. Han, Y.S., Salomaa, K., Wood, D.: Operational state complexity of prefix-free regular languages. In: Ésik, Z., Fülöp, Z. (eds.) Automata, Formal Languages, and Related Topics, Inst. of Informatics, pp. 99–115. University of Szeged, Hungary (2009)
9. Holzer, M., König, B.: On deterministic finite automata and syntactic monoid size. Theoret. Comput. Sci. 327(3), 319–347 (2004)

10. Hoyer, M.: Verallgemeinerung zweier sätze aus der theorie der substitutionengruppen. Math. Ann. 46, 539–544 (1895)
11. Krawetz, B., Lawrence, J., Shallit, J.: State complexity and the monoid of transformations of a finite set (2003), http://arxiv.org/abs/math/0306416v1
12. Maslov, A.N.: Estimates of the number of states of finite automata. Dokl. Akad. Nauk SSSR 194, 1266–1268 (1970) (Russian); English translation: Soviet Math. Dokl. 11, 1373–1375 (1970)
13. Myhill, J.: Finite automata and representation of events. Wright Air Development Center Technical Report, 57–624 (1957)
14. Nerode, A.: Linear automaton transformations. Proc. Amer. Math. Soc. 9, 541–544 (1958)
15. Piccard, S.: Sur les fonctions définies dans les ensembles finis quelconques. Fundamenta Mathematicae 24, 298–301 (1935)
16. Piccard, S.: Sur les bases du groupe symétrique et du groupe alternant. Commentarii Mathematici Helvetici 11, 1–8 (1938)
17. Pin, J.E.: Syntactic Semigroups. In: Handbook of Formal Languages. Word, Language, Grammar, vol. 1, Springer-Verlag New York, Inc., New York (1997)
18. Sierpiński, W.: Sur les suites infinies de fonctions définies dans les ensembles quelconques. Fund. Math. 24, 209–212 (1935)
19. Yu, S.: State complexity of regular languages. J. Autom. Lang. Comb. 6, 221–234 (2001)

Geometrical Regular Languages and Linear Diophantine Equations

Jean-Marc Champarnaud[1], Jean-Philippe Dubernard[1], Franck Guingne[2], and Hadrien Jeanne[1]

[1] LITIS, Université de Rouen, France
{jean-marc.champarnaud,jean-philippe.dubernard}@univ-rouen.fr,
hadrien.jeanne@univ-rouen.fr
[2] I3S, Université de Nice - Sophia Antipolis & CNRS, France
franck.guingne@i3s.unice.fr

Abstract. We present a new method for checking whether a regular language over an arbitrarily large alphabet is semi-geometrical or whether it is geometrical. This method makes use first of the partitioning of the state diagram of the minimal automaton of the language into strongly connected components and secondly of the enumeration of the simple cycles in each component. It is based on the construction of systems of linear Diophantine equations the coefficients of which are deduced from the the the set of simple cycles. This paper addresses the case of a strongly connected graph.

1 Introduction

A d-dimensional geometrical figure is a (possibly infinite) set of sites of the d-dimensional oriented site square lattice connected by a network of nearest neighbour bonds. It turns out that a finite geometrical figure is an animal [12]. A main interest of the study of the d-dimensional geometrical figures comes from the problem of tiling such a figure by an animal. This problem is close to the problem of tiling the cell lattice by a polyomino [12] that has been much studied. An equivalent definition of a geometrical figure is given in [1], where an application to the modeling of real-time task systems [11] is mentioned. Let $\Sigma = \{a_1, \ldots, a_d\}$ be an ordered alphabet with d symbols. The Parikh mapping [21] $c : \Sigma^* \mapsto \mathbb{N}^d$ maps a word $w \in \Sigma^*$ to its coordinate vector $(|w|_{a_1}, \ldots, |w|_{a_d}) \in \mathbb{N}^d$, which allows us to transform a geometrical figure F into a labeled graph: if P and Q are neighbours w.r.t. the kth direction, with $1 \leq k \leq d$, i.e. if $Q = P + c(a_k)$, then there exists a (P, a_k, Q) labeled arc in the graph. As a consequence, the geometrical figure of a prefix closed language is the set of the Parikh images of its words. Conversely, the language of a geometrical figure is the set of the words that are labels of a path going from the origin in the figure. Any prefix closed language is a subset of the language of its geometrical figure, but the reciprocal is false. This property leads to the definition of two sub-families of prefix closed languages: a geometrical language is equal to the

M. Holzer, M. Kutrib, and G. Pighizzini (Eds.): DCFS 2011, LNCS 6808, pp. 107–120, 2011.
© Springer-Verlag Berlin Heidelberg 2011

language of its geometrical figure; a semi-geometrical language is such that two words with the same Parikh image define identical left residuals.

The study of geometrical figures is facilitated by making use of the properties of their languages. For example, the problem of tiling a geometrical figure by an animal is easier to solve if the figure is generated by a regular language [5]. However, even for the regular case, there exists no polynomial-time algorithm for checking whether a language is semi-geometrical or whether it is geometrical, except for $d \leq 2$ (see [4]).

Our aim is to design a new method for checking whether a regular language over an arbitrarily large alphabet is semi-geometrical or whether it is geometrical. This method is based on first the partitioning of the state diagram of the minimal automaton of the language into strongly connected components [24], secondly on the enumeration of the simple cycles in each component [25] and thirdly on the construction of a set of systems of linear Diophantine equations [16] the coefficients of which are deduced from the set of simple cycles. For both tests (is the language semi-geometrical? is the language geometrical?), the answer depends on the existence or not of a solution for such systems.

As far as complexity is concerned, the new method involves two non polynomial-time steps: the NFA determinisation, at least if the data is a regular expression denoting the language, and the enumeration of the simple cycles of a strongly connected graph. Moreover it is based on the resolution of a set of systems of linear Diophantine equations. However, the only method independent of the size of the alphabet known till now [1] presents a similar drawback since it is based on two non polynomial-time steps: the conversion of a finite automaton into a regular expression (whose size is known to be non polynomial-time) and the intersection of Parikh coordinate sets [1]. Beyond the theoretical interest of this new method, the hope is that powerful tools to solve linear Diophantine equation systems such as the Polylib library [26] or the LinBox library [13] would yield good results. Notice that an approach of a similar nature has been successfully developed in [10] where a SAT solver is used to attack the NFA reduction problem.

In this paper, we consider the case of a strongly connected graph. The next section recalls notation and definitions concerning languages, automata and geometrical figures. Section 3 contains a study of the set of paths of a d-ary strongly connected graph and Section 4 is devoted to the design of a semi-geometrical test and of a geometrical test inside such a graph. The last section reports some experimental results.

2   Preliminaries

2.1   Languages, Automata and Graphs

Let us first review basic notions concerning regular languages and finite automata. For a comprehensive treatment of this domain, the reference [9] can be consulted. Let Σ be a nonempty finite set of symbols, called the *alphabet*. An alphabet is said to be *ordered* if it is equipped with an order relation. A *word* over Σ is a finite sequence of symbols, usually written $x_1 x_2 \cdots x_n$. The *length* of a word u, denoted by $|u|$, is the number of symbols in u. The number of occurrences of a symbol a in u is denoted by $|u|_a$. The *empty word*, denoted by ε, has a null length. If $u = x_1 \cdots x_n$ and $v = y_1 \cdots y_m$ are two words over the alphabet Σ, their concatenation $u \cdot v$, usually written uv, is the word $x_1 \cdots x_n y_1 \cdots y_m$. Let Σ^* be the set of words over Σ. Given two words u and w in Σ^*, u is said to be a *prefix* of w if there exists a word v in Σ^* such that $uv = w$. A *language* L over Σ is a subset of Σ^*. The *left residual* of a language L w.r.t. a word $u \in \Sigma$ is the set $u^{-1}L = \{v \in \Sigma^* \mid uv \in L\}$. A language is said to be *prefix closed* if it is equal to the set $\mathrm{Pref}(L)$ of its prefixes. The set of *regular* languages over an alphabet Σ contains the empty set and the set $\{a\}$ for all $a \in \Sigma$ and it is closed under concatenation, union and star.

A *deterministic finite automaton* (DFA) is a 5-tuple $\mathcal{A} = (Q, \Sigma, \delta, s_0, T)$ where Q is a finite nonempty *set of states*, δ is a mapping from $Q \times \Sigma$ to Q, $s_0 \in Q$ is the *initial state* and $T \subseteq Q$ is the *set of final states*. For all $(p, x) \in Q \times \Sigma$, we will write $p \cdot x$ instead of $\delta(p, x)$; for all $Q' \subset Q$ and for all $x \in \Sigma$, the set $\{p \cdot x \mid p \in Q'\}$ is denoted by $Q' \cdot x$. The 3-tuple (p, x, q) in $Q \times \Sigma \times Q$ is said to be *a transition* if and only if $q = p \cdot x$. A DFA $\mathcal{A}$ is said to be *complete* if for any $q \in Q$ and any $a \in \Sigma$, $|q \cdot a| = 1$. In a complete DFA there may exist a *sink state* σ such that $\sigma \notin T$ and, for all $x \in \Sigma$, $\sigma \cdot x = \sigma$.

The *state diagram* of the automaton $\mathcal{A} = (Q, \Sigma, \delta, s_0, T)$ is the *graph* $\mathcal{G} = (Q, U, \Sigma)$, where Q is the set of *vertices* and $U \subset Q \times \Sigma \times Q$ is the set of *labeled arcs*, with $U = \delta$. We say that $(p, q) \in Q \times Q$ is an *arc* if there exists $a \in \Sigma$ such that $(p, a, q) \in U$. By definition the state diagram of an automaton is an *oriented* graph and a *labeled* one. Let $d = |\Sigma|$. The automaton $\mathcal{A}$ and the state diagram $\mathcal{G}$ are said to be *unary* if $d = 1$, *binary* if $d = 2$ and *d-ary* otherwise.

The following notions are actually defined on the state diagram $\mathcal{G}$ of the DFA. Let $p \in Q$ and $u = u_1 \cdots u_t \in \Sigma^*$. The *path* (p, u) of length t starting from p and labeled by u is the sequence of transitions $((p_0, u_1, p_1), \ldots, (p_{t-1}, u_t, p_t)$, with $p_0 = p$. The state p_0 (resp. p_t) is said to be *the head* (resp. *the tail*) of the path. The word $u = u_1 \cdots u_t \in \Sigma^*$ is said to be the *label* of the path. A path $((p_0, u_1, p_1), \ldots, (p_{t-1}, u_t, p_t)$ is said to be *simple* if the states $p_0, \ldots, p_t$ are pairwise distinct. A *cycle* is a path where the head and the tail are the same state. A cycle $((p_0, u_1, p_1), \ldots, (p_{t-1}, u_t, p_t)$, with $p_t = p_0$, is *simple* if the states $p_0, \ldots, p_{t-1}$ are pairwise distinct. A DFA $\mathcal{A}$ is said to be *accessible* if for any $q \in Q$ there exists a path from s_0 to q. A DFA is said to be *strongly connected* if for all $(i, j) \in Q \times Q$ with $i \neq j$, there exist a path going from i to j and a path going from j to i.

A path is said to be *successful* if $p = s_0$ and $p \cdot u \in T$. The language $L(\mathcal{A})$ *recognized* by the DFA $\mathcal{A}$ is the set of words that are labels of successful paths. Kleene's theorem [15] states that a language is recognized by a DFA if and only if it is regular. The *left language* $\overleftarrow{L}_q^{\mathcal{A}}$ (resp. *right language* $\overrightarrow{L}_q^{\mathcal{A}}$) of a state q is the set of words w such that there exists a path in $\mathcal{A}$ from s_0 to the state q (resp. from q to a final state) with w as label. A complete and accessible DFA $\mathcal{A}$ is *minimal* if and only if any two distinct states of $\mathcal{A}$ have distinct right languages.

According to the theorem of Myhill-Nerode [18,19], the minimal DFA of a regular language is unique up to an isomorphism.

2.2   Geometrical Figures and Their Languages

We consider the d-dimensional oriented site square lattice (site lattice for short).

Definition 1. *A d-dimensional geometrical figure F is a (possibly infinite) set of sites of the site lattice connected by a network of nearest neighbour bonds.*

Definition 1 is equivalent to the definition given in [1]. We denote by $\mathcal{O}$ the point with coordinate $(0, \ldots, 0)$. The *level* of the point $P = (x_1, \ldots, x_d)$ is $\text{level}(P) = x_1 + \ldots + x_d$. Notice that 2-dimensional geometrical figures (such as the one of Figure 1) are drawn so that points with the same level lie on a same horizontal line.

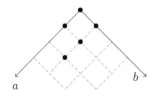

Fig. 1. $F_1 = \{(0,0), (0,1), (1,0), (1,1), (2,1)\}$

Let us consider a d-dimensional geometrical figure $F = (S, U)$, where $S \subset \mathbb{N}^d$ is the (possibly infinite) set of vertices or *points* and $U \subset S \times S$ is the implicit set of arcs defined by the only d authorized steps (that are the South-East and South-West steps for the 2-dimensional figure of Figure 1). It is easy to make F be a labeled figure by considering an ordered alphabet $\Sigma = \{a_1, \ldots, a_d\}$ with d symbols each of which is associated to a direction of the site lattice. More precisely, the Parikh mapping [21] $c : \Sigma^* \mapsto \mathbb{N}^d$ maps a word $w \in \Sigma^*$ to its coordinate vector $c(w) = (|w|_{a_1}, \ldots, |w|_{a_d})$. Hence the following definition: the *geometrical figure of a prefix closed language L* is the figure $\mathcal{F}(L) = \bigcup_{w \in L} c(w)$.

In a geometrical figure, a path (P, u), with $P \in F$ and $u \in \Sigma^*$ is called a *trajectory*. Let $\text{Traj}(\mathcal{O}, F)$ be the set of trajectories of F starting from $\mathcal{O}$. The *language of a geometrical figure F* is the language $\mathcal{L}(F) = \{u \mid (\mathcal{O}, u) \in \text{Traj}(\mathcal{O}, F)\}$. For any language L, it holds that $L \subseteq \mathcal{L}(\mathcal{F}(L))$. Some languages however are such that $\mathcal{L}(\mathcal{F}(L)) \nsubseteq L$. For instance, the two languages $L_1 = \{\varepsilon, a, b, ba\}$ and $L_2 = \{\varepsilon, a, b, ab, ba\}$ over the alphabet $\Sigma = \{a, b\}$ have the same geometrical figure F; it can be checked that $\mathcal{L}(F) = L_2$ whereas $\mathcal{L}(F) \nsubseteq L_1$ since ab is in $\mathcal{L}(F)$ but is not in L_1. Hence the definition of the two following families of languages:

Definition 2. *A prefix closed language L is geometrical if $L = \mathcal{L}(\mathcal{F}(L))$.*

Definition 3. *A prefix closed language L is* semi-geometrical *if, for all u and v in L, the condition $c(u) = c(v) \Rightarrow u^{-1}L = v^{-1}L$ is satisfied.*

2.3 Arithmetic

Given two integers a and b we write $a|b$ if a is a divisor of b. The greatest common divisor of n integers $a_1, \ldots, a_n$ is denoted by $\gcd(a_1, \ldots, a_n)$.

Theorem 4 (Brauer theorem [2]). *Let r be a positive integer and $l_1, l_2, \ldots, l_r$ be r integers such that $0 < l_1 < l_2 < \ldots < l_r$ and $\gcd(l_1, l_2, \ldots, l_r) = 1$. Let us set $m_0 = (l_1 - 1)(l_r - 1)$. Then every integer $m \geq m_0$ is a linear combination with non-negative coefficients of the integers $l_1, \ldots, l_r$.*

If the integers $l_1, \ldots, l_r$ are not mutually prime, let us set $p = \gcd(l_1, l_2, \ldots, l_r)$. Brauer theorem can be applied to the r integers $\frac{l_1}{p}, \frac{l_2}{p}, \ldots, \frac{l_r}{p}$ that are such that $0 < \frac{l_1}{p} < \frac{l_2}{p} < \ldots < \frac{l_r}{p}$ and $\gcd(\frac{l_1}{p}, \frac{l_2}{p}, \ldots, \frac{l_r}{p}) = 1$.

Corollary 5. *Let r be a positive integer and $l_1, l_2, \ldots, l_r$ be r integers such that $0 < l_1 < l_2 < \ldots < l_r$ and $p = \gcd(l_1, l_2, \ldots, l_r)$. Let us set $m_0 = (\frac{l_1}{p} - 1)(\frac{l_r}{p} - 1)$. Then for all integer $m \geq m_0$, mp is a linear combination with non-negative coefficients of the integers $l_1, \ldots, l_r$.*

The two following corollaries address the case where the r integers are not necessarily distinct or not necessarily non null. Since they are straightforward consequences of Corollary 5, the proof is omitted.

Let us consider now r integers $l_1, l_2, \ldots, l_r$ that are not necessarily distinct.

Corollary 6. *Let r be a positive integer and $l_1, l_2, \ldots, l_r$ be r integers. We assume that there exists an integer i such that $1 \leq i \leq r - 1$ and $0 < l_1 < l_2 < \ldots < l_i = l_{i+1} < \ldots < l_r$. Let $p = \gcd(l_1, l_2, \ldots, l_r)$ and $m_0 = (\frac{l_1}{p} - 1)(\frac{l_r}{p} - 1)$. Then for all integer $m \geq m_0$, mp is a linear combination with non-negative coefficients of the integers $l_1, \ldots, l_r$.*

Corollary 7. *Let r be a positive integer, $l_1, l_2, \ldots, l_r$ be r non-negative integers, and $(l_{i_1}, \ldots, l_{i_s})$, with $s \leq r$, a sub-sequence of positive integers of the sequence $(l_1, \ldots, l_r)$. Let $p = \gcd(l_{i_1}, \ldots, l_{i_s})$ and $m_0 = (\frac{l_{i_1}}{p} - 1)(\frac{l_{i_s}}{p} - 1)$. Then for all integer $m \geq m_0$, mp is a linear combination with non-negative coefficients of the integers $l_1, \ldots, l_r$.*

Definition 8. *A system of linear Diophantine equations is a system $Ax = b$, where $A = (a_{i,j})$ is an $m \times n$ matrix with integer entries, b is an $m \times 1$ column vector with integer components and x is an $n \times 1$ solution vector with integer components.*

As far as the resolution of a linear Diophantine equation $a_1 x_1 + a_2 x_2 + \ldots + a_n x_n = b$ is concerned, a well-known result is that integer solutions exist if and only if $\gcd(a_1, a_2, \ldots, a_n)|b$. Moreover, the problem of finding any or all of the solutions of a system of linear Diophantine equations is solved thanks to linear algebra tools such as the Hermite normal form or the Smith normal form of a matrix [23]. However, there exists no polynomial-time algorithm straightforwardly deduced from the computation of these normal forms.

3   Strongly Connected Graphs

Our aim is to characterize the geometrical properties of a prefix closed regular language L through properties of its minimal deterministic automaton $\mathcal{A}$. It turns out that these properties can be formulated in terms of graphs, by considering the state diagram $\mathcal{G} = (Q, U, \Sigma)$ of $\mathcal{A}$. We therefore first study some graph properties. More precisely, we assume that $\mathcal{G}$ is a d-ary strongly connected graph and given two distinct vertices i and j, we focus on the set of paths going from i to j.

This study is a generalization of results that are described in [14,6] and used in [7] in the frame of unary strongly connected graphs. The case of strongly connected graphs is important for two reasons: first it is the basic case in the study of general graphs, and secondly, for a large enough d, the ratio of accessible n-state DFAs over an alphabet with d symbols having a strongly connected state diagram is conjectured to be asymptotically equal to 1.

Let $D_{(d,n)}$ be the number of accessible and complete n-state DFAs over an alphabet with d symbols and $F_{(d,n)}$ be the number of such DFAs having a strongly connected state diagram. Then, the following conjecture holds:

Conjecture 9. [22] The two following conditions aymptotically hold:

$$D_{(d,n)} = n^{dn}\gamma_d^n(1 + o(1)),$$

with $\gamma_d = \frac{(1-c_d)^{\frac{1-c_d}{c_d}}}{c_d^{d-1}}$ and c_d is the root of the equation $c_d = 1 - e^{-dc_d}$, and

$$F_{(d,n)} \equiv c_d D_{(d,n)}$$

As reported in [20], we have: $c_2 = 0.7968$, $c_3 = 0.9405$ and $1 - 10^{-10} < c_{24} < 1$. Hence, for $d > 24$, the ratio of accessible n-state DFAs over an alphabet with d symbols having a strongly connected state diagram is asymptotically equal to 1.

In order to shorten notation, we consider an alphabet $\Sigma = \{1, \ldots, d\}$. Given a symbol $x \in \Sigma$, the vertex j is said to be the x-*successor* of the vertex i if there exists a labeled arc (i, x, j) in U. By abuse of notation the set of x-successors of a set of vertices $X \subset Q$ is denoted by $X \cdot x$.

Let $\mathcal{C}$ be the set of simple cycles of $\mathcal{G}$ and r the number of elements of $\mathcal{C}$. Any sequence $((\alpha_i, c_i))_{1 \le i \le r}$ with, for all $1 \le i \le r$, $\alpha_i \in \mathbb{N}$ and $c_i \in \mathcal{C}$ is said to be a *combination of simple cycles*. Any cycle is a combination of simple cycles. Let i and j be two vertices of Q. The set of paths going from i to j is denoted by $\Gamma_{i,j}$.

Let γ be a path of $\Gamma_{i,j}$ and u be the label of γ. Besides the length of γ that is equal to the length $|u|$ of the word u, we define the following notions.

Definition 10. (1) *For all $x \in \Sigma$, the x-length l^x of the path γ is the number $|u|_x$ of occurrences of x in the word u.*
(2) *The Parikh-length $l(\gamma)$ of the path γ is the vector $(l^1, \ldots, l^d)$ of $\mathbb{N}^d$. It will be denoted by l if there is no ambiguity.*

For all $c_k \in \mathcal{C}$, and for all $x \in \Sigma$, the x-length of the cycle c_k is denoted by l_k^x. The Parikh-length of the cycle c_k is the vector $l_k = (l_k^1, \ldots, l_k^d)$ of $\mathbb{N}^d$. Notice that for a unary graph, the Parikh-length of a path is equal to its length.

Let $a = (a_1, \ldots, a_d)$, $b = (b_1, \ldots, b_d)$ and $r = (r_1, \ldots, r_d)$ be three elements of $\mathbb{N}^d$. The following relations are defined on $\mathbb{N}^d$.

$$a \geq b \Leftrightarrow \forall x \mid 1 \leq x \leq d,\ a_x \geq b_x$$

$$a = r \pmod{b} \Leftrightarrow \forall x \mid 1 \leq x \leq d,\ a_x = r_x \pmod{b_x}$$

Lemma 11. *Let $\mathcal{G} = (Q, U, \Sigma)$ be a d-ary strongly connected graph and i and j two distinct vertices of Q.*

(1) There exists a path $\gamma_0 \in \Gamma_{i,j}$ going through all the vertices of Q.
(2) The path obtained by adding to the path γ_0 any combination of simple cycles of $\mathcal{G}$ belongs to $\Gamma_{i,j}$.

Proof. (1) It is a straightforward consequence of the fact that $\mathcal{G}$ is strongly connected.

(2) Since the path γ_0 goes through all the vertices of Q, it is possible to augment it by any combination of simple cycles of G. The resulting path is obviously in $\Gamma_{i,j}$. $\square$

Given two distinct vertices i and j, any path $\gamma \in \Gamma_{i,j}$ going through all the vertices of Q is said to be a *basic path*. For any simple cycle in $\mathcal{G}$, its length is different from 0 and its Parikh-length is different from the null vector. In contrast, given a symbol $x \in \Sigma$, the x-length of an simple cycle can be null. Hence the following definition of period is useful.

Definition 12. *Let $x \in \Sigma$. Let us consider the sequence $(l_1^x, \ldots, l_r^x)$, where l_i^x, $1 \leq i \leq r$, is the x-length of the simple cycle c_i, and the sub-sequence $(t_k^x)_{1 \leq k \leq s}$ of its non-null elements.*

(1) The x-period p_x of $\mathcal{G}$ is equal to $\gcd(t_1^x, \ldots, t_s^x)$ if the sequence $(t_k^x)_{1 \leq k \leq s}$ is not empty and to 0 otherwise.
(2) The period p of $\mathcal{G}$ is the vector $(p_1, \ldots, p_d)$ of $\mathbb{N}^d$.

Lemma 13. *Let i and j be two vertices in Q. Then the Parikh-lengths of the paths of $\Gamma_{i,j}$ are all equal modulo p.*

Proof. The Parikh-length of any cycle of $\mathcal{G}$ is a linear combination with non-negative coefficients of the Parikh-lengths $l_1, \ldots, l_r$. Consequently, for all $x \in \Sigma$, the x-length of any cycle of $\mathcal{G}$ is a multiple of p_x. Let i and j be two distinct vertices of Q and let γ and γ' be two paths in $\Gamma_{i,j}$. Since $\mathcal{G}$ is strongly connected, there exists a path $\gamma'' \in \Gamma_{j,i}$. The paths $\gamma\gamma''$ and $\gamma'\gamma''$ are cycles that go through i. Let l (resp. l', l'') be the Parikh-length of the path γ (resp. γ', γ''). For all $x \in \Sigma$, the condition $l^x + l''^x = l'^x + l''^x \pmod{p_x}$ is satisfied and consequently $l^x = l'^x \pmod{p_x}$. $\square$

For all $x \in \Sigma$, the set of x-lengths of paths of $\Gamma_{i,j}$ is denoted by $\Lambda_x(i,j)$. We consider the subset $\Lambda_x^{+t}(x,y)$ (resp. $\Lambda_x^{-t}(x,y)$ of x-lengths not less than (resp. less than) a threshold t. The next proposition shows that there exists, for all $x \in \Sigma$, a threshold h_x beyond which the x-length vector has a periodic behaviour. The threshold vector is denoted by $h = (h_1, \ldots, h_d)$. The set of Parikh-lengths of paths of $\Gamma_{i,j}$ is denoted by $\Lambda(i,j)$. We consider the subset $\Lambda^{+t}(x,y)$ (resp. $\Lambda^{-t}(x,y)$) of Parikh-lengths not less than (resp. less than) a threshold t.

If there is no ambiguity, the following abbreviations are used: Λ_x, Λ_x^{+h}, Λ_x^{-h}; and similarly, Λ, Λ^{+h} and Λ^{-h}.

Proposition 14. *For all $x \in \Sigma$ such that $p_x \neq 0$, there exists an integer h_x such that $\Lambda_x^{+h_x} = \{h_x + mp_x \mid m \geq 0\}$.*

Proof. Let $x \in \Sigma$. Consider the sequence $(t_1^x, \ldots, t_s^x)$, with $s \leq r$, of non-null x-lengths. Without loss of generality, we can assume that $t_1^x = \min(t_1^x, \ldots, t_s^x)$ and $t_s^x = \max(t_1^x, \ldots, t_s^x)$.

Let us set $m_x = (\frac{t_1^x}{p_x} - 1)(\frac{t_s^x}{p_x} - 1)$. According to Corollary 7, for all integer $m \geq m_x$, mp_x is a linear combination with non-negative coefficients of the integers $l_1^x, \ldots, l_r^x$. Since $\mathcal{G}$ is strongly connected, according to Lemma 11 there exists a path $\gamma_0 \in \Gamma_{i,j}$ having a Parikh-length l_0, such that for any linear combination with non-negative coefficients of the Parikh-lengths of the simple cycles $d = \sum_{k=1}^{r} \alpha_k l_k$, there exists a path of $\Gamma_{i,j}$ having a Parikh-length equal to $l_0 + d$.

Hence, for all $m \geq m_x$, there exists a path of $\Gamma_{i,j}$ having a x-length equal to $l_0^x + mp_x$. Setting $h_x = l_0^x + m_x p_x$, we obtain $\{mp_x \mid m \geq 0\} \subset \Lambda_x^{+h_x}$. Moreover, according to Lemma 13, two paths of $\Gamma_{i,j}$ have equal x-lengths modulo p_x. As a consequence, the set of x-lengths of paths of $\Gamma_{i,j}$ having a value greater than or eqal to $h_x = l_0^x + m_x p_x$ is the set of integers $\{h^x + mp_x \mid m \geq 0\}$. $\square$

Lemma 15. *We assume that for all $x \in \Sigma$, it holds that $p_x \neq 0$. Then there exists a partition $\Pi(G)$ of the set Q of vertices of $\mathcal{G}$ into $p_1 \times p_2 \ldots \times p_d$ subsets T_r such that for all $k \in \Sigma$, $T_{(r_1,\ldots,r_d)} \cdot k = T_{(r_1',\ldots,r_d')}$, with $r_k' = r_k + 1 \pmod{p_k}$ and, for all $m \neq k$, $r_m' = r_m$.*

Proof. Let i be an arbitrarily chosen vertex of $\mathcal{G}$. For all $r = (r_1, \ldots, r_d) \in \{0, \ldots, p_1 - 1\} \times \ldots \{0, \ldots, p_d - 1\}$, let T_r be the set of vertices j such that the Parikh-length of any path going from i to j is equal to r modulo p. According to Lemma 13 the sets T_r for $r = (0, \ldots, 0)$ to $r = (p_1 - 1, \ldots, p_d - 1)$, define a partition of Q such that $i \in T_{(0,\ldots,0)}$. For all $k \in \Sigma$, the set of k-successors of $T_{(r_1,\ldots,r_d)}$ is the set $T_{(r_1',\ldots,r_d')}$, with $r_k' = r_k + 1 \pmod{p_k}$ and, for all $m \neq k$, $r_m' = r_m$. $\square$

The reasoning is similar if there exists $x \in \Sigma$ such that $p_x = 0$, by taking r in the product $\{0, \ldots, p_1 - 1\} \times \ldots \{0, \ldots, p_{x-1} - 1\} \times \{0, \ldots, p_{x+1} - 1\} \times \ldots \{0, \ldots, p_d - 1\}$.

Definition 16. (1) *The partition $\Pi(G)$ is the* standard partition *of $\mathcal{G}$.*
(2) *Two states j and j' that belong to a same class of $\Pi(G)$ are said to be* congruent.

4   Geometry of Strongly Connected Graphs

In this section, the graph $\mathcal{G}$ is assumed to be a strongly connected one.

Definition 17. *Two distinct vertices j and j' are compatible ($j \equiv j'$) if for any path $\gamma \in \Gamma_{i,j}$ and any path $\gamma' \in \Gamma_{i,j'}$, γ and γ' have a different Parikh-length. That is*

$$j \equiv j' \Leftrightarrow \Lambda(i,j) \cap \Lambda(i,j') = \emptyset$$

Lemma 18. *If two vertices are congruent, then they are compatible.*

Proof. As a consequence of Lemma 13, the Parikh-length l (resp. l') of any path $\gamma \in \Gamma_{i,j}$ (resp. $\gamma' \in \Gamma_{i,j'}$) is equal to some $r \in \mathbb{N}^d$ (resp. r') modulo p. It implies that, if $r \neq r'$ then $j \equiv j'$. $\qquad\qquad\square$

Proposition 19. *Let L be a regular language and $\mathcal{A}$ be its minimal automaton. We assume that the state diagram of $\mathcal{A}$ is a strongly connected graph. Then the language L is semi-geometrical if and only if the states of $\mathcal{A}$ are pairwise compatible.*

Proof. Let u and u' be two distinct words of L. We set $j = s_0 \cdot u$ and $j' = s_0 \cdot u'$. Since $\mathcal{A}$ is the deterministic minimal automaton of L, we have: $u^{-1}L = u'^{-1}L \Leftrightarrow \overrightarrow{L}_j^A = \overrightarrow{L}_{j'}^A \Leftrightarrow j = j'$. Hence the condition $c(u) = c(u') \Rightarrow u^{-1}L = u'^{-1}L$ of Definition 3 is equivalent to $c(u) = c(u') \Rightarrow j = j'$ (Condition 1). Let γ be a successful path in $\Gamma_{i,j}$ and γ' a successful path in $\Gamma_{i,j'}$. The condition $j \equiv j' \Leftrightarrow \Lambda(i,j) \cap \Lambda(i,j') = \emptyset$ of Definition 17 is equivalent to $l(\gamma) = l(\gamma') \Rightarrow j = j'$ (Condition 2). Let $w \in \Sigma^*$ be the label of a successful path γ of $\mathcal{A}$; then we have $l(\gamma) = c(w)$. By consequence, the Condition 1 and the Condition 2 are equivalent. $\qquad\square$

Definition 20. *Let x and y be two symbols in Σ such that $x < y$. Let j and j' be two distinct vertices of Q. The pair (j, j') is said to be a pair of (x, y)-neighbours if there exists a path $\gamma \in \Gamma_{i,j}$ and a path $\gamma' \in \Gamma_{i,j'}$ with respective Parikh-lengths l and l', satisfying the following conditions:*

(1) $l^x = l'^x + 1$ and $l^y = l'^y - 1$,
(2) *For any symbol z different from x and different from y, $l^z = l'^z$.*

Proposition 21. *Let L be a regular language and $\mathcal{A}$ be its minimal automaton. We assume that the state diagram of $\mathcal{A}$ is a strongly connected graph. Then the language L is geometrical if and only if for every pair (j, j') of (x, y)-neighbours the condition $j \cdot y = j' \cdot x$ is satisfied.*

Proof. Let γ be a successful path in $\Gamma_{i,j}$ and γ' be a successful path in $\Gamma_{i,j'}$. Let u (resp. u') be the word in L that is the label of γ (resp. γ'). Since the pair (j, j') is a pair of (x, y)-neighbours we have $c(uy) = c(u'x)$. Let us consider the states k and k' such that $k = j \cdot y$ and $k' = j' \cdot x$. There are two cases where transitions from j by k' and from j' by x have the same effect on the languages L

and $\mathcal{L}(\mathcal{F}(L))$. Case 1: if $k \neq \sigma \wedge k' \neq \sigma$, the words uy and $u'x$ belong to both L and to $\mathcal{L}(\mathcal{F}(L))$. Since $c(uy) = c(u'x)$ we have $k = k'$ in this case. Case 2: if $k = k' = \sigma$, the words uy and $u'x$ do not belong to L nor to $\mathcal{L}(\mathcal{F}(L))$. Otherwise, if for example $k \neq \sigma \wedge k' = \sigma$, the word $u'x$ is in $\mathcal{L}(\mathcal{F}(L))$ but is not in L.   □

In the case of a binary graph, with $\Sigma = \{a, b\}$, Proposition 21 can be simplified as follows. A pair (j, j') is a *pair of neighbours* if there exists a path $\gamma \in \Gamma_{i,j}$ and a path $\gamma' \in \Gamma_{i,j'}$ with respective Parikh-lengths l and l', such that $l^a = l'^a + 1$ and $l^b = l'^b - 1$. The language L is geometrical if and only if for every pair (j, j') of neighbours the condition $j \cdot b = j' \cdot a$ is satisfied.

4.1   Case of Unary Strongly Connected Graphs

Let L be a prefix closed unary regular language and $\mathcal{A}$ be its minimal automaton. Then, if L is an infinite language, we have $L = \Sigma^*$ and the state diagram of $\mathcal{A}$ reduces to a loop. Otherwise, $L = \{\varepsilon, a, aa, \ldots, a^t\}$ for some integer t and the state diagram is made of t components (each of which is reduced to one state). In both cases, the language L is semi-geometrical. Testing whether L is geometrical makes no sense since no vertex has a neighbour.

We now show that the geometry properties of a prefix closed unary regular language L can be characterized on any deterministic automaton $\mathcal{A}$ recognizing L. We assume that the state diagram $\mathcal{G}$ of $\mathcal{A}$ is a strongly connected unary graph.

The period of $\mathcal{C}$ is the integer $p = \gcd(l_1, \ldots, l_r)$. The set Λ (resp. Λ') is the set of lengths of paths in $\Gamma_{i,j}$ (resp. $\Gamma_{i,j'}$). The threshhold h (resp. h') is an integer and Λ^{+h} (resp. $\Lambda'^{+h'}$) is the subset of Λ (resp. Λ') of the lengths that are greater than or equal to h (resp. h'). The path $\gamma_0 \in \Gamma_{i,j'}$ (resp. $\gamma'_0 \in \Gamma_{i,j'}$) is a basic path for the couple (i, j) (resp. (i, j')).

Lemma 22. *Let L be a prefix closed unary regular language and $\mathcal{A}$ be a deterministic automaton recognizing L. We assume that the state diagram of $\mathcal{A}$ is a strongly connected graph. Then the language L is semi-geometrical if and only if its standard partition is trivial.*

Proof. According to Lemma 18, we need only to check compatibility of congruent vertices. Let us show that any two congruent vertices j and j' are not compatible. According to Proposition 14, there exist two integers $h_0 = l_0 + m_0 p$ and $h'_0 = l'_0 + m_0 p$ such that $\Lambda^{+h_0} = \{h_0 + mp \mid m \geq 0\}$ and $\Lambda^{+h'_0} = \{h'_0 + mp \mid m \geq 0\}$. Since h_0 and h'_0 are equal modulo p, it holds that $\Lambda^{+h_0} \cap \Lambda^{+h'_0} \neq \emptyset$. Hence $\Lambda \cap \Lambda' \neq \emptyset$ and thus the two vertices j et j' are not compatible.   □

4.2   Case of d-Ary Strongly Connected Graphs

Semi-Geometrical Test

Proposition 23. *Let L be a regular d-ary language and $\mathcal{A}$ be its minimal automaton. We assume that the state diagram of $\mathcal{A}$ is a strongly connected graph.*

Then the language L is semi-geometrical if and only if for all couple (j, j') of congruent vertices the two following conditions are satisfied :

(1) *Let us consider the following system $\mathcal{S}(j, j')$ of linear Diophantine equations (with coefficients in $\mathbb{N}$ and variables in $\mathbb{Z}$):*

$$(l_0^1, \ldots, l_0^d) + \sum_{1 \leq k \leq r} \alpha_k (l_k^1, \ldots, l_k^d) = (l'^1_0, \ldots, l'^d_0) + \sum_{1 \leq k \leq r} \alpha'_k (l'^1_k, \ldots, l'^d_k)$$

The first condition is that the set of solutions Δ of $\mathcal{S}(j, j')$ is empty.

(2) *The second condition is that $\Lambda_x^{-g_x} \cap \Lambda'^{-g_x}_x = \emptyset$, with for all $x \in \Sigma$, $g_x = \max(h_x, h'_x)$.*

Proof. According to Lemma 18, we only need to check compatibility for couples (j, j') of congruent states.

(1) Let γ (resp. γ') be any path of $\Gamma_{i,j}$ (resp. $\Gamma_{i,j'}$). Let l (resp. l') be the Parikh-length of γ (resp. γ'). Each solution of $\mathcal{S}(j, j')$ is associated to a couple (l, l') such that $l = l'$; however, there may exist couples (l, l'), with $l = l'$, that are not a solution of $\mathcal{S}$. Indeed, according to Proposition 14, for all $x \in \Sigma$, we have $\Lambda_x^{+h_x} \subset \{l^x \mid l^x = l_0^x + \sum_{1 \leq k \leq r} \alpha_k l_k^x\}$. Consequently, $\Lambda^{+h} \subset \{l \mid l = l_0 + \sum_{1 \leq k \leq r} \alpha_k l_k\}$. Similarly it holds that $\Lambda'^{+h'} \subset \{l' \mid l' = l'_0 + \sum_{1 \leq k \leq r} \alpha_k l'_k\}$. Hence the set of couples (l, l') such that the conditions $l \geq h$, $l' \geq h'$ and $l = l'$ are satisfied is a subset of the set of solutions of the system $\mathcal{S}(j, j')$. Thus we have $\Delta = \emptyset \Rightarrow \Lambda^{+h} \cap \Lambda'^{+h'} = \emptyset$.

(2) If for all $x \in \Sigma$, $\Lambda_x^{-g_x} \cap \Lambda'^{-g_x}_x = \emptyset$, then we have $\Lambda^{-h} \cap \Lambda'^{-h'} = \emptyset$. Finally, if the conditions (1) et (2) are satisfied, then it holds that $\Lambda \cap \Lambda' = \emptyset$, which implies that the vertices j et j' are compatible. The reciprocal is straightforward. $\square$

The algorithm for testing semi-geometricty first checks the condition (2), and then, if it is satisfied, solves the system $\mathcal{S}(j, j')$. In the worst case, there are $O(n^2)$ systems to be solved.

Geometricity Test

Proposition 24. *Let L be a regular d-ary language and $\mathcal{A}$ be its minimal automaton. We assume that the state diagram of $\mathcal{A}$ is a strongly connected graph. Let $(j, j', x, y) \in Q \times Q \times \Sigma \times \Sigma$, with $x < y$. Let z be a vector of $\mathbb{N}^d$, with $z_x = 1$, $z_y = -1$ and for all $m \neq x \wedge m \neq y$, $z_m = 0$. Let us consider the following system $\mathcal{S}'(j, j', x, y)$ of linear Diophantine equations:*

$$(l_0^1, \ldots, l_0^d) + \sum_{1 \leq k \leq r} \alpha_k (l_k^1, \ldots, l_k^d) = (l'^1_0, \ldots, l'^d_0) + \sum_{1 \leq k \leq r} \alpha'_k (l'^1_k, \ldots, l'^d_k) + z$$

Then the language L is geometrical if and only if for all (j, j', x, y) with $x < y$, the condition $j \cdot y = j' \cdot x$ is satisfied whenever the set of solutions of the system $\mathcal{S}'(j, j', x, y)$ is nonempty.

Proposition 24 is a straightforward consequence of Proposition 21. There are at most $O(d^2 n^2)$ systems to be solved. In the case of a binary graph, Proposition 24 is simplifed as follows.

Corollary 25. *Let $\Sigma = \{a, b\}$ (with $a < b$) and $(j, j') \in Q \times Q$. Let us consider the following system $\mathcal{S}'(j, j')$ of linear Diophantine equations:*

$$(l_0^1, l_0^2) + \sum_{1 \leq k \leq r} \alpha_k (l_k^1, l_k^2) = (l_0'^1, l_0'^2) + \sum_{1 \leq k \leq r} \alpha_k' (l_k'^1, l_k'^2) + (1, -1)$$

Then the language L is geometrical if and only if for all (j, j'), the condition $j \cdot b = j' \cdot a$ is satisfied whenever the set of solutions of the system $\mathcal{S}'(j, j')$ is nonempty.

Example 26. Let us consider the expression $E = (aab + baa)^*$ over the alphabet $\Sigma = \{a, b\}$. Let us check whether the language $L = \mathrm{Pref}(L(E))$ is semigeometrical or whether it is geometrical. Let $\mathcal{A}$ be the minimal automaton of L (see Figure 2).

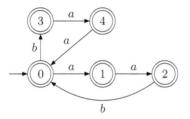

Fig. 2. The minimal automaton of L

The state diagram $\mathcal{G}$ of $\mathcal{A}$ has two cycles $c_1 = 012$ and $c_2 = 034$ such that $l_1 = l_2 = (2, 1)$. The basic paths $\gamma_0(0, j)$, for $1 \leq j \leq 4$, are shown in Table 1.a. The standard partition $\Pi_{\mathcal{G}}$ is shown in Table 1.b.

Table 1. (a) The basic paths $\gamma_0(0, j)$. (b) The standard partition $\Pi_{\mathcal{G}}$.

(a)

j	1	2	3	4
$\gamma_0(0, j)$	a	aa	b	ba
$l(\gamma_0(0, j))$	$(1, 0)$	$(2, 0)$	$(0, 1)$	$(1, 1)$

(b)

$(0, 0)$	$\{2, 3\}$
$(1, 0)$	$\{1, 4\}$

The two systems $\mathcal{S}_{(2,3)}$: $(2, 0) + \alpha_1(2, 1) = (0, 1) + \alpha_2(2, 1)$ and $\mathcal{S}_{(1,4)}$: $(1, 0) + \alpha_1(2, 1) = (0, 1) + \alpha_2(2, 1)$ have no solution. Therefore the states 2 and 3 are compatible and so are the states 1 and 4. Moreover the condition (2) of Proposition 23 is satisfied since for $1 \leq j \leq 4$, the basic path $\gamma_0(0, j)$ has a minimal Parikh-length. By consequence, the language L is semi-geometrical.

The system $\mathcal{S}'_{(1,3)}$: $(1, 0) + \alpha_1(2, 1) = (0, 1) + \alpha_2(2, 1) + (1, -1)$ has a nonempty set of solutions. Moreover $1 \cdot b = \sigma \neq 4 = 3 \cdot a$. By applying Corollary 25, one immediately gets that the language L is not geometrical.

5   Experimental Study

An application has been developed [3] in order to check the new method. Let L be the language to be tested and $\mathcal{A}$ be the minimal automaton of L. Actually, the data is a regular expression denoting L that is converted into a finite automaton; this automaton is then determinized and minimized. Let $\mathcal{G}$ be the state diagram of $\mathcal{A}$. The graph $\mathcal{G}$ is first partitioned into strongly connected components. The method being used thus far is limited to a graph reduced to a unique strongly connected component. Let us assume that $\mathcal{G}$ is reduced to such a graph. The list of the simple cycles of $\mathcal{G}$ is computed, as well as its standard partition. Then, if we consider for example the test of semi-geometricity, for all the couples (j, j') of confluent states, the system $\mathcal{S}(j, j')$ is constructed and given as a data to the algorithms of the Polylib library [26]. As soon as the solver finds a solution for one of these systems, the language L is declared to be not semi-geometrical. A precise analysis of the performance of each step of this method is in progress. Yet, it appears that the resolution of Diophantine equation systems is a greedy step.

6   Conclusion

We have introduced a new method for testing whether a regular language is semi-geometrical or is geometrical. This method will be completed by considering the case of graphs made of several strongly connected components. We intend also to deepen the theoretical relation that exists with the first method [1] as well as with the geometrical solution obtained for the 2-dimensional case. Actually, for both tests, we need not to know the solution itself; we only need to know if there exists a solution. Recent studies address the problem of proving that there is no solution [8,17] and the LinBox library [13] is expected to provide a response to this question. We intend to use this library in our future experiments.

References

1. Blanpain, B., Champarnaud, J.-M., Dubernard, J.P.: Geometrical languages. In: Martin-Vide, C. (ed.) International Conference on Language Theory and Automata (LATA 2007). GRLMC Universitat Rovira I Virgili, vol. 35(07), pp. 127–138 (2007)
2. Brauer, A.: On a problem of partitions. Amer. J. Math. 64, 299–312 (1942)
3. Carpentier, F.: Systèmes d'équations diophantiennes et test de géométricité sur un langage rationnel. Rapport de master, Université de Rouen, France (2008)
4. Champarnaud, J.-M., Dubernard, J.P., Jeanne, H.: Geometricity of binary regular languages. In: Dediu, A.-H., Fernau, H., Martín-Vide, C. (eds.) LATA 2010. LNCS, vol. 6031, pp. 178–189. Springer, Heidelberg (2010)
5. Champarnaud, J.-M., Dubernard, J.P., Jeanne, H.: Regular geometrical languages and tiling the plane. In: Domaratzki, M., Salomaa, K. (eds.) CIAA 2010. LNCS, vol. 6482, pp. 69–78. Springer, Heidelberg (2011)
6. Champarnaud, J.-M., Hansel, G.: Puissances des matrices booléennes. Unsubmitted manuscript, Université de Rouen, France (2005)

7. Chrobak, M.: Finite automata and unary languages. Theor. Comput. Sci. 47(3), 149–158 (1986)
8. d'Alessandro, F., Intrigila, B., Varricchio, S.: On some counting problems for semi-linear sets. CoRR, abs/0907.3005 (2009)
9. Eilenberg, S.: Automata, languages and machines, vol. B. Academic Press, New York (1976)
10. Geldenhuys, J., van der Merwe, B., van Zijl, L.: Reducing nondeterministic finite automata with SAT solvers. In: Yli-Jyrä, A., Kornai, A., Sakarovitch, J., Watson, B. (eds.) FSMNLP 2009. LNCS, vol. 6062, pp. 81–92. Springer, Heidelberg (2010)
11. Geniet, D., Largeteau, G.: WCET free time analysis of hard real-time systems on multiprocessors: A regular language-based model. Theor. Comput. Sci. 388(1-3), 26–52 (2007)
12. Golomb, S.W.: Polyominoes: Puzzles, patterns, problems, and packings. Princeton Academic Press, London (1996)
13. LinBox Group. Linbox project: Exact computational linear algebra (2002), http://www.linalg.org
14. Holladay, J.C., Varga, R.S.: On powers of non negative matrices. Proc. Amer. Math. Soc. 9(4), 631–634 (1958)
15. Kleene, S.: Representation of events in nerve nets and finite automata. Automata Studies 34, 3–41 (1956); Ann. Math. Studies
16. Mordell, L.: Diophantine equations. Academic Press, London (1969)
17. Mulders, T., Storjohann, A.: Certified dense linear system solving. J. Symb. Comput. 37(4), 485–510 (2004)
18. Myhill, J.: Finite automata and the representation of events. WADD TR-57-624, 112–137 (1957)
19. Nerode, A.: Linear automata transformation. Proceedings of AMS 9, 541–544 (1958)
20. Paranthoën, T.: Génération aléatoire et structure des automates à états finis. PhD, Université de Rouen, France (2004)
21. Parikh, R.: On context-free languages. J. ACM 13(4), 570–581 (1966)
22. Robinson, R.W.: Counting strongly connected finite automata. In: Alavi, Y., et al. (eds.) Graph Theory with Applications to Algorithms and Computer Science, pp. 671–685. Wiley, New York (1985)
23. Schrijver, A.: Theory of Linear and Integer Programming. John Wiley and Sons, New York (1986)
24. Tarjan, R.E.: Depth-first search and linear graph algorithms. SIAM J. Comput. 1(2), 146–160 (1972)
25. Tarjan, R.E.: Enumeration of the elementary circuits of a directed graph. SIAM J. Comput. 2, 211–216 (1973)
26. The Polylib Team. Polylib User's Manual. IRISA, France (2002), www.irisa.fr/polylib/doc/

On the Number of Components and Clusters of Non-returning Parallel Communicating Grammar Systems

Erzsébet Csuhaj-Varjú* and György Vaszil

Computer and Automation Research Institute, Hungarian Academy of Sciences
Kende u. 13-17, H-1111 Budapest, Hungary
{csuhaj,vaszil}@sztaki.hu

Abstract. In this paper, we study the size complexity of non-returning parallel communicating grammar systems. First we consider the problem of determining the minimal number of components necessary to generate all recursively enumerable languages. We present a construction which improves the currently known best bounds of seven (with three predefined clusters) and six (in the non-clustered case) to five, in both cases (having four clusters in the clustered variant). We also show that in the case of unary languages four components are sufficient. Then, by defining systems with dynamical clusters, we investigate the minimal number of different query symbols necessary to obtain computational completeness. We prove that for this purpose three dynamical clusters (which means two different query symbols) are sufficient in general, which (although the number of components is higher) can also be interpreted as an improvement in the number of necessary clusters when compared to the case of predefined clusters.

1 Introduction

Due to their theoretical and practical importance, computational models of distributed problem solving systems have been in the focus of interest for a long time. A challenging area of research concerning these systems is to elaborate syntactic frameworks to describe the behavior of communities of communicating agents which cooperate in solving a common problem, where the framework is sufficiently sophisticated but relatively easy to handle. The theory of grammar systems ([8], [3]) offers several constructs for this purpose. One of them is the parallel communicating (PC) grammar system (introduced in [15]), a model for communities of cooperating problem solving agents which communicate with each other by dynamically emerging requests.

In these systems, several grammars perform rewriting steps on their own sentential forms in a synchronized manner until one or more query symbols, that

---

* Also affiliated with the Department of Algorithms and Their Applications, Faculty of Informatics, Eötvös Loránd University, Pázmány Péter sétány 1/c, 1117 Budapest, Hungary.

M. Holzer, M. Kutrib, and G. Pighizzini (Eds.): DCFS 2011, LNCS 6808, pp. 121–134, 2011.

is, special nonterminals corresponding to the components, are introduced in the strings. Then the rewriting process stops and one or more communication steps are performed by substituting all occurrences of the query symbols with the current sentential forms of the component grammars corresponding to the given symbols. Two types of PC grammar systems are distinguished: In the case of returning systems, the queried component returns to its start symbol after the communication and begins to generate a new string. In non-returning systems the components continue the rewriting of their current sentential forms. The language defined by the system is the set of terminal words generated by a dedicated component grammar, the master. In this framework, the grammars represent problem solving agents, the nonterminals open problems to be solved, the query symbols correspond to questions addressed to the agents, and the generated language represents the problem solution. Non-returning systems describe the case when the agent after communication preserves the information obtained so far, while in the case of returning systems, the agent starts its work again from the beginning after communicating information. The reader may notice that the framework of PC grammar systems is also suitable for describing other types of distributed systems, for example, networks with information providing nodes.

During the years, parallel communicating grammar systems have been the objects of a detailed study, which is confirmed by the considerable number of publications in the area. The investigations mainly concentrated on their power and on examining how this power is influenced by changes in their basic characteristics: the way of communication, the synchronization among the components, their way of functioning.

It has been shown that although no explicit context control is given in the framework, returning parallel communicating grammar systems consisting of only five context-free components [6] and non-returning parallel communicating grammar systems consisting of six context-free grammars [7] are able to generate any recursively enumerable language. The results prove that a very few number of simple, but not too simple grammars communicating by dynamically emerging requests is able to reach the power of Turing machines. We note, however, sharp bounds for both types of systems are still objects of investigations.

Throughout the paper, we consider parallel communicating grammar systems with context-free components, and we refer to the returning variants as RPC grammar systems and to the non-returning variants as NPC grammar systems. We note that this notation slightly differs from the customary notations in the literature, we use it to help the legibility.

Returning to the original motivation, namely, to the description of the behavior of communities of problem solving agents, several natural problems arise. One of them is to study systems where clusters or teams of agents represent themselves as separate units in the problem solving process. Notice that this question is also justified by the area of computer-supported team work or cluster computing. The idea of teams has already been introduced in the theory of grammar systems for so-called cooperating distributed (CD) grammar systems and eco-grammar systems, with the meaning that a team is a collection of components which act simultaneously (see [10],[14], [12], [1], [2], [4], [11]).

Inspired by these considerations, in [5] we introduced the notion of a parallel communicating grammar system with clusters of components (a clustered PC grammar system, for short) where instead of individual components, each query symbol refers to a set of components, a (predefined) cluster. Contrary to the original model where any addressee of the issued query is precisely identified, i.e., any query symbol refers to exactly one component, here a cluster is queried, and anyone of its components is allowed to reply. This means that the clusters of components behave as separate units, that is, the individual members of the clusters cannot be distinguished at the systems' level.

Answering the natural question, whether or not the clustered organization implies changes in the properties of PC grammar systems, we studied the generative power of clustered NPC systems. In [5] it was shown that these constructs with only three clusters and seven components are as powerful as Turing machines. Thus, although the number of components does not increase significantly when compared to the non-clustered case, the maximal power can also be obtained with queries to groups of agents instead of queries to precisely identified individuals.

In the present paper we show that any recursively enumerable language can be generated by a clustered NPC grammar system with four (predefined) clusters and five components, thus, there seems to be a trade-off between the number of components and the number of clusters. Although the start point of our proof is the same as that of [7] (and [5]), namely, we simulate two-counter machines, there is no direct tool for distinguishing the members of the clusters during the work of the system, therefore, to select the configurations which correspond steps of the correct simulation extra efforts are needed.

The above results on clustered systems also imply the improvement of the upper bound of the number of components necessary to obtain computational completeness for standard NPC grammar systems from six to five, to the same bound as needed in the case of returning systems.

A natural idea is to examine the case when the clusters are not fixed in advance, as in [5], but formed dynamically in each configuration when query symbols appear. This approach is also motivated by clustered problem solving systems where the clusters are formed according to the (actual) competence levels of the agents. Furthermore, this concept is closely related to the observation that the number of different query symbols which appear in the actual configurations of the system is a significant parameter. If this number is one, then the query may represent a broadcast (any agent who knows the answer may reply), if it is, say k, then k different questions are distributed. Based on these considerations, we introduce the concept of a dynamically clustered PC grammar system, where if the number of query symbols in the actual configuration is k, then at least $k + 1$ clusters are formed non-deterministically (at least one component should belong to a cluster which is not queried).

We show that dynamically clustered NPC grammar systems are as powerful as Turing machines with six components and three clusters. This means that the use of only two different query symbols is sufficient to generate any recursively enumerable language. It is an open question whether systems with only one query symbol are enough to obtain this computational power.

We also deal with the generation of unary languages by clustered NPC grammar systems. In this case only the length of the string, no other information on the structure of the word is given. We show that to generate a recursively enumerable language over a unary alphabet, (clustered) NPC grammar systems with four components (and four predefined clusters) are sufficient. If dynamical clustering is considered, then five components and three dynamical clusters, i.e., two query symbols are enough.

We close the paper with conclusions and some open problems.

2   Preliminaries and Definitions

The reader is assumed to be familiar with the basic notions of formal language theory. The set of non-empty words over an alphabet V is denoted by V^+; the empty word is λ, and $V^* = V^+ \cup \{\lambda\}$. A set $L \subseteq V^*$ is called a language over V. For a word $w \in V^*$ and a set of symbols $A \subseteq V$, we denote the length of w by $|w|$, and the number of occurrences of symbols from A in w by $|w|_A$. If A is a singleton set, i.e., $A = \{a\}$, then we write $|w|_a$ instead of $|w|_{\{a\}}$.

A two-counter machine $M = (\Sigma \cup \{Z, B\}, E, R, q_0, q_F)$, $n \geq 1$, is a 3-tape Turing machine where Σ is an *alphabet*, E is a set of *internal states* with two distinct elements $q_0, q_F \in E$, and R is a set of *transition rules*. The machine has a read-only input tape and two semi-infinite storage tapes. The alphabet of the storage tapes contains only two symbols, Z and B (blank), while the alphabet of the input tape is $\Sigma \cup \{B\}$. The symbol Z is written on the leftmost cell of each storage tape, and may never appear on any other cell. It is scanned initially by the corresponding tape head. An integer t can be stored by moving the tape head t cells to the right of Z. A stored number can be incremented or decremented by moving the tape head right or left. If the symbol scanned by a storage tape head is Z, then the value stored in the corresponding counter is *zero*.

The rule set R contains transition rules of the form $(q, x, c_1, c_2) \rightarrow (q', e_1, e_2)$ where $x \in \Sigma \cup \{B\} \cup \{\lambda\}$ corresponds to the symbol scanned on the input tape in state $q \in E$, and $c_1, c_2 \in \{Z, B\}$ correspond to the symbols scanned on the storage tapes. By a rule of the above form, M enters state $q' \in E$, and the counters are modified according to $e_1, e_2 \in \{-1, 0, +1\}$. If $x \in \Sigma \cup \{B\}$, then the machine scanned x on the input tape, and the head moves one cell to the right; if $x = \lambda$, then the machine performs the transition irrespectively of the scanned input symbol, and the reading head does not move. A word $w \in \Sigma^*$ is accepted by the two-counter machine if starting in the initial state q_0, the input head reaches and reads the rightmost non-blank symbol on the input tape, and the machine is in the accepting state q_F.

Two-counter machines are able to recognize any recursively enumerable language (see [9]).

Remark 1. Without the loss of generality, we may assume for any $(q, x, c_1, c_2) \to (q_F, e_1, e_2) \in R$ that $c_1 = c_2 = Z$ and $e_1 = e_2 = 0$. We also may assume the following: For any transition rule $(q, x, c_1, c_2) \to (r, e_1, e_2) \in R$, if for some $i \in \{1, 2\}$ it holds that $c_i = B$ and $e_i \in \{0, +1\}$, then there exists another transition $(q, x, c'_1, c'_2) \to (r, e_1, e_2) \in R$ such that $c'_i = Z$. To see this consider the following. If there is a transition rule $(q, x, B, c_2) \to (r, e_1, e_2) \in R$ with $e_1 \in \{0, +1\}$, such that there is no $(q, x, Z, c_2) \to (r, e_1, e_2) \in R$, then we can add the new states q', q'' to the state set, modify the rule as $(q, x, B, c_2) \to (q', -1, 0)$, and add the new transition rules $(q', \lambda, B, c_2) \to (q'', +1, 0)$, $(q', \lambda, Z, c_2) \to (q'', +1, 0)$, $(q'', \lambda, B, c_2) \to (r, e_1, e_2)$, $(q'', \lambda, Z, c_2) \to (r, e_1, e_2)$ to the set of transitions.

We also define a variant of the above notion, the notion of a *register machine*. It is a 5-tuple $M = (E, \mathcal{A}, q_0, q_F, R)$, where E is a finite non-empty set of states, $\mathcal{A} = \{A_1, \ldots, A_k\}$, $k \geq 1$, is a set of registers, $q_0, q_F \in E$ are the initial and the final states, respectively, and R is a set of instructions of the forms: $(p, A+, q)$, $(p, A-, q)$, and $(p, A0, q)$ where $p, q \in E, A \in \mathcal{A}$, called an increment, a decrement, and a zero check instruction, respectively. A transition of the register machine consists of updating the number stored in a register and of changing the current state, according to one of the instructions. A zero check $(p, A0, q)$ can only be executed if the register A stores the value zero.

A register machine $M = (E, \mathcal{A}, q_0, q_F, R)$ with k registers, given as above, generates a non-negative integer j if starting from the initial configuration, that is, from the initial state and empty registers, it eventually enters the final state with all registers being empty, except the first one which stores j. For further details on register machines the reader is referred to [13]. It is known that with two registers they can compute all recursively enumerable sets of non-negative integers, that is, the length sets of all recursively enumerable languages over a unary alphabet.

Now we present the notion of a parallel communicating grammar system with (predefined) clusters of components [5], and then we introduce the concept of a dynamically clustered PC grammar system. The original notion of a PC grammar system ([15,3,8]) can be obtained as a special case of the variant with predefined clusters where each component belongs to a different cluster having just one element.

A (context-free) *parallel communicating grammar system* with m *(predefined) clusters* and n components (a *clustered parallel communicating grammar system*) is an $(m + n + 3)$-tuple $\Gamma = (N, K, \Sigma, G_1, \ldots, G_n, \mathcal{C}_1, \ldots, \mathcal{C}_m)$, $n, m \geq 1$, where N is a *nonterminal alphabet*, Σ is a *terminal alphabet*, and $K = \{Q_1, \ldots, Q_m\}$ is an alphabet of *query symbols*. The sets N, Σ, and K are pairwise disjoint; $G_i = (N \cup K, \Sigma, P_i, S_i)$, $1 \leq i \leq n$, called a *component* of Γ, is a context-free grammar with nonterminal alphabet $N \cup K$, terminal alphabet Σ, set of rewriting rules $P_i \subset N \times (N \cup K \cup \Sigma)^*$, and *axiom* (or start symbol) $S_i \in N$. The set $\mathcal{C}_j \subseteq \{G_i \mid 1 \leq i \leq n\}$, $1 \leq j \leq m$, is a *cluster* of components. One of the clusters, $\mathcal{C}_k$, $1 \leq k \leq m$, is distinguished and called the *master cluster* of Γ.

An n-tuple $(x_1, \ldots, x_n)$, where $x_i \in (N \cup \Sigma \cup K)^*$, $1 \leq i \leq n$, is called a *configuration* of Γ; $(S_1, \ldots, S_n)$ is said to be the *initial configuration*. We say that $(x_1, \ldots, x_n)$ *directly derives* $(y_1, \ldots, y_n)$, denoted by $(x_1, \ldots, x_n) \Rightarrow (y_1, \ldots, y_n)$, if one of the following two cases holds:

1. There is no x_i which contains any query symbol, that is, $x_i \in (N \cup \Sigma)^*$ for all $1 \leq i \leq n$. Then, for each i, $1 \leq i \leq n$, $x_i \Rightarrow_{G_i} y_i$ (y_i is obtained from x_i by a direct derivation step in G_i) for $x_i \notin \Sigma^*$ and $x_i = y_i$ for $x_i \in \Sigma^*$.

2. There is some x_i, $1 \leq i \leq n$, which contains at least one occurrence of a query symbol. Then, for each x_i, $1 \leq i \leq n$, with $|x_i|_K \neq 0$ we write $x_i = z_1 Q_{i_1} z_2 Q_{i_2} \ldots z_t Q_{i_t} z_{t+1}$, where $z_j \in (N \cup \Sigma)^*$, $1 \leq j \leq t+1$, and $Q_{i_l} \in K$, $1 \leq l \leq t$. If for all l, $1 \leq l \leq t$, and for every sentential form x_k of G_k, $1 \leq k \leq n$, $G_k \in C_{i_l}$, it holds that $|x_k|_K = 0$, then $y_i = z_1 x_{i_1} z_2 x_{i_2} \ldots z_t x_{i_t} z_{t+1}$ where $x_{i_l} \in \{x_k \mid G_k \in C_{i_l}\}$, that is, any one of the components in the queried cluster is allowed to reply if none of the current sentential forms of the components in the cluster contains a query symbol. Furthermore, (a) in *returning* systems $y_{i_l} = S_{i_l}$, while (b) in *non-returning* systems $y_{i_l} = x_{i_l}$, $1 \leq l \leq t$. If on the other hand, for some l, $1 \leq l \leq t$, there is a $G_k \in C_{i_l}$, $1 \leq k \leq n$, such that $|x_k|_K \neq 0$ then $y_{i_l} = x_{i_l}$. For all i', $1 \leq i' \leq n$, for which y'_i is not specified above, $y'_i = x'_i$.

A clustered RPC or NPC grammar system works in the h (*homogeneous*) communication mode, if the same (non-deterministically chosen) component in C_j replies to all queries $Q_j \in K$, $1 \leq j \leq m$ appearing in a given configuration, i.e., for $Q_{i_h} = Q_{i_g}$, $1 \leq g, h \leq t$, above, both Q_{i_h} and Q_{i_g} are replaced with x_{i_h}, where $|x_{i_h}|_K = 0$ and x_{i_h} is the sentential form of $G_k \in C_{i_h}$ for some k, $1 \leq k \leq n$.

For a fixed i, $1 \leq i \leq n$, let the language $L(G_i)$ generated by the component G_i be defined as $L(G_i) = \{x \in \Sigma^* \mid (S_1, \ldots, S_i, \ldots, S_n) \Rightarrow^* (x_1, \ldots, x_i, \ldots, x_n)$ for some $x_1, \ldots, x_n \in (N \cup \Sigma \cup K)^*$ such that $x = x_i\}$ where $\Rightarrow^*$ denote the reflexive and transitive closure of $\Rightarrow$. The *language generated* by Γ is $\bigcup_{G_i \in C_j} L(G_i)$ where C_j is the master cluster of Γ for some j, $1 \leq j \leq m$.

A (context-free) *parallel communicating grammar system* with n components and *dynamic clusters* (a *dynamically clustered parallel communicating grammar system*) is an $(n+3)$-tuple $\Gamma = (N, K, \Sigma, G_1, \ldots, G_n)$, $n \geq 1$, where N, Σ, and $G_i, 1 \leq i \leq n$ are defined as in the case of clustered parallel communicating grammar systems above, the set of query symbols, however, is $K \subseteq \{Q_1, \ldots, Q_n\}$, and instead of a master cluster, a master component is given.

The rewriting steps are defined in the same way as above, the communication steps, however, are performed differently. If k different query symbols appear in a configuration, $Q_1, \ldots, Q_k$, $k \geq 1$, then the components are grouped into l arbitrary clusters, $C_1, \ldots, C_l$, in such a way that $l \geq k$, and there is no component in C_i with Q_i occurring in its sentential form for any $1 \leq i \leq k$. Then each cluster C_i corresponds to the query symbol Q_i in the sense that Q_i can be replaced by the sentential forms of one of the components from the cluster C_i.

More formally, we say that a configuration $c = (x_1, \ldots, x_n)$ *directly derives* the configuration $c' = (y_1, \ldots, y_n)$ by a communication step, if there is some x_i, $1 \leq i \leq n$, which contains at least one occurrence of a query symbol. Let

$K_c = \{Q \in K \mid |x_i|_Q \geq 1, 1 \leq i \leq n\}$, and let $k = |K_c|$, that is, let k be the number of different query symbols occurring in the configuration c. Let also $\mathcal{C}_j \subseteq \{G_1, \ldots, G_n\}$, $1 \leq j \leq l$ for some $l \geq k$, such that $\bigcup_{1 \leq j \leq l} \mathcal{C}_j = \{G_1, \ldots, G_n\}$ and for $j_1 \neq j_2$, $\mathcal{C}_{j_1} \cap \mathcal{C}_{j_2} = \emptyset$, and moreover, for all $1 \leq s \leq n$ and $G_s \in \mathcal{C}_j$ it holds that $|x_s|_{Q_j} = 0$.

Then, we write $x_i = z_1 Q_{i_1} z_2 Q_{i_2} \ldots z_t Q_{i_t} z_{t+1}$ for each x_i, $1 \leq i \leq n$, with $|x_i|_K \neq 0$ where $z_j \in (N \cup \Sigma)^*$, $1 \leq j \leq t+1$, and $Q_{i_m} \in K_c$, $1 \leq m \leq t$. If for all i_m, $1 \leq m \leq t$, and for every sentential form x_s of $G_s \in \mathcal{C}_{i_m}$, $1 \leq s \leq n$, it holds that $|x_s|_K = 0$, then $y_i = z_1 x_{i_1} z_2 x_{i_2} \ldots z_t x_{i_t} z_{t+1}$ where $x_{i_l} \in \{x_s \mid G_s \in \mathcal{C}_{i_m}\}$, that is, each cluster is assigned to the corresponding query symbol and any of the components in the assigned cluster is allowed to reply if none of the current sentential forms of the components of the cluster contains a query symbol.

Furthermore, (a) in *returning* systems $y_{i_m} = S_{i_m}$, while (b) in *non-returning* systems $y_{i_m} = x_{i_m}$, $1 \leq m \leq t$. If on the other hand, for some m, $1 \leq m \leq t$, there is a $G_s \in \mathcal{C}_{i_m}$, $1 \leq s \leq n$, such that $|x_s|_K \neq 0$ then $y_{i_m} = x_{i_m}$. For all i', $1 \leq i' \leq n$, for which y_i' is not specified above, $y_i' = x_i'$. The h (*homogeneous*) communication mode is defined in the same way as in the case of predefined clusters.

Unlike in the case of predefined (static) clustering, we require here that the clusters are disjoint, otherwise any query symbol could always be replaced by any query free sentential form.

The *language generated* by Γ is $L(G_i)$ where G_i is the master component.

Let the class of languages generated in the homogeneous communication mode by context-free RPC and NPC grammar systems having at most m predefined clusters and n components, $n \geq m \geq 1$, be denoted by $\mathcal{L}(RPC_{m/n}CF)$ and $\mathcal{L}(NPC_{m/n}CF)$, respectively. If $m = n$ then we put n in the subscript instead of n/n. Let also $\mathcal{L}(X_*CF) = \bigcup_{i,j \geq 1} \mathcal{L}(X_{i/j}CF)$, $X \in \{RPC, NPC\}$. If the clusters are formed dynamically, then we use $DRPC$ and $DNPC$ instead of RPC and NPC, respectively.

If the families of context-free languages and recursively enumerable languages are denoted by $\mathcal{L}(CF)$ and $\mathcal{L}(RE)$, respectively, then we can summarize the results obtained so far on the generative power of context-free RPC and NPC grammar systems as follows (for details, see [3,6,7,8,5]). For $X \in \{RPC, NPC\}$,

$$\mathcal{L}(CF) \subset \mathcal{L}(X_2 CF) \subseteq \mathcal{L}(RPC_5 CF) = \mathcal{L}(RPC_* CF) =$$
$$\mathcal{L}(NPC_6 CF) = \mathcal{L}(NPC_{3/7} CF) = \mathcal{L}(NPC_* CF) = \mathcal{L}(RE).$$

3   The Number of Components and Clusters

Now we show that every recursively enumerable language can be generated by a context-free clustered NPC grammar system with five components and four predefined (static) clusters or six components with three dynamical clusters, that is, with two different query symbols.

Theorem 2. $\mathcal{L}(NPC_{4/5} CF) = \mathcal{L}(RE)$ and $\mathcal{L}(DNPC_{3/6} CF) = \mathcal{L}(RE)$.

Proof. Let $L \in \mathcal{L}(RE)$ over an alphabet Σ, and let $M = (\Sigma \cup \{Z, B\}, E, R, q_0, q_F)$ be a two-counter machine with $L(M) = L$. We assume that M satisfies the properties described in Remark 1.

Let us define $\mathcal{I} = \{[q, x, c_1, c_2, q', e_1, e_2] \mid (q, x, c_1, c_2) \to (q', e_1, e_2) \in R\}$, and let us introduce for any $\alpha = [q, x, c_1, c_2, q', e_1, e_2] \in \mathcal{I}$ the following notation: $State(\alpha) = q$, $Read(\alpha) = x$, $NextState(\alpha) = q'$, and $Store(\alpha, i) = c_i$, $Action(\alpha, i) = e_i$, where $i = 1, 2$. We also define for $c', c'' \in \{B, Z\}$ subsets of $\mathcal{I}$ as $\mathcal{I}_{(c', c'')} = \{\alpha \in \mathcal{I} \mid \alpha = [q, x, c', c'', q', e_1, e_2]\}$. We construct clustered NPC grammar systems generating L by simulating the transitions of M.

For the first equality, let $\Gamma = (N, K, \Sigma, G_{sel}, G_{c_1}, G_{c_2}, G_{ch}, G_{gen}, \mathcal{C}_1, \ldots, \mathcal{C}_4)$, where $G_\gamma = (N \cup K, \Sigma, P_\gamma, S)$, $\gamma \in \{sel, c_1, c_2, gen, ch\}$ is a component grammar, and $\mathcal{C}_4$ is the master cluster.

Let $N = \mathcal{I} \cup \{D_{i,\alpha}, E_{i,\alpha}, H_{i,\alpha}, H_{i,\alpha,j}, X_{i,\alpha,j} \mid \alpha \in \mathcal{I}, 1 \leq i \leq 3, 1 \leq j \leq 2\} \cup \{F_{c,i,j}, F_{gen,j}, F_{ch,j} \mid 1 \leq i \leq 2, 1 \leq j \leq 5\} \cup \{S, A, F, C_1, C_2, C_3, W_1, W_2\}$.

The simulation is based on representing the states and the transitions of M with nonterminals from $\mathcal{I}$ and the values of the counters by strings of nonterminals containing as many symbols A as the value stored in the given counter.

Let the clusters and the rule sets of the components be defined as follows. Let $\mathcal{C}_1 = \{G_{sel}\}$, and let

$$P_{sel} = \{S \to \alpha \mid \alpha \in \mathcal{I}, State(\alpha) = q_0\} \cup \{F \to F_{sel}, F_{sel} \to F_{sel}\} \cup$$
$$\{\alpha \to D_{1,\alpha}, D_{1,\alpha} \to D_{2,\alpha}, D_{2,\alpha} \to D_{3,\alpha} \mid \alpha \in \mathcal{I}\} \cup$$
$$\{D_{3,\alpha} \to \beta \mid \alpha, \beta \in \mathcal{I}, NextState(\alpha) = State(\beta)\} \cup$$
$$\{D_{3,\alpha} \to F \mid \alpha \in \mathcal{I}, NextState(\alpha) = q_F\}.$$

This component selects the transition of M to be simulated. The axiom, S, introduces a symbol denoting an initial transition, when symbol F appears, then the simulation of the last transition has been finished.

Next we define $\mathcal{C}_2 = \{G_{c_1}, G_{c_2}\}$. Let for $i \in \{1, 2\}$,

$$P_{c_i} = \{S \to Q_1 W_i, F \to F_{c,i,1}, F_{c,i,3} \to F_{c,i,3}, F_{c,i,j} \to F_{c,i,j+1} \mid 1 \leq j \leq 2\} \cup$$
$(1, i)$ $\{\alpha \to X_{1,\alpha,i}, X_{1,\alpha,i} \to X_{2,\alpha,i}, X_{2,\alpha,i} \to y_{\alpha,i}, A \to Q_1 \mid \alpha \in \mathcal{I},$
       $Store(\alpha, i) = B, y_{\alpha,i} = \sigma(Action(\alpha, i), B)\} \cup$
$(2, i)$ $\{\alpha \to H_{1,\alpha,i}, H_{1,\alpha,i} \to H_{2,\alpha,i}, H_{2,\alpha,i} \to H_{3,\alpha,i}, H_{3,\alpha,i} \to y_{\alpha,i} Q_1 \mid \alpha \in \mathcal{I},$
       $Store(\alpha, i) = Z, y_{\alpha,i} = \sigma(Action(\alpha, i), Z)\},$

where $\sigma : \{1, 0, -1\} \times \{B, Z\} \to \{\lambda, A, AA\}$ is a partial mapping defined as $\sigma(1, B) = AA$, $\sigma(0, B) = \sigma(1, Z) = A$, and $\sigma(-1, B) = \sigma(0, Z) = \lambda$.

These components simulate the change in the contents of the counters which is represented by a string consisting of as many letters A as the actual stored number in the counter. Let $\mathcal{C}_3 = \{G_{ch}\}$, and let

$P_{ch} = \{S \to Q_1\} \cup$
(3) $\{\alpha \to E_{1,\alpha}, E_{1,\alpha} \to Q_2, H_{2,\alpha,1} \to Q_2, H_{3,\alpha,2} \to Q_1 \mid \alpha \in \mathcal{I}_{(Z,Z)}\} \cup$
(4) $\{\alpha \to E_{1,\alpha}, E_{1,\alpha} \to E_{2,\alpha}, E_{2,\alpha} \to Q_2, H_{3,\alpha,1} \to Q_1 \mid \alpha \in \mathcal{I}_{(Z,B)}\} \cup$

(5) $\{\alpha \to E_{1,\alpha}, E_{1,\alpha} \to E_{2,\alpha}, E_{2,\alpha} \to Q_2, H_{3,\alpha,2} \to Q_1 \mid \alpha \in \mathcal{I}_{(B,Z)}\} \cup$

(6) $\{\alpha \to E_{1,\alpha}, E_{1,\alpha} \to E_{2,\alpha}, E_{2,\alpha} \to E_{3,\alpha}, E_{3,\alpha} \to Q_1 \mid \alpha \in \mathcal{I}_{(B,B)}\} \cup$

(7) $\{F \to F_{ch,1}, F_{ch,4} \to F_{ch,4}\} \cup \{F_{ch,j} \to F_{ch,j+1} \mid 1 \le j \le 3\}.$

This component assists in checking whether the respective counter is zero if it is required by the transition to be performed. This is done by requesting the string of component G_{c_1} and/or G_{c_2} from $\mathcal{C}_2$. If the obtained string represents an empty counter, then it must not have an occurrence of A.

Finally, we define $\mathcal{C}_4 = \{G_{gen}\}$, and

$$P_{gen} = \{S \to Q_1, C_1 \to C_2, C_2 \to C_3, C_3 \to Q_1\} \cup$$
$$\{\alpha \to xC_1 \mid \alpha \in \mathcal{I}, Read(\alpha) = x\} \cup$$
$$(8) \quad \{F \to Q_2, F_{c,1,1} \to Q_2, F_{c,2,2} \to Q_3, F_{ch,3} \to \lambda, W_1 \to \lambda, W_2 \to \lambda\}.$$

This component generates the string accepted by the counter machine by adding the symbol $x = Read(\alpha)$ for each $\alpha \in \mathcal{I}$ (chosen by the selector component G_{sel}) using the rule $\alpha \to xC_1$.

Next we discuss the work of Γ in more detail. After the first rewriting step and the following communication, we obtain a configuration $(\alpha, \alpha W_1, \alpha W_2, \alpha, \alpha)$, where $State(\alpha) = q_0$, and then Γ simulates the transition corresponding to α.

To see how the simulation is done, let us consider a configuration of the form $(\alpha, u_1 \alpha u_2 W_1, v_1 \alpha v_2 W_2, \bar{z}_1 \alpha \bar{z}_2, w\alpha)$ where $u_1 u_2, v_1 v_2 \in \{A\}^*$, $\bar{z}_1 \bar{z}_2 \in \{W_1, W_2\}^*$, and $w \in \Sigma^*$. Suppose that up to transition α the simulation of the work of M was correct, that is, $State(\alpha)$ corresponds to the state of M, w corresponds to the string read by M, and $u_1 u_2, v_1 v_2$ contain the same number of As as stored on the counter tapes of M. Depending on c_1 and c_2 in $\alpha = [q, x, c_1, c_2, q', e_1, e_2]$, we discuss the next steps of Γ separately.

Let $\alpha = [q, x, B, Z, q', e_1, e_2] \in \mathcal{I}$, where $x \in \Sigma \cup \{\lambda\}$, $q, q' \in E$, and $e_1 \in \{-1, 0, +1\}$, $e_2 \in \{0, +1\}$. Furthermore, let $\beta \in \mathcal{I}$ with $NextState(\alpha) = State(\beta)$.

In the next rewriting step, α changes to $D_{1,\alpha}$ at component G_{sel}, then in the second and third rewriting steps, $D_{1,\alpha}$ to $D_{2,\alpha}$, $D_{2,\alpha}$ to $D_{3,\alpha}$. Similarly, $w\alpha$ at G_{gen} changes to wxC_1, then to wxC_2, and finally wxC_3, where $x = Read(\alpha)$.

Let us examine now $u_1 \alpha u_2 W_1$ which represents the contents of the first counter. If $e_1 = -1$, then due to the simulated transition, the counter must store a non-negative integer, $u_1 u_2$ should have at least one occurrence of A. If this is not the case, then the rule $A \to Q_1$ in $(1,1)$ cannot be applied since $y_{\alpha,1} = \lambda$. Thus, after the third step, the derivation is blocked since there is no rule to be applied.

If $e_1 \in \{0, +1\}$, then $y_{\alpha,1} \in \{A, AA\}$, which means that the derivation can also continue in the case when u does not contain any symbol A. The simulation remains correct, however, as we have assumed that $\alpha = [q, x, B, Z, q', e_1, e_2]$ for $e_1 \in \{0, +1\}$ implies that $\alpha' = [q, x, Z, Z, q', e_1, e_2]$ is also a possible transition (see Remark 1).

If the derivation is not blocked, then after three rewriting steps performed on $u_1 \alpha u_2 W_1$ and the communication following them, the next cases may hold: The only nonterminal in the new sentential form is W_1 (rules $\alpha \to X_{1,\alpha,1}$, $X_{1,\alpha,1} \to$

$X_{2,\alpha,1}$, and $X_{2,\alpha,1} \to y_{\alpha,1}$ were applied) or an occurrence of $D_{j,\alpha}$, $1 \le j \le 3$, is in the new string (rule $A \to Q_1$ was applied). Since symbols $D_{j,\alpha}$ cannot be erased in the further derivation steps from the string sent at the end of the derivation to the component G_{gen}, Γ can generate a terminal word only if no occurrence of A is rewritten in the first three steps. Therefore, after the fourth rewriting step starting from $u_1 \alpha u_2 W_1$, we must have a string of the form $u_1' Q_1 u_2' W_1$ where $u_1' A u_2' = u_1 y_{\alpha,1} u_2$ and $y_{\alpha,1}$ corresponds to $e_1 = Action(\alpha, 1)$ for $\alpha = [q, x, B, Z, q', e_1, e_2]$ as follows: if $e_1 = -1$, then $y_{\alpha,1} = \lambda$, if $e_1 = 0$, then $y_{\alpha,1} = A$, if $e_1 = +1$, then $y_{\alpha,1} = AA$.

Let us consider now $v_1 \alpha v_2 W_2$, i.e., the string representing the contents of the second counter. In this case, $v_1 v_2$ must not have any occurrence of A. If this is the case, then only the rules in $(2, 2)$ can be applied. After the third rewriting step, the new string will be of the form $v_1 H_{3,\alpha,2} v_2 W_2$ which will be forwarded to component G_{ch} (this is guaranteed by the rules of G_{ch}) and stored there until the end of the derivation when it is sent to G_{gen} in the master cluster $\mathcal{C}_4$. Since G_{gen} does not have rules for erasing As, terminal words can only be generated if G_{ch} received a string representing an empty counter. Notice that G_{c_1} and G_{c_2} are in the same cluster, so G_{ch} might receive the sentential form of any of them. However, if a string not containing $H_{3,\alpha,2}$, i.e., the string of G_{c_1} is forwarded to G_{ch}, then the derivation is blocked, since G_{ch} cannot continue its work.

Assume now that $v_1 v_2$ contains at least one copy of A. Then, after three rewriting steps the following cases may appear: No occurrence of A is rewritten, thus the obtained string, $v_1 H_{3,\alpha,2} v_2 W_2$, contains at least one A. In this case no terminal word can be generated, as we discussed before. If at least one occurrence of A is rewritten, then at least one of the symbols $D_{j,\alpha}$, $1 \le j \le 3$, is introduced in the string. This case leads to a blocking situation, since the string is sent to G_{ch} which has no rule for continuing the rewriting.

Thus, the string obtained from $v_1 \alpha v_2 W_2$ after the fourth rewriting step must be $y_{\alpha,2} Q_1 W_2$, where $y_{\alpha,2}$ corresponds to $e_2 = Action(\alpha, 2)$. Since no A could be deleted, $y_{\alpha,2} = \lambda$ if $e_2 = 0$, and $y_{\alpha,2} = A$ if $e_2 = +1$ (the case $e_2 = -1$ is not applicable, since the counter stores zero, $Store(\alpha, 2) = Z$).

Continuing the derivation, the prescribed communication step results in the configuration $(\beta, u_1' \beta u_2' W_1, v' \beta W_2, z_1' \beta z_2', w' \beta)$ where $u_1' u_2', v', \in \{A\}^*$, $z_1' z_2' \in \{W_1, W_2\}^*$, $w' \in T^*$, and $\beta \in \mathcal{I}$ is a transition with $NextState(\alpha) = State(\beta)$. Now, similarly as above, the simulation of the transition corresponding to the symbol $\beta \in \mathcal{I}$ can be performed.

It is easy to see that the case $\alpha = [q, x, Z, B, q', e_1, e_2]$ can be treated in the same way, with changing the discussion concerning components G_{c_1} and G_{c_2}. If $\alpha = [q, x, B, B, q', e_1, e_2]$, then we use the same reasoning for G_{c_2} as we did for G_{c_1} above. The case $\alpha = [q, x, Z, Z, q', e_1, e_2]$ can be obtained similarly: The simulation can proceed if the sentential form of G_{ch} contains $H_{2,\alpha,1}$ after the second, and $H_{3,\alpha,2}$ after the third derivation step, and has no occurrence of A.

Now we discuss how the derivation terminates. Suppose that $NextState(\alpha) = q_F$ and G_{sel} changes the nonterminal $D_{3,\alpha}$ to F. Then, in the next four derivation steps the sentential forms of G_{c_1}, G_{c_2}, and G_{ch} are forwarded to component

G_{gen} in this order, or the derivation is blocked. The simulation is successful, if by erasing $F_{ch,3}$ and applying rules $W_1 \to \lambda$ and $W_2 \to \lambda$ as many times as necessary, G_{gen} obtains a terminal word.

Thus, we have shown that $\mathcal{L}(NPC_{4/5}CF) \supseteq \mathcal{L}(RE)$. Since due to the Church thesis, $\mathcal{L}(NPC_{4/5}CF) \subseteq \mathcal{L}(RE)$ holds as well, we proved the result.

For the second equality, let $\Gamma = (N, K, \Sigma, G_{sel}, G_{c_1}, G_{c_2}, G_{ch}, G_{ass}, G_{gen})$, where the components are $G_\gamma = (N \cup K, \Sigma, P_\gamma, S)$, $\gamma \in \{sel, c_1, c_2, ch, ass, gen\}$, and G_{gen} is the master grammar. Let $N = N' \cup \{F_{ass}\}$ where N' contains the same symbols as the nonterminals of the system above. Let $K = \{Q_1, Q_2\}$ and let us define the sets of productions $P_{sel}, P_{c_1}, P_{c_2}, P_{ch}, P_{gen}$ exactly as in the previous case. The rules of the newly added assistant component are as follows.

$$P_{ass} = \{S \to Q_1, \alpha \to Q_1, D_{1,\alpha} \to Q_1, D_{2,\alpha} \to Q_1, D_{3,\alpha} \to Q_1 \mid \alpha \in \mathcal{I}\} \cup$$
$$\{F \to F_{ass}, F_{ass} \to F_{ass}\}.$$

The dynamically clustered NPC system Γ works very similarly to the system with the predefined clusters. The newly added component G_{ass} has rewriting rules only for the sentential forms of G_{sel}, thus, when it introduces in each rewriting step the query symbol Q_1, it makes sure that all occurring symbols Q_1 have to be assigned to a dynamically formed cluster $\mathcal{C}_1$ which contains G_{sel}, and moreover, all occurring symbols Q_1 have to be replaced by the sentential form of G_{sel}. (Note that Γ works in the homogeneous communication mode.)

It is left to the reader to check that this is sufficient to see that Γ also simulates the work of the two-counter machine M and also to show that the reverse inclusion, for the equality, holds.

As (static) clustered NPC grammar systems are special cases of non-clustered systems, that is, $\mathcal{L}(NPC_n CF) = \mathcal{L}(NPC_{n/n} CF)$ by definition, Theorem 2 also implies an improvement of the currently known best bound (six) on the number of components of non-clustered NPC grammar systems.

Corollary 3. $\mathcal{L}(NPC_5 CF) = \mathcal{L}(RE)$.

Proof. Notice that for any $n \geq k$, $\mathcal{L}(NPC_{k/n} CF) \subseteq \mathcal{L}(NPC_{n/n} CF)$. To see this, consider a clustered NPC grammar system with n components and k clusters where $n > k$, and consider a modified system with n clusters which are formed from the n components and with each rule introducing queries being replaced by several rules in the following way: if $\mathcal{C}_i = \{G_{i_1}, \ldots, G_{i_k}\}$ is a cluster, then any rule $X \to uQ_i v$ is replaced with the rules $X \to uQ_{i_1} v, \ldots, X \to uQ_{i_k} v$. (If more than one query symbols are present, then all possible combinations are added.)

4   Unary Languages

Let $\mathcal{L}(NRE)$ denote the class of recursively enumerable languages over unary alphabets.

Theorem 4. $\mathcal{L}(\mathrm{NRE}) \subseteq \mathcal{L}(NPC_4CF)$ *and* $\mathcal{L}(\mathrm{NRE}) \subseteq \mathcal{L}(DNPC_{3/5}CF)$.

Proof. Let $L \in \mathcal{L}(\mathrm{NRE})$ over a unary alphabet $\Sigma = \{a\}$, and consider the register machine $M = (E, \mathcal{A}, q_0, q_F, R)$ with two registers $\mathcal{A} = \{A_1, A_2\}$ and with $L(M) = L$. Let us define the set of symbols $\mathcal{I}$ as follows.

$$
\begin{aligned}
\mathcal{I} = \ & \{[q, c_1, c_2; 0, +1, q'] \mid (q, A_2+, q') \in R, \ c_1, c_2 \in \{B, Z\}\} \cup \\
& \{[q, c_1, c_2; +1, 0, q'] \mid (q, A_1+, q') \in R, \ c_1, c_2 \in \{B, Z\}\} \cup \\
& \{[q, c_1, B; 0, -1, q'] \mid (q, A_2-, q') \in R, \ c_1 \in \{B, Z\}\} \cup \\
& \{[q, B, c_2; -1, 0, q'] \mid (q, A_1-, q') \in R, \ c_2 \in \{B, Z\}\} \cup \\
& \{[q, Z, c_2; 0, 0, q'] \mid (q, A_10, q') \in R, \ c_2 \in \{B, Z\}\} \cup \\
& \{[q, c_1, Z; 0, 0, q'] \mid (q, A_20, q') \in R, \ c_1 \in \{B, Z\}\}.
\end{aligned}
$$

Analogously to the previous proof, we also introduce for any $\alpha \in \mathcal{I}$ with $\alpha = [q, c_1, c_2; e_1, e_2, q']$, the notations: $State(\alpha) = q$, $NextState(\alpha) = q'$, $Store(\alpha, i) = c_i$, $Action(\alpha, i) = e_i$, where $i = 1, 2$, and we also define for $c', c'' \in \{B, Z\}$ subsets of $\mathcal{I}$ as $\mathcal{I}_{(c', c'')} = \{\alpha \in \mathcal{I} \mid \alpha = [q, c', c''; , e_1, e_2, q']\}$. To prove the first inclusion, we construct a clustered NPC grammar system generating L by simulating the transitions of M.

Let $\Gamma = (N, K, \Sigma, G_{sel}, G_{c_1}, G_{c_2}, G_{ch}, \mathcal{C}_{sel}, \mathcal{C}_{c_1}, \mathcal{C}_{c_2}, \mathcal{C}_{ch})$, where $G_\gamma = (N \cup K, \Sigma, P_\gamma, S)$, $\gamma \in \{sel, c_1, c_2, ch\}$ are the component grammars, and $\mathcal{C}_\gamma = \{G_\gamma\}$ are the clusters, $\mathcal{C}_{sel}$ is the master cluster. The construction of Γ is similar to the one found in the proof of Theorem 2. Let $N = \mathcal{I} \cup \{D_{i,\alpha}, E_{i,\alpha}, H_{i,\alpha}, H_{i,\alpha,j}, X_{i,\alpha,j} \mid \alpha \in \mathcal{I}, 1 \leq i \leq 3, 1 \leq j \leq 2\} \cup \{S, A_1, A_2, F, F_{sel}, F_{c,1}, F_{ch}, W_1, W_2\}$.

The states and the transitions of M are represented with nonterminals from $\mathcal{I}$, the values of the counters by strings of nonterminals containing as many symbols A_i, as the value stored in the counter c_i, $1 \leq i \leq 2$.

Let the components of Γ be defined as follows.

$$
P_{sel} = P'_{sel} \cup \{F_{sel} \rightarrow Q_{c_2}Q_{ch}, W_1 \rightarrow \lambda, W_2 \rightarrow \lambda, F_{ch} \rightarrow \lambda, F_{c_1} \rightarrow \lambda\}
$$

where P'_{sel} contains the same rules as the set P_{sel} in the proof of Theorem 2. Let

$$
P_{c_1} = P'_{c_1} \cup \{F \rightarrow F_{c,1}, F_{c,1} \rightarrow F_{c,1}\}, \quad P_{c_2} = P'_{c_2} \cup \{F \rightarrow Q_{c_1}, A_1 \rightarrow a, F_{c,1} \rightarrow F_{c,1}\}
$$

where for $i \in \{1, 2\}$,

$$
\begin{aligned}
P'_{c_i} = \ & \{\alpha \rightarrow X_{1,\alpha,i}, X_{1,\alpha,i} \rightarrow X_{2,\alpha,i}, X_{2,\alpha,i} \rightarrow y_{\alpha,i}, A_i \rightarrow Q_{sel} \mid \alpha \in \mathcal{I}, \\
& Store(\alpha, i) = B, y_{\alpha,i} = \sigma(Action(\alpha, i), B, i)\} \cup \\
& \{\alpha \rightarrow H_{1,\alpha,i}, H_{1,\alpha,i} \rightarrow H_{2,\alpha,i}, H_{2,\alpha,i} \rightarrow H_{3,\alpha,i}, H_{3,\alpha,i} \rightarrow y_{\alpha,i}Q_{sel} \mid \alpha \in \mathcal{I}, \\
& Store(\alpha, i) = Z, y_{\alpha,i} = \sigma(Action(\alpha, i), Z, i)\} \cup \{S \rightarrow Q_{sel}W_i\},
\end{aligned}
$$

with $\sigma : \{1, 0, -1\} \times \{B, Z\} \times \{1, 2\} \rightarrow \{\lambda, A_1, A_2, A_1A_1, A_2A_2\}$ is a partial mapping defined as $\sigma(1, B, i) = A_iA_i$, $\sigma(0, B, i) = \sigma(1, Z, i) = A_i$, and $\sigma(-1, B, i) = \sigma(0, Z, i) = \lambda$, $i \in \{1, 2\}$.

These components simulate the change in the contents of the counters as in the case of the proof of Theorem 2, the only difference being that for the representation of the two registers A_1 and A_2, they use two different symbols, A_1 and A_2, respectively.

Let also $P_{ch} = P'_{ch} \cup \{F \rightarrow F_{ch}, F_{ch} \rightarrow F_{ch}\}$ where P'_{ch} contains the rules of P_{ch} from the proof of Theorem 2 with the exception of the rules (7).

The simulation of M is also done in a similar way. After the initial rewriting step and the following communication, a configuration $(\alpha_0, \alpha_0 W_1, \alpha_0 W_2, \alpha_0)$ is obtained where $\alpha_0 \in \mathcal{I}$ corresponds to a transition with $State(\alpha_0) = q_0$.

Then a computation is simulated by executing the transitions corresponding to the chosen symbols from $\mathcal{I}$, and eventually $(F, u_1 F u_2 W_1, v_1 F v_2 W_2, zF)$ is reached, a configuration which corresponds to a final configuration of M, that is, if the simulation was correct, then $u_1 u_2 = A_1^j$ for some $j \geq 0$ stores the value j computed by M, $v_1 v_2 = \lambda$, and $z \in \{W_1, W_2\}^*$. The checking of the correctness of the simulation and the generation of the terminal string a^j is done by entering the configuration $(F_{sel}, u_1 F_{c,1} u_2 W_1, v_1 Q_{c_1} v_2 W_2, z F_{ch})$, and then after performing the communication $(F_{sel}, u_1 F_{c,1} u_2 W_1, v_1 u_1 F_{c,1} u_2 W_1 v_2 W_2, z F_{ch})$. Now, the symbols A_1 in $u_1 u_2$ are changed to a by the rule of P_{c_2}, and then the resulting string is transferred to G_{sel} together with the sentential form of G_{ch}. If erasing the nonterminals $W_1, W_2, F_{ch}, F_{c,1}$ results in a terminal string a^j, then the simulation of M computing the value j was correct.

For the second inclusion, we modify this construction similarly to the second part of the proof of Theorem 2. Let $\Gamma = (N, K, \Sigma, G_{sel}, G_{c_1}, G_{c_2}, G_{ch}, G_{ass})$, where $G_\gamma = (N \cup K, \Sigma, P_\gamma, S)$, $\gamma \in \{sel, c_1, c_2, ch, ass\}$ are the component grammars, and G_{sel} is the master grammar. Let $N = N' \cup \{F_t\}$ where N' contains the same symbols as the nonterminals of the system in the previous part of the proof, and let $K = \{Q_1, Q_2\}$. The sets of productions $P_{sel}, P_{c_1}, P_{c_2}$, and P_{ch} are defined as above, but replacing $Q_{sel}, Q_{c_1}, Q_{c_2}$ in the rules by Q_1, and Q_{ch} by Q_2. The rule $F_{c_1} \rightarrow F_{c_1}$ of P_{c_1} is replaced by $F_{c_1} \rightarrow F_t$ and $F_t \rightarrow F_t$. The rules of the newly added assistant component are as follows.

$$P_{ass} = \{S \rightarrow Q_1, \alpha \rightarrow Q_1, D_{1,\alpha} \rightarrow Q_1, D_{2,\alpha} \rightarrow Q_1, D_{3,\alpha} \rightarrow Q_1 \mid \alpha \in \mathcal{I}\} \cup$$
$$\{F \rightarrow Q_1, F_{c_1} \rightarrow F_t, F_t \rightarrow F_t\}.$$

This dynamically clustered NPC system works very similarly to the one in the second part of the proof of Theorem 2. The newly added component G_{ass} makes sure that all occurring symbols Q_1 have to be assigned to a dynamically formed cluster $\mathcal{C}_1$ which contains G_{sel} during the instruction simulating phase, or G_{c_1} in the final phase of the simulation.

5 Conclusion

In this paper we have improved the best known bound for the number of components needed to generate any recursively enumerable language by clustered and standard NPC grammar systems, and demonstrated a trade-off between the number of necessary clusters and components. We introduced the concept of dynamical clustering, and showed that three dynamical clusters, that is, two different query symbols and six component grammars are sufficient to obtain the same generative power. Important open problems are to find the sharp bounds, for example, to learn whether or not systems with exactly one query symbol are computationally complete.

References

1. ter Beek, M.H.: Teams in grammar systems: hybridity and weak rewriting. Acta Cybernetica 12(4), 427–444 (1996)
2. ter Beek, M.H.: Teams in grammar systems: sub-context-free cases. In: Păun, G., Salomaa, A. (eds.) New Trends in Formal Languages. LNCS, vol. 1218, pp. 197–216. Springer, Heidelberg (1997)
3. Csuhaj-Varjú, E., Dassow, J., Kelemen, J., Păun, G.: Grammar Systems: A Grammatical Approach to Distribution and Cooperation. Topics in Computer Mathematics, vol. 5. Gordon and Breach Science Publishers, Yverdon (1994)
4. Csuhaj-Varjú, E., Mitrana, V.: Dynamical Teams in Eco-Grammar Systems. Fundamenta Informaticae 44(1-2), 83–94 (2000)
5. Csuhaj-Varjú, E., Oswald, M., Vaszil, G.: PC grammar systems with clusters of components. International Journal of Foundations of Computer Science 22(1), 203–212 (2011)
6. Csuhaj-Varjú, E., Păun, G., Vaszil, G.: PC grammar systems with five context-free components generate all recursively enumerable languages. Theoretical Computer Science 299(1-3), 785–794 (2003)
7. Csuhaj-Varjú, E., Vaszil, G.: On the size complexity of non-returning context-free PC grammar systems. In: Dassow, J., Pighizzini, G., Truthe, B. (eds.) Proceedings Eleventh International Workshop on Descriptional Complexity of Formal Systems, Electronic Proceedings in Theoretical Computer Science, vol. 3, pp. 91–101 (2009)
8. Dassow, J., Păun, G., Rozenberg, G.: Grammar systems. In: Salomaa, A., Rozenberg, G. (eds.) Handbook of Formal Languages, vol. II, ch. 4, pp. 155–213. Springer, Heidelberg (1997)
9. Fischer, P.C.: Turing machines with restricted memory access. Information and Control 9, 364–379 (1966)
10. Kari, L., Mateescu, A., Păun, G., Salomaa, A.: Teams in cooperating grammar systems. Journal of Experimental and Theoretical Artificial Intelligence 7, 347–359 (1995)
11. Lázár, K., Csuhaj-Varjú, E., Lőrincz, A., Vaszil, G.: Dynamically formed Clusters of Agents in Eco-grammar Systems. International Journal of Foundations of Computer Science 20(2), 293–311 (2009)
12. Mateescu, A., Mitrana, V., Salomaa, A.: Dynamical teams of cooperating grammar systems. Analele Universitatii Bucuresti. Matematica Inform. 42(43), 3–14 (1993)
13. Minsky, M.: Computation – Finite and Infinite Machines. Prentice Hall, Englewood Cliffs (1967)
14. Păun, G., Rozenberg, G.: Prescribed teams of grammars. Acta Informatica 31(6), 525–537 (1994)
15. Păun, G., Sântean, L.: Parallel communicating grammar systems: The regular case. Annals of the University of Bucharest, Mathematics-Informatics Series 38(2), 55–63 (1989)

On Contextual Grammars
with Subregular Selection Languages

Jürgen Dassow, Florin Manea*, and Bianca Truthe

Otto-von-Guericke-Universität Magdeburg, Fakultät für Informatik
PSF 4120, D-39016 Magdeburg, Germany
{dassow,manea,truthe}@iws.cs.uni-magdeburg.de

Abstract. In this paper, we study the power of external contextual grammars with selection languages from subfamilies of the family of regular languages. If we consider families $\mathcal{F}_n$ which are obtained by restriction to n states or nonterminals or productions or symbols to accept or to generate regular languages, we obtain four infinite hierarchies of the corresponding families of languages generated by external contextual grammars with selection languages in $\mathcal{F}_n$. Moreover, we give some results on the power of external contextual grammars with regular commutative, regular circular, definite, suffix-free, ordered, combinational, nilpotent, and union-free selection languages.

1 Introduction

Contextual grammars were introduced by S. Marcus in [3] as a formal model that might be used in the generation of natural languages. The derivation steps consist in adding contexts to given well formed sentences, starting from an initial finite basis. Formally, a context is given by a pair (u, v) of words and the external adding to a word x gives the word uxv whereas an internal adding gives all words $x_1 u x_2 v x_3$ when $x = x_1 x_2 x_3$. Obviously, by linguistic motivation, a context can only be added if the words x or x_2 satisfy some given conditions. Thus, it is natural to define contextual grammars with selection in a certain family $\mathcal{F}$ of languages, where it is required that x or x_2 have to belong to a set of $\mathcal{F}$ which is associated with the context. Mostly, the family $\mathcal{F}$ is taken from the families of the Chomsky hierarchy (see [2,5,4], and the references therein).

In [1], the study of external contextual grammars with selection in special regular sets was started. Finite, combinational, definite, nilpotent, regular suffix-closed, regular commutative languages and languages of the form V^* for some alphabet V were considered. In this paper, we continue this line of research. More precisely, we obtain some new results on the effect of regular commutative, regular circular, definite, regular suffix-closed, ordered, combinational, nilpotent, and union-free selection languages on the generative power of external contextual grammars.

---

* Also at: *Faculty of Mathematics and Computer Science, University of Bucharest, Str. Academiei 14, RO-010014 Bucharest, Romania (*flmanea@fmi.unibuc.ro*).* His work is supported by the *Alexander von Humboldt Foundation.*

M. Holzer, M. Kutrib, and G. Pighizzini (Eds.): DCFS 2011, LNCS 6808, pp. 135–146, 2011.
© Springer-Verlag Berlin Heidelberg 2011

Moreover, we consider families of regular languages which are defined by restrictions on the resources used to generate or to accept them. As measures we
consider the number of states necessary to accept the regular languages and the
number of nonterminals, productions or symbols needed to generate the regular
languages. We prove that in all cases infinite hierarchies are obtained.

It is worth mentioning that our research is part of the study of problems and
processes connected with regular sets. In the last years, a lot of results were
reported in which, for such problems and processes, the effect of going from
arbitrary regular sets to special regular sets was studied.

2   Definitions

Throughout the paper, we assume that the reader is familiar with the basic concepts of the theory of automata and formal languages. For details we refer to [5].
Here we only recall some notation and the definition of contextual grammars
with selection which form the central notion of the paper.

Given an alphabet V, V^* and V^+ denote the set of all words and of all nonempty words over V, respectively. The empty word is denoted by λ. Given a
word $w \in V^*$ and a letter $a \in V$, by $|w|$ and $\#_a(w)$ we denote the length of w
and the number of occurrences of a in w, respectively.

For a language L over V, we set

$$Comm(L) = \{a_{\pi(1)}a_{\pi(2)} \ldots a_{\pi(n)} \mid a_i \in V \text{ for } 1 \leq i \leq n, \ a_1 a_2 \ldots a_n \in L,$$
$$\pi \text{ is a permutation of } \{1, 2, \ldots, n\}\},$$
$$Circ(L) = \{yx \mid xy \in L \text{ for some } x, y \in V^*\},$$
$$Suf(L) = \{y \mid xy \in L \text{ for some } x \in V^*\}.$$

It is known that $Suf(L)$ and $Circ(L)$ are regular for a regular language L, whereas
$Comm$ does not preserve regularity.

Let V be an alphabet. We say that a language L over V is

- *combinational* iff it can be represented in the form $L = V^*A$ for some finite
  non-empty subset $A \subseteq V \cup \{\lambda\}$,
- *definite* iff it can be represented in the form $L = A \cup V^*B$ where A and B
  are finite subsets of V^*,
- *nilpotent* iff L is finite or $V^* \setminus L$ is finite,
- *commutative* iff $Comm(L) = L$,
- *circular* iff $Circ(L) = L$,
- *suffix-closed* (or *fully initial* or a *multiple-entry* language) iff $Suf(L) = L$,
- *ordered* iff L is accepted by some finite automaton $\mathcal{A} = (Z, V, \delta, z_0, F)$ where
  $(Z, \preceq)$ is a totally ordered set and, for any $a \in V$, the relation $z \preceq z'$ implies
  the relation $\delta(z, a) \preceq \delta(z', a)$,
- *union-free* iff L can be described by a regular expression which is only built
  by product and star.

It is obvious that combinational, definite, nilpotent, ordered, and union-free languages are regular, whereas non-regular languages of the other three types exist.

We denote by REG the class of regular languages. By FIN, $COMB$, DEF, NIL, $COMM$, $CIRC$, SUF, ORD, and UF we denote the families of all finite, combinational, definite, nilpotent, regular commutative, regular circular, regular suffix-closed, ordered, and union-free languages, respectively.

Let $G = (N, T, P, S)$ be a regular grammar (specified by finite sets N and T of nonterminals and terminals, respectively, a finite set of productions of the form $A \rightarrow wB$ or $A \rightarrow w$ with $A, B \in N$ and $w \in T^*$ as well as $S \in N$). Further, let $A = (X, Z, z_0, F, \delta)$ be a deterministic finite automaton (specified by sets X and Z of input symbols and states, respectively, an initial state z_0, a set F of accepting states, and a transition function δ) and L be a regular language. Then we define

$$State(A) = card(Z), Var(G) = card(N), Prod(G) = card(P),$$

$$Symb(G) = \sum_{A \rightarrow w \in P} (|w| + 2),$$

$$State(L) = \min\{State(A) \mid A \text{ is a det. finite automaton accepting } L\},$$

$$Var(L) = \min\{Var(G) \mid G \text{ is a regular grammar generating } L\},$$

$$Prod(L) = \min\{Prod(G) \mid G \text{ is a regular grammar generating } L\},$$

$$Symb(L) = \min\{Symb(G) \mid G \text{ is a regular grammar generating } L\},$$

and, for $K \in \{State, Var, Prod\}$, we set

$$REG_n^K = \{L \mid L \text{ is a regular language with } K(L) \leq n\}.$$

Remark. We note that if we restricted ourselves to rules of the form $A \rightarrow aB$ and $A \rightarrow \lambda$ with $A, B \in N$ and $a \in T$, then we would have $State(L) = Var(L)$.

We now introduce the central notion of this paper.

Let $\mathcal{F}$ be a family of languages. A *contextual grammar with selection in $\mathcal{F}$* is a construct

$$G = (V, (P_1, C_1), (P_2, C_2), \ldots, (P_n, C_n), B)$$

where

- V is an alphabet,
- for $1 \leq i \leq n$, P_i is a language over V in $\mathcal{F}$ and C_i is a finite set of pairs (u, v) with $u \in V^*$, $v \in V^*$,
- B is a finite subset of V^*.

The set V is called the basic alphabet; the languages P_i and the sets C_i, $1 \leq i \leq n$, are called the selection languages and the sets of contexts of G, respectively; the elements of B are called axioms.

We now define external derivation for contextual grammars with selection.

Let $G = (V, (P_1, C_1), (P_2, C_2), \ldots, (P_n, C_n), B)$ be a contextual grammar with selection. A direct *external derivation step* in G is defined as follows: $x \Longrightarrow y$

holds if and only if there is an integer i, $1 \leq i \leq n$, such that $x \in P_i$ and $y = uxv$ for some $(u, v) \in C_i$. Intuitively, we can only wrap the context $(u, v) \in C_i$ around a word x, if x belongs to the corresponding language P_i.

By $\Longrightarrow^*$ we denote the reflexive and transitive closure of $\Longrightarrow$, respectively, and the *external language generated by* G is defined as

$$L(G) = \{z \mid x \Longrightarrow^* z \text{ for some } x \in B\}.$$

By $\mathcal{L}(EC, \mathcal{F})$ we denote the family of all external languages generated by contextual grammars with selection in $\mathcal{F}$. When we speak about contextual grammars in this paper, we mean contextual grammars with external derivation (also called external contextual grammars).

Obviously, the following lemma holds (see [1], Lemma 4.1).

Lemma 1. *For any two language classes* X *and* Y *with* $X \subseteq Y$, *we have* $\mathcal{L}(EC, X) \subseteq \mathcal{L}(EC, Y)$. □

3   Selection with Bounded Resources

First we prove that we obtain an infinite hierarchy with respect to the number of states.

Theorem 2. *For any natural number* $n \geq 1$, *we have the proper inclusion*

$$\mathcal{L}(EC, REG_n^{State}) \subset \mathcal{L}(EC, REG_{n+1}^{State}).$$

Proof. Let $n \geq 1$ and $V = \{a\}$ be a unary alphabet. We set

$$B_n = \{a^i \mid 0 \leq i \leq n\}, \ U_n = \{a^{n+1}\}^*, \text{ and } L_n = B_n \cup U_n.$$

The contextual grammar

$$G_n = (V, (U_n, \{(\lambda, a^{n+1})\}), B_n \cup \{a^{n+1}\})$$

generates the language L_n. This can be seen as follows. The only axiom to which a context can be added, is a^{n+1}. From this, we get the unique derivation

$$a^{n+1} \Longrightarrow a^{2(n+1)} \Longrightarrow a^{3(n+1)} \Longrightarrow \cdots.$$

It is easy to see that the set U_n is accepted by the automaton

$$A_n = (V, \{z_0, z_1, \ldots, z_n\}, z_0, \{z_0\}, \delta_n)$$

with the transition function δ_n satisfying $\delta_n(z_i, a) = z_{i+1}$ for $0 \leq i \leq n - 1$ and $\delta_n(z_n, a) = z_0$. Hence, we have $L_n \in \mathcal{L}(EC, REG_{n+1}^{State})$.

We now prove that $L_n \notin \mathcal{L}(EC, REG_n^{State})$.

Let $G = (V, (P_1, C_1), (P_2, C_2), \ldots, (P_m, C_m), B)$ be a contextual grammar with selection in REG such that $L(G) = L_n$.

Let $k' = \max\{|uv| \mid (u,v) \in C_i, 1 \le i \le m\}$, $k'' = \max\{|z| \mid z \in B\}$, and $k = k' + k''$. We consider the word $w = a^{k(n+1)} \in L_n$. Obviously, $w \notin B$. Thus w is obtained from some word $w' \in L_n$ by adding a context $(u,v) \in C_i$ for some index i with $1 \le i \le m$ and $w' \in P_i$. Then $w = uw'v$. For the length of the word w', we obtain

$$|w'| = |w| - |uv| = (k' + k'')(n+1) - |uv| \ge k'n + k''(n+1) > n.$$

Hence $w' \notin B_n$ which implies $w' = a^{j(n+1)}$ for some j with $1 \le j < k$ and $uv = a^{(k-j)(n+1)}$. Therefore, P_i contains some element of $\{a\}^+$. Further, if P_i contains a word z of B_n, then also $uzv \in L_n$. But $z \in B_n$ implies $|z| = s$ with $1 \le s \le n$, and thus $|uzv| = s + (k-j)(n+1)$ is greater than $n+1$ but not a multiple of $n+1$. This is impossible for words in L_n. Hence, the set P_i does not contain a word of B_n. Let $r = \min\{l \mid a^l \in P_i, a^l \ne \lambda\}$. Then $r \ge n+1$. We set $z_i = a^{r-i}$ for $0 \le i \le r$. Then we have the relations $a^i z_i \in P_i$ and $a^j z_i \notin P_i$ for $1 \le j < i \le r$ because $a^i z_i = a^r$ and $|a^j z_i| < r$ for $1 \le j < i \le r$.

Therefore the words $a, a^2, \ldots, a^r$ are pairwise not in the Myhill-Nerode relation. Thus, the minimal deterministic finite automaton accepting P_i has at least $r \ge n+1$ states. □

We now consider the measures Var and $Prod$.

To begin with, it is not hard to show that $\mathcal{L}(EC, REG_1^{Prod}) = FIN$.

Theorem 3. *Any language $L \in \mathcal{L}(EC, REG)$ over a unary alphabet is in the set $\mathcal{L}(EC, REG_1^{Var}) \cap \mathcal{L}(EC, REG_2^{Prod})$.*

Proof. By Corollary 8.2 of [4], any language in $\mathcal{L}(EC, REG)$ is linear. Thus, any language $L \in \mathcal{L}(EC, REG)$ over a unary alphabet is regular (since all context-free languages over a unary alphabet are regular, see [5], Volume 1, Chapter 3, Theorem 2.6). Therefore,

$$L = \{a^{i_1}, a^{i_2}, \ldots a^{i_r}\} \cup \{a^p\}^* \{a^{j_1}, a^{j_2}, \ldots, a^{j_s}\}$$

for some numbers $r \ge 0$, $s \ge 0$, $p \ge 1$, $i_1, i_2, \ldots, i_r$, $j_1, j_2, \ldots, j_s$ with

$$0 \le i_1 < i_2 < \cdots < i_r < p \le j_1 < j_2 < \cdots < j_s < 2p.$$

Thus, L can be generated by the contextual grammar

$$(\{a\}, (\{a^p\}^* \{a^{j_1}\}, \{(\lambda, a^p)\}), \ldots, (\{a^p\}^* \{a^{j_s}\}), \{(\lambda, a^p)\}), B)$$

with $B = \{a^{i_1}, a^{i_2}, \ldots, a^{i_r}, a^{j_1}, a^{j_2}, \ldots, a^{j_s}\}$. Moreover, each selection language $\{a^p\}^* \{a^{j_\ell}\}$, with $1 \le \ell \le s$, is generated by the regular grammar

$$(\{S\}, \{a\}, \{S \to a^p S, S \to a^{j_\ell}\}, S).$$

Thus, $L \in \mathcal{L}(EC, REG_1^{Var}) \cap \mathcal{L}(EC, REG_2^{Prod})$. □

Moreover, the above proof shows that, in fact, the class of unary languages from $\mathcal{L}(EC, REG)$ equals the class of all unary regular languages.

Let p be a positive natural number. For each natural number $n > 1$, we define the language

$$L_n = \{a(ab^{k_1})\ldots(ab^{k_{n-1}})ab^p \mid k_i > p \text{ for } 1 \le i \le n-1\}$$
$$\cup \{a(ab^{k_1})\ldots(ab^{k_\ell}) \mid 1 \le \ell < n, k_i > p \text{ for } 1 \le i \le \ell\}$$

The parentheses are used above only to highlight the repetitive structure of the language.

Lemma 4. *For $n > 1$, we have $L_n \in \mathcal{L}(EC, REG_{n-1}^{Var})$.*

Proof. First, we assume that $n \ge 3$. Consider the following regular grammars:

- G_1 having $n-1$ nonterminals $S, A_3, A_4, \ldots, A_n$ where S is the axiom and having the rules $S \to aabA_3$, $S \to bS$, $S \to \lambda$, and $A_i \to bA_i$, $A_i \to abA_{i+1}$ for $3 \le i \le n-1$ and $A_n \to bA_n$, $A_n \to abS$.
- G_2 having $n-1$ nonterminals $S, A_3, A_4, \ldots, A_n$ where S is the axiom and having the rules $S \to aabA_3$ and $A_i \to bA_i$, $A_i \to \lambda$, $A_i \to abA_{i+1}$ for $3 \le i \le n-1$ and $A_n \to bA_n$, $A_n \to \lambda$.

The languages generated by the above grammars are:

- $L_1 = L(G_1) = \{a\}(\{a\}\{b\}^+)^{n-1} \cup L_1' \cup L_1'' \cup \{\lambda\}$ where L_1' is a regular language that contains only words with at least $n+2$ a-symbols and at least two distinct factors aa and L_1'' is a regular language that contains only words that start with b.
- $L_2 = L(G_2) = \bigcup_{1 \le \ell < n-1} \{a\}(\{a\}\{b\}^+)^\ell.$

In what follows we show that L_n is generated by the contextual grammar

$$G_n = (V, (L_1, \{(\lambda, b)\}), (L_1, \{(\lambda, ab^p)\}), (L_2, \{(\lambda, b)\}), (L_2, \{(\lambda, ab^{p+1})\}), B)$$

with $V = \{a, b\}$ and $B = \{aab^{p+1}\}$.

First, consider a word $a(ab^{k_1})\ldots(ab^{k_\ell})$ with $1 \le \ell < n$ and $k_i > p$ for $1 \le i \le \ell$. This word is generated starting from the axiom aab^{p+1} by wrapping the context (λ, b) selected by L_2 around the current word until aab^{k_1} is obtained. Then, if $\ell > 1$, the context (λ, ab^{p+1}) selected by L_2 is added and we get $aab^{k_1}ab^{p+1}$. The process continues in the same way: First we add several times (λ, b) selected by L_2, then we add (λ, ab^{p+1}) selected by L_2. At some point, the word $a(ab^{k_1})\ldots(ab^{k_{\ell-1}})(ab^{p+1})$ will be generated. Then, the context (λ, b) selected by L_1 (if $\ell = n-1$) or L_2 (if $\ell < n-1$) is added until the word $a(ab^{k_1})\ldots(ab^{k_\ell})$ is obtained.

Now consider the word $a(ab^{k_1})\ldots(ab^{k_{n-1}})ab^p$. First, we generate the word $a(ab^{k_1})\ldots(ab^{k_{n-2}})ab^{p+1}$ exactly as above. This word is in $L_1 \setminus L_2$. We continue by wrapping the context (λ, b) selected by L_1 around the current word until we obtain $a(ab^{k_1})\ldots(ab^{k_{n-1}})$; to end the derivation, we add the context (λ, ab^p) selected by L_1 and obtain $a(ab^{k_1})\ldots(ab^{k_{n-1}})ab^p$.

It is not hard to see that only words of these forms can be obtained. Using the contextual rules that have L_2 as selector, we only obtain words of the form $a(ab^{k_1})\ldots(ab^{k_\ell})$ or $a(ab^{k_1})\ldots(ab^{k_\ell})(ab^{p+1})$ with $1 \le \ell < n-1$ and $k_i > p$ for $1 \le i \le \ell$. Using additionally the contextual rules that have L_1 as selector, we obtain further the words of the form $a(ab^{k_1})\ldots(ab^{k_\ell})$ or $a(ab^{k_1})\ldots(ab^{k_\ell})(ab^p)$ with $1 \le \ell < n$ and $k_i > p$ for $1 \le i \le \ell$. The words of the first type can be further derived, while the words of the second type cannot be derived anymore as they are not in $L_1 \cup L_2$. Thus, $L_i \in REG_{n-1}^{Var}$ for $i \in \{1,2\}$.

Now consider that $n = 2$. We define the grammar G_1 with one nonterminal S and the rules $S \to aabS$, $S \to bS$, and $S \to \lambda$. The language generated by this grammar is $L_1 = L(G_1) = \{aa\}\{b\}^+ \cup L_1' \cup L_1'' \cup \{\lambda\}$ where L_1' is a regular language that contains at least two distinct factors aa and L_1'' is a regular language that contains only words that start with b. The language L_n is generated by the grammar $G_n = (V, ((\lambda, b), L_1), ((\lambda, ab^p), L_1), B)$. Hence, we have $L_n \in \mathcal{L}(EC, REG_{n-1}^{Var})$ in this case, too. $\square$

Lemma 5. *For $n > 1$, we have that $L_n \notin \mathcal{L}(EC, REG_{n-2}^{Var})$.*

Proof. Assume that $G = (V, (P_1, \{(u_1, v_1)\}), \ldots, (P_\ell, \{(u_\ell, v_\ell)\}), B)$ is a contextual grammar that generates L_n and that $G_1, \ldots, G_\ell$ are regular grammars that generate $P_1, \ldots, P_\ell$, respectively.

We first note that $u_i = \lambda$ for $1 \le i \le \ell$. All the words derived by G have the form aaw with $w \in \{a, b\}^*$. Further, if a context has the form (u_i, v_i) with $u_i \ne \lambda$, then wrapping this context around a certain word derived by G yields a word of the language that contains the factor aa not as a prefix or at least twice. But this is a contradiction.

Now, denote by M the maximum length of the right hand sides of the productions of the grammars $G_1, \ldots, G_\ell$ and denote by M' the maximum length of the words v_i for $1 \le i \le \ell$ and of the words from B. Then $M' \ge p$; otherwise, one could not generate all the words of the set

$$\{a(ab^{k_1})\ldots(ab^{k_{n-1}})ab^p \mid k_i \in \mathbb{N}, k_i > p \text{ for } 1 \le i \le n-1\}.$$

Let $N = M + 2M' + 1$ and consider now the word $w = a(ab^N)\ldots(ab^N)ab^p$ where $|w|_a = n+1$. It does not belong to the set B since it is longer than any word of B. Thus, it is obtained by adding a context, denoted (λ, v_i), to another word w' of L_n. We note that this context is of the form $(\lambda, b^x ab^p)$ with $x \ge 0$ (by the choice of N sufficiently large and because $w' \in L_n$). Hence, $w' = a(ab^N)^{n-2}ab^m$ with $M + M' + 1 \le m \le N$.

In what follows, we show that the grammar G_i generating the selection language P_i of the contextual rule $(P_i, \{(\lambda, v_i)\})$ has at least $n-1$ nonterminals. Let us assume the opposite: The grammar G_i has at most $n-2$ nonterminals.

A possible derivation of the word $w' \in P_i$ has the form

$$S \Longrightarrow^* aab^{k_1} A_1 \Longrightarrow^* aab^N ab^{k_2} A_2 \Longrightarrow^* \cdots \Longrightarrow^* a(ab^N)^{i-1} ab^{k_i} A_i \Longrightarrow^* \cdots$$
$$\Longrightarrow^* a(ab^N)^{n-2} ab^{k_{n-1}} A_{n-1} \Longrightarrow^* a(ab^N)^{n-2} ab^m$$

where $A_1, \ldots, A_{n-1}$ are nonterminals and $k_i \leq M$ for $1 \leq i \leq n-1$. Since G has at most $n-2$ nonterminals by our assumption, there exist numbers i and j such that $1 \leq i < j \leq n-1$ and $A_i = A_j$. Hence, we can also derive by the grammar G_i a word that has at most $t \leq n-1$ symbols a and has the form $a(ab^{l_1}) \ldots (ab^{l_{t-1}})$ with $l_s > p$ for $1 \leq s \leq t-1$ (we derive $a(ab^N)^{i-1}ab^{k_i}A_i$ and then rewrite A_i as we rewrote A_j in the derivation above). In a word obtained in this way, every group of b symbols contains more than p symbols, because we basically decreased the number of symbols in such a group by at most M. Hence, $a(ab^{l_1}) \ldots (ab^{l_{t-1}}) \in P_i$ and the context $(\lambda, b^x ab^p)$ can be added which yields the word $a(ab^{l_1}) \ldots (ab^{l_{t-1}})ab^p$ with $t \leq n-1$ and $l_s > p$ for $1 \leq s \leq t-1$. This is a contradiction to the definition of L_n. Therefore, G_i has at least $n-1$ nonterminals. This concludes our proof. $\qquad\square$

From the previous two lemmas we obtain the following result:

Theorem 6. *For any natural number $n \geq 1$, we have the proper inclusion*

$$\mathcal{L}(EC, REG_n^{Var}) \subset \mathcal{L}(EC, REG_{n+1}^{Var}). \qquad\square$$

The generation of the language L_n for a natural number $n > 1$ requires at least $2(n-2) + 1$ productions in each component (each nonterminal different from the axiom has at least two productions; otherwise, we could substitute each occurrence of a nonterminal A which appears in only one rule $A \to w$ by w in all right hand sides and ignore the nonterminal A and its rule, which would give a regular grammar with a smaller number of nonterminals). From the proof of Lemma 4, we have $L_n \in \mathcal{L}(EC, REG_{3n-6}^{Prod})$ for $n \geq 5$. Hence, together, we obtain $L_n \in \mathcal{L}(EC, REG_{3n-6}^{Prod}) \setminus \mathcal{L}(EC, REG_{2n-4}^{Prod})$ for $n \geq 5$, from which immediately follows that the families $\mathcal{L}(EC, REG_n^{Prod})$ for $n \geq 1$ form an infinite chain with respect to inclusion. If we do not restrict the size of the alphabet we get the following stronger result.

Theorem 7. *For any natural number $n \geq 1$, we have the proper inclusion* $\mathcal{L}(EC, REG_n^{Prod}) \subset \mathcal{L}(EC, REG_{n+1}^{Prod}).$ $\qquad\square$

We now consider the measure $Symb$. Clearly, $Symb(L) \geq 2$, for any L.

Lemma 8. *Let L be an infinite regular language. Let k be the minimal length of non-empty words in L. Then $Symb(L) \geq k+5$.*

Proof. Let G be a regular grammar generating L. Let us consider a derivation

$$S \Longrightarrow x_1 A_1 \Longrightarrow x_1 x_2 A_2 \Longrightarrow \cdots \Longrightarrow x_1 x_2 \ldots x_{n-1} A_{n-1} \Longrightarrow x_1 x_2 \ldots x_n = w$$

of a word $w \in L$ of length k.

If $n = 1$, then $S \Longrightarrow w$. The rule $S \to w$ contributes $k+2$ symbols. There is also a rule $A \to z$ with $z \notin T^*$ since L is infinite. Hence, $Symb(G) \geq k+5$.

If $n \geq 2$, we have rules $S \to x_1 A_1$, $A_i \to x_{i+1} A_{i+1}$ for $1 \leq i \leq n-2$ and $A_{n-1} \to x_n$. Then we have $Symb(G) = k + 5 + 3(n-2) \geq k+5$. $\qquad\square$

One can show the following theorem.

Theorem 9. $\mathcal{L}(EC, REG_k^{Symb}) = FIN$, for all $2 \leq k \leq 5$.

Finally, we also obtain the following result.

Theorem 10. *For any number* $n \geq 6$, $\mathcal{L}(EC, REG_{n-1}^{Symb}) \subset \mathcal{L}(EC, REG_n^{Symb})$.

Proof. We consider $L_n = \{a, a^2, \ldots, a^n\} \cup \{a^{n+1}\}^+$ of the proof of Theorem 2. Again, the grammar G_n generates L_n. Because U_n is generated by the regular grammar $(\{S\}, \{a\}, \{S \rightarrow a^{n+1}S, \ S \rightarrow \lambda\}, S)$, we have $L_n \in \mathcal{L}(EC, REG_{n+6}^{Symb})$.

We now prove that $L_n \notin \mathcal{L}(EC, REG_{n+5}^{Symb})$. Assume the contrary, i. e., there is a contextual grammar $G = (V, (P_1, C_1), (P_2, C_2), \ldots, (P_m, C_m), B)$ with selection in REG such that $L(G) = L_n$. We define k', k'', and k as in the proof of Theorem 2 and consider the words $w_p = a^{pk(n+1)}$ for $p \geq 1$. Again, there are words w_p' such that $w_p = u_p w_p' v_p$ for some context (u_p, v_p) associated with some regular set P_{i_p}, $1 \leq i_p \leq m$, and

$$pk(n+1) = |w_p| > |w_p'| = p(k' + k'')(n+1) - |u_p v_p|$$
$$\geq p(k' + k'')(n+1) - k' > (p-1)k(n+1).$$

Thus, all these words w_p' are different and each of them belongs to at least one of the sets P_j, $1 \leq j \leq m$. Therefore at least one of the sets P_j, $1 \leq j \leq m$, say P_i, is infinite. As in the proof of Theorem 2, we can show that the shortest non-empty word of P_i has a length $r \geq n + 1$. Now we get from Lemma 8 that $Symb(P_i) \geq n + 6$. □

We make some final remarks on the results of this section. We have shown that, for $K \in \{State, Var, Prod\}$, we obtain infinite dense hierarchies, i. e., for any $n \geq 1$, $\mathcal{L}(EC, REG_{n+1}^K) \setminus \mathcal{L}(EC, REG_n^K) \neq \emptyset$. However, these results hold for all alphabets with respect to *State*; in case of *Var*, it is valid for all alphabets with at least two letters (if the alphabet is unary, we have only one level in the hierarchy); and for *Prod* we need alphabets of arbitrary size. It is an open question whether the results hold for *Prod* and a fixed alphabet size. For *Symb*, we get a dense hierarchy over all alphabets, but starting with $n = 6$.

4   Circular, Ordered, and Union-Free Selection

We start with some results on circular selection languages.

Theorem 11. *We have the proper inclusion* $\mathcal{L}(EC, COMM) \subset \mathcal{L}(EC, CIRC)$.

Proof. By Lemma 1, we obtain $\mathcal{L}(EC, COMM) \subseteq \mathcal{L}(EC, CIRC)$. Let

$$P_1 = \{ abc^n \mid n \geq 1 \}, \ P_2 = \{ c^n ba \mid n \geq 1 \}, \ \text{and} \ L = P_1 \cup P_2.$$

The language L is generated by the contextual grammar with circular selection

$$G = (\{ a, b, c \}, (Circ(P_1), \{ (\lambda, c) \}), (Circ(P_2), \{ (c, \lambda) \}), \{ abc, cba \}).$$

If the language L is also generated by a contextual grammar where all selection languages are commutative, then there is a context (λ, c^x) for a number $x \geq 1$ such that c^x is appended to a word abc^n for some number $n \geq 1$. But since the corresponding selection language also contains the word $c^n ba \in L$, we would obtain the word $c^n bac^x \notin L$ which is a contradiction. Thus, $L \notin \mathcal{L}(EC, COMM)$ which yields the proper inclusion $\mathcal{L}(EC, COMM) \subset \mathcal{L}(EC, CIRC)$. □

Theorem 12. *The class $\mathcal{L}(EC, CIRC)$ is incomparable with each of the classes $\mathcal{L}(EC, DEF)$ and $\mathcal{L}(EC, SUF)$.*

Proof. Let $V = \{a, b, c\}$ and $L_1 = \{a^n b^n \mid n \geq 1\} \cup \{cb^n \mid n \geq 1\}$. The language L_1 can be generated by the contextual grammar with circular selection

$$G = (V, (P_1, \{(a, b)\}), (P_2, \{(\lambda, b)\}), \{ab, cb\})$$

with $P_1 = \{w \mid w \in V^* \text{ and } |w|_c = 0\}$ and $P_2 = V^* \setminus P_1$. However, the language does not belong to the class $\mathcal{L}(EC, DEF)$ according to [1].

Let $L_2 = \{ab^n \mid n \geq 1\} \cup \{b\}$. The language L_2 can be generated by the contextual grammar

$$G = (\{a, b\}, (Circ(\{ab^n \mid n \geq 1\}), \{(\lambda, b)\}), \{ab, b\})$$

with circular selection. However, the language does not belong to the class $\mathcal{L}(EC, SUF)$ according to [1].

Let $L_3 = \{ab^n \mid n \geq 1\} \cup \{b^n a \mid n \geq 1\}$. According to [1], the language L_3 belongs to both the classes $\mathcal{L}(EC, DEF)$ and $\mathcal{L}(EC, SUF)$. If the language L_3 is also generated by a contextual grammar where all selection languages are circular, then there is a context (λ, b^x) for a number $x \geq 1$ such that b^x is appended to a word ab^n for some number $n \geq 1$. But since the corresponding selection language also contains the word $b^n a \in L$, we would obtain the word $b^n ab^x \notin L$ which is a contradiction. Thus, $L_3 \notin \mathcal{L}(EC, CIRC)$.

The languages L_1, L_2, and L_3 are witnesses for the claimed incomparability. □

The language $L_3 = \{ab^n \mid n \geq 1\} \cup \{b^n a \mid n \geq 1\}$ from the proof of the previous theorem also belongs to the class $\mathcal{L}(EC, REG)$. This yields the following statement.

Corollary 13. *We have the proper inclusion $\mathcal{L}(EC, CIRC) \subset \mathcal{L}(EC, REG)$.* □

We now give some results on the class of languages generated by contextual grammars with ordered selection.

Let $P_1 = \{a^n b^n \mid n \geq 1\}$, $P_2 = \{b^n \mid n \geq 1\}$, and $L = P_1 \cup P_2$. The language L is generated by the contextual grammar

$$G = (\{a, b\}, (P_1', \{(a, b)\}), (P_2, \{(\lambda, b)\}), \{ab, b\})$$

with $P_1' = \{b\}^* \{a\} \{a, b\}^*$. The set P_1' can be accepted by the finite automaton

$$A = (\{z_0, z_1\}, \{a, b\}, \delta, z_0, \{z_1\})$$

with the transition function δ defined by $\delta(z_0, a) = \delta(z_1, a) = z_1$ and $\delta(z_i, b) = z_i$ for $0 \leq i \leq 1$. Both the sets P_1' and P_2 are ordered. Thus, the language L belongs to the class $\mathcal{L}(EC, ORD)$.

Theorem 14. *There exists a language in the set* $\mathcal{L}(EC, ORD) \setminus \mathcal{L}(EC, DEF)$.

Proof. Similarly to the proof that the language L_1 from the proof of Theorem 12 does not belong to the class $\mathcal{L}(EC, DEF)$ one can also show that L does not belong to $\mathcal{L}(EC, DEF)$. Since we have $L \in \mathcal{L}(EC, ORD)$, we obtain the statement.   □

By Lemma 1, the class $\mathcal{L}(EC, COMB)$ is a subset of the class $\mathcal{L}(EC, DEF)$ (in [1], even its properness was shown) and of the class $\mathcal{L}(EC, ORD)$. This yields the following result.

Corollary 15. *The proper inclusion* $\mathcal{L}(EC, COMB) \subset \mathcal{L}(EC, ORD)$ *holds.*   □

We use the language L given above to show the next statement.

Theorem 16. *The proper inclusion* $\mathcal{L}(EC, NIL) \subset \mathcal{L}(EC, ORD)$ *holds.*

Proof. By Lemma 1, we know the inclusion $\mathcal{L}(EC, NIL) \subseteq \mathcal{L}(EC, ORD)$. Let us consider the language $L \in \mathcal{L}(EC, ORD)$ given above.

Assume, $L \in \mathcal{L}(EC, NIL)$. Then there is a contextual grammar

$$G = (\{a, b\}, (P_1, C_1), (P_2, C_2), \ldots, (P_m, C_m), B)$$

where all sets P_i $(1 \leq i \leq m)$ are nilpotent.

Let μ be the maximal length of all words in the base set B and the finite sets P_i:

$$\mu = \max\{|w| \mid w \in B \text{ or } w \in P_i \text{ and } \#(P_i) < \infty, 1 \leq i \leq m\}.$$

Let κ be the maximal length of all contexts:

$$\kappa = \max\{|u| + |v| \mid (u, v) \in C_i, 1 \leq i \leq m\}.$$

We now consider a word $a^n b^n \in L$ with $n > \mu + \kappa$. Then there exists a word $z \in L(G)$, an index i with $1 \leq i \leq m$, and a context $(u, v) \in C_i$ such that $z \in P_i$ and $a^n b^n = uzv$. Since $n > \kappa \geq |u|$ and $n > |v|$ there are numbers $s \geq 0$ and $t \geq 0$ such that $u = a^s$, $v = b^t$, and $s + t \geq 1$.

Because of the choice of n, we further have $|z| > \mu$. Hence, P_i is infinite (in the finite selection languages, there is no word with a length greater than μ). Since it is nilpotent, the set $C = \{a, b\}^* \setminus P_i$ is finite. Hence, the set C contains only finitely many words of the form $a^k b^k$ or b^k. Thus, the set P_i contains infinitely many words of the form $a^k b^k$ and infinitely many words of the form b^k. If $s \neq t$, we obtain from a word $a^k b^k \in P_i$ a word which is not in the language L. Hence, $s = t$. But then from a word $b^k \in P_i$ we can derive the word $ub^k v = a^s b^{k+s}$ which is due to $s \geq 1$ not a word of the language L. Thus, $L \notin \mathcal{L}(EC, NIL)$.   □

We now discuss union-free languages. By the classical theorem by Kleene we know that every regular language over an alphabet V can be constructed from the sets $\{x\}$ for $x \in V$ and the empty set by finitely many operations of union, concatenation and Kleene-star. We now present a version of this statement using union-free sets.

Lemma 17. *Every regular language can be represented by a finite union of union-free languages.* □

Obviously, there exist non-union-free regular languages. However, the previous statement helps us show that the restriction to union-free selection languages does not imply a restriction of the generative capacity of contextual grammars.

Theorem 18. *We have the equality $\mathcal{L}(EC, UF) = \mathcal{L}(EC, REG)$.*

Proof. According to Lemma 1, we have $\mathcal{L}(EC, UF) \subseteq \mathcal{L}(EC, REG)$. Hence, we only have to show that the inclusion $\mathcal{L}(EC, REG) \subseteq \mathcal{L}(EC, UF)$ also holds.

Let $L \in \mathcal{L}(EC, REG)$ and $G = (V, (P_1, C_1), (P_2, C_2), \dots, (P_n, C_n), B)$ be a contextual grammar generating L where the sets $P_1, P_2, \dots, P_n$ are arbitrary regular languages. By Lemma 17, every language P_i $(1 \le i \le n)$ can be represented as a union $P_i = Q_{i,1} \cup Q_{i,2} \cup \cdots \cup Q_{i,n_i}$ of union-free languages $Q_{i,j}$ with $1 \le j \le n_i$ for a natural number $n_i \ge 1$. The contextual grammar

$$G' = (V, (Q_{1,1}, C_1), \dots, (Q_{1,n_1}, C_1), \dots, (Q_{n,1}, C_n), \dots, (Q_{n,n_n}, C_1), B)$$

generates the same language as G because any context can by added by G if and only if it can be added by G'. Thus, for any language $L \in \mathcal{L}(EC, REG)$, there is also a contextual grammar that generates the language L and has only union-free selection languages. This proves the inclusion $\mathcal{L}(EC, REG) \subseteq \mathcal{L}(EC, UF)$. □

Note that the results of this section come as an extension of the hierarchy of classes of languages generated by contextual grammars with subregular choice reported in [1]. Once again, it is worth mentioning that all these results are valid for alphabets that contain at least two letters, except for Theorem 11, where three letters are needed; it remains to be settled whether these bounds are optimal. It also seems interesting how the hierarchies defined in the previous section can be compared with the hierarchy developed in [1] and here. It seems interesting to see if results similar to the ones shown in this and the previous section can be derived for internal contextual grammars with subregular selection.

References

1. Dassow, J.: Contextual grammars with subregular choice. Fundamenta Informaticae 64 (1-4), 109–118 (2005)
2. Istrail, S.: Gramatici contextuale cu selectiva regulata. Stud. Cerc. Mat. 30, 287–294 (1978)
3. Marcus, S.: Contextual grammars. Revue Roum. Math. Pures Appl. 14, 1525–1534 (1969)
4. Păun, G.: Marcus Contextual Grammars. Kluwer Publ. House, Dordrecht (1998)
5. Rozenberg, G., Salomaa, A. (eds.): Handbook of Formal Languages. Springer, Berlin (1997)

Remarks on Separating Words

Erik D. Demaine[1], Sarah Eisenstat[1], Jeffrey Shallit[2], and David A. Wilson[1]

[1] MIT Computer Science and Artificial Intelligence Laboratory
32 Vassar Street, Cambridge, MA 02139, USA
{edemaine,seisenst,dwilson}@mit.edu
[2] School of Computer Science, University of Waterloo
Waterloo, ON N2L 3G1, Canada
shallit@cs.uwaterloo.ca

Abstract. The *separating words problem* asks for the size of the smallest DFA needed to distinguish between two words of length $\leq n$ (by accepting one and rejecting the other). In this paper we survey what is known and unknown about the problem, consider some variations, and prove several new results.

1 Introduction

Imagine a computing device with very limited powers. What is the simplest computational problem you could ask it to solve? It is not the addition of two numbers, nor sorting, nor string matching — it is telling two inputs apart: distinguishing them in some way.

Take as our computational model the deterministic finite automaton or DFA. As usual, it consists of a 5-tuple, $M = (Q, \Sigma, \delta, q_0, F)$, where Q is a finite nonempty set of states, Σ is a nonempty input alphabet, $\delta : Q \times \Sigma \to Q$ is the transition function (assumed to be *complete*, or defined on all members of its domain), $q_0 \in Q$ is the initial state, and $F \subseteq Q$ is a set of final states.

We say that a DFA M *separates* w and x if M accepts one but rejects the other. Given two distinct words w, x we let $\mathrm{sep}(w, x)$ be the number of states in the smallest DFA accepting w and rejecting x. For example, the DFA below separates 0010 from 1000.

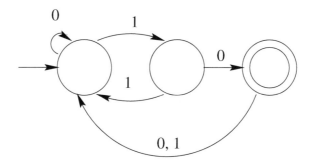

M. Holzer, M. Kutrib, and G. Pighizzini (Eds.): DCFS 2011, LNCS 6808, pp. 147–157, 2011.

However, by a brief computation, we see that no 2-state DFA can separate these two words. So $\text{sep}(1000, 0010) = 3$. Note that $\text{sep}(w, x) = \text{sep}(x, w)$, because the language of a DFA can be complemented by swapping the reject and accept states.

We let $S(n) = \max\limits_{\substack{w \neq x \\ |w|, |x| \leq n}} \text{sep}(w, x)$. The *separating words problem* is to determine good upper and lower bounds on $S(n)$. This problem was introduced 25 years ago by Goralčík and Koubek [5], who proved $S(n) = o(n)$. It was later studied by Robson [7,8], who obtained the best upper bound so far: $S(n) = O(n^{2/5}(\log n)^{3/5})$.

As an additional motivation, the separating words problem can be viewed as an inverse of a classical problem from the early days of automata theory: given two DFAs accepting different languages, what length of word suffices to distinguish them? More precisely, given two DFAs M_1 and M_2, with m and n states, respectively, with $L(M_1) \neq L(M_2)$, what is a good bound on the length of the shortest word accepted by one but not the other? The usual cross-product construction quickly gives an upper bound of $mn - 1$ (make a DFA for $L(M_1) \cap \overline{L(M_2)}$). But the optimal upper bound of $m + n - 2$ follows from the usual algorithm for minimizing automata. Furthermore, this bound is best possible [9, Thm. 3.10.6]. For NFAs the bound is exponential in m and n [6].

From the following result, already proved by Goralčík and Koubek [5], we know that the challenging case of word separation comes from words of equal length:

Proposition 1. *Suppose* $|w|, |x| \leq n$ *and* $|w| \neq |x|$. *Then* $\text{sep}(w, x) = O(\log n)$. *Furthermore, there is an infinite class of examples where* $\text{sep}(w, x) = \Omega(\log n)$.

We use the following lemma [10]:

Lemma 2. *If* $0 \leq i, j \leq n$ *and* $i \neq j$, *then there is a prime* $p \leq 4.4 \log n$ *such that* $i \not\equiv j \pmod{p}$.

Proof. (of Proposition 1) Let's prove the upper bound. If $|w| \neq |x|$, then by Lemma 2 there exists a prime $p \leq 4.4 \log n$ such that $|w| \bmod p \neq |x| \bmod p$. Hence a simple cycle of p states serves to distinguish w from x.

For the other direction, we first recall that a sequence $(p_i)_{i \geq 0}$ is said to be *ultimately periodic* if there exist integers $r \geq 0, s \geq 1$ such that $p_i = p_{r+i}$ for all $i \geq s$. In this case s is called the *preperiod* and r the *period*.

Now we claim that no DFA with n states can distinguish

$$0^{n-1} \quad \text{from} \quad 0^{n-1+\text{lcm}(1,2,...,n)}.$$

To see this, let $p_i = \delta(q_0, 0^i)$ for $i \geq 0$. Then p_i is ultimately periodic with period $\leq n$ and preperiod at most $n - 1$. Thus $p_{n-1} = p_{n-1+\text{lcm}(1,2,...,n)}$. Since, from the prime number theorem, we have $\text{lcm}(1, 2, \ldots, n) = e^{n(1+o(1))}$, the $\Omega(\log n)$ lower bound follows. □

Example 3. Suppose $|w| = 22$ and $|x| = 52$. Then $|w| \equiv 1 \pmod 7$ and $|x| \equiv 3 \pmod 7$. So we can accept w and reject x with a DFA that uses a cycle of size 7, as follows:

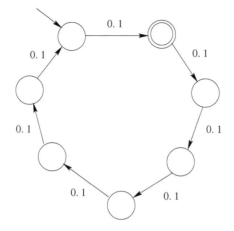

In what follows, then, we only consider the case of equal-length words, and we redefine $S(n) = \max\limits_{\substack{w \neq x \\ |w|=|x|=n}} \text{sep}(w, x)$. The goal of the paper is to survey what is known and unknown, and to examine some variations on the original problem. Our main new results are Theorems 11 and 16.

Notation: in what follows, if x is a word, we let $x[j]$ denote the j'th symbol of x (so that $x[1]$ is the first symbol).

2   Independence of Alphabet Size

As we have defined it, $S(n)$ could conceivably depend on the size of the alphabet Σ. Let $S_k(n)$ be the maximum number of states needed to separate two length-n words over an alphabet of size k. Then we might have a different value $S_k(n)$ depending on $k = |\Sigma|$. The following result shows this is not the case for $k \geq 2$. This result was stated in [5] without proof; we supply a proof here.

Proposition 4. *For all $k \geq 2$ we have $S_k(n) = S_2(n)$.*

Proof. Suppose x, y are distinct length-n words over an alphabet Σ of size $k > 2$. Then x and y must differ in some position, say for $a \neq b$,

$$x = x' \, a \, x'',$$
$$y = y' \, b \, y'',$$

for $|x'| = |y'|$.

Now map a to 0, b to 1 and map all other letters of Σ to 0. This gives two new distinct binary words X and Y of length n. If X and Y can be separated by an m-state DFA, then so can x and y, by renaming transitions of the DFA to be over $\Sigma \backslash b$ and $\{b\}$ instead of 0 and 1, respectively. Thus $S_k(n) \leq S_2(n)$. But clearly $S_2(n) \leq S_k(n)$, since every binary word can be considered as a word over the larger alphabet Σ. So $S_k(n) = S_2(n)$. □

3 Average Case

One frustrating aspect of the separating words problem is that nearly all pairs of words can be easily separated. This means that bad examples cannot be easily produced by random search.

Proposition 5. *Consider a pair of words (w, x) selected uniformly from the set of all pairs of unequal words of length n over an alphabet of size k. Then the expected number of states needed to separate w from x is $O(1)$.*

Proof. With probability $1 - 1/k$, two randomly-chosen words will differ in the first position, which can be detected by an automaton with 3 states. With probability $(1/k)(1 - 1/k)$ the words will agree in the first position, but differ in the second, etc. Hence the expected number of states needed to distinguish two randomly-chosen words is bounded by $\sum_{i \geq 1} (i+2)(1/k)^{i-1}(1-1/k) = (3k-2)/(k-1) \leq 4$.

□

4 Lower Bounds for Words of Equal Length

First of all, there is a lower bound analogous to that in Proposition 1 for words of *equal* length. This does not appear to have been known previously.

Theorem 6. *No DFA of at most n states can separate the equal-length binary words $w = 0^{n-1}1^{n-1+\mathrm{lcm}(1,2,\ldots,n)}$ and $x = 0^{n-1+\mathrm{lcm}(1,2,\ldots,n)}1^{n-1}$.*

Proof. In pictures, we have

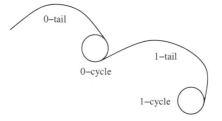

More formally, let M be any DFA with n states, let q be any state, and let a be any letter. Let $p_i = \delta(q; a^i)$ for $i \geq 0$. Then p_i is ultimately periodic with period $\leq n$ and preperiod ("tail") at most $n - 1$. Thus $p_{n-1} = p_{n-1+\mathrm{lcm}(1,2,\ldots,n)}$.

It follows that after processing 0^{n-1} and $0^{n-1+\operatorname{lcm}(1,2,\ldots,n)}$, M must be in the same state. Similarly, after processing

$$0^{n-1}1^{n-1+\operatorname{lcm}(1,2,\ldots,n)} \quad \text{and} \quad 0^{n-1+\operatorname{lcm}(1,2,\ldots,n)}1^{n-1},$$

M must be in the same state. So no n-state machine can separate w from x. $\square$

We now prove a series of very simple results showing that if w and x differ in some "easy-to-detect" way, then $\operatorname{sep}(w,x)$ is small.

4.1   Differences Near the Beginning or End of Words

Proposition 7. *Suppose w and x are words that differ in some symbol that occurs d positions from the start. Then $\operatorname{sep}(w,x) \le d + 2$.*

Proof. Let t be a prefix of length d of w. Then t is not a prefix of x. We can accept the language $t\Sigma^*$ using $d + 2$ states; such an automaton accepts w and rejects x. $\square$

For example, to separate

$$01010011101100110000$$

from

$$01001111101011100101$$

we can build a DFA to recognize words that begin with 0101:

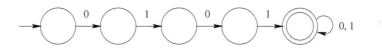

(Transitions to a dead state are omitted.)

Proposition 8. *Suppose w and x differ in some symbol that occurs d positions from the end. Then $\operatorname{sep}(w,x) \le d + 1$.*

Proof. Let the DFA M be the usual pattern-recognizing automaton for the length-d suffix s of w, ending in an accepting state if the suffix is recognized. Then M accepts w but rejects x. States of M correspond to prefixes of s, and $\delta(t,a) = $ the longest suffix of ta that is a prefix of s. $\square$

For example, to separate

$$11111010011001010101$$

from

$$11111011010010101101$$

we can build a DFA to recognize those words that end in 0101:

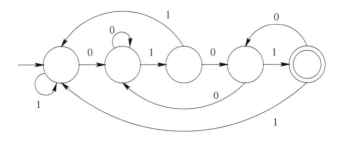

4.2   Fingerprints

Define $|w|_a$ as the number of occurrences of the symbol a in the word w.

Proposition 9. *If $|w|, |x| \leq n$ and $|w|_a \neq |x|_a$ for some symbol a, then* $\mathrm{sep}(w, x) = O(\log n)$.

Proof. By the prime number theorem, if $|w|, |x| = n$, and w and x have k and m occurrences of a respectively ($k \neq m$), then there is a prime $p = O(\log n)$ such that $k \not\equiv m \pmod p$. So we can separate w from x just by counting the number of a's, modulo p. $\square$

Analogously, we have the following result.

Proposition 10. *If there is a pattern of length d occurring a different number of times in w and x, with $|w|, |x| \leq n$, then* $\mathrm{sep}(w, x) = O(d \log n)$.

4.3   Pairs with Low Hamming Distance

The previous results have shown that if w and x have differing "fingerprints", then they are easy to separate. By contrast, the next result shows that if w and x are very similar, then they are also easy to separate.

The *Hamming distance* $H(w, x)$ between two equal-length words w and x is defined to be the number of positions where they differ.

Theorem 11. *Let w and x be words of length n. If $H(w, x) \leq d$, then* $\mathrm{sep}(w, x) = O(d \log n)$.

Proof. Without loss of generality, assume x and y are binary words, and x has a 1 in some position where y has a 0. Consider the following picture:

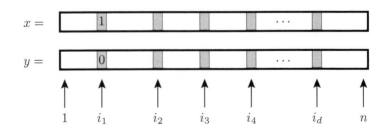

Let $i_1 < i_2 < \ldots < i_d$ be the positions where x and y differ. Now consider $N = (i_2 - i_1)(i_3 - i_1) \cdots (i_d - i_1)$. Then $N < n^{d-1}$. By the prime number theorem, there exists some prime $p = O(\log N) = O(d \log n)$ such that N is not divisible by p. So $i_j \not\equiv i_1 \pmod{p}$ for $2 \leq j \leq d$.

Define $a_{p,k}(x) = \left(\displaystyle\sum_{j \equiv k \pmod{p}} x[j] \right) \bmod 2$. This value can be calculated by a DFA consisting of two connected rings of p states each. We use such a DFA calculating a_{p,i_1}. Since p is not a factor of N, none of the positions $i_2, i_3, \ldots, i_d$ are included in the count a_{p,i_1}, and the two words x and y agree in all other positions. So x contains exactly one more 1 in these positions than y does, and hence we can separate the two words using $O(d \log n)$ states. $\qquad\square$

5   Special Classes of Words

5.1   Reversals

It is natural to think that pairs of words that are related might be easier to separate than arbitrary words; for example, it might be easy to separate a word from its reversal. No better upper bound is known for this special case. However, we still have a lower bound of $\Omega(\log n)$ for this restricted problem:

Proposition 12. *There exists a class of words w for which $\mathrm{sep}(w, w^R) = \Omega(\log n)$ where $n = |w|$.*

Proof. Consider separating

$$w = 0^{t-1} 10^{t-1+\mathrm{lcm}(1,2,\ldots t)}$$

from

$$w^R = 0^{t-1+\mathrm{lcm}(1,2,\ldots t)} 10^{t-1}.$$

Then, as before, no DFA with $\leq t$ states can separate w from w^R. $\qquad\square$

Must $\mathrm{sep}(w^R, x^R) = \mathrm{sep}(w, x)$? No, for $w = 1000$, $x = 0010$, we have

$$\mathrm{sep}(w, x) = 3$$

but

$$\mathrm{sep}(w^R, x^R) = 2.$$

Open Problem 13. *Is $\left| \mathrm{sep}(x, w) - \mathrm{sep}(x^R, w^R) \right|$ unbounded?*

5.2   Conjugates

Two words w, w' are *conjugates* if one is a cyclic shift of the other. For example, the English words enlist and listen are conjugates. Is the separating words problem any easier if restricted to pairs of conjugates?

Proposition 14. *There exist a infinite class of pairs of words w, x such that w, x are conjugates, and $\mathrm{sep}(w, x) = \Omega(\log n)$ for $|w| = |x| = n$.*

Proof. Consider again

$$w = 0^{t-1}10^{t-1+\mathrm{lcm}(1,2,\dots t)}1$$

and

$$w' = 0^{t-1+\mathrm{lcm}(1,2,\dots t)}10^{t-1}1.$$

□

6 Nondeterministic Separation

We can define $\mathrm{nsep}(w, x)$ in analogy with sep: the number of states in the smallest NFA accepting w but rejecting x. There do not seem to be any published results about this measure.

Now there is an asymmetry in the inputs: $\mathrm{nsep}(w, x)$ need not equal $\mathrm{nsep}(x, w)$. For example, the following 2-state NFA accepts $w = 000100$ and rejects $x = 010000$, so $\mathrm{nsep}(w, x) \leq 2$.

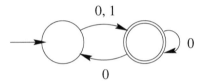

However, an easy computation shows that there is no 2-state NFA accepting x and rejecting w, so $\mathrm{nsep}(x, w) \geq 3$.

Open Problem 15. *Is $|\mathrm{nsep}(x, w) - \mathrm{nsep}(w, x)|$ unbounded?*

A natural question is whether NFAs give more separation power than DFAs. Indeed they do, since $\mathrm{sep}(0001, 0111) = 3$ but $\mathrm{nsep}(0001, 0111) = 2$. However, a more interesting question is the *extent* to which nondeterminism helps with separation — for example, whether it contributes only a constant factor or there is any asymptotic improvement in the number of states required.

Theorem 16. *The quantity $\mathrm{sep}(w, x)/\mathrm{nsep}(w, x)$ is unbounded.*

Proof. Consider once again the words

$$w = 0^{t-1+\mathrm{lcm}(1,2,\dots,t)}1^{t-1} \quad \text{and} \quad x = 0^{t-1}1^{t-1+\mathrm{lcm}(1,2,\dots,t)}$$

where $t = n^2 - 3n + 2$, $n \geq 4$.

We know from Theorem 6 that any DFA separating these words must have at least $t + 1 = n^2 - 3n + 3$ states.

Now consider the following NFA M:

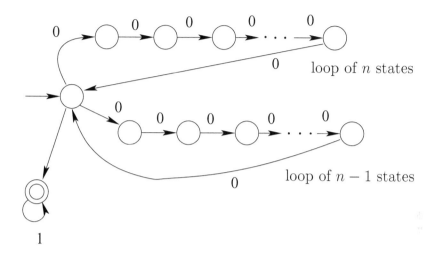

The language accepted by this NFA is $\{0^a : a \in A\}1^*$, where A is the set of all integers representable by a non-negative integer linear combination of n and $n-1$. But $t-1 = n^2 - 3n + 1 \notin A$, as can be seen by computing $t-1$ modulo $n-1$ and modulo n. On the other hand, every integer $\geq t$ is in A. Hence $w = 0^{t-1+\text{lcm}(1,2,\ldots,t)}1^{t-1}$ is accepted by M but $x = 0^{t-1}1^{t-1+\text{lcm}(1,2,\ldots,t)}$ is not.

Now M has $2n = \Theta(\sqrt{t})$ states, so $\text{sep}(x,w)/\text{nsep}(x,w) = \Omega(\sqrt{t}) = \Omega(\sqrt{\log|x|})$, which is unbounded. $\qquad \square$

Open Problem 17. *Find better bounds on* $\text{sep}(w,x)/\text{nsep}(w,x)$.

We can also get an $\Omega(\log n)$ lower bound for nondeterministic separation.

Theorem 18. *No NFA of n states can separate*

$$0^{n^2-1}1^{n^2-1+\text{lcm}(1,2,\ldots,n)}$$

from

$$0^{n^2-1+\text{lcm}(1,2,\ldots,n)}1^{n^2-1}.$$

Proof. A result of Chrobak [1], as corrected by To [11], states that every unary n-state NFA is equivalent to one consisting of a "tail" of at most $O(n^2)$ states, followed by a single nondeterministic state that leads to a set of cycles, each of which has at most n states. The size of the tail was proved to be at most $n^2 - 2$ by Geffert [3].

Now we use the same argument as for DFAs above. $\qquad \square$

Open Problem 19. *Find better bounds on* $\text{nsep}(w,x)$ *for* $|w| = |x| = n$, *as a function of n.*

Theorem 20. *We have* $\mathrm{nsep}(w, x) = \mathrm{nsep}(w^R, x^R)$.

Proof. Let $M = (Q, \Sigma, \delta, q_0, F)$ be an NFA with the smallest number of states accepting w and rejecting x. Now create a new NFA M' with initial state equal to any single state in $\delta(q_0, w) \cap F$ and final state q_0, and all other transitions of M reversed. Then M' accepts w^R. But M' rejects x^R. For if M' accepted x^R then M would also accept x, since the input string and transitions are reversed.   □

7   Separation by 2DPDA's

In [2], the authors showed that words can be separated with small context-free grammars (and hence small PDA's). In this section we observe

Proposition 21. *Two distinct words of length n can be separated by a 2DPDA of size $O(\log n)$.*

Proof. Recall that a 2DPDA is a deterministic pushdown automaton, with end-markers surrounding the input, and two-way access to the input tape. Given distinct strings w, x of length n, they must differ in some position p with $1 \le p \le n$. Using $O(\log p)$ states, we can reach position p on the input tape and accept if (say) the corresponding character equals $w[p]$, and reject otherwise.

Here is how to access position p of the input. We show how to go from scanning position i to position $2i$ using a constant number of states: we move left on the input, pushing two symbols per move on the stack, until the left endmarker is reached. Now we move right, popping one symbol per move, until the initial stack symbol is reached. Using this as a subroutine, and applying it to the binary expansion of p, we can, using $O(\log p)$ states, reach position p of the input.   □

8   Permutation Automata

We conclude by relating the separating words problem to a natural problem of algebra.

Instead of arbitrary automata, we could restrict our attention to automata where each letter induces a permutation of the states ("permutation automata"), as suggested by Robson [8]. He obtained an $O(n^{1/2})$ upper bound in this case.

For an n-state automaton, the action of each letter can be viewed as an element of $\mathcal{S}_n$, the symmetric group on n elements.

Turning the problem around, then, we could ask: what is the shortest pair of distinct equal-length binary words w, x, such that for all morphisms $\sigma : \{0, 1\}^* \to \mathcal{S}_n$ we have $\sigma(w) = \sigma(x)$? Although one might suspect that the answer is $\mathrm{lcm}(1, 2, \ldots, n)$, for $n = 4$, there is a shorter pair (of length 11): 00000011011 and 11011000000.

Now if $\sigma(w) = \sigma(x)$ for all σ, then (if we define $\sigma(x^{-1}) = \sigma(x)^{-1}$) we have that $\sigma(wx^{-1}) =$ the identity permutation for all σ.

Call any nonempty word y over the letters $0, 1, 0^{-1}, 1^{-1}$ an *identical relation* if $\sigma(y) =$ the identity for all morphisms σ. We say y is *nontrivial* if y contains no occurrences of 00^{-1} and 11^{-1}.

What is the length ℓ of the shortest nontrivial identical relation over $\mathcal{S}_n$? Recently Gimadeev and Vyalyi [4] proved $\ell = 2^{O(\sqrt{n} \log n)}$.

Acknowledgments

Thanks to Martin Demaine and Anna Lubiw, who participated in the open problem session at MIT where these problems were discussed.

We thank the DCFS 2011 referees for their helpful suggestions.

References

1. Chrobak, M.: Finite automata and unary languages. Theoret. Comput. Sci. 47, 149–158 (1986); Erratum 302, 497–498 (2003)
2. Currie, J., Petersen, H., Robson, J.M., Shallit, J.: Separating words with small grammars. J. Automata, Languages, and Combinatorics 4, 101–110 (1999)
3. Geffert, V.: Magic numbers in the state hierarchy of finite automata. Inform. Comput. 205, 1652–1670 (2007)
4. Gimadeev, R.A., Vyalyi, M.N.: Identical relations in symmetric groups and separating words with reversible automata. In: Ablayev, F., Mayr, E.W. (eds.) CSR 2010. LNCS, vol. 6072, pp. 144–155. Springer, Heidelberg (2010)
5. Goralčík, P., Koubek, V.: On discerning words by automata. In: Kott, L. (ed.) ICALP 1986. LNCS, vol. 226, pp. 116–122. Springer, Heidelberg (1986)
6. Nozaki, A.: Equivalence problem of non-deterministic finite automata. J. Comput. System Sci. 18, 8–17 (1979)
7. Robson, J.M.: Separating strings with small automata. Inform. Process. Lett. 30, 209–214 (1989)
8. Robson, J.M.: Separating words with machines and groups. RAIRO Inform. Théor. App. 30, 81–86 (1996)
9. Shallit, J.: A Second Course in Formal Languages and Automata Theory. Cambridge University Press, Cambridge (2009)
10. Shallit, J., Breitbart, Y.: Automaticity I: Properties of a measure of descriptional complexity. J. Comput. System Sci. 53, 10–25 (1996)
11. To, A.W.: Unary finite automata vs. arithmetic progressions. Inform. Process. Lett. 109, 1010–1014 (2009)

State Complexity of Four Combined Operations Composed of Union, Intersection, Star and Reversal[*]

Yuan Gao and Sheng Yu

Department of Computer Science, The University of Western Ontario
London, Ontario, Canada N6A 5B7
{ygao72,syu}@csd.uwo.ca

Abstract. In this paper, we study the state complexities of union and intersection combined with star and reversal, respectively. We obtain the exact bounds for these combined operations on regular languages and show that, as usually, they are different from the mathematical compositions of the state complexities of their individual participating operations.

1 Introduction

State complexity is one of the fundamental topics in automata theory, which is important from both theoretical aspect and implications in automata applications. State complexity is a worst-case complexity based on the number of states in a minimal deterministic finite automaton (DFA). The state complexity of an operation also gives an upper bound of both time and space complexity of the operation. For example, the programmer should know the largest possible number of states that would be generated before they program an operation of automata in an application since they need to allocate enough space for the computation and make an estimate of the time it takes.

The research on state complexity can be recalled to 1950's [20]. However, most results on state complexity came out since the 1990s [3–6, 11, 13–15, 19, 22–24]. The research was focused on individual operations, e.g. union, intersection, star, catenation, reversal, etc, until the mid of 2000s when the state complexities of combined operations were initiated [21, 26]. In the following years, many papers were published on this topic, e.g., [1, 2, 7–10, 16, 17].

State complexities of combined operations are not only fundamental and interesting theoretically, but also important in practice. Instead of only one operation is used, a sequence of operations are commonly used in an application. For example, several operations are often applied in a certain order in language searching and processing.

---

[*] This work was supported by the Natural Science and Engineering Council of Canada grant 41630.

M. Holzer, M. Kutrib, and G. Pighizzini (Eds.): DCFS 2011, LNCS 6808, pp. 158–171, 2011.
© Springer-Verlag Berlin Heidelberg 2011

The study of state complexity of individual operations cannot replace the study of state complexity of combined operations. The mathematical composition of the state complexities of individual participating operations is usually far greater than the exact state complexity of the combined operation, due to the fact that the resulting languages of the worst case of one operation may not be among the worst case input languages of the next operation [9, 16, 17, 21]. Clearly, state complexities of combined operations should be considered as an important topic in automata research.

In [21], two combined operations were investigated: $(L(M) \cup L(N))^*$ and $(L(M) \cap L(N))^*$, where M and N are m-state and n-state DFAs, respectively. In [17], Boolean operations combined with reversal were studied, including: $(L(M) \cup L(N))^R$ and $(L(M) \cap L(N))^R$. One natural question is what are the state complexities of these combined operations if we exchange the orders of the composed individual operations. An interesting observation would be how the state complexity of a combined operation changes when the order of the individual operations changes. Note that the study of many of those operations still has the same motivations. For example, we perform star or reversal first and then perform union or intersection. So, in this paper, we investigate four particular combined operations: $L(M)^* \cup L(N)$, $L(M)^* \cap L(N)$, $L(M)^R \cup L(N)$ and $L(M)^R \cap L(N)$.

We show that the state complexities of $L(M)^* \cup L(N)$ and $L(M)^* \cap L(N)$ are both $\frac{3}{4}2^m \cdot n - n + 1$ for $m, n \geq 2$, which have a gap of $n - 1$ with the mathematical compositions of the state complexities of their component operations. For $L(M)^R \cup L(N)$ and $L(M)^R \cap L(N)$, we prove that their state complexities are also the same: $2^m \cdot n - n + 1$ for $m, n \geq 2$. The gap between the mathematical compositions and state complexities is $n - 1$ as well.

In the next section, we introduce the basic notation and definitions used in this paper. In Sections 3, 4, 5 and 6, we investigate the state complexities of $L(M)^* \cup L(N)$, $L(M)^* \cap L(N)$, $L(M)^R \cup L(N)$ and $L(M)^R \cap L(N)$, respectively. In Section 7, we conclude the paper.

2   Preliminaries

An alphabet Σ is a finite set of letters. A word $w \in \Sigma^*$ is a sequence of letters in Σ, and the empty word, denoted by ε, is the word of length 0.

A *deterministic finite automaton* (DFA) is usually denoted by a 5-tuple $A = (Q, \Sigma, \delta, s, F)$, where Q is the finite and nonempty set of states, Σ is the alphabet, $\delta : Q \times \Sigma \rightarrow Q$ is the state transition function, $s \in Q$ is the initial state, and $F \subseteq Q$ is the set of final states. A DFA is said to be *complete* if δ is a total function. Complete DFAs are the basic model used in the study of state complexity. Without specific mentioning, all DFAs are assumed to be complete in this paper. We extend δ to $Q \times \Sigma^* \rightarrow Q$ in the usual way. Then the automaton accepts a word $w \in \Sigma^*$ if $\delta(s, w) \cap F \neq \emptyset$. Two states in a DFA are said to be *equivalent* if and only if for every word $w \in \Sigma^*$, if A is started in either state with w as input, it either accepts in both cases or rejects in both cases. The language accepted by a DFA A is denoted by $L(A)$. A language is accepted by many DFAs but there is only one essentially unique *minimal* DFA for the language which has the minimum number of states.

A *nondeterministic finite automaton* (NFA) is also denoted by a 5-tuple $B = (Q, \Sigma, \delta, s, F)$, where Q, Σ, s, and F are defined the same way as in a DFA and $\delta : Q \times \Sigma \rightarrow 2^Q$ maps a pair consisting of a state and an input symbol into a set of states rather than a single state. An NFA may have multiple initial states, in which case an NFA is denoted by $(Q, \Sigma, \delta, S, F)$ where S is the set of initial states. An NFA can always be transformed into an equivalent DFA by performing subset construction. So, a language L is accepted by an NFA if and only if L is accepted by a DFA, and such a language is called a *regular language*. Two finite automata are said to be equivalent if they accepts the same regular language. The reader may refer to [12, 25] for more details about regular languages and automata theory.

The *state complexity* of a regular language L is the number of states of the minimal, complete DFA accepting L. The state complexity of a class of regular languages is the worst among the state complexities of all the languages in the class. The state complexity of an operation on regular languages is the state complexity of the resulting languages from the operation. For example, we say that the state complexity of union of an m-state DFA language and an n-state DFA language is mn. This implies that the largest number of states of the minimal, complete DFAs that accept the union of an m-state DFA language and an n-state DFA language is mn, and such languages exist. Thus, state complexity is a worst-case complexity.

3   State Complexity of $L_1^* \cup L_2$

We first consider the state complexity of $L_1^* \cup L_2$, where L_1 and L_2 are regular languages accepted by m-state and n-state DFAs, respectively. It has been proved that the state complexity of L_1^* is $\frac{3}{4}2^m$ and the state complexity of $L_1 \cup L_2$ is mn [18, 24]. The mathematical composition of them is $\frac{3}{4}2^m \cdot n$. In the following, we show that the state complexity of this combined operation is slightly lower.

Theorem 1. *For any m-state DFA $M = (Q_M, \Sigma, \delta_M, s_M, F_M)$ and n-state DFA $N = (Q_N, \Sigma, \delta_N, s_N, F_N)$ such that $|F_M - \{s_M\}| = k \geq 1$, $m \geq 2$, $n \geq 1$, there exists a DFA of at most $(2^{m-1} + 2^{m-k-1}) \cdot n - n + 1$ states that accepts $L(M)^* \cup L(N)$.*

Proof. Let $M = (Q_M, \Sigma, \delta_M, s_M, F_M)$ be a complete DFA of m states. Denote $F_M - \{s_M\}$ by F_0. Then $|F_0| = k \geq 1$. Let $N = (Q_N, \Sigma, \delta_N, s_N, F_N)$ be another complete DFA of n states. Let $M' = (Q_{M'}, \Sigma, \delta_{M'}, s_{M'}, F_{M'})$ be a DFA where

$$s_{M'} \notin Q_M \text{ is a new initial state,}$$
$$Q_{M'} = \{s_{M'}\} \cup \{P \mid P \subseteq (Q_M - F_0) \;\&\; P \neq \emptyset\}$$
$$\cup \{R \mid R \subseteq Q_M \;\&\; s_M \in R \;\&\; R \cap F_0 \neq \emptyset\},$$
$$F_{M'} = \{s_{M'}\} \cup \{R \mid R \subseteq Q_M \;\&\; R \cap F_M \neq \emptyset\},$$

for $a \in \Sigma$,

$$\delta_{M'}(s_{M'}, a) = \begin{cases} \{\delta_M(s_M, a)\}, & \text{if } \delta_M(s_M, a) \in F_0; \\ \{\delta_M(s_M, a)\} \cup \{s_M\}, & \text{otherwise,} \end{cases}$$

and for $R \in Q_{M'} - \{s_{M'}\}$,

$$\delta_{M'}(R, a) = \begin{cases} \delta_M(R, a), & \text{if } \delta_M(R, a) \cap F_0 = \emptyset; \\ \delta_M(R, a) \cup \{s_M\}, & \text{otherwise.} \end{cases}$$

It is clear that M' accepts $L(M)^*$. In the second term of the union for $Q_{M'}$ there are $2^{m-k} - 1$ states. And in the third term, there are $(2^k - 1)2^{m-k-1}$ states. So M' has $2^{m-1} + 2^{m-k-1}$ states in total. Now we construct another DFA $A = (Q, \Sigma, \delta, s, F)$ where

$$s = \langle s_{M'}, s_N \rangle,$$
$$Q = \{\langle i, j \rangle \mid i \in Q_{M'} - \{s_{M'}\}, j \in Q_N\} \cup \{s\},$$
$$\delta(\langle i, j \rangle, a) = \langle \delta_{M'}(i, a), \delta_N(j, a) \rangle, \ \langle i, j \rangle \in Q, \ a \in \Sigma,$$
$$F = \{\langle i, j \rangle \mid i \in F_{M'} \text{ or } j \in F_N\}.$$

We can see that

$$L(A) = L(M') \cup L(N) = L(M)^* \cup L(N).$$

Note $\langle s_{M'}, j \rangle \notin Q$, for $j \in Q_N - \{s_N\}$, because there is no transition going into $s_{M'}$ in the DFA M'. So there are at least $n-1$ states in Q that are not reachable. Thus, the number of states of minimal DFA that accepts $L(M)^* \cup L(N)$ is no more than

$$|Q| = (2^{m-1} + 2^{m-k-1}) \cdot n - n + 1. \qquad \square$$

If s_M is the only final state of M $(k = 0)$, then $L(M)^* = L(M)$.

Corollary 2. *For any m-state DFA $M = (Q_M, \Sigma, \delta_M, s_M, F_M)$ and n-state DFA $N = (Q_N, \Sigma, \delta_N, s_N, F_N)$, $m > 1$, $n > 0$, there exists a DFA A of at most $\frac{3}{4}2^m \cdot n - n + 1$ states such that $L(A) = L(M)^* \cup L(N)$.*

Proof.   Let k be defined as in the above proof. There are two cases in the following.

(I) $k = 0$. In this case, $L(M)^* = L(M)$. Then A simply needs at most $m \cdot n$ states, which is less than $\frac{3}{4}2^m \cdot n - n + 1$ when $m > 1$.

(II) $k \geq 1$. The claim is clearly true by Theorem 1. $\qquad \square$

Next, we show that the upper bound $\frac{3}{4}2^m \cdot n - n + 1$ is reachable.

Theorem 3. *Given two integers $m \geq 2$, $n \geq 2$, there exist a DFA M of m states and a DFA N of n states such that any DFA accepting $L(M)^* \cup L(N)$ needs at least $\frac{3}{4}2^m \cdot n - n + 1$ states.*

Proof. Let $M = (Q_M, \Sigma, \delta_M, 0, \{m-1\})$ be a DFA, where $Q_M = \{0, 1, \ldots, m-1\}$, $\Sigma = \{a, b, c\}$ and the transitions of M are

$$\delta_M(i, a) = i + 1 \bmod m, \ i = 0, 1, \ldots, m - 1,$$
$$\delta_M(0, b) = 0, \ \delta_M(i, b) = i + 1 \bmod m, \ i = 1, \ldots, m - 1,$$
$$\delta_M(i, c) = i, \ i = 0, 1, \ldots, m - 1.$$

The transition diagram of M is shown in Figure 1.

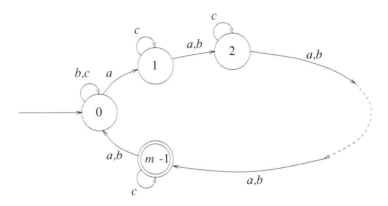

Fig. 1. Witness DFA M for Theorems 3 and 7

Let $N = (Q_N, \Sigma, \delta_N, 0, \{n-1\})$ be another DFA, where $Q_N = \{0, 1, \ldots, n-1\}$ and

$$\delta_N(i, a) = i, \ i = 0, 1, \ldots, n - 1,$$
$$\delta_N(i, b) = i, \ i = 0, 1, \ldots, n - 1,$$
$$\delta_N(i, c) = i + 1 \bmod n, \ i = 0, 1, \ldots, n - 1.$$

The transition diagram of N is shown in Figure 2.

It has been proved in [24] that the minimal DFA that accepts the star of an m-state DFA language has $\frac{3}{4}2^m$ states in the worst case. M is a modification of the worst-case example given in [24] by adding a c-loop to every state. So we design a $\frac{3}{4}2^m$-state, minimal DFA $M' = (Q_{M'}, \Sigma, \delta_{M'}, s_{M'}, F_{M'})$ that accepts $L(M)^*$, where

$$s_{M'} \notin Q_M \text{ is a new initial state,}$$
$$Q_{M'} = \{s_{M'}\} \cup \{P \mid P \subseteq \{0, 1, \ldots, m - 2\} \ \& \ P \neq \emptyset\}$$
$$\cup \{R \mid R \subseteq \{0, 1, \ldots, m - 1\} \ \& \ 0 \in R \ \& \ m - 1 \in R\},$$
$$F_{M'} = \{s_{M'}\} \cup \{R \mid R \subseteq \{0, 1, \ldots, m - 1\} \ \& \ m - 1 \in R\},$$

and for $R \subseteq Q_M$ and $a \in \Sigma$,

$$\delta_{M'}(s_{M'}, a) = \{\delta_M(0, a)\},$$

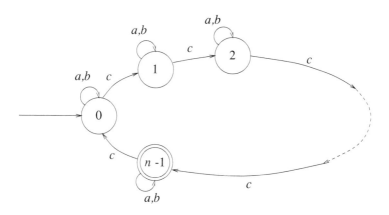

Fig. 2. Witness DFA N for Theorems 3 and 7

$$\delta_{M'}(R, a) = \begin{cases} \delta_M(R, a), & \text{if } m - 1 \notin \delta_M(R, a); \\ \delta_M(R, a) \cup \{0\}, & \text{otherwise.} \end{cases}$$

Then we construct the DFA $A = (Q, \Sigma, \delta, s, F)$ that accepts $L(M)^* \cup L(N)$ exactly as described in the proof of Theorem 1, where

$$s = \langle s_{M'}, 0 \rangle,$$
$$Q = \{\langle i, j \rangle \mid i \in Q_{M'} - \{s_{M'}\}, j \in Q_N\} \cup \{s\},$$
$$\delta(\langle i, j \rangle, a) = \langle \delta_{M'}(i, a), \delta_N(j, a) \rangle, \langle i, j \rangle \in Q, a \in \Sigma,$$
$$F = \{\langle i, j \rangle \mid i \in F_{M'} \text{ or } j = n - 1\}.$$

Now we need to show that A is a minimal DFA.

(I) All the states in Q are reachable.

For an arbitrary state $\langle i, j \rangle$ in Q, there always exists a string $w_1 w_2$ such that $\delta(\langle s'_M, 0 \rangle, w_1 w_2) = \langle i, j \rangle$, where

$$\delta_{M'}(s_{M'}, w_1) = i, w_1 \in \{a, b\}^*,$$
$$\delta_N(0, w_2) = j, w_2 \in \{c\}^*.$$

(II) Any two different states $\langle i_1, j_1 \rangle$ and $\langle i_2, j_2 \rangle$ in Q are distinguishable.

1. $i_1 \neq i_2, j_2 \neq n - 1$. There exists a string w_1 such that

$$\delta(\langle i_1, j_1 \rangle, w_1) \in F,$$
$$\delta(\langle i_2, j_2 \rangle, w_1) \notin F,$$

where $w_1 \in \{a, b\}^*$, $\delta_{M'}(i_1, w_1) \in F_{M'}$ and $\delta'_M(i_2, w_1) \notin F'_M$.

2. $i_1 \neq i_2, j_2 = n - 1$. There exists a string w_1 such that

$$\delta(\langle i_1, j_1 \rangle, w_1 c) \in F,$$
$$\delta(\langle i_2, j_2 \rangle, w_1 c) \notin F,$$

where $w_1 \in \{a, b\}^*$, $\delta_{M'}(i_1, w_1) \in F_{M'}$ and $\delta_{M'}(i_2, w_1) \notin F_{M'}$.

3. $i_1 = i_2 \notin F_{M'}$, $j_1 \neq j_2$. For this case, the string c^{n-1-j_1} distinguishes the two states, since $\delta(\langle i_1, j_1 \rangle, c^{n-1-j_1}) \in F$ and $\delta(\langle i_2, j_2 \rangle, c^{n-1-j_1}) \notin F$.
4. $i_1 = i_2 \in F_{M'}$, $j_1 \neq j_2$. The string $b^m c^{n-1-j_1}$ distinguishes them, because $\delta(\langle i_1, j_1 \rangle, b^m c^{n-1-j_1}) \in F$ and $\delta(\langle i_2, j_2 \rangle, b^m c^{n-1-j_1}) \notin F$.

Since all the states in A are reachable and distinguishable, the DFA A is minimal. Thus, any DFA that accepts $L(M)^* \cup L(N)$ has at least $\frac{3}{4}2^m \cdot n - n + 1$ states. □

This result gives a lower bound for the state complexity of $L(M)^* \cup L(N)$. It coincides with the upper bound in Corollary 2. So we have the following Theorem 4.

Theorem 4. *For any integer* $m \geq 2$, $n \geq 2$, $\frac{3}{4}2^m \cdot n - n + 1$ *states are both sufficient and necessary in the worst case for a DFA to accept* $L(M)^* \cup L(N)$, *where M is an m-state DFA and N is an n-state DFA.*

4 State Complexity of $L_1^* \cap L_2$

Since the state complexity of intersection on regular languages is the same as that of union [24], the mathematical composition of the state complexities of star and intersection is also $\frac{3}{4}2^m \cdot n$. In this section, we show that the state complexity of $L(M)^* \cap L(N)$ is $\frac{3}{4}2^m \cdot n - n + 1$ which is the same as the state complexity of $L(M)^* \cup L(N)$.

Theorem 5. *For any m-state DFA* $M = (Q_M, \Sigma, \delta_M, s_M, F_M)$ *and n-state DFA* $N = (Q_N, \Sigma, \delta_N, s_N, F_N)$ *such that* $|F_M - \{s_M\}| = k \geq 1$, $m > 1$, $n > 0$, *there exists a DFA of at most* $(2^{m-1} + 2^{m-k-1}) \cdot n - n + 1$ *states that accepts* $L(M)^* \cap L(N)$.

Proof.   We construct the DFA A for $L(M)^* \cap L(N)$ which is the same as in the proof of Theorem 1, except that its set of final states is

$$F = \{\langle i, j \rangle \mid i \in F_{M'}, \, j \in F_N\}.$$

Thus, after removing the $n - 1$ unreachable states $\langle s_{M'}, j \rangle \notin Q$, for $j \in Q_N - \{s_N\}$, the number of states of A is sill no more than $(2^{m-1} + 2^{m-k-1}) \cdot n - n + 1$. □

Similarly to the proof of Corollary 2, we consider both the case when M has no other final state except s_M ($L(M)^* = L(M)$) and the case when M has some other final states (Theorem 5). Then we obtain the following corollary.

Corollary 6. *For any m-state DFA* $M = (Q_M, \Sigma, \delta_M, s_M, F_M)$ *and n-state DFA* $N = (Q_N, \Sigma, \delta_N, s_N, F_N)$, $m > 1$, $n > 0$, *there exists a DFA A of at most* $\frac{3}{4}2^m \cdot n - n + 1$ *states such that* $L(A) = L(M)^* \cap L(N)$.

Next, we show that this general upper bound of state complexity of $L(M)^* \cap L(N)$ can be reached by some witness DFAs.

Theorem 7. *Given two integers $m \geq 2$, $n \geq 2$, there exist a DFA M of m states and a DFA N of n states such that any DFA accepting $L(M)^* \cap L(N)$ needs at least $\frac{3}{4}2^m \cdot n - n + 1$ states.*

Proof.   We use the same DFAs M and N as in the proof of Theorem 3. Construct the DFA $M' = (Q_{M'}, \Sigma, \delta_{M'}, s_{M'}, F_{M'})$ that accepts $L(M)^*$ in the same way.

Then we construct the DFA $A = (Q, \Sigma, \delta, s, F)$ that accepts $L(M)^* \cap L(N)$ exactly as described in the proof of Theorem 3 except that

$$F = \{\langle i, n-1 \rangle \mid i \in F_{M'}\}.$$

Now let us prove that A is minimal. We omit the proof for the reachability of an arbitrary state $\langle i, j \rangle$ in A, because it is the same as that in the proof of Theorem 3. In the following, we prove that any two different states $\langle i_1, j_1 \rangle$ and $\langle i_2, j_2 \rangle$ of A are distinguishable.

1. $i_1 \neq i_2$.
   We can find a string w_1 such that
   $$\delta(\langle i_1, j_1 \rangle, w_1 c^{n-1-j_1}) \in F,$$
   $$\delta(\langle i_2, j_2 \rangle, w_1 c^{n-1-j_1}) \notin F,$$
   where $w_1 \in \{a, b\}^*$, $\delta_{M'}(i_1, w_1) \in F_{M'}$ and $\delta_{M'}(i_2, w_1) \notin F_{M'}$.
2. $i_1 = i_2 \notin F_{M'}$, $j_1 \neq j_2$.
   There exists a string w_2 such that
   $$\delta(\langle i_1, j_1 \rangle, w_2 c^{n-1-j_1}) \in F,$$
   $$\delta(\langle i_2, j_2 \rangle, w_2 c^{n-1-j_1}) \notin F,$$
   where $w_2 \in \{a, b\}^*$ and $\delta_{M'}(i_1, w_2) \in F_{M'}$.
3. $i_1 = i_2 \in F_{M'}$, $j_1 \neq j_2$.
   $$\delta(\langle i_1, j_1 \rangle, c^{n-1-j_1}) \in F,$$
   $$\delta(\langle i_2, j_2 \rangle, c^{n-1-j_1}) \notin F.$$

From (I) and (II), A is a minimal DFA with $\frac{3}{4}2^m \cdot n - n + 1$ states which accepts $L(M)^* \cap L(N)$.   □

This lower bound coincides with the upper bound in Corollary 6. Thus, the bounds are tight.

Theorem 8. *For any integer $m \geq 2$, $n \geq 2$, $\frac{3}{4}2^m \cdot n - n + 1$ states are both sufficient and necessary in the worst case for a DFA to accept $L(M)^* \cap L(N)$, where M is an m-state DFA and N is an n-state DFA.*

5   State Complexity of $L_1^R \cup L_2$

In this section, we study the state complexity of $L_1^R \cup L_2$, where L_1 and L_2 are regular languages. It has been proved that the state complexity of L_1^R is

2^m and the state complexity of $L_1 \cup L_2$ is mn [18, 24]. Thus, the mathematical composition of them is $2^m \cdot n$. In this section we will prove that this upper bound of state complexity of $L_1^R \cup L_2$ cannot be reached in any case. We will first try to lower the upper bound in the following.

Theorem 9. *Let L_1 and L_2 be two regular language accepted by an m-state and n-state DFAs, respectively. Then there exists a DFA of at most $2^m \cdot n - n + 1$ states that accepts $L_1^R \cup L_2$.*

Proof.   Let $M = (Q_M, \Sigma, \delta_M, s_M, F_M)$ be a complete DFA of m states and $L_1 = L(M)$. Let $N = (Q_N, \Sigma, \delta_N, s_N, F_N)$ be another complete DFA of n states and $L_2 = L(N)$. Let $M' = (Q_M, \Sigma, \delta_{M'}, F_M, \{s_M\})$ be an NFA with multiple initial states. $\delta_{M'}(p, a) = q$ if $\delta_M(q, a) = p$ where $a \in \Sigma$ and $p, q \in Q_M$. Clearly, $L(M') = L(M)^R = L_1^R$. After performing subset construction, we can get a 2^m-state DFA $A = (Q_A, \Sigma, \delta_A, s_A, F_A)$ that is equivalent to M'. Since A has 2^m states, one of its final state must be Q_M. Now we construct a DFA $B = (Q_B, \Sigma, \delta_B, s_B, F_B)$, where

$$Q_B = \{\langle i, j \rangle \mid i \in Q_A, j \in Q_N\},$$
$$s_B = \langle s_A, s_N \rangle,$$
$$F_B = \{\langle i, j \rangle \in Q_B \mid i \in F_A \text{ or } j \in F_N\},$$
$$\delta_B(\langle i, j \rangle, a) = \langle i', j' \rangle, \text{ if } \langle i, j \rangle \in Q_B, \delta_A(i, a) = i', \delta_N(j, a) = j', a \in \Sigma.$$

We can see that $\delta_B(\langle Q_M, j \rangle, a) \in F_B$ for any $j \in Q_N$ and $a \in \Sigma$. This is because M is a complete DFA and an a-transition is defined for every state in Q_M. Therefore, in the transition function of A which is reversed from δ_M, we have $\delta_A(Q_M, a) = Q_M \in F_A$. Then we know that for any $j \in Q_N$, $w \in \Sigma^*$,

$$\delta_B(\langle Q_M, j \rangle, w) = \langle Q_M, j' \rangle \in F_B$$

where $\delta_N(j, w) = j'$. This means all the states (two-tuples) starting with Q_M are equivalent. There are n such states in total. Thus, the minimal DFA accepting $L_1^R \cup L_2$ has no more than $2^m \cdot n - n + 1$ states.   □

This result gives an upper bound of state complexity of $L_1^R \cup L_2$. Now let's see if this bound is reachable.

Theorem 10. *Given two integers $m \geq 2$, $n \geq 2$, there exist a DFA M of m states and a DFA N of n states such that any DFA accepting $L(M)^R \cup L(N)$ needs at least $2^m \cdot n - n + 1$ states.*

Proof.   Let $M = (Q_M, \Sigma, \delta_M, 0, \{0\})$ be a DFA, where $Q_M = \{0, 1, \ldots, m-1\}$, $\Sigma = \{a, b, c, d\}$ and the transitions are

$$\delta_M(0, a) = m - 1, \delta_M(i, a) = i - 1, i = 1, \ldots, m - 1,$$
$$\delta_M(0, b) = 1, \delta_M(i, b) = i, i = 1, \ldots, m - 1,$$
$$\delta_M(0, c) = 1, \delta_M(1, c) = 0, \delta_M(j, c) = i, j = 2, \ldots, m - 1,$$
$$\delta_M(k, d) = k, k = 0, \ldots, m - 1.$$

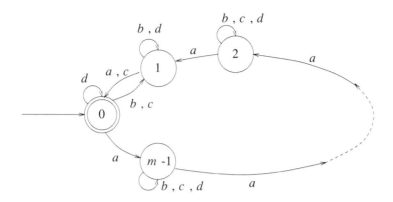

Fig. 3. The transition diagram of the witness DFA M of Theorem 10

The transition diagram of M is shown in Figure 3. Let $N = (Q_N, \Sigma, \delta_N, 0, \{0\})$ be another DFA, where $Q_N = \{0, 1, \ldots, n-1\}$, $\Sigma = \{a, b, c, d\}$ and the transitions are

$$\delta_N(i, a) = i,\ i = 0, \ldots, n-1,$$
$$.\ \delta_N(i, b) = i,\ i = 0, \ldots, n-1,$$
$$\delta_N(i, c) = i,\ i = 0, \ldots, n-1,$$
$$\delta_N(i, d) = i+1 \bmod n,\ i = 0, \ldots, n-1.$$

The transition diagram of N is shown in Figure 4.

Note that M is a modification of worst case example given in [24] for reversal, by adding a d-loop to every state. Intuitively, the minimal DFA accepting $L(M)^R$ should also have 2^m states. Before using this result, we will prove it first. Let $A = (Q_A, \Sigma, \delta_A, \{0\}, F_A)$ be a DFA, where

$$Q_A = \{q \mid q \subseteq Q_M\},$$
$$\Sigma = \{a, b, c, d\},$$
$$\delta_A(p, e) = \{j \mid \delta_M(j, e) = i, i \in p\},\ p \in Q_A,\ e \in \Sigma,$$
$$F_A = \{q \mid 0 \in q, q \in Q_A\}.$$

Clearly, A has 2^m states and it accepts $L(M)^R$. Now let's prove it is minimal.

(i) Every state $i \in Q_A$ is reachable.

1. $i = \emptyset$.
   $|i| = 0$ if and only if $i = \emptyset$. $\delta_A(\{0\}, b) = i = \emptyset$.
2. $|i| = 1$.
   Assume that $i = \{p\}$, $0 \le p \le m-1$. $\delta_A(\{0\}, a^p) = i$.
3. $2 \le |i| \le m$.
   Assume that $i = \{i_1, i_2, \ldots, i_k\}$, $0 \le i_1 < i_2 < \ldots < i_k \le m-1$, $2 \le k \le m$. $\delta_A(\{0\}, w) = i$, where

   $$w = ab(ac)^{i_k - i_{k-1} - 1} ab(ac)^{i_{k-1} - i_{k-2} - 1} \cdots ab(ac)^{i_2 - i_1 - 1} a^{i_1}.$$

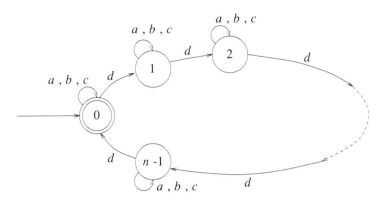

Fig. 4. The transition diagram of the witness DFA N of Theorem 10

(ii) Any two different states i and j in Q_A are distinguishable.
   Without loss of generality, we may assume that $|i| \geq |j|$. Let $x \in i - j$. Then
   a string a^{m-x} can distinguish these two states because

$$\delta_A(i, a^{m-x}) \in F_A,$$
$$\delta_A(j, a^{m-x}) \notin F_A.$$

Thus, A is a minimal DFA with 2^m states which accepts $L(M)^R$. Now let $B = (Q_B, \Sigma, \delta_B, \langle\{0\}, 0\rangle, F_B)$ be a DFA, where

$$Q_B = \{\langle p, q \rangle \mid p \in Q_A - \{Q_M\}, q \in Q_N\} \cup \{\langle Q_M, 0\rangle\},$$
$$\Sigma = \{a, b, c, d\},$$
$$F_B = \{\langle p, q \rangle \mid p \in F_A \text{ or } q \in F_N, \langle p, q \rangle \in Q_B\},$$

and for $\langle p, q \rangle \in Q_B$, , $e \in \Sigma$

$$\delta_B(\langle p, q \rangle, e) = \begin{cases} \langle p', q' \rangle & \text{if } \delta_A(p, e) = p', \delta_N(q, e) = q', p' \neq Q_M, \\ \langle Q_M, 0\rangle & \text{if } \delta_A(p, e) = Q_M. \end{cases}$$

As we mentioned in last proof, all the states (two-tuples) starting with Q_M are equivalent. Thus, we replace them with one state: $\langle Q_M, 0\rangle$. It is easy to see that B accepts the language $L(M)^R \cup L(N)$. It has $2^m \cdot n - n + 1$ states. Now lets see if B is a minimal DFA.

(I) All the states in Q_B are reachable.
   For an arbitrary state $\langle p, q \rangle$ in Q_B, there always exists a string $d^q w$ such that $\delta_B(\langle\{0\}, 0\rangle, d^q w) = \langle p, q \rangle$, where $w \in \{a, b, c\}^*$ and $\delta_A(\{0\}, w) = p$.

(II) Any two different states $\langle p_1, q_1 \rangle$ and $\langle p_2, q_2 \rangle$ in Q_B are distinguishable.
   1. $q_1 = q_2$.
   We can easily find a string $d^i w$ such that

$$\delta_B(\langle p_1, q_1 \rangle, d^i w) \in F_B,$$
$$\delta_B(\langle p_2, q_2 \rangle, d^i w) \notin F_B,$$

where $i + q_1 \bmod n \neq 0$, $w \in \{a, b, c\}^*$, $\delta_A(p_1, w) \in F_A$ and $\delta_A(p_2, w) \notin F_A$.

2. $p_1 = p_2$, $q_1 \neq q_2$.

A string $d^{n-q_1}w$ can distinguish these two states where $w \in \{a,b,c\}^*$ and $\delta_A(p_1, w) \notin F_A$, because

$$\delta_B(\langle p_1, q_1 \rangle, d^{n-q_1}w) \in F_B,$$
$$\delta_B(\langle p_2, q_2 \rangle, d^{n-q_1}w) \notin F_B.$$

3. $p_1 \neq p_2$, $q_1 \neq q_2$.

We first find a string $w \in \{a,b,c\}^*$ such that $\delta_A(p_1, w) \in F_A$ and $\delta_A(p_2, w) \notin F_A$. Then it is clear that

$$\delta_B(\langle p_1, q_1 \rangle, d^{n-q_1}w) \in F_B,$$
$$\delta_B(\langle p_2, q_2 \rangle, d^{n-q_1}w) \notin F_B.$$

Since all the states in B are reachable and distinguishable, DFA B is minimal. Thus, any DFA accepting $L(M)^R \cup L(N)$ needs at least $2^m \cdot n - n + 1$ states. □

This result gives a lower bound for the state complexity of $L(M)^R \cup L(N)$. It coincides with the upper bound. So we have the following Theorem 11.

Theorem 11. *For any integer $m \geq 2$, $n \geq 2$, $2^m \cdot n - n + 1$ states are both sufficient and necessary in the worst case for a DFA to accept $L(M)^R \cup L(N)$, where M is an m-state DFA and N is an n-state DFA.*

6   State Complexity of $L_1^R \cap L_2$

The state complexity of $L_1^R \cap L_2$ is the same as that of $L_1^R \cup L_2$, namely, $2^m \cdot n - n + 1$, since

$$L_1^R \cap L_2 = \overline{\overline{L_1^R} \cup \overline{L_2}} = \overline{\overline{L_1}^R \cup \overline{L_2}}$$

according to De Morgan's laws and $\overline{L^R} = \overline{L}^R$, where $\overline{L}$ denotes the complementation of L, and the state complexity of the complementation of an n-state DFA language is n. Thus, we have the following theorem.

Theorem 12. *For any integer $m \geq 2$, $n \geq 2$, $2^m \cdot n - n + 1$ states are both sufficient and necessary in the worst case for a DFA to accept $L(M)^R \cap L(N)$, where M is an m-state DFA and N is an n-state DFA.*

Note that we cannot use the same method to prove the state complexity of $L_1^* \cap L_2$ is the same as that of $L_1^* \cup L_2$, because $\overline{L^*} \neq \overline{L}^*$.

7   Conclusion

In this paper, we have studied the state complexities of union and intersection combined with star and reversal. We have obtained the state complexities of four particular combined operations that are $L(M)^* \cup L(N)$, $L(M)^* \cap L(N)$,

$L(M)^R \cup L(N)$ and $L(M)^R \cap L(N)$ for $m \geq 2$ and $n \geq 2$. Note that they are all $n-1$ less than the mathematical compositions of the state complexities of their component operations. The gap for $L(M)^* \cup L(N)$ and $L(M)^* \cap L(N)$ exists due to the $n-1$ unreachable states because there are no ingoing transitions for the new initial state which is added for star operation. For $L(M)^R \cup L(N)$ and $L(M)^R \cap L(N)$, we have the same gap because there are $n-1$ equivalent states after construction, which is caused by the resulting languages of reversal operation to reach the worst case.

Considering other known results on the state complexities of combined operations, an interesting question is why the state complexities of $L(M)^* \cup L(N)$ and $L(M)^* \cap L(N)$ are the same whereas the state complexities of $(L(M) \cup L(N))^*$ and $(L(M) \cap L(N))^*$ are different.

Acknowledgement

We would like to thank the anonymous referees of DCFS 2011 for their careful reading and valuable suggestions.

References

1. Cui, B., Gao, Y., Kari, L., Yu, S.: State complexity of catenation combined with star and reversal. In: Proceedings of Descriptional Complexity of Formal Systems 12th Workshop, Saskatoon, pp. 74–85 (2010)
2. Cui, B., Gao, Y., Kari, L., Yu, S.: State complexity of catenation combined with union and intersection. In: Domaratzki, M., Salomaa, K. (eds.) CIAA 2010. LNCS, vol. 6482, pp. 95–104. Springer, Heidelberg (2011)
3. Câmpeanu, C., Culik, K., Salomaa, K., Yu, S.: State complexity of basic operations on finite languages. In: Boldt, O., Jürgensen, H. (eds.) WIA 1999. LNCS, vol. 2214, pp. 60–70. Springer, Heidelberg (2001)
4. Campeanu, C., Salomaa, K., Yu, S.: Tight lower bound for the state complexity of shuffle of regular languages. Journal of Automata, Languages and Combinatorics 7(3), 303–310 (2002)
5. Daley, M., Domaratzki, M., Salomaa, K.: State complexity of orthogonal catenation. In: Proceedings of Descriptional Complexity of Formal Systems 10th Workshop, Charlottetown, pp. 134–144 (2008)
6. Domaratzki, M.: State complexity and proportional removals. Journal of Automata, Languages and Combinatorics 7, 455–468 (2002)
7. Domaratzki, M., Okhotin, A.: State complexity of power. Theoretical Computer Science 410(24-25), 2377–2392 (2009)
8. Ésik, Z., Gao, Y., Liu, G., Yu, S.: Estimation of State Complexity of Combined Operations. Theoretical Computer Science 410(35), 3272–3280 (2008)
9. Gao, Y., Salomaa, K., Yu, S.: The state complexity of two combined operations: star of catenation and star of Reversal. Fundamenta Informaticae 83(1-2), 75–89 (2008)
10. Gao, Y., Yu, S.: State complexity approximation. Electronic Proceedings in Theoretical Computer Science 3, 121–130 (2009)

11. Holzer, M., Kutrib, M.: State complexity of basic operations on nondeterministic finite automata. In: Champarnaud, J.-M., Maurel, D. (eds.) CIAA 2002. LNCS, vol. 2608, pp. 148–157. Springer, Heidelberg (2003)

12. Hopcroft, J.E., Motwani, R., Ullman, J.D.: Introduction to Automata Theory, Languages, and Computation, 2nd edn. Addison Wesley, Reading (2001)

13. Jirásek, J., Jirásková, G., Szabari, A.: State complexity of concatenation and complementation of regular languages. International Journal of Foundations of Computer Science 16, 511–529 (2005)

14. Jirásková, G.: State complexity of some operations on binary regular languages. Theoretical Computer Science 330, 287–298 (2005)

15. Jirásková, G., Okhotin, A.: State complexity of cyclic shift. In: Proceedings of Descriptional Complexity of Formal Systems 7th Workshop, Como, pp. 182–193 (2005)

16. Jirásková, G., Okhotin, A.: On the state complexity of star of union and star of intersection, Turku Center for Computer Science TUCS Technical Report No. 825 (2007)

17. Liu, G., Martin-Vide, C., Salomaa, A., Yu, S.: State complexity of basic language operations combined with reversal. Information and Computation 206, 1178–1186 (2008)

18. Maslov, A.N.: Estimates of the number of states of finite automata. Soviet Mathematics Doklady 11, 1373–1375 (1970)

19. Pighizzini, G., Shallit, J.O.: Unary language operations, state complexity and Jacobsthal's function. International Journal of Foundations of Computer Science 13, 145–159 (2002)

20. Rabin, M., Scott, D.: Finite automata and their decision problems. IBM Journal of Research and Development 3(2), 114–125 (1959)

21. Salomaa, A., Salomaa, K., Yu, S.: State complexity of combined operations. Theoretical Computer Science 383, 140–152 (2007)

22. Salomaa, A., Wood, D., Yu, S.: On the state complexity of reversals of regular languages. Theoretical Computer Science 320, 293–313 (2004)

23. Yu, S.: State complexity of regular languages. Journal of Automata, Languages and Combinatorics 6(2), 221–234 (2001)

24. Yu, S., Zhuang, Q., Salomaa, K.: The state complexity of some basic operations on regular languages. Theoretical Computer Science 125, 315–328 (1994)

25. Yu, S.: Regular languages. In: Rozenberg, G., Salomaa, A. (eds.) Handbook of Formal Languages, vol. 1, pp. 41–110. Springer, Heidelberg (1997)

26. Yu, S.: On the state complexity of combined operations. In: Ibarra, O.H., Yen, H.-C. (eds.) CIAA 2006. LNCS, vol. 4094, pp. 11–22. Springer, Heidelberg (2006)

k-Local Internal Contextual Grammars*

Radu Gramatovici[1] and Florin Manea[1,2]

[1] Faculty of Mathematics and Computer Science, University of Bucharest
Str. Academiei 14, RO-010014 Bucharest, Romania
[2] Otto-von-Guericke-Universität Magdeburg, Fakultät für Informatik
PSF 4120, D-39016 Magdeburg, Germany
{radu.gramatovici,flmanea}@fmi.unibuc.ro

Abstract. In this paper we propose a generalization of the local internal contextual grammars, introduced by Ilie in 1997, namely the k-local internal contextual grammars. These grammars are, in fact, classical internal contextual grammars, but their only permitted derivations are those that can be described in a restricted manner (that depends on the number k). Using this formalism we define different classes of languages, and obtain a series of language theoretic results for them. Also, we show that the membership problem for k-local internal contextual grammars with polynomial choice can be solved in polynomial time. This seems interesting to us, as it shows that the descriptional restrictions on the derivations of a grammar reflect on the computational efficiency of accepting the language generated by that grammar.

Keywords: Internal contextual grammars, k-Local Derivation, Hierarchy of languages, Membership problem.

1 Introduction

Contextual grammars were introduced in [1] by Solomon Marcus as an attempt to transform in generative devices some procedures developed within the framework of analytical models. Although a series of linguistic motivations and applications of the contextual grammars formalism are presented in [2, Chapter 5]), the problem of finding classes of Marcus contextual grammars suitable for natural language processing (discussed in [3, Chapter 7]) is still on going, following the introduction and study of contextual tree-like structures [4], parsing algorithms [5,6,7,8,9,10], or language properties, such as ambiguity and syntactic complexity, see, e.g., [3] and the references therein, and [11,12].

To this end, one of the most important tasks seems to be the design of efficient acceptors/parsers for the analysis of contextual languages. Such algorithms are extensively used in linguistic applications and the primary condition they must fulfill is to be time-efficient. From the theoretical point of view, this means to have a polynomial (of a reasonable degree) time complexity.

The first approaches to efficient contextual languages recognition/parsing were developed by Harbusch, in a series of papers [9,10]. However, the parsers for

---

* The work of Florin Manea is supported by the *Alexander von Humboldt Foundation*.

M. Holzer, M. Kutrib, and G. Pighizzini (Eds.): DCFS 2011, LNCS 6808, pp. 172–183, 2011.
© Springer-Verlag Berlin Heidelberg 2011

internal contextual grammars with context-free selectors reported in these papers are not completely defined and they were not proved to be correct or to have polynomial complexity.

Local internal contextual grammars were introduced by Ilie in [13]; "local", in this context, stands for the localization of the derivation of words with respect to the position of the previously inserted context. A similar condition was defined by Gramatovici in [5], under the name of "derivation that preserves the selectors". In [13], Ilie showed that the class of languages generated by local internal contextual grammars with regular choice can be recognized in polynomial time. However, this result was not effective: it was obtained indirectly, and no practical algorithm was proposed for the recognition of local internal contextual grammars with regular choice. The result of Ilie was improved in [7] in two directions: first the result was extended for local internal contextual grammars with context-free choice and, second, it was obtained by effectively constructing a polynomial algorithm that recognizes any word of length N in $\mathcal{O}(N^7)$ time; the time complexity of this algorithm was further improved to $\mathcal{O}(N^4)$ in [8].

In this paper, we generalize local contextual grammars to k-local contextual grammars. Similar to the case of the local contextual grammars, the derivation is localized, but a newly inserted context has to be adjacent to at least to one of the previously inserted k contexts. The localization condition previously defined in [13] is obtained in our model by taking $k = 1$. As an initial result, we show that this generalization is not trivial since k-local internal contextual grammars generate different classes of languages for different values of k. Further, a series of language theoretic results are given for k-local internal contextual grammars, showing how the descriptive restrictions imposed on the derivations reflect in the generative power of the model. Finally, we show that the languages generated by k-local internal contextual grammars with polynomial choice can be recognized in polynomial time.

2   Preliminaries

We assume that the reader is familiar with the basic concepts of formal languages theory (see, e.g., [2]). In this section we only give the definitions, notations and some examples regarding the generative models we use; for further details concerning contextual grammars the reader is referred to the monograph [3].

For an alphabet V, we denote by V^* and V^+ the set of all words and of all non-empty words over V, respectively. The empty word is denoted by λ. Given a word $w \in V^*$ and a symbol $a \in V$, we denote by $|w|$ and $|w|_a$ the length of w and the number of occurrences of a in w, respectively. For $w \in V^*$ and V' an alphabet, the word $w|_{V'}$ is obtained from w by erasing the symbols not contained in V'; $w|_{V'}$ is called the projection of w to V. For a word w, $w[i..j]$ denotes the factor of w starting at position i and ending at position j, $1 \le i \le j \le |w|$. If $i = j$, then $w[i..j]$ is the i-th symbol of w, which is simply denoted by $w[i]$.

By *FIN*, *REG*, *CF*, *CS* and *P* we denote the classes of finite, regular, context-free, context-sensitive and deterministic polynomial languages, respectively. Let $\mathcal{F}$ be one of these classes.

An *internal contextual grammar with selection* from $\mathcal{F}$ (or, simpler, with $\mathcal{F}$-choice) is a construct $G = (V, A, (L_1, c_1), \ldots, (L_n, c_n))$, where:

- V is an alphabet,
- A is a finite language over V, called the set of *axioms*,
- for $i \in \{1, \ldots, n\}$, (L_i, c_i) is a *contextual rule* with the *selection language* L_i, where $L_i \subseteq V^*$ and $L_i \in \mathcal{F}$, and the *context* $c_i = (u_i, v_i) \in V^* \times V^*$.

When the class $\mathcal{F}$ follows from the context we dot mention it not explicitly.

The derivation in the internal contextual grammar G is defined as $x \Rightarrow y$ if and only if there is a contextual rule $(L_i, (u_i, v_i))$ such that $x = x_1 x_2 x_3$ with $x_2 \in L_i$ and $y = x_1 u_i x_2 v_i x_3$. Let $\overset{*}{\Rightarrow}$ denote the reflexive and transitive closure of $\Rightarrow$. The language generated by G is $L(G) = \{w \in V^* \mid \exists \alpha \in A, \alpha \overset{*}{\Rightarrow} w\}$.

We say that a word w can be derived by a sequence of contexts (w_1, t_1), $(w_2, t_2), \ldots, (w_p, t_p)$ in the contextual grammar G, if there exists the derivation:
$$\alpha \Rightarrow x_{1,1} w_1 x_{2,1} t_1 x_{3,1} \Rightarrow x_{1,2} w_2 x_{2,2} t_2 x_{3,2} \Rightarrow \ldots \Rightarrow x_{1,p} w_p x_{2,p} t_p x_{3,p} = w,$$
such that $\alpha = x_{1,1} x_{2,1} x_{3,1}$ is an axiom from A, $(L_{r_i}, (w_i, t_i))$ is a contextual rule of the grammar G for $1 \leq i \leq p$, $x_{1,i} w_i x_{2,i} t_i x_{3,i} = x_{1,i+1} x_{2,i+1} x_{3,i+1}$ and $x_{2,i} \in L_{r_i}$ for all $1 \leq i \leq p-1$. The sequence of contexts $(w_1, t_1), (w_2, t_2), \ldots, (w_p, t_p)$ is called the *control sequence* of the above derivation.

It is not hard to see that the derivation of a word is not fully characterized by its control sequence, as one could insert the contexts in various positions in the words obtained during such a derivation. An accurate characterization of a derivation as the above is given by the *description* of the derivation:
$$\alpha; x_{1,1}(w_1) x_{2,1}(t_1) x_{3,1}; x_{1,2}(w_2) x_{2,2}(t_2) x_{3,2}; \ldots; x_{1,p}(w_p) x_{2,p}(t_p) x_{3,p}.$$

In this paper, we introduce the marked description of a derivation. Consider the infinite set of symbols $\{(_i,)_i, [_i,]_i \mid i \in \mathbb{N}\}$, and assume that none of its symbols belongs to V. A *marked description* of the above derivation of w from α, in the grammar G, is a sequence:
$$\alpha; y_{1,1}(_1 w_1)_1 y_{2,1}[_1 t_1]_1 y_{3,1}; y_{1,2}(_2 w_2)_2 y_{2,2}[_2 t_2]_2 y_{3,2}; \ldots; y_{1,p}(_p w_p)_p y_{2,p}[_p t_p]_p y_{3,p},$$
where $y_{j,i}|_V = x_{j,i}$, for all $1 \leq i \leq p$, $\alpha = y_{1,1} y_{2,1} y_{3,1}$, and $y_{1,i}(_i w_i)_i y_{2,i}[_i t_i]_i y_{3,i} = y_{1,i+1} y_{2,i+1} y_{3,i+1}$ for any $1 \leq j \leq 3$ and $1 \leq i \leq p-1$. The *marked descriptor* of w with respect to the given derivation is the word $\beta = y_{1,p}(_p w_p)_p y_{2,p}[_p t_p]_p y_{3,p}$.

A marked descriptor β of a word w, with respect to one of its derivations in G, characterizes completely that derivation. Indeed, one can easily obtain from β the marked description of the respective derivation of w (see [14]).

Example 1. Note that a word w may have several different marked descriptors with respect to its different derivations in an internal contextual grammar with choice, even if we start all the derivations with the same axiom. Indeed, consider the grammar $G = (\{a, b\}, \{a^2 b^3\}, (a^* b^*, (a^3, b^3)))$. Then the words:

1. $a(_1 aa(_2 aaa)_2 a)_1 abb[_1 bbb[_2 bbb]_2]_1 b$,
2. $(_1 aaa)_1 a(_2 aaa)_2 ab[_1 bbb]_1 bb[_2 bbb]_2$,
3. $(_1 aaa(_2 aaa)_2)_1 aabb[_1 bbb]_1[_2 bbb]_2 b$, and
4. $aa(_1 aaa(_2 aaa)_2[_2 bbb]_2)_1 bbb[_1 bbb]_1$

are all marked descriptors of the same word $a^8 b^9$, with respect to four different two-steps derivations of this word from the axiom $a^2 b^3$.

The main notion that we introduce in this paper is defined in the following:

Definition 2. *Let k be a positive integer and $G = (V, A, (L_1, c_1), \ldots, (L_n, c_n))$ be an internal contextual grammar with choice. Consider the following derivation of w from α:*

$$\alpha \Rightarrow x_{1,1}w_1x_{2,1}t_1x_{3,1} \Rightarrow x_{1,2}w_2x_{2,2}t_2x_{3,2} \Rightarrow \ldots \Rightarrow x_{1,p}w_px_{2,p}t_px_{3,p} = w,$$

where $\alpha = x_{1,1}x_{2,1}x_{3,1}$, $(w_i, t_i) = c_{r_i}$ where $r_i \in \{1, \ldots, n\}$ for all $1 \leq i \leq p$, $x_{1,i}w_ix_{2,i}t_ix_{3,i} = x_{1,i+1}x_{2,i+1}x_{3,i+1}$ and $x_{2,i} \in L_{r_i}$ for all $1 \leq i \leq p - 1$. This derivation is called k-local if it has the marked description:

$$\alpha; y_{1,1}(_1w_1)_1y_{2,1}[_1t_1]_1y_{3,1}; y_{1,2}(_2w_2)_2y_{2,2}[_2t_2]_2y_{3,2}; \ldots; y_{1,p}(_pw_p)_py_{2,p}[_pt_p]_py_{3,p},$$

that fulfills the conditions:

- *for any q, with $k < q \leq p$, there exists r, with $q - k \leq r < q$, such that $(_r$ is in $y_{1,q}$, $)_r$ and $[_r$ are in $y_{2,q}$, and $]_r$ is in $y_{3,q}$.*
- *for any q and r, with $1 \leq r < q \leq p$, if $(_r$ is in $y_{1,q}$ and $)_r$ is in $y_{2,q}y_{3,q}$, then $)_r$ and $[_r$ are in $y_{2,q}$ and $]_r$ is in $y_{3,q}$; if $[_r$ is in $y_{1,q}y_{2,q}$ and $]_r$ is in $y_{3,q}$, then $(_r$ is in $y_{1,q}$, $)_r$ is in $y_{2,q}$ and $[_r$ is in $y_{2,q}$.*

A k-local derivation of w from α is denoted by $\alpha \overset{*}{\Rightarrow}_{k-loc} w$.

The language generated by the grammar G by k-local derivation is

$$L_{k-loc}(G) = \{w \in V^* \mid \exists \alpha \in A, \alpha \overset{*}{\Rightarrow}_{k-loc} w\}.$$

Intuitively, in a k-local derivation only the first k derivation steps can be performed arbitrarily with respect to the previous steps, while all the other contexts are inserted such that they are adjacent to one of the previously k inserted contexts. Moreover, if the left side of a context is inserted adjacently to the left side of some previously inserted context, then also the right side of the new context is inserted adjacently to the right side of the previously inserted context. For instance, in Example 1 the first marked descriptor corresponds to a k-local derivation with $k \geq 1$, the second corresponds to a k-local derivation with $k \geq 2$, while the others do not correspond to k-local derivations for any $k \geq 1$.

For simplicity, we may call an internal contextual grammar k-local internal contextual grammar when we are interested only in its k-local derivation.

We denote by $ICC(\mathcal{F})$ the class of languages generated by internal contextual grammars with $\mathcal{F}$-choice by usual derivation, by $ICC_{k-loc}(\mathcal{F})$ we denote the class of languages generated by internal contextual grammars with $\mathcal{F}$-choice by k-local derivation, and by $ICC_{\infty-loc}(\mathcal{F})$ we denote the union of the all these classes $ICC_{\infty-loc}(\mathcal{F}) = \bigcup_{k \geq 1} ICC_{k-loc}(\mathcal{F})$.

Since the definition of 1-local derivation is clearly equivalent to the definition of local derivation from [13] we write $ICC_{loc}(\mathcal{F})$ instead of $ICC_{1-loc}(\mathcal{F})$ (see the technical report [14] for more details).

3   Language Theoretic Properties

We begin this section with several examples that will become useful in the sequel.

Example 3. Let k be an positive integer, and let $G_k = (\{a, b_1, \ldots, b_k\}, \{b_1 \ldots b_k\}, (\{b_1, \ldots, b_k\}, (\lambda, a)))$ be an internal contextual grammar with *FIN*-choice. First, the language generated by G_k by usual derivation is the regular language L_k described by the regular expression $b_1 a^* b_2 a^* \ldots b_k a^*$. Second, it is not hard to see that the language generated by G_k by ℓ-local derivation equals, as well, L_k for $\ell \geq k$. Finally, the language generated by G_k by m-local derivation for $m < k$, denoted $L_{k,m}$, is different from L_k. Indeed,

$$L_{k,m} = \{b_1 a^{n_1} \ldots b_k a^{n_k} \mid n_1, \ldots, n_k \in \mathbb{N}, \text{ and } \exists \ell, \text{ such that } k - m \leq \ell \leq k,$$
$$\text{and } \exists r_1, r_2, \ldots, r_\ell \in \{1, \ldots, k\}, \text{ with } n_{r_1} = n_{r_2} = \ldots = n_{r_\ell} = 0\}.$$

That is, in any word from $L_{k,m}$, at most m groups of a symbols are non-empty.

Example 4. Let k be a positive integer, and let $G'_k = (\{a, b_1, b_2, \ldots, b_{2k-1}\}, \{b_1 b_2 \ldots b_{2k-1}\}, (\{b_1, b_3 \ldots, b_{2k-1}\}, (a, a)))$ be an internal contextual grammar with *FIN*-choice. The language generated by G'_k by usual derivation is, clearly, the context-free language:
$$L'_k = L(G'_k) = \{a^{n_1} b_1 a^{n_1} b_2 a^{n_2} b_3 a^{n_2} \ldots a^{n_k} b_{2k-1} a^{n_k} \mid n_1, \ldots, n_k \geq 0\}.$$
Further, it is not hard to see that the languages generated by G'_k by ℓ-local derivation are also equal to L'_k for $\ell \geq k$. On the other hand, the language $L'_{k,m}$ generated by G'_k by m-local derivation is different from L'_k for $m < k$. Indeed,

$$L'_{k,m} = \{ a^{n_1} b_1 a^{n_1} b_2 a^{n_2} b_3 a^{n_2} \ldots a^{n_k} b_{2k-1} a^{n_k} \mid n_1, \ldots, n_k \geq 0, \text{ and }$$
$$\exists \ell, \text{ such that } k - m \leq \ell \leq k, \text{ and } \exists r_1, r_2, \ldots, r_\ell, \text{ such that }$$
$$1 \leq r_1 < r_2 < \ldots < r_\ell \leq k \text{ and } n_{r_1} = n_{r_2} = \ldots = n_{r_\ell} = 0\}.$$

We show, in the following, that L'_k cannot be generated by an internal contextual grammar with $\mathcal{F}$-choice by m-local derivation for any $m < k$ and any class of languages $\mathcal{F}$.

Example 5. Let $G'' = (\{a, b, c\}, \{abc\}, (\{ab^n \mid n \in \mathbb{N}, n \geq 1\}, (a, bc)))$ be an internal contextual grammar with regular choice. For $k \geq 1$, the language generated by the grammar G by k-local derivation, denoted L''_k, is a non-context-free language. Indeed, it is not hard to see that $L''_k \cap a^* b^* c^* = \{a^n b^n c^n \mid n \geq 1\}$, which is not a context-free language. Thus, L''_k is also non-context-free.

Remark 6. If $x_{1,1} x_{2,1} x_{3,1} \Rightarrow x_{1,1} w_1 x_{2,1} t_1 x_{3,1} \Rightarrow \ldots \Rightarrow x_{1,p} w_p x_{2,p} t_p x_{3,p}$ is a k-local derivation in an internal contextual grammar G and t is a positive integer with $1 < t \leq p$, then $x_{1,t} x_{2,t} x_{3,t} \Rightarrow x_{1,t} w_t x_{2,t} t_t x_{3,t} \Rightarrow \ldots \Rightarrow x_{1,p} w_p x_{2,p} t_p x_{3,p}$ is also a k-local derivation in G.

Proof. Assume that $y_{1,1} y_{2,1} y_{3,1}$, $y_{1,1} (_1 w_1)_1 y_{2,1} [_1 t_1]_1 y_{3,1}$, $y_{1,2} (_2 w_2)_2 y_{2,2} [_2 t_2]_2 y_{3,2}$, $\ldots$, $y_{1,p} (_p w_p)_p y_{2,p} [_p t_p]_p y_{3,p}$, is a marked description of the initial derivation $x_{1,1} x_{2,1} x_{3,1} \overset{*}{\Rightarrow} x_{1,p} w_p x_{2,p} t_p x_{3,p}$. We define the alphabet $V' = V \cup \{(_j,)_j, [_j,]_j | t \leq j \leq p\}$ and the words $\alpha_i = y_{1,i} (_i w_i)_i y_{2,i} [_i t_i]_i y_{3,i} |_{V'}$ for all i such that $t \leq i \leq p$. Then, for all i such that $t \leq i \leq p$, define the words β_{i-t+1} as α_i in which we replace the index j of all parentheses $(_j,)_j, [_j,]_j$ by $j - t + 1$. It is rather clear that the sequence $x_{1,t}x_{2,t}x_{3,t}, \beta_1, \ldots, \beta_{p-t+1}$ is a marked description of the derivation $x_{1,r}x_{2,r}x_{3,r} \overset{*}{\Rightarrow} x_{1,p}w_px_{2,p}t_px_{3,p}$.

From *Definition 2*, it follows that for the marked description $y_{1,1}y_{2,1}y_{3,1}$, $y_{1,1}(_1w_1)_1y_{2,1}[_1t_1]_1y_{3,1}$, $y_{1,2}(_2w_2)_2y_{2,2}[_2t_2]_2y_{3,2}$, $\ldots$, $y_{1,p}(_pw_p)_py_{2,p}[_pt_p]_py_{3,p}$, the following holds: for any q, with $k < q \leq p$, there exists r, with $q - k \leq r < q$, such that $(_r$ belongs to $y_{1,q}$, $)_r$ and $[_r$ belong to $y_{2,q}$ and $]_r$ belongs to $y_{3,q}$.

From the way in which it was constructed and from the fact that the above property relies only on the previously inserted k contexts, it results that the same property is true for the marked description $x_{1,t}x_{2,t}x_{3,t}, \beta_1, \ldots, \beta_{p-t+1}$. Clearly, the second condition from the the definition of k-local derivation holds canonically for this marked description. Thus, the derivation $x_{1,r}x_{2,r}x_{3,r} \overset{*}{\Rightarrow} x_{1,p}w_px_{2,p}t_px_{3,p}$, given by the above marked description, is also a k-local. $\square$

The following result is immediate:

Proposition 7. *For any two classes of languages* $\mathcal{F}$ *and* $\mathcal{F}'$, *if* $\mathcal{F} \subseteq \mathcal{F}'$ *then* $ICC_{k-loc}(\mathcal{F}) \subseteq ICC_{k-loc}(\mathcal{F}')$.

Further, we present a series of generative properties of k-local internal contextual grammars.

Proposition 8. $ICC_{(k+1)-loc}(\mathcal{F}) \setminus ICC_{k-loc}(\mathcal{F}) \neq \emptyset$ *for all* $k \geq 1$ *and all the classes of languages* $\mathcal{F}$ *that contain* FIN.

Proof. Consider the language L'_{k+1} defined in Example 4,
$$L'_{k+1} = \{a^{n_1}b_1a^{n_1}b_2a^{n_2}b_3a^{n_2} \ldots a^{n_{k+1}}b_{2k+1}a^{n_{k+1}} \mid n_1, \ldots, n_{k+1} \geq 0\}.$$
From Example 4 it follows that L'_{k+1} is generated by the grammar G'_{k+1} which has FIN-choice by $(k+1)$-local derivation. Thus, $L'_{k+1} \in ICC_{(k+1)-loc}(FIN)$, and, consequently, $L'_{k+1} \in ICC_{(k+1)-loc}(\mathcal{F})$ for all the classes of languages $\mathcal{F}$ that contain FIN.

For the second part of the proof, we show that $L'_{k+1} \notin ICC_{k-loc}(\mathcal{F})$ for any class of languages $\mathcal{F}$.

Let us assume the opposite: there exists a class of languages $\mathcal{F}$ such that $L'_{k+1} \in ICC_{k-loc}(F)$. Consequently, there exists an internal contextual grammar with $\mathcal{F}$-choice $G = (V, A, (L_1, c_1), \ldots, (L_n, c_n))$ such that $L_{k-loc}(G) = L'_{k+1}$.

For $1 \leq i \leq k+1$, denote by $N_i = 1 + \max\{n_i \mid$ there exist $n_1, \ldots, n_{i-1}, n_{i+1}, \ldots, n_{k+1}$, such that $a^{n_1}b_1a^{n_1}b_2a^{n_2}b_3a^{n_2} \ldots a^{n_i}b_{2i-1}a^{n_i} \ldots a^{n_{k+1}}b_{2k+1}a^{n_{k+1}} \in A\}$.

Consider $w = a^{N_1}b_1a^{N_1}b_2a^{N_2}b_3a^{N_2} \ldots a^{N_{k+1}}b_{2k+1}a^{N_{k+1}}$. By the definition of the language L'_{k+1} we have $w \in L'_{k+1} \setminus A$. Therefore, there exists a k-local derivation $\alpha \overset{*}{\Rightarrow}_{k-loc} w$, where $\alpha \in A$. Now, it is not hard to see that no context of the grammar, that is used in the derivation of w, contains any of the symbols $b_1, b_2, \ldots, b_k$; otherwise we could easily obtain words that contain more than one symbol b_i for some $i \in \{1, \ldots, k\}$. Moreover, each of the $2k + 2$ groups of symbols a of w can be obtained only after the insertion of at least one context. Also, the only possibility for the sides of a context to be inserted simultaneously in two such groups of a-s would be to insert it around a word of the form $a^\ell b_i a^e$ for some $\ell, r \in \mathbb{N}$ and $i \in \{1, \ldots, k\}$. Now, if w would be derived by a k-local derivation we would obtain that the sides of the contexts could be inserted in at most $2k$ of the symbol a groups. But this is a contradiction.

Thus $L'_{k+1} \notin ICC_{k-loc}(\mathcal{F})$ for any class of languages F. $\qquad\square$

Proposition 9. $ICC_{k-loc}(\mathcal{F})$ *is incomparable with REG for all $k \geq 1$ and all the classes of languages $\mathcal{F}$ that contain FIN.*

Proof. Let $k \geq 1$ be a positive integer. Consider the regular language L_{2k+1} defined in Example 3. Similarly to the second part of the proof of Proposition 8, one can show that $L_{2k+1} \notin ICC_{k-loc}(\mathcal{F})$ for any class of languages $\mathcal{F}$.

According to the previous examples we see that $ICC_{k-loc}(FIN)$ contains several regular languages. Moreover, if $\mathcal{F}$ contains FIN then $ICC_{k-loc}(\mathcal{F})$ also contains languages as L'_k, defined in Example 4, which is a context-free non-regular language. $\qquad\square$

In fact, for any $k \geq 1$ and any class of languages F that contains REG, $ICC_{k-loc}(\mathcal{F})$ may contain even non-context-free languages. Example 5 presents a class of non-context-free languages which can be generated by an internal contextual grammar with REG-choice by k-local derivation for all $k \geq 1$.

The following result answers an open problem from [13, page 43].

Proposition 10. *For any class of languages $\mathcal{F}$, the class of regular languages REG is not included in $ICC_{loc}(\mathcal{F})$.*

Proof. It follows as in the second part of the proof of Proposition 8 for $k = 1$, and using the equivalence between the 1-local derivation and the local derivation. $\quad\square$

We conclude this section by giving a result on the upper bound of the class of languages generated by k-local internal contextual grammars having at most CS-choice.

Proposition 11. *For any class of languages $\mathcal{F}$ contained in the class of context-sensitive languages, we have $ICC_{\infty-loc}(\mathcal{F}) \subset CS$.*

Proof. Given an internal contextual grammar G, with at most context-sensitive choice, one can easily construct a Turing machine working in linear space and accepting $L_{k-loc}(G)$.

Further, recall that a language $L \subseteq V^*$ fulfills the *internal bounded step* property if there is a constant p such that for each $w \in L$ with $|w| > p$, there exists $y \in L$ such that $x = x_1 u x_2 v x_3$, $y = x_1 x_2 x_3$ and $0 < |uv| \leq p$ (see [2, page 243]). Clearly, any internal contextual grammar G with at most CS-choice generates, by k-local derivation, only languages having the internal bounded step property, while CS contains also languages that do not fulfill the IBS property. Hence, the inclusion $ICC_{\infty-loc}(\mathcal{F}) \subset CS$ is strict. This concludes our proof. $\qquad\square$

4   Computational Aspects

For the rest of the paper we fix an internal contextual grammar $G = (V, A, (L_1, (u_1, v_1)), \ldots, (L_n, (u_n, v_n)))$ with P-choice. The problem that we try to solve in this section is the membership problem for the language generated by the grammar G: given a word $w \in V^*$ and $k \in I\!N$ we must decide whether w was generated by G or not by k-local derivation.

We may assume, without losing generality, that if (u_i, v_i) is a context of this grammar then $u_i v_i \neq \lambda$. Clearly, the derivation of a word w in such a grammar has at most $|w|$ steps. Also, note that, since L_i is in P, the language $u_i L_i v_i$ is in P as well for all $i \in \{1, \ldots, n\}$.

Our approach is based on a bottom-up strategy: we try to identify the rules that were used in the possible derivations of w, in the reverse order of their application, and we accept if and only if we obtain in this way a derivation that started with an axiom of G. Clearly, a direct implementation of this approach runs in exponential time and it is generally unknown whether the membership problems for languages generated by unrestricted internal contextual grammars with P-choice can be solved in polynomial time. We show here that when we are interested in checking whether w can be derived by k-local derivation, we can implement the general idea mentioned above in polynomial time; however, degree of the polynomial bounding the running time of this algorithm depends on k. In the following, we provide only a few basic ideas on how this algorithm works; a more detailed presentation can be found in [14].

First note that, due to the locality of the derivation, it is important to identify and memorize the exact place and derivation step in which each a context was inserted during a derivation, not only to identify and store the contextual rules that were used in that derivation. Thus, we use the following approach: each time a valid context is identified, it is marked. More precisely we proceed as in the case of the marked description of the derivation: we insert (and) around the left side of an identified context, respectively, [and] around the right side of the context. Moreover, we associate with an identified context the number of contexts previously found in the input word, to which we add 1. For example, assuming that m derivation steps are performed in a derivation of w from an axiom α of the grammar, the first identified context (which is, in fact, the last context inserted in the derivation $\alpha \overset{*}{\Rightarrow}_{k-loc} w$) is associated with 1, the second with 2, and so on; the last identified context (which is actually the first context inserted in the derivation) is associated with m. Thus, the sequence of the numbers associated with the identified contexts is the reversed sequence of numbers associated with the contexts in the marked description of the derivation. For simplicity, the symbol $\beta[i]$ of the word β, which was obtained from w by marking several contexts, is said to be (-marked (respectively, [-marked) if there exist j and ℓ such that $j < i < \ell$, $\beta[j] = (_q$, and $\beta[\ell] =)_q$ (respectively, $\beta[j] = [_q$ and $\beta[\ell] =]_q$) for some $q \in I\!N$; a factor $\beta[i..i']$ of β is said to be (-marked ([-marked) if there exist j and ℓ such that $j < i \leq i' < \ell$, $\beta[j] = (_q$, and $\beta[\ell] =)_q$ (respectively, $\beta[j] = [_q$ and $\beta[\ell] =]_q$) for some $q \in I\!N$. A (-marked ([-marked) factor of a word in which several contexts were identified and marked is said to be maximal if it is there is no other (-marked ([-marked) factor of the same word that contains it.

We say that a word x is correctly parenthesized if the following hold:

- the word x contains at most one symbol $(_j$ and one symbol $)_j$ for all $j \in I\!N$; also, x contains at most one symbol $[_j$ and one symbol $]_j$ for all $j \in I\!N$;
- if x contains one symbol from $\{(_j,)_j, [_j,]_j\}$, then it contains all the symbols from this set, and $x = x'(_jy')_jz'[_ju']_jv'$;
- if $x[i_1] = (_l, x[i_2] = (_j$ and $x[i_3] =)_j$, such that $i_2 < i_1 < i_3$, then there exist i_4 such that $w[i_4] =)_l$ and $i_2 < i_1 < i_4 < i_3$; if $x[i_1] = [_l, x[i_2] = [_j$ and $x[i_3] =]_j$, such that $i_2 < i_1 < i_3$, then there exist i_4 such that $w[i_4] =]_l$ and $i_2 < i_1 < i_4 < i_3$.

It is not hard to see that the marked descriptor of a word z, with respect to a derivation of the grammar G, is correctly parenthesized. On the other hand, the words we obtain, by identifying the contexts inserted in a word and associating numbers with them, are also correctly parenthesized.

Now we briefly describe how a new context is identified in a word in which several contexts were identified and marked. Assume that we have a word x in which $q - 1$ contexts were identified and marked, so far. We search for the factors usv of the word formed by the unmarked symbols of x provided that $c = (u, v)$ is a context of the grammar and s is a selector of that context; if we find an occurrence of usv we insert $(_q$ and $)_q$ around the symbols corresponding to u, respectively, $[_q$ and $]_q$ around the symbols corresponding to v. Note that we may insert $(_q$ and $)_q$ (respectively, $[_q$ and $]_q$) around several already marked symbols of the initial word, and the corresponding parentheses. In this respect, the insertion of the new parentheses is made such that the newly obtained word remains correctly parenthesized; if there are more possibilities to do the marking of a context then all of them are analyzed.

Let β be a word obtained after q contexts were identified. We check whether the derivation constructed so far (which, in fact, consists in inserting the marked contexts) is k-local; we assume that the insertion of the previously found $q - 1$ contexts formed a k-local derivation. Hence, we must check only whether there exists r with $q > r \geq q - k$, such that $\beta[i_1] = (_r, \beta[i_2] =)_r, \beta[i_3] = (_q$, and $\beta[i_4] =)_q$ with $i_3 < i_1 < i_2 < i_4$, and $\beta[j_1] = [_r, \beta[j_2] =]_r, \beta[j_3] = [_q$, and $\beta[j_4] =]_q$ with $j_3 < j_1 < j_2 < j_4$ (that is, the parentheses indexed by r are placed between the parentheses of the same type indexed by q). To this end, if β is a word obtained from w after at least r context were identified, we say that the index r is satisfied if there exists an index q, with $r + k \geq q > r$, such that $\beta[i_1] = (_r, \beta[i_2] =)_r, \beta[i_3] = (_q$, and $\beta[i_4] =)_q$ with $i_3 < i_1 < i_2 < i_4$, and $\beta[j_1] = [_r, \beta[j_2] =]_r, \beta[j_3] = [_q$, and $\beta[j_4] =]_q$ with $j_3 < j_1 < j_2 < j_4$. Assume that, at some point, we succeeded to identify $r + k$ contexts; these derivation steps form a k-local derivation if and only if after the $(r + k)^{th}$ context was identified, and the corresponding parentheses inserted, all the unsatisfied indices are strictly greater than r. Clearly, the indices of the parentheses limiting the maximal marked factors are unsatisfied, and no other unsatisfied indices exist.

Now we are able to describe formally the main step of our algorithm.

Remark 12. Let $\gamma \in (V \cup \{(_j,)_j, [_j,]_j \mid j \leq |w|\})^*$ be a word such that:

- γ is correctly parenthesized;
- $\gamma \mid_V = w$ and the unmarked symbols of γ form a word y;
- γ has m maximal (-marked factors and m' maximal [-marked factors where both m and m' are less or equal to k;

Then the following equivalence holds:

- w is obtained from y by a p-steps k-local derivation and
- γ can be obtained from w by marking the symbols of the contexts inserted in the above derivation, in reverse order of their insertion, and
- the unsatisfied indices of the parentheses appearing in γ are greater than $p - k$.

if and only if there exists $\beta \in (V \cup \{(_j,)_j, [_j,]_j \mid j \leq |y|\})^*$ such that:

- $\beta \mid_V = w$, the unmarked symbols of β form the word z, and w is obtained from z by a $(p-1)$-steps k-local derivation,
- β has j maximal (-marked sequences and j' maximal [-marked sequences with $j, j' \leq k$; moreover, β can be obtained from w by marking the contexts inserted in the above derivation, in reverse order of their insertion,
- each of not-satisfied indices in β are greater than $p - 1 - k$, and
- there exists a context $c = (u, v)$ of the grammar and one of its selectors s, such that γ can be obtained from β by identifying in z an occurrence of the sequence usv (in this order), and marking the symbols corresponding to the context c in β.   □

Note that at any moment of an analysis that confirms that the w can be generated by the rules of G starting from some word by k-local derivation there exist at most k unsatisfied indices (at most k maximal (-marked factors and k maximal [-marked factors can be obtained), and the difference between any two such indices is less than k. Consequently, we can use, instead of the real value of the indices, their value modulo k. In this setting, we state that the derivation steps defined by the contexts marked until a given moment in w do not form a k-local derivation if and only if at some point two unsatisfied indices, associated with the parentheses used to mark these contexts, which are equal modulo k are obtained; that is, the derivation of w is not k-local if and only if there exists q such that the indices of the parentheses associated with the $(q - k)^{th}$ context were not satisfied after the qth context was identified. According to the above, one should memorize only the unsatisfied indices, the position of the parentheses associated with these indices and the number of contexts identified until that moment in the input word.

According to Remark 12, we can decide whether w can be generated by G as follows: perform a "breadth-first" search in the space of all the words that fulfill the conditions in Remark 12, starting from the word w, and trying to find a word α, whose unmarked symbols form an axiom of G. Following Remark 12, the transition, in such a search, between two words β and γ is possible if and only if γ can be obtained from β by marking the sides of a context correctly selected.

The basic data structure used in our algorithm is called *item*, and it is a pair (γ, m) with $m \in \mathbb{N}$ such that $m \leq |w|$ and $\gamma \in (V \cup \{(_i,)_i, [_i,]_i \mid 0 \leq i \leq k-1\})^*$ such that γ contains t maximal (-marked sequences and t' maximal [-marked sequences with $t, t' \leq k$ and no other parentheses than the ones marking the maximal marked factors. Every word γ which fulfills the properties stated in Remark 12 can be encoded as the item $(\overline{\gamma}, m)$ where m is the number of contexts identified in γ and $\overline{\gamma}$ is obtained from γ by deleting the parentheses with satisfied indices and by replacing each index with its value modulo k.

Now we are able to give an exact insight on how our algorithm works.

Remark 13. To decide whether w can be generated by G a breadth-first search in the space of all the possible items is performed:

- The starting item of the search is $(w, 0)$;
- The transition from (β, a) towards (γ, b) is possible when $b = a + 1$ and γ is obtained from β by identifying and marking (as described before) the sides of a context correctly selected, and, then, by deleting all the parentheses with satisfied indices (note that (γ, b) must still be a correct item);
- If we reach, during this search, an item (α, a), such that the unmarked symbols of α form an axiom of the grammar, then the algorithm stops and accepts. Otherwise, the algorithm stops and rejects the input word.

It is not hard to see that this algorithm stops after a finite number of steps. Indeed, for a given word w, the graph defined by the items and the transitions connecting them is a directed acyclic graph, each path in this graph having at most $|w|$ items on it. Also, we have to explore only the items obtained from w by marking several contexts, using markings indexed over the set $\{0, \ldots, k-1\}$. □

Finally, we remark that the complexity of our algorithmic approach is polynomial: every item has at most k (-marked maximal factors and at most k [-maximal marked factors. So, in order to memorize an item we only need to memorize the starting point and the ending point of each such factor, and the index associated with the parentheses that mark it. But there are polynomially many such possibilities. Thus, the number of items is polynomially bounded, and, consequently, the search described above takes only a polynomial number of steps; however, the degree of this polynomial clearly depends on k, as the number of items is given by a polynomial whose degree depends on k. Moreover, the graph defined by the items and the transitions between them can be used to obtain a derivation of the input word from an axiom of G, as well (see [14]).

The following result can be stated.

Proposition 14. *For an internal contextual grammar G with P-choice, the membership problem can be solved in polynomial time by the algorithm described in Remark 13.*   □

5   Conclusions

The generalization of local contextual grammars proposed in this paper is supported by the fact that such grammars have rather poor generative properties.

Proposition 10 answers an open question given by Ilie in [13]: there are regular languages that cannot be generated by local internal contextual grammars with finite or regular choice. A similar result is proved in Proposition 9 for any k-local internal contextual grammar with a fixed $k \geq 1$. It remains an open problem whether any regular language can be generated by a k-local internal contextual grammar for some k depending on that regular language.

The problem of recognizing k-local internal contextual languages with only finite, regular or context-free choice should be considered; it seems interesting to see whether the particular form of the selectors permits a more efficient implementation of our entire strategy, or only the identification of the contexts and their selectors can be performed faster. It is worth seeing if our approach works for other types of (linguistically motivated) contextual grammars.

References

1. Marcus, S.: Contextual grammars. Revue Roum. Math. Pures Appl. 14, 1525–1534 (1969)
2. Rozenberg, G., Salomaa, A. (eds.): Handbook of Formal Languages. Springer, Berlin (1997)
3. Păun, G.: Marcus Contextual Grammars. Kluwer Publ. House, Dordrecht (1998)
4. Gramatovici, R., Martín-Vide, C.: Sorted dependency insertion grammars. Theor. Comput. Sci. 354(1), 142–152 (2006)
5. Gramatovici, R.: An efficient parser for a class of contextual languages. Fundam. Inform. 33, 211–238 (1998)
6. Enguix, G.B., Gramatovici, R.: Parsing with active p automata. In: Martín-Vide, C., Mauri, G., Păun, G., Rozenberg, G., Salomaa, A. (eds.) WMC 2003. LNCS, vol. 2933, pp. 31–42. Springer, Heidelberg (2004)
7. Gramatovici, R., Manea, F.: Parsing local internal contextual languages with context-free choice. Fundam. Inform. 64, 171–183 (2005)
8. Gramatovici, R., Manea, F.: A cyk-based parser for local internal contextual grammars with context-free choice. In: Proc. AFL 2005, pp. 31–42 (2005)
9. Harbusch, K.: An efficient online parser for contextual grammars with at most context-free selectors. In: Gelbukh, A. (ed.) CICLing 2003. LNCS, vol. 2588, pp. 168–179. Springer, Heidelberg (2003)
10. Harbusch, K.: Parsing contextual grammars with linear, regular and context-free selectors. In: Grammars and Automata for String Processing. Topics in Computer Mathematics, vol. 9, pp. 45–54. Taylor and Francis, Abington (2003)
11. Jancar, P., Mráz, F., Plátek, M., Procházka, M., Vogel, J.: Restarting automata, marcus grammars and context-free languages. Developments in Language Theory, 102–111 (1995)
12. Mráz, F., Plátek, M., Procházka, M.: Restarting automata, deleting and marcus grammars. In: Recent Topics in Mathematical and Computational Linguistics, pp. 218–233. Romanian Academy Publishing House (2000)
13. Ilie, L.: On computational complexity of contextual languages. Theor. Comput. Sci. 183(1), 33–44 (1997)
14. Gramatovici, R., Manea, F.: k-Local Internal Contextual Grammars. Technical report, Otto-von-Guericke-Universität Magdeburg, Fakultät für Informatik (2011), http://theo.cs.uni-magdeburg.de/pubs/preprints/pp-afl-2011-06.pdf

On Synchronized Multitape and
Multihead Automata

Oscar H. Ibarra[1] and Nicholas Q. Tran[2]

[1] Department of Computer Science
University of California, Santa Barbara, CA 93106, USA
ibarra@cs.ucsb.edu
[2] Department of Mathematics & Computer Science
Santa Clara University, Santa Clara, CA 95053, USA
ntran@math.scu.edu

Abstract. Motivated by applications to verification problems in string manipulating programs, we look at the problem of whether the heads in a multitape automaton are synchronized. Given an n-tape pushdown automaton M with a one-way read-only head per tape and a right end marker \$ on each tape, and an integer $k \geq 0$, we say that M is k-synchronized if at any time during any computation of M on any input n-tuple $(x_1, \ldots, x_n)$ (whether or not it is accepted), no pair of input heads that are not on \$ are more than k cells apart. This requirement is automatically satisfied if one of the heads has reached \$. Note that an n-tuple $(x_1, \ldots, x_n)$ is accepted if M reaches the configuration where all n heads are on \$ and M is in an accepting state. The automaton can be deterministic (DPDA) or nondeterministic (NPDA) and, in the special case, may not have a pushdown stack (DFA, NFA). We obtain decidability and undecidability results for these devices for both one-way and two-way versions. We also consider the notion of k-synchronized one-way and two-way multihead automata and investigate similar problems.

Keywords: multitape automata, multihead automata, synchronized, reversal-bounded counters.

1 Introduction

Applications of finite and infinite-state automata to verification problems have been investigated in various contexts. Recently, they have been used in the verification of string manipulation operations (see, e.g., [6,7,8]). Here, the set of reachable configurations of a string variable is represented as the language accepted by an automaton, e.g., by a one-tape single-track DFA. In order to check the relationships between many string variables, restricted versions of one-tape multi-track automata (i.e., the input alphabet consists of many tracks, where a track symbol is of the form $(a_1, ..., a_n)$, where some a_i's may be λ, a special symbol denoting *blank*) have been employed. The use of these machines improve the precision of string analysis and enables verification of properties that were not previously verifiable with one-tape single-track automata.

M. Holzer, M. Kutrib, and G. Pighizzini (Eds.): DCFS 2011, LNCS 6808, pp. 184–197, 2011.

A one-tape multi-track DFA is equivalent to a multitape DFA (i.e., an automaton with multiple one-way single-track input tapes with one head/tape) in the following sense: a set of n-tuples is accepted by a multitape DFA if and only if the tuple components, when appropriately interleaved with λ symbols and stacked vertically to form multi-track inputs, are accepted by a one-tape multi-track DFA. In recent papers, restricted versions of one-tape multi-track finite automata (or equivalently, multitape finite automata) have been found useful in the verification of string manipulating programs [8]. These are the so-called "aligned" or "synchronized" one-tape multi-track (or multitape) DFAs, which we define below.

A (one-way) n-tape deterministic finite automaton (DFA) M is a finite automaton with n-tapes where each tape contains a strings over input alphabet Σ. Each tape is read-only and has an associated one-way input head. We assume that each tape has a right end marker $\$$ (not in Σ). On a given n-tuple input $x = (x_1, \ldots, x_n) \in \Sigma^+ \times \cdots \times \Sigma^+$ (n times), where each x_i is delimited on the right by $\$$, M starts in initial state q_0 with all the heads on the first symbols of their respective tapes. The transition function of M consists of rules of the form $\delta(q, a_i, \ldots, a_n) = (p, d_1, \ldots, d_n)$ (resp. $= \varnothing$). This rule means that if M is in state q, with head H_i on symbol a_i, then the machine moves H_i in direction 1 or 0 (for right move or stationary move), and enters state p (resp., halts). When a head reaches the end marker $\$$, that head has to remain on the end marker. The input x is accepted if M reaches the configuration where all n heads are on $\$$ and M eventually enters an accepting state.

Let M be an n-tape DFA and $k \geq 0$. M is k-synchronized if at any time during the computation on any input n-tuple $(x_1, \ldots, x_n)$ (accepted or not), no two heads that are both on symbols in Σ are more than k "tape cells apart". Notice that, since the condition in the definition concerns pairs of heads that are both on symbols in Σ, if one of these two heads is on $\$$, then we can stipulate that the condition is automatically satisfied, irrespective of the distance between the heads. Note that if $k = 0$, then all heads move to the right synchronously at the same time (except for heads that reach the right end marker early). M is $finitely$-$synchronized$ if it is k-synchronized for some k.

A 0-synchronized n-tape DFA M can be represented by a one-tape n-track DFA M' as follows: An n-tuple input $x = (x_1, \ldots, x_n)$ to M, is represented by an n-track tape $x' = t_1 \ldots t_s$, where $s = \max \{|x_1|, \ldots, |x_n|\}$, and for $1 \leq j \leq s$, t_j is an n-track symbol consisting of symbols in position j of each x_i, with the convention that when $j > |x_i|$, the symbol in the i-th track is λ. We will also use this equivalent representation of 0-synchronized n-tape DFAs in the sequel.

The above definitions generalize to n-tape nondeterministic finite automata (NFAs). Now, k-synchronized requires that for any computation on any input n-tuple $(x_1, \ldots, x_n)$ (accepted or not), no two heads that are both on symbols in Σ are more than k tape cells apart.

The definitions can also be generalized to n-tape deterministic pushdown automata (DPDAs) and n-tape nondeterministic pushdown automata (NPDAs), which may even be augmented with a finite number of reversal-bounded counters. At each step, each counter can be incremented by 1, decremented by 1, or left unchanged and can be tested for zero. The counters are reversal-bounded in the sense that during any computation, no counter can change mode from increasing to decreasing and vice-versa more than a specified fixed number of times.

We show the following:

1. It is decidable to determine, given an n-tape NPDA M, whether it is k-synchronized for some k, and if this is the case, the smallest such k can be found.
2. Any k-synchronized n-tape NPDA M can be converted to a 0-synch-synchronized NPDA. In the special case of DFA, we show that a k-synchronized n-tape DFA with s states and input alphabet size t can be converted to an equivalent 0-synchronized n-tape DFA M' (in the sense that they accept the same set of n-tuples) with $O(s \cdot t^{k \cdot (n-1)})$ states, and this bound is tight.

We also obtain decidability and undecidability results for two-way multitape NFAs and DFAs. We then consider the notion of k-synchronized one-way and two-way multihead automata and investigate similar problems.

Note: All input n-tuples $(x_1, \ldots, x_n)$ are delimited by a right end marker $ on each tape. Sometimes the end markers are not shown, but they are assumed to be present.

We will need the following result from [3]:

Theorem 1. *The emptiness (Is $L(M) = \varnothing$?) and infiniteness (Is $L(M)$ infinite?) problems for 1-tape NPDAs with reversal-bounded counters are decidable.*

Corollary 2. *The emptiness and infiniteness problems for multitape NPDAs with reversal-bounded counters are decidable.*

Proof. Let M is an n-tape NPDA with reversal-bounded counters. For $1 \leq i \leq n$, construct a 1-tape NPDA with reversal-bounded counters M_i by projection on the i-th tape (i.e., M_i guesses the symbols of tapes $1, \ldots, i-1, i+1, \ldots n$) Then $L(M) = \varnothing$ if and only if $L(M_1) = \varnothing$, and $L(M)$ is infinite if and only if $L(M_i)$ is infinite for some i. $\qquad\square$

2   One-Way Multitape NPDAs

Theorem 3. *It is decidable to determine, given an n-tape NPDA M, whether it is finitely-synchronized for some k.*

Proof. Let M be an n-tape NPDA. Clearly, M is not finitely-synchronized if for any given $d \geq 0$, there is an input $x = (x_1, \ldots, x_n)$ and some $1 \leq i < j \leq n$ such that on input x, M has a computation in which head H_i (on tape i) has processed some portion y_i of x_i and head H_j has processed some portion of y_j

of x_j (note that the the last symbol of y_i and y_j are not the right end marker) such that $|y_i - y_j| \geq d$.

We construct a 1-tape NPDA M' with two 1-reversal counters C_1 and C_2 that are initially zero. Given a unary input $w = 1^d$, M', without moving on the unary input, simulates the computation of M on $(x_1, \ldots, x_n)$, by guessing the symbols that the heads of M reads on each tape (a new symbol is guessed when the head has moved right until the right end marker $\$$ is guessed when thereafter, no new symbol is guessed for that head). Before the simulation, M' also guesses some $1 \leq i < j \leq n$ and during the computation, counter C_1 (resp., counter C_2) is incremented every time head H_i (resp., head H_j) moves right, provided the end marker $\$$ has not yet been guessed by the heads.

At some point, M' terminates the simulation of M and checks and accepts 1^d if $d \leq |v_1 - v_2|$, where v_1 (resp., v_2) is the value of counter C_1 (resp., counter C_2). Checking this condition is accomplished by decrementing the counters until one of them becomes zero and then verifying that the remaining value of the other counter is at least d. It follows that M is not finitely-synchronized if and only if M' accepts an infinite language, which is decidable by Theorem 1.   □

Corollary 4. *It is decidable to determine, given an n-tape NPDA M and an integer $k \geq 0$, whether M is k-synchronized.*

Proof. The construction in the proof of Theorem 3 applies. In fact, since k is fixed, M' does not need the 1-reversal counters. M' can simply keep track of the "distance" between heads H_i and H_j in the state. So M is just an ordinary NPDA.   □

The following follows from the previous two results.

Corollary 5. *It is decidable to determine, given an n-tape NPDA M, whether it is k-synchronized for some k. Moreover, if it is, we can effectively determine the smallest such k.*

Clearly, the above results generalize to machines with reversal-bounded counters. In particular to the following:

Theorem 6. *It is decidable to determine, given an n-tape NPDA M augmented with reversal-bounded counters, whether it is k-synchronized for some k. Moreover, if it is, we can effectively determine the smallest such k.*

The results above are best possible in the sense that they do not hold if the NPDA is augmented with an unrestricted counter. In fact, we have:

Theorem 7. *It is undecidable to determine, given a two-tape DFA augmented with two unrestricted counters (i.e., non-reversal bounded), whether it is 0-synchronized.*

Proof. It is known that the halting problem for 2-counter machines (where both counters are initially zero) is undecidable [5]. Given any such machine M, we construct a 2-tape DFA M' over a unary alphabet, augmented with two counters. Given input (x_1, x_2), M' first simulates the computation of M on the two counters. Clearly, if M does not halt, M is 0-synchronized (since the heads on the two tapes of M' are not moved). If M halts, then M' moves the head on x_1 to the right end marker and then moves the head on x_2 to the right end marker. Since x_1 and x_2 are arbitrary unary strings, M' is not 0-synchronized; in fact, it is not k-synchronized for any k. The result follows.   □

3   One-Way Multitape DFAs

3.1   Precise Bound on k

We will show that if a multitape DFA M is k-synchronizable, then k is smaller than the number of states of M, i.e., there is a "gap" between $q - 1$- and q-synchronizability for machines with q states:

Lemma 8. *Let M be an n-tape DFA with q states. If M is not $(q-1)$-synchronized, then M not k-synchronized for any $k \geq 0$.*

Proof. Since M is not $(q - 1)$-synchronized, there is an input $x = (x_1, \ldots, x_n)$ and $1 \leq i < j \leq n$ such that on input x, M has a computation in which head H_i (on tape i) has processed some portion y_i of x_i and head H_j has processed some portion of y_j of x_j, where:

1. The last symbol of y_i of y_j are not the right end marker;
2. $|y_i| - |y_j| \geq q$.

We will modify x by "pumping" the components x_m, $1 \leq m \leq n$ *separately* to obtain longer inputs x' witnessing the fact that M is not k-synchronized for any $k \geq 0$.

First, write each input component $x_m = w_{m,0} w_{m,1} \ldots w_{m,q}$ for $1 \leq m \leq n$ so that during the computation of M on x, the distance between heads H_i and H_j first becomes c when each head H_m is reading the first symbol of $w_{m,c}$, and M is in state s_c, $0 \leq c \leq q$. In other words, take a snapshot of M's head positions and state the first time H_i and H_j are c apart for $0 \leq c \leq q$. These positions exist since M is not $(q - 1)$-synchronized by hypothesis.

Because M has only q states, two of the states $s_0, s_1, \ldots, s_q$ must be identical, say s_a and s_b, where $a < b$. Define x' to be the n-tuple obtained by adding the segment $w_{m,a} \ldots w_{m,b-1}$ to each input component x_m as follows: $x'_m = w_{m,0} \ldots w_{m,a} \ldots w_{m,b-1} \mathbf{w_{m,a}} \ldots \mathbf{w_{m,b-1}} w_{m,b} \ldots w_{m,q}$. It is clear that after reading the extra segments, M is back in the same state s_a, but the distance between H_i and H_j has increased by at least 1. Hence, x' witnesses that M is not q-synchronized either.

The added segments can be repeated to show that M is not k-synchronized for any $k \geq 0$.   □

3.2 Converting a k-Synchronized n-Tape DFA to a 0-Synchronized n-Tape DFA

Theorem 9. *Any k-synchronized n-tape DFA M with s states and input alphabet size t can be converted to a 0-synchronized n-tape DFA M' with $O(s \cdot t^{k \cdot (n-1)})$ states.*

Proof. The initial state of M' is $[q_0, \varepsilon, \ldots, \varepsilon]$. We describe the transition function of M', denoted by δ':

1. The states of M' will be of the form $[q, \$, \ldots, \$]$, or of the form $[q, x_1, \ldots, x_n]$ satisfying the following conditions:
   (a) Each x_i is in $\Sigma^* \cup \Sigma^*\$$.
   (b) For $1 \leq i \leq n$, $0 \leq |x_i| \leq k$. (Note that if $|x_i| = 0$, then $x_i = \varepsilon$.)
   (c) q is a state of M with its head H_i on the first symbol, say b_i, of x_i if $x_i \neq \varepsilon$. If $x_i = \varepsilon$, then H_i is on the symbol of the tape it is currently on.
   (d) If not all of the x_i's are $\$$, at least one $x_i = \varepsilon$
   Clearly, the initial state, $[q_0, \varepsilon, \ldots, \varepsilon]$ satisfies the conditions (a) – (d).
2. If M' is in state $[q, \$, \ldots, \$]$, then $\delta'([q, \$, \ldots, \$], \$, \ldots, \$) = (\alpha, +1, \ldots, +1)$, where α is a new symbol representing accepting state, provided M in state q with its heads on the $\$$'s enters an accepting state.
3. Suppose M' is in state $[q, x_1, \ldots, x_n]$ and not all of the x_i's are $\$$ and, hence, satisfies conditions (a) – (d) in item 1 above. Then on input $(c_1, \ldots, c_n)$, define the rule $\delta'([q, x_1, \ldots, x_n], c_1, \ldots, c_n) = ([p, y_1, \ldots, y_n], d_1, \ldots, d_n)$ provided the following holds:

   (a) If $x_i \in \Sigma^*\$$, then $c_i = \$$.
   (b) If $x_i \in \Sigma^*\$$. then $d_i = 0$.
   (c) If $x_i \in \Sigma^*$, then $d_i = +1$.
   (d) Let $x_i' = x_i$ if $x_i \in \Sigma^*\$$ (hence, $c_i = \$$) and $x_i' = x_i c_i$ if $x_i \in \Sigma^*$. Then M in configuration $(q, x_1', \ldots, x_n')$ reaches the configuration $(p, y_1, \ldots, y_n)$ (after a finite number of moves) , where y_i is a (not-necessarily proper) suffix of x_i' and at least one of the y_i's is ε. Clearly, the state $[p, y_1, \ldots, y_n]$ again satisfies (a) – (d) of item 1. In particular, $0 \leq |y_i| \leq k$, since M is k-synchronized.

It is straightforward to verify that M' is equivalent to M (i.e., they accept the same set of n-tuples). Since the states of M' of the form $[q, x_1, \ldots, x_n]$ are such that at least one of the x_i's has length 1, the number of possible such states is $O(s \cdot t^{k \cdot (n-1)})$, where s is the number of states of M. $\qquad\square$

3.3 Tightness of the Upper Bound

We now show that the exponential (in $k(n-1)$) bound in Theorem 9 is tight.
   Let Σ be an alphabet with cardinality t. For $k \geq 1$, denote by Σ^k the set of all strings in Σ^* of length k.

Let $n \geq 1$ and $x_1, \ldots, x_n$ be strings in Σ^k. For $1 \leq i \leq n$, let $x_i = a_{i1} \cdots a_{ik}$, where $a_{ij} \in \Sigma$ for $1 \leq j \leq k$. The shuffle of $x_1, \ldots, x_n$ is defined to be the string $S(x_1, \ldots, x_n) = a_{11} a_{21} \cdots a_{n1} \cdots a_{1k} a_{2k} \cdots a_{nk}$.

Let $\#$ be a new symbol not in Σ. Consider the set of n-tuples $L(n, k) = \{(x_1 \# S(x_2, \ldots, x_n), x_2, \ldots, x_n) \mid x_i \in \Sigma^k\}$. $L(n, k)$ can be accepted by a k-synchronized n-tape DFA M with $O(k)$ states as follows, given an n-tuple $(x_1 \# y, x_2, \ldots, x_n)$ (note that each string in the tuple is delimited by a right end marker $\$$): without moving the heads on tapes 2 to n, M reads the the first tape and checks that the string before $\#$ has length k. (This uses $O(k)$ states). Then M' checks that the string after the $\#$ is the shuffle of the strings on tapes 2 to n, while also checking that these strings of length k. This uses $O(nk)$ states).

Hence by Theorem 9 $L(n, k)$ is accepted by some 0-synchronized n-tape DFA; equivalently, there is a one-tape DFA M' accepting the n-track version of $L(n, k)$. We claim that M' must have at least $t^{(n-1)k}$ states. Otherwise, there will be two n-tuples $\quad u \quad = \quad (x_1 \# S(x_2, \ldots, x_n), x_2, \ldots, x_n) \quad$ and $\quad$ moreover $v = (x_1 \# S(x'_2, \ldots, x'_n), x'_2, \ldots, x'_n)$, such that M' when processing the n-track version of u will reach $\#$ in the same state as when M' reaches $\#$ when processing the n-track version of v. This is because there are $t^{(n-1)k}$ $n-1$-tuples of strings of length k. It follows that M' will also accept the n-track version of $w = (x_1 \# S(x_2, \ldots, x_n), x'_2, \ldots, x'_n)$. This contradicts the assumption that M' accepts exactly the n-track version of $L(n, k)$.

3.4   Synchronizability of n-Tape DFA/NFA

Theorem 10. *For any $n \geq 2$, there exists an n-tape DFA M that cannot be converted to an equivalent synchronized n-tape DFA M'.*

Proof. Let $L = \{(a^i c^k, c^k) \mid i, k \geq 1\}$. Clearly, L can be accepted by a 2-tape DFA. Suppose L can be accepted by a synchronized 2-tape DFA. Then, by Theorem 9, it can also be accepted by a 0-synchronized 2-tape DFA. Then this DFA can be represented as a one-tape 2-track DFA M'. Let M' have s states. Consider the two-track string

$$w = \begin{pmatrix} a^{s+1} c^{s+1} \\ c^{s+1} \lambda^{s+1} \end{pmatrix}.$$

Then w is accepted by M'. Then there exist $i, k \geq 0$ and $j \geq 1$ such that w decomposes into

$$w = \begin{pmatrix} a^i a^j a^{s+1-i-j} c^{s+1} \\ c^i c^j c^{s+1-i-j} \lambda^{s+1} \end{pmatrix}$$

and

$$\begin{pmatrix} a^i a^{mj} a^{s+1-i-j} c^{s+1} \\ c^i c^{mj} c^{s+1-i-j} \lambda^{s+1} \end{pmatrix}$$

is accepted by M' for every $m \geq 0$. Let $m = 2$. Then

$$w' = \begin{pmatrix} a^i a^{2j} a^{s+1-i-j} c^{s+1} \\ c^i c^{2j} c^{s+1-i-j} \lambda^{s+1} \end{pmatrix}$$

is accepted by M'. But now, the first track of w' contains the string $a^{s+1+j}c^{s+1}$, and the second track contains c^{s+1+j}. Since $j \geq 1$, this is a contradiction since the number of c's in the first track is less than the number of c's in the second track. $\qquad\square$

On the other hand, there are examples of non-synchronized n-tape DFAs which can be converted to synchronized n-tape DFAs. Consider, e.g., the set $L = \{(a^i, a^j) \mid i, j \geq 1\}$. We can construct a 2-tape DFA M which reads the first tape until its head reaches the end marker, and then reads the second tape until its head reaches the end marker, and then M accepts. This machine is not synchronized. But, we can construct a 0-synchronized 2-tape DFA M, which when given, (a^i, a^j), the two heads move to the right reading (a, a)'s until one of the head reaches the end marker. Then M' reads the remaining a's on the other tape and accepts. Thus, the following is an interesting problem:

Open: Is it decidable to determine, given an n-tape DFA M, whether there exists a synchronized n-tape DFA M' such that $L(M') = L(M)$?

We conjecture that the answer to the above problem is yes. On the other hand, the following theorem shows that the corresponding problem for NFA is undecidable:

Theorem 11. *It is undecidable to determine, given a 2-tape NFA M, whether there exists a 2-tape NFA M' such that $L(M') = L(M)$ and M' is 0-synchronized (resp., k-synchronized for a given k, k-synchronized for some k).*

Proof. We reduce this problem to the halting problem for single-tape Turing machines on blank input. Note that if such a machine Z has a halting sequence of configurations, the sequence is unique. Without loss of generality, we may assume that the number of steps is odd, and that the Turing machine does not write blank symbols. Hence if C is a configuration and D is its valid successor configuration, then the length of D is at most one more than the length of C. Thus, the unique halting sequence of configuration has the form

$$C_1 \# D_1 \# C_2 \# D_2 \# C_3 \# D_3 \# \ldots \# C_k \# D_k$$

where:

- $k \geq 1$;
- D_i is the successor of configuration C_i for $i = 1, 2, \ldots, k$;
- C_{i+1} is the successor of configuration D_i for $i = 1, 2, \ldots, k-1$;
- C_1 is the initial configuration and D_k is a halting configuration.

Let d be a new symbol. Construct a 2-tape NFA M_Z which, when given a tuple $w = (d^j x, y)$, operates by nondeterministically selecting one of the processes below to execute:

1. M_Z checks and accepts $w = (d^j x, y)$ if (x, y) is *not* of the form

$$(C_1 \# C_2 \# \ldots \# C_k, D_1 \# D_2 \# \ldots \# D_k)$$

where the C's and D's are configurations and the difference in lengths between C_i and D_i is at most 1, and C_1 is the initial configuration, and D_k is a halting configuration. Since inputs with the wrong format are accepted by this process, we may assume in the other processes that (x, y) has the correct format.

2. M_Z checks that in $w = (d^j x, y)$, D_i is not the successor of C_i for some i and then accepts.

3. M_Z checks that in $w = (d^j x, y)$, C_{i+1} is not the successor of D_i for some i and then accepts.

Let L be the set of tuples accepted by M_Z. If the Turing machine Z does not halt on blank tape, L consists of all tuples of the form $(d^j x, y)$ (for any j, x, y), and it is straightforward to construct a 0-synchronized 2-tape NFA to accept L.

However, if Z halts on blank tape, and

$$C_1 \# D_1 \# C_2 \# D_2 \# C_3 \# D_3 \# \ldots \# C_k \# D_k$$

is the halting sequence of configurations of Z, then M_Z will not accept

$$(d^j C_1 \# C_2 \# C_3 \ldots \# C_k, D_1 \# D_2 \# D_3 \# \ldots \# D_k)$$

for any j. We now show that L cannot be accepted by any 0-synchronized 2-tape NFA.

To see this, recall that a 0-synchronized 2-tape NFA N is equivalent to a one-tape two-track NFA N' in the following sense: N accepts a pair (x, y) if and only if N' accepts the two-track input $\binom{x}{y}$ obtained by stacking vertically left-justified x and y and padding the shorter string with λ's so that they have the same length. Define $L' = \{\binom{x}{y} \mid (x, y) \in L\}$. Our claim is equivalent to showing that L' is not regular.

Suppose L' is accepted by some NFA N' with q states, so N' rejects the input

$$\begin{pmatrix} d^{q+1} C_1 \# C_2 \# C_3 \ldots \# C_k \\ D_1 \# D_2 \# D_3 \# \ldots \# D_k \end{pmatrix}.$$

(To simplify notation, we omit above the padded λ's needed for the two tracks to have the same length.) Clearly, there must be some $i < j \leq q + 1$ such that N' is in the same state when it reads the ith and j^{th} symbols of this input. Let $s = \begin{pmatrix} d^{j-i+1} \\ \alpha \end{pmatrix}$ be the substring starting at position i and ending at position j inclusive. It is clear that N' must also reject all inputs obtained by repeating s k times for any k.

If the lower-track component α of s contains a $\#$, then repeating s causes the lower track of such a "pumped" input to have more $\#$'s than the upper track. Since such input does not have the correct format, it should be in L'. On the other hand, if α does not contain a $\#$, then it must be a substring of some D_l for some $l \leq q$. Again, repeating s twice will cause D_l to have length more than the length of C_l plus 1, so the result is again a string that does not have the correct format and hence should be in L'. In both cases, we obtain a contradiction, since N' rejects a string that is in L'. $\square$

Corollary 12. *It is undecidable to determine, given a 2-tape NFA M and $s \geq 5$, whether there is a 0-synchronized 2-tape NFA M' with at most s states such that $L(M') = L(M)$.*

Proof. From the proof of Theorem 11, if the TM Z does not halt on blank tape, then $L(M) = \{(d^j x, y) \mid$ for any $j, x, y\}$ can clearly be accepted by a 0-synchronized 2-tape DFA M' with $s = 5$ states. If the TM Z halts, then there is no 0-synchronized 2-tape NFA M' (with any number of states) such that $L(M') = L(M)$. □

In contrast, for n-tape DFAs, we have:

Proposition 13. *It is decidable to determine, given an n-tape DFA M and $s \geq 1$, whether there is a 0-synchronized n-tape DFA M' with at most s states such that $L(M') = L(M)$.*

Proof. This follows from the fact that equivalence of multitape DFAs is decidable [1] and the observation that we can systematically enumerate all 0-synchronized n-tape DFAs and check if one of them is equivalent to M. □

4   Two-Way Multitape NFAs

In this section, we consider the synchronization problem for two-way multitape NFAs. A two-way n-tape NFA M is a generalization of an n-tape NFA in that the input heads can now move two-way $(-1, 0, +1)$ on their respective input tapes which are provided with left end marker # and right end marker \$. Initially, all heads are on #. M accepts an n-tuple $(\#x_1\$, \ldots, \#x_n\$)$ if all heads reach \$, and the machine eventually enters an accepting state. M is k-synchronized if at any time during any computation on any input n-tuple (accepted or not), no two heads that are not on \$ are more than k cells apart (as measured from their left end marker #). M is finitely-synchronized if it is k-synchronized for some k.

Theorem 14. *It is undecidable to determine, given a two-way 2-tape DFA (hence, also for two-way 2-tape NFA) M, whether M is finitely-synchronized.*

Proof. It is well-known that it is undecidable to determine, given a deterministic 2-counter machine Z, where both counters are initially zero (there is no input tape), whether Z will halt. Furthermore, it is well-known that it is undecidable to determine, given a deterministic 2-counter machine Z, whether Z will halt [5]. (There is no input tape.) A close look at the proof of the undecidability of the halting problem, where initially one counter has value d_1 and the other counter is zero in [5] reveals that the counters behave in a regular pattern. Z operates in phases in the following way. Let C_1 and C_2 be its counters. Then the machine's operation can be divided into phases, where each phase starts with one of the counters equal to zero and the other counter equal to some positive integer d_i. During the phase, the first counter is increasing, while the second counter is decreasing. The phase ends with the first counter having value d_{i+1}

and the second counter having value 0. Then in the next phase the modes of the counters are interchanged. We can also assume that if Z does not halt, the values of counters during the computation are increasing, i.e., the d_i's cannot be bounded by a constant. It follows that if Z goes into an infinite loop, the difference between the values of the counters will grow unboundedly.

We construct a two-way 2-tape DFA M which, when given the input $(\#a^i\$, \#a^j\$)$ where $i, j \geq 0$ with both heads on $\#$, simulates Z faithfully using the two tapes to simulate the counters (thus, the heads on the tapes move right for increment and move left for decrement). When Z halts, M then moves both heads simultaneously to the right until one head reaches $\$$ and then moves the other head to $\$$ and then accepts. If one of the heads of M reaches $\$$ before Z halts, M moves the other head to $\$$ and accepts.

Clearly, if Z halts after at most k steps (for some k), then M accepts all tuples in $\#a^*\$ \times \#a^*\$$ and the heads are at most k cells apart during any computation.

If Z does not halt, then M also accepts all tuples in $\#a^*\$ \times \#a^*\$$, but the distance between the two heads cannot be bounded by any constant during all computations.

It follows that M finitely-synchronized if and only if Z halts, which is undecidable. $\qquad\square$

On the other hand, for given k, the k-synchronizability problem is decidable.

Theorem 15. *It is decidable to determine, given a two-way n-tape NFA M and a nonnegative integer k, whether M is k-synchronized.*

Proof. Given M, we construct a two-way 1-tape NFA M' operating on an input string that has n-tracks. If the input to M is $(\#x_1\$, \ldots, \#x_k\$)$, then the input string y to M' consists of n tracks, where track i is the string $\#x_i\lambda^{d_i}\$$ for some $d_i \geq 0$ (where λ is a new symbol representing a *blank*), such that that the x_i's are left-justified and blank-filled so that the lengths of the tracks are all the same.

Clearly, M' with only one head can simulate the computation and keep track of the movements of the n heads of M, using a finite buffer in its state. If, during the simulation, a pair of heads attempts to "separate" more than k cells apart, M' accepts the input. It follows that M is not k-synchronized if and only if M' accepts a nonempty language, which is decidable since M' accepts a regular set. $\qquad\square$

5   Multihead Automata

In this section, we look at finitely-synchronized multihead automata. Like an n-tape automaton, an n-head automaton has n independent heads that operate either one-way or two-way on one input tape with end markers. The automaton is k-synchronized if at any time during the computation on any input, no two heads are more than k cells apart. It is finitely-synchronized if it is k-synchronized for some k.

5.1   One-Way Model

Theorem 16. *It is undecidable to determine, given a one-way 2-head DFA M, whether M is finitely-synchronized.*

Proof. We will use the fact that it is undecidable to determine, given a single-tape Turing machine Z, whether it will halt on an initially blank tape. We may assume that if Z loops (does not halt), it does not loop on a finite amount of tape. Thus, if Z loops, and $C_1 \# C_2 \# C_3 \# \cdots$ (where C_1 is the initial configuration of Z on blank tape, and C_{i+1} is a direct successor of C_i for $i \geq 1$) is the non-halting computation of Z, then for every r, there is a C_s such that the length of $C_s > r$.

We construct a one-way 2-head DFA M which, on input w, uses the two heads to check if w is a halting computation of Z on blank tape, i.e., $w = C_1 \# \cdots \# C_n$, where C_1 is the initial configuration, C_n is a halting configuration, and C_{i+1} is a direct successor of C_i for $1 \leq i \leq n-1$. Note that in the computation of M, one head is lagging behind the other head by one configuration. We omit the details.

Clearly, if Z halts on blank tape, then there exists a k such that it is k-synchronized. If Z does not halt on blank tape, M will not be k-synchronized for any k.   □

However, for restricted multihead automata, we can prove a positive result:

Theorem 17. *It is decidable to determine, given a one-way n-head NPDA M whose inputs come from $w_1^* \cdots w_t^*$ for some (not necessarily distinct) non-null strings $w_1, \ldots, w_t$, whether M is finitely-synchronized.*

Proof. First consider the case when $w_1, \ldots, w_t$ are distinct symbols $a_1, \ldots, a_t$. Given M with heads $H_1, \ldots, H_n$, we construct an n-head NPDA M' with the same heads as M. Let b be a new symbol different from $a_1, \ldots, a_t$. The input to M' is a string of the form yb^r, where y is in $a_1^* \cdots a_t^*$, and $r \geq 1$. Initially, all heads are on the left end of y.

M' simulates M on y with heads $H_1, \ldots, H_n$. At some point (nondeterministically chosen), M' terminates the simulation. M' guesses $1 \leq i, j \leq n$ with $i \neq j$ and checks that H_i and H_j have not reached symbol b. It then moves both heads simultaneously to the right and accepts if one of these heads reaches the right end marker \$ at the same time that the other head reaches the first b of the input segment b^r (indicating that distance between heads H_i and H_j when the simulation of M was terminated was r).

Now M' accepts a bounded language $L(M) \subseteq a_1^* \cdots a_t^* b^*$. It is known that the Parikh map of the bounded language accepted by a multihead NPDA is an effectively computable semilinear set $Q \subseteq N^{t+1}$ [2]. It follows that the projection of this semilinear set on the last coordinate (corresponding to the multiplicity r of symbol b) is also an effectively computable semilinear set Q'. Clearly, M is finitely-synchronized if and only if Q' is finite, which is decidable since finiteness of semilinear sets is decidable.

The result for the general case follows from the observation that given M whose inputs come from $w_1^* \cdots w_t^*$, we can construct an n-head NPDA M' whose inputs come from $a_1^* \cdots a_t^*$ such that $L(M') = \{a_1^{i_1} \cdots a_t^{i_t} \mid w_1^{i_1} \cdots w_t^{i_t}$ is in $L(M)\}$, and M' is finitely-synchronized if and only if M is finitely-synchronized. $\qquad\square$

We showed in Theorem 16 that it is undecidable to determine, given a one-way 2-head DFA M, whether it is finitely-synchronized and, obviously, this is true when M is a one-way 2-head DPDA. In contrast when k is given, we have:

Theorem 18. *It is decidable to determine, given a one-way n-head NPDA M augmented with reversal-bounded counters and an integer k, whether M is k-synchronized.*

Proof. Construct a 1-head NPDA M' augmented with reversal-bounded counters that simulates the n heads of M in its finite control. M' accepts an input x if at least two heads of M on x become separated by more than k cells during the computation. Clearly, M' is k-synchronized if and only if $L(M')$ is empty, which is decidable by Theorem 1. $\qquad\square$

5.2   Two-Way Model

(a) Finite-Turn Case

If in the two-way model, the n-heads of the NPDA M are finite-turn in the sense that the heads can make turns on the input tape (which is provided with left and right end markers) at most a fixed number of times, then the proof of Theorem 17 generalizes since the Parikh map of the bounded language (i.e., inputs coming from $a_1^* \cdots a_t^* b^*$) accepted by a multihead NPDA whose input heads are two-way finite turn is also an effectively computable semilinear set [2]. Then we have:

Theorem 19. *It is decidable to determine, given a two-way finite-turn n-head NPDA M whose inputs come from $w_1^* \cdots w_t^*$ for some strings $w_1, \ldots w_t$, whether M is finitely-synchronized.*

(b) Unrestricted-Turn Case

Theorem 20. *It is decidable to determine, given a two-way multihead NFA M and an integer k, whether M is k-synchronized.*

Proof. Similar to the proof of Theorem 18, but now M' is a two-way one-head NFA. The result follows since the emptiness problem of two-way 1-head NFAs is decidable. $\qquad\square$

The above theorem does not hold for two-way multihead NPDA. In fact, we can prove that it does not hold even for two-way 2-head DCMs (deterministic one-counter machines)

Theorem 21. *It is undecidable to determine, given a two-way 2-head DCM M and an integer k, whether M is k-synchronized.*

Proof. Let M be a two-way 1-head DCM. It is known that the emptiness problem for these machines is undecidable (this follows from the undecidabilty of halting for 2-counter machines [5]). Construct a two-way two-head DCM M' which operates as follows: If x is an input to M, the input to M' is $x\#^d$, where $\#$ is a new symbol and $d \geq 0$. So for a given x, there are are infinitely many inputs to M'. The two heads of M' move simultaneously (with no separation) as a pair simulating the single head of M. If M accepts x, then the first head of M remains on the last symbol of x and the other head moves to the end of $\#^d$. If M does not halt or M rejects, the two heads are not separated. It follows that M' is k-synchronized (in fact 0-synchronized) if and only if $L(M)$ is empty, hence, the result.   □

Corollary 22. *It is undecidable to determine, given a two-way 2-head DPDA M, and an integer k, whether M is k-synchronized.*

Finally, in contrast to Theorem 21, since the emptiness problem for two-way 1-head DCMs whose counter is reversal-bounded is decidable [4], we have the following result using an argument similar to the proof of Theorem 20:

Theorem 23. *It is decidable to determine, given a two-way 2-head DCM M whose counter is reversal-bounded and an integer k, whether M is k-synchronized.*

Acknowledgment

We would like to thank Zhe Dang, Bala Ravikumar, and Fang Yu for helpful comments on this work.

References

1. Harju, T., Karhumki, J.: The equivalence problem of multitape finite automata. Theor. Comput. Sci. 78, 347–355 (1991)
2. Ibarra, O.H.: A note on semilinear sets and bounded-reversal multihead pushdown automata. Inf. Process. Lett. 3, 25–28 (1974)
3. Ibarra, O.H.: Reversal-bounded multicounter machines and their decision problems. J. Assoc. Comput. Mach. 25, 116–133 (1978)
4. Ibarra, O.H., Jiang, T., Tran, N.Q., Wang, H.: New decidability results concerning two-way counter machines. SIAM J. Comput. 24, 123–137 (1995)
5. Minsky, M.: Recursive unsolvability of Post's problem of Tag and other topics in the theory of Turing machines. Ann. of Math. 74, 437–455 (1961)
6. Yu, F., Bultan, T., Cova, M., Ibarra, O.H.: Symbolic string verification: an automata-based approach. In: Havelund, K., Majumdar, R. (eds.) SPIN 2008. LNCS, vol. 5156, pp. 306–324. Springer, Heidelberg (2008)
7. Yu, F., Bultan, T., Ibarra, O.H.: Symbolic string verification: Combining string analysis and size analysis. In: Kowalewski, S., Philippou, A. (eds.) TACAS 2009. LNCS, vol. 5505, pp. 322–336. Springer, Heidelberg (2009)
8. Yu, F., Bultan, T., Ibarra, O.H.: Relational string verification using multi-track automata. In: Domaratzki, M., Salomaa, K. (eds.) CIAA 2010. LNCS, vol. 6482, pp. 290–299. Springer, Heidelberg (2011)

State Complexity of Projected Languages

Galina Jirásková[1,*] and Tomáš Masopust[2,3,**]

[1] Mathematical Institute, Slovak Academy of Sciences
Grešákova 6, 040 01 Košice, Slovak Republic
jiraskov@saske.sk
[2] CWI, P.O. Box 94079, 1090 GB Amsterdam, The Netherlands
[3] Institute of Mathematics, Czech Academy of Sciences
Žižkova 22, 616 62 Brno, Czech Republic
masopust@math.cas.cz

Abstract. This paper discusses the state complexity of projected regular languages represented by incomplete deterministic finite automata. It is shown that the known upper bound is reachable only by automata with one unobservable transition, that is, a transition labeled with a symbol removed by the projection. The present paper improves this upper bound by considering the structure of the automaton. It also proves that the new bounds are tight, considers the case of finite languages, and presents several open problems.

1 Introduction

Projections, also called natural projections since they can be seen as natural transformations of category theory, or abstractions, play an important role in many fields of computer science and engineering, such as verification, diagnoses, and supervisory control [1,16,17,18,30]. Given a regular language L and a projection P, it is well-known that the minimal deterministic finite automaton (dfa) accepting language $P(L)$ can be of exponential size in comparison with the dfa accepting language L. The known upper bound for projection is $3 \cdot 2^{n-2} - 1$ [29]. On the other hand, however, this result does not consider the structure of the automaton, which is of interest because, as shown in this paper, this upper bound is reachable only for automata with one *unobservable transition*, that is, a transition that is labeled with a symbol removed by the projection. Note that several unobservable transitions connecting the same two states in the same direction (called unobservable multi-transitions) are considered as only one unobservable transition, that is, we disregard unobservable multi-transitions.

In this paper, we improve the upper bound by considering the structure of the automaton. Specifically, we study the state complexity with respect to the

---

* Research supported by the Slovak Research and Development Agency under contract APVV-0035-10 "Algorithms, Automata, and Discrete Data Structures".
** Research supported by the European Community's 7th Framework Programme grant no. INFSO-ICT-224498, and by the GAČR grant no. 202/11/P028.

M. Holzer, M. Kutrib, and G. Pighizzini (Eds.): DCFS 2011, LNCS 6808, pp. 198–211, 2011.

structure of unobservable transitions. This parameter turns out to be more convenient than the number of unobservable transitions. We show that, given a projection and a minimal incomplete dfa with n states, the minimal incomplete dfa accepting the projected language has no more than $2^{n-1} + 2^{n-m} - 1$ states, where m is the number of states incident with unobservable transitions. This bound is reachable if the number of unobservable transitions is $m-1$. However, any additional unobservable transition can introduce a new unreachable subset, which means that the bound is not tight if there are more than $m-1$ unobservable transitions. Therefore, we also discuss the case the automaton has at least m unobservable transitions, and show that in this case the tight upper bound is $3 \cdot 2^{n-3} + 2^{n-m} - 1$.

The paper also discusses the case of projected finite languages, and shows that the upper bounds on the number of states correspond to the upper bounds on the nfa to dfa conversion [26].

For several operations, $op(\cdot)$, such as the determinization of nfa's, it has been shown that for all integers n and α with $f(n) \leq \alpha \leq g(n)$, where $f(n)$ and $g(n)$ are the tight lower and upper bounds for $op(\cdot)$, there exists a regular language L represented by a minimal dfa of size n such that the minimal dfa for $op(L)$ is of size α. A number α for which no such language exists is called *magic* for n with respect to $op(\cdot)$. For instance, there are no magic numbers for the determinization of nfa's with the input alphabet of cardinality at least three, where $f(n) = n$ and $g(n) = 2^n$. During the last few years, this topic has widely been discussed in the literature. The reader is referred to [6,8,10,11,12,13,15,28] for more information. Our last theorem solves the magic number problem for projections using the result on magic numbers for stars of regular languages [14].

We conclude the paper with a short overview of open problems concerning projected regular languages.

2   Preliminaries and Definitions

We assume that the reader is familiar with automata theory, and for all unexplained notions, we refer the reader to [27,31].

For an alphabet (finite nonempty set) Σ, denote by Σ^* the set of all finite strings over the alphabet Σ including the empty string ε. A *language* over Σ is any subset of Σ^*. A language L is *finite* if L is a finite set.

Let $\Sigma_o \subseteq \Sigma$. A homomorphism $P : \Sigma^* \to \Sigma_o^*$ is called the *(natural) projection* if it is defined so that $P(a) = \varepsilon$ if $a \in \Sigma \setminus \Sigma_o$, and $P(a) = a$ if $a \in \Sigma_o$.

An *(incomplete) dfa* is a quintuple $A = (Q, \Sigma, \delta, s, F)$, where Q is a finite set of *states*, Σ is an *input alphabet*, $\delta : Q \times \Sigma \to Q$ is a *(partial) transition function*, $s \in Q$ is the *initial state*, and $F \subseteq Q$ is the set of *final states*. In the usual way, transition function δ can be extended to the domain $Q \times \Sigma^*$. The language *accepted* by A is defined as the set $L(A) = \{w \in \Sigma^* \mid \delta(s, w) \in F\}$. A transition $\delta(p, a) = q$ is said to be *unobservable* with respect to P if $a \in \Sigma \setminus \Sigma_o$, that is, if $P(a) = \varepsilon$.

For a regular language L, we denote by $\|L\|$ the smallest number of states in any incomplete dfa accepting L.

In comparison with complete dfa's, each incomplete dfa represents two languages. The language accepted by the dfa as defined above, also called a *marked language*, and the language of all strings that the dfa can read called a *generated language*, that is, the strings for which the corresponding transitions are defined. For complete dfa's, the latter language is equal to Σ^*.

Considering complete automata, the corresponding upper bounds can be derived from the results for incomplete automata by considering only those unobservable transitions that are not incident with the *dead* or *sink* state. For this reason, we only discuss the case of incomplete dfa's in this paper.

3   DFAs as Graphs

Here we concentrate our attention on the number of states potentially reachable in the subset automaton constructed from a given dfa after applying a projection. For simplification, we consider the important parts of automata as graphs.

A *directed graph* is a pair $G = (V, E)$, where V is a finite set of nodes, and $E \subseteq V \times V$ is a set of edges. An edge $(u, v) \in E$ is called a *loop* if $u = v$. Let $u \in V$ be a node, then *in-degree* and *out-degree* of v are the sizes of sets $\{u \in V \mid (u, v) \in E\}$ and $\{w \in V \mid (v, w) \in E\}$, respectively. A node with in-degree 0 and out-degree 1, or with in-degree 1 and out-degree 0 is called a *leaf*. This definition requires that the node is incident to an edge. Thus, a node incident to no edge is not considered to be a leaf.

A *path* is a sequence of nodes $v_0, v_1, \ldots, v_k$ such that $v_i \neq v_j$ if $i \neq j$, and (v_i, v_{i+1}) is an edge in E for $i = 0, 1, \ldots, k-1$. A *non-oriented path* is a sequence $v_0, v_1, \ldots, v_k$ such that $v_i \neq v_j$ if $i \neq j$, and either (v_i, v_{i+1}) or (v_{i+1}, v_i) is an edge in E for $i = 0, 1, \ldots, k-1$. A graph G is *connected* if for all nodes u, v in V, there is a non-oriented path from u to v. For a node v in V, let $G \setminus \{v\}$ denote the graph constructed from G by removing node v and all edges incident to v.

A subset X of V is said to be *bad* in graph $G = (V, E)$ if there exists an edge (u, v) in E such that $u \in X$ and $v \notin X$. A set is said to be *good* if it is not bad; thus a good subset of V is closed under outgoing transitions. Let $b(G)$ denote the number of bad subsets in G, and $g(G)$ the number of good subsets in G. We first study the number of bad subsets in a graph.

Lemma 1. *Let $m, n \geq 2$ and let $G = (V, E)$ be a directed graph without loops with n nodes. Let $U = \{u, v \in V \mid (u, v) \in E\}$ and assume that U is of size m. Then $b(G) \geq (2^{m-1} - 1)\, 2^{n-m}$.*

Proof. Let G and U be as assumed in the theorem, and consider a special case where the edges involved in nodes of U go only from $m - 1$ different nodes to the last m-th node. This means that there exists a node v in V such that for each node u in $U \setminus \{v\}$, the edge (u, v) is in E, while for each node z in V, the edge (z, u) is not in E. Then there are $2^{m-1} - 1$ nonempty subsets of U which do not contain node v, and so are bad. This gives $b(G) \geq (2^{m-1} - 1)\, 2^{n-m}$.

Now, we will show the theorem to be true in general, and not just under the assumption that the edges in U go only from $m - 1$ different nodes to the last m-th node as was done in the paragraph above. The proof is by induction on m.

If $m = 2$, then U involves either one or two edges. Note first that if X is a bad subset in G, then X is bad after addition of any number of edges to G. Thus, we can consider that there is only one edge because the other one cannot decrease the number of bad subsets. Then, if we have one edge, say (a, b), we can have a along with any combination of elements of $V \setminus \{a, b\}$ in a bad subset, and thus we have $b(G) \geq 2^{n-2} = (2^{2-1} - 1) 2^{n-2}$. Assume that the statement holds for all sets U of size less than m, and consider the case U is of size m. There are two possibilities. Either the number of edges is strictly less than m, or it is greater then or equal to m. In the former case, consider the number of edges and denote it by t, and in the latter case, consider the subset of edges of size t forming the minimal spanning tree (forest). Thus $t < m$ and there is a leaf v in U such that v is connected with a node u in $U \setminus \{v\}$. Then, either (i) all nodes in $U \setminus \{v\}$ are incident with some of the t edges, or (ii) node u was connected only with v and now it is not incident with any other node in $U \setminus \{v\}$.

In case (i), the set $U \setminus \{v\}$ is of size $m - 1$, and by the induction hypothesis, there are at least $2^{m-2} - 1$ bad subsets of $U \setminus \{v\}$. If $(v, u) \in E$, then for each subset A of $U \setminus \{v\}$ that is bad in $U \setminus \{v\}$, the sets A and $A \cup \{v\}$ are bad in U, and $\{v\}$ is a new bad set. This gives $b(G) \geq (2^{m-2} - 1 + 2^{m-2} - 1 + 1) 2^{n-m}$. Similarly, if $(u, v) \in E$, then for each subset A of $U \setminus \{v\}$ that is bad in $U \setminus \{v\}$, the sets A, $A \cup \{v\}$ are bad in U, and the set $U \setminus \{v\}$ is a new bad set.

In case (ii), the set $U \setminus \{u, v\}$ is of size $m - 2$, and so, there are at least $2^{m-3} - 1$ bad subsets of $U \setminus \{u, v\}$. We now have $m \geq 4$. The sets $\emptyset$ and $U \setminus \{u, v\}$ are not bad. Thus $\{v\}$ or $\{u\}$, and $U \setminus \{u\}$ or $U \setminus \{v\}$, depending on the direction of the edge connecting u and v, are two new bad subsets. Moreover, all bad subsets of $U \setminus \{u, v\}$ are also bad in U. If there is at least one more proper non-empty good subset B of $U \setminus \{u, v\}$, then $B \cup \{u\}$ or $B \cup \{v\}$ is the third new bad subset of U. Summarized, this gives $b(G) \geq (2^2 (2^{m-3} - 1) + 3) 2^{n-m} = (2^{m-1} - 1) 2^{n-m}$. If there are only two good subsets of $U \setminus \{u, v\}$, namely $\emptyset$ and $U \setminus \{u, v\}$, then the number of bad subsets of $U \setminus \{u, v\}$ is $2^{m-2} - 2$, which, since $m \geq 4$, gives $b(G) \geq 2^2(2^{m-2} - 2) 2^{n-m} = (2^{m-1} - 1 + 2^{m-1} - 7) 2^{n-m} \geq (2^{m-1} - 1) 2^{n-m}$. □

Consider the statement of Lemma 1. Then the number of all the subsets of $V \setminus U$ is 2^{n-m} while the number of bad subsets of U is $2^{m-1} - 1$. Moreover, there is a graph $G = (V, E)$ with U of size $|E| - 1$, for which the equality holds. However, if $m \leq |E|$, each additional transition can introduce a new bad subset. This problem is discussed in the following result.

Lemma 2. *Let $m, n \geq 2$ and let $G = (V, E)$ be a directed graph without loops with n nodes. Let $U = \{u, v \in V \mid (u, v) \in E\}$ and assume that $|U| = m \leq |E|$. Then $b(G) \geq (5 \cdot 2^{m-3} - 1) 2^{n-m}$.*

Proof. The proof is by induction on m. If $m = 2$, then the graph consists of two nodes connected by two edges. This gives two bad subsets of U, which results in $b(G) = 2 \cdot 2^{n-m} \geq 3/2 \cdot 2^{n-m}$. Assume that the statement holds for all sets U of cardinality less then m, and consider the case U is of cardinality m. Recall that $m \leq |E|$. Consider a subset of m edges forming a minimal spanning tree (forest). Then there is a leaf v in U. If $|U \setminus \{v\}| \leq |E(G \setminus \{v\})|$ then by the induction hypothesis, the set $U \setminus \{v\}$ has at least $5 \cdot 2^{m-4} - 1$ bad subsets. Otherwise, by Lemma 1, the set $U \setminus \{v\}$ has at least $2^{m-2} - 1$ bad subsets.

In the former case, if $(v, u) \in E$, then for each bad subset A of $U \setminus \{v\}$, the set $A \cup \{v\}$ is a new bad subset of U and, in addition, $\{v\}$ is a new bad subset of U. If $(u, v) \in E$, then for each bad subset A of $U \setminus \{v\}$, the set $A \cup \{v\}$ is a new bad subset of U and, in addition, the set $U \setminus \{v\}$ is a new bad subset of set U. Thus $b(G) \geq (5 \cdot 2^{m-4} - 1 + 5 \cdot 2^{m-4}) 2^{n-m} = (5 \cdot 2^{m-3} - 1) 2^{n-m}$.

In the latter case, notice that there are at least two edges connecting v and $U \setminus \{v\}$ in G. We have three possibilities:

(i) Node v is connected with $U \setminus \{v\}$ by edges (v, u_1) and (v, u_2) with $u_1 \neq u_2$. Then the sets $A \cup \{v\}$, $A \cup \{v, u_1\}$, and $A \cup \{v, u_2\}$ are bad in U for every subset A of $U \setminus \{v, u_1, u_2\}$. Hence we have at least $3 \cdot 2^{m-3}$ new bad subsets in U.

(ii) Node v is connected with $U \setminus \{v\}$ by edges (u_1, v) and (u_2, v). Then for each subset A of $U \setminus \{u_1, u_2, v\}$, if $A \cup \{u_1\}$ is bad in $U \setminus \{v\}$, then $A \cup \{v, u_1\}$ is bad in U, otherwise $A \cup \{u_1\}$ is bad in U; if $A \cup \{u_2\}$ is bad in $U \setminus \{v\}$, then $A \cup \{v, u_2\}$ is bad in U, otherwise $A \cup \{u_2\}$ is bad in U; if $A \cup \{u_1, u_2\}$ is bad in $U \setminus \{v\}$, then $A \cup \{u_1, u_2, v\}$ is bad in U, otherwise $A \cup \{u_1, u_2\}$ is bad in U. Summarized, there are $3 \cdot 2^{m-3}$ new bad subsets in U.

(iii) Node v is connected with $U \setminus \{v\}$ by edges (u_1, v) and (v, u_2). Then the sets $A \cup \{v\}$ and $A \cup \{u_1, v\}$ are bad in U for each subset A of $U \setminus \{u_1, u_2, v\}$. In addition, if $A \cup \{u_1, u_2\}$ is bad in $U \setminus \{v\}$, then the set $A \cup \{u_1, u_2, v\}$ is a new bad subset of U. Otherwise, the set $A \cup \{u_1, u_2\}$ is a new bad subset of U. Thus there are at least $3 \cdot 2^{m-3}$ new bad subsets of U.

This gives $b(G) \geq (2^{m-2} - 1 + 3 \cdot 2^{m-3}) 2^{n-m} = (5 \cdot 2^{m-3} - 1) 2^{n-m}$. □

4   State Complexity of Projected Regular Languages

Recall that it is shown in [29] that the worst-case tight upper bound on projected regular languages is $2^{n-1} + 2^{n-2} - 1$, where n is the number of states of the minimal incomplete dfa recognizing the given language.

Theorem 3 ([29]). *Let $n \geq 2$ and L be a regular language over Σ with $\|L\| = n$. Let $\Sigma_o \subseteq \Sigma$ and P be the projection of Σ^* onto Σ_o^*. The tight upper bound on the size of the minimal incomplete dfa for projected language $P(L)$ is $3 \cdot 2^{n-2} - 1$.*

In what follows, we improve the upper bound by taking into account the structure of nonloop unobservable transitions. More specifically, we consider the number of states that are incident with nonloop unobservable transitions. Note that it follows from the results that the previous bound is reachable only by dfa's with one unobservable transition, up to unobservable multi-transitions.

Theorem 4. *Let $m, n \geq 2$, $\Sigma_o \subseteq \Sigma$, and P be the projection of Σ^* onto Σ_o^*. Let L be a regular language over alphabet Σ with $\|L\| = n$, and $(Q, \Sigma, \delta, s, F)$ be the minimal incomplete dfa recognizing language L, in which*

$$|\{p, q \in Q \mid p \neq q \text{ and } q \in \delta(p, \Sigma \setminus \Sigma_o)\}| = m.$$

Then $\|P(L)\| \leq 2^{n-1} + 2^{n-m} - 1$.

Proof. Consider the minimal incomplete dfa $(Q, \Sigma, \delta, s, F)$ accepting L, and construct a directed graph $G = (Q, E)$ without loops so that E contains an edge (p, q) in $Q \times Q$ if and only if $p \neq q$ and there is a transition $\delta(p, a) = q$ for some unobservable symbol a in $\Sigma \setminus \Sigma_o$. Construct an nfa for language $P(L)$ from dfa A by replacing all the unobservable transitions with ε-transitions. Observe that each subset of Q that contains p, but not q, is not reachable in the corresponding subset automaton because every string leading the nfa to state p also leads the automaton to state q. This means that no subset of Q that is bad in graph G is reachable. By Lemma 1, for the number $g(G)$ of good subsets (that is, subsets closed under outgoing transitions) we have $g(G) = 2^n - b(G) \leq 2^n - (2^{m-1} - 1)\, 2^{n-m} = 2^{n-1} + 2^{n-m}$. Good subsets of Q in graph G correspond to potentially reachable states in the subset automaton. This number is decreased by one because the empty set (the dead state) is potentially reachable but it is not present in the minimal incomplete dfa.   □

Notice that Theorem 3 is a consequence of Theorem 4 since $\|P(L)\|$ is maximal if $m = 2$. The next result shows that the bound $2^{n-1} + 2^{n-m} - 1$ is tight.

Theorem 5. *Let $m, n \geq 2$ and P be the projection of $\{a, b, c\}^*$ onto $\{a, b\}^*$. There exists a regular language L over $\{a, b, c\}$ with $\|L\| = n$, such that the minimal incomplete dfa accepting L has $m - 1$ unobservable nonloop transitions connecting m states, and $\|P(L)\| = 2^{n-1} + 2^{n-m} - 1$.*

Proof. Let L be the language over $\{a, b, c\}$ accepted by the incomplete dfa shown in Fig. 1. After applying the projection onto $\{a, b\}$ and removing ε-transitions, we get the n-state nfa shown in Fig. 2. The nfa accepts the string b^n only from state $n - 1$, and the string $a^i b^n$ only from state $n - 1 - i$ $(0 \leq i \leq n - 1)$. It follows that the states in the corresponding subset automaton are pairwise distinguishable. To prove the theorem, we only need to show that the subset automaton has $2^{n-1} + 2^{n-m} - 1$ reachable non-empty states.

We first prove by induction that every subset of $\{0, 1, \ldots, n - 1\}$ containing state 0 is reachable. The initial state $\{0\}$ goes to state $\{n - m\}$ by a^{n-m}, then by a string in b^* to states $\{0, i\}$ with $n - m + 1 \leq i \leq n - 2$. State $\{0, n - 2\}$ goes to state $\{0, 1, n - 1\}$ by a, and then by a string in b^* to states $\{0, i, n - 1\}$ with $1 \leq i \leq n - 2$. State $\{0, n - 2, n - 1\}$ goes to $\{0, n - 1\}$ by b, and then to $\{0, 1\}$ by a. By a string in b^*, state $\{0, 1\}$ goes to states $\{0, i\}$ with $1 \leq i \leq n - m$. Thus each subset of size 2 containing state 0 is reachable. Now let $X = \{0, i_1, i_2, \ldots, i_t\}$ be

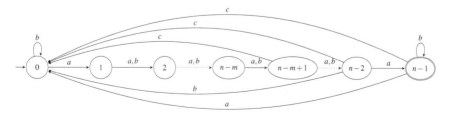

Fig. 1. The minimal incomplete dfa for a language L with $\|P(L)\| = 2^{n-1} + 2^{n-m} - 1$

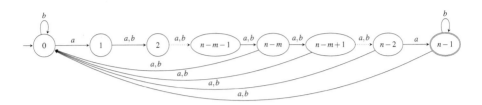

Fig. 2. An nfa accepting the projection of the language from Fig. 1

a set of size $t + 1$, where $2 \leq t \leq n - 1$ and $1 \leq i_1 < i_2 < \cdots < i_t \leq n - 1$. Consider two cases:

(i) $i_t = n - 1$. Then X is reached from $\{0, i_2 - i_1, \ldots, i_{t-1} - i_1, n - 2\}$ by $ab^{i_1 - 1}$, and the latter set of size t is reachable by the induction hypothesis.

(ii) $i_t < n - 1$. Then X is reached from $\{0, i_2 - i_1, \ldots, i_t - i_1, n - 1\}$ by $ab^{i_1 - 1}$, and the latter set of size $t + 1$ contains state $n - 1$, and is reachable by (i).

This proves reachability of all subsets containing state 0. Next, if $\{i_1, i_2, \ldots, i_t\}$ is a non-empty subset of the set $\{1, 2, \ldots, n - m\}$, then it is reached from the set $\{0, i_2 - i_1, i_3 - i_1, \ldots, i_t - i_1\}$ containing state 0 by a^{i_1}. This gives $2^{n-1} + 2^{n-m} - 1$ reachable non-empty states, and completes our proof.   □

In the theorems above, the number of unobservable transitions is considered to be less than the size of the set $\{p, q \in Q \mid p \neq q \text{ and } q \in \delta(p, \Sigma \setminus \Sigma_o)\}$. However, an additional unobservable transition may introduce a new unreachable subset. The following example shows that if the size of this set is less than or equal to the number of unobservable nonloop transitions, then the upper bound is not tight. The precise upper bound for this case is open.

Example 6. Let $m, n \geq 2$. Consider a minimal incomplete dfa $(Q, \Sigma, \delta, s, F)$ of n states. Let the incomplete automaton have at least m unobservable transitions. Let $U = \{p, q \in Q \mid p \neq q \text{ and } q \in \delta(p, \Sigma \setminus \Sigma_o)\}$ and assume that $|U| = m$. Construct a directed graph $G = (Q, E)$ without loops so that the set E contains an edge (p, q) in $Q \times Q$ if and only if $p \neq q$ and there is a transition $\delta(p, a) = q$ for some unobservable symbol a in $\Sigma \setminus \Sigma_o$.

In the case of $m = 2$, there must be a cycle of length two in G. In this case, however, we have $g(G) = 2^n - 2 \cdot 2^{n-2} = 2^{n-1}$.

In the case of $m = 3$, there are three possibilities: (i) if U contains a cycle of length three, then there are at least 6 subsets that are bad for U because all but the empty set and the whole set U are bad; (ii) if U contains a cycle with one transition reversed, then there are at least 4 bad subsets of U; (iii) if U contains a cycle of length two and an edge to (or from) the third node, then there are at least 5 bad subsets of U. In all three cases, we get $g(G) \leq 2^n - 4 \cdot 2^{n-3} = 2^{n-1}$.

Since only non-empty good subsets for G can be reached in the incomplete dfa for the projected language, we get the bound $2^{n-1} - 1$ on the size of this dfa in both cases. This is strictly less than $2^{n-1} + 2^{n-m} - 1$ given by Theorem 4.   □

Finally, the situation is significantly different for projections of regular languages with one-letter co-domains.

Theorem 7. *Let a be a symbol in an alphabet Σ and P be the projection of strings in Σ^* to strings in a^*. Let L be a regular language over Σ with $\|L\| = n$. Then $\|P(L)\| \leq e^{(1+o(1))\sqrt{n \ln n}}$.*

Proof. Replace all the transitions unobservable for projection P in the minimal incomplete dfa recognizing language L with ε-transitions to get an n-state unary nfa for language $P(L)$. This unary nfa can be simulated by a dfa with no more than $e^{(1+o(1))\sqrt{n \ln n}}$ states [2,6,20], and the upper bound follows.   □

The following theorem discusses a special case that gives an idea how to treat the cases with more and more unobservable transitions.

Theorem 8. *Let $m, n \geq 2$ and $\Sigma_o \subseteq \Sigma$. Let P be the projection of strings in Σ^* to strings in Σ_o^*. Let L be a regular language over alphabet Σ with $\|L\| = n$, and $(Q, \Sigma, \delta, s, F)$ be the minimal incomplete dfa recognizing language L, in which $|\{p, q \in Q \mid p \neq q \text{ and } q \in \delta(p, \Sigma \setminus \Sigma_o)\}| = m$. If at least m transitions in the dfa are unobservable for the projection, then $\|P(L)\| \leq 2^{n-2} + 2^{n-3} + 2^{n-m} - 1$.*

Proof. Consider the minimal incomplete dfa $(Q, \Sigma, \delta, s, F)$ for L, and construct a directed graph $G = (Q, E)$ without loops so that E contains an arc (p, q) if and only if $p \neq q$ and there is a transition $\delta(p, a) = q$ for some unobservable symbol a in $\Sigma \setminus \Sigma_o$. Construct an nfa for language $P(L)$ from the dfa for L by replacing all the unobservable transitions with ε-transitions. Then every subset that is reachable in the corresponding subset automaton must be good for G. By Lemma 2, we have $g(G) \leq 2^n - (5 \cdot 2^{m-3} - 1) 2^{n-m} = 2^{n-2} + 2^{n-3} + 2^{n-m}$. This number is decreased by one because of the empty set (the dead state).   □

The next result proves the tightness of the bound $2^{n-2} + 2^{n-3} + 2^{n-m} - 1$ in the case of a four-letter domain alphabet.

Theorem 9. *Let $n \geq 2$ and P be the projection of $\{a, b, c, d\}^*$ onto $\{a, b, c\}^*$. There exists a regular language L over $\{a, b, c, d\}$ with $\|L\| = n$ such that the minimal incomplete dfa accepting L has m unobservable nonloop transitions on no more than m states, and $\|P(L)\| = 2^{n-2} + 2^{n-3} + 2^{n-m} - 1$.*

Proof. Consider the language L over the alphabet $\{a, b, c, d\}$ accepted by the incomplete n-state dfa shown in Fig. 3. Construct an nfa for language $P(L)$ from the dfa for L by replacing all the unobservable transitions with ε-transitions. After removing the ε-transitions, we get the n-state nfa for $P(L)$ shown in Fig. 4.

Notice that this nfa accepts string a^{n-i} with $2 \leq i \leq n$ only from state i, and string ca^{n-2} only from state 1. It follows that all the states in the corresponding subset automaton are pairwise distinguishable. Thus it is enough to show that the subset automaton has $2^{n-2} + 2^{n-3} + 2^{n-m}$ reachable states including the empty set.

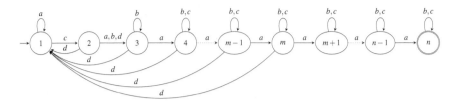

Fig. 3. The incomplete dfa over $\{a, b, c, d\}$ with m unobservable transitions on m states meeting the bound $2^{n-2} + 2^{n-3} + 2^{n-m} - 1$ on the projection onto $\{a, b, c\}$

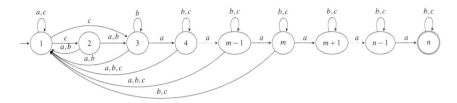

Fig. 4. The nfa for the projection of the language from Fig. 3

State $\{1\}$ is the start state of the subset automaton. Each set $\{1, i_1, i_2, \ldots, i_t\}$ of size $t + 1$, where $3 \le i_1 < i_2 < \cdots < i_t \le n$ and $1 \le t \le n - 1$, is reached from the set $\{1, i_2 - (i_1 - 3), \ldots, i_t - (i_1 - 3)\}$ of size t by string $cba^{i_1 - 3}$. Thus, by induction, each state $\{1\} \cup X$ with $X \subseteq \{3, 4, \ldots, n\}$ is reachable. Next, such a state $\{1\} \cup X$ goes to state $\{1, 2, 3\} \cup X$ by c. Finally, if X is a subset of $\{m + 1, m + 2, \ldots, n\}$, then state $\{1\} \cup X$ goes to state X by b. This proves the reachability of the desired number of states, and concludes our proof.   □

5   State Complexity of Projected Finite Languages

In this section, we consider the state complexity of projected finite languages. First, let us consider the case of projections with co-domains of size one.

Proposition 10. *Let a be a symbol in an alphabet Σ and let P be the projection of Σ^* onto a^*. If L is a finite regular language over Σ, then $\|P(L)\| \le \|L\|$.*

Proof. Consider the minimal complete dfa with n states accepting language L. Since L is finite, there must exist a string that leads the dfa to the dead state. Hence the minimal incomplete dfa accepting L has $n-1$ states. After replacing all the unobservable transitions with ε-transitions and eliminating ε-transitions, the resulting nfa with $n - 1$ states accepts finite language $P(L)$. Therefore, this nfa can be simulated by an n-state complete dfa [26]. Again, some string must lead this complete dfa to the dead state, which implies that the minimal incomplete dfa accepting $P(L)$ has at most $n - 1$ states. Thus $\|P(L)\| \le \|L\|$.   □

The following theorem deals with finite languages and binary co-domain alphabets.

Theorem 11. *Let a and b be symbols in an alphabet Σ and P be the projection of Σ^* onto $\{a, b\}^*$. Let L be a finite language over Σ with $\|L\| = n$. Then*

$$\|P(L)\| \leq \begin{cases} 2 \cdot 2^{\lfloor n/2 \rfloor} - 2 & \text{if } n \text{ is even,} \\ 3 \cdot 2^{\lfloor n/2 \rfloor} - 2 & \text{if } n \text{ is odd.} \end{cases}$$

In addition, the bound is tight in the case of a ternary domain alphabet.

Proof. We first prove the upper bound. Consider an incomplete dfa accepting language L, and construct an n-state nfa for $P(L)$ by replacing all the unobservable transitions with ε-transitions, and eliminating the ε-transitions. The n-state nfa for finite language $P(L)$ can be simulated by a complete dfa of $2^{n/2+1} - 1$ states if n is even, or of $3 \cdot 2^{\lfloor n/2 \rfloor} - 1$ states if n is odd [26]. Since some string must lead this complete dfa to the dead state, this state is removed from the minimal incomplete dfa representation of $P(L)$.

For tightness, consider the ternary finite regular language recognized by the incomplete dfa shown in Fig. 5, where $k = \lceil n/2 \rceil - 1$. The application of the projection P results in the language

$$P(L) = \bigcup_{i=0}^{\lceil n/2 \rceil - 1} (a+b)^i a (a+b)^{\lfloor n/2 \rfloor - 1}$$

that can be written as $P(L) = \{uav \in \{a, b\}^* \mid |uav| < n \text{ and } |v| = \lfloor n/2 \rfloor - 1\}$. However, the minimal complete dfa accepting $P(L)$ has $2^{n/2+1} - 1$ states if n is even, or $3 \cdot 2^{\lfloor n/2 \rfloor} - 1$ states if n is odd, as shown in [26]. Since $P(L)$ is finite, the minimal incomplete dfa for $P(L)$ has one less state than the complete dfa. Hence the bounds are tight. $\qquad\square$

In the next theorem, we consider the case of projections of finite languages with co-domains of size k with $k \geq 2$. In comparison with the previous result, where the sizes of the domain and co-domain differ by one, note that the size of the domain of the projection is required to be of linear size with respect to the number of states. It remains open if it can be limited by a constant.

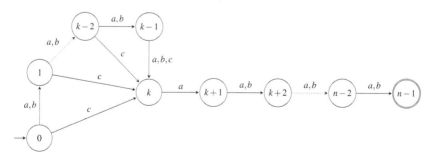

Fig. 5. The minimal incomplete dfa over $\{a, b, c\}$ accepting a finite language meeting the upper bound on the projection onto $\{a, b\}$; $k = \lceil n/2 \rceil - 1$

Theorem 12. *Let $k, n \geq 2$. There exist alphabets Σ and Σ_o with $\Sigma_o \subseteq \Sigma$ and $|\Sigma_o| = k$, and a finite language L over Σ with $\|L\| = n$ such that*

$$\|P(L)\| = (k^{\lfloor n/(\log k+1) \rfloor + 1} - 1)/(k - 1) - 1,$$

where P is the projection of strings in Σ^* onto strings in Σ_o^*. In addition, the upper bound is $(k^{\lceil (n/(\log k+1) \rceil + 1} - 1)/(k - 1) - 1$.

Proof. The upper bound follows from [26, Theorem 5] in a similar way as shown in the proof of Theorem 11. To prove the lower bound, let $t = \lceil \log k \rceil$ and let $m = \lfloor n/(t+1) \rfloor$. Let $\Sigma_o = \{0, 1, \ldots, k-1\}$, let $\Sigma = \{a_1, a_2, \ldots, a_{n-m-1}\} \cup \Sigma_o$, and let P be the projection of Σ^* onto Σ_o^*.

Set $S_i = \{j \in \Sigma_o \mid j \bmod 2^i \geq 2^{i-1}\}$ for $i = 1, 2, \ldots, t$. Notice that a symbol j is in S_i if and only if the i-th digit from the end in the binary notation of j is 1.

Now let L' be the language over Σ_o consisting of all strings of length $n-1$ that have a symbol from S_i in position $i\,m$ from the end ($i = 1, 2, \ldots, t$). Language L' is accepted by an n-state incomplete dfa A' over Σ_o with states $0, 1, \ldots, n-1$, of which 0 is the initial state, and $n-1$ is the sole final state.

Construct an incomplete dfa A over Σ from dfa A' by adding an unobservable transition on a_ℓ from the initial state 0 to state ℓ for $\ell = 1, 2, \ldots, n-m-1$. Let L be the language over Σ recognized by A. The projected language $P(L)$ consists of all suffixes of length at least m of strings in L'. As shown in [25,26], every incomplete dfa for $P(L)$ needs at least $(k^{\lfloor n/(\log k+1) \rfloor + 1} - 1)/(k - 1)$ states.   □

Our last result shows that the size of the minimal dfa for a projected language may reach an arbitrary value from 1 up to the upper bound $2^{n-1} + 2^{n-2} - 1$. Hence there are no magic numbers for projections of regular languages.

Theorem 13. *Let $n \geq 2$ and $1 \leq \alpha \leq 2^{n-1} + 2^{n-2} - 1$. There exist an alphabet Σ, a projection P of strings in $(\Sigma \cup \{\#\})^*$ onto strings in Σ^* with $\# \notin \Sigma$, and a regular language L over $\Sigma \cup \{\#\}$ with $\|L\| = n$ such that $\|P(L)\| = \alpha$.*

Proof. If $1 \leq \alpha \leq n - 2$, then take the minimal incomplete dfa of Fig. 6 with $\Sigma = \{a\}$. The projected language is $\{a^i \mid i \geq \alpha - 1\}$, for which the minimal incomplete dfa has α states.

If $\alpha = n - 1$, then take the incomplete dfa of Fig. 7 with $\Sigma = \{a\}$. The projected language is $(a^{n-1})^*$, for which the minimal incomplete dfa has $n - 1$ states.

Now let $n \leq \alpha \leq 2^{n-1} + 2^{n-2} - 1$. Then $n + 1 \leq \alpha + 1 \leq \frac{3}{4} \cdot 2^n$, and so $\alpha + 1$ can be expressed as $\alpha + 1 = n - k + \frac{3}{4} \cdot 2^k + m$, where $2 \leqslant k \leqslant n$ and

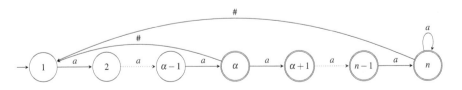

Fig. 6. The incomplete n-state dfa A over $\{a, \#\}$ with $\|P(L(A))\| = \alpha$; $1 \leq \alpha \leq n - 2$

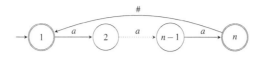

Fig. 7. The incomplete n-state dfa A over $\{a, \#\}$ with $\|P(L(A))\| = n - 1$

$0 \leqslant m \leqslant 2^{k-1} + 2^{k-2} - 2$. It is shown in [14, Lemma 9 and Lemma 10] that there exists a minimal n-state dfa $M_{n,k,m}$ over an alphabet Σ with states $1, 2, \ldots, n$, of which 1 is the initial state, and k is the sole final state (and no state is dead) such that the minimal dfa for the star of language $L(M_{n,k,m})$ has $\alpha + 1$ states.

Let us modify the dfa $M_{n,k,m}$ by adding an unobservable transition by symbol $\#$ from the final state k to the initial state 1. Then in the subset automaton for the projected language, all the states that were reachable in the subset automaton for star will be again reachable, except for the initial state $\{q_0\}$ that was added in the construction of an nfa for star in [14] . All the reachable states will be pairwise distinguishable. Therefore, the minimal incomplete dfa for the projected language has exactly α states.   □

6   Conclusion

The dfa accepting a projected language is obtained from the dfa accepting an input language by replacing unobservable transitions with ε-transitions and by applying the subset construction to the resulting nfa. The minimal dfa for the projected language, however, may be of exponential size in comparison with the input automaton [9,19,21,22]. This observation gives rise to a challenging open problem. How to characterize classes of dfa's, for which the minimal dfa for the projections is of a linear (polynomial, logarithmic) size?

Problem 14. Let P be a projection, and let $\mathbb{A}_P^f$ denote the class of all minimal dfa's such that $A \in \mathbb{A}_P^f$ if and only if the minimal dfa accepting $P(L(A))$ has no more than $f(n)$ states, where f is a (recursive) upper bound state-space function. Given a projection P and a function f, characterize the class $\mathbb{A}_P^f$.

It follows from the results of this paper that the class $\mathbb{A}_P^f$ does not include all minimal acyclic dfa's for any reasonable upper bound f (such as linear or polynomial). Note that there exists a property called an *observer property* [29] ensuring that the minimal automaton for the projected language has no more states than the minimal automaton for the input language, see also [23]. This property is well known and widely used in supervisory control of hierarchical and distributed discrete-event systems, and, as mentioned in [24], also in compositional verification [5] and modular synthesis [3,7]. If the projection does not satisfies the property, the co-domain of the projection can be extended so that it satisfies it. However, the computation of such a minimal extension is NP-hard. Nevertheless, there exists a polynomial-time algorithm that finds an acceptable extension [4]. A different approach with further references can be found in [24]. Although we know that the result is of polynomial size, the problem is how to compute it in polynomial time. Consider the determinization procedure of an nfa. This procedure can produce an exponential number of states where most of the states are equivalent. In [29], a polynomial-time algorithm running in $O(n^7 m^2)$, where n is the number of states and m is the cardinality of the co-domain of the projection satisfying the observer property, has been proposed. However, the precise time complexity of this problem is open.

Problem 15. How to compute the minimal dfa accepting the projected language when the projection satisfies the observer property?

Acknowledgement

We would like to thank Professor Jan H. van Schuppen for his useful comments.

References

1. Cassandras, C.G., Lafortune, S.: Introduction to discrete event systems, 2nd edn. Springer, Heidelberg (2008)
2. Chrobak, M.: Finite automata and unary languages. Theoret. Comput. Sci. 47(2), 149–158 (1986); Errata: Theoret. Comput. Sci. 302, 497–498 (2003)
3. Feng, L., Wonham, W.M.: Computationally efficient supervisor design: Abstraction and modularity. In: Proc. of WODES 2006, Ann Arbor, USA, pp. 3–8 (2006)
4. Feng, L., Wonham, W.M.: On the computation of natural observers in discrete-event systems. Discrete Event Dyn. Syst. 20, 63–102 (2010)
5. Flordal, H., Malik, R.: Compositional verification in supervisory control. SIAM J. Control Optim. 48(3), 1914–1938 (2009)
6. Geffert, V.: Magic numbers in the state hierarchy of finite automata. Inf. Comput. 205(11), 1652–1670 (2007)
7. Hill, R.C., Tilbury, D.M.: Modular supervisory control of discrete event systems with abstraction and incremental hierarchical construction. In: Proc. of WODES 2006, Ann Arbor, USA, pp. 399–406 (2006)
8. Holzer, M., Jakobi, S., Kutrib, M.: The magic number problem for subregular language families. In: Proc. of DCFS 2010. EPTCS, vol. 31, pp. 110–119 (2010)
9. Holzer, M., Kutrib, M.: Descriptional complexity – an introductory survey. In: Scientific Applications of Language Methods, vol. 2, Imperial College Press, London (2010)
10. Iwama, K., Kambayashi, Y., Takaki, K.: Tight bounds on the number of states of DFAs that are equivalent to n-state NFAs. Theoret. Comput. Sci. 237, 485–494 (2000)
11. Iwama, K., Matsuura, A., Paterson, M.: A family of NFAs which need $2^n - \alpha$ deterministic states. Theoret. Comput. Sci. 301, 451–462 (2003)
12. Jirásek, J., Jiráskova, G., Szabari, A.: Deterministic blow-ups of minimal nondeterministic finite automata over a fixed alphabet. IJFCS 19, 617–631 (2008)
13. Jiráskova, G.: Note on minimal finite automata. In: Sgall, J., Pultr, A., Kolman, P. (eds.) MFCS 2001. LNCS, vol. 2136, pp. 421–431. Springer, Heidelberg (2001)
14. Jiráskova, G.: On the state complexity of complements, stars, and reversals of regular languages. In: Ito, M., Toyama, M. (eds.) DLT 2008. LNCS, vol. 5257, pp. 431–442. Springer, Heidelberg (2008), http://im3.saske.sk/~jiraskov/star/

15. Jirásková, G.: Magic numbers and ternary alphabet. In: Diekert, V., Nowotka, D. (eds.) DLT 2009. LNCS, vol. 5583, pp. 300–311. Springer, Heidelberg (2009)
16. Komenda, J., Masopust, T., van Schuppen, J.H.: Supervisory control synthesis of discrete-event systems using a coordination scheme. CoRR 1007.2707 (2010), http://arxiv.org/abs/1007.2707
17. Komenda, J., Masopust, T., Schuppen, J.H.v.: Synthesis of safe sublanguages satisfying global specification using coordination scheme for discrete-event systems. In: Proc. of WODES 2010, Berlin, Germany, pp. 436–441 (2010)
18. Komenda, J., van Schuppen, J.H.: Coordination control of discrete event systems. In: Proc. of WODES 2008, Göteborg, Sweden, pp. 9–15 (2008)
19. Lupanov, O.B.: Über den vergleich zweier typen endlicher quellen. Probl. Kybernetik 6, 328–335 (1966), translation from Probl. Kibernetiki 9, 321–326 (1963)
20. Lyubich, Y.I.: Estimates for optimal determinization of nondeterministic autonomous automata. Sib. Matemat. Zhu. 5, 337–355 (1964) (in Russian)
21. Meyer, A.R., Fischer, M.J.: Economy of description by automata, grammars, and formal systems. In: Proc. of FOCS 1971, pp. 188–191. IEEE, Los Alamitos (1971)
22. Moore, F.R.: On the bounds for state-set size in the proofs of equivalence between deterministic, nondeterministic, and two-way finite automata. IEEE Trans. Comput. 20(10), 1211–1214 (1971)
23. Pena, P.N., Cury, J.E.R., Lafortune, S.: Polynomial-time verification of the observer property in abstractions. In: Proc. of ACC 2008, Seattle, USA, pp. 465–470 (2008)
24. Pena, P.N., Cury, J.E.R., Malik, R., Lafortune, S.: Efficient computation of observer projections using OP-verifiers. In: Proc. WODES 2010, pp. 416–421 (2010)
25. Salomaa, K.: NFA to DFA conversion for finite languages over a k-letter alphabet. Personal Communication (2011)
26. Salomaa, K., Yu, S.: NFA to DFA transformation for finite languages. In: Raymond, D.R., Yu, S., Wood, D. (eds.) WIA 1996. LNCS, vol. 1260, pp. 149–158. Springer, Heidelberg (1997)
27. Sipser, M.: Introduction to the theory of computation. PWS Publishing Company, Boston (1997)
28. Szabari, A.: Descriptional Complexity of Regular Languages. Ph.D. thesis, Mathematical Institute, Slovak Academy of Sciences, Košice, Slovakia (2010)
29. Wong, K.: On the complexity of projections of discrete-event systems. In: Proc. of WODES 1998, Cagliari, Italy, pp. 201–206 (1998)
30. Wonham, W.M.: Supervisory control of discrete-event systems, Lecture Notes, Dept. of Electrical and Computer Engineering, Univ. of Toronto, Canada (2009)
31. Yu, S.: Regular languages. In: Handbook of Formal Languages, vol. I, pp. 41–110. Springer, Heidelberg (1997)

Note on Reversal of Binary Regular Languages[*]

Galina Jirásková[1] and Juraj Šebej[2]

[1] Mathematical Institute, Slovak Academy of Sciences,
Grešákova 6, 040 01 Košice, Slovakia
jiraskov@saske.sk
[2] Institute of Computer Science, P.J. Šafárik University,
Jesenná 5, 041 54 Košice, Slovakia
juraj.sebej@gmail.com

Abstract. We present binary deterministic finite automata of n states that meet the upper bound 2^n on the state complexity of reversal. The automata have a single final state and are one-cycle-free-path, thus the witness languages are deterministic union-free. This result allows us to describe a binary language such that the nondeterministic state complexity of the language and of its complement is n and $n + 1$, respectively, while the state complexity of the language is 2^n. We also show that there is no regular language with state complexity 2^n such that both the language and its complement have nondeterministic state complexity n.

Keywords: Regular languages, reversal, state complexity, nondeterministic state complexity, deterministic union-free languages.

1 Introduction

Reversal is an operation on formal languages defined as $L^R = \{w^R \mid w \in L\}$, where w^R stands for the string w written backwards. The operation preserves regularity as shown already by Rabin and Scott in 1959 [10]. A nondeterministic finite automaton for the reverse of a regular language can be obtained from an automaton recognizing the given language by swapping the role of initial and final states, and by reversing the transitions. This gives the upper bound 2^n on the state complexity of reversal, that is, on the number of states that are sufficient and necessary in the worst case for a deterministic finite automaton to accept the reversal of a language represented by a deterministic finite automaton of n states.

In 1966, Mirkin [9] pointed out that the Lupanov's ternary witness automaton for nfa-to-dfa conversion presented in 1963 [7] proves the tightness of the upper bound in the ternary case since the ternary nondeterministic automaton is a reverse of a deterministic automaton.

Another ternary witness example for the reversal was given in 1981 by Leiss [6], who also proved the tightness of the upper bound in the binary case. However, his binary automata have $n/2$ final states.

---

[*] Research supported by VEGA grant 2/0183/11.

M. Holzer, M. Kutrib, and G. Pighizzini (Eds.): DCFS 2011, LNCS 6808, pp. 212–221, 2011.
© Springer-Verlag Berlin Heidelberg 2011

In 2004, the authors of [11, Theorem 3] claimed a binary worst-case example with a single accepting state. Unfortunately, the result does not hold: in the case of $n = 8$, with the initial and final state 1, the number of reachable states in the subset automaton for the reversal is 252 instead of 256. A similar problem arises whenever $n = 8 + 4k$ for a non-negative integer k. This result has been used in the literature several times, so our first aim is to present correct binary witness automata with a single final state.

We start with an observation that all the states in the subset automaton corresponding to the reverse of a minimal deterministic automaton are pairwise distinguishable [1,9]. This allows us to avoid the proof of distinguishability of states throughout the paper. Then we present a ternary worst-case example with a very simple proof of reachability of all the subsets. In a more difficult way, we prove our main result that the upper bound 2^n can be met by a binary n-state deterministic finite automaton with a single final state. Our witness automata are uniformly defined for all integers n, and can be used in all the cases where the incorrect result from [11] has been used.

The binary witnesses allow us to prove the tightness of the upper bound also in the case of reversal of deterministic union-free languages, that is, languages represented by so called one-cycle-free-path deterministic automata, in which from each state there exists exactly one cycle-free accepting path [5]. This was our first motivation for finding binary worst-case examples with a single final state. We also need such examples to be able to describe a *binary* language such that the nondeterministic state complexity of the language and its complement is n and $n + 1$, respectively, while the state complexity of the language (and of its complement) is 2^n. In both these cases, the existence of a sole final state in the binary witness automaton for reversal is crucial. In the latter case we also prove that except for the case of $n = 2$, there is no regular language such that both language and its complement have nondeterministic state complexity n, while the state complexity of the language would be 2^n.

2   Preliminaries

This section gives some basic definitions, notations, and preliminary results used throughout the paper. For further details, we refer the reader to [12,14].

Let Σ be a finite alphabet and Σ^* the set of all strings over the alphabet Σ including the empty string ε. A language is any subset of Σ^*. For a language L, we denote by L^c the complement of L, that is, the language $\Sigma^* \setminus L$. The cardinality of a finite set A is denoted by $|A|$ and its power-set by 2^A.

A *deterministic finite automaton* (dfa) is a quintuple $M = (Q, \Sigma, \delta, s, F)$, where Q is a finite set of states, Σ is a finite input alphabet, δ is the transition function that maps $Q \times \Sigma$ to Q, s is the initial (start) state, $s \in Q$, and F is the set of final states, $F \subseteq Q$. In this paper, all dfa's are assumed to be complete. The transition function δ is extended to the domain $Q \times \Sigma^*$ in a natural way. The *language accepted by* dfa M is the set $L(M) = \{w \in \Sigma^* \mid \delta(s, w) \in F\}$.

A *nondeterministic finite automaton* (nfa) is a quintuple $M = (Q, \Sigma, \delta, S, F)$, where Q, Σ, and F are defined the same way as for a dfa, S is the set of initial states, and δ is the nondeterministic transition function that maps $Q \times \Sigma$ to 2^Q. The transition function can be naturally extended to the domain $2^Q \times \Sigma^*$. The *language accepted by* nfa M is $L(M) = \{w \in \Sigma^* \mid \delta(S, w) \cap F \neq \emptyset\}$.

Two automata are *equivalent* if they accept the same language. A dfa (an nfa) M is *minimal* if every dfa (every nfa, respectively) that is equivalent to M has at least as many states as M. It is well-known that a dfa is minimal if all its states are reachable from the initial state, and no two different states are equivalent.

The *state complexity* of a regular language L, $sc(L)$, is the number of states in the minimal dfa accepting language L. The *nondeterministic state complexity* of a regular language L, $nsc(L)$, is defined as the number of states in a minimal nfa with a single initial state for language L.

An nfa $(Q, \Sigma, \delta, S, F)$ can be converted to an equivalent dfa $(2^Q, \Sigma, \delta', S, F')$ by the subset construction [10]: The transition function δ' is defined by $\delta'(R, a) = \bigcup_{r \in R} \delta(r, a)$, and a state R in 2^Q is in F' if $R \cap F \neq \emptyset$. We call the resulting dfa the *subset automaton* corresponding to the given nfa. The subset automaton need not be minimal since some states may be unreachable or equivalent.

The *reverse* w^R *of a string* w is defined as follows: $\varepsilon^R = \varepsilon$ and if $w = va$ for a string v in Σ^* and a symbol a in Σ, then $w^R = av^R$. The *reverse of a language* L is the language $L^R = \{w^R \mid w \in L\}$.

The *reverse of a dfa* $A = (Q, \Sigma, \delta, s, F)$ is the nfa A^R obtained from A by reversing all the transitions and by swapping the role of initial and final states, that is, $A^R = (Q, \Sigma, \delta^R, F, \{s\})$, where $\delta^R(q, a) = \{p \in Q \mid \delta(p, a) = q\}$.

Proposition 1. *The reverse of a dfa A recognizes the language $L(A)^R$.*   □

Proposition 2. *Let L be a regular language with $sc(L) = n$. Then $sc(L^R) \leqslant 2^n$.*

Proof. The reverse A^R of the minimal dfa A for language L is an n-state nfa (possibly with multiple initial states) for language L^R. After applying the subset construction to nfa A^R, we get a dfa for language L^R of at most 2^n states.   □

For the sake of completeness, we give a short proof of the fact that in the subset automaton corresponding to the reverse of a minimal deterministic finite automaton, all states are pairwise distinguishable [1,4,9].

Proposition 3 ([1,4,9]). *All the states of the subset automaton corresponding to the reverse of a minimal dfa are pairwise distinguishable.*

Proof. Let A^R be the reverse of a minimal dfa A, and let q be an arbitrary state of nfa A^R. Since state q is reachable in dfa A, there is a string w_q that is accepted in nfa A^R from state q. Moreover, string w_q is not accepted by nfa A^R from any other state because otherwise there would be two distinct computations of dfa A on string w_q^R. It follows that in the subset automaton corresponding to nfa A^R, all states are pairwise distinguishable since two different subsets of the state set of nfa A^R must differ in a state q of the nfa, and so the string w_q distinguishes the two subsets.   □

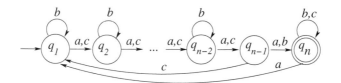

Fig. 1. The ternary n-state dfa meeting the upper bound 2^n for reversal

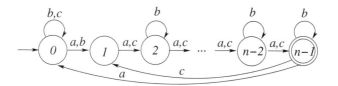

Fig. 2. The reverse of the dfa from Fig. 1 with renamed states

We first present a ternary language meeting the upper bound 2^n for reversal with a very easy proof of reachability of all subsets in the subset automaton. Let us recall that, as pointed by Mirkin in 1966 [9], the ternary Lupanov's witness automaton for nfa-to-dfa conversion from 1963 [7] is the reverse of a dfa which follows that the bound 2^n for reversal is tight. The ternary witness presented in [15] with b and c interchanged is the same as Lupanov's example. A similar ternary witness language was given by Leiss [6]. The following example is a bit different.

Proposition 4. *Let* $n \geqslant 2$. *There exists a ternary regular language* L *with* $\mathrm{sc}(L) = n$ *such that* $\mathrm{sc}(L^R) = 2^n$.

Proof. Consider the ternary language accepted by the dfa of Fig. 1. Construct an nfa for the reverse of the recognized language from the dfa by reversing all the transitions, and swapping the role of the initial and final states. For the purpose of the proof, rename its states using numbers $0, 1, \ldots, n-1$ as shown in Fig. 2.

Let us show that the corresponding subset automaton has 2^n reachable states. The proof is by induction on the size of subsets of the state set $\{0, 1, \ldots, n-1\}$. All the singleton sets are reached from the initial state $\{0\}$ by strings in a^*, and the empty set is reached from state $\{1\}$ by b. Next, each set $\{i_1, i_2, \ldots, i_k\}$ of size k, where $2 \leqslant k \leqslant n$ and $0 \leqslant i_1 < i_2 < \cdots < i_k \leqslant n-1$, is reached from the set $\{0, i_3 - i_2 + 1, \ldots, i_k - i_2 + 1\}$ of size $k - 1$ by string $bc^{i_2 - i_1 - 1}a^{i_1}$. All the states are pairwise distinguishable by Proposition 3. $\square$

3 Binary Witness Languages for Reversal

The authors of paper [11] present binary dfa scheme depicted in Fig. 3, and claim that every dfa A resulting from the scheme and satisfying $L(A) \neq \emptyset$ and $L(A) \neq \Sigma^*$ requires 2^n deterministic states for the reverse of language $L(A)$.

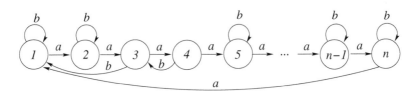

Fig. 3. The dfa scheme from [11, Theorem 3]

Unfortunately, the example does not work: in the case of $n = 8$, and with the initial and sole accepting state 1, the resulting dfa has 252 reachable states instead of 256: Notice that the sets $\{1, 4, 5, 8\}$, $\{8, 3, 4, 7\}$, $\{7, 2, 3, 6\}$, $\{6, 1, 2, 5\}$, are not reachable in the subset automaton corresponding to the reverse of the dfa since each of them contains exactly one of the states 1 and 3, and therefore cannot be reached from any set by b. Moreover, in the subset automaton, we have $\{6, 1, 2, 5\} \xrightarrow{a} \{7, 2, 3, 6\} \xrightarrow{a} \{8, 3, 4, 7\} \xrightarrow{a} \{1, 4, 5, 8\} \xrightarrow{a} \{6, 1, 2, 5\}$, and no other state goes to one of the four sets by a. It follows that none of these sets is reachable. A similar argument holds for each integer n with $n = 8 + 4k$, where the set $\{1, 4, 5, 8, 9, \ldots, n-4, n-3, n\}$ and all its shifts by a are not reachable.

The correct binary witnesses with a single final state, uniformly defined for every n with $n \geq 2$, have been recently presented by Šebej in [13]. The next theorem gives an alternative proof for slightly modified Šebej's automata. Notice that the dfa's in the theorem below are so called one-cycle-free-path dfa's, that is, from each state of the dfa, there exists exactly one cycle-free accepting path, and so the resulting languages are deterministic union-free [5]. This shows that the upper bound 2^n on reversal is met by *binary deterministic union-free languages*, which improves a result from [5].

Theorem 5. *Let $n \geq 2$. There exists a binary (deterministic union-free) regular language L with $\mathrm{sc}(L) = n$ such that $\mathrm{sc}(L^R) = 2^n$.*

Proof. Consider the binary n-state dfa A of Fig. 4 with states $1, 2, \ldots, n$, of which 1 is the initial state, and state n is the sole final state. By a, state 3 goes to state 1, state n goes to state 4, and every other state i goes to state $i + 1$. By b, state 2 goes to state 1, state 3 goes to state 4, state 4 goes to state 3, and every other state goes to itself.

If $n = 2$, then state 2 goes to 1 by a. If $n = 3$, then state 3 goes to itself by b. In these two cases, after applying subset construction to the reverse of dfa A, we get a four-state minimal dfa if $n = 2$, and an eight-state minimal dfa if $n = 3$.

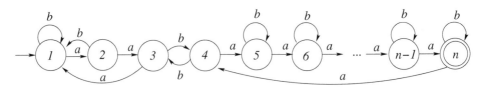

Fig. 4. The binary n-state dfa meeting the upper bound 2^n for reversal

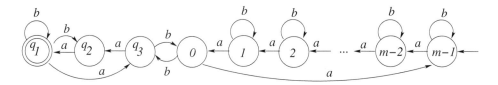

Fig. 5. The reverse of the dfa from Fig. 4 with renamed states

Now let $n \geqslant 4$. Construct an nfa for the reverse of language $L(A)$ from dfa A by swapping the role of the initial and final states, and by reversing all the transitions. To simplify the proof, let us rename the states of the resulting nfa as shown in Fig. 5: The first three states are now denoted by q_1, q_2, and q_3, and the remaining states are numbered by $0, 1, \ldots, m-1$ with $m = n-3$. We are going to show that the corresponding subset automaton has 2^n reachable states.

Notice that in the nfa, by bb state q_1 goes to $\{q_1, q_2\}$, state q_2 goes to the empty set, and every other state goes to itself.

In the corresponding subset automaton, all the singleton sets are reached from the initial state $\{m-1\}$ by strings in a^*ba^*, and the empty set is reached from state $\{q_2\}$ by b.

We now show that each state $\{q_1, q_2, q_3\} \cup X$ with $X \subseteq \{0, 1, \ldots, m-1\}$ is reachable. The proof is by induction on the size of X. The set $\{q_1, q_2, q_3\}$ is reached from state $\{q_1\}$ by $babb$. State $\{q_1, q_2, q_3\}$ goes by b to state $\{q_1, q_2\} \cup \{0\}$, and then by string abb to state $\{q_1, q_2, q_3\} \cup \{m-1\}$, from which each state $\{q_1, q_2, q_3\} \cup \{j\}$ with $0 \leqslant j \leqslant m-1$ can be reached by a string in a^*. Next, each state $\{q_1, q_2, q_3\} \cup \{i_1, i_2, \ldots, i_k\}$, where $0 \leqslant i_1 < i_2 < \cdots < i_k \leqslant m-1$, is reached from state $\{q_1, q_2, q_3\} \cup \{i_2 - i_1, \ldots, i_k - i_1\}$ by $babba^{m-1-i_1}$. It follows that each state $\{q_1, q_2, q_3\} \cup X$ with $X \subseteq \{0, 1, \ldots, m-1\}$ is reachable.

We next show that each state $\{q_3\} \cup X$ with $X \subseteq \{0, 1, \ldots, m-1\}$ is reachable. For a subset X of $\{0, 1, \ldots, m-1\}$ and a number i, denote by $X \oplus i$ the set that goes to X by a^i, that is, $X \oplus i = \{(x+i) \bmod m \mid x \in X\}$. We have $|X \oplus i| = |X|$. Consider several cases (here the arithmetic is modulo m):

  (i) Let $m-2 \in X$. Take $X' = X \setminus \{m-2\}$. Then $0 \notin X' \oplus 2$. Therefore, state $\{q_1, q_2, q_3\} \cup (X' \oplus 2)$, which is reachable as shown above, goes to state $\{q_3\} \cup \{m-2\} \cup X' = \{q_3\} \cup X$ by $baabb$.
  (ii) Let there exists an integer k such that $(m-2) - 3k$ is in X. Then state $\{q_3\} \cup (X \ominus 3k)$ containing $m-2$ is reachable as shown in case (i), and goes to state $\{q_3\} \cup X$ by a^{3k}.
  (iii) Let there exists a k such that $(m-2) - 3k - 1$ is in X. Then $\{q_3\} \cup (X \oplus 4)$ is reachable as shown in case (ii), and goes to $\{q_3\} \cup X$ by $aabbaabb$.
  (iv) Let there exists a k such that $(m-2) - 3k - 2$ is in X. Then $\{q_3\} \cup (X \oplus 4)$ is reachable as shown in case (iii), and goes to $\{q_3\} \cup X$ by $aabbaabb$.
  (v) State $\{q_3\}$ is reachable.

Thus each state $\{q_3\} \cup X$ with $X \subseteq \{0, 1, \ldots, m-1\}$ is reachable. It follows that each state $\{q_1\} \cup X$, as well as each state $\{q_2\} \cup X$, is reachable since each

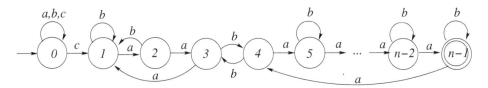

Fig. 6. A left ideal meeting the bound $2^{n-1} + 1$ for reversal; unspecified transitions on c go to state 1

state $\{q_3\} \cup (X \oplus 1)$ goes to $\{q_2\} \cup X$ by a, and each state $\{q_3\} \cup (X \oplus 2)$ goes to $\{q_1\} \cup X$ by aa. Now, each state $\{q_1\} \cup X$ goes to $\{q_1, q_2\} \cup X$ by bb, and similarly as above also each state $\{q_2, q_3\} \cup X$ and $\{q_1, q_3\} \cup X$ with $X \subseteq \{0, 1, \ldots, m-1\}$ can be reached. Finally, each state $\{q_2\} \cup X$ goes to state $\emptyset \cup X$ by bb.

Hence we have shown that all the subsets of the state set $\{q_1, q_2, q_3\} \cup \{0, 1, \ldots, m-1\}$ are reachable. By Proposition 3, they are pairwise distinguishable, and our proof is complete. $\square$

4   Binary Witnesses for Reversal in Some Other Results

The incorrect result from [11] has been used for the reversals of left ideal languages and suffix-closed languages [2,3]. We now restate these results, and present correct witnesses. Recall that a language L over an alphabet Σ is a left ideal if $L = \Sigma^* L$, and is suffix-closed if for every string w in L, every suffix of w is in L.

Theorem 6 ([2], Theorem 15, Reversal of Left Ideals). *Let $n \geqslant 3$ and let L be a left ideal with $\mathrm{sc}(L) = n$. Then $\mathrm{sc}(L^R) \leqslant 2^{n-1} + 1$, and the bound is tight in the ternary case.*

Proof. The upper bound is from [2]. For tightness, consider the ternary language accepted by the dfa of Fig. 6, where unspecified transitions on c go to state 1. The language is a left ideal. Consider the subset automaton corresponding to the reverse of the dfa. By Theorem 5, all the subsets of $\{1, 2, \ldots, n-1\}$ are reachable from the initial state $\{n-1\}$. State $\{0\}$ is reached from state $\{1\}$ by c. All the states are pairwise distinguishable by Proposition 3. $\square$

Theorem 7 ([3], Theorem 5, Reversal of Suffix-Closed Languages). *Let $n \geqslant 3$ and let L be a suffix-closed regular language with $\mathrm{sc}(L) = n$. Then $\mathrm{sc}(L^R) \leqslant 2^{n-1} + 1$, and the bound is tight in the ternary case.*

Proof. The operation of reversal commutes with complementation, and the complement of a suffix-closed language is a left ideal. Thus the upper bound follows. For tightness consider the complement of the languages accepted by the dfa of Fig. 6. The language is suffix-free and meets the upper bound as shown in the proof above. $\square$

Fig. 7. The 2-state nfa's for a language L and L^c, respectively, with $\mathrm{sc}(L) = 4$

We now use the binary witnesses for reversal described in the previous section to strengthen the following result by Mera and Pighizzini [8].

Theorem 8 ([8]). *Let $n \geqslant 1$. There exists a regular language L over the alphabet $\{a, b, c\}$ such that*

- $\mathrm{nsc}(L) \ = \ n,$
- $\mathrm{sc}(L) \ = \ 2^n,$
- $\mathrm{nsc}(L^c) \leqslant \ n + 1.$

Our first question is if $\mathrm{nsc}(L^c)$ in the above theorem can be decreased to n. Fig. 7 shows that in the case of $n = 2$, this can indeed happen. The complement of the 2-state nfa language of Fig. 7 (left) is accepted by the 2-state nfa of Fig. 7 (right), while the state complexity of the language (and of its complement) is 4. However, the next theorem shows that this is only an exception.

Theorem 9. *Let $n \neq 2$. There is no regular language L such that*

- $\mathrm{nsc}(L) \ = \ n,$
- $\mathrm{sc}(L) \ = \ 2^n,$
- $\mathrm{nsc}(L^c) = \ n.$

Proof. If $n = 1$, then one of the language or its complement must be empty, thus the other one is Σ^*. Both are 1-state dfa languages. Assume that there is a language L with $\mathrm{sc}(L) = 2^n$ and $\mathrm{nsc}(L) = \mathrm{nsc}(L^c) = n$ and $n \geqslant 3$.

Let M be an n-state nfa for the language L with states $q_1, \ldots, q_n$, of which q_1 is the single initial state. Let N be an n-state nfa for the complement L^c with states $p_1, \ldots, p_n$, of which p_1 is a single initial state. Let M' and N' be the 2^n-state dfa's obtained from nfa's M and N, respectively, by the subset construction. Since both nfa's M and N have at least one final state, both dfa's M' and N' have at least 2^{n-1} final states. Since the sum of final states in dfa M and N is 2^n, it follows that both nfa's M and N must have exactly one final state. Moreover, exactly one of the initial states of nfa's M and N is accepting. Without loss of generality, q_1 is accepting, and so p_1 is rejecting. Since q_1 is the only accepting state in nfa M, we have

$$\text{if } u \in L \text{ and } v \in L, \text{ then also } uv \in L. \tag{1}$$

Let p_2 be the final state of nfa N. Since $n \geqslant 3$, and nfa N has exactly one final state, state p_3 is rejecting. Since rejecting state $\{p_1, p_3\}$ is reachable in the subset automaton N', there is a string u such that the initial state $\{p_1\}$ goes by u to the rejecting state $\{p_1, p_3\}$ in dfa N' for language L^c. This means that string u is in language L. We are now going to show that in dfa N', the rejecting states $\{p_1, p_3\}$ and $\{p_1\}$ must be equivalent.

If a string v is accepted by dfa N' from state $\{p_1\}$, then it is also accepted from state $\{p_1, p_3\}$. If a string v is rejected by dfa N' from state $\{p_1\}$, then v must be in language L. But then, by (1), we have that $uv \in L$, and so $uv \notin L^c$. This means that v must be rejected by dfa N' from state $\{p_1, p_3\}$; recall that $\{p_1\}$ goes to $\{p_1, p_3\}$ by u. Hence states $\{p_1\}$ and $\{p_1, p_3\}$ are equivalent, which is a contradiction with $\mathrm{sc}(L) = \mathrm{sc}(L^c) = 2^n$. $\qquad\square$

Now, using the fact that the binary witnesses for reversal from Fig. 4 on page 216 have a single final state, we can prove the following theorem.

Theorem 10. *Let $n \neq 2$. There exists a* binary *regular language L such that*

- $\mathrm{nsc}(L) \quad = \quad n,$
- $\mathrm{sc}(L) \quad\ = \quad 2^n,$
- $\mathrm{nsc}(L^c) = \quad n + 1.$

Proof. If $n = 1$, then take $L = \{\varepsilon\}$. Let $n \geqslant 3$. Let A be the binary n-state dfa from Theorem 5 meeting the upper bound 2^n on its reversal and shown in Fig. 4 on page 216. Set $L = L(A)^R$. Then language L is accepted by n-state nfa A^R that has a single initial state, and theorem 5 shows that $\mathrm{sc}(L) = \mathrm{sc}(L(A^R)) = 2^n$. Hence $\mathrm{nsc}(L) = n$.

We next have $L^c = (L(A)^R)^c = (L(A)^c)^R$. A dfa for language $L(A)^c$ is obtained from dfa A by interchanging the accepting and rejecting states. The reverse of this dfa is an nfa that has multiple initial states, and so we add a new initial state to get an nfa with a single initial state for language $(L(A)^c)^R$. Therefore, taking into account the above theorem, we have $\mathrm{nsc}(L^c) = n + 1$. $\qquad\square$

5   Conclusions

We examined the state complexity of reversals of regular languages. We first presented an easy proof that the upper bound 2^n is tight in the ternary case. Then we described binary n-state dfa languages with a single final state meeting the upper bound on the state complexity of reversal. Moreover, the dfa's are one-cycle-free-path, and so the binary witness languages are deterministic union-free which improves a result from [5]. Using presented witnesses, we described a binary language such that the nondeterministic state complexity of the language and of its complement is n and $n + 1$, respectively, while the state complexity of the language (and of its complement) is 2^n. We also proved that there is no regular language with state complexity 2^n such that both the language and its complement would have nondeterministic state complexity n, except for $n = 2$.

Acknowledgement

We would like to thank Jozef Štefan Jirásek from Charles University in Prague for his help with the computational verification of our examples.

References

1. Brzozowski, J.A.: Canonical Regular Expressions and Minimal State Graphs for Definite Events. In: Proceedings of the Symposium on Mathematical Theory of Automata, New York, NY, April 24-26 (1962); Fox, J. (ed.) MRI Symposia Series, vol. 12, pp. 529–561. Polytechnic Press of the Polytechnic Institute of Brooklyn, Brooklyn, NY (1963)

2. Brzozowski, J., Jirásková, G., Li, B.: Quotient complexity of ideal languages. In: López-Ortiz, A. (ed.) LATIN 2010. LNCS, vol. 6034, pp. 208–221. Springer, Heidelberg (2010)

3. Brzozowski, J., Jirásková, G., Zou, C.: Quotient complexity of closed languages. In: Ablayev, F., Mayr, E.W. (eds.) CSR 2010. LNCS, vol. 6072, pp. 84–95. Springer, Heidelberg (2010)

4. Champarnaud, J.-M., Khorsi, A., Paranthoën, T.: Split and join for minimizing: Brzozowski's algorithm, http://jmc.feydakins.org/ps/c09psc02.ps

5. Jirásková, G., Masopust, T.: Complexity in union-free regular languages. In: Gao, Y., Lu, H., Seki, S., Yu, S. (eds.) DLT 2010. LNCS, vol. 6224, pp. 255–266. Springer, Heidelberg (2010)

6. Leiss, E.: Succinct representation of regular languages by Boolean automata. Theoret. Comput. Sci. 13, 323–330 (1981)

7. Lupanov, U.I.: A comparison of two types of finite automata. Problemy Kibernetiki 9, 321–326 (1963) (in Russian)

8. Mera, F., Pighizzini, G.: Complementing unary nondeterministic automata. Theor. Comput. Sci. 330, 349–360 (2005)

9. Mirkin, B.G.: On dual automata. Kibernetika (Kiev) 2, 7–10 (1966) (in Russian); English translation: Cybernetics 2, 6–9 (1966)

10. Rabin, M., Scott, D.: Finite automata and their decision problems. IBM Res. Develop. 3, 114–129 (1959)

11. Salomaa, A., Wood, D., Yu, S.: On the state complexity of reversals of regular languages. Theoret. Comput. Sci. 320, 315–329 (2004)

12. Sipser, M.: Introduction to the theory of computation. PWS Publishing Company, Boston (1997)

13. Šebej, J.: Reversal of regular languages and state complexity. In: Pardubská, D. (ed.) Proc. 10th ITAT, pp. 47–54. Šafárik University, Košice (2010)

14. Yu, S.: Chapter 2: Regular languages. In: Rozenberg, G., Salomaa, A. (eds.) Handbook of Formal Languages, vol. I, pp. 41–110. Springer, Heidelberg (1997)

15. Yu, S., Zhuang, Q., Salomaa, K.: The state complexity of some basic operations on regular languages. Theoret. Comput. Sci. 125, 315–328 (1994)

State Complexity of Operations
on Two-Way Deterministic Finite Automata
over a Unary Alphabet

Michal Kunc[1,*] and Alexander Okhotin[2,3,**]

[1] Masaryk University, Czech Republic
kunc@math.muni.cz
[2] Department of Mathematics, University of Turku, Finland
[3] Academy of Finland
alexander.okhotin@utu.fi

Abstract. The paper determines the number of states in a two-way deterministic finite automaton (2DFA) over a one-letter alphabet sufficient and in the worst case necessary to represent the results of the following operations: (i) intersection of an m-state 2DFA and an n-state 2DFA requires between $m + n$ and $m + n + 1$ states; (ii) union of an m-state 2DFA and an n-state 2DFA, between $m + n$ and $2m + n + 4$ states; (iii) Kleene star of an n-state 2DFA, $(g(n) + O(n))^2$ states, where $g(n) = e^{\sqrt{n \ln n}(1+o(1))}$ is the maximum value of $\mathrm{lcm}(p_1, \ldots, p_k)$ for $\sum p_i \leqslant n$, known as Landau's function; (iv) k-th power of an n-state 2DFA, between $(k - 1)g(n) - k$ and $k(g(n) + n)$ states; (v) concatenation of an m-state and an n-state 2DFAs, $e^{(1+o(1))\sqrt{(m+n)\ln(m+n)}}$ states.

1 Introduction

The study of state complexity of operations on one-way deterministic finite automata (1DFA) dates back to Maslov [11], who showed that a concatenation of an m-state 1DFA with an n-state 1DFA may require a 1DFA with up to exactly $m \cdot 2^n - 2^{n-1}$ states, Kleene star of an n-state 1DFA requires up to $\frac{3}{4}2^n$ states, etc. For the case of a one-letter alphabet $\Sigma = \{a\}$, Yu, Zhuang and K. Salomaa [16] showed that the complexity of most operations is significantly different from the case of larger alphabets: for instance, Kleene star requires $(n - 1)^2 + 1$ states. For one-way nondeterministic automata (1NFA), both over unary and larger alphabets, the complexity of operations was determined by Holzer and Kutrib [5]. The first results of this kind for the intermediate family of unambiguous finite automata (1UFA) were recently obtained by Okhotin [13].

State complexity of operations on two-way automata (2DFA) is more difficult to investigate, because of the lack of any general lower bound methods. An attempt to study the complexity of operations on 2DFA using the constructions

---

* Supported by the project MSM0021622409 of the Ministry of Education of the Czech Republic and by Grant 201/09/1313 of the Grant Agency of the Czech Republic.
** Supported by the Academy of Finland under grant 134860.

M. Holzer, M. Kutrib, and G. Pighizzini (Eds.): DCFS 2011, LNCS 6808, pp. 222–234, 2011.

and the lower bound techniques developed for 1DFAs was made by Jirásková and Okhotin [6], and predictably led to very rough estimations, such as a $\frac{1}{n}2^{\frac{n}{2}-1}$ lower bound and a $2^{O(n^{n+1})}$ upper bound on the state complexity of Kleene star. These results essentially relied upon an alphabet of exponential size.

This paper is aimed to determine the state complexity of basic operations on 2DFAs in the special case of a one-letter alphabet. The study of unary 2DFAs began with a paper by Chrobak [1], who showed that the language generated by an n-state 2DFA is ultimately periodic with period $\mathrm{lcm}(p_1, \ldots, p_k)$, for some numbers $p_1, \ldots, p_k \geqslant 1$ with $p_1 + \cdots + p_k \leqslant n$. The authors' [8] recent analysis of 2DFAs over a one-letter alphabet refined this understanding with a precise estimation of the starting point of periodicity, known as the *length of the tail* of the minimal 1DFA, or the *index* of the corresponding semigroup: a unary language recognized by an n-state 2DFA has period $\mathrm{lcm}(p_1, \ldots, p_k)$ beginning from ℓ, for some numbers $p_1, \ldots, p_k, \ell \geqslant 1$ with $p_1 + \cdots + p_k + \ell \leqslant n+1$ [8, Cor. 6]. The greatest value of the least common multiple of partitions of a number n is known as *Landau's function* $g(n)$, estimated as $g(n) = e^{\sqrt{n \ln n}(1+o(1))}$ [10], and the exact number of states in a 1DFA needed to simulate an n-state unary 2DFA is accordingly expressed as $\max_{1 \leqslant \ell \leqslant n} g(n+1-\ell) + \ell$.

The state complexity of Boolean operations is addressed in Section 3. For the *intersection*, the obvious $(m+n+1)$-state upper bound is matched by an almost tight lower bound of $m+n$ states, obtained by intersecting a language with a long period and no tail, with a language with period 2 and a long tail. The *union* of two 2DFAs can be directly represented, as long as one of them halts on every input. The latter condition can be ensured by the authors' [9] upcoming result that every n-state unary 2DFA can be transformed to a *reversible* 2DFA with $2n+3$ states. This leads to a $(2m+n+4)$-state upper bound for the union. A lower bound of $m+n$ states is proved similarly to the case of intersection.

The rest of the paper is concerned with concatenation and the derived operations: Kleene star and power. The effect of these operations on unary 1DFAs was first studied by Yu et al. [16], who showed that the worst-case complexity is achieved when the arguments are cyclic languages and the result is a co-finite language. Since 2DFAs for co-finite languages are as large as 1DFAs, this method can be extended to showing the state complexity of operations on 2DFAs. For *Kleene star*, discussed in Section 4, the resulting complexity is $(g(n) + O(n))^2$, and the next Section 5 shows that concatenating k copies of a language—the *k-th power* operation—has state complexity between $(k-1)g(n) - k$ and $kg(n) + O(kn)$. For the case of *concatenation* of two unary languages given by 2DFAs, its worst-case complexity is explained in terms of a variant of Landau's function, $g(m, n)$, which is in turn found to have growth rate $g(m, n) = e^{\sqrt{(m+n)\ln(m+n)}(1+o(1))}$.

2   Unary 2DFAs and Their Expressive Power

A 1DFA over a unary alphabet is just a directed graph of out-degree 1. It has a unique path from the initial state, which eventually converges to a *cycle*. Zero or more states visited before entering the cycle are called the *tail* of the 1DFA.

Computations of 2DFAs are more complicated and more challenging to understand, even in the unary case. Given an input string w, a 2DFA operates on a tape containing the string $\vdash w \dashv$, where $\vdash$ and $\dashv$ are special symbols known as the left-end marker and the right-end marker, respectively. According to the standard definition, a 2DFA begins its computation at the left-end marker and accepts at the right-end marker. In this paper, as well as in the authors' previous work [8], the definition is extended to allow acceptance on both sides: this leads to symmetric constructions and allows avoiding some awkward exceptions in the results. Changing the mode of acceptance affects the size of an automaton at most by one state.

A *2DFA (with two-sided acceptance)* is defined as a sextuple $\mathcal{A} = (\Sigma, Q, q_0, \delta, F_\vdash, F_\dashv)$, in which Σ is a finite alphabet with $\vdash, \dashv \notin \Sigma$, Q is a finite set of states, $q_0 \in Q$ is the initial state, $\delta \colon Q \times (\Sigma \cup \{\vdash, \dashv\}) \rightarrow Q \times \{-1, +1\}$ is a partially defined transition function, and $F_\vdash, F_\dashv \subseteq Q$ are sets of states accepting on $\vdash$ and on $\dashv$, respectively. When $\mathcal{A}$ is in a state q and observes a square of the tape with a symbol $a \in \Sigma \cup \{\vdash, \dashv\}$, the value $\delta(q, a)$ indicates the next state and the direction of motion. The computation of $\mathcal{A}$ on an input string $\vdash w \dashv = \vdash a_1 \ldots a_\ell \dashv$, with $\ell \geqslant 0$ and $a_1, \ldots, a_\ell \in \Sigma$, begins in state q_0, with the head observing $\vdash$. If it eventually reaches an accepting state in $F_\vdash$ or in $F_\dashv$ while on the corresponding end-marker, the string is accepted; otherwise, it either encounters an undefined transition or gets into an infinite loop. The set of strings accepted by a 2DFA $\mathcal{A}$ is denoted by $L(\mathcal{A})$.

Every 2DFA can be transformed to an equivalent 1DFA, which is often much larger than the original 2DFA. In terms of the structure of the minimal 1DFA, there are essentially two possibilities for a 2DFA to provide a more succinct description. First, a 2DFA can count divisibility separately for several numbers, while an equivalent 1DFA would need to count modulo the least common multiple of those numbers.

Example 1. Let $p_1, \ldots, p_k \geqslant 2$ be any integers and denote $p = \mathrm{lcm}(p_1, \ldots, p_k)$. Take an arbitrary $f \in \{0, \ldots, p-1\}$. Then the language $L = a^f (a^p)^*$ is recognized by a $(p_1 + \cdots + p_k)$-state 2DFA, although the minimal 1DFA for L has p states. For $p_1 = 2$, $p_2 = 3$ and $f = 0$, this gives a 5-state 2DFA recognizing the language $(a^6)^*$, which has the set of states $Q = \{q_0, q_1, r_0, r_1, r_2\}$, transitions $\delta(q_0, \vdash) = (q_0, +1)$, $\delta(q_i, a) = (q_{(i+1) \bmod 2}, +1)$, $\delta(r_i, a) = (r_{(i+1) \bmod 3}, -1)$, $\delta(q_0, \dashv) = (r_0, -1)$, and $F_\vdash = \{r_0\}$, $F_\dashv = \varnothing$.

Secondly, a 2DFA can generate a language with tail of length $\ell+1$ by counting up to ℓ, and then using one of the cycles to distinguish the string of length ℓ from longer strings.

Example 2. Let $p \geqslant 2$, $f \in \{0, \ldots, p-1\}$ and $\ell \geqslant 1$ be any numbers with $\ell \not\equiv f$ (mod p). Then the language $L = a^f(a^p)^* \cup \{a^\ell\}$ is recognized by a $(p+\ell)$-state 2DFA with acceptance only on the right-end marker, although the minimal 1DFA recognizing L has $p + \ell + 1$ states. A 2DFA recognizing such a language L with $p = 2$, $f = 1$ and $\ell = 2$ is illustrated below:

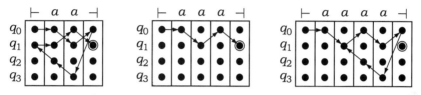

The following result recently established by the authors [8] asserts that the minimal 1DFA equivalent to an n-state unary 2DFA cannot have any other tail-cycle structure than in the above examples.

Proposition 3 ([8]). *Let $\mathcal{A}$ be an n-state 2DFA over $\Sigma = \{a\}$. Then there exist $k \geqslant 1$ and numbers $p_1, \ldots, p_k \geqslant 1$ and $\ell \geqslant 1$, with $p_1 + \cdots + p_k + \ell \leqslant n + 1$, such that there exists a 1DFA for $L(\mathcal{A})$ with tail of length ℓ and period $p = \mathrm{lcm}(p_1, \ldots, p_k)$.*

This result can also be presented in the following equivalent form.

Proposition 4 ([8]). *Let $L \subseteq a^*$ be a regular language with the minimal 1DFA with tail of length ℓ and period p. Let $p = p_1 \cdots p_k$, where $p_1, \ldots, p_k$ are powers of distinct primes, be the prime factorization of p (for $p = 1$, assume that $1 = 1$ is a prime factorization). Then, every 2DFA recognizing L must have at least $p_1 + \cdots + p_k + \max(\ell, 1) - 1$ states.*

In particular, this result implies that a language with a long tail requires a 2DFA with as many states as the length of the tail. This will be used in Sections 4–6 to prove lower bounds using co-finite languages.

How large could a least common multiple of numbers $p_1, \ldots, p_k$ be, if the sum of these numbers is bounded by n? As a function of n, this number

$$g(n) = \max\{\,\mathrm{lcm}(p_1, \ldots, p_k) \mid k \geqslant 1,\ p_1 + \cdots + p_k \leqslant n\,\}$$

is known as *Landau's function*, as its $e^{(1+o(1))\sqrt{n \ln n}}$ asymptotics was determined by Landau [10] (see also Miller [12] for a more accessible argument). Furthermore, the numbers $p_1, \ldots, p_k$, on which the maximum is reached, can be assumed to be powers of distinct primes.

For any positive integer n, the number $g(n)$ is the longest period of a language accepted by an n-state unary 2DFA. In order to take the length of the tail in the corresponding minimal 1DFAs into account, define $g'(n) = \max_{0 \leqslant \ell < n} g(n - \ell) + \ell$. In terms of this function, the 2DFA–1DFA tradeoff is expressed as follows.

Proposition 5 ([8]). *Let $n \geqslant 1$. Then, for every unary two-way deterministic automaton $\mathcal{A}$ with n states, there exists an equivalent complete 1DFA with $g'(n) + 1$ states. For $n \geqslant 3$, this bound is tight already for the transformation of 2DFAs to 1NFAs.*

3   Union and Intersection

Intersection of an m-state and an n-state 1DFAs can be represented by a 1DFA with mn states. This number of states is necessary already for a unary alphabet, as long as m and n are relatively prime, because under this assumption $(a^m)^* \cap (a^n)^* = (a^{mn})^*$. When m and n are not relatively prime, intersection of unary 1DFAs sometimes has a lower complexity, witnessed by languages of a different form [14].

For 2DFAs, intersection can always be represented with $m + n + 1$ states, and the only known lower bound of $m + n - o(m + n)$ states was established using an alphabet of enormous size [6]. This paper improves the lower bound to $m + n$ using only unary alphabet. The main idea is to choose one of the languages being intersected to be of the form presented in Example 1, with a period obtained as a prime factorization and with no tail, and let the other 2DFA be of the form as in Example 2, using period 2 and a tail as long as possible. If everything works as planned, the intersection should have both a long period and a long tail.

The period of the first 2DFA will be obtained using the following result:

Proposition 6 (Dressler [3]). *Every number greater than 9 is representable as a sum of distinct odd primes.*

The almost tight bounds on the intersection are now established for all values of m and n greater than one, with only two exceptions.

Theorem 7. *For every $m, n \geqslant 2$ with $(m, n) \notin \{(2, 2), (6, 6)\}$, the state complexity of intersection of an m-state 2DFA and an n-state 2DFA over a unary alphabet is at least $m + n$. It is at most $m + n + 1$ for all $m, n \geqslant 1$, for a general alphabet.*

Proof. The construction of an $(m + n + 1)$-state 2DFA for the intersection is straightforward [6]. Given two 2DFAs $\mathcal{A}$ and $\mathcal{B}$ with the sets of states Q and R, respectively, the new 2DFA $\mathcal{C}$ has the set of states $Q \cup \{q_\leftarrow\} \cup R$. It begins its computation by simulating $\mathcal{A}$, and whenever $\mathcal{A}$ would accept, $\mathcal{C}$ gets back to the left-end marker in the special state $q_\leftarrow$, and then proceeds with simulating $\mathcal{B}$, until it accepts or rejects.

Turning to the lower bound argument, first assume that the numbers m and n are not both in $\{2, 4, 6\}$. Without loss of generality, let $n \notin \{2, 4, 6\}$, and let $m \geqslant 2$ be any number. If $n \geqslant 10$, then, by Proposition 6, there is a partition $n = p_1 + \cdots + p_k$, where $p_1, \ldots, p_k \geqslant 3$ are pairwise distinct primes; for $n \in \{3, 5, 7\}$, such a partition is given by $k = 1$ and $p_1 = n$; finally, for $n = 9$, let $k = 1$ and $p_1 = 3^2$, and for $n = 8$, let $k = 2$, $p_1 = 3$ and $p_2 = 5$. In each case, n has been represented as $n = p_1 + \cdots + p_k$, where $p_1, \ldots, p_k \geqslant 3$ are powers of pairwise distinct odd primes. Consider the languages

$$K = \{\, a^\ell \mid \ell \not\equiv m \ (\mathrm{mod}\ 2) \ \text{or} \ \ell = m - 2 \,\} = a^{1-(m\ \mathrm{mod}\ 2)}(a^2)^* \cup \{a^{m-2}\}$$

and

$$L = \{\, a^\ell \mid \ell \equiv m - 2 \ (\mathrm{mod}\ p_1 \cdots p_k) \,\} = a^{(m-2)\ \mathrm{mod}\ p_1 \cdots p_k}(a^{p_1 \cdots p_k})^*,$$

which are recognized by an m-state 2DFA as in Example 2, and by an n-state 2DFA from Example 1, respectively. Their intersection is

$$K \cap L = a^j (a^{2 \cdot p_1 \cdots p_k})^* \cup \{a^{m-2}\},$$

where j is the least non-negative integer with $j \not\equiv m \ (\mathrm{mod}\ 2)$ and $j \equiv m - 2$ $(\mathrm{mod}\ p_1 \cdots p_k)$. The minimal 1DFA for this language has tail of length $m-1$ and period $p = 2 \cdot p_1 \cdots p_k$. Since the latter is a prime factorization of p, Proposition 4 is applicable, and it asserts that every 2DFA recognizing this intersection must have at least $2 + p_1 + \cdots + p_k + \max(m - 1, 1) - 1 = m + n$ states.

Consider the remaining cases of $(m, n) \in \{(4, 2), (4, 4), (6, 2), (6, 4)\}$, and let the two languages be $K = \{\, a^\ell \mid \ell \equiv m + 1 \ (\mathrm{mod}\ 3) \,\} \cup \{a^{m-3}\}$ and $L = \{\, a^\ell \mid \ell \equiv m - 3 \ (\mathrm{mod}\ n) \,\}$, with an m-state and an n-state 2DFA from Example 2 and Example 1, respectively. The intersection of these languages is

$$K \cap L = \{\, a^\ell \mid \ell \equiv m + 1 \ (\mathrm{mod}\ 3) \ \text{and} \ \ell \equiv m - 3 \ (\mathrm{mod}\ n) \,\} \cup \{a^{m-3}\},$$

The minimal 1DFA for this language has tail of length $m-2$ and period $p = 3 \cdot n$. Since the latter is a prime factorization of p, by Proposition 4, every 2DFA recognizing $K \cap L$ has at least $3 + n + \max(m - 2, 1) - 1 = m + n$ states.   ☐

Turning to the union operation, representing a union of two 2DFAs is straightforward, if one of them always halts. Geffert et al. [4] showed that any n-state 2DFA can be transformed to an equivalent $4n$-state 2DFA that halts on every input. From this result, Jiráskova and Okhotin [6] inferred a $(4m+n+const)$-state upper bound on the complexity of union for 2DFAs, which was accompanied by a lower bound of $m + n - o(m + n)$ states.

For the unary case, there is a stronger result on transforming 2DFAs to *reversible 2DFAs*, which is established in an upcoming paper by the authors. The proof develops the idea of the construction by Kondacs and Watrous [7] for transforming a 1DFA to a reversible 2DFA.

Proposition 8 ([9]). *For every n-state 2DFA over a unary alphabet, there exists an equivalent reversible 2DFA with $2n + 3$ states (which, in particular, halts on every input).*

This reversibility construction yields an improved upper bound on the state complexity of union for unary 2DFAs mentioned in the next theorem. The lower bound is analogous to Theorem 7.

Theorem 9. *For every $m, n \geqslant 2$ with $(m, n) \notin \{(2, 2), (6, 6)\}$, the state complexity of union of an m-state 2DFAs and an n-state 2DFA over a unary alphabet is at least $m + n$. For all $m, n \geqslant 1$, it is at most $2m + n + 4$.*

Proof. The construction for the upper bound is explained above.

The lower bound is proved similarly to the proof of Theorem 7. Consider first the case of $n \notin \{2, 4, 6\}$ and arbitrary $m \geqslant 2$, and represent n as $n = p_1 + \cdots + p_k$, where $p_1, \ldots, p_k \geqslant 3$ are powers of pairwise distinct odd primes. Consider the language $K = a^{1-(m \bmod 2)}(a^2)^* \cup \{a^{m-2}\}$, recognized by an m-state 2DFA as in Example 2, and another language $L = \{a^\ell \mid \ell \not\equiv m - 2 \pmod{p_1 \cdots p_k}\}$, representable by an n-state 2DFA; note that L is the complement of the language from Example 1, used in the proof of Theorem 7. Their union is

$$K \cup L = \{a^\ell \mid \ell \not\equiv m - 2 \pmod{p_1 \cdots p_k} \text{ or } \ell \not\equiv m \pmod 2\} \cup \{a^{m-2}\}.$$

The minimal 1DFA for this language has tail of length $m - 1$ and period $p = 2 \cdot p_1 \cdots p_k$. Since the latter is a prime factorization of p, Proposition 4 is applicable, and it asserts that every 2DFA recognizing this union must have at least $2 + p_1 + \cdots + p_k + \max(m - 1, 1) - 1 = m + n$ states.

The remaining cases of $(m, n) \in \{(4, 2), (4, 4), (6, 2), (6, 4)\}$ can be handled in the very same way as for intersection, again using the complement of L.   □

The gap between the lower bound $m + n$ and the upper bound $2m + n + 4$ is still large, and narrowing it requires further studies. On the one hand, the only known method of obtaining a 2DFA for union relies on Proposition 8, and $2n + 3$ is the best known number of states in this transformation. On the other hand, the lower bound techniques of Proposition 4 apply only to the lengths of the tail and the cycle, and this cannot yield any lower bound higher than $m + n$.

4   Kleene Star

For 1DFAs, the state complexity of the Kleene star is $\frac{3}{4}2^n$ for alphabets containing at least two letters [11], but only $(n - 1)^2 + 1$ for the unary alphabet [16]. The latter result is implied by the following two properties:

Proposition 10 (Yu et al. [16]). *(i) Let A be a unary 1DFA with n states. Then there is a 1DFA for $L(A)^*$ with $(n - 1)^2 + 1$ states.*

(ii) For every $n \geqslant 2$, the language $L = a^{n-1}(a^n)^*$ has an n-state 1DFA, but the language L^* is co-finite, and its minimal 1DFA has tail of length $(n - 1)^2$ and period 1.

This result can be "lifted" to 2DFAs, in the following sense. First, the star of a 2DFA can be represented by first converting it to a 1DFA and then applying the construction of Proposition 10(i). Secondly, the periodic witness language in Proposition 10(ii) can be inflated to $L = a^{g(n)-1}(a^{g(n)})^*$ using a 2DFA with n states, and then the language L^* requires a large 2DFA, because it is co-finite. This leads to the following asymptotically tight bounds:

Theorem 11. *The Kleene star of every n-state unary 2DFA can be represented by a 2DFA with $(g'(n))^2+1$ states. Conversely, the language $L = a^{g(n)-1}(a^{g(n)})^*$ is representable by an n-state 2DFA, but every 2DFA accepting L^* has at least $(g(n)-1)^2$ states.*

Proof. To show the upper bound, consider an arbitrary n-state unary 2DFA. By Proposition 5, there exists a 1DFA with $g'(n)+1$ states recognizing the same language. The latter 1DFA can be transformed, according to Proposition 10(i), to another 1DFA with $(g'(n))^2+1$ states recognizing the language L^*.

Turning to the lower bound, let $n \geqslant 1$ and $g(n) = p_1 \cdots p_k$, where p_i are powers of distinct primes, and consider the language $L = a^{g(n)-1}(a^{g(n)})^*$. This language is recognized by a 2DFA with $p_1 + \cdots + p_k \leqslant n$ states, which checks that the length of the input string is congruent to $p_i - 1$ modulo each p_i. At the same time, according to Lemma 10(ii), the minimal 1DFA for the language L^* has tail of length $(g(n)-1)^2$ and period 1. Therefore, by Proposition 4, every 2DFA for L^* requires at least $(g(n)-1)^2$ states.   □

Accordingly, the state complexity of Kleene star for unary 2DFAs equals $g(n)^2(1+o(1)) = e^{\sqrt{n \ln n}(2+o(1))}$.

5   Power

Viewing concatenation as a product of languages, one can consider the k-th power of a language, defined as the concatenation of k of its copies, $L^k = L \cdots L$. For 1DFAs over a general alphabet, Domaratzki and Okhotin [2] demonstrated that the k-th power operation requires $\Theta(n2^{(k-1)n})$ states. In the unary case, Rampersad [15] proved that the state complexity of L^k for 1DFAs is exactly $kn - k + 1$. More precisely, the following facts are known.

Proposition 12 (Rampersad [15]). *(i) For every $k \geqslant 1$ and for every unary 1DFA A with n states (tail $\ell \geqslant 0$, period $p \geqslant 1$), the language $L(A)^k$ is represented by a 1DFA with $kn - k + 1$ states (tail $k\ell + (k-1)p - k + 1$, period p).*

(ii) The language $L = a^{n-1}(a^n)^*$ is recognized by an n-state 1DFA, but the minimal 1DFA for L^k has $kn - k + 1$ states, with tail $(k-1)(n-1)$ and period n.

These properties will now be lifted to 2DFAs similarly to the case of the Kleene star.

Theorem 13. *Let $k \geqslant 2$. The state complexity of L^k for unary 2DFAs is at least $(k-1)g(n) - k$ and at most $kg'(n) + 1$.*

Proof. For the lower bound, let $p_1, \ldots, p_m \geqslant 2$ be the numbers from the definition of Landau's function for n, which satisfy $p_1 + \cdots + p_m \leqslant n$ and $\mathrm{lcm}(p_1, \ldots, p_m) = g(n)$. Then there is an n-state 2DFA recognizing the language $L = a^{g(n)-1}(a^{g(n)})^*$. By Proposition 12(ii), the minimal 1DFA for L^k has tail of length $(k-1)(g(n)-1)$ and period $g(n)$. Then, by Proposition 4, every 2DFA for L^k must have at least $p_1 + \cdots + p_m + (k-1)(g(n)-1) - 1 \geqslant (k-1)g(n) - k$ states.

Upper bound: Let L be recognized by an n-state 2DFA. By Proposition 5, there is an equivalent 1DFA with $g'(n) + 1$ states. Then Proposition 12 asserts that there is a 1DFA for L^k with $kg'(n) + 1$ states.   □

Unfortunately, the bounds in Theorem 13 do not lead to any asymptotical estimation better than $\Theta(g(n))$. The reason can be traced to the limitations of the lower bound method of Propositions 3–4, which estimate the number of states needed to represent period $g(n)$ only as $\Omega(n)$. On the other hand, in all upper bound arguments, such a period cannot in general be represented using fewer than $g(n)$ states.

6   Concatenation

The state complexity of concatenation for unary 1DFAs is proved by the methods much like those used for the star and the power. In particular, the lower bound is witnessed by two cyclic languages with a co-finite concatenation.

Proposition 14 (Yu et al. [16]). *For all relatively prime m and n, the languages $K = a^{m-1}(a^m)^*$ and $L = a^{n-1}(a^n)^*$ are recognized by an m-state 1DFA and an n-state 1DFA, respectively, while their concatenation KL is a co-finite language, for which the minimal 1DFA has tail $mn - 1$ and period 1.*

Yu et al. [16] also gave a matching upper bound of mn states in a 1DFA representing a concatenation of an m-state and an n-state 1DFA. The following more refined upper bound also reflects the dependence of tail and cycle lengths of the minimal 1DFA for concatenation on the tails and the cycles of the arguments.

Proposition 15 (Pighizzini and Shallit [14]). *Let $K \subseteq a^*$ be represented by a 1DFA with tail k and period p, and let $L \subseteq a^*$ have a 1DFA with tail ℓ and period q. Then there is a 1DFA recognizing KL with tail $k + \ell + \mathrm{lcm}(p, q) - 1$ and period $\mathrm{lcm}(p, q)$.*

Attempting to lift the lower bound in Proposition 14 to 2DFAs in the same way as in Sections 4–5 leads to the following ultimately unsuccessful argument. Given m and n, one would choose one set of cycle lengths $p_1, \ldots, p_k$ with $p_1 + \cdots + p_k \leqslant m$ and $g(m) = p_1 \cdots p_k$, as well as another set of cycle lengths $q_1, \ldots, q_\ell$ with $q_1 + \cdots + q_\ell \leqslant n$ and $g(n) = q_1 \cdots q_\ell$, and construct a pair of an m-state and an n-state 2DFA with these cycle lengths, that recognize the languages $K = a^{g(m)-1}(a^{g(m)})^*$ and $L = a^{g(n)-1}(a^{g(n)})^*$, expecting to find a lower bound $g(m)g(n)$ on their concatenation. However, the last step would not work out, because the numbers $g(m)$ and $g(n)$ are almost never relatively prime, and their greatest common divisor is typically large. The latter, according to Proposition 15, would imply that the concatenation KL can be represented by a 1DFA with a much shorter tail than intended, which would in turn diminish the lower bound on a 2DFA for this language.

For this argument to work, for every pair of numbers m, n, one has to find partitions of each of these numbers into powers of distinct primes, so that no primes are shared between the partitions. Landau's function as it is does not provide such partitions, and hence its variant needs to be defined:

$$g(m, n) = \max\{\, \mathrm{lcm}(p_1, \ldots, p_k, q_1, \ldots, q_\ell) \mid p_1 + \cdots + p_k \leqslant m, \ q_1 + \cdots + q_\ell \leqslant n \,\}$$

As in the definition of $g(n)$, one can assume that $p_1, \ldots, p_k, q_1, \ldots, q_\ell$ are relatively prime: there is no loss of generality in this assumption, because for each two numbers p and p' in this list, one of them can be divided by $\gcd(p, p')$ without affecting the least common multiple.

It turns out that $\ln g(m, n)$ is asymptotically equivalent to $\ln g(m + n)$.

Lemma 16. $g(m, n) = e^{(1+o(1))\sqrt{(m+n)\ln(m+n)}}$.

Proof. The argument follows the general outline of Miller's [12] proof of Landau's [10] asymptotics of $g(n)$.

Let π_i denote the i-th prime, and define a variant of Landau's function, in which the cycle lengths are preset to be the first primes:

$$f(n) = \pi_1 \cdots \pi_k,$$

where k is the greatest number with $\pi_1 + \cdots + \pi_k \leqslant n$. Denote the next prime by

$$h(n) = \pi_{k+1}.$$

The proof given by Miller [12] proceeds by showing that $\ln g(n) \sim \ln f(n)$ and $\ln f(n) \sim \sqrt{n \ln n}$. The latter argument also contains an estimation of h as $h(n) \sim \sqrt{n \ln n}$.

Following the same course, consider a variant of $g(m, n)$, in which as many first primes as possible are used for the partition for m, and the subsequent primes are used for n:

$$f(m, n) = \pi_1 \cdots \pi_k \cdot \pi_{k+1} \cdots \pi_\ell,$$

where k is the greatest number with $\pi_1 + \cdots + \pi_k \leqslant m$, and ℓ is the greatest number with $\pi_{k+1} + \cdots + \pi_\ell \leqslant n$.

This function can be tightly bounded as follows:

$$\frac{f(m+n)}{h(m+n)} \leqslant f(m, n) \leqslant f(m+n),$$

where the upper bound holds by definition, and the denominator $h(m+n)$ in the lower bound reflects that at most one prime is unused due to the partition of the number $m+n$ into m and n. To prove the lower bound, let k be the largest integer with $\pi_1 + \cdots + \pi_k \leqslant m$, and write $f(m+n)$ as $f(m+n) = \pi_1 \cdots \pi_k \cdot \pi_{k+1} \cdots \pi_\ell$.

Then $f(m,n)$ equals either $f(m+n)$ or $\pi_1 \cdots \pi_k \cdot \pi_{k+1} \cdots \pi_{\ell-1}$, since $\pi_{k+1} + \cdots + \pi_{\ell-1} \leqslant \pi_{k+2} + \cdots + \pi_\ell \leqslant n$. Consequently, $f(m,n) \geqslant \frac{f(m+n)}{\pi_\ell} \geqslant \frac{f(m+n)}{h(m+n)}$.

Turning to the function $g(m,n)$, it can now be estimated as follows:

$$\frac{f(m+n)}{h(m+n)} \leqslant f(m,n) \leqslant g(m,n) \leqslant g(m+n),$$

where the last inequality is by taking the same numbers within the definition of $g(m+n)$. Since both the upper and the lower bounds are asymptotically $e^{(1+o(1))\sqrt{(m+n)\ln(m+n)}}$, so is $g(m,n)$. $\qquad\square$

Theorem 17. *The state complexity of concatenation of an m-state 2DFA and an n-state 2DFA over a unary alphabet is at least $g(m,n) - 1$ and at most $2g(m,n) + m + n$. It is accordingly estimated as $e^{(1+o(1))\sqrt{(m+n)\ln(m+n)}}$.*

Proof.
Lower bound: According to the definition of $g(m,n)$, let $p_1, \ldots, p_k \geqslant 2$ and $q_1, \ldots, q_\ell \geqslant 2$ be the relatively prime numbers with $p_1 + \cdots + p_k \leqslant m$ and $q_1 + \cdots + q_\ell \leqslant n$, for which $g(m,n) = \operatorname{lcm}(p_1, \ldots, p_k, q_1, \ldots, q_\ell)$. The numbers $\operatorname{lcm}(p_1, \ldots, p_k) = p_1 \cdots p_k$ and $\operatorname{lcm}(q_1, \ldots, q_\ell) = q_1 \cdots q_\ell$ are relatively prime as well.

Consider the languages $K = a^{p_1 \cdots p_k - 1}(a^{p_1 \cdots p_k})^*$ and $L = a^{q_1 \cdots q_\ell - 1}(a^{q_1 \cdots q_\ell})^*$, recognized by an m-state 2DFA and an n-state 2DFA, respectively (both as in Example 1). Since their periods are relatively prime, by Proposition 14, the minimal 1DFA for their concatenation KL has tail of length $p_1 \cdots p_k \cdot q_1 \cdots q_\ell - 1 = g(m,n) - 1$ and period 1. Then, by Proposition 4, every 2DFA for this language requires at least $g(m,n) - 1$ states.

Upper bound: Given a 2DFA A with m states, by Proposition 3 there exists an equivalent 1DFA A' with tail of length ℓ and period $\operatorname{lcm}(p_1, \ldots, p_k)$, where $k \geqslant 1$ and $p_1, \ldots, p_k, \ell \geqslant 1$ satisfy $p_1 + \cdots + p_k + \ell \leqslant m + 1$. Similarly, for a 2DFA B with n states, let B' be an equivalent 1DFA with tail of length ℓ' and period $\operatorname{lcm}(q_1, \ldots, q_{k'})$, where $k' \geqslant 1$ and $q_1, \ldots, q_{k'}, \ell' \geqslant 1$ are such that $q_1 + \cdots + q_{k'} + \ell' \leqslant n + 1$.

Then, by Proposition 15, the language $L(A')L(B')$ has a 1DFA with tail of length $\ell + \ell' + \operatorname{lcm}(p_1, \ldots, p_k, q_1, \ldots, q_{k'}) - 1$ and period $\operatorname{lcm}(p_1, \ldots, p_k, q_1, \ldots, q_{k'})$. The total number of states in this 1DFA is at most

$$\ell + \ell' + 2\operatorname{lcm}(p_1, \ldots, p_k, q_1, \ldots, q_{k'}) \leqslant m + n + 2g(m,n). \qquad\square$$

Corollary 18. *The state complexity of concatenation of an m-state 2DFA and an n-state 2DFA is $\Theta(g(m,n)) = e^{(1+o(1))\sqrt{(m+n)\ln(m+n)}}$.*

7 Summary

The state complexity of operations over a unary alphabet for 1DFAs, 1NFAs and 2DFAs is compared in the following table. The operations listed are: complementation ($\sim$), intersection ($\cap$), union ($\cup$), concatenation ($\cdot$), star (*) and k-th power (^{k}).

	1DFA	1NFA	**2DFA**
$\sim$	n	$g(n) + O(n^2)$ [5]	$n \leqslant \cdot \leqslant 2n + 4$ [9]
$\cap$	mn	mn	$m + n \leqslant \cdot \leqslant m + n + 1$
$\cup$	mn	$m + n + 1$ [5]	$m + n \leqslant \cdot \leqslant 2m + n + 4$
$\cdot$	mn [16]	$m + n - 1 \leqslant \cdot \leqslant m + n$ [5]	$e^{(1+o(1))\sqrt{(m+n)\ln(m+n)}}$
$*$	$(n-1)^2 + 1$ [16]	$n + 1$ [5]	$(g(n) - 1)^2 \leqslant \cdot \leqslant g'(n)^2 + 1$
k	$kn - k + 1$ [15]	?	$(k-1)g(n) - k \leqslant \cdot \leqslant kg'(n) + 1$

Comparing the new results on unary 2DFAs to the known results for multiple-letter alphabets by Jiráskova and Okhotin [6], the new lower bounds for union and for intersection improve over the known bound $m + n - o(m+n)$, and do so using only a unary alphabet, vs. an alphabet of exponential size. Turning to the concatenation, star and power operations, their state complexity for multiple-letter alphabets is $2^{\Omega(n)}$ [6], while the complexity for a unary alphabet is tied to Landau's function and is therefore smaller.

References

1. Chrobak, M.: Finite automata and unary languages. Theoretical Computer Science 47, 149–158 (1986); Errata 302, 497–498 (2003)
2. Domaratzki, M., Okhotin, A.: State complexity of power. Theoretical Computer Science 410(24-25), 2377–2392 (2009)
3. Dressler, R.E.: A stronger Bertrand's postulate with an application to partitions. Proceedings of the AMS 33(2), 226–228 (1972)
4. Geffert, V., Mereghetti, C., Pighizzini, G.: Complementing two-way finite automata. Information and Computation 205(8), 1173–1187 (2007)
5. Holzer, M., Kutrib, M.: Nondeterministic descriptional complexity of regular languages. International Journal of Foundations of Computer Science 14, 1087–1102 (2003)
6. Jiráskova, G., Okhotin, A.: On the state complexity of operations on two-way finite automata. In: Ito, M., Toyama, M. (eds.) DLT 2008. LNCS, vol. 5257, pp. 443–454. Springer, Heidelberg (2008)
7. Kondacs, A., Watrous, J.: On the power of quantum finite state automata. In: 38th Annual Symposium on Foundations of Computer Science (FOCS 1997), Miami Beach, Florida, USA, October 19-22, pp. 66–75. IEEE, Los Alamitos (199719-22)
8. Kunc, M., Okhotin, A.: Describing periodicity in two-way deterministic finite automata using transformation semigroups. In: Leporati, A. (ed.) DLT 2011. LNCS, vol. 6795, pp. 324–336. Springer, Heidelberg (2011)
9. Kunc, M., Okhotin, A.: Reversible two-way finite automata over a unary alphabet (manuscript in preparation)
10. Landau, E.: Über die Maximalordnung der Permutationen gegebenen Grades (On the maximal order of permutations of a given degree). Archiv der Mathematik und Physik, Ser. 3(5), 92–103 (1903)
11. Maslov, A.N.: Estimates of the number of states of finite automata. Soviet Mathematics Doklady 11, 1373–1375 (1970)
12. Miller, W.: The maximum order of an element of a finite symmetric group. American Mathematical Monthly 94(6), 497–506 (1987)

13. Okhotin, A.: Unambiguous finite automata over a unary alphabet. In: Hliněný, P., Kučera, A. (eds.) MFCS 2010. LNCS, vol. 6281, pp. 556–567. Springer, Heidelberg (2010)
14. Pighizzini, G., Shallit, J.: Unary language operations, state complexity and Jacobsthal's function. International Journal of Foundations of Computer Science 13(1), 145–159 (2002)
15. Rampersad, N.: The state complexity of L^2 and L^k. Information Processing Letters 98, 231–234 (2006)
16. Yu, S., Zhuang, Q., Salomaa, K.: The state complexity of some basic operations on regular languages. Theoretical Computer Science 125, 315–328 (1994)

Kleene Theorems for Product Systems

Kamal Lodaya[1], Madhavan Mukund[2], and Ramchandra Phawade[1]

[1] The Institute of Mathematical Sciences
CIT Campus, Chennai 600113, India
[2] Chennai Mathematical Institute
H1, SIPCOT IT Park, Siruseri 603103, India

Abstract. We prove Kleene theorems for two subclasses of labelled product systems which are inspired from well-studied subclasses of 1-bounded Petri nets. For product T-systems we define a corresponding class of expressions. The algorithms from systems to expressions and in the reverse direction are both polynomial time. For product free choice systems with a restriction of structural cyclicity, that is, the initial global state is a feedback vertex set, going from systems to expressions is still polynomial time; in the reverse direction it is polynomial time with access to an NP oracle for finding deadlocks.

1 Introduction

The descriptional complexity of regular expressions versus automata is well known: the Kleene construction from expressions to automata can be carried out in DLOGSPACE [JR91], while for the converse translation exponential size lower bounds are known [EZ76, GH08]. In this paper we seek to extend these results to the class of 1-bounded free choice Petri net systems and their subclass, 1-bounded T-systems [CHEP71, GL73, Hack72, DE95].

In [Lod06a], we gave a syntactic characterization of Mazurkiewicz's recognizable trace languages [Maz77, Och85, DR95], seen as behaviours of labelled product automata [BeSh83, Arn94]. Our expression syntax was borrowed from Grabowski [Gra81] and Garg and Ragunath [GR92], ultimately deriving from Campbell and Haberman's path expressions [CH74] and Hoare's CSP [Hoa85] by extending regular expressions with a parallel operation (equivalent to shuffle on words), a parallel mixed with intersection (or shuffle with synchronization) and renaming a letter by another.

Zielonka's theorem [Zie87] shows that 1-bounded Petri nets can be viewed as such products. Hence we work with product systems. We are able to extend known constructions on finite automata to syntactically characterize live and structurally cyclic product free choice systems and live product T-systems. The next section gives definitions for these classes, borrowing from Petri nets. Unlike the earlier paper [Lod06a] we do not use Zielonka's theorem in our proofs. Going from automata to expressions we get polynomial time algorithms, which might appear surprising, but the benefit is derived from the condition of structural cyclicity.

M. Holzer, M. Kutrib, and G. Pighizzini (Eds.): DCFS 2011, LNCS 6808, pp. 235–247, 2011.

In our earlier paper, we used renaming to disambiguate synchronization, but some subtleties remain. For example the system shown in the figure might seem to be described by the expression $(a_1||a_1a_2||a_2)[a/a_1, a/a_2]$, but in fact the example is *not* a labelled product system (see the definitions in the next section) and the expression is not valid, since the labelling, and the renaming operator, have to preserve the process structure: synchronizations between different sets of processes cannot get the same label.

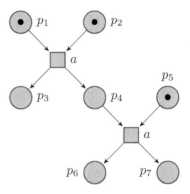

However its behaviour is just the single word aa and the system is a labelled 1-bounded Petri net which even satisfies the "trace labelling" condition of Thiagarajan [Thi96]. Our basic results do not use the renaming operator, consequently we bear the burden of using labellings which preserve process structure.

The largest proper subclass of nets where we are aware of earlier results are on 1-bounded SR-systems [LRR03, RL03], which use an algebraic structure of series and parallel operations [LW00], with only a simple "fork-join" type of synchronization mechanism. Even T-systems are not included in SR-systems since they provide a genuine multi-way synchronization (or "rendezvous") mechanism for communication. The algebraic approach has been very successful at classifying subclasses of regular languages (see [Weil04, TT07] for surveys emphasizing this aspect). However, partially commutative monoids which are used to characterize recognizable trace languages have not so far yielded any results on free choice systems and their subclass of T-systems. Ours is the first work in this direction.

2   Labels and Products

Following [Lod06a] we define a **rendezvous alphabet** to be a tuple $(A, |, 0, loc)$ where A is a finite alphabet A containing a dummy action 0, $| : A \times A \to A$ is a commutative and associative **rendezvous** operation over A with 0 as an absorbing element and $loc : A \to \wp(Loc)$ maps actions to locations such that

- $loc(0) = \emptyset$ and $loc^{-1}(\emptyset) = 0$.
- If $loc(a)$ and $loc(b)$ are not disjoint, $a|b = 0$.
- If $loc(a)$ and $loc(b)$ are disjoint and $a|b \neq 0$, $loc(a|b) = loc(a) \cup loc(b)$.
- If $loc(c) = r \cup s$ for disjoint r and s then there exist a, b such that $c = a|b$, with $loc(a) = r, loc(b) = s$.

Actions in A with a single location are called local, and nonzero actions a such that for every b, $a|b = 0$ are global. Thus, a global action is either a local action that does not rendezvous at all, or a "full" synchronization $a_1|a_2| \cdots |a_k$ whose "partial" subsets such as a_3, $a_1|a_k, \ldots$ are not global since further rendezvous will be carried out. Let $G(A)$ be the global actions in A.

A **renaming** between rendezvous alphabets is a relation ρ that is *Loc*-respecting and |-**stable**: that is, if $a\rho b$ then $loc(a) = loc(b)$ and for all c, $(a|c)\rho(b|c)$. The expression in the Introduction does not have a*Loc*-respecting renaming.

Let ρ be a renaming which is an equivalence relation over alphabet A. $C = (G(A)/\rho, loc)$ is called a **distributed alphabet** where $loc([a]) \overset{\text{def}}{=} loc(a)$ is well defined. We also write ρ as the function $\rho(a) = [a]$.

Definition 1 ([Lod06a]). *Let* $A_i \overset{\text{def}}{=} \{a \in A \mid i \in loc(a)\}$. *A* **product system of automata** N *over the alphabet* $(A, |, 0, loc)$ *is given by automata* $N_i = (P_i, p_0^i, \rightarrow_i)$ *(called* places, initial places *and* local transitions*) over the alphabet* A_i, *for each* i *in Loc. We call* $\Pi_{i \in Loc} p_0^i$ *the* initial global state. *Given a renaming* ρ *defining a distributed alphabet* C, *a* **labelled product system of automata** $N[\rho]$ *is a product system* N *over* C.

A product system runs on a word w over the global actions (or $\rho(w)$ over the distributed alphabet) by associating global states from $\Pi_{i \in Loc} P_i$ to prefixes of w: the empty word is assigned the initial global state, and for every prefix va of w, if $\Pi_{i \in Loc} p_i$ is the global state reached after v, then the state $\Pi_{i \in Loc} q_i$ reached after va satisfies, for every $j \in loc(a)$, $p_j \overset{a}{\rightarrow}_i q_j$ in M_i, and for every other j, $p_j = q_j$. Thus every action transforms the places of the locations it affects, the other places remaining fixed. We call $t = \Pi_{i \in Loc} p_i \overset{a}{\rightarrow}_i q_i$ a **global transition** if there is some word wa such that t describes the change in global state from w to wa for some run of N on wa.

The **language** of the product system is the set of maximal words (finite or infinite), where a system keeps on running as long as possible and, in addition, each global transition which is infinitely often enabled occurs infinitely often in the run. Since a product system can be simulated by a finite automaton, its accepted language is regular and we call it a **recognizable shuffle language** [Moh99].

Traces. Let I be an irreflexive symmetric relation over A called **independence** defined by aIb if $loc(a)$ and $loc(b)$ are disjoint. Let its reflexive transitive closure on A^* be $\sim_I$, called **trace congruence**. For instance, if aIb then $wabx \sim_I wbax$ (a and b commute).

Notice that if a product system has a run (or an accepting run) on a word $wabx$ and aIb, then it has a run (respectively, an accepting run) on the word $wbax$ as well. Hence a recognizable shuffle language is a recognizable trace language over $(G(A), I)$ in the sense of Mazurkiewicz [Maz77]. Zielonka showed that the converse is not true [Zie87].

Let I be the independence relation over A above extended to C. Using the properties of ρ, the languages accepted by labelled product automata continue to be recognizable trace languages over (C, I). But they need no longer be recognizable shuffle languages. Every recognizable trace language is accepted by a labelled product system.

In a product system, we say the local transition $p \overset{a}{\rightarrow}_i q_1$ is **conflict-equivalent** to the local transition $p' \overset{a}{\rightarrow}_j q_1'$ if $loc(a) = loc(b)$, for every other local transition $p \xrightarrow{b}_i q_2$, there is a local transition $p' \xrightarrow{b}_j q_2'$ and, conversely, transitions from p' are matched by transitions from p.

A product system N has a natural representation as a (labelled) 1-safe Petri net (P, T, F, λ, M_0), with places P, net transitions T, flow relation $F \subseteq (P \times T) \cup (T \times P)$, labelling $\lambda : T \to A$ and initial marking $M_0 \subseteq P$, as follows:

- $P = \bigcup_{i \in Loc} P_i$,
- $T = \{t = \Pi_{i \in Loc(a)} p_i \xrightarrow{a}_i q_i \mid t \text{ is a global transition of } N\}$,
- $F = \{(p, t), (t, q) \mid \exists t = \Pi_{i \in Loc(a)} p_i \xrightarrow{a}_i q_i : \exists i \in Loc(a) : p = p_i, q = q_i\}$,
- $\lambda(\Pi_{i \in Loc(a)} p_i \xrightarrow{a}_i q_i) = a$, and
- $M_0 = \bigcup_{i \in Loc} \{p_0^i\}$.

We now borrow some definitions from Petri nets into the framework of product systems [CHEP71, GL73, Hack72, DE95]. First on the structural side, and then on the behavioural:

Definition 2. *A product system is **free choice**, more briefly an **FC-product**, if for every a such that $|loc(a)| > 1$, every pair of a-labelled local transitions is conflict-equivalent. We will also use **FC-dag** for FC-products which are acyclic and just **dag** for acyclic and rooted finite automata. A **product T-system (T-product)** is one where every place has at most one input transition and at most one output transition.*

Definition 3. *A global state is **live** if for any run from it and any global transition $t = \Pi_{i \in Loc(a)} p_i \xrightarrow{a}_i q_i$, the run can be extended so that transition t occurs. A product system is **live** if its initial global state is live. It is **deadlock-free** if for every i, from a place p_i in a reachable global state $\Pi_{j \in Loc} p_j$ and a local transition $p_i \xrightarrow{a}_i q_i$, there is a run in which a global transition $\Pi_{j \in Loc} p_j \xrightarrow{a}_j q_j$ occurs.*

The above definition is weaker than the usual one, an empty product system (with no transitions) is deadlock-free. The next definition is new to this paper and identifies a restriction needed for our results. It is stronger than the net-theoretic definition of a net being **cyclic** when its initial global state is a home state [BV84, DE95] (reachable from any reachable global state)—that is, the set of reachable markings is strongly connected. But it is weaker in the sense that acyclic nets are included.

Definition 4. *We say that a product system N is **structurally cyclic** if the initial global state $\Pi_{i \in Loc} p_0^i$ is a **feedback vertex set** (that is, removing that set of places from N makes the resulting system acyclic).*

The adjacent figure shows a product system (actually an automaton) which is live and 1-bounded. The initial state p_1 is a home state, so the system is cyclic. Removing p_1 does not eliminate all cycles in the reachable global states, so it is not structurally cyclic.

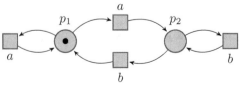

Live and 1-bounded FC-net systems have a characterization [Hack72] which shows that they can be covered by S-components (strongly connected components which are finite automata).

Theorem 5 (Hack). *A live FC-system (N, M_0) is 1-bounded iff it is covered by S-components.*

3   Expressions and Languages

Let A be a finite alphabet. We will consider finite as well as infinite words on this alphabet, and languages over them.

For a word w (or any kind of expression defined below), and $a \in A$, $|w|_a$ denotes the number of occurrences of the letter a that appear in w. The alphabet of an expression or word w is $\alpha(w) = \{a \in A \mid |w|_a > 0\}$. The projection $\downarrow$ over the subalphabet $B \subseteq A$ is given as the homomorphism from A^* to B^* which retains all letters in B and deletes all letters outside B. The shuffle of two words $w\|x$ is a language, defined as usual. It is an associative and commutative operation. Now we define the synchronized shuffle over a subalphabet $X \subseteq A$.

Let $w, v \in A^*$ such that $w{\downarrow}X = v{\downarrow}X = a_1 \ldots a_n$. Let $w = w_0 a_1 w_1 \ldots a_n w_n$, with $w_i \in (A \setminus X)^*$, and $v = v_0 a_1 v_1 \ldots a_n v_n$, with $v_i \in (A \setminus X)^*$. Then $w\|_X v$ is defined to be the language $(w_0\|v_0) a_1 (w_1\|v_1) \ldots a_n (w_n\|v_n)$. If $w{\downarrow}X \neq v{\downarrow}X$, $w\|_X v$ is undefined.

Definition 6. *Our expressions come in three syntactic sorts: **sums, connected expressions** and **ω-expressions**. If the operation $+$ is not used, we call them **T-sequences, connected T-expressions** and **ω-T-expressions**, respectively.*

Sums	$s ::= a \in A \mid s_1 s_2 \mid s_1 + s_2$
Connected expressions	$c ::= 0 \mid s \mid fsync(c_1, c_2)$
ω-expressions	$e ::= c^\omega \mid par(e_1, e_2)$

For a syntactic expression x, we use $\alpha(x)$ to denote its alphabet—the set of letters of A occurring in x—and $wd(x)$ for its alphabetic width—the total number of occurrences of letters of A in x. For instance, the connected expression $fsync(aabab, abab)$ has an alphabet $\{a, b\}$ and alphabetic width 9.

The semantics of each of these expressions is a language over A. For sums s it is a nonempty language of nonempty finite words, for connected expressions c it is a language of nonempty finite words, for ω-expressions e it is a language of infinite words. The languages are closed under an independence relation which we will define from the expressions themselves, so that we have languages of Mazurkiewicz traces [DR95].

3.1   Sums

To begin with, the language associated with a letter $a \in A$ is $\{a\}$. Formally, $Lang(a) = \{a\}$, $Lang(s_1 s_2)$ is the concatenation and $Lang(s_1 + s_2)$ the union, as usual. The alphabet $\alpha(s)$ and projection $s{\downarrow}B$ of a sum are well-defined. We also use the sets $Init(s) \subseteq A$ for the initial actions of a sum, and also Antimirov derivatives $Der_a(s)$ [Ant96]. (Briefly, the Brzozowski a-derivative of $ab + ac$ is the expression $b + c$ [BMc63], the Antimirov a-derivative of $ab + ac$ is the set of expressions $\{b, c\}$.) For the derivatives we will need an extra syntactic entity ϵ standing for the empty word.

3.2 Connected Expressions

Now we come to the semantics of connected expressions. Let Loc be the set of all maximal sums occurring in the given expression. Each letter a is located at the sum in which it occurs. We will inductively maintain the following **clustering** property: for initial actions $a, b \in Init(s)$ of a sum s, $loc(a) = loc(b)$. We use $Der_a^{\{l\}}(s)$ instead of $Der_a(s)$ to emphasize that the derivatives are taken at the set of locations $\{l\}$.

Define two occurrences of letters in a connected expression, say a and b, to be **independent**, if $loc(a)$ and $loc(b)$ are disjoint. (Thus our clustering property implies that initial letters in a sum are **dependent**.) We define **trace equivalence** for words over an alphabet with an independence relation, as before. Our semantics for the connected expressions yields unions of trace equivalence classes. Clearly this is so for a sum s since there are no independent letters.

For the connected expression 0, we have $Lang(0) = \alpha(0) = \emptyset$ and $0{\downarrow}B = 0$.

Let c_1, c_2 be connected expressions and L_1, L_2 be disjoint sets of locations such that loc_1 maps c_1 to L_1 and loc_2 maps c_2 to L_2. Their free choice synchronization $fsync(c_1, c_2)$ is over the locations $L_1 \cup L_2$, where for every letter $a \in X = \alpha(c_1) \cap \alpha(c_2)$: $loc(a) = loc_1(a) \cup loc_2(a)$. For the other letters in A, $loc(a)$ is inherited from loc_1 or loc_2, as appropriate. So inductively we have the loc function mapping occurrences of letters in an expression $\alpha(e)$ to nonempty subsets of Loc.

Now we inductively define the derivatives and the semantics of the operation $fsync(c_1, c_2)$. For a letter $a \notin X$ (say a occurs in c_1) we have $Der_a^{L_1 \cup L_2}(fsync(c_1, c_2)) = \{fsync(c', c_2) \mid c' \in Der_a^{L_1}(c_1)\}$, and symmetrically for the case when a appears in c_2. Otherwise suppose that for every sum s in c_1 and c_2, $Init(s) \cap X \neq \phi$ implies $Init(s) \subseteq X$. We say that this synchronization on the common letters X is **clustered** and define $Der_a^{L_1 \cup L_2}(fsync(c_1, c_2)) = \{fsync(c'_1, c'_2) \mid c'_1 \in Der_a^{L_1}(c_1), c'_2 \in Der_a^{L_2}(c_2)\}$. It is possible that a synchronization is clustered but has no derivatives, for example in $fsync(ab, ba)$.

We can keep taking derivatives in this fashion for all letters, but only finitely many times since the derivatives become shorter. The number of such derivatives can blow up exponentially in the number of $+$ operators in the expression.

If every synchronization we encounter is clustered we say that the $fsync$ operation itself is **clustered** and we define its language as:

$$Lang(fsync(c_1, c_2)) = \bigcup \{w_1 \|_X w_2 \mid w_1 \in Lang(c_1),\ w_2 \in Lang(c_2)\}.$$

But it might be that at some derivative of c_1 or c_2, we have a sum s with a choice between an action $a \in Init(s) \cap X$ and an action $b \in Init(s) \setminus X$. (This cannot happen if s is a T-sequence which has $|Init(s)| = 1$.) Then we say that the $fsync$ is not clustered and declare by fiat that $Lang(fsync(c_1, c_2)) = \emptyset$.

A short proof shows that $fsync$ is an associative operation (see, for example, Hoare's CSP [Hoa85]).

The alphabet of $fsync(c_1, c_2)$ is empty if its language is empty and the union of the alphabets of c_1 and c_2 otherwise. In the former case, $fsync(c_1, c_2){\downarrow}B$ is 0, otherwise it is $fsync(c_1{\downarrow}B, c_2{\downarrow}B)$, which is recursively defined.

We call a connected expression **clustered** if every $fsync$ operation in it is clustered. Connected T-expressions are clustered and "deterministic" (there is at most one derivative given an expression and a letter). We will call an FC-product **clustered** if at every reachable global state, if actions a and b are enabled, either they have the same set of locations or they have disjoint locations.

3.3   Omega-Power and Shuffle

Consider now the expression c^ω. Assume associated with the connected expression c is a function loc over the locations Loc. The independence relation is the one computed for the expression c. $Lang(c^\omega) = [(Lang(c))^\omega]$, the trace closure under our independence relation, where $K^\omega = \{w_1 w_2 \cdots \mid \forall i, w_i \in K\}$. Each equivalence class is a set of infinite words.

Finally the semantics of the par operator is defined to be shuffle of languages.

4   From Expressions to Product Automata

In this section we construct product automata for our syntactic entities. The first result is well known (see, for example, [BeSe86, JR91]).

Lemma 7. *A sum s over A is the language accepted by an acyclic rooted finite automaton, which we call a **dag**. (In case s is a T-sequence, the automaton consists of a single directed path.) The size of the automaton is $O(wd(s))$ (for example, using derivatives as states), and it can be computed in linear time and* DLOGSPACE.

4.1   Connected Expressions

Now we come to connected expressions, for which we will construct a product of automata. Before that we look for deadlocks.

Lemma 8. *The emptiness of the language of a connected expression c can be checked in* NP, *and of a connected T-expression in time $O(wd(c)^2)$.*

Proof. The complexity bound for a connected T-expression holds because we track at most $wd(c)$ tokens (represented by pointers in the expression) through a word of length at most $wd(c)$ to determine whether we reach the end of each T-sequence. This does not work for connected expressions: for example, $fsync(ab + ac, ad + ae + af)$ has six runs beginning with a in the resultant product. Now we use nondeterminism to guess the word letter-by-letter and move tokens. On any letter, if there is a derivative in one component of an $fsync$ but none in another, we have a deadlock.   □

Lemma 9. *Let c be a connected expression. Then there exists a deadlock-free clustered connected FC-dag (N, M_0) accepting $Lang(c)$ which is covered by a set Loc of dags. The size of the constructed system is $O(wd(c))$ and it can be computed using a polynomial time algorithm with access to an NP oracle. For connected T-expressions, the time bound is $O(wd(c)^2)$.*

Proof. We use the preceding lemma to check for a deadlock using an NP oracle query. If the answer is yes, we return the empty product system, covered by the empty set of dags!

If the oracle says there is no deadlock, we use Lemma 7 as the base case of an induction producing a deadlock-free clustered FC-dag that is covered by dags. We let the set Loc stand for these dags. Thus, for a dag constructed above, we pick a fresh location $l \in Loc$ and we locate every letter a labelling a transition in the dag by $loc(a) = \{l\}$. As an aside, note that the generated independence relation is empty, every transition in the path is dependent on the other transitions and on itself.

Inductively, consider connected expressions c_1 and c_2, and assume we have corresponding deadlock-free clustered FC-dags, covered by the dags in L_1 and L_2, with the independence relation of the FC-dags matching those of the expressions.

For the expression $fsync(c_1, c_2)$, we construct using the derivatives the FC-dag that is the synchronization of these two FC-dags, which are assumed to be covered by disjoint dags. The resulting automaton will be acyclic and covered by the dags $L_1 \cup L_2$. Because of the clustering property of the expressions, the resulting FC-dag will be clustered. Its size is $O(wd(c_1) + wd(c_2))$.

The trace equivalence generated from the locations is such that the language K of the constructed automaton is trace-closed. We can now verify that K is obtained by performing the $fsync$ operation on the languages of the two component automata.   □

4.2   Omega-Power and Shuffle

For the expression c^ω we map in linear time the ω-power operation to the construction of an FC-product.

Lemma 10. *Let $e = c^\omega$ be an expression over alphabet A with $Lang(c)$ a nonempty language of nonempty words. Then there exists a live and structurally cyclic FC-product accepting $Lang(e)$. The size of the constructed system is $O(wd(c))$ and it can be computed using a polynomial time algorithm with access to an NP oracle. For ω-T-expressions, the time bound is $O(wd(c)^2)$.*

Proof. For the expression c^ω, consider the deadlock-free clustered connected FC-dag N for c, covered by the dags in Loc and accepting the language K, obtained from the previous lemma. Recall that the trace equivalence generated from the independence relation of N saturates K, that is, $K = [K]$.

For each dag $l \in Loc$, we fuse the initially marked places of l with its sink places (which are different since K does not have the empty word). Call the new product system N'. The product satisfies the following properties:

(1) Each node of N was covered by some dag $l \in Loc$. So N' is an FC-product.
(2) It is structurally cyclic since by construction the initial global state is a feedback vertex set.
(3) Fusing the sink and source places makes each dag of N strongly connected in N', in fact a strongly connected component of N', since N was connected and deadlock-free. By Theorem 5, N' is live.

We now show that the language of N' is $Lang(e) = [Lang(c)^\omega]$.

By construction $K^\omega \subseteq Lang(N')$. Since N' has the same locations as N, it generates the same trace equivalence and hence we have that $[K^\omega] \subseteq [Lang(N')] = Lang(N')$.

To prove the converse inclusion, $Lang(N') \subseteq [K^\omega]$, suppose not and we have w accepted by N' but not in $[K^\omega]$. We can remove prefixes of w which are in $[K]$, so let us assume $w = uav$, u is a proper prefix of K and ua is not a prefix of a word in $[K^\omega]$. Since N was deadlock-free, there is some extension ub that is a prefix of K such that b is enabled after executing u. If a and b are dependent and they are both enabled, in a clustered FC-dag they have the same locations, and ua would be a prefix of K as well. Hence a and b are independent and we can commute them. We apply this argument repeatedly to increase the length of the prefix; but since K is a finite language, after some point we will find that $w = uav$ for some $u \in [K]$ after which a is enabled, hence a is enabled at the initial global state of N. We can remove this prefix and again continue the argument. This shows that w is in $[K^\omega]$, a contradiction. $\qquad\square$

For the expression $par(e_1, e_2)$, all occurrences of letters in e_1 are independent of those in e_2, so that the net corresponding to them is obtained by taking the disjoint union of the two subnets, and its language is the shuffle of the two sublanguages. Clearly the size of the constructed system is $O(wd(e_1)) + O(wd(e_2))$. So we conclude:

Theorem 11. *For every ω-expression e, there is a live and structurally cyclic FC-product of size $O(wd(e))$ accepting $Lang(e)$.*

We put this together with our earlier result on connected expressions. The FC-products constructed are not necessarily live.

Corollary 12. *For every expression e which is a shuffle of connected expressions and ω-expressions, there is a structurally cyclic FC-product accepting $Lang(e)$. Further, the emptiness of the language of such expressions can be checked in NP. For ω-T-expressions, the time complexity is $O(wd(e)^2)$.*

5   FC-Products to Expressions

In this section we discuss how to build language equivalent expressions for a given FC-product. We follow the same strategy as in the previous section, working through dags and FC-dags before tackling the general case.

Lemma 13. *Let $N = (P, \rightarrow, p_0)$ be a dag. Then there exists an equivalent sum s for its language. The alphabetic width of this expression is quadratic in N and it can be computed in time quadratic in N.*

Proof. First, we delete all nodes unreachable from p_0 and then apply Kleene's theorem. Each transition appears in a path and the length of each path is linear in N which gives a quadratic upper bound. □

Next, we construct expressions for FC-dags. We do not check whether the expression has deadlocks.

Lemma 14. *Let $N[\rho]$ be a connected FC-dag. There is a connected clustered expression c for $Lang(N[\rho])$ of alphabetic width $O(|N|^2)$ which can be computed in $O(|N|^3)$ time.*

Proof. Using Lemma 13, we obtain in quadratic time equivalent sum expressions s_i of size quadratic in the alphabetic width, for each component of the product. The renaming ρ satisfies the property that transitions labelled the same have the same locations. Hence we can consider the expression formed by taking $fsync$ expressions of the s_i, taken in some order. Since the FC-dag was a free choice net, each synchronization will be clustered. Its alphabetic width is quadratic in the size of N. □

Finally we have a cubic time algorithm from live structurally cyclic FC-products to ω-expressions.

Theorem 15. *Let $N[\rho]$ be a live, structurally cyclic product FC-automaton. Then we can compute in cubic time an ω-expression of alphabetic width $O(|N|^2)$ for the accepted language.*

Proof. Consider $N[\rho]$ a given live, structurally cyclic FC-product. We first divide it up into strongly connected components and deal with them separately. This can be done in time $O(|N|)$.

Now we adopt a small trick. Make a copy P_0' of the places P_0 in the initial global state and change the system so that the edges coming into P_0 are replaced by edges into the corresponding places of P_0'. Since P_0 is a feedback vertex set, the resulting net system $N'[\rho]$ is a connected deadlock-free FC-dag of size $O(|N|)$.

By Lemma 14 we can compute in $O(|N|^3)$ time a connected expression c of alphabetic width $O(|N|^2)$ for this FC-dag. We claim the expression c^ω describes the language of the original net system (N, M_0). The proof follows the same arguments as in Lemma 10.

For each SCC, use the argument above, and then use the *par* operator to obtain the shuffle of the languages. This preserves both the time complexity and the expression's alphabetic width. □

We can extend the result above to deal with product systems which are not necessarily live, but structural cyclicity is crucially used. The constructed expression is not checked for deadlocks.

Corollary 16. *Let $N[\rho]$ be a structurally cyclic product FC-system. Then we can compute in polynomial time a shuffle of connected and ω-expressions, of alphabetic width polynomial in $|N|$, for the accepted language.*

Proof. If a dag synchronizes with a strongly connected product, the initial global state of the resulting system will not be live. We unfold the given product into a dag. For example, if path abc synchronizes with circuit $debfcgh$ on b and c, we replace the circuit by the path $debfcghde$ where the d and e transitions can occur twice, but the synchronizations occur once.

When repeating this process, some synchronizations might occur more than once. For example, if the erstwhile circuit $debfcgh$ synchronized with circuit $xyzd$ on d, the second circuit is now replaced by path $xyzdxyzdxyz$ with two occurrences of the synchronization d.

Using this idea, we can modify the algorithm in the proof of Theorem 15 to first cover the reachable parts of the given product system with dags and strongly connected components, then convert the non-live part into equivalent dags, finally obtaining an FC-product which is divided into connected dags which are not live (which might blow up this part of the net to a size $O(|N|^2)$), and live strongly connected components with a feedback vertex set as initial state, which are not modified. Now we use the two preceding theorems to provide connected expressions and ω-expressions. The final expression is a shuffle of these.   □

Finally, the algorithms of this section can be seen to produce T-sequences, connected T-expressions and ω-T-expressions in case we are given a product T-system which is path-like, a T-dag and live, respectively, since T-systems are structurally cyclic. Thus we have efficient Kleene characterizations for product T-systems as well.

6   Conclusion

In this paper we have shown Kleene theorems for the class of acyclic product T-systems and live product T-systems, and also over the corresponding subclasses of FC-products with a restriction to structural cyclicity. Using in one direction a Berry-Sethi type algorithm [BeSe86] we have obtained a polynomial time algorithm with access to an NP oracle. In the other direction we have made use of the condition of structural cyclicity to obtain a polynomial time algorithm.

There are several avenues for further research. Perhaps the complexity can be improved from FP^{NP}. We would like to extend our work to deal with cyclic free choice product systems; from a conceptual viewpoint we are interested in seeing if the polynomial time reachability algorithms for live, cyclic and 1-bounded free choice nets can fall out of this kind of algebraic structure. It is not clear if the same idea extends to all 1-bounded free choice nets.

References

[Ant96]   Antimirov, V.: Partial derivatives of regular expressions and finite automaton constructions. Theoret. Comput. Sci. 155, 291–319 (1996)

[Arn94]   Arnold, A.: Finite transition systems. Prentice-Hall, Englewood Cliffs (1994)

[BeSe86]   Berry, G., Sethi, R.: From regular expressions to deterministic automata. Theoret. Comp. Sci. 48(3), 117–126 (1986)

[BeSh83]   Best, E., Shields, M.: Some equivalence results for free choice and simple nets and on the periodicity of live free choice nets. In: Ausiello, G., Protasi, M. (eds.) CAAP 1983. LNCS, vol. 159, pp. 141–154. Springer, Heidelberg (1983)

[BV84]   Best, E., Voss, K.: Free choice systems have home states. Acta Inform. 21, 89–100 (1984)

[BMc63]   Brzozowski, J.A., McCluskey, E.J.: Signal flow graph techniques for sequential circuit state diagrams. IEEE Trans. Electr. Comput. EC-12, 67–76 (1963)

[CH74]   Campbell, R.H., Habermann, A.N.: The specification of process synchronization by path expressions. In: Gelenbe, E., Kaiser, C. (eds.) Proc. Operating Systems Conference. LNCS, vol. 16, pp. 89–102 (1974)

[CHEP71]   Commoner, F., Holt, A.W., Even, S., Pnueli, A.: Marked directed graphs. J. Comp. Syst. Sci. 5(5), 511–523 (1971)

[DE95]   Desel, J., Esparza, J.: Free choice Petri nets, Cambridge (1995)

[DR95]   Diekert, V., Rozenberg, G. (eds.): The book of traces. World Scientific, Singapore (1995)

[EZ76]   Ehrenfeucht, A., Zeiger, P.: Complexity measures for regular expressions. J. Comp. Syst. Sci. 12, 134–146 (1976)

[GR92]   Garg, V.K., Ragunath, M.T.: Concurrent regular expressions and their relationship to Petri nets. Theoret. Comp. Sci. 96(2), 285–304 (1992)

[GL73]   Genrich, H.J., Lautenbach, K.: Synchronisationsgraphen. Acta Inform. 2, 143–161 (1973)

[Gra81]   Grabowski, J.: On partial languages. Fund. Inform. IV(2), 427–498 (1981)

[GH08]   Gruber, H., Holzer, M.: Finite automata, digraph connectivity, and regular expression size. In: Aceto, L., Damgård, I., Goldberg, L.A., Halldórsson, M.M., Ingólfsdóttir, A., Walukiewicz, I. (eds.) ICALP 2008, Part II. LNCS, vol. 5126, pp. 39–50. Springer, Heidelberg (2008)

[Hack72]   Hack, M.H.T.: Analysis of production schemata by Petri nets. Project MAC Report TR-94. MIT (1972)

[Hoa85]   Hoare, C.A.R.: Communicating sequential processes. Prentice-Hall, Englewood Cliffs (1985)

[JR91]   Jiang, T., Ravikumar, B.: A note on the space complexity of some decision problems for finite automata. Inf. Proc. Lett. 40(1), 25–31 (1991)

[Kle56]   Kleene, S.C.: Representation of events in nerve nets and finite automata. In: Shannon, C.E., McCarthy, J. (eds.) Automata Studies, Princeton, pp. 3–41 (1956)

[Lod06a]   Lodaya, K.: Product automata and process algebra. In: Pandya, P.K., Hung, D.v. (eds.) Proc. 4th SEFM, Pune, pp. 128–136. IEEE, Los Alamitos (2006)

[Lod06b]   Lodaya, K.: A regular viewpoint on processes and algebra. Acta Cybernetica 17(4), 751–763 (2006)

[LRR03]   Lodaya, K., Ranganayakulu, D., Rangarajan, K.: Hierarchical structure of
          1-safe petri nets. In: Saraswat, V.A. (ed.) ASIAN 2003. LNCS, vol. 2896,
          pp. 173–187. Springer, Heidelberg (2003)
[LW00]   Lodaya, K., Weil, P.: Series-parallel languages and the bounded-width
          property. Theoret. Comp. Sci. 237(1-2), 347–380 (2000)
[Maz77]   Mazurkiewicz, A.: Concurrent program schemes and their interpretations.
          DAIMI Report PB-78 (1977)
[Mil89]   Milner, R.: Communication and concurrency. Prentice-Hall, Englewood
          Cliffs (1989)
[Moh99]   Mohalik, S.K.: Local presentations for finite state distributed systems, PhD
          thesis, University of Madras (1999)
[MR02]   Mohalik, S., Ramanujam, R.: Distributed automata in an assumption-
          commitment framework. Sādhanā 27, part 2, 209–250 (2002)
[MS97]   Mukund, M., Sohoni, M.A.: Keeping track of the latest gossip in a dis-
          tributed system. Distr. Comp. 10(3), 117–127 (1997)
[Och85]   Ochmański, E.: Regular behaviour of concurrent systems. Bull. EATCS 27,
          56–67 (1985)
[Pet62]   Petri, C.-A.: Fundamentals of a theory of asynchronous information flow.
          In: Popplewell, C.M. (ed.) Proc. IFIP, Munich, pp. 386–390. North-
          Holland, Amsterdam (1962)
[RL03]   Ranganayukulu, D., Lodaya, K.: Infinite series-parallel posets of 1-safe
          nets. In: Thangavel, P. (ed.) Proc. Algorithms and Artificial Systems,
          Chennai, pp. 107–124. Allied (2003)
[TT07]   Tesson, P., Thérien, D.: Logic meets algebra: the case of regular languages.
          Log. Meth. Comput. Sci. 3(1) (2007)
[TV84]   Thiagarajan, P.S., Voss, K.: A fresh look at free choice nets. Inf.
          Contr. 61(2), 85–113 (1984)
[Thi96]   Thiagarajan, P.S.: Regular trace event structures. BRICS Report RS-96-
          32. Dept. of Computer Science, Aarhus University (1996)
[Weil04] Weil, P.: Algebraic recognizability of languages. In: Fiala, J., Koubek, V.,
          Kratochvíl, J. (eds.) MFCS 2004. LNCS, vol. 3153, pp. 149–175. Springer,
          Heidelberg (2004)
[Zie87]   Zielonka, W.: Notes on finite asynchronous automata. RAIRO Inform. Th.
          Appl. 21(2), 99–135 (1987)

Descriptional Complexity of Two-Way Pushdown Automata with Restricted Head Reversals[*]

Andreas Malcher[1], Carlo Mereghetti[2], and Beatrice Palano[2]

[1] Institut für Informatik, Universität Giessen
Arndtstr. 2, 35392 Giessen, Germany
malcher@informatik.uni-giessen.de
[2] Dipartimento di Scienze dell'Informazione, Università degli Studi di Milano
via Comelico 39/41, 20135 Milano, Italy
{mereghetti,palano}@dsi.unimi.it

Abstract. Two-way nondeterministic pushdown automata (2PDA) are classical nondeterministic pushdown automata (PDA) enhanced with two-way motion of the input head. In this paper, the subclass of 2PDA accepting bounded languages and making at most a constant number of input head turns is studied with respect to descriptional complexity aspects. In particular, the effect of reducing the number of pushdown reversals to a constant number is of interest. It turns out that this reduction leads to an exponential blow-up in case of nondeterministic devices, and to a doubly-exponential blow-up in case of deterministic devices. If the restriction on boundedness of the languages considered and on the finiteness of the number of head turns is dropped, the resulting trade-offs are no longer bounded by recursive functions, and so-called non-recursive trade-offs are shown.

Keywords: two-way pushdown automata; bounded head reversals; descriptional complexity; bounded languages.

1 Introduction

Descriptional complexity is an area of theoretical computer science in which one of the main questions is how succinctly a formal language can be described by a formalism in comparison with other formalisms. A fundamental result is the exponential trade-off between nondeterministic and deterministic finite automata [18]. A further exponential trade-off is known to exist between unambiguous and deterministic finite automata, whereas the trade-offs between alternating and deterministic finite automata [13] as well as between deterministic pushdown automata (PDA) and deterministic finite automata [21] are bounded by doubly-exponential functions. Other doubly-exponential trade-offs exist between

---

[*] Partially supported by CRUI/DAAD under the project "Programma Vigoni: Descriptional Complexity of Non-Classical Computational Models".

M. Holzer, M. Kutrib, and G. Pighizzini (Eds.): DCFS 2011, LNCS 6808, pp. 248–260, 2011.

the complement of a regular expression and conventional regular expressions [8], and between constant height PDA and deterministic finite automata [2].

Apart from such trade-offs bounded by recursive functions, Meyer and Fischer [18] first showed the existence of trade-offs which cannot be bounded by any recursive function – so-called non-recursive trade-offs – between context-free grammars generating regular languages and finite automata. Nowadays, many non-recursive trade-offs are known, and surveys on recursive and non-recursive trade-offs may be found in [3,7].

In this paper, we study the descriptional complexity of two-way pushdown automata (2PDA) which are conventional PDA with the possibility of moving the input head in both directions. 2PDA are a strong computational model: it is currently unknown whether their computational power equals that of linear bounded automata. Moreover, it is not known whether or not nondeterministic and deterministic variants describe the same language class. Thus, we consider here the subclass of those 2PDA where the number of reversals of the input head is bounded by some fixed constant. These head-turn bounded 2PDA have nice decidable properties when the languages accepted are letter-bounded (bounded, for short), i.e., they are subsets of $a_1^* a_2^* \cdots a_m^*$, where $a_1, a_2, \ldots, a_m$ are pairwise distinct symbols. In this case, the languages accepted are semilinear [11] and, due to decidability results on semilinear languages shown in [4], one obtains that the questions of emptiness, universality, inclusion, and equivalence are decidable. It is shown in [12] that these questions are decidable also for deterministic 2PDA where the number of turns of the pushdown store is bounded by some constant.

This paper is organized as follows. In Section 2, we formally introduce 2PDA, their size, and recall notions on context-free grammars. In Section 3, we obtain two recursive trade-offs for 2PDA accepting bounded languages. First, we consider the nondeterministic case and compare head-turn bounded 2PDA versus head-turn bounded and pushdown-turn bounded 2PDA. It turns out that the reduction of pushdown reversals leads to an exponential trade-off. This generalizes a similar result for one-way PDA: the trade-off between PDA and PDA with a fixed finite number of pushdown reversals is non-recursive when arbitrary languages are considered [16] whereas the trade-off becomes exponential in case of bounded languages [17]. As a second result, we convert head-turn bounded nondeterministic and deterministic 2PDA into equivalent deterministic devices which are additionally pushdown-turn bounded, obtaining a doubly-exponential trade-off. The main idea in the conversion is to reduce membership of bounded languages generated by context-free grammars to solving linear systems of Diophantine equations, which is shown to be manageable by deterministic 2PDA. In a second step, we generalize this result for the conversion of 2PDA with certain properties.

Finally, in Section 4 we consider arbitrary languages instead of bounded languages. We get non-recursive trade-offs between two-way and one-way devices. Furthermore, non-recursive trade-offs exist between 2PDA with an arbitrary and a constant number of head reversals both in the deterministic and nondeterministic case.

2   Preliminaries and Definitions

We assume that the reader is familiar with basic notions in formal language theory (see, e.g., [10]). The set of natural numbers, with 0, is here denoted by $\mathbb{N}$. Let Σ^* denote the set of all words over the finite alphabet Σ. The empty word is denoted by λ, and $\Sigma^+ = \Sigma^* \setminus \{\lambda\}$. The reversal of a word w is denoted by w^R, and for the length of w we write $|w|$.

The following definition adapts the definition for two-way multi-head automata given in [9] to two-way pushdown automata. A two-way pushdown automaton can be obtained by equipping a finite automaton with a pushdown storage. We have a single read-only input tape whose inscription is the input word in between two end markers. The input head can move freely on the tape but not beyond the end markers. Formally:

Definition 1. *A nondeterministic two-way pushdown automaton (2PDA) is a system* $\mathcal{M} = \langle Q, \Sigma, \Gamma, \delta, \triangleright, \triangleleft, q_0, Z_0, F \rangle$, *where:*

1. *Q is the finite set of internal states,*
2. *Σ is the set of input symbols,*
3. *Γ is the set of pushdown symbols,*
4. *$\triangleright \notin \Sigma$ and $\triangleleft \notin \Sigma$ are the left and right end markers, respectively,*
5. *$q_0 \in Q$ is the initial state,*
6. *$Z_0 \in \Gamma$ is the initial pushdown symbol,*
7. *$F \subseteq Q$ is the set of accepting states, and*
8. *δ is the partial transition function mapping $Q \times (\Sigma \cup \{\triangleright, \triangleleft\}) \times \Gamma$ into the subsets of $Q \times \Gamma^* \times \{-1, 0, 1\}$, where 1 means to move the head one square to the right, -1 means to move it one square to the left, and 0 means to keep the head on the current square. Whenever $(q', \gamma', d) \in \delta(q, a, \gamma)$ is defined, then $d \in \{0, 1\}$ if $a = \triangleright$, and $d \in \{-1, 0\}$ if $a = \triangleleft$.*

A 2PDA starts with its head on the first square of the tape. It *halts* when the transition function is not defined for the current situation.

A *configuration* of a 2PDA $\mathcal{M} = \langle Q, \Sigma, \Gamma, \delta, \triangleright, \triangleleft, q_0, Z_0, F \rangle$ at a given time $t \geq 0$ is a 4-tuple $c_t = (w, q, \gamma, p)$ where $w \in \Sigma^*$ is the input, $q \in Q$ is the current state, $\gamma \in \Gamma^*$ is the current pushdown content, and $p \in \{0, 1, \ldots, |w| + 1\}$ gives the current head position. If p is 0, then the head is scanning the symbol $\triangleright$, if it satisfies $1 \leq p \leq |w|$, then the head is scanning the pth letter of w, and if it is $|w| + 1$, then the head is scanning the symbol $\triangleleft$. The *initial configuration* for input w is set to $(w, q_0, Z_0, 1)$. Along its computation, $\mathcal{M}$ runs through a sequence of configurations. One step from a configuration to one of its successor configurations is denoted by $\vdash$. Let $w = a_1 a_2 \cdots a_n$ be the input, $a_0 = \triangleright$, $a_{n+1} = \triangleleft$, and $Z \in \Gamma$ be the topmost pushdown symbol. Then, we set $(w, q, Z\gamma, p) \vdash (w, q', \gamma'\gamma, p + d)$ if and only if $(q', \gamma', d) \in \delta(q, a_p, Z)$. As usual we define the reflexive, transitive closure of $\vdash$ by $\vdash^*$. Note that, due to the restriction of the transition function, the head cannot move beyond the end markers.

The language accepted by the 2PDA $\mathcal{M}$ is precisely the set of words w on which $\mathcal{M}$ has some computation on $\triangleright w \triangleleft$ halting in an accepting state:

$$L(\mathcal{M}) = \{\, w \in \Sigma^* \mid (w, q_0, Z_0, 1) \vdash^* (w, f, \gamma, p), \text{ with } f \in F$$
$$\text{and } \mathcal{M} \text{ halts in } (w, f, \gamma, p) \,\}.$$

If, on any element of $Q \times (\Sigma \cup \{\triangleright, \triangleleft\}) \times \Gamma$, the transition function δ is either undefined or a singleton, then the two-way pushdown automaton is said to be *deterministic*. Deterministic two-way pushdown automata are denoted by 2DPDA. In case the head never moves to the left, the pushdown automaton is said to be *one-way*. Nondeterministic and deterministic one-way pushdown automata are denoted by PDA and DPDA, respectively. The family of all languages accepted by a device of some type X is denoted by $\mathscr{L}(X)$, where $X \in \{\text{DPDA}, \text{PDA}, \text{2DPDA}, \text{2PDA}\}$.

A two-way pushdown automaton is said to be *head-turn bounded* (denoted by the prefix *htb*) if the number of reversals the input head makes is bounded by some constant. A pushdown automaton is said to be *pushdown-turn bounded* (denoted by the prefix *ptb*), if the number of alternations between increasing and decreasing the pushdown is bounded by some constant. The prefix *(htb,ptb)* denotes pushdown automata which are both head-turn bounded and pushdown-turn bounded.

In this paper, we measure the size $|\mathcal{M}|$ of a PDA $\mathcal{M}$ by the product of the number of states, the number of pushdown symbols, the number of input symbols, and the maximum length $\mu(\mathcal{M})$ of pushdown symbols appearing in the transition rules, i.e., $|\mathcal{M}| = |Q| \cdot |\Gamma| \cdot |\Sigma| \cdot \mu(\mathcal{M})$. (See also the discussion in [7] on PDA size measuring). Furthermore, we consider PDA and 2PDA in a certain normal form, and we make, without loss of generality, the following assumptions about pushdown automata (see [20]):

1. At the start of the computation the pushdown store contains only the start symbol Z_0; this symbol is never pushed on or popped from the stack;
2. the input is accepted if and only if the automaton reaches a final state, the pushdown store only contains Z_0 and all the input has been scanned;
3. if the automaton moves the input head, then no operations are performed on the stack;
4. every push operation adds exactly one symbol on the stack.

The transition function δ of a PDA is then a mapping from $Q \times (\Sigma \cup \{\lambda\}) \times \Gamma$ into the subsets of $Q \times (\{-, pop\} \cup \{push(A) \mid A \in \Gamma\})$, where '$-$' means that the stack is not modified. The partial transition function δ of a 2PDA is a mapping from $Q \times (\Sigma \cup \{\triangleright, \triangleleft\}) \times \Gamma$ into the subsets of $Q \times (\{-, pop\} \cup \{push(A) \mid A \in \Gamma\}) \times \{-1, 0, 1\}$. By introducing new states for every transition of a given pushdown automaton, the following lemma can be shown (see also [7]):

Lemma 2. *Let $\mathcal{M} = \langle Q, \Sigma, \Gamma, \delta, \triangleright, \triangleleft, q_0, Z_0, F \rangle$ be a 2PDA, 2DPDA, or PDA. Then, an equivalent 2PDA, 2DPDA, or PDA, respectively, in normal form of size $O(|\mathcal{M}|)$ can be constructed.*

A *context-free grammar* (CFG) is a 4-tuple $\mathcal{G} = (V, \Sigma, P, S)$, where V is the set of variables, Σ is the set of terminals, V and Σ are disjoint sets, $S \in V$ is the initial symbol and $P \subseteq V \times (V \cup \Sigma)^*$ is the finite set of productions. A production $(A, \alpha) \in P$ is denoted by $A \rightarrow \alpha$. The relations $\Rightarrow$, $\overset{*}{\Rightarrow}$, and $\overset{+}{\Rightarrow}$ are defined in the usual way (see, e.g., [10]). The language generated by $\mathcal{G}$ is the set $L(\mathcal{G}) = \{x \in \Sigma^* \mid S \overset{*}{\Rightarrow} x\}$. Given $\alpha, \beta \in (V \cup \Sigma)^*$, if θ is a derivation of β from α, then we write $\theta : \alpha \overset{*}{\Rightarrow} \beta$. A useful representation of derivations of context-free grammars is provided by *parse trees*. A parse tree (or *tree*, for short) for the context-free grammar $\mathcal{G}$ is a labeled tree satisfying the following conditions:

1. Each internal node is labeled by a variable in V,
2. each leaf is labeled by either a variable, a terminal, or λ; however, if the leaf is labeled λ, then it must be the only child of its parent,
3. if an internal node is labeled with a variable A, and its children, from left to right, are labeled with $X_1, X_2, \cdots, X_k \in V \cup \Sigma$, then $A \rightarrow X_1 X_2 \cdots X_k$ is a production of $\mathcal{G}$.

If T is a parse tree whose root is labeled with a variable $A \in V$ and such that the labels of the leaves, from left to right, form a string $\alpha \in (V \cup \Sigma)^*$, then we write $T : A \overset{*}{\Rightarrow} \alpha$. Furthermore, we indicate as $\nu(T)$ the set of variables which appear as labels of some nodes in T.

3   Head Turns on Bounded Languages

In this section, we analyze the size of several variants of head-turn bounded pushdown automata when accepting bounded languages. We recall that a *(letter) bounded* language is any set $L \subseteq a_1^* a_2^* \cdots a_m^*$, for pairwise distinct symbols $a_1, a_2, \ldots, a_m$; the *size of L* is m.

Let us begin by showing an analog to a result given in [17]. There it is shown that, given a language $L \subseteq a_1^* a_2^* \cdots a_m^*$ accepted by a PDA of size n, then L can also be accepted by a PDA with $m - 1$ pushdown turns and having size $2^{O(n^2)}$. Here, we generalize this result by considering a wider class of bounded languages.

Theorem 3. *Let $L \subseteq a_1^* a_2^* \cdots a_m^*$ be accepted by some htb-2PDA of size n performing at most k head turns. Then, L can also be accepted by some (htb,ptb)-2PDA of size $2^{O(n^2)}$ with k head turns and $(m + 1)(k + 1)$ pushdown turns.*

Proof. (sketch) Let $\mathcal{M}$ be an htb-2PDA of size n performing k head turns and accepting L. Without loss of generality, we may assume that $\mathcal{M}$ is *sweeping*, i.e., it performs head turns at the end markers only. We also may assume that $\mathcal{M}$ accepts exactly when reading $\triangleright$, after an odd number of head turns. It is easy to see that both assumptions increase the size of $\mathcal{M}$ at most by some linear factor.

Since $\mathcal{M}$ performs k head turns, the input read by $\mathcal{M}$ can be understood in a linearized form as a subset of $I = I_1 I_2 \cdots I_{(k+1)/2} \triangleleft$, where, for $1 \leq i \leq (k+1)/2$, $I_i = \triangleright_i a_{1,i,1}^* a_{2,i,1}^* \cdots a_{m,i,1}^* \triangleleft_i a_{m,i,2}^* a_{m-1,i,2}^* \cdots a_{1,i,2}^*$. All symbols occurring in the sets I_i are chosen to be pairwise distinct. It is easy to construct a one-way PDA $\mathcal{M}_1$ simulating $\mathcal{M}$ while reading an input from I and interpreting symbols $a_{j,i,1}$, $a_{j,i,2}$, $\triangleright_i$, and $\triangleleft_i$ as symbols a_j, $\triangleright$, and $\triangleleft$ for $1 \leq j \leq m$ and $1 \leq i \leq (k+1)/2$. Clearly, $\mathcal{M}_1$ has size $O(n)$ and accepts a bounded context-free language of size $\frac{k+1}{2}(2m+2)+1 = (m+1)(k+1)+1$. In particular, all words accepted by $\mathcal{M}$ are accepted by $\mathcal{M}_1$ as well by using the above interpretation. Owing to a result on bounded context-free languages given in [17], we can turn $\mathcal{M}_1$ into an equivalent finite-turn PDA $\mathcal{M}_2$ of size $2^{O(n^2)}$ performing at most $(m+1)(k+1)$ many pushdown turns.

Now, we can construct an (htb,ptb)-2PDA $\mathcal{M}_3$ on input $\triangleright x \triangleleft$ where $x \in a_1^* a_2^* \cdots a_m^*$, which simulates $\mathcal{M}_2$ on the linearized input which is a subset of I. Observe that $\mathcal{M}_3$ performs k head turns and at most $(m+1)(k+1)$ many pushdown turns. Furthermore, $\mathcal{M}_3$ has size $2^{O(n^2)}$.   □

Thus, we get an exponential upper bound for the reduction of pushdown turns also in the two-way case.

The next questions we are going to tackle concern the following trade-offs:

(1) htb-2PDA $\longrightarrow$ htb-2DPDA,
(2) htb-2PDA $\longrightarrow$ (htb,ptb)-2DPDA,
(3) (htb,ptb)-2PDA $\longrightarrow$ (htb,ptb)-2DPDA,
(4) htb-2DPDA $\longrightarrow$ (htb,ptb)-2DPDA.

To approach problem (2), we again recall some notions and results from [17].

Let us consider an alphabet $\Sigma = \{a_1, a_2, \ldots, a_m\}$ and a CFG $\mathcal{G} = (V, \Sigma, P, S)$ in Chomsky normal form with h variables, generating a subset of $a_1^* a_2^* \cdots a_m^*$. Without loss of generality, we can suppose that each variable of $\mathcal{G}$ is *useful*, i.e., for each $A \in V$, there exist terminal strings u, v, w, such that $S \overset{*}{\Rightarrow} uAw \overset{*}{\Rightarrow} uvw$. The following property is proved for $\mathcal{G}$:

Lemma 4. *For each variable $A \in V$, an index $1 \leq l \leq m$ $(1 \leq r \leq m$, resp.$)$ exists such that if $A \overset{+}{\Rightarrow} uAv$, with $u, v \in \Sigma^*$, then $u \in a_l^*$ $(v \in a_r^*$, resp.$)$. Furthermore, if at least one derivation $A \overset{+}{\Rightarrow} uAv$ exists with $u \neq \lambda$, $(v \neq \lambda$, resp.$)$ then such an l $(r$, resp.$)$ is unique.*

A *partial derivation tree* (or *partial tree*, for short) $U : A \overset{*}{\Rightarrow} vAx$ is a parse tree whose root is labeled with a variable A and all the leaves, with the exception of one whose label is the same variable A, are labeled with terminal symbols. Given a partial tree $U : A \overset{*}{\Rightarrow} vAx$, any derivation tree $T : S \overset{*}{\Rightarrow} z$ with $A \in \nu(T)$ can be "pumped" using U, by replacing a node labeled A in T with the subtree U. In this way, a new tree $T' : S \overset{*}{\Rightarrow} z'$ is obtained, where $z' = uvwxy$, such that $z = uwy$, $S \overset{*}{\Rightarrow} uAy$, and $A \overset{*}{\Rightarrow} w$. Moreover, $\nu(T') = \nu(T) \cup \nu(U)$.

On the other hand, any derivation tree producing a sufficiently long terminal string can be obtained by pumping a derivation tree of a shorter string with a partial tree. By applying the pumping lemma for context–free languages (see, e.g., [10]) several times, one can prove that any derivation tree can be obtained by starting from a derivation tree of a "short" string (namely, a string of length at most 2^{h-1}) and iteratively pumping it with "small" partial trees:

Lemma 5. *Let $\mathcal{G}$ be a CFG in Chomsky normal form having h variables, and $T : S \overset{*}{\Rightarrow} z$ be a derivation tree of a string $z \in \Sigma^*$. If $|z| > 2^{h-1}$, then we can write $z = uvwxy$, with $0 < |vx| < 2^h$, such that trees $T' : S \overset{*}{\Rightarrow} uwy$ and $T'' : A \overset{\pm}{\Rightarrow} vAx$ exist satisfying $A \in \nu(T')$, $A \overset{\pm}{\Rightarrow} w$ and $\nu(T) = \nu(T') \cup \nu(T'')$.*

This lemma and the following definition enable us to settle a counting argument that will turn out to be useful in our constructions:

Definition 6. *Let $\mathcal{G}$ be a CFG in Chomsky normal form having h variables. Let $T : S \overset{*}{\Rightarrow} z$ be a derivation tree for a string $z \in L(\mathcal{G})$ of length at most 2^{h-1}. Then, $\nu^*(T)$ denotes the set of all variables occurring in T plus those variables occurring in partial trees which can be pumped into T. Finally, $\tau(\mathcal{G}) = \{(z, \nu^*(T)) \mid T : S \overset{*}{\Rightarrow} z \text{ and } |z| \leq 2^{h-1} \text{ for some tree } T\}$.*

The cardinality of $\tau(\mathcal{G})$ can be upper bounded by the number of variables in $\mathcal{G}$ and the size of bounded language:

Lemma 7. *Let $\mathcal{G}$ be a CFG in Chomsky normal form having h variables, such that $L(\mathcal{G}) \subseteq a_1^* a_2^* \cdots a_m^*$. Then, $|\tau(\mathcal{G})| \leq 2^{h(m+1)}$.*

Proof. Clearly, there exist at most 2^h different sets $\nu^*(T)$. Let us now evaluate the number of all possible initial terminal strings in $L(\mathcal{G})$ of length not exceeding 2^{h-1}. Such a number is clearly bounded by the cardinality of the set $A = \{a_1^{x_1} a_2^{x_2} \cdots a_m^{x_m} \mid x_i \in \mathbb{N} \text{ and } x_1 + x_2 + \cdots + x_m \leq 2^{h-1}\}$. Moreover, it is easy to see that the number of strings in A of length i coincides with the number of non-negative solutions of the equation $x_1 + x_2 + \cdots + x_m = i$, which is $\binom{i+m-1}{i}$ (see, e.g., [19]). Thus, we get $|A| = \sum_{i=0}^{2^{h-1}} \binom{i+m-1}{i} = \binom{2^{h-1}+m}{2^{h-1}} \leq (2^{h-1}+1)(2^{h-1})^{m-1} \leq 2^{hm}$, since $\frac{2^{h-1}+i}{i} \leq \frac{2^{h-1} \cdot i}{i} = 2^{h-1}$ for every $i \geq 2$ and using the formula $\sum_{k=0}^{m} \binom{k+n}{k} = \binom{n+m+1}{m}$ (see, e.g., [19]). Hence, the claimed result follows. □

We are now ready to show how the number of variables in $\mathcal{G}$ and the size of $L(\mathcal{G})$ may bound the size of an equivalent 2DPDA and the number of its head and pushdown turns:

Theorem 8. *Let $\mathcal{G}$ be a CFG in Chomsky normal form having h variables, such that $L(\mathcal{G}) \subseteq a_1^* a_2^* \cdots a_m^*$. Then, an equivalent (htb,ptb)-2DPDA $\mathcal{M}$ can be constructed whose size, as well as number of head and pushdown turns, is bounded by a doubly-exponential function of h.*

Proof. The key idea is to consider all derivation trees for strings in $L(\mathcal{G})$ of length up to 2^{h-1}. According to Lemma 5, any string in $L(\mathcal{G})$ is obtained by pumping these derivation trees with suitable partial derivation trees. Now, let $(z, \nu^*(T))$ be an element of $\tau(\mathcal{G})$. The words which can be derived by pumping from T are the initial string z with $|z| \leq 2^{h-1}$ and all the strings which can be obtained by pumping some variable $A \in \nu^*(T)$ with a partial derivation tree. By Lemma 4, any such variable can insert strings v_A and w_A, each one built on a different symbol from $\{a_1, a_2, \ldots, a_m\}$ (unless, of course, $v_A = \lambda$ or $w_A = \lambda$). Furthermore, by Lemma 5, the length of $v_A w_A$ is bounded by $2^h - 1$. Thus, the number of different lengths for v_A and w_A is easily seen to be bounded by $\sum_{i=1}^{2^h-1}(i+1) \leq 2^{2h}$. Considering this bound for all variables in $\nu^*(T)$, we obtain at most $h \cdot 2^{2h}$ pairs of different lengths which may be inserted.

Let us now discuss how a 2DPDA may check whether an input string $w = a_1^{n_1} a_2^{n_2} \cdots a_m^{n_m}$ belongs to $L(\mathcal{G})$. We know that $w \in L(\mathcal{G})$ implies that w can be derived starting with some pair $(z, \nu^*(T))$ from $\tau(\mathcal{G})$. So, let $z = a_1^{z_1} a_2^{z_2} \cdots a_m^{z_m}$ and $(s_1, t_1), (s_2, t_2), \ldots, (s_k, t_k)$, with $k \leq h \cdot 2^{2h}$, be an enumeration of strings that may be inserted by pumping some variable from $\nu^*(T)$. It is not hard to see that membership of w in $L(\mathcal{G})$ can be tested by solving a suitable linear system of Diophantine equations. Indeed, for $1 \leq i \leq m$, we define $\alpha_i : \Sigma^* \to \mathbb{N}$ as $\alpha_i(x) = |x|$, if $x \in a_i^*$, and $\alpha_i(x) = 0$ otherwise. Consider the following system of m equations with variables $m_1, m_2, \ldots, m_k$:

$$n_1 = z_1 + m_1\left(\alpha_1(s_1) + \alpha_1(t_1)\right) + \cdots + m_k\left(\alpha_1(s_k) + \alpha_1(t_k)\right)$$
$$n_2 = z_2 + m_1\left(\alpha_2(s_1) + \alpha_2(t_1)\right) + \cdots + m_k\left(\alpha_2(s_k) + \alpha_2(t_k)\right)$$
$$\cdots$$
$$n_m = z_m + m_1\left(\alpha_m(s_1) + \alpha_m(t_1)\right) + \cdots + m_k\left(\alpha_m(s_k) + \alpha_m(t_k)\right).$$

If the above system has a solution in natural numbers then w can be generated by $\mathcal{G}$. Furthermore, w can be generated by $\mathcal{G}$ if and only if there exists a pair $(z, \nu^*(T))$ from $\tau(\mathcal{G})$ such that its corresponding system of equations has a solution in natural numbers. Thus, we have to construct a 2DPDA which tests sequentially all systems corresponding to pairs $(z, \nu^*(T))$ from $\tau(\mathcal{G})$.

Next, we describe a procedure how a 2DPDA can test whether one linear system of Diophantine equations has a solution in natural numbers. The procedure is sketched in [5,14]. Here, it will be rephrased in a modified way together with an estimation of the size of the corresponding 2DPDA.

The above system of equations can be written as $A \cdot x = b$, where A is a matrix with m rows and k columns containing the lengths of strings to be inserted by pumping, $x = (m_1, m_2, \ldots m_k)^T$, and $b = (n_1 - z_1, n_2 - z_2, \ldots, n_m - z_m)^T$. Now, let r be the rank of A. Then, the system has $k-r$ free variables. It has been shown in [5,14] that if the equation $A \cdot x = b$ has a solution in natural numbers, then it has also a solution in natural numbers where all free variables are bounded by the maximal absolute value Ψ of the determinants of all $r \times r$ submatrices of A. By standard linear algebra, the system $A \cdot x = b$ is transformed into the system

$$\sum_{j=1}^{k} a_{ij}x_j = b_i, \qquad \text{for } i = 1, 2, \ldots, r \quad (*)$$

$$0 = b_i^*, \qquad \text{for } i = r+1, r+2, \ldots, m.$$

We let B be the matrix consisting of the coefficients a_{ij} in $(*)$, b_i^* a sum of b_i and suitably scaled entries b_j, with $1 \leq j \leq r$. We let $b^* = (b_1, \ldots, b_r, b_{r+1}^*, \ldots, b_m^*)^T$. This transformation enables an implementation on 2DPDA.

Let S be an enumeration of all subsets of $\{1, 2, \ldots, k\}$ having cardinality r; clearly, $|S| = \binom{k}{r} \leq k^r$. For all elements $s \in S$ corresponding to sets $L_s = \{l_1, l_2, \ldots, l_r\} \subseteq \{1, 2, \ldots, k\}$, we compute the determinant Δ_s of the submatrix D_s of B formed by the columns in L_s as well as the determinants δ_{ij}^s of D_{ij}^s, where D_{ij}^s is the submatrix formed from D_s by deleting the ith row and jth column $(1 \leq i, j \leq r)$. To test whether the equation $A \cdot x = b$ has a solution in natural numbers for the choice $s \in S$ of variables, a 2DPDA $\mathcal{M}$ works on input $w = a_1^{n_1} a_2^{n_2} \cdots a_m^{n_m}$ as follows. For every combination of integral values $0 \leq y_t < |\Delta_s|$ for the variables x_t, with $t \notin L_s$, $\mathcal{M}$ tries to calculate a non-negative integral value y_j for the variables x_j, with $j \in L_s$, by using Cramer's rule. In detail, $\mathcal{M}$ has to check whether $y_{l_j} = d_j/\Delta_s$, for $l_j \in L_s$, where $d_j = \sum_{i=1}^{r}(-1)^{i+j}\delta_{ij}^s b_i'$ and $b_i' = b_i - \sum_{t \notin L_s} a_{it} y_t$ is a non-negative integer.

To this end, we assume that $\mathcal{M}$ starts from the first input symbol and moves to the right while reading all input symbols a_i which belong to a positive sign $(-1)^{i+j}$ in the sum d_j. For each input symbol read, an appropriate number of symbols is pushed onto the pushdown. This number depends on the value δ_{ij}^s, the choice of values $0 \leq y_t < |\Delta_s|$ for $t \notin L_s$, and on the values a_{it} for $t \notin L_s$. All these values are stored into the states of $\mathcal{M}$. When the input head has reached the right end marker, it reverts its direction and moves to the left while reading all input symbols a_i which belong to a negative sign $(-1)^{i+j}$ in the sum d_j. For each input symbol read, an appropriate number of symbols is popped from the pushdown. Again, this number depends on values stored into the states. When the pushdown store becomes empty while reading the input, d_j is a negative number and the integral test of y_j can be stopped. Otherwise, d_j is a non-negative number which is counted on the pushdown store. Then, y_j can be checked to be a non-negative integer by iteratively popping Δ_s symbols until the pushdown store is empty. We can observe that we need one head-turn and one pushdown-turn for this check. Next, we want to count the number of states needed. Since Δ_s, r values z_i, r signs $(-1)^{i+j}$, r values δ_{ij}^s, $k - r$ values y_t, and $k - r$ values a_{it} have to be stored, we obtain $c_1 \Psi r 2^{h-1} r r \Psi (k-r) \Psi (k-r) 2^h \leq c_1 \Psi^3 r^3 (k-r)^2 2^{2h}$, for some constant c_1, as an upper bound. To test all y_j to be non-negative, we need at most r head turns, at most r pushdown turns, and at most $c_1 \Psi^3 m^4 k^2 2^{2h}$ states, since $r \leq m$. Finally, we have to check whether the values b_i^* are zero for $r+1 \leq i \leq m$. This can be done for each i with one head turn and one pushdown turn analogously to the above construction. Since each b_i^* is a sum of suitably scaled input values n_j and z_i, where the scale factor of each addend is bounded by $\left(2^h\right)^r = 2^{hr}$, we increase the pushdown store adequately when moving from left to right and reading symbols n_j corresponding to a positive sign in the sum of b_i^*. Then, we decrease the pushdown store adequately when moving from right to left and reading symbols n_j corresponding to a negative sign. Finally, the pushdown store is tested for emptiness to decide whether b_i^* is zero. This behavior needs at most $c_2(r+1)2^{hr}$ states for each b_i^* and some constant c_2, and, altogether, at most $c_3(m-r)(r+1)2^{hr}$ states for some constant c_3. Moreover, at most $m - r$ head turns and pushdown turns are needed.

The just described procedure has to be repeated for every combination of integral values $0 \leq y_t < |\Delta_s|$ for the variables x_t, with $t \notin L_s$. This can be done by a 2DPDA which successively repeats the procedure for every combination. Thus, the number of states is increased by the factor $|\Delta_s|^{k-r} \leq \Psi^{k-r}$, and the resulting 2DPDA performs $m\Psi^{k-r}$ head turns and pushdown turns.

Additionally, we have to consider this procedure for every $s \in S$. This increases the number of states, head turns, and pushdown turns by the factor k^r. Finally, we have to consider this procedure also for every $(z, \nu^*(T))$ in $\tau(\mathcal{G})$. By Lemma 7, this increases the number of states, head turns, and pushdown turns by the factor $2^{h(m+1)}$. It is noted in [5] that

$$\Psi \leq r! \max \left\{ \prod_{t=1}^{r} a_{i_t j_t} \mid 1 \leq i_1 < \cdots < i_r \leq r, 1 \leq j_1 < \cdots < j_r \leq k \right\} \leq m! \cdot 2^{hm}.$$

Thus, the number of states needed is bounded by

$$2^{h(m+1)} k^r \Psi^{k-r} \left(c_1 \Psi^3 m^4 k^2 2^{2h} + c_3 m^2 2^{hr} \right) \leq c_4 h^{2m} m^4 \left(m! \right)^{2^{3h}} 2^{m2^{4h}},$$

for some constant c_4, whereas the number of head turns and pushdown turns are both bounded by $m2^{h(m+1)} k^r \Psi^{k-r} \leq m \left(m! \right)^{2^{3h}} h^m 2^{4hm}$. Thus, the number of states as well as the number of head turns and pushdown turns is bounded by a doubly-exponential function of h. □

Theorem 9. *Let $L \subseteq a_1^* a_2^* \cdots a_m^*$ be accepted by some htb-2PDA of size n. Then L can also be accepted by some (htb,ptb)-2DPDA whose size is bounded by a doubly-exponential function of $O(n^2)$.*

Proof. (sketch) Let L be accepted by some htb-2PDA $\mathcal{M}$ in normal form of size n, performing k head turns. As in the proof of Theorem 3, we may assume that $\mathcal{M}$ is sweeping and accepts exactly when reading $\triangleright$ after an odd number of head turns.

Since $\mathcal{M}$ performs k head turns, the input read by $\mathcal{M}$ can be interpreted in a linearized form as a subset of $I = I_1 I_2 \cdots I_{(k+1)/2} \triangleleft$, where, for $1 \leq i \leq (k+1)/2$, $I_i = \triangleright_i a_{1,i,1}^* a_{2,i,1}^* \cdots a_{m,i,1}^* \triangleleft_i a_{m,i,2}^* a_{m-1,i,2}^* \cdots a_{1,i,2}^*$. It is easy to construct a one-way PDA $\mathcal{M}_1$ simulating $\mathcal{M}$ while reading an input from I and interpreting suitably the symbols read. Clearly, $\mathcal{M}_1$ has size $O(n)$ and accepts a bounded context-free language of size $\frac{k+1}{2}(2m+2) + 1 = (m+1)(k+1) + 1$. Again, $\mathcal{M}_1$ accepts at least those suitably interpreted words which are accepted by $\mathcal{M}$, and it can be transformed into an equivalent CFG $\mathcal{G}$ by the standard construction. It may be observed that the resulting CFG $\mathcal{G}$ is nearly in Chomsky normal form due to the fact that $\mu(\mathcal{M}) = \mu(\mathcal{M}_1) = 2$. So, $\mathcal{G}$ can be easily transformed into Chomsky normal form. The number of nonterminals of $\mathcal{G}$ is $O(n^2)$.

Next, we apply Theorem 8 and get an equivalent (htb,ptb)-2DPDA $\mathcal{M}'$. The size of $\mathcal{M}'$ as well as the number of head turns and pushdown turns is bounded by doubly-exponential functions of $O(n^2)$. Now, we can construct an (htb,ptb)-2DPDA $\mathcal{M}''$ on input $\triangleright x \triangleleft$ where $x \in a_1^* a_2^* \cdots a_m^*$ which simulates $\mathcal{M}'$ on an input from I. We observe that the size of $\mathcal{M}''$ and the number of head turns and pushdown turns is bounded by a doubly-exponential function of $O(n^2)$. □

Thus, the reduction of pushdown turns and determinization results in a doubly-exponential blow-up which gives an upper bound for the trade-off in problem (2). Obviously, we also obtain doubly-exponential upper bounds for the conversion problems (1), (3), and (4). An immediate question is whether these results can be improved. Since only one resource, namely either nondeterminism or pushdown turns is reduced, one would expect only a single exponential upper bound. Thus, an interesting task would be either to show an exponential upper bound or to establish a doubly-exponential lower bound.

4   Non-Recursive Trade-Offs

In the previous section, we have obtained doubly-exponential, and thus recursive, trade-offs between several variants of head-turn bounded pushdown automata accepting bounded languages. If we remove the restriction of boundedness of the languages considered, then the resulting trade-offs are no longer bounded by a recursive function. We obtain so-called *non-recursive trade-offs* (see [6,7]), i.e., every recursive function cannot represent an upper bound for the trade-offs.

A method to prove non-recursive trade-offs is proposed by Hartmanis and makes use of the set of valid computations of a Turing machine. Details are presented in [6,7,10], and quickly recalled here. Let $\mathcal{M} = (Q, \Sigma, T, \delta, q_0, B, F)$ be a deterministic one-tape one-head Turing machine (DTM), where T is the set of tape symbols including the set of input symbols Σ and the blank symbol B, Q is the finite set of states and $F \subseteq Q$ is the set of final states. The initial state is q_0 and δ is the transition function. Without loss of generality, we assume that Turing machines can halt only after an odd number of moves, accept by halting, make at least three moves, and cannot print blanks. At any instant during a computation, $\mathcal{M}$ can be completely described by an *instantaneous description* (ID) which is a string $tqt' \in T^*QT^*$ with the following meaning: $\mathcal{M}$ is in the state q, the non-blank tape content is the string tt', and the head is scanning the first symbol of t'. The initial ID of $\mathcal{M}$ on input $x \in \Sigma^*$ is $\mathrm{ID}_0(x) = q_0 x$. An ID is accepting whenever it belongs to T^*FT^*. The set VALC($\mathcal{M}$) of valid (accepting) computations of $\mathcal{M}$ (see [1]) consists of all finite strings $\mathrm{ID}_0(x)\#\mathrm{ID}_2(x)\# \cdots \#\mathrm{ID}_{2n}(x)\$\mathrm{ID}_{2n+1}^R(x)\# \cdots \#\mathrm{ID}_3^R(x)\#\mathrm{ID}_1^R(x)$ such that $\mathrm{ID}_i(x)$ leads to its successor $\mathrm{ID}_{i+1}(x)$ according to δ, and $\mathrm{ID}_{2n+1}(x)$ is an accepting ID. Following a generalization of Hartmanis's technique given in [15] (see also [7]), we obtain non-recursive trade-offs between two types D_1 and D_2 of pushdown automata if for every DTM $\mathcal{M}$ a language $L_\mathcal{M}$ exists such that a PDA of type D_1 for $L_\mathcal{M}$ can be effectively constructed and $L_\mathcal{M} \in \mathscr{L}(D_2)$ if and only if $L(\mathcal{M})$ is finite. To apply this technique in our context, we first need a technical lemma. The proof is omitted here.

Lemma 10. *Let $\mathcal{M}$ be a Turing machine accepting a subset of Σ^* and $a \notin \Sigma$ be a new symbol. Then, the following holds:*

(1) VALC($\mathcal{M}$) belongs to $\mathscr{L}((htb,ptb)\text{-}2DPDA)$ and a (htb,ptb)-2DPDA can be effectively constructed.

(2) VALC($\mathcal{M}$) belongs to $\mathscr{L}(PDA)$ if and only if $L(\mathcal{M})$ is a finite set.

(3) $L(\mathcal{M}) = \{a^{2^{|w|}} w \mid w \in VALC(\mathcal{M})\}$ belongs to $\mathscr{L}(2DPDA)$ and a 2DPDA can be effectively constructed.

(4) $L(\mathcal{M})$ belongs to $\mathscr{L}(htb\text{-}2PDA)$ if and only if $L(\mathcal{M})$ is a finite set.

Thus, we immediately obtain the following non-recursive trade-offs.

$$\text{PDA} \overset{non\text{-}rec}{\longrightarrow} \text{DPDA}, \text{2DPDA} \overset{non\text{-}rec}{\longrightarrow} \text{DPDA}, \text{ and 2PDA} \overset{non\text{-}rec}{\longrightarrow} \text{PDA}.$$

The first non-recursive trade-off is already shown in [22]. The remaining two trade-offs can be shown to be non-recursive by using (1) and (2) in Lemma 10. In particular, we obtain

$$\text{(htb,ptb)-2DPDA} \overset{non\text{-}rec}{\longrightarrow} \text{DPDA and (htb,ptb)-2PDA} \overset{non\text{-}rec}{\longrightarrow} \text{PDA}.$$

Clearly, all commonly studied decidability questions such as emptiness, finiteness, inclusion, or equivalence are not semidecidable for all automata classes containing (htb,ptb)-2DPDA that may perform at least one head turn and at least two pushdown turns. The latter fact can be observed from the construction of a (htb,ptb)-2DPDA accepting VALC($\mathcal{M}$) which is omitted here.

It is currently unknown whether or not 2PDA and 2DPDA have the same computational power. Thus, it is not clear whether there is a recursive or non-recursive trade-off between 2PDA and 2DPDA.

If we additionally remove the restriction on the boundedness of the head turns, we obtain machines which may accept non-semilinear bounded languages and obtain the following non-recursive trade-offs by applying (3) and (4) in Lemma 10:

$$\text{2DPDA} \overset{non\text{-}rec}{\longrightarrow} \text{htb-2DPDA and 2PDA} \overset{non\text{-}rec}{\longrightarrow} \text{htb-2PDA}.$$

References

1. Baker, B.S., Book, R.V.: Reversal-Bounded multipushdown machines. Journal of Computer and System Sciences 8, 315–322 (1974)
2. Geffert, V., Mereghetti, C., Palano, B.: More concise representation of regular languages by automata and regular expressions. Information and Computation 208, 385–394 (2010)
3. Goldstine, J., Kappes, M., Kintala, C.M.R., Leung, H., Malcher, A., Wotschke, D.: Descriptional complexity of machines with limited resources. Journal of Universal Computer Science 8, 193–234 (2002)
4. Ginsburg, S.: The Mathematical Theory of Context-Free Languages. McGraw-Hill, New York (1966)
5. Gurari, E.M., Ibarra, O.H.: The complexity of the equivalence problem for two characterizations of Presburger sets. Theoretical Computer Science 13, 295–314 (1981)
6. Hartmanis, J.: On the succinctness of different representations of languages. SIAM Journal on Computing 9, 114–120 (1980)

7. Holzer, M., Kutrib, M.: Descriptional complexity—an introductory survey. In: Martín-Vide, C. (ed.) Scientific Applications of Language Methods, pp. 1–58. Imperial College Press, London (2010)
8. Holzer, M., Kutrib, M.: The complexity of regular(-like) expressions. In: Gao, Y., Lu, H., Seki, S., Yu, S. (eds.) DLT 2010. LNCS, vol. 6224, pp. 16–30. Springer, Heidelberg (2010)
9. Holzer, M., Kutrib, M., Malcher, A.: Complexity of multi-head finite automata: origins and directions. Theoretical Computer Science 412, 83–96 (2011)
10. Hopcroft, J.E., Ullman, J.D.: Introduction to Automata Theory, Language, and Computation. Addison-Wesley, Reading (1979)
11. Ibarra, O.H.: A note on semilinear sets and bounded-reversal multihead pushdown automata. Information Processing Letters 3, 25–28 (1974)
12. Ibarra, O.H., Jiang, T., Tran, N., Wang, H.: New decidability results concerning two-way counter machines. SIAM Journal on Computing 24, 123–137 (1995)
13. Leiss, E.: Succinct representation of regular languages by Boolean automata. Theoretical Computer Science 13, 323–330 (1981)
14. Liu, L.Y., Weiner, P.: Finite-reversal pushdown automata and semi-linear sets. In: Proc. of Sec. Ann. Princeton Conf. on Inf. Sciences and Systems, pp. 334–338 (1968)
15. Malcher, A.: Descriptional complexity of cellular automata and decidability questions. Journal of Automata, Languages and Combinatorics 7, 549–560 (2002)
16. Malcher, A.: On recursive and non-recursive trade-offs between finite-turn pushdown automata. Journal of Automata, Languages and Combinatorics 12, 265–277 (2007)
17. Malcher, A., Pighizzini, G.: Descriptional complexity of bounded context-free languages. In: Harju, T., Karhumäki, J., Lepistö, A. (eds.) DLT 2007. LNCS, vol. 4588, pp. 312–323. Springer, Heidelberg (2007); http://arxiv.org/abs/0905.1045 (for an extended version)
18. Meyer, A.R., Fischer, M.J.: Economy of descriptions by automata, grammars, and formal systems. In: IEEE Symposium on Foundations of Computer Science, pp. 188–191 (1971)
19. Rosen, K.H.: Handbook of discrete and combinatorial mathematics. CRC Press, Boca Raton (2000)
20. Pighizzini, G., Shallit, J., Wang, M.W.: Unary context-free grammmars and pushdown automata, descriptional complexity and auxiliary space lower bounds. Journal of Computer and System Sciences 65, 393–414 (2002)
21. Valiant, L.G.: Regularity and related problems for deterministic pushdown automata. Journal of the ACM 22, 1–10 (1975)
22. Valiant, L.G.: A note on the succinctness of descriptions of deterministic languages. Information and Control 32, 139–145 (1976)

State Trade-Offs in Unranked Tree Automata

Xiaoxue Piao and Kai Salomaa

School of Computing, Queen's University
Kingston, Ontario K7L3N6, Canada
{piao,ksalomaa}@cs.queensu.ca

Abstract. A common definition of tree automata operating on un-ranked trees uses a set of vertical states that define the bottom-up computation, and the transitions on vertical states are determined by so called horizontal languages recognized by finite automata on strings. It is known that, in this model, a deterministic tree automaton with the smallest total number of states (that is, vertical states and states used for automata to define the horizontal languages) does not need to be unique nor have the smallest possible number of vertical states. We consider the question by how much we can reduce the total number states by introducing additional vertical states. We give an upper bound for the state trade-off for deterministic tree automata where the horizontal languages are defined by DFAs (deterministic finite automata). Also, we give a lower bound construction that reduces the number of horizontal states, roughly, from 4^n to $8n$ by doubling the number of vertical states. The lower bound is close to the worst-case upper bound in the case where the number of vertical states is multiplied by a constant.

We show that deterministic tree automata where the horizontal languages are specified by NFAs (nondeterministic finite automata) can have no trade-offs between the numbers of vertical states and horizontal states, respectively. We study corresponding trade-offs also for nondeterministic tree automata.

Keywords: tree automata, unranked trees, state complexity, determinism and nondeterminism.

1 Introduction

Modern applications of tree automata, such as XML document processing [3,4,18], use automata operating on unranked trees. In unranked trees, the label of a node does not determine the number of children and there is no a priori bound on the number of children of a node. Due to this reason, the set of transitions of an unranked tree automaton is, in general, infinite and the transitions are usually specified in terms of a regular language, which is called a *horizontal language*. Thus, in addition to the finite set of *vertical states* used in the bottom-up computation, an unranked tree automaton needs for each vertical state q and input symbol σ a finite string automaton to recognize the horizontal language consisting of strings of states defining the transitions associated to q and σ [3]. The

M. Holzer, M. Kutrib, and G. Pighizzini (Eds.): DCFS 2011, LNCS 6808, pp. 261–274, 2011.

total state size of a tree automaton is defined by the number of vertical states and the number of horizontal states used by automata to specify the horizontal languages [3,11,16].

We get different unranked tree automaton models depending on whether the bottom-up computation is nondeterministic or deterministic and whether the horizontal languages are recognized by an NFA or a DFA ((non-)deterministic finite automaton). We use DTA(DFA) and DTA(NFA) (respectively, NTA(DFA) and NTA(NFA)) to denote the class of deterministic (respectively, nondeterministic) unranked tree automata where the horizontal languages are specified, respectively, by a DFA or an NFA.

It is known that a regular tree language does not, in general, have a unique minimal DTA(DFA) [11], and in particular, the DTA(DFA) with the smallest total number of states does not need to have the smallest possible number of vertical states (see e.g., Example 4.1 in [15]). On the other hand, by defining an equivalence relation for the set of vertical states (as in the case for tree automata on ranked trees) it is easy to see that any regular tree language has a unique DTA(DFA) with the smallest number of vertical states. By a *state trade-off* we mean a situation where we add to a DTA(DFA) additional vertical states in a way that reduces the total number of states. Since minimization of the total number of states of a DTA(DFA) is NP-complete [11], questions of state trade-offs can be expected to be hard.

We establish upper bounds for the maximal state trade-offs in DTA(DFA)s by considering, roughly speaking, how much smaller can be a set of DFAs whose disjoint union recognizes a regular language defined by a given DFA. Finding the worst-case upper bound leads to questions that are related, but not the same, as the question of maximizing the product of summands considered by Krause [10]. We also give an exponential lower bound for the state trade-offs using a fixed size alphabet. With a variable sized alphabet we give an improved lower bound that by, roughly, doubling the number of vertical states reduces the number of horizontal states from 4^n to $8n$. Also by relying on nondeterministic state complexity of regular languages [6] we show that for DTA(NFA)s there can be no trade-offs between the number of vertical and horizontal states, that is, any regular tree language has a minimal DTA(NFA) that has also the smallest possible number of vertical states. However, this does not mean that a minimal DTA(NFA) would be unique, because it is well known that a minimal NFA for a regular language need not be unique [19,20].

We also consider corresponding state trade-offs for nondeterministic tree automata. Here the situation becomes more involved due to the fact that also the bottom-up computations with a minimal number of vertical states can be constructed in very different ways. For trade-offs in NTA(DFA)s we give an exponential lower bound, however, establishing lower bounds for NTA(NFA)s is more challenging. We give a lower bound example for NTA(NFA)s where the number of horizontal states is reduced from $O(n^2)$ to $O(n)$ by adding one vertical state.

To conclude this section, we mention some related work. In contrast to the situation with DTA(DFA)s, there are two alternative definitions of determinism for unranked tree automata that guarantee that the minimal automaton is unique, namely syntactically deterministic automata [4,17], and stepwise tree automata [2,11]. The syntactically deterministic automata are called also *strongly deterministic* tree automata [15]. The state complexity of transformations between different unranked tree automaton models, as well as operational state complexity has been considered in [15,16]. Recent work on state complexity of nested word automata, which can be viewed as generalizations of tree automata can be found in [13,14]. General references on state complexity of finite automata include [7,8,20], and more references can be found therein.

The paper is organized as follows. We briefly recall definitions and related notations for tree automata operating on unranked trees in Section 2. We study the maximal state trade-offs of DTA(DFA)s in Section 3 and prove that there can be no state trade-offs for DTA(NFA)s in Section 4. In the following sections we investigate the state trade-offs for NTA(DFA)s and NTA(NFA)s, respectively.

2 Preliminaries

The set of non-negative integers is $\mathbb{N}$. A *tree domain* is a prefix-closed subset D of $\mathbb{N}^*$ such that if $ui \in D$, $u \in \mathbb{N}^*$, $i \in \mathbb{N}$ then $uj \in D$ for all $j < i$. The set of nodes of a tree t is represented in the well-known way as a tree domain $\mathrm{dom}(t)$ and the node labeling is given by a mapping $\mathrm{dom}(t) \to \Sigma$ where Σ is a finite alphabet of symbols. The label of a node does not determine the number of children, and thus, we use labeled ordered unranked trees. The set of all Σ-labeled trees is T_Σ.

We introduce the following notation for trees. For $i \geq 0$, $a \in \Sigma$ and $t \in T_\Sigma$, we denote by $a^i(t) = a(a(...a(t)...))$ a tree, where the nodes ε, 1, $\ldots$, 1^{i-1} are labelled by a and the subtree at node 1^i is t. When $a \in \Sigma$, $w = b_1 b_2 ... b_n \in \Sigma^*$, we use $a(w)$ to denote the tree $a(b_1, b_2, ..., b_n)$.

For a string w over an alphabet Σ, $|w|_\sigma$, $\sigma \in \Sigma$ denotes the number of occurrences of σ in w. For a regular language L, we denote by $sc(L)$ (respectively, $nsc(L)$) the number of the states of the minimal DFA (respectively, a minimal NFA) recognizing L.

Next we briefly recall some notations used for automata operating on unranked trees. For more details the reader is referred, e.g., to [3,15]. An early reference on regular unranked tree languages is [1].

A *nondeterministic* unranked bottom-up tree automaton (NTA) is a 4-tuple $A = (Q, \Sigma, \delta, F)$ where Q is a finite set of states, Σ is the alphabet, $F \subseteq Q$ is the set of final states, δ is a mapping from $Q \times \Sigma$ to the subsets of Q^* which satisfies the condition that, for each $q \in Q$, $\sigma \in \Sigma$, the language $\delta(q, \sigma)$ is regular. The language $\delta(q, \sigma)$ is called the *horizontal language* associated with q and σ. The tree language recognized by A, $L(A)$, consists of all $t \in T_\Sigma$, such that some computation of A reaches the root of t in a state of F.

A nondeterministic unranked tree automaton $A = (Q, \Sigma, \delta, F)$ is said to be *deterministic*, a DTA, if for any two states $q_1, q_2 \in Q$, $q_1 \neq q_2$, and $\sigma \in \Sigma$, we have $\delta(q_1, \sigma) \cap \delta(q_2, \sigma) = \emptyset$. The above condition guarantees that the state assigned by A to a node u of an input tree is unique (but A need not assign any state to u if the computation becomes blocked below u).

An NTA(NFA) (respectively, NTA(DFA)) is a nondeterministic unranked tree automaton where each horizontal language is specified by an NFA (respectively a DFA). Similarly, a deterministic tree automaton is a DTA(DFA) (respectively, a DTA(NFA)) if each horizontal language is specified by a DFA (respectively an NFA). The DFAs (respectively NFAs) recognizing horizontal languages are called *horizontal DFAs (respectively NFAs)* and their states are called *horizontal states*. The states in Q are called *vertical states*.

We define the *(state) size of A*, size(A), as a pair of integers $[|Q|; n]$, where n is the sum of the sizes of all horizontal automata associated with A. We denote as $tsize(A)$ the total number of vertical and horizontal states, that is, $|Q| + n$.

We say that a DTA(DFA) A is *v-minimal* if A has the smallest number of vertical states among all the DTA(DFA)s that recognize $L(A)$, and A is *t-minimal* if A has the smallest total number of states.

A regular tree language does not need to have a unique t-minimal DTA(DFA) [11]. In particular, it is possible that an automaton with the smallest total number of states does not have the smallest possible number of vertical states, and we will consider the question by how much we can reduce the number of horizontal states by adding more vertical states, that is, we will consider trade-offs between the numbers of vertical and horizontal states.

By extending the Nerode congruence from words to trees, we can define the v-minimal DTA(DFA) for a regular tree language where the states consist of the congruence classes [4][1], and hence the v-minimal DTA(DFA) is unique. Note that once the vertical states are determined by the congruence classes, the minimal DFAs for the corresponding horizontal languages are also unique. The extension of the Nerode congruence is called the top-congruence in [1], and the corresponding construction for tree languages over ranked alphabets can be found in [5]. A Myhill-Nerode theorem for stepwise automata on unranked trees can be found in [11].

Proposition 1. *The v-minimal DTA(DFA) of a regular tree language is unique.*

We conclude this section with some further notation associated with computations of a tree automaton A. For $t \in T_\Sigma$, $t^A \subseteq Q$ denotes the set of states that in some bottom-up computation A may reach at the root of t. We extend this notation for a string $w \in \Sigma^*$, by setting $w^A \in Q^*$ to denote the string of states that A reaches at leaves labeled by elements of the string w.

For $t \in T_\Sigma$, a leaf u of t, and $q \in Q$ we denote by $t(u \leftarrow q)$ the tree obtained from t by replacing the label of u by q. We say that states q_1 and q_2 of a DTA(DFA) A are *equivalent* if for any $t \in T_\Sigma$ and any leaf u of t, the computation of A accepts $t(u \leftarrow q_1)$ if and only if it accepts $t(u \leftarrow q_2)$.

---

[1] As noted in [1,4], for unranked tree languages in addition to the congruence having a finite index we need further conditions to guarantee regularity of the horizontal languages. However, in Proposition 1 we just need a v-minimal deterministic automaton for a tree language that is known to be regular, and we do not need to consider the additional conditions.

3 Maximal Trade-Off in DTA(DFA)

In this section, we first investigate the upper bounds on the state trade-offs in a DTA(DFA). After that we give two lower bound results, with a fixed size and a non-fixed size alphabet, respectively.

Lemma 2. *Let $A = (Q, \Sigma, \delta, F)$ be an arbitrary DTA(DFA) with n vertical states, $Q = \{1, \ldots, n\}$, and for each $\sigma \in \Sigma$, let $L_{i,\sigma}$, $1 \leq i \leq n$ be the horizontal language associated with σ and state i. Assume that $L_{i,\sigma} = \bigoplus_{j=1}^{k_i} L_{i,\sigma,j}$, where $\bigoplus$ denotes disjoint union.*

Then there exists a DTA(DFA) B equivalent with A where state i is replaced by k_i equivalent states and the transitions of B associated with symbol σ need at most $\sum_{i=1}^{n} \sum_{j=1}^{k_i} sc(L_{i,\sigma,j})$ horizontal states.

Proof.   Let $B = (Q', \Sigma, \delta', F')$, where $Q' = \{(i, j) \mid 1 \leq i \leq n, 1 \leq j \leq k_i\}$, and the δ'-transitions are defined for each $\sigma \in \Sigma$ and $(i, j) \in Q'$ by setting

$$\delta'((i, j), \sigma) = \{ (i_1, j_1)(i_2, j_2) \cdots (i_m, j_m) \mid m \geq 0, \ i_1 i_2 \cdots i_m \in L_{i,\sigma,j} \}.$$

A state (i, j) is in F' if $i \in F$. Since by our assumption the languages L_{i,σ,j_1} and L_{i,σ,j_2} are always disjoint when $j_1 \neq j_2$, the tree automaton B is deterministic.

The total number of horizontal states needed for transitions associated with σ is $\sum_{i=1}^{n} \sum_{j=1}^{k_i} sc(L_{i,\sigma,j})$. $\square$

Since the state complexity of a regular language $L_{i,\sigma}$ may be considerably larger than $\sum_{j=1}^{k_i} sc(L_{i,\sigma,j})$, Lemma 2 gives a method to reduce the total number of states in a DTA(DFA). In order to establish an upper bound for the worst-case state trade-off, we first observe that any trade-off for a v-minimal DTA(DFA) has to be based on a construction where a given vertical state and it's horizontal language are replaced by equivalent vertical states with disjoint horizontal languages.

Suppose that A is the unique v-minimal DTA(DFA) (as given by Proposition 1), and B is any DTA(DFA) that is equivalent to A. By considering the standard equivalence relation among vertical states of B (as defined in the previous section), it is easy to see that B is a "refinement" of A where each vertical state of A has been replaced by one or more equivalent vertical states. Thus, when considering the trade-off between the number of vertical and horizontal states, it is sufficient to restrict consideration to situations where in a v-minimal DTA(DFA) we replace each vertical state by a number of states that are equivalent (in terms of the vertical computation), as described in the statement of Lemma 2.

In the following we want to identify the maximal reduction of the total number states that may result when we replace one vertical state i of a v-minimal DTA(DFA) A by k_i vertical states. Recalling the state-complexity of (disjoint) union [20] and using the notations of Lemma 2, the maximal number of horizontal states corresponding of i and $\sigma \in \Sigma$ in A is $\Pi_{j=1}^{k_i} sc(L_{i,\sigma,j})$ and in the modified DTA(DFA) B these are replaced by $\sum_{j=1}^{k_i} sc(L_{i,\sigma,j})$ horizontal states and $k_i - 1$ additional vertical states. Thus the question of finding the maximal trade-off amounts to finding $k_i \geq 1$ and horizontal languages $L_{i,\sigma,j}$, $1 \leq j \leq k_i$, such that the

value $\Pi_{j=1}^{k_i} \mathrm{sc}(L_{i,\sigma,j})$ is maximized as a function of $\displaystyle\sum_{j=1}^{k_i} (\mathrm{sc}(L_{i,\sigma,j}) + 1)$.   (1)

We note that Krause [10] considers a related, but different, problem of maximizing the product of integers $\Pi_{j=1}^{k} d_j$ as a function of their sum $\sum_{j=1}^{k} d_j$. Our solution is inspired by the solution given in [10], but the case analysis for our problem turns out to be a bit more complicated.

In order to solve (1), define $\{x_1, \ldots, x_k\}$, $x_i \in \mathbb{N}$, $i = 1, \ldots, k$, $k \geq 1$ to be a *partition* of $s \in \mathbb{N}$ if $s = \sum_{i=1}^{k} (x_i + 1)$. A partition is *a winning partition* if $\prod_{i=1}^{k} x_i$ is maximal among all partitions of s. We observe that the following properties hold for a winning partition.

1. No winning partition can contain a one (except when $s = 2$). If $x_i = 1$, we just take it out and add two to some other x_j.
2. No winning partition needs to contain a six because a six can be replaced by a two and a three. (Note an extra vertical state is needed.)
3. No x_i can be greater than six. If $x_i > 6$ is even, then $x/2(x/2 - 1) > x$. If $x_i > 6$ is odd, then $(x-1)/2 \cdot (x-1)/2 > x$. In both cases P is not a winning partition.
4. P cannot contain a two and a five because they could be replaced by a three and a four.
5. P cannot contain a two and a four because they could be replaced by two three's.
6. P cannot contain two two's because they could be replaced by a five.
7. P cannot contain a two, and two three's because they could be replaced by a four and a five.

The above means that $x_i = 2$ can only occur in P when $P = \{2, 3\}$ and $s = 7$, or $P = \{2\}$ and $s = 3$.

The winning partitions for small values of s can be calculated easily, and in the following we restrict consideration to cases $s \geq 12$. Up to now we have concluded that the only numbers that can occur in P are three, four and five.

8. P cannot contain two five's because they could be replaced by three three's.
9. P cannot contain a three and a five because they could be replaced by two four's.

Now we know that either P contains only four's and one five, or only three's and four's.

10. P cannot contain two four's and a five because they could be replaced by four three's.

Thus, the number five can occur only in cases $s = 11$ and $s = 6$.

11. P cannot contain five three's because they could be replaced by four four's.

Thus, we know that when $s \geq 12$, P contains only three's and four's, and at most four three's.

Clearly if P is a winning partition, the sum of $(x_i + 1)$'s is exactly s (because otherwise we could add one to one of the x_i's).

Putting the above together means that writing $s = \sum_{j=1}^{k}(\text{sc}(L_{\sigma,j})+1)$, $s \geq 12$, and $t = \Pi_{j=1}^{k}\text{sc}(L_{\sigma,j})$, we have exactly one possible solution for (1) that is determined as follows:

- If $s \equiv 0 \pmod{5}$, then t is maximized to $4^{s/5}$ when each $\text{sc}(L_{\sigma,j}) = 4$,
- If $s \equiv 1 \pmod{5}$, then t is maximized to $3^4 \cdot 4^{(s-16)/5}$ when four of the $\text{sc}(L_{\sigma,j})$'s are equal to 3, and the rest of the $\text{sc}(L_{\sigma,j})$'s are equal to 4,
- If $s \equiv 2 \pmod{5}$, then t is maximized to $3^3 \cdot 4^{(s-12)/5}$ when three of the $\text{sc}(L_{\sigma,j})$'s is equal to 3, and the rest of the $\text{sc}(L_{\sigma,j})$'s are equal to 4,
- If $s \equiv 3 \pmod{5}$, then t is maximized to $3^2 \cdot 4^{(s-8)/5}$ when two of the $\text{sc}(L_{\sigma,j})$'s is equal to 3, and the rest of the $\text{sc}(L_{\sigma,j})$'s are equal to 4,
- If $s \equiv 4 \pmod{5}$, then t is maximized to $3 \cdot 4^{(s-4)/5}$ when one of the $\text{sc}(L_{\sigma,j})$'s is equal to 3, and the rest of the $\text{sc}(L_{\sigma,j})$'s are equal to 4.

The above analysis allows us to give an upper bound for the worst-case trade-off that can be obtained based on the method of Lemma 2.

Theorem 3. *Using the notations of Lemma 2, let $s_i = \sum_{j=1}^{k_i}(\text{sc}(L_{i,\sigma,j}) + 1)$, $1 \leq i \leq n$,[2] and assume that $s_i \geq 12$. Let $X, Y, Z, U, V \subseteq \{1, 2, \ldots, n\}$ be the sets of s_i's defined by the conditions*

- $s_x \equiv 0 \pmod{5}$, $x \in X$, $s_y \equiv 1 \pmod{5}$, $y \in Y$, $s_z \equiv 2 \pmod{5}$, $z \in Z$,
- $s_u \equiv 3 \pmod{5}$, $u \in U$, $s_v \equiv 4 \pmod{5}$, $v \in V$.

The maximal trade-off (corresponding to (1)) occurs when the tree automata A and B (as in Lemma 2) have the following numbers, respectively, of vertical and horizontal states:

$$size(A) = [n;\ \sum_{x \in X} 4^{s_x/5} + \sum_{y \in Y} 3^4 \cdot 4^{(s_y-16)/5} + \sum_{z \in Z} 3^3 \cdot 4^{(s_z-12)/5} +$$
$$\sum_{u \in U} 3^2 \cdot 4^{(s_u-8)/5} + \sum_{v \in V} 3 \cdot 4^{(s_v-4)/5}]$$

and

$$size(B) = [\sum_{x \in X} s_x/5 + \sum_{y \in Y}(4 + (s_y - 16)/5) + \sum_{z \in Z}(3 + (s_z - 12)/5) +$$
$$\sum_{u \in U}(2 + (s_u - 8)/5) + \sum_{v \in V}(1 + (s_v - 4)/5);\ \sum_{i=1}^{n} s'_i],$$

where

$$s'_i = \begin{cases} \frac{4}{5}s_i & \text{if } s_i \equiv 0 \pmod{5}, \\ \frac{4}{5}(s_i - 16) + 12 & \text{if } s_i \equiv 1 \pmod{5}, \\ \frac{4}{5}(s_i - 12) + 9 & \text{if } s_i \equiv 2 \pmod{5}, \\ \frac{4}{5}(s_i - 8) + 6 & \text{if } s_i \equiv 3 \pmod{5}, \\ \frac{4}{5}(s_i - 4) + 3 & \text{if } s_i \equiv 4 \pmod{5}. \end{cases} \quad 1 \leq i \leq n.$$

For $s_i < 12$, the maximal trade-offs are omitted due to the length restriction.

----

[2] To be completely general the values s_i depend, in addition to $i \in Q$ also on a symbol $\sigma \in \Sigma$. We have omitted σ in the notation to avoid making the formulas even more complicated.

3.1   Lower Bound Results

We first present a lower bound result for an alphabet of fixed size and afterwards give a better lower bound result on an alphabet depending on n.

Lemma 4. *There exists a tree language T over alphabet $\Sigma = \{a, b, c\}$ where any v-minimal DTA(DFA) for T has at least three vertical states and at least 2^n, $n \geq 2$ horizontal states, and T is recognized by a DTA(DFA) B with $size(B) = [n + 1; n^2 + n]$.*

Proof.   We define the tree language $T = \{c^i(w) \mid i \geq 1, w \in L\}$, where L is the union of the languages accepted by DFAs $A_1, A_2, \ldots, A_{n-1}$ shown in Figure 1.

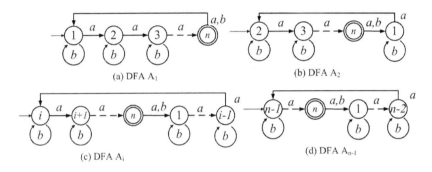

(a) DFA A_1

(b) DFA A_2

(c) DFA A_i

(d) DFA A_{n-1}

Fig. 1. DFAs A_i

Let $A = (Q, \Sigma, \delta, F)$ be a v-minimal DTA(DFA) with three vertical states that recognizes T. Clearly A must assign different states q_a and q_b to leaves labeled by a and b, respectively. Assume that A assigns q_a to the root of a tree $c(w)$, $w \in \{a, b\}^*$. This means that A would have to accept trees obtained from $t \in T$ by replacing the leaves labeled by a with $c(w)$, and we conclude that A would not recognize T. In exactly the same way we see that A cannot assign q_b to the root of any tree $c(w)$, $w \in \{a, b\}^*$. Thus, A has only one state q such that $\delta(q, c) \neq \emptyset$. This argument also establishes that any DTA(DFA) for T needs at least three vertical states. Since A recognizes T, we conclude that $\delta(q, c) \cap Q^+ = q + \{w^A \mid w \in \cup_{i=1}^{n-1} L(A_i)\}$. The horizontal language $\{w^A \mid w \in \cup_{i=1}^{n-1} L(A_i)\}$ can be accepted by a $(n - 1)$-entry DFA, and any equivalent DFA has at least $2^n - 2$ states according to Lemma 3 in [9]. Then a DFA needs at least 2^n states to recognize $\delta(q, c)$. Thus, we have that A has at least three vertical states and 2^n horizontal states.

Let $B = (Q', \{a, b, c\}, \delta', F')$, where $Q' = \{p_1, p_2, \ldots, p_{n-1}, p_a, p_b\}$, $F' = \{p_1, p_2, \ldots, p_{n-1}\}$, $\delta'(p_a, a) = \epsilon$, $\delta'(p_b, b) = \epsilon$, $\delta'(p_i, c) = p_i + \{s^B \mid s \in L(A_i)\}$. It is obvious that $L(B) = T$. Since $L(A_i) \cap L(A_j) = \emptyset$ when $i \neq j$, the tree automaton B is a DTA(DFA). Each horizontal DFA needs at least $n + 2$ states to recognize $\delta'(p_i, c)$, and two horizontal states are needed in total to recognize $\delta'(p_a, a)$ and $\delta'(p_b, b)$. We have $size(B) = [n+1; n^2 + n]$. Although all the vertical states $\{p_1, p_2, \ldots, p_{n-1}\}$ are equivalent in B, B has a total size that is much smaller than A.   □

The upper bound in Theorem 3 and the lower bound in Lemma 4 do not match. We can get a better lower bound using an alphabet that depends on n.

Lemma 5. *Let* $\Sigma = \{a_0, a_1, \ldots, a_n\}$, $n \geq 1$. *There exists a tree language* T *over* Σ *such that any v-minimal DTA(DFA)* A *for* T *has* $n + 1$ *vertical states and at least* $2^{2n+1} - 3^n - 1 + n$ *horizontal states, and* T *has a DTA(DFA)* B *such that* $size(B) = [2n; 8n]$.

Proof.   We define the tree language $T = \{a_0^i(w) \mid i \geq 1, w \in L\}$, where L is the union of the languages $L_i = \{wa_i \in \{a_1, \ldots, a_n\}^* \mid |w|_{a_i} \equiv 0 \bmod 4\}$, $1 \leq i \leq n$.

Let $A = (Q, \Sigma, \delta, F)$ be a v-minimal DTA(DFA) with $n+1$ vertical states that recognizes T. Clearly A must assign different states q_i, $1 \leq i \leq n$ to leaves labeled by a_i. Assume that A assigns q_i to the root of a tree $a_0(w)$, $w \in \{a_1, \ldots, a_n\}^*$. This means that A would have to accept trees obtained from $t \in T$ by replacing the leaves labeled by a_i with $a_0(w)$, and we conclude that A would not recognize T. Thus, A has only one state q_0 such that $\delta(q_0, a_0) \neq \emptyset$. This argument also establishes that any DTA(DFA) for T needs at least $n+1$ vertical states. Since A recognizes T, we conclude that $\delta(q_0, a_0) = q_0 + \{w^A \mid w \in \cup_{i=1}^n L_i\}$. The minimal DFA H for the horizontal language $\{w^A \mid w \in \cup_{i=1}^n L_i\}$ has $2^{2n+1} - 3^n - 1$ states. H has non-final states $(j_1, \ldots, j_n)$ where each $j_i \in \{0, 1, 2, 3\}$ keeps track of the number of symbols a_i mod 4, and the last seen symbol was some a_k where $j_k \neq 1$. There are $4^n - 1$ such states (since the state $(1, 1, \ldots, 1)$ is unreachable). H has final states $(j_1, \ldots, j_n, f)$ where each j_i keeps track of the number of symbols a_i mod 4, and the last seen symbol was some a_k where $j_k = 1$. The last component f is used just to differentiate the state from the corresponding non-final state $(j_1, \ldots, j_n)$. There are $4^n - 3^n$ such states. It is easy to see that all states of H are pairwise inequivalent. Since A needs a singleton DFA for the horizontal language associated with q_i, $1 \leq i \leq n$, A has in total at least $2^{2n+1} - 3^n - 1 + n$ horizontal states.

Let $B = (Q', \Sigma, \delta', F')$, where $Q' = \{p_1, p_2, \ldots, p_n, h_1, \ldots, h_n\}$, $F' = \{p_1, p_2, \ldots, p_n\}$, $\delta'(p_i, a_0) = p_i + \{s^B \mid s \in L_i\}$ and $\delta(h_i, a_i) = \epsilon$ for $1 \leq i \leq n$. It is obvious that $L(B) = T$. Since $L_i \cap L_j = \emptyset$ when $i \neq j$, the tree automaton B is a DTA(DFA). We have $size(B) = [2n; 8n]$.   □

The lower bound construction of Lemma 5 can be compared with the worst case upper bound of Theorem 3 as follows. Consider A and B as in the statement of Theorem 3. Denote by n the number of vertical states of A and suppose that the number of vertical states of B is $c \cdot n$ (in the construction of Lemma 5 we have $c = 2$). In this case the difference between the numbers of horizontal states, respectively, of A and of B would be at most constant times 4^n.

Thus, at least for the particular numbers of vertical states given by the construction of Lemma 5, the lower bound is reasonably close to the worst-case upper bound. However, Lemma 5 uses an alphabet of size n and for a fixed sized alphabet in Lemma 4 the conversion from A to B increases the number of vertical states by a non-constant factor while the number of horizontal states of A is only $2^{\sqrt{m}}$ where m stands for the number of horizontal states of B.

4   Results for DTA(NFA)

Compared with a DTA(DFA), it is interesting that it turns out that there are no trade-offs between the numbers of vertical and horizontal states in a DTA(NFA). For any regular tree language there exists a v-minimal DTA(NFA) that is also a t-minimal DTA(NFA).

Theorem 6. *For any DTA(NFA) A whose number of vertical states is not minimal, there always exists an equivalent DTA(NFA) B such that*

(1) B has a minimal number of vertical states,
(2) $tsize(B) \leq tsize(A)$.

Proof.   Let T be an arbitrary regular tree language, and $A = \{Q, \Sigma, \delta, F\}$ be a DTA(NFA) recognizing T such that the number of vertical states in A is not minimal. Since the number of vertical states in A is not minimal, there exist at least two states $q, q' \in Q$ that are equivalent [3]. Without loss of generality, we assume that for $\sigma \in \Sigma$, $\delta(q, \sigma) = L_1$ and $\delta(q', \sigma) = L_2$. Now construct a DTA(NFA) $B = \{Q', \Sigma, \delta', F'\}$, where $Q' = Q - \{q, q'\} + \{p\}$. The transition function δ' is defined as same as δ except that

1) transition rules $\delta(q, \sigma) = L_1$ and $\delta(q', \sigma) = L_2$ are replaced by $\delta'(p, \sigma) = L_1 \cup L_2$,
2) all occurrences of q, q' in δ are replaced by p.

The final set of states $F' = F$ if $q, q' \notin F$, and $F' = F - \{q, q'\} + \{p\}$ if $q, q' \in F$. (Note that since q, q' are equivalent states, either both of them are final or neither of them is final.) It is easy to see that A is equivalent to B. According to the results in [6], we know that

$$nsc(L_1 \cup L_2) \leq nsc(L_1) + nsc(L_2) + 1.$$

Now we have that

$$tsize(A) - tsize(B) = |Q| + nsc(L_1) + nsc(L_2) - (|Q| - 1 + nsc(L_1 \cup L_2)) \geq 0.$$

We repeat the above process if the number of vertical states in B is not minimal.

$\square$

The following corollary is immediate.

Corollary 7. *Any regular tree language has a DTA(NFA) A that is both v-minimal and t-minimal, and A can be effectively constructed.*

5   Results for NTA(DFA)

We state a lower bound construction.

Example 8. Let $\Sigma = \{a, b, c\}$. Consider a tree language $T = \{c^i(w) \mid 1 \le i \le m - 2, w \in L\}$ $(m \ge 3)$ where L is the language recognized by an NFA A_0 shown in Figure 2.

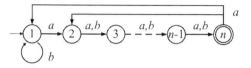

Fig. 2. NFA A_0

T has an NTA(DFA) $M = (\{q_a, q_b, q_0, q_1, \ldots, q_{m-3}\}, \Sigma, \delta, \{q_0, q_1, \ldots, q_{m-3}\})$ where

- $\delta(q_a, a) = \epsilon$, $\delta(q_b, b) = \epsilon$, $\delta(q_{m-3}, c) = \{s^M \mid s \in L\}$,
- $\delta(q_{j-1}, c) = q_j$, where $1 \le j \le m - 3$.

M is v-minimal. The horizontal language $\delta(q_{m-3}, c)$ is recognized by an NFA A_1 shown in Figure 3. According to [12], any DFA equivalent to A_1 needs at least

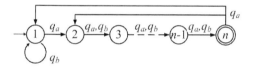

Fig. 3. The NFA A_1 for the horizontal language $\delta(q_{m-3}, c)$

2^n states. Thus, we have $size(M) = [m, 2^n + 2m - 4]$.

The tree language T has also the following NTA(DFA). Define

$$N = (\{p_a, p_b, p_x, p_0, p_1, \ldots, p_{m-3}\}, \Sigma, \delta', \{p_0, p_1, \ldots, p_{m-3}\})$$

where

- $\delta'(p_a, a) = \epsilon$, $\delta'(p_b, b) = \epsilon$, $\delta'(p_x, a) = \epsilon$, $\delta'(p_{m-3}, c) = \{s^N \mid s \in L\}$,
- $\delta'(p_{j-1}, c) = p_j$, where $1 \le j \le m - 3$.

The horizontal language $\delta'(p_{m-3}, c)$ is recognized by a DFA shown in Figure 4. Thus, we have $size(N) = [m + 1; n + 2m - 3]$.

Using the fact that the minimal syntactically deterministic bottom-up automaton is unique [4], and the conversions between NTA(DFA)s and syntactically deterministic automata [15], we can get an upper bound for the trade-off

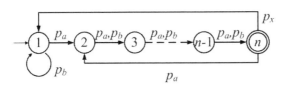

Fig. 4. The DFA for the horizontal language $\delta'(p_{m-3}, c)$

that is exponential in the total number of states (vertical and horizontal states). Note that the syntactically deterministic automata of [4] are called "strongly deterministic" in [15]. Since also the nondeterministic vertical computatation of an NTA(DFA) (or NTA(NFA)) with a smallest number of vertical states can be constructed in very different ways, we do not have a good upper bound for the trade-offs in these cases.

6   Results for NTA(NFA)

In the same way as described at the end of the previous section, we can get a computable upper bound for state trade-offs in NTA(NFA)s, but again we do not have a good upper bound. Also finding lower bounds turns out to be more difficult in the case of NTA(NFA)s. Note that the construction used in Example 8 relies essentially on the property that the horizontal languages are recognized by a DFA and similar constructions do not seem to work for NTA(NFA)s.

In Example 9 below, we give a construction that reduces the number of horizontal states from $O(n^2)$ to $O(n)$ by adding only one vertical state.

Example 9. Let $\Sigma = \{a, c, d\}$ be the alphabet, $p_1, \ldots, p_n$ be any integers and $P = p_1 \cdot \ldots \cdot p_n$. Define tree language T to consist of trees

$$\{a^i(d^m) \mid 1 \le i \le n, \ m \equiv 0 (\bmod\ p_i)\} \cup \{a^i c(d^m) \mid 1 \le i \le n, \ m \equiv 0 (\bmod\ P)\}.$$

T can be recognized by an NTA(NFA) $A = (\{q_1, \ldots, q_n, q_d\}, \Sigma, \delta, \{q_1\})$, where δ-transition is defined as:

- $\delta(q_d, d) = \epsilon,$ $\delta(q_i, a) = (q_d^{p_i})^* + q_{i+1}$, for $1 \le i \le n-1,$
- $\delta(q_n, a) = (q_d^{p_n})^*,$ $\delta(q_i, c) = (q_d^P)^*$, for $1 \le i \le n,$

It is easy to verify that A has the smallest number of vertical states. To count the number of a's, A needs at least n states. (The number of a's is from 1 to n.) A needs a state for leaf nodes labeled by d. If A assigned any other state in $\{q_1, \ldots, q_n\}$ to a node labeled by d, the automaton will accept some trees that are not in T. For instance, if A assigns q_2 to a leaf node labeled by d, A will accepts tree $a(d)$, which is not in T. (Node labeled by d is assigned with state q_2 and according to $\delta(q_1, a) = q_2$, a final state is assigned to the root of $a(d)$.)

Any NFA for $\delta(q_i, a) = (q_d^{p_i})^* + q_{i+1}$ needs at least $p_i + 2$ states. Thus, the size of A is

$$size(A) = [n + 1; \ nP + \sum_{i=1}^{n} p_i + 2n - 1].$$

By adding one more vertical state q_c to A, we can construct an equivalent NTA(NFA) $B = (\{q_1, \ldots, q_n, q_d, q_c\}, \Sigma, \delta', \{q_1\})$, where δ'-transition is defined as:

- $\delta'(q_d, d) = \epsilon,$ $\delta'(q_i, a) = (q_d^{p_i})^* + q_{i+1} + q_c,$ for $1 \leq i \leq n - 1,$
- $\delta'(q_n, a) = (q_d^{p_n})^* + q_c,$ $\delta'(q_c, c) = (q_d^P)^*.$

The size of B is

$$size(B) = [n + 2; \ P + \sum_{i=1}^{n} p_i + 2n + 1].$$

By choosing $n = P$, we have that $tsize(A) = O(n^2)$ and $tsize(B) = O(n)$, which means that in the worst case the number of horizontal states can be reduced to the square root by adding one more vertical state.

7 Conclusion

We have investigated the state trade-offs in unranked tree automaton models. For state trade-offs in DTA(DFA)s we have given a lower bound construction that is close to the corresponding worst-case upper bound. Although a DTA(NFA) is a more general model than a DTA(DFA), we proved that there are no state trade-offs in DTA(NFA)s. We gave a lower bound example where by adding one vertical state to an NTA(NFA), the number of horizontal states is reduced to the square root. However, the lower bound remains very far away from the upper bound. The state trade-offs for nondeterministic unranked tree automata are a topic for further research.

References

1. Brüggemann-Klein, A., Murata, M., Wood, D.: Regular tree and hedge languages over unranked alphabets. HKUST Research Report, HKUST-TCSC-2001-05, http://hdl.handle.net/1783.1/738
2. Carme, J., Niehren, J., Tommasi, M.: Querying unranked trees with stepwise tree automata. In: van Oostrom, V. (ed.) RTA 2004. LNCS, vol. 3091, pp. 105–118. Springer, Heidelberg (2004)
3. Comon, H., Dauchet, M., Gilleron, R., Jacquemard, F., Lugiez, D., Löding, C., Tison, S., Tommasi, M.: Tree Automata Techniques and Applications (2007), electronic book available at tata.gforge.inria.fr
4. Cristau, J., Löding, C., Thomas, W.: Deterministic automata on unranked trees. In: Liśkiewicz, M., Reischuk, R. (eds.) FCT 2005. LNCS, vol. 3623, pp. 68–79. Springer, Heidelberg (2005)

5. Gécseg, F., Steinby, M.: Tree languages. In: Handbook of Formal Languages, vol. III, pp. 1–68. Springer, Heidelberg (1997)
6. Holzer, M., Kutrib, M.: Nondeterministic descriptional complexity of regular languages. International Journal of Foundations of Computer Science 14, 1087–1102 (2003)
7. Holzer, M., Kutrib, M.: Descriptional and computational complexity of finite automata. In: Dediu, A.H., Ionescu, A.M., Martín-Vide, C. (eds.) LATA 2009. LNCS, vol. 5457, pp. 23–42. Springer, Heidelberg (2009)
8. Holzer, M., Kutrib, M.: Nondeterministic finite automata – Recent results on the descriptional and computational complexity. International Journal of Foundations of Computer Science 20(4), 563–580 (2009)
9. Holzer, M., Salomaa, K., Yu, S.: On the state complexity of k-entry deterministic finite automata. Journal of Automata, Languages and Combinatorics 6(4), 453–466 (2001)
10. Krause, F.E.: Maximizing the product of summands; minimizing the sum of factors. Mathematics Magazine 69(4), 270–278 (1996)
11. Martens, W., Niehren, J.: On the minimization of XML schemas and tree automata for unranked trees. Journal of Computer and System Sciences 73, 550–583 (2007)
12. Moore, F.R.: On the bounds for state-set size in the proofs of equivalence between deterministic, nondeterministic, and two-way finite automata. IEEE Transactions on Computers 20, 1211–1214 (1971)
13. Okhotin, A., Salomaa, K.: Descriptional complexity of unambiguous nested word automata. In: Dediu, A.-H., Inenaga, S., Martín-Vide, C. (eds.) LATA 2011. LNCS, vol. 6638. Springer, Heidelberg (to appear, 2011)
14. Piao, X., Salomaa, K.: Operational state complexity of nested word automata. Theoretical Computer Science 410, 3290–3302 (2009)
15. Piao, X., Salomaa, K.: Transformations between different models of unranked bottom-up tree automata. In: Proc. of DCFS 2010, pp. 193–204 (2010); Full version to appear in Fundamenta Informaticae
16. Piao, X., Salomaa, K.: Operational state complexity of deterministic unranked tree automata. In: Proc. of DCFS 2010, pp. 181–192 (2010)
17. Raeymaekers, S., Bruynooghe, M.: Minimization of finite unranked tree automata (2004) (manuscript)
18. Schwentick, T.: Automata for XML,– a survey. Journal of Computer and System Sciences 73, 289–315 (2007)
19. Shallit, J.: A Second Course in Formal Languages and Automata Theory. Cambridge University Press, Cambridge (2009)
20. Yu, S.: Regular languages. In: Handbook of Formal Languages, vol. I, pp. 41–110. Springer, Heidelberg (1997)

A $\Sigma_2^P \cup \Pi_2^P$ Lower Bound Using Mobile Membranes

Shankara Narayanan Krishna[1] and Gabriel Ciobanu[2]

[1] IIT Bombay, Powai, Mumbai, India 400 076
krishnas@cse.iitb.ac.in
[2] Romanian Academy, Institute of Computer Science
and A.I.Cuza University of Iaşi, Romania
gabriel@info.uaic.ro

Abstract. One of the interesting applications of membrane computing is the ability to solve intractable problems in polynomial time. The existing variants with active membranes have several powerful features like polarizations, dissolution, evolution and communication rules as well as non-elementary membrane division. We propose a simple variant which uses elementary membrane division and communication only in the form of mobility of membranes. We show that this variant has $\Sigma_2^P \cup \Pi_2^P$ as lower bound. This is the first known treatment of the complexity classes Σ_2^P, Π_2^P using active membranes without the features of polarizations, non elementary membrane division.

1 Introduction

The area of membrane computing originated 12 years ago, when Gh. Păun attempted to formulate a model of computation motivated by the structure and functioning of the living cell. Initial research in the area focussed on computability aspects of various biological operations modelled in the context of membranes; in the later years, focus has shifted to applications of membrane computing and relationship with complexity classes. The first known model to give a semi-uniform solution to an **NP**-complete problem (SAT) is the one with active membranes and polarizations [15]. The operation of membrane division used in this model, motivated by *mitosis* in living cells, was crucial to solve **NP**-complete problems. After [15], several researchers gave semi-uniform/uniform solutions to a host of hard problems (**NP**-complete/**PSPACE**-complete). Since P systems with active membranes, polarizations, dissolution, and non-elementary membrane division are too powerful and would be computationally equivalent to Parallel Random Access Machines (PRAMs), efforts were made for weaker variants of P systems for solving hard problems. Notable among these are:

1. [10] gives two uniform solutions for SAT: (1) using polarizations, communication rules, evolution rules and separation rules, and (2) no polarizations, but allowing label change, communication rules, evolution rules and separation rules. Separation rules are similar to division rules in that they create

M. Holzer, M. Kutrib, and G. Pighizzini (Eds.): DCFS 2011, LNCS 6808, pp. 275–288, 2011.

two new membranes; however, they can have different objects unlike division. [11] gives a semi-uniform solution for SAT without polarizations, label change, but using separation, release and merge rules. Release is a form of dissolution, while merge combines the contents of two membranes. [9] gives a uniform solution for SAT using division for elementary membranes, evolution rules involving bi-stable catalysts, dissolution and communication. No polarizations were used. [2] gives a uniform solution to SAT using elementary division, evolution rules, communication rules, dissolution and two polarizations. [1] gives a semi-uniform solution for SAT using P systems without polarizations, dissolution, but using non-elementary division of membranes, and evolution, communication rules, while [17] gives a semi-uniform solution to SAT without polarizations, evolution and communication rules but using non-elementary division and dissolution rules.

2. [3] and [13] : [13] gives a polynomial time solution to a **PP**-complete problem using polarizations, elementary membrane divison and communication of objects across membranes, while [3] solves a #**P**-complete problem in polynomial time using two polarizations, rewriting rules, communication of objects out of membranes as well as elementary membrane division. However, [3] requires either cooperative evolution rules, or post processing of data of exponential size (when expressed in unary).

3. [7] presents a semi-uniform solution to QBF-3-SAT using polarizationless P systems without communication and evolution, but using dissolution and non-elementary division.

In the literature, the complexity classes that have been studied in the context of active membranes are $\mathbf{P}, \mathbf{NP}, \mathbf{coNP}, \mathbf{L}, \mathbf{NL}, \mathbf{PP}, \mathbf{PSPACE}$. The interested reader can look at [12] for more details on these complexity classes. Characterizations of $\mathbf{P}$ have been obtained for P systems with active membranes without polarizations that do not make use of dissolution, as well as for P systems with active membranes which do not have membrane division [16]. The classes $\mathbf{L}, \mathbf{NL}$ have been characterized [16] by polarizationless P systems with active membranes under tighter uniformity conditions (reductions computable in $\mathbf{AC^0}$ as opposed to $\mathbf{P}$).

The complexity classes in levels greater than 1 of the polynomial hierarchy (PH) have not been characterized so far by any P system with active membranes. It is known that the lowest level of the polynomial hierarchy is given by $\Sigma_0^P = \Pi_0^P = \Delta_0^P = \mathbf{P}$. Also, $\Delta_{i+1}^P = \mathbf{P}^{\Sigma_i^P}$, $\Sigma_{i+1}^P = \mathbf{NP}^{\Sigma_i^P}$ and $\Pi_{i+1}^P = \mathbf{coNP}^{\Sigma_i^P}$, $i \geq 0$. Thus, the classes $\mathbf{P}, \mathbf{NP}, \mathbf{coNP}$ are at level 1 of the polynomial hierarchy, while $PH \subseteq PSPACE$. In [16] it is stated that there is no known variant of P systems with active membranes that can solve NP-complete problems without using any of the features of polarizations, non-elementary division and dissolution. Likewise, *no variant of polarizationless P systems with active membranes* has gone beyond the first level of the polynomial hierarchy using only the operations of communication and elementary membrane division.

We propose a variant of enhanced mobile membranes [5,6] which uses only the operations of elementary membrane division as well as the operation of mobility of membranes. Our membranes do not have polarization. An elementary membrane can move in and move out of its adjacent membrane. There are two forms of mobility: (i) an elementary membrane while moving in/out of an adjacent membrane can replace an object in itself while moving - we refer to this form of mobility by the rules *endocytosis* and *exocytosis*; (ii) an elementary membrane moves in/out of an adjacent membrane in the absence of some object(s) in the adjacent membrane. No replacement of objects takes place in either membrane. This form of mobility is referred to as *inhibitive endocytosis* and *inhibitive exocytosis*. Our contribution is two fold: we show that this variant (1) using only elementary division, endocytosis and exocytosis can solve SAT in polynomial time, and (2) using elementary division and mobility, solve a **coNP**$^{\mathbf{NP}}$-complete problem (2QBF) in polynomial time, thereby going to the second level in the polynomial hierarchy. *It is our belief that this is the first variant of polarizationless P systems with active membranes which uses only elementary membrane division and communication in solving an* **NP**-*complete problem and a* **coNP**$^{\mathbf{NP}}$-*complete problem.*

2   Mobile Membranes

We assume the reader is familiar with membrane computing; for the state of the art, see [16]. We follow the notations used in [5,6] for our class of P systems. We call our variant *P systems with mobile membranes and controlled mobility*. Such a system is a construct $\Pi = (V, H, \mu, w_1, \ldots, w_n, R, i)$, where: $n \geq 1$ (the initial *degree* of the system); V is a finite alphabet (its elements are called *objects*); H is a finite set of *labels* for membranes; μ is a *membrane structure*, consisting of n membranes, labelled with elements of H; $w_1, w_2, \ldots, w_n$ are strings over V, describing the initial *multisets of objects* placed in the n regions of μ, i is the output membrane of the system, and R is a finite set of *developmental rules* of the following forms:

(a) $[a]_h [\ ]_m \rightarrow [[w]_h]_m$, for $h, m \in H, a \in V, w \in V^*$ *endocytosis*
an elementary membrane labeled h containing a enters the adjacent membrane labeled m (m is not necessarily an elementary membrane) ; the labels h and m remain unchanged during this process; however, the object a is modified to w during the operation.

(b) $[[a]_h]_m \rightarrow [w]_h [\ ]_m$, for $h, m \in H, a \in V, w \in V^*$ *exocytosis*
an elementary membrane labeled h containing a is sent out of a membrane labeled m (membrane m is not necessarily elementary); the labels of the two membranes remain unchanged; however the object a from membrane h is modified to w during this operation;

(c) $[a]_h [\ ]_{m/\neg S} \rightarrow [[a]_h]_m$, for $h, m \in H, a \in V, S \subseteq V$ *inhibitive endocytosis*
an elementary membrane labeled h containing a can enter m provided m does not contain any object from S; the object a does not evolve in the process; the labels h, m of the membranes also remain unchanged. The objects of S are *inhibitors* that prevent membrane h from entering membrane m whenever h contains the object a.

(d) $[[b]_h]_{m/\neg S} \rightarrow [\ ]_m[b]_h$, for $h, m \in H, b \in V, S \subseteq V$ *inhibitive exocytosis*
an elementary membrane labeled h containing b can come out of m provided m does not contain any object from S; the object b does not evolve in the process; the labels h, m of the membranes also remain unchanged. The objects of S are *inhibitors* that prevent membrane h from leaving membrane m whenever h contains the object b.

(e) $[a]_j \rightarrow [u]_j[v]_j$, for $j \in H, a, u, v \in V$ *elementary division*
in reaction with an object a, the elementary membrane labeled j is divided into two membranes labeled j, with the object a replaced in the two new membranes by possibly new objects; the other objects remain unchanged in the new copies.

The rules are applied according to the following principles:

1. All the rules are applied in parallel, non-deterministically choosing the rules, the membranes, and the objects, but in such a way that the parallelism is maximal; this means that in each step we apply a multiset of rules such that no further rule can be added to the multiset, no further membranes and objects can evolve at the same time.
2. The membrane m from each type (a) – (d) of rules as above is said to be *passive*, while the membrane h is said to be *active*. In any step of a computation, a membrane can either be active or passive or neither, but not both. In any step of a computation, any active membrane and object in an active membrane can be involved in at most one rule, the passive membranes are not considered involved in the use of rules (hence they can be used by several rules at the same time);
3. The membrane j in rule (e) is called a *divider*. A *divider* cannot be active in the same step it divides; it can be passive in the same step it divides.
4. The semantics of rules endocytosis is as follows: if membranes m, h are adjacent, with h elementary, and there are objects $a_1, \ldots, a_k$ in membrane h for which an endocytosis rule is enabled - then non-deterministically, the rule corresponding to one of the objects a_i is used. Similar for exocytosis rules.
5. If there are two elementary adjacent membranes h, m that have mutual endocytosis rules enabled - that is, there are rules $[a]_h[\ ]_m \rightarrow [[a']_h]_m$ and $[b]_m[\ ]_h \rightarrow [[b']_m]_h$ with h containing a and m containing b, then non-deterministically, one of them is used.
6. The semantics of inhibitive endocytosis is as follows: Let membranes m, h be adjacent, with h elementary. Let $a_1, \ldots, a_n$ be the distinct objects in h (the contents of h could be several copies of each a_i). Let $[a_i]_h[\ ]_{m/\neg S_i} \rightarrow [[a_i]_h]_m$ for $1 \leq i \leq n$ be the rules of type(c) associated with the objects a_i in h, $1 \leq i \leq n$ and membrane m. Then h enters m using inhibitive endocytosis provided m has no symbols from $\bigcup_{i=1}^n S_i$. The semantics of inhibitive exocytosis is similar.
7. Let m, k and h be adjacent membranes with h elementary.
   - If in the current step, h is enabled to move into m or k using inhibitive endocytosis, then a non-deterministic choice is made; h enters into one of m, k.

- If h, m are children of j and if h is enabled to enter m using inhibitive endocytosis or come out of j using inhibitive exocytosis in a step, then again a non-deterministic choice is made - h either enters m or comes out of j.
- If there is a situation where h is enabled to (i) use an endocytosis rule and enter m (and in the process a symbol a in h is replaced with b) and (ii) use inhibitive endocytosis and enter either m or k, then a non-deterministic choice is made - h can either enter m using the endocytosis rule replacing a or choose to enter one of m, k (with no replacement of any symbol in h).
- In case there is a situation where there is an object c in m, an object a in h and (i) h has an enabled endocytosis rule $[a]_h[\ ]_m \rightarrow [[b]_h]_m$, and (ii) there is a rule $[a]_h[\ ]_{m/\neg S} \rightarrow [[a]_h]_m$, with $c \in S$, then h can enter m using the endocytosis rule replacing a by b.

8. The evolution of objects and membranes takes place in a bottom-up manner. After having a (maximal) multiset of rules chosen, they are applied starting from the innermost membranes, level by level, up to the skin membrane (all these sub-steps form a unique evolution step, called a *transition* step).
9. When a membrane is moved across another membrane, by rules (a)-(d), its whole contents (its objects) are moved.
10. All objects and membranes which do not evolve at a given step (for a given choice of rules which is maximal) are passed unchanged to the next configuration of the system.

By using the rules in this way, we get transitions among the configurations of the system. A sequence of transitions is a computation, and a computation is successful if it halts (it reaches a configuration where no rule can be applied).

At the end of a halting computation, the number of objects from a special membrane called output membrane is considered as the result of the computation.

We denote by *endo* and *exo* the operations endocytosis and exocytosis; *iendo, iexo* represent inhibitive endocytosis and inhibitive exocytosis while *div* represents elementary membrane division. When we restrict $|w| = 1$ in rules (a),(b), we call the operations *rendo, rexo*, where r stands for "restricted".

The mobile membranes considered in [5] differ from the above definition in the following respects: (i) [5] allows object evolution rules of the kind $[a \rightarrow v]_h$, $a \in V, v \in V^*$ and contextual evolution rules of the kind $[[a]_j[b]_h]_k \rightarrow [[w]_j[b]_h]_k$ for $h, j, k \in H, a, b \in V, w \in V^*$, (ii) [5] allows forced endocytosis and forced exocytosis, (iii) [5] does not have inhibitive endocytosis and exocytosis *iendo, iexo*.

We provide an example of a *P systems with mobile membranes and controlled mobility* that will clarify the semantics of the mobility and division operations. Consider the configuration $[[pq[abc]_1 [abb]_2 [cde]_3 [sr]_9]_4 [aa]_5 [ef]_6 [uv]_7]_8$ with rules

(a) $[a]_2[\ ]_{3/\neg\{c\}} \rightarrow [[a]_2]_3$ *iendo*

(b) $[b]_2[\ ]_{3/\neg\{f\}} \rightarrow [[b]_2]_3$ *iendo*

$$(c) \ [a]_2[\ ]_3 \rightarrow [[d]_2]_3 \qquad\qquad\qquad endo$$
$$(d) \ [a]_2[\ ]_{1/\neg\{t\}} \rightarrow [[a]_2]_1 \qquad\qquad iendo$$
$$(e) \ [a]_1[\ ]_{2/\neg\{n\}} \rightarrow [[a]_1]_2 \qquad\qquad iendo$$
$$(f) \ [a]_5 \rightarrow [b]_5[c]_5 \qquad\qquad\qquad\quad div$$
$$(g) \ [e]_6[\ ]_5 \rightarrow [[f]_6]_5 \qquad\qquad\qquad endo$$
$$(h) \ [[r]_9]_{4/\neg\{s\}} \rightarrow [r]_9[\ ]_4 \qquad\qquad iexo$$
$$(i) \ [u]_7[\ ]_{4/\neg\{p,o\}} \rightarrow [[u]_7]_4 \qquad\qquad iendo$$

First we summarize the rules and their effects: (i) Membrane 2 cannot enter membrane 3 using *iendo* since rule (a) is violated. The distinct objects of membrane 2 are a, b, and there is an inhibitor in membrane 3 with respect to a. However, membrane 2 can enter membrane 3 using the endocytosis rule (c). (ii) Membrane 2 can enter membrane 1 using *iendo*, likewise, membrane 1 can enter membrane 2 using *iendo* - the relevant rules are (d),(e). However, exactly one of them can be used in a step. (iii) Membrane 5 divides. Membrane 6 has an *endo* rule to enter membrane 5 at the same step - it enters a copy of membrane 5 non-deterministically. The relevant rules are (f),(g). (iv) Membrane 9 can leave membrane 4 using *iexo* using rule (h). (v) Membrane 7 cannot enter membrane 4 using *iendo*. Look at rule (i).

A possible next configuration using rules (c), (f),(g)and (h) is

$$[[pq[abc]_1 \ [cde[dbb]_2]_3 \ ]_4 \ [sr]_9 \ [ba]_5 \ [ca[ff]_6]_5 \ [uv]_7 \ ]_8$$

Another possible next configuration using rules (e), (f),(g) and (h) is

$$[[pq \ [abb[abc]_1]_2 \ [cde]_3 \ ]_4 \ [sr]_9 \ [ba]_5 \ [ca[ff]_6]_5 \ [uv]_7 \ ]_8$$

Another possible next configuration using rules (d), (f),(g)and (h) is

$$[[pq \ [abc[abb]_2]_1 \ [cde]_3 \ ]_4 \ [sr]_9 \ [ba]_5 \ [ca[ff]_6]_5 \ [uv]_7 \ ]_8$$

3   Complexity of Mobile Membranes

Complexity classes for P systems with mobile membranes [5], [6] have not yet been studied; we start the study here for the variant considered in this paper. When we treat mobile membrane systems as language deciding devices to solve decision problems, we call these *recognizer systems with mobile membranes and controlled mobility* (recognizer systems for short from hereon). Formally, a *recognizer membrane system Π* is such that (1) All computations halt, (2) there exist objects $yes, no \in V$, and (3) One of the objects yes, no "appear" (may be multiple copies) in the halting configuration. The computation is accepting if the *yes* object arrives in the halting configuration and rejecting if the *no* object arrives.

Uniformity and Semi-Uniformity. A family of P systems with mobile membranes and controlled mobility $\mathbf{\Pi}$ is a collection of recognizer systems. The family $\mathbf{\Pi}$ solves a decision problem if for each instance of the problem there is a member of the family to solve it. We can think of each instance of the decision problem to be encoded as a string x over a suitable alphabet Σ. Let $X = \{x_1, x_2, \ldots\}$ be a language of encoded instances of the given problem. The member of $\mathbf{\Pi}$ which solves the instance x is denoted by $\Pi(x)$. In case a member of $\mathbf{\Pi}$ is used to solve all instances of a fixed length n, then we denote that member by Π_n. The family $\mathbf{\Pi}$ decides X if for any string $x \in \Sigma^*$, the P system $\Pi(x)$ (or Π_n for all instances x, $|x| = n$) accepts whenever $x \in X$ and rejects otherwise. Thus, each instance of the problem is solved by some family member of $\mathbf{\Pi}$. The family $\mathbf{\Pi}$ is *sound* with respect to X when, for each $x \in \Sigma^*$, if there exists an accepting computation of $\Pi(x)$ (Π_n), then $x \in X$. The family $\mathbf{\Pi}$ is *complete* with respect to X when, for each $x \in \Sigma^*$, if $x \in X$, then every computation of $\Pi(x)$ (Π_n) is accepting.

The notion of *uniformity* was first introduced by Borodin [4] for boolean circuits. If we can invest unbounded amounts of computation in order to construct each member of the family $\mathbf{\Pi}$, it can potentially solve uncomputable problems. To ensure that the function that constructs each member of the family does not increase the set of problems decided by the family, we impose that the constructing function is computable within certain restricted resources (time/space). When the function maps an instance size to a membrane system that decides all instances of that length, then the function is called a *uniformity condition*. When the function maps a single instance to a membrane system that decides that instance, then the function is called a *semi-uniformity* condition. The notions of uniformity and semi-uniformity were first applied to membrane systems in [8].

Class of problems solved by a uniform family: Let $\mathcal{R}$ be a family of recognizer systems and let $t : \mathbf{N} \to \mathbf{N}$ be a (total) function. Let E, F be classes of functions. Let $X = \{x_1, x_2 \ldots\}$ be a set of problem instances. If

(a) There exists a F-uniform family of membrane systems $\mathbf{\Pi} = \{\Pi_1, \Pi_2, \ldots\}$ of type $\mathcal{R}$: what this means is that, there exists a function $f \in F$, $f : \{1\}^* \to \mathbf{\Pi}$ such that $f(1^n) = \Pi_n$ (all instances x_k of length n are solved by Π_n; such a Π_n can be constructed by a function $f \in F$),

(b) There exists an input encoding function $e \in E$ such that $e(x)$ is the input multiset of Π_n, for $|x| = n$,

(c) $\mathbf{\Pi}$ is t-efficient : Π_n halts in $t(n)$ steps. Thus, for example if $t(n)$ is polynomial in n for all n, then we can call $\mathbf{\Pi}$ as polynomial efficient.

(d) The family $\mathbf{\Pi}$ is sound with respect to (X, e, f): if there is an accepting computation of $\Pi_{|x|}$ on input $e(x)$, then $x \in X$,

(e) The family $\mathbf{\Pi}$ is complete with respect to (X, e, f): for each $x \in X$, every computation of $\Pi_{|x|}$ on input $e(x)$ must be accepting.

then we say that the class of problems X is solved by an (E, F)-uniform family of membrane systems $\mathcal{R}$ in time t, and denote this family by (E, F)-$MC_{\mathcal{R}}(t)$. The set of languages decided by a uniform family of membrane systems in polynomial time is defined as (E,F)-$PMC_{\mathcal{R}} = \bigcup_{k \in \mathbf{N}}(E,F) - MC_{\mathcal{R}}(n^k)$.

Semi-uniformity is a generalization of uniformity. Let H be a class of functions. In this case, the members of $\mathbf{\Pi}$ are denoted $\Pi(x)$ for each problem instance x. The class of problems solved by a (H)-semi-uniform family of membrane systems of type $\mathcal{R}$ in time t denoted (H)-$MC_{\mathcal{R}}^*(t)$ contains all problems X such that:

(a) There exists a H-semi-uniform family $\mathbf{\Pi} = \{\Pi_{x_1}, \Pi_{x_2}, \ldots\}$ of membrane systems of type $\mathcal{R}$: what this means is that, there exists a function $h \in H$, $h : X \cup \overline{X} \to \mathbf{\Pi}$ such that $h(x_i) = \Pi_{x_i}$,
(b) $\mathbf{\Pi}$ is t-efficient : Π_n halts in $t(|x_n|)$ steps,
(c) The family $\mathbf{\Pi}$ is sound with respect to (X, h): for each $x \in X \cup \overline{X}$, if there is an accepting computation of Π_x, then $x \in X$,
(d) The family $\mathbf{\Pi}$ is complete, with respect to (X, h): for each $x \in X$, every computation of Π_x is accepting.

The set of languages decided by a semi-uniform family of membrane systems in polynomial time is defined as (H)-$PMC_{\mathcal{R}}^* = \bigcup_{k \in \mathbf{N}}(H)$-$MC_{\mathcal{R}}^*(n^k)$. In our case, $\mathcal{R}$ will be substituted with classes of P systems with mobile membranes and controlled mobility. Our class of recognizer systems is denoted $\mathcal{MM}^0(\alpha)$ (the superscript 0 stands for polarizationless) and the parameter α is as follows: $\alpha \subseteq \{div, rendo, rexo, iendo, iexo\}$.

3.1 Solving SAT

The SAT problem checks the satisfiability of a propositional logic formula in conjunctive normal form (CNF). Let $\{x_1, x_2, \ldots, x_n\}$ be a set of propositional variables. A formula in CNF is of the form $\varphi = C_1 \wedge C_2 \wedge \ldots \wedge C_m$ where each $C_i, 1 \leq i \leq m$ is a disjunction of the form $C_i = y_1 \vee y_2 \vee \ldots \vee y_r, r \leq n$, and each y_j is either a variable x_k or its negation $\neg x_k$. In this section, we propose a semi-uniform polynomial time solution to the SAT problem using the operations of $rendo$, $rexo$ and div (for any instance of SAT with n variables and m clauses, we construct a system $\Pi_{n,m}$ which solves it). Consider the formula $\varphi = C_1 \wedge C_2 \wedge \ldots C_m$, over the variables $\{x_1, \ldots, x_n\}$. Construct $\Pi_{m,n} = (V, H, \mu, w_0, \ldots, w_{m+1}, R, -)$ where $\mu = [[\ldots[[c_0]_J[\ ]_K[c]_L]_1 \ldots]_m[a_1 \ldots a_n]_0]_{m+1}$. The output membrane is not important for our purposes since we are answering a decision question. $V = \{a_i, t_i, f_i \mid 1 \leq i \leq n\} \cup \{c_i \mid 0 \leq i \leq m+n\} \cup \{c, d, yes, no\}$. Membranes 1 to m correspond to clauses C_1 to C_m. The rules R are as follows:

1. $[a_i]_0 \to [t_i]_0[f_i]_0$ div
   (Generation of all the 2^n assignments, n steps)
2. $[c_i]_J[\ ]_K \to [[c_{i+1}]_J]_K, 0 \leq i \leq n+m-1$, $rendo$
   $[[c_i]_J]_K \to [c_{i+1}]_J[\ ]_K, 0 \leq i \leq n+m-1$, $rexo$
   $[[c_{n+m}]_J]_K \to [d]_J[\ ]_K, [c_{n+m}]_J[\ ]_K \to [[c_{n+m}]_J]_K$ $rexo, rendo$
   (The counter keeps track of the number of steps)

3. $[t_j]_0[\ ]_i \to [[t_j]_0]_i$, if clause C_i contains the literal x_j,   *rendo*
   $[f_j]_0[\ ]_i \to [[f_j]_0]_i$, if clause C_i contains the literal $\neg x_j$ *rendo*
4. $[c]_L[\ ]_0 \to [[yes]_L]_0, [d]_J[\ ]_L \to [[no]_J]_L$ *rendo*

n steps are required for generating the assignments, and m steps for the satisfying assignments to reach the innermost membrane. If at the end of $n + m$ steps, the membrane 1 contains any membrane labeled 0, then the SAT instance has a solution, otherwise not. The counter c_i evolves to c_{n+m} and into d. A "yes" is created by replacing the object c when membrane L enters some membrane 0 in the $(n + m + 1)$th step. If no membranes 0 reach the membrane 1, then there is no question of replacing c as explained; a "no" is created by replacing d in step $(n + m + 2)$ or $(n + m + 3)$ when membrane J enters membrane L. A "no" is created in step $(n + m + 2)$ or $(n + m + 3)$ iff a "yes" is not created in step $(n + m + 1)$. Note that the system can produce exactly one of the objects "yes" or "no" at the end of a halting configuration.

Note that the non-determinism of the system coming from rules 1,3 does not affect the correctness. It is possible that after k applications of rule 1, $(1 \le k < n)$, rule 3 is used for a few steps. The condition for propagation of a membrane 0 into an inner membrane ensures that the membranes 0 that have reached a level j, $m \ge j \ge 1$ contain assignments that satisfy $C_m, \ldots, C_j$. Membrane 0 will divide further at a later stage depending on requirement (it is possible that the inward propagation has happened from membrane m to j, none of the clauses $C_i, j \le i \le m$ contained x_r or $\neg x_r$, a_r is still present in the membranes 0 that have reached so far upto membrane j, and further propagation of the membranes 0 into membrane $j - 1$ requires t_r or f_r). In the worst case, the membranes 0 will divide and replace the remaining a_i after they have reached the inner most membrane 1. Irrespective of any order between rules 1 and 3, a maximum of $m + n$ steps are needed to reach the innermost membrane, after replacing all the a_i's.

3.2   Analysis

The number of membranes in the initial configuration is $m + 4$. The number of rules in the above system: n rules of type 1, $n + m + 2$ rules of type 2, $2mn$ rules of type 3, and 2 rules of type 4. Hence, total number of rules is $\mathcal{O}(mn)$. We do not go into the details to show that

- the above construction is semi-uniform : it is straightforward;
- sound and complete : Π says "yes" iff the given SAT instance is satisfiable;
- the function H required for the above construction is **P**.

This result, along with the observation that $\textbf{P-}PMC_{\mathcal{R}}^*$ is closed under complements and polynomial time reductions gives us the following result:

Theorem 1. $\textbf{NP} \cup \textbf{coNP} \subseteq \textbf{P-}\mathcal{PMC}^*{}_{\mathcal{MM}^0(\{rendo, rexo, div\})}.$

3.3   Solving 2QBF

In this section, we propose a polynomial time semi-uniform solution for solving satisfiability of 2QBF using the operations $rendo, rexo, iendo$ and div. A quantified boolean formula is said to be in 2QBF if it is of the form $\varphi = \forall X \exists Y \psi$ or $\exists X \forall Y \psi$ where ψ is in CNF and X, Y partition the variables of ψ. ψ is called the quantifier free part of φ. For 2QBF formulae of the form $\exists X \forall Y \psi$, satisfiability simplifies to the SAT problem $\exists X \psi'$ where ψ' is the CNF obtained from ψ by removing all occurrences of universal literals. *Hence we deal only with 2QBF of the form* $\varphi = \forall X \exists Y \psi$. Satisfiability of 2QBF of the form $\forall X \exists Y \psi$ is Π_2^p (or **coNP^{NP}**)-complete, while it is Σ_2^p (or **NP^{NP}**)-complete if it is of the form $\varphi = \exists X \forall Y \psi$.

For example, consider the 2QBF formula $\varphi_1 = \forall X \exists Y$ $((x_1 \vee \neg x_3) \wedge (\neg x_1 \vee \neg x_2))$, with $X = \{x_1, x_2\}, Y = \{x_3\}$. φ_1 is not true, since for the case $x_1 = x_2 = T$, there is no assignment of values to x_3 which can make φ_1 true. On the other hand, the formula $\varphi_2 = \forall X \exists Y ((x_1 \vee x_3) \wedge (\neg x_1 \vee x_2 \vee x_3))$ where $X = \{x_1, x_2\}, Y = \{x_3\}$, is true. The idea we use in checking whether a 2QBF is true is as follows: First find all satisfying assignments of ψ, the quantifier-free part of the 2QBF; prune these solutions to check if they contain all possible 2^k assignments to the variables $x_1, \ldots, x_k$ of X. For example, in the case of φ_1, the assignments satisfying the quantifier-free part $((x_1 \vee \neg x_3) \wedge (\neg x_1 \vee \neg x_2))$ are $\{TFT, TFF, FFF, FTF\}$. When this set is pruned to check whether all the 2^2 assignments corresponding to x_1, x_2 are there, we find that it is not the case since there is no string TTT or TTF; our system outputs "no".

Consider the formula $\varphi = \forall X \exists Y \psi$ where $\psi = (C_1 \wedge C_2 \ldots \wedge C_m)$. Let $X = \{x_1, \ldots, x_k\}$ and $Y = \{x_{k+1}, \ldots, x_n\}$, $X \cap Y = \emptyset$, and each C_i is a clause (disjunction of literals x_i or $\neg x_i$). Construct $\Pi_{m,n} = (V, H, \mu, w_0, \ldots, w_{m+1}, R, -)$ where

$$\mu = [[[\ldots [[\ldots [[a_1 \ldots a_n]_0]_{1'} \ldots]_{k'}]_1 \ldots]_m [b_1 b_2 \ldots b_k]_L]_{m+1} [c_0]_J[]_K]_{m+2},$$

$V = \{a_i, t_i, f_i, b_j \mid 1 \leq i \leq n, 1 \leq j \leq k\} \cup \{c_i \mid 0 \leq i \leq n + k + m\} \cup \{c, d, e, d_1, d_2, yes, no\}$. Membranes labeled 1 to m correspond to clauses C_1 to C_m. The rules R are

1. $[a_i]_0 \rightarrow [t_i]_0 [f_i]_0, 1 \leq i \leq n$ $\hfill div$
2. $[b_i]_L \rightarrow [t_i]_L [f_i]_L, 1 \leq i \leq k$ $\hfill div$
   (Rule 1 : generation of all the 2^n assignments corresponding to the n variables in ψ, takes n steps. Rule 2 produces all 2^k assignments corresponding to variables in X. This is used later in checking the $\forall$ part of the formula)
3. $[[d_i]_0]_{i'} \rightarrow [\ ]_{i'} [d_i]_0$ for $d_i \in \{t_i, f_i\}, 1 \leq i \leq k$ $\hfill rexo$
   (The k membranes $1'$ to k' which surround the membranes 0 ensure that the a_i's for $1 \leq i \leq k$ are replaced with t_i, f_i after division before they reach the membrane 1. When the membranes 0 reach membrane 1, there will be no symbols a_i for $1 \leq i \leq k$; however, it is possible to have a_i for $k + 1 \leq i \leq n$. This takes k steps)

4. For $1 \leq j \leq n$, $1 \leq i \leq m$,

$[[t_j]_0]_i \rightarrow [t_j]_0[\ ]_i$, if clause C_i contains the literal x_j,   (rexo)

$[[f_j]_0]_i \rightarrow [f_j]_0[\ ]_i$, if clause C_i contains the literal $\neg x_j$ (rexo)

(Checking if ψ has any solutions, takes m steps. The membranes 0 which contain a solution for ψ will travel out of the membranes i, $1 \leq i \leq m$, and reach membrane $m + 1$. It takes m steps for the membranes 0 to reach membrane $m + 1$ from membrane 1)

5. $[c_i]_J[\ ]_K \rightarrow [[c_{i+1}]_J]_K$, $0 \leq i \leq n + k + m - 1$ (rendo)

   $[[c_i]_J]_K \rightarrow [c_{i+1}]_J[\ ]_K$, $0 \leq i \leq n + k + m - 2$ (rexo)

   $[[c_{n+k+m-1}]_J]_K \rightarrow [c]_J[\ ]_K$,   (rexo)

   $[[c_{n+k+m}]_J]_K \rightarrow [c]_J[\ ]_K$,   (rexo)

(A counter c_i keeps track of the number of steps incurred until solutions of ψ reach membrane $m + 1$. The earliest membranes 0 can reach membrane $m + 1$ is at the end of $k + k + m$ steps - k steps spent in replacing all the a_i's $1 \leq i \leq k$ with t_i, f_i by division using rule 1, k steps in crossing over membranes $1'$ to k', and then m steps to cross over membranes 1 to m; the latest membranes 0 can reach membrane $m + 1$ is at the end of $n + k + m$ steps - n steps spent in replacing all the a_i's $1 \leq i \leq n$ with t_i, f_i by division using rule 1, k steps to cross over membranes $1'$ to k' and then m steps to cross over membranes 1 to m. If $n + k + m$ is odd, then membrane J with c_{n+k+m} will be inside membrane K. $c_{n+k+m-1}$ is replaced with c in case $n + k + m$ is even, and c_{n+k+m} is replaced with c in case $n + k + m$ is odd, and membrane J comes out of K. Rule 5 happens in parallel with rules 1-4. Maximum number of steps needed till now is $n + k + m + 1$)

6. $[t_i]_0[\ ]_{L/\neg\{f_i\}} \rightarrow [[t_i]_0]_L$, $1 \leq i \leq k$ (iendo)

   $[f_i]_0[\ ]_{L/\neg\{t_i\}} \rightarrow [[f_i]_0]_L$, $1 \leq i \leq k$ (iendo)

(Once satisfying assignments of ψ have reached membrane $m + 1$, we start checking if the $\forall$ quantifier is met. Due to the non-determinism created by rules 1,4, it is possible to obtain satisfying assignments in membrane $m + 1$ even before all the a_i's for $k + 1 \leq i \leq n$ are replaced. However, all the b_i's in membranes L would have been replaced at the end of the first k steps of the computation of Π. Between the $(k + k + m + 1)$th and the $(n + k + m + 1)$th step, we use the *iendo* rules 6 to check which copies of membrane 0 can enter a copy of membrane L. Let there be a copy of membrane 0 containing $d_1 d_2 \ldots d_k d_{k+1} \ldots d_n$ where $d_i \in \{t_i, f_i, a_i\}$, $k + 1 \leq i \leq n$, and $d_i = t_i$ for $1 \leq i \leq k$. This copy of membrane 0 can only enter the copy of membrane L containing $t_1 t_2 \ldots t_k$. This is because f_i in L is an inhibitor of t_i in 0 for $1 \leq i \leq k$. Thus, a copy of membrane 0 containing some assignment $\mathcal{A}$ of $x_1, \ldots, x_k, x_{k+1} \ldots, x_n$ will enter a copy of membrane L containing an assignment $\mathcal{B}$ of $x_1, \ldots, x_k$ iff $\mathcal{A}$ and $\mathcal{B}$ agree on $x_1, \ldots, x_k$. Thus, each of the 2^k copies of membrane L will have atleast a copy of membrane 0 inside them provided the $\forall$ quantifier is met : that is, if among the solutions of ψ, we indeed have all 2^k assignments of variables $x_1, \ldots, x_k$. Otherwise, some copies of L will remain elementary. Rule 6 takes a single step of execution:

at the end of the step, a membrane 0 enters a membrane L which has no inhibitors with respect to its distinct objects)

7. $[c]_J \rightarrow [d]_J[e]_J$ (div)
8. $[e]_J[\ ]_{m+1} \rightarrow [[no]_J]_{m+1}$ $(rendo)$
9. $[d]_J \rightarrow [d_1]_J[d_2]_J$ (div)
10. $[\alpha]_L[\ ]_J \rightarrow [[\alpha]_L]_J, \alpha \in \{t_k, f_k\}$ $(rendo)$
11. $[d_1]_J[\ ]_{m+1} \rightarrow [[d_1]_J]_{m+1}$ $(rendo)$
12. $[no]_J[\ ]_J \rightarrow [[yes]_J]_J$ $(rendo)$

(Now to say a "yes" or "no". Membrane J having c divides into two copies with d, e. Next, rules 8,9 are applied in parallel : the membrane J with e enters membrane $m + 1$, replacing e with no, while membrane J containing d divides into two copies with d_1, d_2. Next, rules 10,11 are applied in parallel : the elementary membranes L (if any) enter membrane J containing "no", and stay there; in parallel, the copy of membrane J with d_1 enters membrane $m+1$. Rule 12 is used only if the copy of membrane J containing "no" remains elementary : this is when rule 10 was not applied in the previous step. What this means is that among the solutions of ψ, all combinations of $x_1, \ldots, x_k$ were present. In this case, by rule 12, the "no" is replaced with "yes". In the case when rule 12 is not applicable, we will have a "no" in the system, and in the case when rule 12 is applicable, we will have a "yes" in the system).

3.4   Analysis

The number of rules in the above system: n rules of type 1, k rules of type 2, $2k$ rules of type 3, $2mn$ rules of type 4, $n + k + m + 1$ rules of type 5, $2k$ rules of type 6. Therefore, the total number of rules is $\mathcal{O}(mn)$. Thus, the system is polynomially constructible. The total number of steps required: n steps for generation of assignments, $k + m$ steps to reach membrane $m + 1$. Counter increases upto $n+k+m+1$: upto $n+k+m+1$ steps are required till completion of rule 6. A maximum of 4 steps for rules 7-12. Thus, the number of steps needed is $\leq n + k + m + 5$. We do not go into the details to show that

- the above construction is semi-uniform: it is clear that the rules depend on k, and encode the clauses C_i. Hence for each 2QBF instance, we have a particular membrane system solving it;
- sound and complete : the system outputs "yes" iff the 2QBF instance is true;
- the function H required for the above construction is in **P**.

This result, along with the observation that **P**-$PMC_{\mathcal{R}}^*$ is closed under complements and polynomial time reductions gives us the following result:

Theorem 2. $\mathbf{NP^{NP}} \cup \mathbf{coNP^{NP}} \subseteq \mathbf{(P)}\text{-}\mathcal{PMC}^*_{\mathcal{MM}^0}(\{rendo, rexo, iendo, div\})$

We conclude with an example. Consider the 2QBF $\varphi_1 = \forall X \exists Y ((x_1 \vee \neg x_3) \wedge (\neg x_1 \vee \neg x_2))$, $X = \{x_1, x_2\}, Y = \{x_3\}$. φ_1 is not true, since for $x_1 = x_2 = T$, there is no satisfying assignment. Here $C_1 = (x_1 \vee \neg x_3), C_2 = (\neg x_1 \vee \neg x_2)$. Let us look at the case of φ_1. In this case, $k = 2, n = 3, m = 2, n + m + k = 7$, we have $\mu = [\ [\ [[\ [[[a_1 a_2 a_3]_0]_{1'}]_{2'}\ ]_1]_2\ [b_1 b_2]_L]_3[c_0]_J[\ ]_K]_4$ with the following steps:

1. $[\,[\,[\,[\quad[\,[\,[[a_1 a_2 a_3]_0]_{1'}]_{2'}\quad]_1]_2\,[b_1 b_2]_L]_3[c_0]_J[\quad]_K]_4$

2. $[\,[\,[\,[\quad[\,[\,[[t_1 a_2 a_3]_0 f_1 a_2 a_3]_0]_{1'}]_{2'}\quad]_1]_2\,[t_1 b_2]_L[f_1 b_2]_L]_3[[c_1]_J]_K]_4$

3. $[\,[\,[\,[\quad[\,[\,[[t_1 t_2 a_3]_0[t_1 f_2 a_3]_0[f_1 t_2 a_3]_0[f_1 f_2 a_3]_0]_{1'}]_{2'}\quad]_1]_2$
   $[t_1 t_2]_L[t_1 f_2]_L[f_1 t_2]_L[f_1 f_2]_L]_3[c_2]_J[\quad]_K]_4$
   (a_1, a_2 have been replaced. In the next step, the membranes 0 start crossing membranes $1', 2'$. Note that this is a non-deterministic decision - we could have waited till a_3 gets replaced, and then started the crossing over)

4. $[\,[\,[\,[\quad[\,[\quad]_{1'}[t_1 t_2 a_3]_0[t_1 f_2 a_3]_0[f_1 t_2 a_3]_0[f_1 f_2 a_3]_0]_{2'}]_1]_2$
   $[t_1 t_2]_L[t_1 f_2]_L[f_1 t_2]_L[f_1 f_2]_L]_3[[c_3]_J]_K]_4$

5. $[\,[\,[\,[\quad[\,[\quad]_{1'}]_{2'}[t_1 t_2 a_3]_0[t_1 f_2 a_3]_0[f_1 t_2 a_3]_0[f_1 f_2 a_3]_0]_1]_2$
   $[t_1 t_2]_L[t_1 f_2]_L[f_1 t_2]_L[f_1 f_2]_L]_3[c_4]_J[\quad]_K]_4$

6. $[\,[\,[\,[\quad[\,[\quad]_{1'}]_{2'}[t_1 t_2 t_3]_0[t_1 t_2 f_3]_0[f_1 t_2 t_3]_0[f_1 t_2 f_3]_0[f_1 f_2 t_3]_0\,[f_1 f_2 f_3]_0]_1$
   $[t_1 f_2 a_3]_0]_2[t_1 t_2]_L[t_1 f_2]_L[f_1 t_2]_L[f_1 f_2]_L]_3[c_5]_J]_K]_4$
   (The assignment $t_1 f_2 a_3$ crosses over membrane 1 since C_1 is satisfied, the same could have been done for $t_1 t_2 a_3$. However, we have illustrated the case when the remaining membranes 0 divide further)

7. $[\,[\,[\,[\quad[\,[\quad]_{1'}]_{2'}[f_1 t_2 t_3]_0[f_1 f_2 t_3]_0\quad]_1[t_1 t_2 t_3]_0[t_1 t_2 f_3]_0[f_1 f_2 t_3]_0[f_1 t_2 f_3]_0]_2$
   $[t_1 f_2 a_3]_0[t_1 t_2]_L[t_1 f_2]_L[f_1 t_2]_L[f_1 f_2]_L]_3[c_6]_J[\quad]_K]_4$
   ($t_1 f_2 a_3$ crosses over membrane 2; among the remaining membranes 0 which divided in the previous step, those which satisfy C_1 cross over membrane 1.)

8. $[\,[\,[\,[\quad[\,[\quad]_{1'}]_{2'}[f_1 t_2 t_3]_0[f_1 f_2 t_3]_0\quad]_1[t_1 t_2 t_3]_0[t_1 t_2 f_3]_0]_2[f_1 f_2 t_3]_0[f_1 t_2 f_3]_0$
   $[t_1 t_2]_L[t_1 f_2[t_1 f_2 a_3]_0]_L[f_1 t_2]_L[f_1 f_2]_L]_3[[c_7]_J]_K]_4$
   ($f_1 f_2 f_3$ and $f_1 t_2 f_3$ cross over membrane 2. Now, all assignments satisfying $((x_1 \vee \neg x_3) \wedge (\neg x_1 \vee \neg x_2))$ have come out of membrane 2. These are $t_1 f_2 a_3, f_1 f_2 f_3, f_1 t_2 f_3$. Clearly, not all possible assignments to x_1, x_2 have made it. In parallel, the assignment $t_1 f_2 a_3$ enters membrane L containing $t_1 f_2$ using the *iendo* rule. For readability, from the next step onward, we will omit the trapped assignments inside membranes 1,2)

9. $[\,[\,[\,[\quad[\,[\quad]_{1'}]_{2'}\quad]_1]_2[t_1 t_2]_L[t_1 f_2[t_1 f_2 t_3]_0[t_1 f_2 f_3]_0]_L$
   $[f_1 t_2[f_1 t_2 f_3]_0]_L[f_1 f_2[f_1 f_2 f_3]_0]_L]_3[c]_J[\quad]_K]_4$
   (The assignments $f_1 t_2 f_3$ and $f_1 f_2 f_3$ enter the respective membranes L; in parallel, the membrane 0 containing $t_1 f_2 a_3$ divides replacing a_3. c_7 is replaced with c)

10. $[\,[\,[\,[\quad[\,[\quad]_{1'}]_{2'}\quad]_1]_2[t_1 t_2]_L[t_1 f_2\,[t_1 f_2 t_3]_0[t_1 f_2 f_3]_0]_L$
    $[f_1 t_2\,[f_1 t_2 f_3]_0]_L[f_1 f_2\,[f_1 f_2 f_3]_0]_L]_3[d]_J[e]_J[\quad]_K]_4$
    (Membrane J divides replacing c with d, e)

11. $[\,[\,[\,[\quad[\,[\quad]_{1'}]_{2'}\quad]_1]_2[t_1 t_2]_L[t_1 f_2\,[t_1 f_2 t_3]_0[t_1 f_2 f_3]_0]_L$
    $[f_1 t_2\,[f_1 t_2 f_3]_0]_L[f_1 f_2\,[f_1 f_2 f_3]_0]_L[no]_J]_3[d_1]_J[d_2]_J[\quad]_K]_4$
    (The copy of membrane J with e enters membrane 3 replacing e with "no". In parallel, the other copy of membrane J with d divides again, with d_1, d_2)

12. $[\,[\,[\,[\quad[\,[\quad]_{1'}]_{2'}\quad]_1]_2[t_1 f_2\,[t_1 f_2 t_3]_0[t_1 f_2 f_3]_0]_L$
    $[f_1 t_2\,[f_1 t_2 f_3]_0]_L[f_1 f_2\,[f_1 f_2 f_3]_0]_L[no\,[t_1 t_2]_L]_J]_3[d_1]_J[d_2]_J[\quad]_K]_4$
    (The elementary copy of membrane L enters membrane J containing "no". In parallel, the copy of membrane J with d_1 enters membrane 3)

There are no more steps and the system halts. The "no" remains in the system. Number of steps $= 11 = n + k + m + 4$.

References

1. Alhazov, A., Pan, L., Păun, G.: Trading Polarizations for Labels in P Systems with Active Membranes. Acta Informatica 41(2-3), 111–144 (2004)
2. Alhazov, A., Freund, R.: On the Efficiency of P systems with Active Membranes and Two Polarizations. In: Mauri, G., Păun, G., Jesús Pérez-Jímenez, M., Rozenberg, G., Salomaa, A. (eds.) WMC 2004. LNCS, vol. 3365, pp. 146–160. Springer, Heidelberg (2005)
3. Alhazov, A., Burtseva, L., Cojocaru, S., Rogozhin, Y.: Solving PP-Complete and #P-complete problems by P systems with active membranes. In: Corne, D.W., Frisco, P., Păun, G., Rozenberg, G., Salomaa, A. (eds.) WMC 2008. LNCS, vol. 5391, pp. 108–117. Springer, Heidelberg (2009)
4. Borodin, A.: On Relating Time and Space to Size and Depth. SIAM Journal of Computing 6(4), 733–744 (1977)
5. Krishna, S.N., Ciobanu, G.: On the Computational Power of Enhanced Mobile Membranes. In: Beckmann, A., Dimitracopoulos, C., Löwe, B. (eds.) CiE 2008. LNCS, vol. 5028, pp. 326–335. Springer, Heidelberg (2008)
6. Krishna, S.N., Ciobanu, G.: Enhanced Mobile Membranes: Computability Results. Theory of Computing Systems 48 (2011), doi:10.1007/s00224-010-9256-9).
7. Leporati, A., Ferretti, C., Mauri, G., Pérez-Jiménez, M.J., Zandron, C.: Complexity Aspects of Polarizationless Membrane Systems. Natural Computing 8(4), 703–717 (2009)
8. Pérez-Jiménez, M.J., Romero-Jiménez, A., Sancho-Caparrini, F.: Complexity Classes in Models of Cellular Computing with Membranes. Natural Computing 2(3), 265–285 (2003)
9. Pérez-Jiménez, M.J., Romero-Jiménez, A.: Trading Polarizations for Bi-stable Catalysts in P Systems with Active Membranes. In: Mauri, G., Păun, G., Jesús Pérez-Jímenez, M., Rozenberg, G., Salomaa, A. (eds.) WMC 2004. LNCS, vol. 3365, pp. 373–388. Springer, Heidelberg (2005)
10. Pan, L., Ishdorj, T.-O.: P systems with Active Membranes and Separation Rules. Journal of Universal Computer Science 10, 630–649 (2004)
11. Pan, L., Alhazov, A., Ishdorj, T.-O.: Further Remarks on P systems with Active Membranes, Separation, Merging, and Release Rules. Soft Computing 9(9), 686–690 (2005)
12. Papadimitriou, C.: Computational Complexity. Addison-Wesley, Reading (1994)
13. Porreca, A.E., Leporati, A., Mauri, G., Zandron, C.: P Systems with Elementary Active Membranes: Beyond NP and coNP. In: Gheorghe, M., Hinze, T., Păun, G., Rozenberg, G., Salomaa, A. (eds.) CMC 2010. LNCS, vol. 6501, pp. 338–347. Springer, Heidelberg (2010)
14. Păun, G.: Computing with Membranes. Journal of Computer and System Sciences 61(1), 108–143 (2000)
15. Păun, G.: P Systems with Active Membranes: Attacking NP-Complete Problems. Journal of Automata, Languages and Combinatorics 6(1), 75–90 (2001)
16. Păun, G., Rozenberg, G., Salomaa, A. (eds.): The Oxford Handbook of Membrane Computing. Oxford University Press, Oxford (2010)
17. Zandron, C., Leporati, A., Ferretti, C., Mauri, G., Pérez-Jiménez, M.J.: On the Computational Efficiency of Polarizationless Recognizer P Systems with Strong Division and Dissolution. Fundamenta Informaticae 87, 79–91 (2008)

Language Classes Generated by Tree Controlled Grammars with Bounded Nonterminal Complexity

Sherzod Turaev[1], Jürgen Dassow[2], and Mohd Hasan Selamat[1]

[1] Faculty of Computer Science and Information Technology
University Putra Malaysia
43400 UPM Serdang, Selangor, Malaysia
{sherzod, hasan}@fsktm.upm.edu.my
[2] Otto-von-Guericke-Universität Magdeburg, Fakultät für Informatik
PSF 4120, D-39016 Magdeburg, Germany
dassow@iws.cs.uni-magdeburg.de

Abstract. A tree controlled grammar can be given as a pair (G, G') where G is a context-free grammar and G' is a regular grammar. Its language consists of all terminal words with a derivation in G such that all levels of the corresponding derivation tree – except the last level – belong to $L(G')$. We define its descriptional complexity $\mathrm{Var}(G, G')$ as the sum of the numbers of nonterminals of G and G'. In [24] we have shown that tree controlled grammars (G, G') with $\mathrm{Var}(G, G') \leq 9$ are sufficient to generate all recursively enumerable languages. In this paper, our main result improves the bound to seven. Moreover, we show that all linear and regular simple matrix languages can be generated by tree controlled grammars with a descriptional complexity bounded by three.

1 Introduction

Since "economical" representation of formal languages has been always important, it is interesting to investigate their grammars from the point of view of descriptional complexity measures such as the number of nonterminals, the number of production rules, and the total number of symbols.

The study of the descriptional complexity with respect to regulated grammars was started in [1,4,5,6,22]. In recent years several interesting results on this topic have been obtained. For instance, [17] demonstrates that four-nonterminal matrix grammars with a certain type of leftmost derivations characterize the family of recursively enumerable languages. The nonterminal complexity of programmed and matrix grammars is studied in [9], where it is shown that three nonterminals for programmed grammars with appearance checking, and four nonterminals for matrix grammars with appearance checking are enough to generate every recursively enumerable language. A more detailed investigation with respect to the appearance checking is given in [10]. There are several papers which study the descriptional complexity of scattered context grammars [2,11,12,18,25], semi-conditional grammars [19,20,22,25], and multi-parallel grammars [16].

M. Holzer, M. Kutrib, and G. Pighizzini (Eds.): DCFS 2011, LNCS 6808, pp. 289–300, 2011.

In this paper we study the nonterminal complexity of tree controlled grammars. A tree controlled grammar can be given as a pair (G, G') where G is a context-free grammar and G' is a regular grammar. Its language consists of all terminal words with a derivation in G such that all levels of the corresponding derivation tree – except the last level – belong to $L(G')$. We define its descriptional complexity $\mathrm{Var}(G, G')$ as the sum of the numbers of nonterminals of G and G'. In contrast to most of the papers cited above, we do not only take the number of nonterminals of G but we also add the number of nonterminals of G', i. e., we also measure the complexity of the control device (however, we note that, for the matrix, programmed and scattered context grammars, it is not clear how one can measure the complexity of the control device in terms of nonterminals). In [24], we have shown that there is an infinite hierarchy with respect to the descriptional complexity, if we consider tree controlled grammars with non-erasing rules only, where the allowance of erasing rules leads to the result that every recursively enumerable language can be generated by a tree controlled grammar with no more than nine nonterminals in G and G'. The main contribution of this paper is the improvement of the bound for recursively enumerable languages from nine to seven. Moreover, we show that all linear and regular simple matrix languages can be generated by tree controlled grammars with the descriptional complexity bounded by three.

2   Definitions

We assume that the reader is familiar with formal language theory (see [7,23]).

Let T^* denote the set of all words over an alphabet T. The empty word is denoted by ε. The cardinality of a set X is denoted by $|X|$.

A context-free grammar is specified as a quadruple $G = (N, T, P, S)$ where N and T are the disjoint alphabets of nonterminals and terminals, respectively. By $\mathrm{Var}(G)$ we denote the number of the nonterminals of a grammar $G = (N, T, P, S)$, i.e., $\mathrm{Var}(G) = |N|$.

With each derivation in a context-free grammar G, one associates a derivation tree. The *level* associated with a node is the number of edges in the path from the root to the node. The *height* of the tree is the largest level number of any node. With a derivation tree t of height k and each number $0 \leq i \leq k$, we associate the *word of level* i which is given by all nodes of level i read from left to right, and we associate the *sentential form of level* i which consists of all nodes of level i and all leaves of level less than i read from left to right. Obviously, if u and v are sentential forms of two successive levels, then $u \Rightarrow^* v$ holds and this derivation is obtained by a parallel replacement of all nonterminals occurring in the sentential form u.

A *tree controlled grammar* is a quintuple $H = (N, T, P, S, R)$ where $G = (N, T, P, S)$ is a context-free grammar and $R \subseteq (N \cup T)^*$ is a regular set. The language $L(H)$ consists of all words w generated by the underlying grammar G such that there is a derivation tree t of w with respect to G, where the words of all levels (except the last one) are in R.

The family of all tree controlled grammars is denoted by $\mathcal{TC}$. It was proved that tree controlled grammars generate all recursively enumerable languages (see [3]).

Since $R = L(G')$ for some regular grammar $G' = (N', T', P', S')$, a tree controlled grammar H can be given as a pair $H = (G, G')$. Then it is natural to define the nonterminal complexity of the tree controlled grammar H as

$$\mathrm{Var}(H) = \mathrm{Var}(G) + \mathrm{Var}(G').$$

By this measure we take into consideration the size of the underlying grammar G as well as the size of control grammar G'.

For a language L, we set

$$\mathrm{Var}_{\mathcal{TC}}(L) = \min\{\mathrm{Var}(H) : H = (G, G'), \text{ where } G \text{ is a context- free grammar,}$$
$$G' \text{ is a regular grammar and } L(H) = L\}.$$

3 A Bound for Recursively Enumerable Languages

In this section we show that the bound for recursively enumerable languages established in [24] can be improved from nine to seven.

In [13], it was shown that every recursively enumerable language is generated by a grammar

$$G = (\{S, A, B, C\}, T, P \cup \{ABC \to \varepsilon\}, S)$$

in the *Geffert normal form* where P contains only context-free rules of the form (a) $S \to uSa$ where $u \in \{A, AB\}^*$, $a \in T$; (b) $S \to uSv$ where $u \in \{A, AB\}^*$, $v \in \{BC, C\}^*$; (c) $S \to uv$ where $u \in \{A, AB\}^*$, $v \in \{BC, C\}^*$.

In addition, any terminal derivation in G is of the form (1) $S \Rightarrow^* w'Sw$ by productions of the form $S \to uSa$, where $w' \in \{A, AB\}^*$ and $w \in T^*$; (2) $w'Sw \Rightarrow^* w_1 w_2 w$ by productions of the form $S \to uSv$ and $S \to uv$, where $w_1 \in \{A, AB\}^*$ and $w_2 \in \{BC, C\}^*$; (3) $w_1 w_2 w \Rightarrow^* w$ by $ABC \to \varepsilon$.

In order to distinguish the phases in a terminal derivation, we use a new nonterminal and slightly modify the rules of the grammar. A grammar G is in the *modified Geffert normal form* if

$$G = (\{S, S', A, B, C\}, T, P \cup \{ABC \to \lambda\}, S)$$

where P contains only context-free rules of the form

(a) $S \to uSa$ where $u \in \{A, AB\}^*$, $a \in T$,
(b) $S \to S'$,
(c) $S' \to uS'v$ where $u \in \{A, AB\}^*$, $v \in \{BC, C\}^*$,
(d) $S' \to \varepsilon$.

In addition, any terminal derivation in G is of the form

(1) $S \Rightarrow^* w'Sw \Rightarrow w'S'w$ by productions of the form $S \to uSa$ and $S \to S'$, where $w' \in \{A, AB\}^*$ and $w \in T^*$,

(2) $w'S'w \Rightarrow^* w_1 S'w_2 w \Rightarrow w_1 w_2 w$ by productions of the form $S' \to uS'v$ and $S' \to \varepsilon$, where $w_1 \in \{A, AB\}^*$ and $w_2 \in \{BC, C\}^*$,

(3) $w_1 w_2 w \Rightarrow^* w$ by $ABC \to \varepsilon$.

Theorem 1. *Every recursively enumerable language can be generated by a tree controlled grammar with not more than seven nonterminals.*

Proof. Let $L \subseteq T^*$ be a recursively enumerable language generated by the grammar

$$G = (\{S, S', A, B, C\}, T, P \cup \{ABC \to \varepsilon\}, S)$$

as above. We define the morphism $\phi : \{A, B, C\}^* \to \{0, \$\}^*$ by setting

$$\phi(A) = 0\$, \quad \phi(B) = 0^2\$, \quad \phi(C) = 0^3\$,$$

and construct a tree controlled grammar $H' = (N', T, P_\phi \cup P'', S, R')$ where

$$N' = \{S, S', 0, 1, \$, \#\},$$

$$P_\phi = \{S \to \phi(u)Sa \mid S \to uSa \in P, u \in \{A, AB\}^*, a \in T\}$$

$$\cup \{S \to S'\}$$

$$\cup \{S' \to \phi(u)S'\phi(v) \mid S' \to uS'v \in P, u \in \{A, AB\}^*, v \in \{BC, C\}^*\}$$

$$\cup \{S' \to \varepsilon\},$$

$$P'' = \{0 \to 0, 0 \to 1, \$ \to \$, \$ \to \#, 1 \to \varepsilon, \# \to \varepsilon\},$$

$$R' = (\{S, S', 0, \$, 1\#1^2\#1^3\#\} \cup T)^*.$$

First we show that any terminal derivation in G can be simulated by a derivation in H. It is clear that the first and second phases of the derivation for $w \in T^*$ in the grammar G

$$S \Rightarrow^* w'Sw \Rightarrow w'S'w \Rightarrow^* w_1 S'w_2 w \Rightarrow w_1 w_2 w,$$

$w', w_1 \in \{A, AB\}^*$, $w_2 \in \{BC, C\}^*$, $w \in T^*$, can be simulated in H using the corresponding rules of P_ϕ and chain rules $0 \to 0$, $\$ \to \$$, which result in the sentential form

$$S \Rightarrow^* \phi(w')Sw \Rightarrow \phi(w')S'w \Rightarrow^* \phi(w_1)S'\phi(w_2)w \Rightarrow \phi(w_1)\phi(w_2)w.$$

Since the rules of P_ϕ generate words from $(\{S, S', 0, \$\} \cup T)^*$, every control word of R in these phases of the derivation is also in $(\{S, S', 0, \$\} \cup T)^*$.

Let

$$z = uABCvw, u \in \{A, AB\}^*, v \in \{BC, C\}^*, w \in T^*,$$

be a sentential form in the third phase of the derivation in G. Then

$$z' = \phi(u)0\$0^2\$0^3\$\phi(v)w, \phi(u) \in \{0, \$\}^*, \phi(v) \in \{0, \$\}^*, w \in T^*,$$

is the corresponding sentential form in the derivation in H, and z' is continued as follows:

$$\phi(u)0\$0^2\$0^3\$\phi(v)w \xrightarrow{\;(0\to1)^6\,(\$\to\#)^3\,(0\to0)^*\,(\$\to\$)^*\;} \phi(u)1\#1^2\#1^3\#\phi(v)w$$

$$\xrightarrow{\;(1\to\varepsilon)^6\,(\#\to\varepsilon)^3\,(0\to0)^*\,(\$\to\$)^*\;} \phi(u)\phi(v)w,$$

which simulates the elimination of the substring ABC in z.

Now we show that $L(H) \subseteq L(G)$ also holds.

Let $D : S \Rightarrow^* w = x_1 x_2 \cdots x_n \in T^*$, $x_1, x_2, \ldots, x_n \in T$, be a derivation in the grammar H.

Since $x_1 x_2 \cdots x_n$ can be generated only by rules $S \to \phi(u)Sa \in P'$,

$$S \Rightarrow^* w'Sx_1x_2 \cdots x_n \Rightarrow^* w''S'x_1x_2 \cdots x_n, \quad w', w'' \in \{0, 1, \$, \#\}^*, \qquad (1)$$

is a phase of the derivation D.

If w', w'' have occurrences of 1 or $\#$, then they must have the subword $1\#1^2\#1^3\#$ by the construction of R. Since rules of the form $S \to \phi(u)Sa$ can generate at most subwords $0\$0^2\$$, i.e., $0^3\$$ cannot be generated. Therefore w', w'' cannot contain the subword $1\#1^2\#1^3\#$. Thus, in this phase, rules of the form $S \to \phi(u)Sa$ and chain rules $0 \to 0$, $\$ \to \$$ are applied. It follows that

$$w' = w'' = \phi(u_n) \cdots \phi(u_2)\phi(u_1)$$

for some $\phi(u_n), \ldots, \phi(u_2), \phi(u_1) \in \{0, \$\}^*$. Then

$$S \Rightarrow^* u_n \cdots u_2 u_1 S x_1 x_2 \cdots x_n \Rightarrow u_n \cdots u_2 u_1 S' x_1 x_2 \cdots x_n$$

is the first phase of a derivation in G, which simulates (1).

Let from S' some sentential form $w_1 w_2 \in \{0, 1, \$, \#\}^*$ be generated, i.e.,

$$S' \Rightarrow^* w_1 S' w_2. \qquad (2)$$

Though the subwords $0\$$, $0^2\$$ and $0^3\$$ can be generated in the first part of this phase, i.e., in $S' \Rightarrow^* w_1 S' w_2$, any sentential form cannot contain a subword $0\$0^2\$0^3\$$, as S' separates subwords $0\$0^2\$$ and $0^3\$$ or $0\$$ and $0^2\$0^3\$$, i.e., $0\$0^2\$S'0^3\$$ and $0\$S'0^2\$0^3\$$ can be possible subwords. Thus a subword $1\#1^2\#1^3\#$ cannot be generated, and in $S' \Rightarrow^* w_1 S' w_2$, only rules of the form $S' \to \phi(u)S'\phi(v)$, $\phi(u), \phi(v) \in \{0, \$\}^*$ and the chain rules $0 \to 0$, $\$ \to \$$ are applied. It follows that

$$w_1 = \phi(u'_m) \cdots \phi(u'_2)\phi(u'_1) \text{ and } w_2 = \phi(v'_1)\phi(v'_2) \cdots \phi(v'_m)$$

for some $\phi(u'_1), \phi(u'_2), \ldots, \phi(u'_m), \phi(v'_1), \phi(v'_2), \ldots, \phi(v'_m) \in \{0, \$\}^*$.

Then

$$u_n \cdots u_2 u_1 S' x_1 x_2 \cdots x_n \Rightarrow^* u_n \cdots u_2 u_1 u'_m \cdots u'_2 u'_1 S' v'_1 v'_2 \cdots v'_m x_1 x_2 \cdots x_n$$

is the second phase of a derivation in G, which simulates (2).

Let us now consider the sentential form

$$w'w_1S'w_2w. \tag{3}$$

As it is stated above, $0\$0^2\$S'0^3\$$ and $0\$S'0^2\$0^3\$$ are possible subwords containing nonterminals S', 0 and $, (3) can be in the form

$$w'_1 0\$S'0^2\$0^3\$w'_2 w, \text{ where } w'_1 0\$ = w'w_1, 0^2\$0^3\$w'_2 = w_2$$

or

$$w'_1 0\$0^2\$S'0^3\$w'_2 w, \text{ where } w'_1 0\$0^2\$ = w'w_1, 0^3\$w'_2 = w_2.$$

By eliminating S', we obtain the sentential form

$$w'w_1w_2w$$

by rules $S' \to \varepsilon$ and $0 \to 0$, $\$ \to \$$ or the sentential form

$$w'_1 1\#1^2\#1^3\#w'_2 w$$

by rules $S' \to \varepsilon$, $0 \to 0$, $\$ \to \$$, and $0 \to 1$, $\$ \to \#$.

Further, the subword $1\#1^2\#1^3\#$ is erased by $1 \to \varepsilon$ and $\# \to \varepsilon$, resulting in $w'_1 w'_2 w$.

In the former case,

$$w'w_1S'w_2w \Rightarrow^* w'w_1w_2w$$

is simulated by

$$uS'vw \Rightarrow uvw, \phi(u) = w'w_1, \phi(v) = w_2,$$

which is obtained by $S' \to \varepsilon$.

In the latter case,

$$w'w_1S'w_2w = \left\{ \begin{array}{l} w'_1 0\$S'0^2\$0^3\$w'_2 w \\ w'_1 0\$0^2 S'\$0^3\$w'_2 w \end{array} \right\} \Rightarrow^* w'_1 w'_2 w$$

is simulated by

$$uS'vw \Rightarrow u'ABCv'w \Rightarrow^* u'v'w,$$

$\phi(u) = w'w_1, \phi(v) = w_2, \phi(u') = w'_1, \phi(v') = w'_2$, which is obtained by $S' \to \varepsilon$ and $ABC \to \varepsilon$.

Any sentential form $z \in \{0, 1, \$, \#\}^*$ of D associated with some level (except the last one) and containing occurrences of 1 and $\#$, must be of the form

$$z = x1\#1^2\#1^3\#yw \text{ for some } x, y \in \{0, \$\}^*$$

by the definition of R'.

Then the possible sentential forms z^- and z^+ associated with the previous and next levels of the derivation tree are

$$z^- \in \{x0\$0^2\$0^3\$yw, \ x0\$S'0^2\$0^3\$yw, \ x0\$0^2\$S'0^3\$yw,$$
$$x0\$1\#1^2\#1^3\#0^2\$0^3\$yw, \ x0\$0^2\$1\#1^2\#1^3\#0^3\$yw\}$$

and

$$z^+ \in \{xyw, \; x'0\$1\#1^2\#1^3\#0^2\$0^3\$y'w, \; x'0\$0^2\$1\#1^2\#1^3\#0^3\$y'w\},$$

respectively, where $x', y' \in \{0, \$\}^*$.

Without loss of generality we can assume that

$$\left.\begin{array}{r} x0\$0^2\$0^3\$yw \\ x0\$S'0^2\$0^3\$yw \\ x0\$1\#1^2\#1^3\#0^2\$0^3\$yw \end{array}\right\} \Rightarrow^* z \Rightarrow^* \left\{\begin{array}{l} xyw \\ x'0\$1\#1^2\#1^3\#0^2\$0^3\$y'w, \end{array}\right.$$

Since the application of rules $0 \to 1$ and $\$ \to \#$ can be delayed without changing z and still generating words of R', we replace

$$x0\$S'0^2\$0^3\$yw \xrightarrow{(S' \to \varepsilon)(0 \to 1)^6(\$ \to \#)^3(0 \to 0)^*(\$ \to \$)^*} x1\#1^2\#1^3\#yw$$

with

$$x0\$S'0^2\$0^3\$yw \xrightarrow{(S' \to \varepsilon)(0 \to 0)^*(\$ \to \$)^*} x0\$0^2\$0^3\$yw$$

$$\xrightarrow{(0 \to 1)^6(\$ \to \#)^3(0 \to 0)^*(\$ \to \$)^*} x1\#1^2\#1^3\#yw.$$

The same changes can be done with the derivation

$$x0\$1\#1^2\#1^3\#0^2\$0^3\$yw \xrightarrow{(1 \to \varepsilon)^6(\# \to \varepsilon)^3}$$

$$\xrightarrow{(0 \to 1)^6(\$ \to \#)^3(0 \to 0)^*(\$ \to \$)^*} x1\#1^2\#1^3\#yw,$$

which is replaced with

$$x0\$1\#1^2\#1^3\#0^2\$0^3\$yw \xrightarrow{(1 \to \varepsilon)^6(\# \to \varepsilon)^3(0 \to 0)^*(\$ \to \$)^*} x0\$0^2\$0^3\$yw$$

$$\xrightarrow{(0 \to 1)^6(\$ \to \#)^3(0 \to 0)^*(\$ \to \$)^*} x1\#1^2\#1^3\#yw.$$

We also do similar changes with the derivation

$$x1\#1^2\#1^3\#yw \xrightarrow{(1 \to \varepsilon)^6(\# \to \varepsilon)^3(0 \to 1)^6(\$ \to \#)^3(0 \to 0)^*(\$ \to \$)^*} x'0\$1\#1^2\#1^3\#0^2\$0^3\$y'w,$$

i.e.,

$$x1\#1^2\#1^3\#yw \xrightarrow{(1 \to \varepsilon)^6(\# \to \varepsilon)^3(0 \to 0)^*(\$ \to \$)^*} x0\$0^2\$0^3\$yw$$

$$\xrightarrow{(0 \to 1)^6(\$ \to \#)^3(0 \to 0)^*(\$ \to \$)^*} x'1\#1^2\#1^3\#y'w.$$

Now, from all cases above, we can see that $z = x1\#1^2\#1^3\#yw$ is generated from $x0\$0^2\$0^3\$yw$, and results in xyw, i.e.,

$$x0\$0^2\$0^3\$yw \Rightarrow^* x1\#1^2\#1^3\#yw \Rightarrow^* xyw.$$

This phase of the derivation D can be simulated by

$$uABCvw \Rightarrow^* uvw, \phi(u) = x, \phi(v) = y,$$

in G by using $ABC \to \varepsilon$.

Thus, for every derivation D in H, we can construct a derivation in G simulating D, i.e., $L(H) \subseteq L(G)$.

Since R' can be generated by the regular grammar $G' = (\{S''\}, T'', P'', S'')$ where

$$T'' = \{S, S', 0, 1, \$, \#\} \cup T,$$
$$P'' = \{S'' \to xS'' : x \in \{S, S', 0, \$, 1\#1^2\#1^3\#\} \cup T\} \cup \{S'' \to \varepsilon\},$$

we have $\mathrm{Var}(H) = 7$ and, consequently, $\mathrm{Var}_{TC}(L) \leq 7$.

Thus every recursively language is generated by a tree controlled grammar with at most seven nonterminals. $\qquad\square$

4   A Bound for Some Other Language Families

In this section, for some classes of languages, we improve the bound seven given in the preceding section to three.

Theorem 2. *For any regular language L, there is a tree controlled grammar H such that $L(H) = L$ and $\mathrm{Var}(H) = 3$.*

Proof. Let L be a regular language and $G = (N, T, P, S)$ a regular grammar which generates L. Let $N = \{A_1, A_2, \ldots, A_n\}$ and $S = A_1$. We now construct the tree controlled grammar $H = (\{A, B\}, T, P', A, R)$ with

$$P' = \{A \to BwA^i \mid A_j \to wA_i \in P \text{ for some } 1 \leq i, j \leq n\}$$
$$\cup \{A \to Bw \mid A_j \to w \in P \text{ for some } 1 \leq j \leq n\}$$
$$\cup \{A \to B, \ B \to \varepsilon\},$$

$$R = \{A\} \cup \{B^j wA^i \mid A_j \to wA_i \in P\} \cup \{B^j w \mid A_j \to w \in P\}.$$

Any derivation in H has the form

$$A \Rightarrow Bw_1 A^{i_1} \Rightarrow^* w_1 B^{i_1} w_2 A^{i_2} \Rightarrow^* w_1 w_2 B^{i_2} w_3 A^{i_3}$$
$$\Rightarrow^* w_1 w_2 \cdots w_{n-2} B^{i_{n-2}} w_{n-1} A^{i_{n-1}} \Rightarrow^* w_1 w_2 \cdots w_{n-2} w_{n-1} B^{i_{n-1}} w_n \qquad (4)$$
$$\Rightarrow^* w_1 w_2 \cdots w_{n-2} w_{n-1} w_n$$

(by the structure of R, in the sentential form $w_1 w_2 \ldots w_{r-1} B^{i_r-1} w_r A^{i_r}$, we have to replace the first $i_r - 1$ occurrences of A by B's and the last occurrence of A by $Bw_{r+1} A^{i_{r+1}}$ or by Bw_n for $r = n - 1$) and the words at the levels of the corresponding derivation tree are

$$A, \ Bw_1 A^{i_1}, \ B^{i_1} w_2 A^{i_2}, \ldots, \ B^{i_{n-2}} w_{n-1} A^{i_{n-1}}, \ B^{i_{n-1}} w_n. \qquad (5)$$

According to R, we have the rules

$$S = A_1 \to w_1 A_{i_1}, \ A_{i_1} \to w_2 A_{i_2}, \ A_{i_2} \to w_3 A_{i_3}, \dots,$$
$$A_{i_{n-2}} \to w_{n-1} A_{i_{n-1}}, \ A_{i_{n-1}} \to w_n \tag{6}$$

in P. Hence we have the derivation

$$S = A_1 \Rightarrow w_1 A_{i_1} \Rightarrow w_1 w_2 A_{i_2} \Rightarrow w_1 w_2 w_3 A_{i_3} \Rightarrow \cdots$$
$$\Rightarrow w_1 w_2 \cdots w_{n-2} A_{i_{n-2}} \Rightarrow w_1 w_2 \cdots w_{n-2} w_{n-1} A_{i_{n-1}} \tag{7}$$
$$\Rightarrow w_1 w_2 \cdots w_{n-2} w_{n-1} w_n$$

in G. Therefore, $L(H) \subseteq L(G)$.

Conversely, it is easy to see that, for any derivation (7) in G, where the rules (6) are applied, there is a derivation (4) with the words given in (5) in the levels. Hence we have $L(G) \subseteq L(H)$.

Since R is a finite set, it can be generated by a regular grammar with one nonterminal (the nonterminal generates all words in one step by a rule). Therefore we have $\mathrm{Var}(G) = 3$. ☐

Remark 3. We note that the existence of an upper bound for the number of nonterminals comes from the control since there are regular languages L_n, $n \geq 0$, which require n nonterminals for the generation by context-free grammars (see [14]).

We now extend Theorem 2 to regular simple matrix grammars. For the sake of completeness, we recall the necessary notions.

A *regular simple matrix grammar of degree* n, $n \geq 1$, is an $(n+3)$-tuple $G = (V_1, V_2, \dots, V_n, T, M, S)$, where $V_1, V_2, \dots, V_n$ are pairwise disjoint alphabets of nonterminals, T is an alphabet of terminals, S is a nonterminal which is not in $\bigcup_{i=1}^{n} V_i$, and M is a set of matrices of the following forms:

1. $(S \to x)$, $x \in T^*$,
2. $(S \to A_1 A_2 \cdots A_n)$, $A_i \in V_i$, $1 \leq i \leq n$,
3. $(A_1 \to x_1 B_1, A_2 \to x_2 B_2, \dots, A_n \to x_n B_n)$, $A_i, B_i \in V_i$, $x_i \in T^*$, $1 \leq i \leq n$,
4. $(A_1 \to x_1, A_2 \to x_2, \dots, A_n \to x_n)$, $A_i \in V_i$, $x_i \in T^*$, $1 \leq i \leq n$.

We say that G is a *regular simple matrix grammar*, if it is a regular simple matrix grammar of some degree n. A regular simple matrix grammar is called *non-erasing* if we require $x_i \in T^+$ for all $1 \leq i \leq n$ in Condition 4 above.

A direct derivation step in a regular simple matrix grammar G is defined by

- $S \Rightarrow z$ if and only if there is a matrix $(S \to z) \in M$,
- $z_1 A_1 z_2 A_2 \cdots z_n A_n \Rightarrow z_1 x_1 B_1 z_2 x_2 B_2 \cdots z_n x_n B_n$ if and only if there exists a matrix $(A_1 \to x_1 B_1, \dots, A_n \to x_n B_n) \in M$,
- $z_1 A_1 z_2 A_2 \cdots z_n A_n \Rightarrow z_1 x_1 z_2 x_2 \cdots z_n x_n$ if and only if there exists a matrix $(A_1 \to x_1, A_2 \to x_2, \dots, A_n \to x_n) \in M$.

The language $L(G)$ generated by a regular simple matrix grammar is defined as $L(G) = \{z \mid z \in T^*,\ S \Rightarrow^* z\}$ where $\Rightarrow^*$ is the reflexive and transitive closure of $\Rightarrow$.

Simple matrix grammar and languages have been introduced by O. Ibarra in [15]. A summary of results on them can be found in Section 5.1 of [7].

Intuitively, a regular matrix grammar of degree n performs in parallel the derivations of n regular grammars. Moreover, in the corresponding derivation tree, the word of any level t is obtained by a concatenation of words of level t of the derivation trees from the regular grammars. Thus it is easy to transform the proof for regular languages (Theorem 2) to the case of non-erasing regular simple matrix grammars. Essentially, we have only to concatenate the words of the levels. The assumption of non-erasing rules in the matrices of type 4 is necessary; otherwise, we can obtain a word $B^{i_1} B^{i_2} \cdots B^{i_m} x_{m+1} B^{i_{m+1}} \cdots x_n B^{i_n}$ by a matrix $(A_{i_1} \to \varepsilon, A_{i_2} \to \varepsilon, \ldots, A_{i_m} \to \varepsilon, A_{i_{m+1}} \to x_{m+1}, \ldots, A_{i_n} \to x_n)$, but we are not able to recognize the exact powers of B, i. e., we cannot ensure the right remembering of the nonterminals. The details are left to the reader. Since non-erasing regular simple matrix grammars are as strong as arbitrary regular simple matrix grammars (see Theorem 1.5.3, [7]), we get the following statement.

Theorem 4. *For any regular simple matrix grammar G, there is a tree controlled grammar H such that $L(H) = L(G)$ and $\mathrm{Var}(H) = 3$.*

Another modification concerns linear languages. Any linear language can be generated by a linear grammar $G = (N, T, P, S)$, where all rules are of the form $A \to wB$ or $A \to Bw$ or $A \to w$ with $A, B \in N$ and $w \in T^+$ (with the exception $S \to \varepsilon$ if the language contains the empty word, but then S does not occur on the right hand side of a rule). We modify the construction of H in the proof of Theorem 2 by defining the set of productions and the control set as follows:

$$
\begin{aligned}
P' = & \{A \to BwA^i \mid A_j \to wA_i \in P \text{ for some } 1 \leq i, j \leq n\} \\
& \cup \{A \to A^i wB \mid A_j \to A_i w \in P \text{ for some } 1 \leq i, j \leq n\} \\
& \cup \{A \to wB \mid A_j \to w \in P \text{ for some } 1 \leq j \leq n\} \\
& \cup \{A \to B,\ B \to \varepsilon\},
\end{aligned}
$$

$$
\begin{aligned}
R = & \{A\} \cup \{B^j wA^i \mid A_j \to wA_i \in P\} \\
& \cup \{A^i wB^j \mid A_j \to A_i w \in P\} \cup \{wB^j \mid A_j \to w \in P\}.
\end{aligned}
$$

This leads to the following statement.

Theorem 5. *For any linear language L, there is a tree controlled grammar H such that $L(H) = L$ and $\mathrm{Var}(H) = 3$.*

5   Conclusions

In this paper we have studied the nonterminal complexity of tree controlled grammars generating recursively enumerable and regular languages. We have proved that every recursively enumerable language can be generated by a tree controlled grammar with no more than seven nonterminals (in the underlying grammar and the control grammar together) and, in the case of linear and regular simple matrix languages, this bound can be reduced to three. But it remains open whether the bounds seven and three are optimal. Moreover, we do not know good bounds for context-free, matrix, or ET0L languages which can be obtained by special choices of control languages (see [8]).

Acknowledgements

This work was partially supported by University Putra Malaysia via RUGS 05-01-10-0896RU.

References

1. Cremers, A.B., Mayer, O., Weiss, K.: On the complexity of regulated rewriting. Information Control 33, 10–19 (1974)
2. Csuhaj-Varjú, E., Vaszil, G.: Scattered context grammars generated any recursively enumerable language with two nonterminals. Information Processing Letters 110(20), 902–907 (2010)
3. Čulik II, K., Maurer, H.: Tree controlled grammars. Computing 19, 129–139 (1977)
4. Dassow, J.: Remarks on the complexity of regulated rewriting. Fundamenta Informaticae 7, 83–103 (1984)
5. Dassow, J., Păun, G.: Further remarks on the complexity of regulated rewriting. Kybernetika 21, 213–227 (1985)
6. Dassow, J., Păun, G.: Some notes on the complexity of regulated rewriting. Bull. Math. Soc. Sci. Math. R.S. Roumanie 30 (1986)
7. Dassow, J., Păun, G.: Regulated rewriting in formal language theory. Springer, Berlin (1989)
8. Dassow, J., Stiebe, R., Truthe, B.: Generative capacity of subregularly tree controlled grammars. International Journal of Foundations of Computer Science 21, 723–740 (2010)
9. Fernau, H.: Nonterminal complexity of programmed grammars. Theoretical Computer Science 296, 225–251 (2003)
10. Fernau, H., Freund, R., Oswald, M., Reinhardt, K.: Refinding the nonterminal complexity of graph-controlled, programmed, and matrix grammars. Journal of Automata, Languages and Combinatorics 12(1), 117–138 (2007)
11. Fernau, H., Meduna, A.: On the degree of scattered context-sensitivity. Theoretical Computer Science 290, 2121–2124 (2003)
12. Fernau, H., Meduna, A.: A simultaneous reduction of several measures of descriptional complexity in scattered context grammars. Information Processing Letters 86, 235–240 (2003)
13. Geffert, V.: Context-free-like forms for phrase-structure grammars. In: Koubek, V., Janiga, L., Chytil, M.P. (eds.) MFCS 1988. LNCS, vol. 324, pp. 309–317. Springer, Heidelberg (1988)
14. Gruska, J.: On a classification of context-free languages. Kybernetika 3, 22–29 (1967)

15. Ibarra, O.: Simple matrix grammars. Inform. Control 17, 359–394 (1970)
16. Masopust, T.: Descriptional complexity of multi-parallel grammars. Information Processing Letters 108, 68–70 (2008)
17. Meduna, A.: On the number of nonterminals in matrix grammars with leftmost derivations. In: Păun, G., Salomaa, A. (eds.) New Trends in Formal Languages. LNCS, vol. 1218, pp. 27–38. Springer, Heidelberg (1997)
18. Meduna, A.: Generative power of three-nonterminal scattered context grammars. Theoretical Computer Science 246, 279–284 (2000)
19. Meduna, A., Gopalaratnam, A.: On semi-conditional grammars with productions having either forbidding or permitting conditions. Acta Cybernetica 11(4), 307–323 (1994)
20. Meduna, A., Švec, M.: Reduction of simple semi-conditional grammars with respect to the number of conditional productions. Acta Cybernetica 15, 353–360 (2002)
21. Păun, G.: On the generative capacity of tree controlled grammars. Computing 21, 213–220 (1979)
22. Păun, G.: Six nonterminals are enough for generating each RE language by a matrix grammar. International Journal of Compuational Mathematics 15, 23–37 (1984)
23. Rozenberg, G., Salomaa, A. (eds.): Handbook of formal languages, vol. I-III. Springer, Berlin (1997)
24. Turaev, S., Dassow, J., Selamat, M.: Nonterminal complexity of tree controlled grammars. Theoretical Computer Science (submitted, 2011)
25. Vaszil, G.: On the descriptional complexity of some rewriting mechanisms regulated by context conditions. Theoretical Computer Science 330, 361–373 (2005)

Transition Function Complexity of Finite Automata

Māris Valdats

University of Latvia, Faculty of Computing
Rga, Raia Bulv. 19, Latvia
d20416@lanet.lv

Abstract. State complexity of finite automata in some cases gives the same complexity value for automata which intuitively seem to have completely different complexities. In this paper we consider a new measure of descriptional complexity of finite automata — BC-complexity. Comparison of it with the state complexity is carried out here as well as some interesting minimization properties are discussed. It is shown that minimization of the number of states can lead to a superpolynomial increase of BC-complexity.

1 Introduction

State complexity of finite automata[2][9] has been analyzed for more than 50 years and since then has been the main measure to estimate the descriptional complexity of finite automata. Minimization algorithm[8] for it was developed as well as methods to prove upper and lower bounds for various languages.

It is hard to find any evidence of any other complexity measure. Transition complexity[10] could be the one, it counts the number of transitions, but there is not much use of it for deterministic automata (it is proportional to state complexity) — it is used in the nondeterministic case. In this paper only deterministic automata are considered.

However further we give some examples from which it can be seen that calculating state complexity of an automaton sometimes is not sufficient and something else is necessary.

Consider an automaton with binary input and output tapes that writes the same data that it reads but shifted right by 200 symbols (or one can say that it copies with delay 200). It can be easily proved that the size of the state space of such an automaton is 2^{200} states: it has to remember last 200 input bits. Such an automaton can easily be implemented by keeping its state space in a 200 bit register with LIFO structure (Fig. 1(a)), which reads input from one end and which writes output from the other. The state complexity of this automaton is 2^{200}.

On the other hand consider a "random" automaton with 2^{200} states. There is essentially no better way to describe it as with its state transition table which consists of 2^{201} lines which as it is widely assumed would be larger than our

M. Holzer, M. Kutrib, and G. Pighizzini (Eds.): DCFS 2011, LNCS 6808, pp. 301–313, 2011.

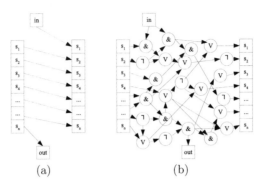

Fig. 1. Circuits that represent the transition function of (a) shift automaton and (b) "random" automaton.

universe. Although the state of this automaton can also be represented as a 200 bit register, the transition function of it represented in any reasonable way (e.g. as a Boolean circuit) would still have a complexity of order 2^{200} (Fig. 1(b)).

It is easy to represent a large number of states by a state register — 2^n states can fit into n state bits of the state register. But the transition function which does some computation on this register can be very easy in some cases and very complex in other cases. Therefore it seems natural to introduce a complexity measure for an automaton which will measure the complexity of its transition function.

In this paper we consider automata with output (transducers). All the basic facts are true also for automata without output, but for them the set of accepting states makes it more complex. For transducers output and next state can be combined in one transition function T which outputs a tuple of output symbol and next state. For acceptors it can be so that the transition function itself is simple while it is hard to say at the end if the state is accepting or rejecting if the characteristic function of the subset of accepting states $\tilde{Q} \subseteq Q$ is hard to compute (this would exactly be the case if one would turn automaton from Example 12 of Sect. 4 into acceptor). Therefore for acceptors complexity of both of these functions (transition function and the characteristic function of the subset of accepting states) have to be considered simultaneously.

2   Preliminaries

2.1   Finite Automata

A finite state (deterministic) transducer (FST)[7] (alternatively called Mealy machine) is a tuple (X, Y, S, T, s_0), where

1. X is the input alphabet (a finite set)
2. Y is the output alphabet (a finite set)
3. S is the state space (a finite set)

4. $T : X \times S \rightarrow Y \times S$ is the transition function
5. $s_0 \in S$ is the start state

Further in the text by an automaton a finite state transducer is assumed.

By T_Y and T_S we denote the projections of the transition function T to the output set Y and state space S respectively. An automaton starts computation in the state s_0 and in each step it reads input symbol $x \in X$, writes output symbol $y \in Y$ and changes its state. If the current state of automaton is $s \in S$ and it reads input symbol $x \in X$ then it moves to state $s' \in S$ and writes output symbol $y \in Y$ such that $(y, s') = T(x, s)$.

In such a way an automaton transforms input sequences $x_1, x_2, \ldots, x_n$ to output sequences $y_1, y_2, \ldots, y_n$ of the same length, so one can say it computes a function $g : \{0, 1\}^* \rightarrow \{0, 1\}^*$. Two automata that compute the same function g are called equivalent.

The state complexity of an automaton is the number of states in the state space $C_s(A) = |S|$. For each automaton a natural task is to minimize its state complexity. The following theorem states that every automaton has a unique minimal automaton.

Theorem 1. [2] *For every FST A there exists a unique (up to an isomorphism) minimal automaton $A_m = M(A)$ such that it is equivalent to A and its state complexity is minimal. There is an algorithm (minimization algorithm) M that for any automaton A constructs its minimal automaton.*

2.2 Boolean Circuits

We will use Boolean circuits to represent transition functions of FST. Here we define them and discuss some basic properties. We will restrict our attention to those circuits that are in the standard base ($\&, \vee, \neg$).

A Boolean circuit is a directed acyclic graph with indegree for any vertex at most 2. The nodes of indegree 0 are called inputs, and are labeled with a variable x_i or with a constant 0 or 1. The nodes of indegree $k \in \{1, 2\}$ are called gates and are labeled with Boolean functions:

1. $\neg$ if $k = 1$
2. $\&$ or $\vee$ if $k = 2$

Some of the nodes are designated as output nodes and are labeled with output symbols $y_1, \ldots, y_m$. The size of the circuit is the number of nodes in the graph.

To make diagrams more readable output nodes are shown as separate objects with unlabelled arrows leading to them. Also sometimes when it is necessary to show intermediate results in the circuit, additional nodes are added to the graph which do not belong to the circuit — they are coloured grey.

Boolean circuit F represents a Boolean function $(y_1, \ldots, y_m) = F(x_1, \ldots, x_n)$ in a natural way. Every node computes from its input(s) the function that it is labeled with — Boolean AND ($\&$), OR ($\vee$) or NOT ($\neg$). The value of m output nodes is the result of the computation.

Each function $f : \{0,1\}^n \rightarrow \{0,1\}^m$ can be represented by a Boolean circuit in (infinitely many) different ways. By the complexity of this function $C(f)$ we will consider the size of the smallest circuit that represents this function.

Two classical results about Boolean circuits state that most of functions $f : \{0,1\}^n \rightarrow \{0,1\}$ has a circuit complexity around $2^n/n$. This can be obtained by counting arguments and found in classical books about Boolean circuits ([3]) so we just state the result.

Theorem 2. *For any Boolean function* $f : \{0,1\}^n \rightarrow \{0,1\}$

$$C(f) \leq \frac{2^n}{n}(1 + O(\frac{\log n}{n}))$$

There exists a Boolean function $f : \{0,1\}^n \rightarrow \{0,1\}$ *such, that*

$$C(f) > \frac{2^n}{n}$$

If we consider Boolean functions with m output nodes, then by taking into account that they can be represented as m separate Boolean functions with just one output node we can conclude that

Corollary 3. *For any Boolean function* $f : \{0,1\}^n \rightarrow \{0,1\}^m$

$$C(f) \leq m\frac{2^n}{n}(1 + O(\frac{\log n}{n}))$$

Actually it can be proved that the complexity of almost all Boolean functions $f : \{0,1\}^n \rightarrow \{0,1\}$ lie in this interval $(\frac{2^n}{n}, \frac{2^n}{n}(1 + \varepsilon))$ and $\varepsilon \rightarrow 0$ when $n \rightarrow \infty$. This effect that most of the functions have a complexity that is close to the maximum is called Shannon effect. By Sh_n we denote the lexicographically first Boolean function on n arguments with the maximal complexity (Shannon function). From Theorem 2 it follows, that $C(Sh_n) > \frac{2^n}{n}$.

Further we will need a circuit that can simulate one step of a Turing machine.

Theorem 4. *Consider a Turing machine which for input data of length n uses at most $s(n)$ cells of the tape. Then any step of such a Turing machine that works on any variable of length n can be simulated by a Boolean circuit of size at most $cs(n)$ elements, where c is a constant that is dependent on TM, but not on n.*

Proof. First we add one additional state $\tilde{q}$ to the set of states of this Turing machine — it will be called the empty state and it will identify, that currently the head of TM is not at this cell.

Circuit works on binary encoded data. Each cell will be represented by its (binary encoded) symbol $i \in X$ and state $q \in Q \cup \{\tilde{q}\}$.

The circuit (Fig. 2) consists of two types of elements — transition elements U and filter elements F. Transition elements describe the change of the tape while filter elements simulate the movement of the head.

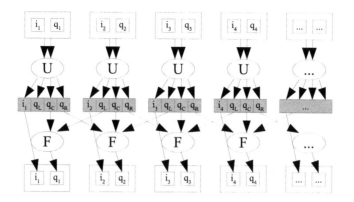

Fig. 2. Simulating one step of a Turing machine

Transition element U reads input (i, q) and outputs i', q_L, q_C, q_R. If $q = \tilde{q}$ then it does nothing: $i' = i$ and $q_L = q_C = q_R = \tilde{q}$. But if $q \in Q$ and the transition for pair (i, q) is $i, q \to j, q'R$ then it calculates $i' = j$, $q_R = q'$ and $q_C = q_L = \tilde{q}$. If the head have to move left (L) or stay (C) then it sets to q' the value of q_L or q_C respectively.

Filter element F checks if the head moves to the current cell from left, right or top. It receives three values q_L, q_C, q_R from left, top and right cell (Fig. 2) and if any of these is not $\tilde{q}$ then it sets value of q to the value of it, otherwise its result is $\tilde{q}$.

The size of elements U and F is constant (for a fixed Turing machine). As for each cell one U element and one F element is necessary, the size of the circuit is $(|U| + |F|)s(n) = cs(n)$.   □

Note that the circuit is the same for any step of the Turing machine. Therefore by concatenating few such circuits together (passing outputs of the previous circuit to the inputs of the next) one can simulate more than one step of a Turing machine.

Corollary 5. *If a Turing machine works in time $T(n)$ then for input length n it can be simulated by a Boolean circuit of size at most $cs(n)T(n)$ where c is a constant that is dependent on the Turing machine.*

Corollary 6. *If a Turing machine works in polynomial time, then it can be simulated by a polynomial size Boolean circuit.*

2.3   Complexity Classes PSPACE and P/Poly

Complexity class PSPACE contains all the decision problems (functions with output 0 or 1) that are computable in polynomial space. It means if $F \in PSPACE$ then there exists a (one tape) Turing machine TM_F and a polynomial $s(n)$ such that if TM_F is given input $x_1 x_2 \ldots x_n$ of length n then it does not use more than $s(n)$ cells for computation and when it halts the value in the first cell on the tape is $F(x_1x_2 \ldots x_n)$.

The working time of a Turing machine is exponentially bounded to the used space. The following theorem is given without a proof:

Theorem 7. *For any decision problem $F \in PSPACE$ there is a polynomial $s(n)$ such that there is a Turing machine solving F using no more than $s(n)$ space and $2^{s(n)}$ time.*

Complexity class PSPACE is a superclass of the polynomial hierarchy PH including P and NP classes.

Complexity class P/Poly contains all the decision problems that have a polynomial size Boolean circuit.

Definition 8. *A decision problem F has a polynomial size Boolean circuit ($F \in P/Poly$) if there exists a polynomial $p(x)$ such that for all n $C(F|_n) \leq p(n)$ where $F|_n : \{0,1\}^n \to \{0,1\}$ is a restriction of F to inputs of size n.*

Karp-Lipton theorem[6] states that if $NP \subseteq P/Poly$ then $PH = \Sigma_2$. In other words it means that if all problems in NP have a polynomial size Boolean circuit then the polynomial hierarchy collapses to its second level ($PH = \Sigma_2$). $PH = \Sigma_2$ is a weaker conjecture than $P = NP$ but is also considered to be unlikely. In Section 5 it is proved that if BC-complexity of a minimal automaton is always polynomially bounded to the BC-complexity of any equivalent automaton then $PSPACE \subset P/Poly$.

3   Representations of Automata

Classical representations of automata are table forms or state transition diagrams. They are essentially the same — state diagram can be thought of as a visualization of a table form. Table form lists automata transition function as a table where each line corresponds to one input (state and input symbol pair) of automaton's transition function. In state transition diagram each state is denoted by a circle and for each transition $(s, i) \to (s', o)$ an arrow is drawn from state s to state s' on which i/o symbols are written (see Fig. 5, for an example of a state transition diagram).

Both of these representations show each state of the automaton separately. In table form a state transition table consists of $|S| \cdot |X|$ lines, each state is represented by $|X|$ lines showing what to do in this state for each input symbol. In state transition diagram each state is represented by a circle and a collection of arrows leading to other states.

But normally to keep a large number of states you do not have to have a separate object for each state. You can encode —S— states into $\lceil \log_2(|S|) \rceil$ state bits which can be kept in a *state register* (In fact we do not restrict the number of state bits to $\lceil \log_2(|S|) \rceil$, this is the lower bound). Its size (number of bits) is logarithmic to the size of the state space (number of states). Also input and output alphabets can be encoded in an input register and output register.

Transition function in this case will take as input the state register and the input register and write result in the output register and the state register. It is thus a Boolean function and a natural way to represent it is with a Boolean circuit. Such a representation has been used before to obtain upper bounds for the circuit complexity of functions computed by transducers[5] or regular languages[4], but as far as we know it has not been studied as a measure for the complexity of an automaton itself.

Definition 9. *Let $A(X, Y, S, T, s_0)$ be a given DFA. We say that a Boolean circuit F with $m_x + m_s$ input variables and $m_y + m_s$ output variables represents it if there exist injective functions $f_X : X \to \{0,1\}^{m_x}$, $f_Y : Y \to \{0,1\}^{m_y}$ and $f_S : S \to \{0,1\}^{m_s}$ such that $f_S(s_0) = 0$ and for all $x \in X$ and $s \in S$ if $T(x, s) = (y, s')$, then*

$$F(f_X(x), f_S(s)) = (f_Y(T_Y(x, s)), f_S(T_S(x, s))).$$

In other words circuit F that represents A reads $f_X(x)$ as first m_x input bits and $f_S(s)$ as following m_s input bits, it writes as output $f_Y(y)$ as first m_y output bits and $f_S(s')$ as following m_s output bits.

Minimal values for m_x, m_y and m_s are $\lceil \log_2(|X|) \rceil$, $\lceil \log_2(|Y|) \rceil$ and $\lceil \log_2(|S|) \rceil$ respectively. This follows from the condition that functions f_x, f_y and f_s are injective. But values of m_x, m_y and m_s can be larger than these minimal values and we do not known if it gives a possibility to construct a smaller circuit for an automaton although the results from Sect. 5 suggests that it is true.

4   BC-Complexity of an Automaton

Each automaton can have (infinitely) many Boolean circuits that represent its transition function. Boolean circuit complexity (BC-complexity) of an automaton $C_{BC}(A)$ is the size of the smallest Boolean circuit that represents automaton A.

$$C_{BC}(A) = \min\{C(F) : F \text{ represents } A\}$$

Although the name "circuit complexity of automata" also sounds reasonable, we use the abbreviation "BC-complexity" to avoid confusion with the circuit complexity of Boolean functions.

Further we continue by setting the upper and lower bounds for BC-complexity compared to the state complexity of an automaton and show that these bounds are closely reachable.

Theorem 10. *If $\lceil \log_2(C_s(A)) \rceil = n$ then*

$$n \leq C_{BC}(A) \leq c2^n$$

where constant c is dependent on the size of input and output alphabets of the automaton.

Proof. Lower bound. Boolean circuit that represents automaton A must have at least n input variables — otherwise function f_s will not be injective. Therefore its complexity is at least n.

Upper bound. Take a Boolean circuit of minimal size with $m_x + n$ input variables and $m_x + n$ output variables where $m_x = \lceil \log_2(|X|) \rceil$ and $m_y = \lceil \log_2(|Y|) \rceil$ that represents this automaton. By Corollary 3 the complexity of this circuit is not larger than

$$(m_y + n) \frac{2^{m_x+n}}{m_x + n}(1 + \varepsilon) \le c2^n$$

where $c = 2^{m_x} \frac{m_y}{m_x}(1 + \varepsilon)$ and $\varepsilon \to 0$ when $n \to \infty$. $\square$

Now we consider two examples which shows that the difference in BC-complexity for automata with the same number of states can indeed be exponential.

Example 11. As a first example we consider already mentioned automaton which shifts its input tape by n bits and denote it A_1^n . It has binary input and output $X = Y = \{0,1\}$ and it writes what it has read n steps ago (0 in first n steps) $y_k = x_{k-n}$. Its state complexity is 2^n, it has to remember all the previous n input symbols.

BC-complexity of this automaton is $n + 1$, nothing more than $n + 1$ input and output argument (one variable for input and n for state) is not necessary for a circuit to represent its transition function (see Fig. 1(a)).

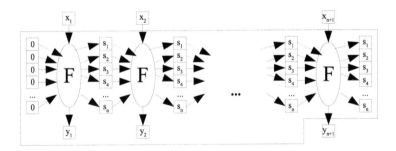

Fig. 3. Construction of a circuit for Shannon function

Example 12. Consider an automaton A_2^n, that writes on the output tape Shannon function Sh_{n+1} of the last $n + 1$ input variables including the current input symbol. Its input and output alphabet again is $X = Y = \{0,1\}$ and output symbol is $y_k = Sh_{n+1}(x_{k-n}, x_{k-n+1}, \ldots, x_{k-1}, x_k)$. For this automaton state complexity is not larger than 2^n, it is enough to remember last n input symbols for what 2^n states is sufficient. But its BC-complexity is at least $\frac{2^{n+1}}{(n+1)^2}$.

Proof. Let F be any Boolean circuit that represents automaton A_2^n. Assume F has one input bit that represents input symbol from the tape and m variables for state bits (m can differ for different circuits). By concatenating $n + 1$ circuits

F together (state bit output of i-th circuit is passed as state bit input of $i+1$-st) one can obtain a circuit whose size is not larger than $(n + 1)C(F)$ (Fig. 3).

If we consider inputs $x_1, x_2, \ldots, x_{n+1}$ and output y_{n+1} then this circuit calculates exactly Shannon function Sh_{n+1}. Therefore by Theorem 2 its size is larger than $\frac{2^{n+1}}{n+1}$. From $(n + 1)C(F) \geq \frac{2^{n+1}}{n+1}$ we get that $C(F) \geq \frac{2^{n+1}}{(n+1)^2}$. $\qquad\square$

The following theorem summarizes previous examples:

Theorem 13. *For every n there exists automata A_1^n and A_2^n such that:*

$$\begin{cases} C_s(A_1^n) = 2^n \\ C_{\mathrm{BC}}(A_1^n) = n + 1 \end{cases} \quad and \quad \begin{cases} C_s(A_2^n) \leq 2^n \\ C_{\mathrm{BC}}(A_2^n) \geq \frac{2^{n+1}}{(n+1)^2} \end{cases}$$

5   Minimization

In this section we discuss one interesting property of BC-complexity — that for some automata A BC-complexity is significantly smaller than for their minimal automata $M(A)$. It means that in some cases by minimizing the number of states (minimizing state complexity) BC-complexity of the transition function can increase superpolynomially. And on the other hand — sometimes allowing equivalent states in the automaton helps to keep BC-complexity small. The theorem is based on the conjecture that $PSPACE \not\subseteq P/Poly$.

Theorem 14. *If there is a polynomial $p(x)$ such that*

$$C_{\mathrm{BC}}(M(A)) < p(C_{\mathrm{BC}}(A))$$

for all automata A then $PSPACE \subset P/Poly$.

Proof. The idea of the proof is following: given a decision problem F construct an automaton A_n such that it computes F on its first n input bits but outputs the result only after an exponentially long time. Such an automaton can be constructed with a polynomial size BC-complexity, by modeling in its state register the Turing machine that computes F. But for the corresponding minimal automaton $M(A_n)$ the value of F is known already after reading first n bits — automaton can be in only one of two states corresponding to two possible values of F. From this assuming $C_{\mathrm{BC}}(M(A_n))$ is polynomially bounded to $C_{\mathrm{BC}}(A_n)$ one can construct a polynomial size circuit for F.

Now, assume that such a polynomial p exists. Take any decision problem $F \in PSPACE$. We have to prove, that there is a polynomial $r(n)$ such that for any n circuit complexity of $F|_n$ — restriction of F to inputs of length n — is at most $r(n)$.

By Theorem 7 there is a Turing machine TM_F, that solves F using at most $q(n)$ cells of tape and in time less than $2^{q(n)}$ where $q(n)$ is a polynomial. Denote $m = q(n)$ and consider the following function $g_{F,n} : 0, 1^* \to 0, 1^*$ that transforms sequence $x_1, x_2, \ldots, x_t$ to $y_1, y_2, \ldots, y_t$ and

$$y_k = \begin{cases} 1 & \text{if } k = n + 2^m \text{ and } F(x_1, \ldots, x_n) = 1 \\ 0 & \text{otherwise} \end{cases}$$

Automaton A_n that computes function $g_{F,n}$ will have $(1+m)+m(2+\log_2(|Q|+1))$ state bits where $|Q|$ is the number of states of TM_F and its BC-complexity will be polynomially bounded in n. The idea of the construction is following — automaton A_n reads in first n symbols and then starts to simulate the Turing machine TM_F. After 2^m steps TM_F has already halted and its output $F(x_1,\ldots,x_n)$ can be written on the output tape.

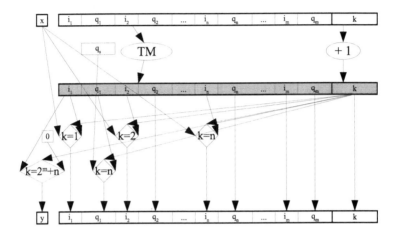

Fig. 4. Boolean circuit of the automaton A_n

"Block diagram" of a Boolean circuit that represents A_n is shown in Fig. 4. x is the input bit from the input tape, block $i_1q_1\ldots i_mq_m$ is used to simulate Turing machine TM_F and block k is a counter. Each i_j contains two bits of binary representation of contents of the i-th cell of the tape of TM_F, each q_j contains $\log(|Q|+1)$ bits of binary representation of the state of TM_F (as in Theorem 4). It is assumed, that Λ (empty cell of TM_F) is encoded as 0 and $\tilde{q}$ (empty state) also is encoded as 0 — therefore the initial state of the register filled with zeros corresponds to an empty tape of TM_F and all states set to empty state $\tilde{q}$. Counter k consists of $m+1$ bit, its initial value also is zero.

This circuit consists of three types of "block elements". "TM" element simulates one step of a Turing machine TM_F (Theorem 4). "+1" element adds 1 to the counter until it reaches its maximal value of $2^{m+1}-1$ after which it does not change. Switching elements "$k=a$"which are denoted as "diamonds" have three inputs: top input where the value of the counter k is passed, left input which is passed to the output if the condition written on the element is true and right input which is passed if the condition is false. Note that switching elements receive the value of the counter after addition of 1 — therefore condition $x=a$ is true exactly in the a-th step of the calculation.

In the first n steps blocks $i_1,\ldots,i_n$ one by one are filled with binary representations of input values $x_1,\ldots,x_n$. It is done by switching elements "$k=j$" which write current input bit into variable i_j iff $k=j$. There are n such switching elements for first n input bits.

After n symbols has been read, switch $k = n$ sets the state block q_1 to the start state of the Turing machine q_s. Till then all the state blocks where set to $\tilde{q}$ and therefore block TM which simulates one step of TM_F did nothing. Now the simulation of TM_F starts.

After 2^m steps TM_F has halted — it means that its output (value of $F(x_1, \ldots, x_n)$) is contained in variable i_1. If $k = 2^m + n$ then one more switching element writes the value of i_1 on the output tape, where otherwise 0 is always written. After this automaton A_n outputs only zeros.

Size of the element "TM" is polynomially bounded to n because of Theorem 4. Although it is possible to explicitly create circuits for switching elements "$k = j$" and addition element "$+1$" to make it shorter we just refer to the Theorem 6 and the evident fact, that all these elements can be calculated by a Turing machine in a polynomial time, to state, that the circuit size for each of them also is polynomially bounded to n.

In total there are $n + 2$ switching elements, one "$+1$" element and one "TM" element — as all of them are polynomially bounded to n then the total size of the circuit is also polynomially bounded. Hence, $C_{BC}(A_n) \leq h(n)$ where $h(n)$ is some polynomial.

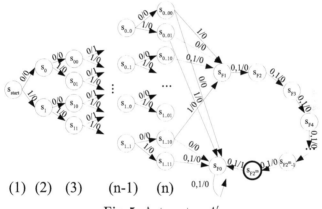

Fig. 5. Automaton A'_n

State transition diagram of another automaton A'_n that calculates the same function $g_{F,n}$ is schematically shown in Fig. 5. In the beginning $n - 1$ input bits are read leading to 2^{n-1} different states which are organized in n-th column. When the n-th input bit is read $F(x_1, \ldots, x_n)$ is calculated and depending on the result automaton leads to the state s_{F1} (if the result is 1) or to the state s_{F0} otherwise. From the state s_{F1} it goes through 2^m states and finally arrives in the only state s_{F2^m} (marked bold) in which it outputs 1. Afterward it moves to the state s_{F0} where it outputs 0 forever.

One can see that after n steps automaton A'_n already contains the information about the value of $F(x_1, \ldots, x_n)$ — it is exactly in one of two states: either s_{F1} or s_{F0} depending on this value. This can be used to construct a circuit for $F(x_1, \ldots, x_n)$ similarly as it was done in Example 12.

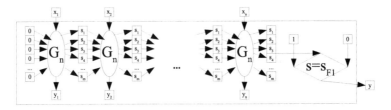

Fig. 6. Construction of a circuit for $F|_n$

Although A'_n is not minimal (it could happen that its "left side" can be minimized) minimization of it can lead only to "glueing" of some states and it is clear that for the minimal automaton $M(A'_n) = M(A_n)$ there also will be two states s_{F0} and s_{F1} that will correspond to those of A'_n in which it can be after n steps and from which value of $F(x_1, \ldots, x_n)$ can be deduced.

By the assumption of the theorem $C_{BC}(M(A_n)) < p(C_{BC}(A_n)) < p(h(n))$ therefore there exists a Boolean circuit G_n that represents automaton $M(A^n)$ and which is polynomially bounded to n.

Using this we construct a polynomial size Boolean circuit for $F|_n$. Concatenate n circuits G_n together (Fig. 6) to obtain a circuit that represents first n steps of the automaton $M(A^n)$. Add one switch "$s = s_{F1}$" and output 1 or 0 depending on the result of it. As after reading n inputs automaton $M(A^n)$ is in state s_{F1} iff $F(x_1 \ldots x_n) = 1$ then this circuit computes exactly function $F|_n$. The complexity of this circuit is $r(n) = n * C(G_n) + C(< s = s_{F1} >)$ which is polynomial to n.   □

6   Conclusions

In this paper a new measure of complexity — BC-complexity of finite automata was considered. It was proved that for some languages BC-complexity is of the same order as state complexity while for other languages it can be exponentially smaller. And the minimization of state complexity can lead to explosion of BC-complexity.

As BC-complexity is based on circuit complexity of Boolean functions then the behavior of it is expected to be similar to the complexity of them — that for most of automata BC-complexity is close to its maximum value (Shannon effect) but for some (which include most of practical instances) it can be exponentially smaller. Some counting argument seems necessary to prove that.

Example in Sect. 5 showed an automaton for which minimization of states leads to increase in BC-complexity. Although this is a correct example, it is impractical from the point of view, that it outputs 1 only in one bit position after exponential number of steps. In first $2^m + n - 1$ steps it outputs only zeros independently on input. But the method used in proof — simulating exponentially long calculation of a Turing machine does not seem to be able to produce a more "practical" example. This is again a field for future research. As is BC-complexity itself.

References

1. Nigmatullin, R.: Complexity of Boolean Functions, Moscow (1986) (in Russian)
2. Barzdins, J., Trakhtenbrot, B.: Finite Automata. Behavior and Synthesis, Moscow (1970) (in Russian)
3. Boppana, R.B.: The complexity of Finite Functions, New York (1989)
4. Straubing, H.: Automata, Formal Logic and Circuit Complexity. Birkhäuser, Basel (1994)
5. Savage, J.E.: Models of Computation: Exploring the Power of Computing. Addison Wesley, Reading (1998)
6. Karp, R.M., Lipton, R.J.: Some connections between nonuniform and uniform complexity classes. In: Proceedings of the Twelfth Annual ACM Symposium on Theory of Computing, STOC 1980 (1980)
7. Mealy, G.H.: A Method to Synthesizing Sequential Circuits. Bell Systems Technical Journal, 1045–1079 (1955)
8. Hopcroft, J.E.: An n log n algorithm for minimizing states in finite automata, Technical Report STAN-CS-71-190. Stanford University, Computer Science Department (1971)
9. Hopcroft, J.E., Ullman, J.D.: Introduction to Automata Theory, Languages and Computation. Addison-Wesley, Reading (1979)
10. Gramlich, G., Schnitger, G.: Minimizing NFAs and regular expressions. In: Diekert, V., Durand, B. (eds.) STACS 2005. LNCS, vol. 3404, pp. 399–411. Springer, Heidelberg (2005)

Complexity of Nondeterministic Multitape Computations Based on Crossing Sequences[*]

Jiří Wiedermann

Institute of Computer Science, Academy of Sciences of the Czech Republic
Pod Vodárenskou věží 2, 182 07 Prague 8, Czech Republic
jiri.wiedermann@cs.cas.cz

Abstract. Developing the concept of crossing sequences for multitape computations proposed in 1979 by G. Wechsung, we derive new relations among complexity measures for nondeterministic multitape computations. Especially, we characterize inherent relations between nondeterministic time and space and other complexity measures related to the notion of crossing sequences. We also show a nondeterministic simulation of nondeterministic computations whose complexity depends on the length of crossing sequences of the simulated machine. To a certain extent our results mirror classical results known to hold for single-tape computations or for deterministic multitape computations.

1 Introduction

The concept of crossing sequences was invented in the 1962 by F.C. Hennie who has used it for proving lower bounds on time and space bounded one-tape off-line Turing machine computations [4]. This concept has turned out to be quite fruitful and become the main tool for proving interesting complexity results about the computational and recognition power of variants of single-tape Turing machines. For instance, Hartmanis [3] has used the idea of crossing sequences as the main analytical tool for proving the lower bounds concerning the recognition of regular languages. The inherent time-space trade-offs between time and space complexity of single-tape machines have later been improved by Paterson [8], Ibarra and Moran [6], and Liśkiewicz and Loryś [7]. The technique based on crossing sequences was also used by Wiedermann for separating the corresponding alternating and nondeterministic complexity classes for the case of single-tape alternating Turing machines [11], [12]. Recently, Pighizzini [9] has studied the computational properties of one-tape off-line nondeterministic Turing machines also by means of crossing sequences. Hence, the notion of crossing sequences has appeared to be a valuable analytic tool for studying various kinds of one-tape computations, indeed.

Unfortunately, as observed already by Hennie [4], it seemed that the concept of crossing sequences cannot be extended for obtaining time lower bounds for multitape Turing machines.

---

[*] This research was carried out within the institutional research plan AV0Z10300504 and partially supported by the GA ČR grant No. P202/10/1333.

M. Holzer, M. Kutrib, and G. Pighizzini (Eds.): DCFS 2011, LNCS 6808, pp. 314–327, 2011.

However, Gerd Wechsung in his 1979 paper [10] proposed a reasonable generalization of the notion of crossing sequences. For the case of nondeterministic two-tape machines Wechsung was able to prove a lemma similar to Hennie's original result allowing mixing of computations with the same crossing sequences. Wechsung used this result for separation of complexity classes depending on the length of crossing sequences, remarking merely that a similar approach can also be used for proving lower bounds on multitape computations.

Our paper builds on Wechsung's approach to the definition of crossing sequences for multitape computations.

In Section 2, we introduce the framework needed for defining the crossing sequences and other related notions. As compared to [10], in our approach we will consider, without loss of generality, the so-called diagonal computations leading to a simpler definition of crossing systems.

Next, in Section 3, we introduce definition of crossing systems and state their basic properties. Based on it, we define crossing sequences. Our definition of crossing sequences differs from the Wechsung's definition since is does not explicitly include the definition of so-called crossing pattern in it. Then, for this modified definition we prove the so-called mixing lemma and its important corollary stating that in any accepting computational tree of a nondeterministic computation there always exists an accepting path in which each crossing sequence occurs at most once. This is a similar statement that has been known to hold for single-tape computations (cf. [3]).

In Section 4, we define two new complexity measures: the crossing complexity $C(n)$ and the number of crossing systems $N(n)$. Then we show inherent relations that under certain technical assumptions must hold for any nondeterministic multitape computations for the latter mentioned measures and time complexity $T(n) : C(n) = \Omega(\log N(n))$ and $T(n) = \Omega(N(n) \log N(n))$. Note that the previous relations are in fact lower-bounds on the growth of $C(n)$ and $T(n)$, respectively. These results can be seen as a validation of Wechsung's original remark on the potential of the crossing sequence approach for proving lower bounds on complexity of computations also in the case of multitape Turing machines. We also prove $N(n) = O(T(n)/\log T(n))$ showing that for nondeterministic multitape Turing machines number of crossing systems is a more powerful computational resource than time. This is to be compared with a similar result holding for the deterministic multitape computations [5] where such a relation is known to hold between space and time complexities.

Finally, in Section 5 we describe a nondeterministic simulation of nondeterministic computations whose complexity depends on the length of crossing sequences of the simulated machine. For the case of single-tape computations a similar theorem was proved in [9].

The results from Section 4 and 5 are new and to a certain extent correspond to the classical results known to hold for single-tape computations or for deterministic multitape computations (cf. [3], [9], [5]). To the best of our knowledge, after more than 30 years the presented results are the first ones employing the concept of crossing sequences in derivation of inherent complexity relations in multitape nondeterministic computations.

2   Preliminaries

In this paper, we consider a standard model of a k-tape nondeterministic Turing machine $\mathcal{N}$, $k \geq 1$, with set of states Q, alphabet Σ, transition relation δ and input w of length n written on the first tape, left justified.

In what follows we will only consider 2-tape machines since it is known that any such machine can simulate any k-tape machine in linear time and space (cf. [2]).

The notions of the *head configuration*, of the *configuration*, of the *computation*, of the *acceptance*, and those of time and space complexity are defined in the usual way (cf. [1]).

Any computation of a two-tape machine can be captured in a three-dimensional *computational diagram*. In it, the x-axis (the y-axis) corresponds to the first (second) tape, while the z-axis represents the flow of time (in discrete steps). A point $[x, y, z]$ in such a diagram corresponds to the situation at time z when the first (second) head scans cell number x (y).

In a computational diagram the movement of heads in any computation can be recirded by a *computational trajectory*. It is an oriented curve starting in point $[1, 1, 1]$ connecting, in chronological order, the centers of those cells in the diagram (which are three-dimensional cubes) that correspond to the tape-cells visited during a computation.

For simplicity, in what follows we will only consider a two-dimensional representation of a computation (in fact, this was the case considered by Hennie and Wechsung). This representation will be a projection of the previous three-dimensional representation into the two-dimensional plane corresponding to axes x and y. In such a notation the time dimension is lost. This dimension can easily be recovered from the trajectory in cases when at least one head performs a move. When a trajectory moves "backwards" along some of its parts the respective segment of a trajectory will be drawn as a curve tightly following that part in the opposite direction. In this way, only cases when for a few subsequent steps both heads do not move are not properly represented in the diagram. Such "no move" cases can last for at most a constant number of steps and w.l.o.g. can be completely avoided by redesigning the transition relation δ of the machine.

In the computational diagram the vertical and horizontal *gridlines* correspond to the boundaries between the neighboring tape cells. Gridline number i corresponds to the boundary between cell i and $i + 1$.

Note that thanks to the fact that a computational curve connects the centers of neighboring squares in a diagram the curve never follows a gridline. A curve can either cross a gridline (in a perpendicular or diagonal manner) or a part of a curve parallels a gridline on either side.

Having the notion of a two-dimensional computational diagram we can extend the concept of crossing sequences known from single-tape computation (cf. [3])

to the two-dimensional case. In principle, in a single move of a two-tape machine one of the following three possibilities might occur: (i) both heads of the machine cross the boundaries on their respective tapes between the currently scanned cell and the neighboring cell, (ii) only one head on one tape crosses the boundary, or (iii) none of the heads crosses any boundary — both heads retain their positions. As noted above, the third mentioned behavior pattern can be avoided by reprogramming the machine at hand.

The situation corresponding to case (i) seen in the computational diagram looks as follows. Let $[i, j]$ be a square in the computational diagram corresponding to the current head positions. Case (i) corresponds to crossing of two perpendicular gridlines whose cut point is in one of the four corners of the cell $[i, j]$. E.g., when the head on tape one moves from cell i to cell $i + 1$ and the head on tape two from cell j to $j - 1$, then both the vertical gridline i and the horizontal gridline $j - 1$ are crossed simultaneously.

Case (ii) was considered in [10] and has lead Wechsung to a relatively complicated definition of crossing systems that had to deal with parts of trajectories moving horizontally or vertically. In order to avoid such complication we will only consider computations of two-tape TMs in which both heads on working tapes move simultaneously in each step. Such machines will be called *diagonal machines* performing *diagonal computations*.

We show that in any computation this assumption can be made without loss of generality.

Theorem 1. *Let $\mathcal{M}$ be a standard deterministic or nondeterministic two-tape Turing machine. Then there exists a diagonal machine $\mathcal{M}'$ of the same type as $\mathcal{M}$ simulating $\mathcal{M}$ in linear time and space.*

Sketch of the proof: For technical reasons the input to $\mathcal{M}'$ (which is the same as the input to $\mathcal{M}$), written on the first tape, must be converted into an equivalent string whose symbols are separated by blanks. The converted string will be written onto the second tape. This is done as follows.

For simplicity, assume that n is an odd number. If this is not the case, then prolong the input by one special symbol. Then $\mathcal{M}$ copies the first input symbol into the first cell on tape two. Now assume that the input string has been converted up to its i-th symbol, for $i = 1, 3, 5, \ldots$ and that the head on tape one scans the i-th cell and the head on tape two the $(2i - 1)$-st cell. We show that in four more steps head one will scan the $(i + 2)$-nd input symbol while head two the $(2i + 3)$-rd symbol, with cell $(2i + 1)$ on the second tape holding the $(i + 1)$-st input symbol. The corresponding moves of both heads, inclusively the direction of their moves over the cells in the conversion process are captured by the following diagram: $\begin{array}{l} i \ \ \rightarrow i+1 \rightarrow \ i+2 \ \leftarrow \ i+1 \ \rightarrow \ i+2 \\ 2i-1 \rightarrow \ 2i \ \rightarrow 2i+1 \rightarrow 2i+2 \rightarrow 2i+3 \end{array}$. In this diagram, in step two, the input symbol just scanned by head one it stored in the state and printed in the next step onto tape two. Thus, after four moves the situation on both tapes is as required. The conversion process terminates when the end of the input is reached. Then both heads return to their initial position at the left end of both tapes, essentially replaying the moves in the reversed order. Note that neither head of $\mathcal{M}'$ has performed a stationary move.

Then the simulation of $\mathcal{M}$'s computation on a given input can begin.

Throughout the simulation the following invariant will be preserved: The i-th tape cell of $\mathcal{M}$ will be represented in the $2i+1$-st cell on the corresponding tape of $\mathcal{M}'$. The even numbered cells in between the occupied cells (holding symbols from the $\mathcal{M}$'s tape) will be empty.

At each step simulating each move of $\mathcal{M}$, $\mathcal{M}'$ scans odd positions of tape heads on both tapes, and keeps track in the state as to whether the current position, or the next position of both tapes is being scanned in $\mathcal{M}$. Furthermore, both heads can move right once, then left once, before simulating a move of $\mathcal{M}$, remembering two characters on both tapes in the state. Then, after a move, each tape head can either i) stay in the same position by moving left once, then right once, ii) move right two cells, iii) move left two cells. This simulation works both for deterministic and nondeterministic machines. $\qquad\square$

3   Crossing Sequences and the Mixing Lemma

Now we proceed to the definition of crossing sequences. Our approach is inspired by that of G. Wechsung [10]. However, due to our concentration on diagonal computations we need not consider special cases of horizontal or vertical moves in the corresponding computational diagrams, and consequently our definition of a crossing sequence can be simplified. This will also bring additional benefits in the form of a simpler proof of the important combining Lemma 8 (which is also due to Wechsung) on which our new results are grounded.

In accordance with [10] we will define a so-called crossing system as a certain set of gridlines crossed in dependence of head movements in a diagonal computation. The respective gridlines connect those coordinates of the computational trajectory which represent the tape-cells whose content is interdependent.

Definition 2. *Let c be a computational curve of a diagonal computation. Let S, $|S| \geq 2$, be a set of gridlines on c such that if a gridline $f \in S$, then for each point in which f cuts c also a gridline g perpendicular to f at that point is in S.*

A crossing system *on c is a minimal set S satisfying the previous condition.*

Note that thanks to the minimality requirement each crossing system is "closed" — S cannot have a proper subset satisfying the condition stated in the definition. Examples of crossing systems can be seen in Fig. 1 and Fig. 2 — their respective gridlines are shown as dotted lines.

Given any gridline f, for a given computational curve c the crossing system S containing f can be constructed as follows: we start with $S = \emptyset$, add f to S, find all cut points of f and c, and add to S all gridlines perpendicular to f in these cut points. Then we proceed recursively with all members of S, until no further cut points emerge (and thus no further gridlines are added to S). Obviously, for a given computation there can be many crossing systems (cf. Fig. 2). From the previous construction it is seen that all of them are disjoint — no two of them can share a common gridline.

The next idea of a computational curve coloring also originates in [10] (cf. Fig. 1):

Proposition 3. *Let c be a diagonal computation, let S be a crossing system on c. Then*

1. *S defines a decomposition of the whole computational area into rectangles with corners in the cut points of gridlines from S; these rectangles partition the area into columns and rows;*
2. *S defines a decomposition of c into segments $c_0, c_1, \ldots, c_n$ such that each segment remains entirely in one of the rectangles and begins and ends in one of its corner squares;*
3. *segments $c_0, c_1, \ldots, c_n$ can be colored by two colors in such a way that*
   (a) along the curve the colors of segments alternate;
   (b) all segments within the same column (row) are of the same color.

Sketch of the proof: See Fig. 1 in which the colors are depicted by segments of different thickness.

The first and the second claim follow from the definition of S.

For the last claim, assume that up to some c_i condition (3) from the above proposition is satisfied. This means that up to c_i the color of segments alternates and the segments in columns (rows) have the same color. When crossing the next boundary, c_{i+1} changes its color and enters the neighboring column. Hence it has the same color as the previous segments in that column. At the same occasion, c_{i+1} also changes the row and, therefore again, it has the same color as the other segments in that row.   □

Definition 4. *Let $S = \{h_1, \ldots, h_k, v_1, \ldots, v_\ell\}$ be a crossing system for a diagonal computation c, with horizontal gridlines $h_1, \ldots, h_k$ and vertical gridlines $v_1, \ldots, v_\ell$, for some $k \geq 1$ and $\ell \geq 1$. Then the sequence $(t_1, \ldots, t_s)$ is called the crossing pattern of S if and only if for all for $1 \leq p \leq s$ it holds: if c crosses gridlines h_{i_p} and v_{j_p} from S for the p-th time then $t_p = (i_p, j_p)$.*

Informally, the crossing pattern captures the sequence of "corners" of rectangles (cf. Proposition 3, item 1 and 2), in a chronological order in which they are crossed by c.

Definition 5. *Point $[i, j]$ on computational curve c is called the* crossing point *for gridline g if and only if c crosses g immediately after leaving $[i, j]$.*

Obviously, a crossing system S for any computation c can also be defined with the help of crossing points from c.

The next definition of a crossing sequence in principle mirrors the original definition by Wechsung, but it deviates from it in two aspects. First, it is adjusted to capture the nondeterministic computations. Second, in the definition of the crossing system elements the indices of the crossed gridlines (the crossing pattern) are omitted.

Definition 6. *Let $(C_1, C_2, \ldots, C_s)$, $s \geq 1$ be a sequence of crossing points, listed in a chronological order, w.r.t. a crossing system S for a diagonal computation c.*

Let α be a function which to each C_i assigns the instruction (i.e., an element of δ) of M that was used by M at time when its heads were leaving C_i.

Then, $\Gamma_{S,c} = (\alpha(C_1), \alpha(C_2), \dots, \alpha(C_s))$ is called the crossing sequence *of c on S. Number s is called the length of the crossing sequence $\Gamma_{S,c}$.*

In the definition of a crossing sequence the relation of crossing sequence elements to the crossing points is lost — an element of a crossing sequence cannot be uniquely assigned back to a crossing point. Note, however, that in our definition of a crossing sequence the crossing pattern is implicitly there, since the sequence of values of function α states in what order, and what manner (i.e., via which corners in the rectangular representation of S) the computational curve c proceeds.

Also note that the representation of $\Gamma_{S,c} = (\alpha(C_1), \alpha(C_2), \dots, \alpha(C_s))$ is of size $\Theta(s)$, whereas the representation à la Wechsung, with the explicit crossing pattern, would be of size $\Omega(s \log s)$, with $\log s$ factor accounting for the crossing pattern. This will be of advantage in the proof of Theorem 13. However, from the viewpoint of the information content, both our new and Wechsung's original definition of crossing sequences are equivalent.

Proposition 7. *Let S be a crossing system on a diagonal computation c inducing a segmentation of c into segments that are colored according to Proposition 3.*

Then, knowing the corresponding crossing sequence $\Gamma_{S,c}$ the equally colored segments of c can be computed independently of the segments colored by the other color.

Sketch of the proof: Consider the sequence of segments of c of the same color, in a chronological order. Each segment in this sequence can be computed over the tape sectors corresponding to the rectangle in which the segment is located. For the first time, the computation is performed over the empty tape sectors. Subsequently, when computing chronologically the next segment of the same color, it is always computed over the tape contents left by the lastly performed computation over these sectors in the equally colored segments. Upon entering a segment, the initial head configuration is always given by the corresponding member of the crossing sequence $\Gamma_{S,c}$. Thus, the only interaction among the differently colored neighboring segments proceeds via the corresponding crossing sequence elements and, therefore, the equally colored segments of c can be computed independently of the segments colored by the other color.   □

From technical reasons we will need the notion of input disjoint crossing systems. We say that a crossing system S is *input disjoint* if and only if none of the gridlines of S is incidental with a cell holding an input element. In what follows the requirement for input disjoint crossing systems will ensure that when manipulating, and possibly deleting parts of computations the original input will remain intact.

Using the previous result, the next lemma states the possibility of mixing two diagonal computations (a similar lemma has originally been proved by Wechsung [10]).

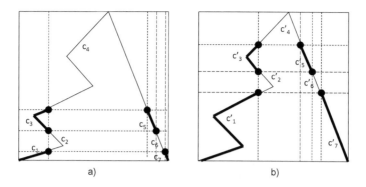

Fig. 1. A computation with two identical crossing sequences

Lemma 8. *Let c and c' be two (not necessarily distinct) diagonal computations of a 2NTM $\mathcal{M}$ and let $\mathcal{S}$ and $\mathcal{S}'$ be input disjoint crossing systems for c and c', respectively.*

If $\Gamma_{\mathcal{S},c} = \Gamma_{\mathcal{S}',c'}$ and $(c_1, \ldots, c_n)$ and $(c'_1, \ldots, c'_n)$ are the decompositions of c and c' induced by $\mathcal{S}$ and $\mathcal{S}'$, respectively, then also the curves $c_1, c'_2, c_3, c'_4, \ldots$ and $c'_1, c_2, c'_3, c_4, \ldots$ represent possible diagonal computations of $\mathcal{M}$.

The proof of this lemma mirrors that of Lemma 4 in [10], since our definition of crossing sequences is equivalent to the original Wechsung's definition. The proof is somewhat simpler since no horizontal and vertical parts of c or c' must be considered.

The following two corollaries seem to be new (they are not stated in [10]):

Corollary 9. *Let c be a diagonal computation of a 2NTM $\mathcal{M}$ and let there exist two different input disjoint crossing systems $\mathcal{S}$ and $\mathcal{S}'$ for c such that $\Gamma_{\mathcal{S},c} = \Gamma_{\mathcal{S}',c}$. Then, there is a diagonal computation c' of $\mathcal{M}$ with only one crossing system and another computation c'' of $\mathcal{M}$ with three crossing systems, with all crossing systems sharing the same crossing sequence $\Gamma_{\mathcal{S},c}$.*

Sketch of the proof: The proof relies on the fact that crossing systems $\mathcal{S}$ and $\mathcal{S}'$ are disjoint and also that gridlines of $\mathcal{S}$ and $\mathcal{S}'$ cannot "interlace" (namely, gridlines of $\mathcal{S}$ cannot be in the rectangle defined by those of $\mathcal{S}'$ or viceversa).

Let $s = c_1, c_2, \ldots$ be a segmentation of c induced by crossing system $\mathcal{S}$ for computation c, and analogously, let $s' = c'_1, c'_2, \ldots$ be a segmentation of c induced by crossing system $\mathcal{S}'$. According to Proposition 3 the segments can be colored by two colors, let us say red and green. Assume that both c_1 and c'_1 are red. Note that in s the gridlines of $\mathcal{S}'$ cut the green segments $c_2, c_4, \ldots$ while in s' the gridlines of $\mathcal{S}$ cut the red segments $c'_1, c'_3, \ldots$ (cf. Fig. 1).

Then, according to the claim of Lemma 8 both $c' = c_1, c'_2, c_3, c'_4, \ldots$ and $c'' = c'_1, c_2, c'_3, c_4, \ldots$ are possible computational curves of $\mathcal{M}$. In both computations the ends of their segments are separated by a crossing system with the same crossing sequence $\Gamma_{\mathcal{S},c}$.

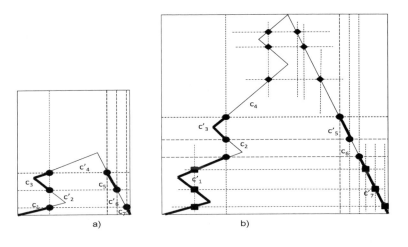

Fig. 2. Two ways of computations mixing

However, the green segments $c_2, c_4, \ldots$ in c'' are cut by gridlines of $\mathcal{S}'$, whereas the red segments $c'_1, c'_3, \ldots$ are cut by gridlines of $\mathcal{S}$. Therefore, computation $c'' = c'_1, c_2, c'_3, c_4, \ldots$, generates three crossing systems with the same crossing sequence $\Gamma_{\mathcal{S},c}$ - cf. Fig. 2 b). Crossing points belonging to the same crossing system are denoted by the same geometrical figure (a circle, a diamond, a square).

Finally, consider computation $c' = c_1, c'_2, c_3, c'_4, \ldots$. In it, neither red nor green segments are cut by gridlines from $\mathcal{S}'$ or from $\mathcal{S}$. Therefore, c' generates but one crossing system (Fig. 2 a)) with crossing sequence $\Gamma_{\mathcal{S},c}$ emerging at the transition points between red and green segments of c'.   □

Now, for a given input, think about all crossing systems in a computational diagram of the corresponding diagonal computation. All such systems must be disjoint and to each of them a unique crossing sequence can be assigned. Thus, to each computation a set of crossing sequences can be assigned. If there were two identical input disjoint crossing sequences in this set then, according to the previous corollary, there would exist an equivalent computation (accepting the same input) with the corresponding set of all crossing sequences no longer containing two identical input disjoint crossing sequences.

Corollary 10. *To any diagonal accepting computation of a 2NTM $\mathcal{M}$ there exists an equivalent accepting computation in which each input disjoint crossing sequence occurs at most once.*

The last corollary allows to reduce from an arbitrary number of input disjoint crossing systems sharing a same crossing sequence, to only one input disjoint crossing system. This is in fact an analog of a similar statement holding for single-tape computations (cf. [4], [3]).

4   Complexity of Nondeterministic Multitape Computations

The result from Corollary 10 enables the derivation of non-trivial lower bound on both the lengths of the crossing sequences and time in nondeterministic computations.

Definition 11. *Let M be a diagonal 2NTM with input w.*

The crossing complexity $C(n)$ of M is the minimum, taken over all accepting computations of M, of the maximal lengths of crossing sequences taken over all inputs w of length n.

The number of crossing systems $N(n)$ of M is the minimum, taken over all accepting computations, of the maximal number of crossing systems generated in a computation of M, taken over all inputs w of length n.

Note that for single-tape computations of space complexity $S(n)$ the corresponding number of crossing systems is $N(n) = S(n)$. For multitape computations we have the following inherent relations:

Proposition 12. *Let M be a diagonal 2NTM of time complexity $T(n)$, space complexity $S(n)$, crossing complexity $C(n)$, and with $N(n)$ crossing systems. Then*

$$1 \leq N(n) \leq S(n),$$
$$n \leq S(n) \leq T(n) \leq N(n)C(n), \text{ and}$$
$$1 \leq C(n) \leq T(n).$$

Among crossing complexity, the number of crossing systems, and time complexity the following non-trivial inherent relations hold:

Theorem 13. *Let M be a diagonal 2NTM of time complexity $T(n)$, crossing complexity $C(n)$, with $N(n)$ crossing systems. If $\lim_{n\to\infty} n/N(n) = 0$, then*

(i) $C(n) = \Omega(\log N(n))$,
(ii) $T(n) = \Omega(N(n) \log N(n))$, and
(iii) $N(n) = O(T(n)/\log T(n))$.

Sketch of the proof: For any $i \geq 1$ the number of crossing sequences of length i is bounded by $(4q^2|\Sigma|^4)^i = d^i$. In the previous bound 4 is the number of possible moves of both heads (stationary moves are excluded), factor q^2 corresponds to the number of different pairs of the current and the new states, and $|\Sigma|^4$ corresponds to the number of possible ways of rewriting the pair of the currently scanned symbols by the new symbols.

Now, in order to upper-bound the number $N(n)$ with the help of Corollary 10 we want to eliminate from computations of M the duplicates of crossing sequences. However, there might be equal crossing sequences related to crossing systems whose gridlines are incidental with the cells holding the input symbols. None of such crossing sequences can be eliminated from any computation of M

since their elimination would shorten the input. Note that there are at most n of such sequences since the corresponding crossing systems (which must all be disjoint) can interfere with at most n first cells holding the input. Now, thanks to Corollary 10 for any computation we may chose a branch in which all crossing sequences, except possibly those incidental with the input, are different. The number $N(n) - n$ of such sequences will at most be equal to the number of all possible different sequences of length $1, 2, \ldots, C(n)$. Then we must have $N(n) - n \leq \sum_{i=0}^{C(n)} d^i \leq d^{C(n)+1}$. Making use of our assumption on the asymptotic growth of $N(n)$ we infer that for a sufficiently large n, $1/2N(n) \leq N(n) - n$ and therefore, $C(n) = \Omega(\log N(n))$.

Further note that in virtue of Corollary 10 $\mathcal{M}$ generates at most $N(n) - n$ different crossing sequences each of length at most $C(n)$. Obviously, $T(n)$ equals the sum of lengths of these sequences and, therefore, $T(n)$ is lower bounded by the sum of lengths of the first $N(n) - n$ members in the series of all lexicographically ordered crossing sequences. Let r be the length of the longest crossing sequence that is minimal such that $\sum_{i=0}^{r} d^i \geq N(n) - n$. Then, $1/2N(n) \leq \sum_{i=0}^{r} d^i = \frac{d^{r+1}-1}{d-1} \leq 2d^r$, for $d \geq 2$, i.e., $r = \Omega(\log N(n))$. Therefore, $T(n) \geq \sum_{i=0}^{r} id^i \geq rd^r \geq \Omega(N(n) \log N(n))$.

Finally, we show that the growth of $N(n) = O(T(n)/\log T(n))$ is a maximal one such that (ii) still holds.

If $N(n) = O(T(n)/\log T(n))$ then, since $T(n) \geq N(n)$, $T(n) = \Omega(N(n) \log T(n)) = \Omega(N(n) \log N(n))$. This means that (ii) holds.

Finally we show that if $N(n)$ grew asymptotically faster than $T(n)/\log T(n)$ then (ii) cannot hold.

To that end assume $\lim_{n\to\infty} T(n)/(N(n) \log T(n)) = 0$. Then for any $\varepsilon > 0$ there exists an n_0 such that for all $n > n_0$ $T(n)/(N(n) \log T(n)) < \varepsilon$. Therefore, $T(n) = \Omega(N(n) \log N(n)) = \Omega(T(n)/(\varepsilon \log T(n)) \log(T(n)/(\varepsilon \log T(n)))) = \Omega(T(n)/\varepsilon[1 - \log(\varepsilon \log T(n))/\log T(n)])$. The last relation cannot hold since for a sufficiently small ε and a sufficiently large n the last Ω-expression cannot be made smaller than $T(n)$. $\square$

To some extent, the results from Theorem 13 correspond to Theorem 3 from [3] that were proved for single-tape off-line machines (with $S(n)$ in place of $N(n)$).

Moreover, the last relation from Theorem 13 is also related to the main result from [5] stating that deterministic time is less powerful than deterministic space. In our case, the result $N(n) = O(T(n)/\log T(n))$ can be interpreted as the claim that in any nondeterministic computation time is a less powerful computational resource than the number of crossing systems.

5   Other Complexity Relations

Theorem 14. *Let $\mathcal{M}$ be a diagonal 2NTM of space complexity $S(n)$ and of crossing complexity $C(n)$ with $N(n)$ crossing systems. Then there is a 2NTM $\mathcal{M}'$ simulating $\mathcal{M}$ in space $O(C(n) \log S(n))$ and in time $O(N(n)C(n) \log S(n))$.*

Sketch of the proof: Imagine the computational diagram of $\mathcal{M}$'s computation with the computational curve c and all crossing systems drawn in this diagram. Any crossing system $\mathcal{S}$ is given by its vertical and horizontal gridlines which cut the x and y axes at certain points called the coordinates of $\mathcal{S}$. A gridline cutting an axis between cell i and $i+1$ will have the coordinate i. Thus, each crossing system $\mathcal{S}$ is given by the list of coordinates of vertical and horizontal gridlines from $\mathcal{S}$. We also say that $\mathcal{S}$ occupies cells corresponding to its coordinates on the respective tapes. Note that thanks to the disjointness of the crossing systems (see the remark following Definition 2) the cells occupied by any two crossing system are also disjoint.

The simulation algorithm works as follows.

Starting from the origin in the computational diagram of $\mathcal{M}$s computation $\mathcal{M}'$ considers, in left to right direction, one after the other the crossing systems in that diagram. That is, for each crossing system $\mathcal{S}$ considered it guesses and writes down, in the chronological order, the coordinates of all cut points (at most $C(n)$) of the gridlines from $\mathcal{S}$ with c. To each of these points $\mathcal{M}'$ also guesses the corresponding crossing sequence element. On each tape the coordinates of the cut points are disjoint but on each tape it may happen that some coordinates lay one next to each other and in such a case $\mathcal{M}'$ only keeps the lower and upper coordinate of the respective tape segment. Such intervals are called occupied segments. System $\mathcal{S}$ is called the old crossing system.

Then $\mathcal{M}'$ proceeds to considering the next crossing system $\mathcal{S}'$ called the new system. For this system, $\mathcal{M}'$ also guesses and writes down the analogous information as it had guessed for system $\mathcal{S}$. Note that the crossing points of the new crossing system are either immediate neighbors of the old crossing points that can be reached in one move or a new crossing point has been guessed by $\mathcal{M}'$ that is not reachable in one move from any previously guessed crossing point.

In the first case, the respective condition is checked by $\mathcal{M}'$ and in the positive case, the previously mentioned occupied segments must grow at either end and occasionally grow together. .

In the second case, $\mathcal{M}'$ opens a new segment for the point(s) at hand.

Finally, $\mathcal{M}'$ deletes the information concerning $\mathcal{S}$ (except that recorded in the occupied segments), $\mathcal{S}'$ becomes the old system and $\mathcal{M}'$ proceeds to considering the next crossing system as in the previous paragraph.

The simulation ends correctly when all checks are positive and all crossing systems have been inspected. The latter fact is recognized by $\mathcal{M}'$ when all occupied segments on both tapes merge together (there are no "holes" among them).

As far as the space complexity of the previous simulation is concerned, note that during the simulation $\mathcal{M}'$ has to keep the elements of two crossing systems and the coordinates of the respective crossing points. The respective information is of size $O(C(n) \log S(n))$. Moreover, there are at most $C(n)$ non-overlapping segments occupied by the so-far inspected crossing systems. Each segment is identified by its lower and upper end. The segments are kept on one of the $\mathcal{M}'$s tapes in a sorted order. If a new segment is to be inserted among the previous segments, the second tape of $\mathcal{M}'$ is used for efficiently creating the necessary gap between the existing segments. Note that there can never be more then $C(n)$ occupied segments since opening the $(C(n) + 1)$-st disjoint segment would mean that a crossing sequence of length greater than $C(n)$ has been guessed/encountered. Thus, asymptotically speaking, the bookkeeping of occupied segments does not increase the originally estimated space complexity.

Processing one crossing system takes time $O(C(n) \log S(n))$ (inclusively a possible creation of a new segment) since at such an occasion the entire information stored on a tape must be traversed and some part of it must be updated. This is repeated $N(n)$ times. $\qquad\square$

Corollary 15. *Let $\mathcal{M}$ be a diagonal 2NTM of crossing complexity $C(n)$ and $N(n)$ crossing systems. Then there is a 2NTM $\mathcal{M}'$ simulating $\mathcal{M}$ in in space $O(C^2(n))$ and in time $O(N(n)C^2(n))$.*

Sketch of the proof: In the complexity estimation of the simulation procedure from the previous theorem the space $O(\log S(n))$ necessary for representing a position on $\mathcal{M}$s tape can be upper bounded as follows. With the different crossing sequences of length at most $C(n)$ we can rewrite a tape up to the distance of at most $\sum_{i=1}^{C(n)} id^i = O(C(n)d^{C(n)})$ (d is as in Theorem 13). Hence, any position on a rewritten part of a tape can be stored in space $O(C(n))$ and therefore $\log S(n) = O(C(n))$. $\qquad\square$

6   Conclusions

Being inspired by the original Wechsung's ideas in defining the crossing sequences we proved a lemma stating that in any accepting computational tree of a nondeterministic computation there always exists an accepting path in which each crossing sequence occurs at most once. This has allowed a derivation of nontrivial lower-bounds on the length of crossing sequences and on time complexity of multitape nondeterministic computations. We have also designed a nondeterministic simulation of that latter computations whose complexity depends on the crossing complexity of the simulated Turing machine.

The main contribution of the paper is a sound extension of the notion of crossing sequences to the multitape case which might prove useful in the future investigations of the properties of multitape machines and automata.

Acknowledgment. The author thanks to anonymous referees for their helpful comments.

References

1. Aho, A.V., Hopcroft, J.E., Ullman, J.D.: The Design and Analysis of Computer Algorithms. Addison-Wesley, Reading (1974)
2. Book, R.V., Greibach, S.A., Wegbreit, B.: Time and tape bounded Turing acceptors and AFL's. J. Comput. Syst. Sci. 4, 606–621 (1970)

3. Hartmanis, J.: Computational Complexity of One-Tape Turing Machine Computations. JACM 15(2), 325–339 (1968)
4. Hennie, F.C.: One-tape, off-line Turing machine computations. Information and Control 8, 553–578 (1965)
5. Hopcroft, J.E., Paul, W.J., Valiant, L.G.: On Time Versus Space. J. ACM 24(2), 332–337 (1977)
6. Ibarra, O.H., Moran, D.: Some Time-Space Tradeoff Results Concerning Single-Tape and Offline TM's. SIAM J. Comput. 12(2), 388–394 (1983)
7. Liśkiewicz, M., Loryś, K.: Fast simulations of time-bounded one-tape Turing machines by space-bounded ones. SIAM J. Comput. 19(3), 511–521 (1990)
8. Paterson, M.: Tape Bounds for Time-Bounded Turing Machines. J. Comput. Syst. Sci. 6(2), 116–124 (1972)
9. Pighizzini, G.: Nondeterministic one-tape off-line Turing machines and their time complexity. Journal of Automata, Languages and Combinatorics 14(1), 107–124 (2010)
10. Wechsung, G.: A Crossing Measure for 2-Tape Turing Machines. In: Becvar, J. (ed.) MFCS 1979. LNCS, vol. 74, pp. 508–516. Springer, Heidelberg (1979)
11. Wiedermann, J.: Speeding-up Single-Tape Nondeterministic Computations by Single Alternation, with Separation Results. In: Meyer auf der Heide, F., Monien, B. (eds.) ICALP 1996. LNCS, vol. 1099, pp. 381–392. Springer, Heidelberg (1996)
12. Wiedermann, J.: Speeding-Up Nondeterministic Single-Tape Off-Line Computations by One Alternation. In: Brim, L., Gruska, J., Zlatuška, J. (eds.) MFCS 1998. LNCS, vol. 1450, pp. 607–615. Springer, Heidelberg (1998)

Author Index

Printed by Publishers' Graphics LLC